Aesthetics

Patrick Maynard teaches philosophical classics at the University of Western Ontario. He is guest editor of the special issue of *The Journal of Aesthetics and Art Criticism*, 'Perspectives on the Arts and Technology' (Spring 1997), and author of *The Engine of Visualization: Thinking Through Photography* (Ithaca, NY, 1997). He is currently writing a book on aspects of drawing, entitled *Drawing Distinctions*.

Susan L. Feagin is Professor of Philosophy at the University of Missouri-Kansas City. She was book review editor for the *Journal of Aesthetics and Art Criticism* from 1988 to 1993 and has served on the Board of Trustees of the American Society for Aesthetics. Recent publications include *Reading with Feeling: The Aesthetics of Appreciation* (Cornell University Press, 1996), 'Paintings and their Places', *Australasian Journal of Philosophy* (1996) (repr. in Stephen Davies (ed.), *Art and its Messages: Meaning, Morality, and Society* (Pennsylvania State University Press, 1997), and 'Feminist Art History and De Facto Significance', in Peggy Zeglin Brand and Carolyn Korsmeyer (eds.), *Feminism and Tradition in Aesthetics* (Pennsylvania State University Press, 1995).

OXFORD **READERS**

The Oxford Readers series represents a unique interdisciplinary resource for students, teachers, and the general reader, offering authoritative collections of primary and secondary sources on core issues and concepts.

OXFORD READERS

Aesthetics

Edited by

Susan L. Feagin *and* Patrick Maynard

OXFORD
UNIVERSITY PRESS

Oxford University Press, Walton Street, Oxford OX2 6DP

Oxford New York

Athens Auckland Bangkok Bogotá Bombay
Buenos Aires Calcutta Cape Town Dar es Salaam
Delhi Florence Hong Kong Istanbul Karachi
Kuala Lumpur Madras Madrid Melbourne
Mexico City Nairobi Paris Singapore
Taipei Tokyo Toronto Warsaw

and associated companies in
Berlin Ibadan

Oxford is a trade mark of Oxford University Press

First published as an Oxford University Press paperback 1997

British Library Cataloguing in Publication Data
Data available

Library of Congress Cataloging in Publication Data
Aesthetics / edited by Susan L. Feagin and Patrick Maynard.
P. cm.—(Oxford readers)
Includes bibliographical references and index.
1 Aesthetics. I. Feagin, Susan L., 1948– . II. Maynard,
Patrick, 1939– . III. Series.
BH39.A286 1997 111'85–dc21 97-29064

ISBN 978-0-19-289275-1

10

Typeset by Pure-Tech India Ltd, Pondicherry
Printed in Great Britain
by the MPG Books Group

Aesthetics

Introduction

From light bulb jokes to the vast and starry heavens above, from tragedies of Sophocles to symphonies of Mozart, from the exquisite lines of a Chinese porcelain bowl to the dynamic sculptures of Michelangelo: we experience amusement, the sublime, sorrow, joy, pleasure, and awe. Experiences such as these are the starting point for aesthetics, the starting point for reflecting on the nature and value of the arts, the quality of our experiences of the arts, of natural and constructed environments and of various aspects of ordinary life.

The word 'aesthetics' derives from a Greek word for perception, and is typically used to refer to what is valuable about experiences as perceptual experiences. It is most commonly used to refer to what is visually pleasing, while philosophically it is used in relation to both visual and auditory experiences, with ongoing debate about whether gustatory and kinaesthetic perceptions should also be thought of as 'aesthetic'. Imagination has also been closely associated with the aesthetic, and at one time was conceived of as the capacity to form (visual) images in the mind, thus ensuring its connection with perception. It is also associated with ideas of creativity and contrasted with reason and logic.

One idea of relevance to aesthetics that has emerged from the psychology of perception is that perception is 'cognitively informed': actually 'formed' or 'shaped' by one's attitudes, beliefs, and past experiences. Any given object, event, or series of events can be experienced in a multitude of ways. One may perceive something differently as one's beliefs change, and also as one imagines being in a different situation or taking a different point of view. In broadening the range of perceptual experiences and exercising imagination one's mind doesn't simply change; it grows. It grows not only because of the variety, but also through deepening and sharing experiences. This collection is organized to show how art, nature, and our experiences of them contribute richness and value to our lives. The questions heading each section were selected because they identify common concerns about the aesthetic, the idea of art, self-expression in art, creativity, understanding art, emotionally responding to and evaluating art. Ultimately, these questions all point to issues of value, sometimes in ways that are fairly obvious: what is valuable about having the kinds of experiences people have called 'aesthetic', and why does it matter whether one accepts that something is a work of art or not? In other cases the significance of the issues is not quite so obvious. Ideas about self-expression are significant because they involve concepts of self-understanding and also cultural identity, the ways one would like to play a role in one's culture, and the relationships among personal freedom, cultural reality, and political necessity. Other questions of general interest include: What does one gain by trying to understand a work of art? Are one's own emotional responses important to appreciate art? Of what use is it to evaluate works of art?

In what follows we first describe how the readings within each section and subsection are set out to explore these issues of value and significance. We then suggest how a number of cross-cutting themes might be identified and further pursued.

1. Themes of Value

(i) Aesthetic perceptions

It may seem appropriate for the first part of an anthology on aesthetics to address what is 'the aesthetic'. The aesthetic is put forward as a value, and accounts have been given of the value the concept is supposed to describe. There are, potentially, multiple aesthetics both within the tradition of Western philosophy and among diverse cultural traditions. The everyday meaning of 'aesthetics' comprises studies of beauty or the aesthetic, taste, and art. Yet many theories of 'aesthetics' are designed to stress the differences, even the oppositions, between art and the aesthetic.

Accounts of art and aesthetic experience will normally take the two to overlap in important ways. Though these ideas overlap, they are not identical: few would deny that nature can produce both the most beautiful and repulsive things, while many would agree that there are works of fine art that derive little of their value from beauty. For one of the authors in Section I, the aesthetic is primarily the artistic; for another it is exclusively artistic, so nature takes its beauties by being experienced through art. By contrast, a third author treats visual artworks as kinds of aesthetic objects among others, both natural and artificial, and still another argues the case for an aesthetics of nature that is not based on paradigms established within the world of art. This debate about the relationships between the aesthetic and art surfaces throughout later parts of the collection—indeed, often as a main theme.

Even on its own, separate from the topic of art, the idea of aesthetics is controversial. Historically 'the aesthetic' appeared as a reformulation of ideas about beauty. It then became a replacement for them: as revealed today even in one everyday use of the term 'aesthetic' to denote cosmetology, a name deriving from 'cosmos', denoting a beauty-enhancing order. On some ancient traditions, beauty, and the perception of beauty, are of cosmic importance. Beauty was and is often associated with delight in perception, yet its older and abiding meaning, associated with order, attributes to it greater significance. In sharp contrast, the 'aesthetic' interpretation of beauty and fineness, as represented in more modern readings, has tended to denote one perceptual pleasure beside others. Thus the effort of modern theories has been, overwhelmingly, to identify that kind of delight, to theorize about its sources, and to estimate its worth among other values.

A view that sees the worth of the aesthetic as superseding all others is what we usually call 'aestheticism', a phenomenon strangely neglected in most treatments of philosophical aesthetics. It is represented here mainly by Oscar Wilde. Aestheticism is known not only for the value it sets on certain kinds of experiences, but equally for how it values a person's discriminative capacities, or sensibilities, for having such experiences. Indeed, the modern notion of 'the aesthetic' may itself be understood as an aspect of 'taste', as defined by Voltaire, like others of the time, as a perceptual accomplishment: taste is 'that perception of beauties and deformities in all the arts; a quick discernment that anticipates reflection, relishes the good, rejects the contrary, and requires force of habit to give it fixed and uniform determination.' There are many different types of perceptual skills, and different ones can be exercised on the same objects, resulting in very different kinds of experiences, each of which has aesthetic validity. Perceptual skills are exercised in the artworld as in other aspects of life. While, to the traditional Masai, the ability to estimate and admire cattle is very important, to the Innu or to a rapper it is probably not.

An important initiative of this collection is to draw attention to the neglected field of multiple aesthetics. Most treatments speak of 'the' aesthetic, as opposed to 'the' practical, 'the' ethical, etc., passing over the different aesthetics that characterize different societies, groups, individuals, or individual styles. In Section I.b. we present evocative accounts of forms of Japanese aesthetics, another of native people of North America, a version of Nietzsche's opposition of Apollonian and Dionysian sensibilities, as well as an investigation of gender sensibility to indicate how broad the field for investigation can be. The term 'an aesthetic' has another standard meaning, that of denoting distinctive artistic principles of form, exemplified here in an essay presenting a photography and film aesthetic.

(ii) The idea of art

It is common for aesthetics collections to present readings under the rubric 'What is art?', and this question is often presented as the most important problem of theoretical interest in aesthetics or philosophy of art. Over a dozen extracts throughout this collection argue substantive answers to that contested question. Yet our approach in Section II is to focus on the neglected question that logically precedes it: Why does it matter to us that something is a work of art? The question 'What is art?' would hardly provoke such wide interest unless it mattered whether something is or is not art.

Something's being art often does matter to us, as does our own ability to appreciate that something is art. Furthermore, to think of oneself as an artist, to prove oneself to be one (or even to be artistic) is an attainment, and perceived as such in most parts of the world today. The historical perspectives provided in Sections II and III, working from the mid-eighteenth century towards the present, show the philosophy of art to consist in attempts to rethink, in relevant ways, very basic questions of the personal and social values of a place and time. Understanding those values requires the work of historians, social scientists, artists, and critics, as well as those of philosophers.

Thus, any philosophical study of the idea of art, or of a kind of art, such as music, the novel, poetry, drama, dance, painting, needs to consider the practices, traditions, and institutions that sustain it. Paul Oskar Kristeller argues that the development of the modern idea of the fine arts occurred at a time when collections and presentations of various arts were becoming more widely available to a much larger public. Not all works of art are like the pyramids of the world: most of them vanish. Where not all we value can be saved, the fraction saved has added significance. Simply preserving things as works of art involves efforts expressive of value; as such, preservation is always selective and often requires large investments of time and money. Contemporary philosophy of art has become increasingly reflective about the values expressed and reinforced by institutions and practices of art collection and presentation, including museums, concerts, film archives, musical notation and recordings, and so forth.

(iii) Expression: self, society, freedom and creativity

In a treatment of 'the diversity of cultures', the anthropologist Ruth Benedict quoted an Amerindian: 'God gave to every people a cup, a cup of clay, and from this cup they drank their life ... Our cup is broken now. It has passed away.' What we now call the arts and aesthetic(s) of a society, like its languages, technologies, beliefs, manners, ceremonies, games, food, and history, are often basic to that society's sense of identity and self-value. Arts thus are self-expressive in that important and much contested way, for ancient, well-developed, and widely recognized societies, as well as for brief and local groups and 'subcultures'. When languages, practices, historical memories, artistic processes are lost or destroyed—inadvertently or by policy and design—such societies may be weakened or destroyed. They may also be strengthened in ways that enable them to survive in a changing world. Similar claims might be made about the more usual idea of individuals engaging in self-expression when certain memories and activities are conceived of as fundamental to their own identities. Nevertheless, individuals, societies, and cultures inexorably change, absorbing from others and discarding aspects of their former selves. Self-expression through art is a phenomenon of many values inextricably enmeshed—of self, of society, of the processes and products of society and self—none of which can be identified in total disregard of the others.

Self-expression understood as an aspect of arts and cultures brings in train notorious difficulties about the understanding of the term 'cultures'. One of the immediate issues for the philosophy of art and aesthetics to which this collection repeatedly points is that of variation within cultures: the historical facts that there are high and low cultures within societies worldwide, that cultures change, and that there are multicultural societies—and that cultures are increasingly, affected by globalization. With the development and spread of the idea of fine art throughout the world, fine arts have become not only self-defining features of societies, but also symbolic means by which societies (or their official representatives), would present themselves to other societies. Not surprisingly, the problems of whose artistic expressions express which society are real, value-laden, and difficult. One of the aims of the collection is to open up these issues for more sustained attention than they have previously received in the field of philosophical aesthetics. Section III is the focus for this project, but extracts from all the other sections bear on it.

(iv) Appreciating art

Though discussion of the natures and values of the aesthetic, an aesthetic art, and self-expression may be a common part of life, most people probably come to the field of philosophical aesthetics because of their appreciation of particular works and kinds of art, such as music or film. Appreciation encompasses the trio of topics that constitutes the second half of the reader: interpretation, emotional response and involvement, evaluation. It is normal to encounter disagreements about what a work means; philosophically, such disagreements lead to questions about the very point, possibility, and validity of interpretations. Indeed, the enormous growth of commentaries, of explanatory and critical practices, and of art institutions in recent times is overwhelming, and has produced a reaction that questions the appropriateness of any interpretative apparatus at all. Selections in Section IV present not merely different conceptions of interpretation or understanding, but also ideas about why it is important to understand an artwork in a particular way, and what one would be missing if one lacked such understanding. The multiple aesthetics introduced in Section I are balanced in Section IV by what we might call multiple epistemics. The challenge is not to sort through all theories of interpretation to decide on which is the one that is right, but to see how each conception of understanding provides a different perspective and alternative experience of works of art. Section IV reflects tensions evident elsewhere in the readings, between approaches that are more perceptual and those that are more cognitive, those that are more audience-based and those that are more artist-based, and those that are more socially, culturally, or historically embedded and those that are more individualistic.

Voltaire's requirement that 'beauty must be felt as well as perceived' may sound quaint to modern ears, but having insightful interpretations about a work of art by any standard presented in Section IV would hardly ever count as sufficient for appreciating it. One may understand a joke even if one is not

amused by it; one may even think it is a good joke. But appreciating something, whether it is a joke, or a film, or a new socket wrench seems to require
not merely understanding but involvement: using it, even imagining using it,
in ways that enable one to experience, that is, appreciate, how good (or bad) it
is. Section V contributes to the theme of valuing art—and valuing our understanding of art—by looking at perceptions, feelings, and emotions produced
through audience participation. Perception itself is an active process, even
when it involves unpleasant or disturbing experiences. 'This suspense is
terrible. I hope it will last', and 'I don't like novels that end happily; they
depress me so much', are well-known lines by Oscar Wilde. The range of
experiences considered appropriate by the authors of selections in this section
extends far beyond the pleasing visual experience implied by the everyday use
of 'aesthetic'. They include or make reference to some of the most profound
and disturbing, yet also some of the most joyous and reinforcing, experiences
people can have. Emotional responses to and participation in art, together
with communication and discussion about art, are ways of constructing and
participating in communities of various sorts.

It is natural that not only perceptions, responses, and interpretations of an
artwork will show variation among individuals, but that evaluative judgements will vary also. Discussions of such differences can be endless, and raise
questions about what is the value of evaluation itself: How does one benefit
from discussing the artistic or aesthetic quality of an artwork? The purposes
of discussion and criticism, whether by interested individuals or professional
critics, are inextricable from issues of value that are emphasized throughout
the reader: with conceptions of the aesthetic and perceptions of works of art,
the value of expression to an individual and within a culture or society, the
nature and value of understanding an artwork, and of responding emotionally to it.

2. Other Themes

Many of the selections in this reader have been heavily edited, in part to focus
on those portions of a book or essay that contribute to the issues identified for
each of its six sections. In addition, shorter selections make it possible for a
greater number of points of view to be represented when they clearly have
relevance to the issues raised. For example, Li Kung-lin comments on expression, Schapiro explores limitations of a certain concept of form, Tanizaki
describes an aesthetic that he associates with pre-World War II Japan. Thus,
historians of the arts, anthropologists, and literary theorists working from a
wide range of cultural backgrounds contribute to a set of dialogues that aim
to understand the values and meanings of art, artistry, and experiences
naturally described as aesthetic. By embedding such selections within philosophical contexts we hope to show that philosophy of art and aesthetics is

enriched by specialist knowledge about a variety of cultures. By exploring the concepts they employ, we hope to foster greater reciprocal understanding about what in the Western world is called 'art', 'artistic', and 'aesthetic', and ideas that go by other names in other traditions.

Selections can be unified in ways that intersect the groupings. Besides well representing definitions of art, the anthology is, first, particularly strong in philosophical considerations of art and culture, society, and politics, as there is hardly a section without serious treatment of those topics. Second, ideas about representation receive extensive treatment in selections from Bell, Ziff, Wilde, Nochlin, Roemer, Kristeller, Batteux, d'Alembert, Pollock, Mill, d'Azevedo, Geertz, Hegel, Hsieh Ho, Elliott, Baxandall, Walton, and Berger. Third, 'form' is particularly well represented by Bell, Carlson, Dewey, Nietzsche, Taylor, Roemer, Geertz, Hegel, Baxandall, Schapiro, Isenberg. Fourth, a unit of debate about art and craft could include aspects of Ziff, Dewey, Kristeller, Batteux, d'Alembert, d'Azevedo, Kant, Poe, and Collingwood. Fifth, a continuous historical reader can be formed from Sections II and III, with classic works added from the other parts. Sixth, in the excerpts and section introductions we attempted to represent empathy and the understanding of others through art, for example, in the selections from Okakura, Tanizaki, Nietzsche, Taylor, Roemer, Higgins, Karp, Geertz, Mill, Tolstoy, Hegel, Collingwood, Wollheim, Baxandall, Elliott, Walton, Nussbaum, and Berger. We are confident that readers will discover additional substantively represented topics.

Finally, the extracts are written in a variety of styles. Besides providing interesting information and interpretations, authors typically attempt to draw insightful distinctions and to frame new conceptions. Often, of course, they provide reasons or evidence to show, logically, why their conclusions are reasonable, and hence why we should accept them. Such arguments may be direct. They may also work indirectly, by stating a problem and arguing against alternative solutions to it, so that theirs solution appears to be best. Arguments in either style usually depend upon interpretations of significant examples, which we have done our best to include.

Sometimes, however, authors write in ways that exemplify the attitudes they advocate, and thereby have the potential to get readers into the position of those who hold them, better to perceive things from such perspectives. For example, the different styles of Wilde, Nietzsche, Okakura, Tanizaki, Batteux, and Barthes enable readers to imagine for themselves distinctive styles of perception. Stylistic characteristics of other selections have significance as well. For example, Bell writes warmly and passionately about 'the cold white peaks of art', responses to which, on his view, are divorced from ordinary emotions. Cohen, drawing an analogy between jokes and art, argues that some jokes both presume and reinforce communities of understanding and experience. As he carefully attributes the sources of the examples he uses, the very footnotes to the paper present its author as participating in a community of friends and acquaintances, not merely philosophers, who understand and assist one another.

The extracts in this book are therefore selected and arranged as encounters with lively minds, pursuing a connected series of issues in aesthetics, all of which focus on questions of value, thereby casting even the most standard readings in new lights. We hope that reading this collection will stimulate, extend, and challenge readers' own thoughts about such questions, and that it will present new possibilities for understanding the arts and varieties of experiences thought of as aesthetic.

Why Describe Anything as Aesthetic?

INTRODUCTION

How do you use the word 'aesthetic'? Some people use it to refer to an object's visually pleasing properties or to what is beautiful, reflecting a concern with the way something looks. Others place less emphasis on the visual, and have used it to refer to what they take to be an important and valuable aspect of human experience, including our experiences of nature, the fine arts, and various aspects of ordinary life. These ordinary employments of 'aesthetic' have their counterparts in writings on philosophical aesthetics. As one might expect, there is no universal agreement about what the aesthetic is, much less why it is valuable.

The opening selection from Clive Bell is one of the most widely known investigations of the topic. Addressing only aesthetic responses to the visual arts, Bell passionately defends the view that we have a special emotion, aesthetic emotion, in response to lines, shapes, and colour when they exhibit 'significant form'. Though Bell says at one point that there is no objective basis for aesthetic judgements—that is, no basis in the properties the object has—it is nevertheless clear that he believes some aesthetic judgements are true (or false), and not merely 'true for me' or 'true for you'.

Bell introduces the concept of the aesthetic in relation to art. As noted, in normal usage 'aesthetic' is not so restricted. Paul Ziff carries the common view to a challenging extreme, maintaining that any sort of thing can be viewed aesthetically—a Leonardo portrait, a sunset, even dried dung. There are several possible explanations why someone might not find something worth attending to aesthetically; Ziff is never content simply to blame the object. Explanations may have to do with the person (one's tastes and preferences, psychological dispositions and anxieties, desires, values, and knowledge), the actions one performs in relation to the object, or the conditions under which one experiences the aesthetic object. These four sets of variables in aesthetic situations do not result in complete value relativism; according to Ziff, value judgements about the objects themselves can be made. For example, if one is interested in colour, a Vuillard painting is more worth attending to aesthetically than a Manet: different objects will better reward different kinds of attention.

Allen Carlson uses Ziff's approach to address important issues concerning the value of the natural environment, where he finds art-based models misleading. Unlike most art, Carlson argues, nature typically provides us an environment rather than objects for perceptual inspection. Thus, to treat nature as only a landscape (a scene to be viewed) or to isolate individual objects from nature (a crystal or a flower) is not to appreciate nature aesthetically, but only some manipulated portion of it. Still, aesthetic appreciation of nature, like that of art, requires understanding and knowledge so that we can identify what the objects and aspects of the experience are.

Paul Ziff once suggested that we could look at nature as if it were art (what Carlson refers to as the Object of Art model): 'Artists teach us to look at the world in new ways. Look at a Mondrian, then look at the world as though it were a Mondrian and you will see what I mean. To do this, you must know how to look at a Mondrian.' He thus inverts the commonplace that you look at art to see a copy or imitation of the world. This inversion was celebrated by Oscar Wilde towards the end of the nineteenth century. Wilde was part of a movement called 'aestheticism' which held, like Ziff, that anything could be a fit object of aesthetic attention.

Wilde also took to task the view that an artwork expresses the spirit of the age in which it was produced. That an artwork expresses the spirit of an age is a view associated especially with Leo Tolstoy, an excerpt from whom is included in Part III, and versions of which are developed by Clifford Geertz and others in II.a. By contrast, Wilde writes: 'The Japanese people are the deliberate self-conscious creation of certain individual artists', anticipating late twentieth-century authors who criticize the ways Europeans and Americans have represented other cultures. (See, for example, the selection below in II.b by Ivan Karp.)

According to John Dewey, aestheticism—as separating, and claiming priority for, one set of values over all others—reflects fragmentation in a society's values. On Dewey's philosophy, the aesthetic does not signify a distinct, competing realm of experience. It is rather the consummate form of many kinds of experiences: biological, practical, ethical, intellectual, religious, political. In most societies the arts arise in affirmation of the aesthetic as it occurs in all these spheres. For Dewey, sharply separating what he calls the standpoints of artists and audiences would mean a loss of wholeness in aesthetic experience.

Sometimes 'aesthetic' functions as a noun: we attribute an aesthetic to an individual or group. Two excerpts from Japanese sources eloquently express how segments of historical cultures, as well as individuals, can be characterized with regard to their aesthetic sensibilities, which may be so tightly woven with other values that the explanation of the one is impossible without exposition of the other. For example, Kakuzo Okakura describes aspects of the Japanese tea ceremony, the cultural role of tea, different 'schools' or ways of thinking about tea, the tea ceremony's connection with Taoism and Zen Buddhism, requirements for the tea-room, the role of flowers in the ceremony, and finally the way a tea master serves as a model of how to conduct one's life. Such elaborate philosophies and rituals and ideas about values and human life are all embedded within an 'aesthetic' of tea, and the more one is familiar with these ideas, so that they infuse and affect the experience one has of taking tea, the more one is able to experience this particular kind of aesthetic. In the selection included here, Okakura describes the tea-room and how to respond to its materials, structure, and location in the process of the tea ceremony.

Jun'ichirō Tanizaki writes in pre-World War II Japan to record an aesthetic that he sees fast fading in the glare of Western technological influences. Not a defined ritual or nameable philosophy, but rather an attitude to sense perception, particularly to vision, expressed through valuing what softly gleams from a matrix of shadows, is presented by this wry, sensitive novelist of modern life. Tanizaki's aesthetic applies to many everyday tools and procedures: the importance of shadow in architecture; the look, sound, and absorbency of writing paper; the action of pen as opposed to brush; and preference for dark, lustrous woods and laquerware.

Multiple 'aesthetics' do not emerge exclusively from different cultural viewpoints. For example, not all Japanese scholars might agree with Tanizaki's analysis of Japanese culture, and Western civilization exhibits many different 'aesthetics', as well. Nietzsche identified two of them, the Apollonian and Dionysian. Very roughly, most of the selections so far have exhibited the Apollonian ideal—beautiful, ordered, something presented as if for our pleasure. By contrast, the Dionysian is engaged, ecstatic, and frenzied, driven by one's individuality, energy, and desire. Nietzsche believed that there is no truth independent of a personal perspective, and hence abandoned any search for rationality and objectivity as illusory goals. His is an aesthetic of participation—not merely viewing a play, but enacting it oneself; not listening to music, but singing it; not watching dancers but dancing. Nietzsche's own style of writing embodies the Dionysian ideal; in one memorable passage he says, 'I write with my blood.'

Working from an interpretative background affected by Nietzsche's dualism of (Apollonian) controlled forms and (Dionysian) impulses to form-obliterating rhythms, Joshua Taylor observes that the decorative aesthetic of native peoples of the North American Northwest Coast provides a surprising coincidence—rather than an attempted reconciliation—of the two motives. There the 'proportional relationships of clearly defined forms' and a ceaseless continuity of movement 'with little concern for beginnings and endings' blurs 'the difference between object and mind, the outer and inner'. The forms also blur the distinction between perceiver and participant in having eyes that seem to look back at us; the viewer is viewed and thus becomes not merely an observer of pictorial forms but also a participant in a process.

Since what one sees, how things look, is affected by one's knowledge, beliefs, and interests, 'an aesthetic' may reflect a psychologically, culturally, or even politically distinctive point of view. Linda Nochlin's discussion of several nineteenth-century French paintings enables us to see how they reflected and reinforced certain assumptions about social roles for women. Describing a feminist point of view such as Nochlin's as providing one more 'aesthetic' is highly controversial. That a feminist point of view can constitute 'an aesthetic' arises out of the position that 'an aesthetic' should not be restricted to the formalist views of Clive Bell and its cousins, but extended to refer to ways of seeing and experiencing things that embody many different attitudes and interests.

Finally, 'an aesthetic' may identify a distinctive approach to a particular art. Michael Roemer argues that the motion picture (and television) medium requires such an aesthetic. This principle is based upon a well-known characteristic of photographic images: 'the medium's capacity for finding meaning in the detail of everyday life'—detail, Roemer writes, of the 'ordinary surfaces' of things. He argues that this characteristic sets camera arts apart from theatre, drawing audiences into a distinctive kind of imaginative 'participation'. Roemer is here representative of artists and theorists of other modern forms who have presented their approaches in terms of alleged basic 'aesthetics' of their media—providing one of the meanings of the controversial phrase 'aesthetic formalism'.

I. a. The Aesthetic

CLIVE BELL

1 The Aesthetic Hypothesis

[handwritten: Experiential]

The starting-point for all systems of aesthetics must be the personal experience of a peculiar emotion. The objects that provoke this emotion we call works of art. All sensitive people agree that there is a peculiar emotion provoked by works of art. I do not mean, of course, that all works provoke the same emotion. On the contrary, every work produces a different emotion. But all these emotions are recognisably the same in kind; so far, at any rate, the best opinion is on my side. That there is a particular kind of emotion provoked by works of visual art, and that this emotion is provoked by every kind of visual art, by pictures, sculptures, buildings, pots, carvings, textiles, &c., &c., is not disputed, I think, by anyone capable of feeling it. This emotion is called the aesthetic emotion; and if we can discover some quality common and peculiar to all the objects that provoke it, we shall have solved what I take to be the central problem of aesthetics. We shall have discovered the essential quality in a work of art, the quality that distinguishes works of art from all other classes of objects. *[handwritten right margin: Visual Art genre]*

For either all works of visual art have some common quality, or when we speak of 'works of art' we gibber. Everyone speaks of 'art,' making a mental classification by which he distinguishes the class 'works of art' from all other classes. What is the justification of this classification? What is the quality common and peculiar to all members of this class? Whatever it be, no doubt it is often found in company with other qualities; but they are adventitious—it is essential. There must be some one quality without which a work of art cannot exist; possessing which, in the least degree, no work is altogether worthless. What is this quality? What quality is shared by all objects that provoke our aesthetic emotions? What quality is common to Sta Sophia and the windows at Chartres, Mexican sculpture, a Persian bowl, Chinese carpets, Giotto's frescoes at Padua, and the masterpieces of Poussin, Piero della Francesca, and Cézanne? Only one answer seems possible—significant form. In each, lines and colours combined in a particular way, certain forms and relations of forms, stir our aesthetic emotions. These relations and combinations of lines and colours, these aesthetically moving forms, I call 'Significant Form'; and 'Significant Form' is the one quality common to all works of visual art. *[handwritten right margin: Its main question]*

At this point it may be objected that I am making aesthetics a purely subjective business, since my only data are personal experiences of a particular emotion. It will be said that the objects that provoke this emotion vary with each individual, and that therefore a system of aesthetics can have no objective validity. It must be replied that any system of aesthetics which pretends to be based on some objective truth is so palpably ridiculous as not to be worth discussing. We have no other means of recognising a work of art than our feeling for it. The objects that provoke aesthetic emotion vary with each individual. Aesthetic judgments are, as the saying goes, matters of taste; and about tastes, as everyone is proud to admit, there is no disputing. A good critic may be able to make me see in a picture that had left me cold things that I had overlooked, till at last, receiving the aesthetic emotion, I recognise it as a work of art. To be continually pointing out those parts, the sum, or rather the combination, of which unite to produce significant form, is the function of criticism. But it is useless for a critic to tell me that something is a work of art; he must make me feel it for myself. This he can do only by making me see; he must get at my emotions through my eyes. Unless he can make me see something that moves me, he cannot force my emotions. I have no right to consider anything a work of art to which I cannot react emotionally; and I have no right to look for the essential quality in anything that I have not *felt* to be a work of art. The critic can affect my aesthetic theories only by affecting my aesthetic experience. All systems of aesthetics must be based on personal experience—that is to say, they must be subjective.

Yet, though all aesthetic theories must be based on aesthetic judgments, and ultimately all aesthetic judgments must be matters of personal taste, it would be rash to assert that no theory of aesthetics can have general validity. For, though A, B, C, D are the works that move me, and A, D, E, F the works that move you, it may well be that x is the only quality believed by either of us to be common to all the works in his list. We may all agree about aesthetics, and yet differ about particular works of art. We may differ as to the presence or absence of the quality x. My immediate object will be to show that significant form is the only quality common and peculiar to all the works of visual art that move me; and I will ask those whose aesthetic experience does not tally with mine to see whether this quality is not also, in their judgment, common to all works that move them, and whether they can discover any other quality of which the same can be said. [. . .]

'Are you forgetting about colour?' someone inquires. Certainly not; my term 'significant form' included combinations of lines and of colours. The distinction between form and colour is an unreal one; you cannot conceive a colourless line or a colourless space; neither can you conceive a formless relation of colours. In a black and white drawing the spaces are all white and all are bounded by black lines; in most oil paintings the spaces are multi-coloured and so are the boundaries; you cannot imagine a boundary line without any content, or a content without a boundary line. Therefore, when I speak of significant form, I mean a combination of lines and colours (counting white and black as colours) that moves me aesthetically.

Some people may be surprised at my not having called this 'beauty.' Of course, to those who define beauty as 'combinations of lines and colours that provoke aesthetic emotion,' I willingly concede the right of substituting their word for mine. But most of us, however strict we may be, are apt to apply the epithet 'beautiful' to objects that do not provoke that peculiar emotion produced by works of art. Everyone, I suspect, has called a butterfly or a flower beautiful. Does anyone feel the same kind of emotion for a butterfly or a flower that he feels for a cathedral or a picture? Surely, it is not what I call an aesthetic emotion that most of us feel, generally, for natural beauty. I shall suggest, later, that some people may, occasionally, see in nature what we see in art, and feel for her an aesthetic emotion; but I am satisfied that, as a rule, most people feel a very different kind of emotion for birds and flowers and the wings of butterflies from that which they feel for pictures, pots, temples and statues. Why these beautiful things do not move us as works of art move us is another, and not an aesthetic, question. For our immediate purpose we have to discover only what quality is common to objects that do move us as works of art. In the last part of this chapter, when I try to answer the question— 'Why are we so profoundly moved by some combinations of lines and colours?' I shall hope to offer an acceptable explanation of why we are less profoundly moved by others. [. . .]

The hypothesis that significant form is the essential quality in a work of art has at least one merit denied to many more famous and more striking—it does help to explain things. We are all familiar with pictures that interest us and excite our admiration, but do not move us as works of art. To this class belongs what I call 'Descriptive Painting'—that is, painting in which forms are used not as objects of emotion, but as means of suggesting emotion or conveying information. Portraits of psychological and historical value, topographical works, pictures that tell stories and suggest situations, illustrations of all sorts, belong to this class. That we all recognise the distinction is clear, for who has not said that such and such a drawing was excellent as illustration, but as a work of art worthless? Of course many descriptive pictures possess, amongst other qualities, formal significance, and are therefore works of art: but many more do not. They interest us; they may move us too in a hundred different ways, but they do not move us aesthetically. According to my hypothesis they are not works of art. They leave untouched our aesthetic emotions because it is not their forms but the ideas or information suggested or conveyed by their forms that affect us.

Few pictures are better known or liked than Frith's *Paddington Station*; certainly I should be the last to grudge it its popularity. Many a weary forty minutes have I whiled away disentangling its fascinating incidents and forging for each an imaginary past and an improbable future. But certain though it is that Frith's masterpiece, or engravings of it, have provided thousands with half-hours of curious and fanciful pleasure, it is not less certain that no one has experienced before it one half-second of aesthetic rapture—and this although the picture contains several pretty passages of colour, and is by no means badly painted. *Paddington Station* is not a work of art; it is an interesting and amusing document. In it line and colour are used to recount anecdotes, suggest ideas, and indicate the manners and customs of an age: they are not used to provoke aesthetic emotion. Forms and the relations of forms were for Frith not objects of emotion, but means of suggesting emotion and conveying ideas.

The ideas and information conveyed by *Paddington Station* are so amusing and so well presented that the picture has considerable value and is well worth preserving. But, with the perfection of photographic processes and of the cinematograph, pictures of this sort are becoming otiose. Who doubts that one of those *Daily Mirror* photographers in collaboration with a *Daily Mail* reporter can tell us far more about 'London day by day' than any Royal Academician? For an account of manners and fashions we shall go, in future, to photographs, supported by a little bright journalism, rather than to descriptive painting. [. . .] Therefore it must be confessed that pictures in the Frith tradition are grown superfluous; they merely waste the hours of able men who might be more profitably employed in works of a wider beneficence. Still, they are not unpleasant, which is more than can be said for that kind of descriptive painting of which *The Doctor* is the most flagrant example. Of course *The Doctor* is not a work of art. In it form is not used as an object of emotion, but as a means of suggesting emotions. This alone suffices to make it nugatory; it is worse than nugatory because the emotion it suggests is false. What it suggests is not pity and admiration but a sense of complacency in our own pitifulness and generosity. It is sentimental. Art is above morals, or, rather, all art is moral because, as I hope to show presently, works of art are immediate means to good. Once we have judged a thing a work of art, we have judged it ethically of the first importance and put it beyond the reach of the moralist. But descriptive pictures which are not works of art, and, therefore, are not necessarily means to good states of mind, are proper objects of the ethical philosopher's attention. Not being a work of art, *The Doctor* has none of the immense ethical value possessed by all objects that provoke aesthetic ecstasy; and the state of mind to which it is a means, as illustration, appears to me undesirable. [. . .]

Most people who care much about art find that of the work that moves them most the greater part is what scholars call 'Primitive.' Of course there are bad primitives. For instance, I remember going, full of enthusiasm, to see one of the earliest Romanesque churches in Poitiers (Notre-Dame-la-Grande), and finding it as ill-proportioned, over-decorated, coarse, fat and heavy as any better class building by one of those highly civilised architects who flourished a thousand years earlier or eight hundred later. But such exceptions are rare. As a rule primitive art is good—and here again my hypothesis is helpful—for, as a rule, it is also free from descriptive qualities.

In primitive art you will find no accurate representation; you will find only significant form. Yet no other art moves us so profoundly. Whether we consider Sumerian sculpture or pre-dynastic Egyptian art, or archaic Greek, or the Wei and T'ang masterpieces, or those early Japanese works of which I had the luck to see a few superb examples (especially two wooden Bodhisattvas) at the Shepherd's Bush Exhibition in 1910, or whether, coming nearer home, we consider the primitive Byzantine art of the sixth century and its primitive developments amongst the Western barbarians, or, turning far afield, we consider that mysterious and majestic art that flourished in Central and South America before the coming of the white men, in every case we observe three common characteristics—absence of representation, absence of technical swagger, sublimely impressive form. Nor is it hard to discover the connection between these three. Formal significance loses itself in preoccupation with exact representation and ostentatious cunning. [. . .]

Let no one imagine that representation is bad in itself; a realistic form may be as significant, in its place as part of the design, as an abstract. But if a representative form has value, it is as form, not as representation. The representative element in a work of art may or may not be harmful; always it is irrelevant. For, to appreciate a work of art we need bring with us nothing from life, no knowledge of its ideas and affairs, no familiarity with its emotions. Art transports us from the world of man's activity to a world of aesthetic exaltation. For a moment we are shut off from human interests; our anticipations and memories are arrested; we are lifted above the stream of life. The pure mathematician rapt in his studies knows a state of mind which I take to be similar, if not identical. He feels an emotion for his speculations which arises from no perceived relation between them and the lives of men, but springs, inhuman or super-human, from the heart of an abstract science. I wonder, sometimes, whether the appreciators of art and of mathematical solutions are not even more closely allied. Before we feel an aesthetic emotion for a combination of forms, do we not perceive intellectually the rightness and necessity of the combination? If we do, it would explain the fact that passing rapidly through a room we recognise a picture to be good, although we cannot say that it has provoked much emotion. We seem to have recognised intellectually the rightness of its forms without staying to fix our attention, and collect, as it were, their emotional significance. If this were so, it would be permissible to inquire whether it was the forms themselves or our perception of their rightness and necessity that caused aesthetic emotion. But I do not think I need linger to discuss the matter here. I have been inquiring why certain combinations of forms move us; I should not have travelled by other roads had I enquired, instead, why certain combinations are perceived to be right and necessary, and why our perception of their rightness and necessity is moving. What I have to say is this: the rapt philosopher, and he who contemplates a work of art, inhabit a world with an intense and peculiar significance of its own; that significance is unrelated to the significance of life.

In this world the emotions of life find no place. It is a world with emotions of
its own.

To appreciate a work of art we need bring with us nothing but a sense of
form and colour and a knowledge of three-dimensional space. That bit of
knowledge, I admit, is essential to the appreciation of many great works, since
many of the most moving forms ever created are in three dimensions. To see
a cube or a rhomboid as a flat pattern is to lower its significance, and a sense
of three-dimensional space is essential to the full appreciation of most
architectural forms. Pictures which would be insignificant if we saw them
as flat patterns are profoundly moving because, in fact, we see them as related
planes. If the representation of three-dimensional space is to be called 'representation,' then I agree that there is one kind of representation which is not
irrelevant. Also, I agree that along with our feeling for line and colour we
must bring with us our knowledge of space if we are to make the most of
every kind of form. Nevertheless, there are magnificent designs to an appreciation of which this knowledge is not necessary: so, though it is not
irrelevant to the appreciation of some works of art it is not essential to the
appreciation of all. What we must say is that the representation of three-
dimensional space is neither irrelevant nor essential to all art, and that every
other sort of representation is irrelevant.

[. . .] Before a work of art people who feel little or no emotion for pure
form find themselves at a loss. They are deaf men at a concert. They know
that they are in the presence of something great, but they lack the power of
apprehending it. [. . .] Instead of going out on the stream of art into a new
world of aesthetic experience, they turn a sharp corner and come straight
home to the world of human interests. For them the significance of a work of
art depends on what they bring to it; no new thing is added to their lives, only
the old material is stirred. A good work of visual art carries a person who is
capable of appreciating it out of life into ecstasy: to use art as a means to the
emotions of life is to use a telescope for reading the news. You will notice that
people who cannot feel pure aesthetic emotions remember pictures by their
subjects; where as people who can, as often as not, have no idea what the
subject of a picture is. They have never noticed the representative element,
and so when they discuss pictures they talk about the shapes of forms and the
relations and quantities of colours. Often they can tell by the quality of a
single line whether or not a man is a good artist. They are concerned only
with lines and colours, their relations and quantities and qualities; but from
these they win an emotion more profound and far more sublime than any
that can be given by the description of facts and ideas.

This last sentence has a very confident ring—over-confident, some may
think. Perhaps I shall be able to justify it, and make my meaning clearer too, if
I give an account of my own feelings about music. I am not really musical. I
do not understand music well. I find musical form exceedingly difficult to

apprehend, and I am sure that the profounder subtleties of harmony and rhythm more often than not escape me. The form of a musical composition must be simple indeed if I am to grasp it honestly. My opinion about music is not worth having. Yet, sometimes, at a concert, though my appreciation of the music is limited and humble, it is pure. Sometimes, though I have poor understanding, I have a clean palate. Consequently, when I am feeling bright and clear and intent, at the beginning of a concert for instance, when something that I can grasp is being played, I get from music that pure aesthetic emotion that I get from visual art. It is less intense, and the rapture is evanescent; I understand music too ill for music to transport me far into the world of pure aesthetic ecstasy. But at moments I do appreciate music as pure musical form, as sounds combined according to the laws of a mysterious necessity, as pure art with a tremendous significance of its own and no relation whatever to the significance of life; and in those moments I lose myself in that infinitely sublime state of mind to which pure visual form transports me. How inferior is my normal state of mind at a concert. Tired or perplexed, I let slip my sense of form, my aesthetic emotion collapses, and I begin weaving into the harmonies, that I cannot grasp, the ideas of life. Incapable of feeling the austere emotions of art, I begin to read into the musical forms human emotions of terror and mystery, love and hate, and spend the minutes, pleasantly enough, in a world of turbid and inferior feeling. At such times, were the grossest pieces of onomatopoeic representation—the song of a bird, the galloping of horses, the cries of children, or the laughing of demons—to be introduced into the symphony, I should not be offended. Very likely I should be pleased; they would afford new points of departure for new trains of romantic feeling or heroic thought. I know very well what has happened. I have been using art as a means to the emotions of life and reading into it the ideas of life. I have been cutting blocks with a razor. I have tumbled from the superb peaks of aesthetic exaltation to the snug foothills of warm humanity. It is a jolly country. No one need be ashamed of enjoying himself there. Only no one who has ever been on the heights can help feeling a little crestfallen in the cosy valleys. And let no one imagine, because he has made merry in the warm tilth and quaint nooks of romance, that he can even guess at the austere and thrilling raptures of those who have climbed the cold, white peaks of art.

About music most people are as willing to be humble as I am. If they cannot grasp musical form and win from it a pure aesthetic emotion, they confess that they understand music imperfectly or not at all. They recognise quite clearly that there is a difference between the feeling of the musician for pure music and that of the cheerful concert-goer for what music suggests. [. . .] Is it too much to ask that others should be as honest about their feelings for pictures as I have been about mine for music? For I am certain that most of those who visit galleries do feel very much what I feel at concerts. They have their moments of pure ecstasy; but the moments are short and unsure. Soon they fall back into the world of human interests and feel emotions, good no doubt, but inferior. I do not dream of saying that what they get from art is bad or nugatory; I say that they do not get the best that art can give. I do not say that they cannot understand art; rather I say that they cannot understand the state of mind of those who understand it best. I do not say that art means nothing or little to them; I say they miss its full significance. I do not suggest for one moment that their appreciation of art is a thing to be ashamed of; the majority of the charming and intelligent people with whom I am acquainted appreciate visual art impurely; and, by the way, the appreciation of almost all great writers has been impure. But provided that there be some fraction of pure aesthetic emotion, even a mixed and minor appreciation of art is, I am sure, one of the most valuable things in the world—so valuable, indeed, that in my giddier moments I have been tempted to believe that art might prove the world's salvation.

Yet, though the echoes and shadows of art enrich the life of the plains, her spirit dwells on the mountains. To him who woos, but woos impurely, she returns enriched what is brought. Like the sun, she warms the good seed in good soil and causes it to bring forth good fruit. But only to the perfect lover does she give a new strange gift—a gift beyond all price. Imperfect lovers bring to art and take away the ideas and emotions of their own age and civilisation. In twelfth-century Europe a man might have been greatly moved by a Romanesque church and found nothing in a T'ang picture. To a man of a later age, Greek sculpture meant much and Mexican nothing, for only to the former could he bring a crowd of associated ideas to be the objects of familiar emotions. But the perfect lover, he who can feel the profound significance of form, is raised above the accidents of time and place. To him the problems of archaeology, history, and hagiography are impertinent. If the forms of a work are significant its provenance is irrelevant. Before the grandeur of those Sumerian figures in the Louvre he is carried on the same flood of emotion to the same aesthetic ecstasy as, more than four thousand years ago, the Chaldean lover was carried. It is the mark of great art that its appeal is universal and eternal.[1] Significant form stands charged with the power to provoke aesthetic emotion in anyone capable of feeling it. The ideas of men go buzz and die like gnats; men change their institutions and their customs as they change their coats; the intellectual triumphs of one age are the follies of another; only great art remains stable and unobscure. Great art remains stable and unobscure because the feelings that it awakens are independent of time and place, because its kingdom is not of this world. To those who have and hold a sense of the significance of form what does it matter whether the forms that move them were created in Paris the day before yesterday or in Babylon fifty centuries ago? The forms of art are inexhaustible; but all lead by the same road of aesthetic emotion to the same world of aesthetic ecstasy.

[*Art* (London and New York: Chatto & Windus / G. P. Putnam's Sons, 1958), 15–34. First published in 1914.]

PAUL ZIFF

2   Anything Viewed

Look at the dried dung!

What for?

If I had said 'Look at the sunset!' would you have asked 'What for?'?

People view sunsets aesthetically. Sunsets are customary objects of aesthetic attention. So are trees rocks wildflowers clouds women leaping gazelles prancing horses: all these are sometime objects of aesthetic attention. But not everything is: not soiled linen greasy dishes bleary eyes false teeth not excrement. *What makes something aesthetic? Is it beauty? No.*

Why not? It's not because they're unbeautiful or even ugly. Beautiful things are no problem for a rambling aesthetic eye but not all objects of aesthetic attention are beautiful: Grünewald's *Crucifixion* isn't neither is Picasso's *Guernica*. Brueghel's rustics aren't lovely. The stark morning light in a Hopper is powerful but it is not beautiful. Not being beautiful needn't matter.

These unbeautiful objects are works of art. By chance some objects of aesthetic attention have been naturally produced. For the rest: they are products of art.

What is a work of art? *defines for us* Something fit to be an object of aesthetic attention. Most likely nowadays (now that didactic art is largely dead) something tailor-made for the purpose designed to be just that. If you want to attend aesthetically to something fix on a work of art as your object: that's the way it's thought to be. Is a work of art the paradigm of an object fit for aesthetic attention? What does a work of art have or lack that dung doesn't?

What is a work of art? Not everything. Leonardo's portrait of Ginevra de' Benci is. A mound of dried dung isn't. Nor is an alligator at least a living gator basking in the sun on a mud bank in a swamp isn't. A reason they are not is plain: nothing is a work of art if it is not an artefact something made by man. *one reason* A gator basking a mound of dried dung are products of nature made or produced by natural forces. Not being made or produced by men they are not classed artefacts. Not being artefacts they are not classed works of art. Such is a common or the common if there is anything that is the common conception of a work of art.

Most likely there is no such thing as the common conception of a work of art: these are vague ill-defined notions. And some say that some objects that are not artefacts are nonetheless works of art. That needn't concern us: undoubtful examples of works of art are all that are wanted here and now and these are easier to come by when one considers artefacts rather than nonartefacts.

When one looks at a gator basking a mound of dried dung is one at once cognizant of the fact that not one or the other is man-made? And does such cognizance at once preclude all possibility of aesthetic attention to the gator basking the mound of dried dung? Though the gator basking is not man-made it is (to invoke the shade of Paley) remarkable in design and structure. By no stretch of the imagination can it be imagined to be less detailed rich intricate in design less complex in structure than an artefact. Given the present state of technology there's no way anyone can actually make a gator basking. But making a mound of dried dung is easy. Conjure up this image: a field in which there are two virtually identical mounds of dried dung. One was and the other was not man-made. Would that fact render the latter less accessible than the former to aesthetic attention?

Imagine this: that the Henry Moore statue at Lincoln Center was in fact not an artefact by Moore but a naturally formed that is nonman-made object found in a desert and transported to Lincoln Center. Would that matter to an appreciation of the statue? Yes enormously. Knowing that one's view of the object would be restructured: one would not in looking at the work look at it as a work. One would not look for manifestations of craftsmanship. One would not look for and see signs of the sculptor's hands: there would be none. But the object would still have shape form mass and balance. The various parts of the object would still be in the spatial relations they are in. The solidity of the volumes would remain unaltered. Nor would the expressive aspects of the object be seriously impaired if impaired at all by its lacking the status of an artefact. It would still possess those physiognomic characteristics which serve to make it an imposing impressive work. That it was not an artefact would not indicate that it was not a fit object for aesthetic attention. That something is not an artefact does not suggest let alone establish that it is therefore unfit to be an object of aesthetic attention. And unless one has a compelling narcissistic obsession with the marks of men's endeavours one can view things in the world aesthetically without being concerned with or inhibited by their lack of status as artefacts.

If a work of art is a paradigm of an object fit for aesthetic attention it is not owing to the status of a work of art as an artefact. Not that just any artefact is classed a work of art: a garden rake a screwdriver a green paper plate are not though they are undoubtful example of artefacts. What if the paper plate were on a pedestal displayed as a piece of sculpture? Would it then be classed a work of art? By some. Not by others. Even so: if one wanted an undoubtful example of a work of art wouldn't one prefer Leonardo's *Ginevra* to the paper plate? An undoubtful example of a work of art is a hand-made work a product of an art a craft: it is an artefact the production of which called for considerable and unmistakable craftsmanship. Look at Leonardo's *Ginevra*: that the craftsmanship displayed is remarkable is obvious. (And that is not belied by the fact that one may wonder whether the portrayed slight strabismus is rightly to be attributed to Ginevra herself.)

This exquisite portrait is incomparably more beautiful than any reproduction can suggest. The marvelous sense of atmosphere surrounding Ginevra, the harmonious unity of landscape and figure, and the incredible delicacy with which minute details are rendered can only be appreciated in the original painting.[1]

Reproductions rarely capture the quality of a work of art of an exquisite and refined craft. That a work does not lend itself to easy reproduction however may be owing either to its being remarkably ordered (so to speak) a product of great craftsmanship or to its being a clear manifestation of entropy. Leonardo's *Ginevra* would be difficult to copy and so would one of Pollock's typically dribbled pieces: to smash an egg is easy but to replicate the appearance of the smashed egg in all perceivable details may be impossible.

A display of craftsmanship may on occasion facilitate aesthetic attention to an object. The lack of that display in no way indicates that an object is unfit for such attention. Consider a typical work by Piet Mondriaan: one of black lines and white ground. Such a work displays virtually nothing of the painter's craft rightly so-called: a tolerably steady hand an ability to apply masking tape judiciously is about all the technical skill required to produce it. Or to reproduce it: a perfect copy would be a matter of a few hours work at most.

That works of art may be artefacts that they may be skillfully hand-made objects here doesn't signify. Figuratively and on occasion literally speaking works of art are framed objects. It is that more than anything else that makes them plausible paradigms of objects fit for aesthetic attention. But both the efficacy and the necessity of a frame are something of an illusion.

Works of art are framed mounted hung illuminated displayed exhibited. The object is supplied with a milieu an environment a background. Presumably all that facilitates aesthetic attention to the works by those concerned to appreciate them. The basic idea would seem to be this: a person *p* performs certain relevant actions *a* in connection with a work of art an entity *e* under conditions *c*. The entity *e* is supposed to be of a kind or character to facilitate and make valuable the performance of *a* by *p* under *c*. If so *e* is then a fit object for aesthetic attention. And what if *e* is dried dung? Then the performance of actions *a* by person *p* under conditions *c* in connection with *e* the dried dung is supposed to be neither facilitated nor rendered valuable by the dried dung. Hence the dried dung is not supposed to be a fit object for aesthetic attention. But obviously all this depends on the person p the actions a and the conditions c.

Aesthetic value is as it were a cooperative affair. If attending aesthetically to an object is worthwhile then the object contributes its presence and possibly the conditions under which one attends to the object contribute their share while the person contributes his: what is wanted is an harmonious relation between the person and the object. It is never the case that such harmony depends solely on the contribution of the object. For despite its presence the conditions of attention may be infelicitous: who could enjoy viewing Klee's *Twittering Machine* while being tortured? (Perhaps a *roshi*.) If both object and conditions make their contribution something about the person may occasion a difficulty: a color blind person may be cut off from an appreciation of a Matisse nude and so conceivably could one psychologically disturbed about sexual matters.

To say of something that it is worth attending to aesthetically is to speak in an abstract way. For in so saying one abstracts from reference to persons actions and the conditions under which the actions are to be performed. On occasion this abstract way of speaking is somewhat fatuous. A case in point: 'Michelangelo's Sistine Chapel murals are worth viewing.' Presumably these are great works of art. Theoretically the viewing of these works is aesthetically worthwhile. In fact it is not. It would be worthwhile if the works were not where they are if the conditions of viewing were altered for example if the Chapel were turned on its side. Where they are high up and almost out of sight they are for all save presbyopes virtually inaccessible to the performance of any relevant aesthetic action. Viewing them is literally a pain in the neck. One can recline on a bench or the floor (if the guards permit and the spectators don't trample) but that position is not conducive to aesthetic attention. Here one should keep in mind the illusion of the full moon on the horizon: the apparent size of the moon is radically reduced by turning one's back to it bending down and viewing it between one's legs with one's head upside down. Evidently the positions in which one views things can serve to alter the apparent size of the things viewed. (It is said that Frank Lloyd Wright hated paintings: that would account for the sloping floors and tilted perspectives of the Guggenheim Museum which serve effectively to sabotage any delicately balanced work.)

A work of art is supposed to retain its identity from frame to frame wall to wall room to room: those who suffer from inept framers know how silly this view is. Seurat took care at times to prepare and paint his own frames. But he could do nothing about the walls floors company his works were forced to keep. Conversely is there any doubt that dried dung displayed by the lighting engineers of the New York Museum of Modern Art could prove to be a fantastically intriguing aesthetic object? With appropriately placed lights and shadows walls of the right tint in the right position of the right height carefully proportioned pedestals anything at all that could be displayed could be a fit object for aesthetic attention.

Would it be the dried dung or the dried dung under special environing conditions that would be a fit object for aesthetic attention? Certainly at least the latter is obviously true and I think also the former but let's focus on the latter for the moment for that's the way it always is anyway with any work of art. Works of art such as paintings and pieces of sculpture are best thought of as scores awaiting realization in actual performance. Viewing a yellow version of Josef Albers' *Hommage to the square* displayed in a yellow frame on a yellow stuccoed wall would be like listening to a Rossini overture performed *con sordini* with all instruments muted.

To say that an object is fit for aesthetic attention is not simply to say that there are or could be environing conditions under which the object would be worth attending to aesthetically. That seems plainly true (to me anyway) and not surprising in the light of twentieth century art and techniques of display. In saying that an object is fit for aesthetic attention one is saying much more namely that the object can be attended to and is worth attending to aesthetically in that such attention to the object is worthwhile and if it is not that it is not is attributable either to interference by the conditions or to something about persons or their actions.

When attention to an object is not aesthetically worthwhile it may be uncertain what the lack is attributable to. If aesthetic attention to a floating clump of seaweed was not worthwhile that may be owing to the fact that while contemplating the clump one was being savaged by a school of sharks. Here conditions may fairly be said to have interfered. But if on a cold dank winter's day in Venice one finds the contemplation of a Tintoretto in a dim unheated church not aesthetically worthwhile is the lack to be attributed to the conditions under which the work is viewed or to a failure of concentration on the part of the person?

As the character of the objects attended to vary the character of the actions the conditions and the requisite qualities skills and capacities of the person may also have to vary if attention to the objects is to be aesthetically worthwhile. Demands made on a person are absolutely minimal in the appreciation of the popular art of his own culture: soap operas rock and roll comic strips western flicks. No special knowledge is called for no special actions are wanted: not even the capacity for continued attention is requisite. (Which is not to deny that from an intercultural point of view these demands can be seen as prodigious: the wonderful world of *Barry McKenzie* a comic strip is not apt to be available to those who haven't lived among the kanga-bloodyroos.) Popular art is popular because it is so readily available to all within the culture. But traditional works of art such as Leonardo's *Ginevra de' Benci Mona Lisa* the madonna on the rocks Botticelli's Venus on the half shell are also popular and for much the same reason: from a western intracultural point of view an appreciation of these works calls for nothing special on the part of the viewer. The same is true of the appreciation of many carefully hand-crafted objects of many beautiful things in general.

When one turns to modern works demands on the person are apt to increase. Elliott Carter's *2nd Quartet* is a work of rare beauty but it is not instantly available to all. If one attempts in listening to the quartet to attend to recurring themes and variations as one would in listening to a work in standard sonata form then one is ready for Beethoven's *C minor Opus 18 No 4* but not for Carter: eighteen seconds of the opening *Allegro fantastico* should be enough to make that clear. Modern works of art often call for prolonged continuous close attention if one is to appreciate them. The same is true of a gator basking in the sun on a mud bank in a swamp. Anything viewed makes demands.

To suppose that anything that can be viewed is a fit object for aesthetic attention is not like supposing that anything one can put in one's mouth is a fit object to eat. It is more like supposing that anything that can be seen can be read. Because it can. It isn't true that one can't read just anything that one can see. Not everything has meaning but anything can be given meaning. One can read a blank piece of paper or a cloud or a sea anemone as some read palms and tea leaves and entrails. One can give meaning to stones but one can't make them edible. And one can see them as displays of solidity as expressive objects.

What's a fit subject to photograph? Anything that can be seen. Or is it not what the photographer photographs but what he makes of it? With his camera and darkroom and skills? What he does with art I can do with my (or maybe you too can with your) eyes. One can look at anything and within limits and depending on one's powers create an appropriate frame and environing conditions for what one sees.

I will describe what I call 'antiaesthetic litter clearance'. A non-aesthetic approach is a simple exercise in futility: the litter is offensive pick it up put it in trash cans sweep and tidy the area. Which owing to the unchanging propensities of the inhabitants will soon almost immediately be covered with litter again. The antiaesthetic approach is to alter one's view to see the original litter not as litter but as an object for aesthetic attention: a manifestation of a fundamental physical factor: entropy. One can look upon the disorder of litter as a form of order a beautiful randomness a precise display of imprecision. (And if you cannot look at litter in this way perhaps you can learn to do so by looking at Pollock Tobey and others.) Garbage strewn about is apt to be as delicately variegated in hue and value as the subtlest Monet. Discarded beer cans create striking cubistic patterns.

Consider a gator basking in the sun on a mud bank in a swamp. Is he a fit object for aesthetic attention? He is and that he is is readily confirmable. Go look and see if you doubt what I say. He is presently to be seen around Chokoloskee Island in the Everglades. What is in question is the American alligator (*Alligator mississipiensis*) not to be confused with a crocodile. Gators have shorter broader heads and more obtuse snouts. The fourth enlarged tooth of a gator's lower jaw fits into a pit formed for it in the upper jaw, whereas a crocodile's fits into an external notch. It helps in viewing a gator to see it as a gator and not as a crocodile. But that requires knowing something about gators.

Seen from the side the gator appears to have a great healthy grin conveying a sense of well-being vitality. When Ginevra's portrait was painted by Leonardo she must have been sick for a long time. The pallor of her face conveys a 'sense of melancholy'.[2] The ossified scutes along his back forming the characteristic dermal armour constitute a powerful curving reticular pattern conveying simultaneously an impression of graceful fluidity and of remorseless solidity. Ginevra's face is 'framed by cascading curls. These ringlets, infinitely varied in their shapes and movement, remind us of Leonardo's drawings of whirling eddies of water'.[3] He has just come out of the water to bask in the sun. His sight is acute as is his power of hearing. But his eyes now have a lazy look being half-closed for he has upper and lower lids as well as a nictitating membrane. Ginevra too stares at us out of half-closed eyes. He is not strabismic. Her eyes are hazel. His seem green and remote despite the great grin.

Anything that can be viewed is a fit object for aesthetic attention. But not everything can be viewed just as not everything can be eaten. And in eating and in viewing the difficulties may be attributed either to the object or to the person. The former are obvious: stones can't be eaten and some gases subatomic particles and so forth can't be viewed because they can't be seen. But what cannot be eaten or cannot be viewed owing to the person is another matter. There are places where a rat foetus is considered a delicacy. The same is true of sheep's eye balls in aspic. In India warm monkey's brains are served up raw. Eskimos are reported to munch with delight on deer droppings (perhaps only in times of stress). Many in my society could not ingest these items: they would be stricken with nausea in the attempt. And there are hideous offensive nauseating objects that one cannot bear to view. Are such objects fit for aesthetic attention?

Yes why not? That I am psychologically incapable of attending aesthetically to a certain object tells you something about me nothing about the aesthetic qualities of the object. The same could be true of a work of art. Suppose Derain had done an heroic portrait of Hitler: I could not attend aesthetically to that work. Hitler was a repulsive nauseating object. That nausea is readily evoked by any lifelike image of the person. But my nausea would not be a criticism of Derain's art. Many of us cannot bear to look at blood particularly our own: that is not to deny that blood may be of a beautiful color and form beautiful patterns as it flows. If there were something that no one was psychologically capable of viewing even though the object was available for viewing then one might wonder whether such a thing was a fit object for aesthetic attention. But as far as I know there is no such thing and even if there were there's no need in theory anyway to countenance a morbid sensitivity that makes one psychologically incapable of viewing something in the world.

If anything that can be viewed is a fit object for aesthetic attention aren't some things more fit than others? No why think it? But granted that both a gator basking and Leonardo's *Ginevra* are fit objects for aesthetic attention isn't *Ginevra* more fit? No. In what way? It would make sense to compare the two only if there were some basis of comparison. But there isn't.

But isn't one painting better than another? In some ways and not in others. Rubens' paintings were superior to those of many of his contemporaries with respect to technique and pigmentation. Ingres' work displays finer draftsmanship than that of David. Vuillard's works have finer color than Manet's. But this isn't to say that Vuillard's works are more fit than those of Manet for aesthetic attention. If you are concerned to attend aesthetically to color then giving such attention to Vuillard's works will prove more worthwhile than giving such attention to Manet's works. But there are other things to attend to in viewing Manet's works. There are always other things to attend to.

For one can attend to anticolor: one can attend to precisely those aspects of hue value saturation of Manet's works which when standing on one's right foot adopting the stance of judge one judges to be inferior to Vuillard's. And one can without losing one's balance adopt a different stance standing on one's left foot one judges Manet's color superior to Vuillard's. And one can stand squarely on both feet and abandon the silliness of aesthetic judgements.

In looking at *Ginevra* one can attend to the display of craftsmanship and the beauty of form and shape: in looking at the gator basking one can attend to the beautiful grinning display of life. Anything that can be viewed can fill the bill of an object fit for aesthetic attention and none does it better than any other. Granted that 2 3 5 7 11 and so forth are primes: are some more so than others? A monk asked Ummon: 'What is Buddha?' Ummon answered him: 'Dried dung.'

['Anything Viewed', in *Antiaesthetics: An Appreciation of the Cow with the Subtle Nose* (Dordrecht: Reidel, 1984 by kind permission of Kluwer Academic Publishers), 129–39.]

ALLEN CARLSON

3 Aesthetic Appreciation of the Natural Environment

I.   The Central Problem of the Aesthetics of Nature

In his classic work, *The Sense of Beauty,* philosopher George Santayana characterizes the natural landscape as follows:

once a landscaper tries to make nature intentionally beautiful & less vague, we are drawn to it.

The natural landscape is an indeterminate object; it almost always contains enough diversity to allow . . . great liberty in selecting, emphasizing, and grouping its elements, and it is furthermore rich in suggestion and in vague emotional stimulus. A landscape to be seen has to be composed . . . then we feel that the landscape is beautiful . . . The promiscuous natural landscape cannot be enjoyed in any other way.[1]

With these few words, Santayana poses the central question of aesthetic appreciation of nature. The natural landscape, he says, is indeterminate and promiscuous. To be appreciated, it must be composed. Yet it is so rich in diversity, suggestion, and emotional stimulus that it allows great liberty in selecting, emphasizing, and grouping. Thus, the problem is that of *what* and *how* to select, emphasize, and group, of what and how to compose, to achieve appropriate appreciation.

bc art is already emphasized & composed

It is significant that there is no parallel problem concerning appreciation of art. With traditional works of art we typically know both the what and the how of appropriate aesthetic appreciation. We know *what* to appreciate in that we know the difference between a work and that which is not it nor a part of it and between its aesthetically relevant qualities and those without such relevance. We know that we are to appreciate the sound of the piano in the concert hall and not the coughing that interrupts it; we know that we are to appreciate a painting's delicacy and balance, but not where it happens to hang. Similarly, we know *how* to appreciate works of art in that we know the modes of appreciation that are appropriate for different kinds of works. We know that we are to listen to the sound of the piano and look at the surface of the painting. Moreover, we know that for different types of paintings, for instance, we must use different approaches. Philosopher Paul Ziff introduces the notion of 'act of aspection,' pointing out that different acts of aspection are appropriate for works of different types:

nature isn't like this

to contemplate a painting is to perform one act of aspection; to scan it is to perform another; to study, observe, survey, inspect, examine, scrutinize, are still other acts of aspection[2]

With art our knowledge of what and how to appreciate is grounded in the fact that works of art are our creations. In making an object we know what we make and thus its parts, its purposes, and what to do with it. In creating a painting, we know that it ends at its frame, that its colors and lines are aesthetically important, and that we are to look at it rather than listen to it. Moreover, works of different types have different kinds of boundaries, different foci of aesthetic significance, and demand different acts of aspection. Thus, in knowing the classification we know what and how to appreciate appropriately. Ziff again:

Generally speaking, a different act of aspection is performed in connection with works belonging to different schools of art, which is why the classification of style is of the essence. Venetian paintings lend themselves to an act of aspection involving attention to balanced masses; contours are of no importance.... The Florentine school demands attention to contours, the linear style predominates. Look for light in a Claude, for color in a Bonnard, for contoured volumes in a Signorelli.[3]

However, the fact that we know what and how to appreciate with art because we have created it does not immediately solve the central problem of aesthetic appreciation of nature. Nature is not art and it is not our creation. Rather it is our whole natural environment, our natural world. It surrounds us and confronts us, in Santayana's words, indeterminately and promiscuously, rich in diversity, suggestion, and stimulus. But what are we to appreciate in all this richness, what are the limits and the proper foci of appreciation; and how are we to appreciate, what are the appropriate modes of appreciation and acts of aspection? Moreover, what are the grounds on which we can justifiably base answers to such questions?

II.   Some Artistic Approaches to Appreciating Nature

Various artistic models of appreciation are typically accepted as the grounds for addressing the question of what and how to aesthetically appreciate with respect to the natural environment.

One such approach may be called the Object of Art Model (OAM). Consider our appreciation of a non-representation sculpture, for example, a Brancusi, such as *Bird In Space* (1919). We appreciate the actual physical object; the aesthetically relevant features are sensuous and design qualities of the object and certain abstract expressive qualities. Such sculpture need not relate to anything external to itself; it is a self-contained aesthetic unit. The Brancusi has no direct representational ties to the rest of reality and no relational connections with its immediate surroundings. Yet it has significant aesthetic qualities: it glistens, has balance and grace, and expresses flight itself. Clearly we can aesthetically appreciate objects of nature in accord with OAM. We can appreciate a rock or a piece of driftwood as we appreciate a Brancusi: we actually or imaginatively remove the object from its surroundings and dwell on its sensuous and possible expressive qualities. Natural objects are often appreciated in precisely this way: mantel pieces are littered with rocks and pieces of driftwood.

Nonetheless, OAM is in many ways inappropriate for aesthetic appreciation of nature. Santayana notes the natural environment's indeterminateness. He also observes that nature contains objects that have determinate forms, but suggests that when appreciation is directed specifically to them, we no longer have genuine aesthetic appreciation of nature. In fact, on one understanding of OAM, the objects of nature when so appreciated become 'readymades' or 'found art.' The natural objects are granted what is called 'artistic enfranchisement,' and they, like artifacts such as Marcel Duchamp's urinal which he enfranchised as a work called *Fountain* (1917), become works of art.[4]

The questions of what and how to aesthetically appreciate are answered, but for art rather than for nature; the appreciation of nature is lost in the shuffle.

OAM does not have to turn natural objects into art objects. It may treat the objects of nature simply by actually or imaginatively removing them from their surroundings. We need not appreciate the rock on our mantel as a readymade sculpture; we can appreciate it only as an aesthetically pleasing object. Yet OAM is still problematic in involving the removal of natural objects from their surroundings. The model is appropriate for art objects that are self-contained aesthetic units such that neither their environment of creation nor their environment of display is aesthetically relevant. However, natural objects are a part of and have been formed within their environments of creation by means of the natural forces at work within them. Thus, for natural objects, environments of creation are aesthetically relevant and, because of this, environments of display are equally relevant in virtue of being either the same as or different from environments of creation.

To appreciate the extent of OAM's problem, consider our rock again: on the mantel it seems gracefully curved and expressive of solidity, but in its environment of creation it has more and different aesthetic qualities—qualities resulting from the connections between it and its environment. It is expressive of the forces that shaped and continue to shape it and displays for aesthetic appreciation its place in and its relationships to its environment. Moreover, it may not express those qualities, such as solidity, that it appears to express on the mantel. The problem for OAM is a dilemma: either we remove the object from its environment or we leave it where it is. If the object is removed, the model answers questions of what and how to appreciate, but results in appreciation of a limited set of aesthetic qualities. On the other hand, if the object is not removed, OAM does not constitute an adequate model for much of the appreciation that is possible.

A second artistic approach to aesthetic appreciation of nature may be called the Landscape or Scenery Model (LSM). In one of its senses 'landscape' means a prospect—usually an imposing prospect—seen from a specific standpoint and distance.[5] The model encourages perceiving and appreciating nature as if it were a landscape painting, as an imposing prospect to be viewed from a specific position and distance. It directs appreciation to artistic and scenic qualities of line, color, and design.

LSM has been historically significant in aesthetic appreciation of nature. It is the direct descendant of the eighteenth century concept of the picturesque. This term literally means 'picture-like' and indicates a mode of appreciation by which the natural world is divided into scenes, each aiming at an ideal dictated by art, especially landscape painting. The concept guided the aesthetic appreciation of early tourists as they pursued picturesque scenery with the help of the 'Claude-glass,' a small, tinted, convex mirror designed for viewing the landscape. Thomas West's popular guidebook to the Lake District (1778) says of the glass:

where the objects are great and near, it removes them to a due distance, and shews them in the soft colours of nature, and most regular perspective the eye can perceive, art teach, or science demonstrate . . . to the glass is reserved the finished picture, in highest colouring, and just perspectives.[6]

In a similar fashion, modern tourists frequently show a preference for LSM by visiting 'scenic viewpoints' where the actual space between tourist and prescribed 'view' constitutes 'a due distance' which aids the impression of 'soft colours of nature, and the most regular perspective the eye can perceive.' And the 'regularity' of the perspective is enhanced by the position of the viewpoint itself. Modern tourists also desire 'the finished picture, in highest colouring, and just perspective'; whether this be the 'scene' framed and balanced in a camera viewfinder, the result of this in the form of a Kodacolor print, or 'artistically' composed postcard and calendar reproductions of the 'scene' which often receive more appreciation than that which they 'reproduce.' Geographer R. Rees characterizes the situation:

the taste has been for a view, for scenery, not for landscape in the original . . . meaning of the term, which denotes our ordinary, everyday surroundings. The average modern sightseer . . . is interested not in natural forms and processes, but in a prospect.[7]

LSM's answers to the what and how questions cause some uneasiness in a number of thinkers. Some individuals, such as human ecologist Paul Shepard, find LSM so misguided that they doubt the wisdom of any aesthetic approach to nature. Others find the model ethically and environmentally worrisome. For example, after contending that modern tourists are only interested in prospects, Rees concludes that the picturesque:

simply confirmed our anthropocentrism by suggesting that nature exists to please as well as to serve us. Our ethics . . . have lagged behind our aesthetics. It is an unfortunate lapse which allows us to abuse our local environments and venerate the Alps and the Rockies.[8]

LSM is also questionable on aesthetic grounds. The model construes the environment as if it were a static, essentially 'two dimensional' representation. [. . .] But the natural environment is not a scene, not a representation, not static, and not two dimensional. In short, the model requires appreciation of the environment not as what it is and with the qualities it has, but as something it is not and with qualities it does not have. Consequently it not only, as OAM, unduly limits appreciation, in this case to certain artistic and scenic qualities, it also misleads it. Philosopher Ronald Hepburn puts the point in general terms:

Supposing that a person's aesthetic education . . . instils in him the attitudes, the tactics of approach, the expectations proper to the appreciation of art works only, such a person will either pay very little aesthetic heed to natural objects or else heed them in the wrong way. He will look—and of course look in vain—for what can be found and enjoyed only in art.[9]

III.   *Some Alternative Approaches to Appreciating Nature*

If traditional artistic approaches to aesthetic appreciation of nature either unduly limit or mislead appreciation, how are we to deal with Santayana's indeterminate natural environment? Perhaps we can learn from the failures of the artistic approaches. These approaches limit and mislead appreciation because they do not adequately acknowledge the true nature of the object of appreciation. It is our natural environment, something both natural and an environment, but OAM, in focusing on particular natural objects, overlooks the environmental dimension, while LSM, in focusing on artistic and scenic features, down plays the natural dimension. Awareness of these failures has inspired some alternative approaches to appreciation of nature that share the conviction that such appreciation requires full recognition of the true nature of its object and cannot simply be assimilated to aesthetic appreciation of art.

alternatives fix the failures

One alternative, alive to the problems of picturesque appreciation and of LSM and seemingly sceptical about aesthetic approaches to nature in general, simply denies the possibility of aesthetic appreciation of nature. This position argues that aesthetic appreciation necessarily involves aesthetic evaluation, which entails judging the object of appreciation as the achievement of its creator and, therefore, since nature, unlike art, is not our creation, indeed is not the product of any designing intellect, appreciation of it is not aesthetic. One version of this position is called the 'Human Chauvinistic Aesthetic' (HCA). Environmental philosopher Robert Elliot elaborates this view, claiming that our appreciative responses to nature do not 'count as aesthetic responses':

Denial

BC nature doesn't have an agreeable creator, it's not aesthetic

[a] judgemental element in aesthetic evaluation serves to differentiate it from environmental evaluation ... [for] ... Evaluating works of art involves explaining them, and judging them, in terms of their author's intentions; ... locating them in some tradition and in some special *milieu* ... [but] ... is not a work of art ...[10]

A second alternative approach to appreciation of nature is more troubled by the limitations of OAM. It argues that traditional aesthetic approaches as exemplified by OAM, and to a lesser extent LSM, presuppose a subject / object dichotomy involving an isolating, distancing, and objectifying stance which is inappropriate for aesthetic appreciation not only of nature but of art as well. This stance wrongly abstracts both natural objects and appreciators from the environments in which they properly belong and in which appropriate appreciation is achieved. One version of this position is termed the 'Aesthetics of Engagement' (AOE) and developed by philosopher Arnold Berleant:

The boundlessness of the natural world does not just surround us; it assimilates us. Not only are we unable to sense absolute limits in nature; we cannot distance the natural world from ourselves.... Perceiving environments from within, as it were, looking not *at* it but being *in* it, nature ... is transformed into a realm in which we live as participants, not observers.... The aesthetic mark of all such times is ... total engagement, a sensory immersion in the natural world.[11]

By highlighting natural and environmental dimensions of the natural environment, HCA and AOE address many of the shortcomings of the traditional artistic models. However, these two approaches have problems of their own.[12] HCA runs counter to both the orthodox view that everything is open to aesthetic appreciation and the common sense idea that at least some instances of appreciation of natural things such as fiery sunsets and soaring birds constitute paradigm cases of aesthetic appreciation. AOE is also problematic. First, since at least some degree of the subject/object dichotomy seems integral to the very nature of aesthetic appreciation, its total rejection may necessitate a rejection of the aesthetic itself, reducing AOE to a version of HCA. Second, AOE seemingly embraces an unacceptable degree of subjectivity in aesthetic appreciation of both nature and art. However, the main problem with both positions is that, in the last analysis, they do not provide adequate answers to the questions of what and how to aesthetically appreciate in nature. Concerning the what question, the HCA's answer is quite simply 'nothing,' while AOE's is seemingly 'everything.' And, therefore, concerning the how question, the former view has nothing more to say, while the latter apparently recommends 'total immersion,' an answer offering less guidance than we might wish.

IV.   A Natural Environmental Model for Appreciating Nature

In spite of the problems inherent in HCA and AOE, both positions point toward a certain kind of paradigm for appreciation of nature. This paradigm is exemplified in the following description by geographer Yi-Fu Tuan:

An adult must learn to be yielding and careless like a child if he were to enjoy nature polymorphously. He needs to slip into old clothes so that he could feel free to stretch out on the hay beside the brook and bathe in a meld of physical sensations: the smell of the hay and of horse dung; the warmth of the ground, its hard and soft contours; the warmth of the sun tempered by breeze; the tickling of an ant making its way up the calf of his leg; the play of shifting leaf shadows on his face; the sound of water over the pebbles and boulders, the sound of cicadas and distant traffic. Such an environment might break all the formal rules of euphony and aesthetics, substituting confusion for order, and yet be wholly satisfying.[13]

Tuan's characterization of how to appreciate nature accords with AOE's answer to the question of what to appreciate, that is, everything. This answer, of course, will not do. We cannot appreciate everything; there must be limits and emphases in appreciation of nature as there are in appreciation of art. Without such limits and emphases our experience of the natural environment would be only 'a meld of physical sensations' without any meaning or significance, what philosopher William James characterises as a 'blooming buzzing confusion.' Such experience would indeed substitute 'confusion for order' and, contra to both Tuan and AOE, would be neither 'wholly satisfying' nor aesthetic. It would be too far removed from aesthetic appreciation of art to merit the label 'aesthetic' or even the label 'appreciation.' Consider again the case of art: the boundaries and foci of aesthetic significance for works of art are a function of the type of art: paintings end at their frames and their lines and colors are significant. Must nature remain indeterminate, promiscuous, and ultimately beyond aesthetic appreciation?

The fact that the natural environment is natural—not our creation—does not mean, of course, that we must be without knowledge of it. Our knowledge, essentially common sense and scientific knowledge, is a plausible candidate for playing the role in appreciation of nature that our knowledge of art forms, types of works, and artistic traditions plays in appreciation of art. Consider Tuan's example: we experience a 'meld of sensations'—the smell of hay and of horse dung, the feel of the ant, the sound of cicadas and of distant traffic. However, if our response is to be aesthetic appreciation rather than just raw experience, the meld cannot remain a 'blooming buzzing confusion.' Rather it must become what philosopher John Dewey calls a consummatory experience: one in which knowledge and intelligence transform raw experience by making it determinate, harmonious, and meaningful. For example, we must recognize the smell of hay and that of horse dung and perhaps distinguish between them; we must feel the ant at least as an insect rather than as, say, a twitch. Such recognizing and distinguishing generate foci of aesthetic significance, natural foci appropriate to the particular natural environment. Likewise knowledge of the environment may yield appropriate boundaries and limits; the sound of cicadas may be appreciated as a proper part of the environment, but the sound of distant traffic excluded much as we ignore coughing in the concert hall.

Common sense and scientific knowledge of natural environments is relevant not only to the question of what to appreciate, but also to that of how to appreciate. Since natural environments, as works of art, differ in type, different natural environments require different acts of aspection; and as with what to appreciate, knowledge of the environments in question indicates how to appreciate, indicates the appropriate act or acts of aspection. Ziff tells us to look for contours in the Florentine school, for light in a Claude, and for color in a Bonnard, to survey a Tintoretto and to scan a Bosch. Likewise, we must survey a prairie, looking at the subtle contours of the land, feeling the wind blowing across the open space, and smelling the mix of prairie grasses and flowers. But such acts of aspection have little place in a dense forest. Here we

[handwritten margin note:] Knowledge of nature will give us a license to appreciate it.

must examine and scrutinize, inspecting the detail of the forest floor, listening carefully for the sounds of birds and smelling carefully for the scent of spruce and pine. Similarly, Tuan's description, in addition to characterizing environmental acts of aspection in general, also indicates the act of aspection appropriate for a particular type of environment—perhaps best classified as pastoral. In appropriate aesthetic appreciation of nature, as in that of art, classification, as Ziff says, is of the essence.[14]

Thus the questions of what and how to appreciate aesthetically with respect to the natural environment may be answered analogously to the parallel questions about art. The difference is that with natural environments the relevant knowledge is common sense and scientific knowledge we have discovered about the environments in question. As the knowledge provided by art critics and art historians equips us to aesthetically appreciate art, that provided by naturalists, ecologists, geologists, and natural historians equips us to aesthetically appreciate nature.[15] Thus the natural and environmental sciences are central to appropriate aesthetic appreciation of nature.

A position which takes natural and environmental science to be the key to aesthetic appreciation of the natural environment may be termed the Natural Environmental Model (NEM). Like HCA and AOE, this model stresses the importance of the fact that the natural environment is both natural and an environment and, unlike OAM and LSM, it does not assimilate natural objects to art objects nor natural environments to scenery. Yet unlike HCA and AOE, NEM does not reject the general and traditional structure of aesthetic appreciation of art as a model for aesthetic appreciation of the natural world. In fact it applies that structure rather directly to nature, making only such adjustments as are necessary in light of the nature of the natural environment. In doing so it avoids the absurdity of deeming appreciation of nature nonaesthetic while promoting aesthetic appreciation of nature for what it is and for the qualities it has.

V. Further Ramifications

NEM suggests that to achieve appropriate aesthetic appreciation, to, as Santayana says, find nature beautiful, the composition must be in terms of common sense / scientific knowledge. In addition to answering the central problem of the aesthetics of nature, this suggestion has a number of other ramifications.

Some of these ramifications concern what is called applied aesthetics, specifically, popular appreciation of nature as practised not only by tourists but by each of us in our daily pursuits. As noted, such appreciation is frequently based on artistic models, especially LSM. However, the picturesque does not have a monopoly on applied aesthetic appreciation; it is in competition with a somewhat different approach. This other mode of appreciation grows from the tradition of thinkers such as Henry David Thoreau and has its paradigmatic realization in John Muir. For Muir, everything in the natural world, all nature and especially all wild nature, is aesthetically beautiful and ugliness exists only where nature is despoiled by human intrusion.[16] This conception, which may be called positive aesthetics, is closely tied to the idea of wilderness preservation and to the appreciation of nature typical of environmentalism. NEM is relevant to positive aesthetics because the model provides theoretical underpinnings of this mode of appreciation. When nature is aesthetically appreciated in virtue of the natural and environmental sciences, positive aesthetic appreciation is singularly appropriate, for, on the one hand, pristine nature is an aesthetic ideal and, on the other, as science increasingly finds, or at least appears to find, unity, order, and harmony in nature, nature itself, appreciated in light of such knowledge, appears more fully beautiful.

Other ramifications of NEM are more clearly environmental and ethical. As noted, the traditional artistic models, and by implication other aesthetic approaches, are frequently condemned as totally anthropocentric, as not only anti-natural but also arrogantly disdainful of environments not conforming to artistic ideals. However, NEM bases aesthetic appreciation on a scientific view of what nature is and of what qualities it has. NEM thereby endows aesthetic appreciation of nature with a degree of objectivity which helps to dispel environmental and moral criticisms, such as that of anthropocentrism. Moreover, the possibility of an objective basis for aesthetic appreciation of nature holds out promise of some direct practical relevance in a world increasingly engaged in environmental assessment. Individuals making such assessments, although typically not worried about anthropocentrism, are yet frequently reluctant to acknowledge the relevance and importance of aesthetic considerations, regarding them simply as at worst completely subjective whims or at best only relativistic, transient, and soft-headed cultural and artistic ideals. Recognizing that aesthetic appreciation of nature has scientific underpinnings helps to meet such doubts.

Another consequence concerns the discipline of aesthetics itself. NEM, in rejecting artistic models in favour of a dependence on common sense / scientific knowledge of nature, provides a blueprint for aesthetic appreciation in general. This model suggests that in aesthetic appreciation of anything, be it people or pets, farmyards or neighbourhoods, shoes or shopping malls, appreciation must be centred on and driven by the object of appreciation itself. This turn away from artistic preconceptions and toward the true nature of objects of appreciation points the way to a general aesthetics, an aesthetics that expands the traditional conception of the discipline, which is so narrow that aesthetics is equated with nothing more than philosophy of art. The upshot is, instead of simply an aesthetics of art, a more universal aesthetics—an aesthetics frequently termed environmental aesthetics.

Lastly, in initiating a more universal and object-centred aesthetics, NEM aids in the alignment of aesthetics with other areas of philosophy, such as ethics, epistemology, and philosophy of mind, in which there is increasingly a rejection of archaic, inappropriate models and a new-found dependence on knowledge relevant to the particular phenomena in question. The challenge implicit in Santayana's remarks—that we confront a natural world that allows great liberty in selecting, emphasizing, and grouping, and that we must therefore compose it in order to appropriately appreciate it—holds out an invitation to do more than simply find that world beautiful.

[This essay is a substantially modified version of 'Appreciation and the Natural Environment', *Journal of Aesthetics and Art Criticism*, 37 (1979), 267–76.]

OSCAR WILDE

4   The New Aesthetics

VIVIAN. [...] All that I desire to point out is the general principle that Life imitates Art far more than Art imitates Life, and I feel sure that if you think seriously about it you will find that it is true. Life holds the mirror up to Art, and either reproduces some strange type imagined by painter or sculptor, or realises in fact what has been dreamed in fiction. Scientifically speaking, the basis of life—the energy of life, as Aristotle would call it—is simply the desire for expression, and Art is always presenting various forms through which this expression can be attained. Life seizes on them and uses them, even if they be to her own hurt. Young men have committed suicide because Rolla did so, have died by their own hand because by his own hand Werther died. Think of what we owe to the imitation of Christ, of what we owe to the imitation of Cæsar.

CYRIL. The theory is certainly a very curious one, but to make it complete you must show that Nature, no less than Life, is an imitation of Art. Are you prepared to prove that?

VIVIAN. My dear fellow, I am prepared to prove anything.

CYRIL. Nature follows the landscape painter, then, and takes her effects from him?

VIVIAN. Certainly. Where, if not from the Impressionists, do we get those wonderful brown fogs that come creeping down our streets, blurring the gas-lamps and changing the houses into monstrous shadows? To whom, if not to them and their master, do we owe the lovely silver mists that brood over our river, and turn to faint forms of fading grace curved bridge and swaying barge? The extraordinary change that has taken place in the climate of

London during the last ten years is entirely due to a particular school of Art. You smile. Consider the matter from a scientific or a metaphysical point of view, and you will find that I am right. For what is Nature? Nature is no great mother who has borne us. She is our creation. It is in our brain that she quickens to life. Things are because we see them, and what we see, and how we see it, depends on the Arts that have influenced us. To look at a thing is very different from seeing a thing. One does not see anything until one sees its beauty. Then, and then only, does it come into existence. At present, people see fogs, not because there are fogs, but because poets and painters have taught them the mysterious loveliness of such effects. There may have been fogs for centuries in London. I dare say there were. But no one saw them, and so we do not know anything about them. They did not exist till Art had invented them. Now, it must be admitted, fogs are carried to excess. They have become the mere mannerism of a clique, and the exaggerated realism of their method gives dull people bronchitis. Where the cultured catch an effect, the uncultured catch cold. And so, let us be humane, and invite Art to turn her wonderful eyes elsewhere. She has done so already, indeed. That white quivering sunlight that one sees now in France, with its strange blotches of mauve, and its restless violet shadows, is her latest fancy, and, on the whole, Nature reproduces it quite admirably. Where she used to give us Corots and Daubignys, she gives us now exquisite Monets and entrancing Pisaros. Indeed there are moments, rare, it is true, but still to be observed from time to time, when Nature becomes absolutely modern. Of course she is not always to be relied upon. The fact is that she is in this unfortunate position. Art creates an incomparable and unique effect, and, having done so, passes on to other things. Nature, upon the other hand, forgetting that imitation can be made the sincerest form of insult, keeps on repeating this effect until we all become absolutely wearied of it. Nobody of any real culture, for instance, ever talks nowadays about the beauty of a sunset. Sunsets are quite old-fashioned. They belong to the time when Turner was the last note in art. To admire them is a distinct sign of provincialism of temperament. Upon the other hand they go on. Yesterday evening Mrs Arundel insisted on my going to the window, and looking at the glorious sky, as she called it. Of course I had to look at it. She is one of those absurdly pretty Philistines to whom one can deny nothing. And what was it? It was simply a very second-rate Turner, a Turner of a bad period, with all the painter's worst faults exaggerated and over-emphasised. Of course, I am quite ready to admit that Life very often commits the same error. She produces her false Renés and her sham Vautrins, just as Nature gives us, on one day a doubtful Cuyp, and on another a more than question-able Rousseau. Still, Nature irritates one more when she does things of that kind. It seems so stupid, so obvious, so unnecessary. A false Vautrin might be delightful. A doubtful Cuyp is unbearable. However, I don't want to be too hard on Nature. I wish the Channel, especially at Hastings, did not look quite so often like a Henry Moore, grey pearl with yellow lights, but then, when Art is more varied, Nature will, no doubt, be more varied also. That she imitates Art, I don't think even her worst enemy would deny now. It is the one thing that keeps her in touch with civilised man. But have I proved my theory to your satisfaction?

CYRIL. You have proved it to my dissatisfaction, which is better. But even admitting this strange imitative instinct in Life and Nature, surely you would acknowledge that Art expresses the temper of its age, the spirit of its time, the moral and social conditions that surround it, and under whose influence it is produced.

VIVIAN. Certainly not! Art never expresses anything but itself. This is the principle of my new æsthetics; and it is this, more than that vital connection between form and substance, on which Mr Pater dwells, that makes music the type of all the arts. Of course, nations and individuals, with that healthy natural vanity which is the secret of existence, are always under the impression that it is of them that the Muses are talking, always trying to find in the calm dignity of imaginative art some mirror of their own turbid passions, always forgetting that the singer of life is not Apollo but Marsyas. Remote from reality, and with her eyes turned away from the shadows of the cave, Art reveals her own perfection, and the wondering crowd that watches the opening of the marvellous, many-petalled rose fancies that it is its own history that is being told to it, its own spirit that is finding expression in a new form. But it is not so. The highest art rejects the burden of the human spirit, and gains more from a new medium or a fresh material than she does from any enthusiasm for art, or from any lofty passion, or from any great awakening of the human consciousness. She develops purely on her own lines. She is not symbolic of any age. It is the ages that are her symbols.

Even those who hold that Art is representative of time and place and people cannot help admitting that the more imitative an art is, the less it represents to us the spirit of its age. The evil faces of the Roman emperors look out at us from the foul porphyry and spotted jasper in which the realistic artists of the day delighted to work, and we fancy that in those cruel lips and heavy sensual jaws we can find the secret of the ruin of the Empire. But it was not so. The vices of Tiberius could not destroy that supreme civilisation, any more than the virtues of the Antonines could save it. It fell for other, for less interesting reasons. The sibyls and prophets of the Sistine may indeed serve to interpret for some that new birth of the emancipated spirit that we call the Renaissance; but what do the drunken boors and brawling peasants of Dutch art tell us about the great soul of Holland? The more abstract, the more ideal an art is, the more it reveals to us the temper of its age. If we wish to understand a nation by means of its art, let us look at its architecture or its music.

CYRIL. I quite agree with you there. The spirit of an age may be best expressed in the abstract ideal arts, for the spirit itself is abstract and ideal.

Upon the other hand, for the visible aspect of an age, for its look, as the phrase goes, we must of course go to the arts of imitation.

VIVIAN. I don't think so. After all, what the imitative arts really give us are merely the various styles of particular artists, or of certain schools of artists. Surely you don't imagine that the people of the Middle Ages bore any resemblance at all to the figures on mediæval stained glass, or in mediæval stone and wood carving, or on mediæval metal-work, or tapestries, or illuminated MSS. They were probably very ordinary-looking people, with nothing grotesque, or remarkable, or fantastic in their appearance. The Middle Ages, as we know them in art, are simply a definite form of style, and there is no reason at all why an artist with this style should not be produced in the nineteenth century. No great artist ever sees things as they really are. If he did, he would cease to be an artist. Take an example from our own day. I know that you are fond of Japanese things. Now, do you really imagine that the Japanese people, as they are presented to us in art, have any existence? If you do, you have never understood Japanese art at all. The Japanese people are the deliberate self-conscious creation of certain individual artists. If you set a picture by Hokusai, or Hokkei, or any of the great native painters, beside a real Japanese gentleman or lady, you will see that there is not the slightest resemblance between them. The actual people who live in Japan are not unlike the general run of English people; that is to say, they are extremely commonplace, and have nothing curious or extraordinary about them. In fact the whole of Japan is a pure invention. There is no such country, there are no such people. One of our most charming painters went recently to the Land of the Chrysanthemum in the foolish hope of seeing the Japanese. All he saw, all he had the chance of painting, were a few lanterns and some fans. He was quite unable to discover the inhabitants, as his delightful exhibition at Messrs Dowdeswell's Gallery showed only too well. He did not know that the Japanese people are, as I have said, simply a mode of style, an exquisite fancy of art. And so, if you desire to see a Japanese effect, you will not behave like a tourist and go to Tokio. On the contrary, you will stay at home and steep yourself in the work of certain Japanese artists, and then, when you have absorbed the spirit of their style, and caught their imaginative manner of vision, you will go some afternoon and sit in the Park or stroll down Piccadilly, and if you cannot see an absolutely Japanese effect there, you will not see it anywhere. Or, to return again to the past, take as another instance the ancient Greeks. Do you think that Greek art ever tells us what the Greek people were like? Do you believe that the Athenian women were like the stately dignified figures of the Parthenon frieze, or like those marvellous goddesses who sat in the triangular pediments of the same building? If you judge from the art, they certainly were so. But read an authority, like Aristophanes for instance. You will find that the Athenian ladies laced tightly, wore high-heeled shoes, dyed their hair yellow, painted and rouged their faces, and were exactly like any silly fashionable or fallen creature of our own day. The fact is that we look back on the ages entirely through the medium of art, and art, very fortunately, has never once told us the truth. [. . .]

CYRIL. [. . .] But in order to avoid making any error I want you to tell me briefly the doctrines of the new æthetics.

VIVIAN. Briefly, then, they are these. Art never expresses anything but itself. It has an independent life, just as Thought has, and develops purely on its own lines. It is not necessarily realistic in an age of realism, nor spiritual in an age of faith. So far from being the creation of its time, it is usually in direct opposition to it, and the only history that it preserves for us is the history of its own progress. Sometimes it returns upon its footsteps, and revives some antique form, as happened in the archaistic movement of late Greek Art, and in the pre-Raphaelite movement of our own day. At other times it entirely anticipates its age, and produces in one century work that it takes another century to understand, to appreciate and to enjoy. In no case does it reproduce its age. To pass from the art of a time to the time itself is the great mistake that all historians commit.

The second doctrine is this. All bad art comes from returning to Life and Nature, and elevating them into ideals. Life and Nature may sometimes be used as part of Art's rough material, but before they are of any real service to art they must be translated into artistic conventions. The moment Art surrenders its imaginative medium it surrenders everything. As a method Realism is a complete failure, and the two things that every artist should avoid are modernity of form and modernity of subject-matter. To us, who live in the nineteenth century, any century is a suitable subject for art except our own. The only beautiful things are the things that do not concern us. It is, to have the pleasure of quoting myself, exactly because Hecuba is nothing to us that her sorrows are so suitable a motive for a tragedy. Besides, it is only the modern that ever becomes old-fashioned. M. Zola sits down to give us a picture of the Second Empire. Who cares for the Second Empire now? It is out of date. Life goes faster than Realism, but Romanticism is always in front of Life.

The third doctrine is that Life imitates Art far more than Art imitates Life. This results not merely from Life's imitative instinct, but from the fact that the self-conscious aim of Life is to find expression, and that Art offers it certain beautiful forms through which it may realise that energy. It is a theory that has never been put forward before, but it is extremely fruitful, and throws an entirely new light upon the history of Art.

It follows, as a corollary from this, that external Nature also imitates Art. The only effects that she can show us are effects that we have already seen through poetry, or in paintings. This is the secret of Nature's charm, as well as the explanation of Nature's weakness.

The final revelation is that Lying, the telling of beautiful untrue things, is the proper aim of Art. But of this I think I have spoken at sufficient length. And now let us go out on the terrace, where 'droops the milk-white peacock like a ghost,' while the evening star 'washes the dusk with silver.' At twilight nature becomes a wonderfully suggestive effect, and is not without loveliness, though perhaps its chief use is to illustrate quotations from the poets. Come! We have talked long enough.

['The Decay of Lying', in *Intentions* (New York: The Nottingham Society, 1909), 40–9, 54–7. First published in 1891.]

JOHN DEWEY

5   The Aesthetic in Experience

Fortunately a theory of the place of the esthetic in experience does not have to lose itself in minute details when it starts with experience in its elemental form. Broad outlines suffice. The first great consideration is that life goes on in an environment; not merely *in* it but because of it, through interaction with it. No creature lives merely under its skin; its subcutaneous organs are means of connection with what lies beyond its bodily frame, and to which, in order to live, it must adjust itself, by accommodation and defense but also by conquest. At every moment, the living creature is exposed to dangers from its surroundings, and at every moment, it must draw upon something in its surroundings to satisfy its needs. The career and destiny of a living being are bound up with its interchanges with its environment, not externally but in the most intimate way. [. . .]

The live animal does not have to project emotions into the objects experienced. Nature is kind and hateful, bland and morose, irritating and comforting, long before she is mathematically qualified or even a congeries of 'secondary' qualities like colors and their shapes. Even such words as long and short, solid and hollow, still carry to all, but those who are intellectually specialized, a moral and emotional connotation. The dictionary will inform any one who consults it that the early use of words like sweet and bitter was not to denote qualities of sense as such but to discriminate things as favorable and hostile. How could it be otherwise? Direct experience comes from nature and man interacting with each other. In this interaction, human energy gathers, is released, dammed up, frustrated and victorious. There are rhythmic beats of want and fulfillment, pulses of doing and being withheld from doing. [. . .]

There are two sorts of possible worlds in which esthetic experience would not occur. In a world of mere flux, change would not be cumulative; it would not move toward a close. Stability and rest would have no being. Equally is it true, however, that a world that is finished, ended, would have no traits of suspense and crisis, and would offer no opportunity for resolution. Where everything is already complete, there is no fulfillment. We envisage with pleasure Nirvana and a uniform heavenly bliss only because they are projected upon the background of our present world of stress and conflict. Because the actual world, that in which we live, is a combination of movement and culmination, of breaks and re-unions, the experience of a living creature is capable of esthetic quality. The live being recurrently loses and reëstablishes equilibrium with his surroundings. The moment of passage from disturbance into harmony is that of intensest life. In a finished world, sleep and waking could not be distinguished. In one wholly perturbed, conditions could not even be struggled with. In a world made after the pattern of ours, moments of fulfillment punctuate experience with rhythmically enjoyed intervals.

Inner harmony is attained only when, by some means, terms are made with the environment. When it occurs on any other than an 'objective' basis, it is illusory—in extreme cases to the point of insanity. Fortunately for variety in experience, terms are made in many ways—ways ultimately decided by selective interest. Pleasures may come about through chance contact and stimulation; such pleasures are not to be despised in a world full of pain. But happiness and delight are a different sort of thing. They come to be through a fulfillment that reaches to the depths of our being—one that is an adjustment of our whole being with the conditions of existence. In the process of living, attainment of a period of equilibrium is at the same time the initiation of a new relation to the environment, one that brings with it potency of new adjustments to be made through struggle. The time of consummation is also one of beginning anew. Any attempt to perpetuate beyond its term the enjoyment attending the time of fulfillment and harmony constitutes withdrawal from the world. Hence it marks the lowering and loss of vitality. But, through the phases of perturbation and conflict, there abides the deep-seated memory of an underlying harmony, the sense of which haunts life like the sense of being founded on a rock. [. . .]

Experience occurs continuously, because the interaction of live creature and environing conditions is involved in the very process of living. Under conditions of resistance and conflict, aspects and elements of the self and the world that are implicated in this interaction qualify experience with emotions and ideas so that conscious intent emerges. Oftentimes, however, the experience had is inchoate. Things are experienced but not in such a way that they are composed into an experience. There is distraction and dispersion; what we observe and what we think, what we desire and what we get, are at odds with each other. We put our hands to the plow and turn back; we start and then we stop, not because the experience has reached the end for the sake of which it was initiated but because of extraneous interruptions or of inner lethargy.

In contrast with such experience, we have *an* experience when the material experienced runs its course to fulfillment. Then and then only is it integrated within and demarcated in the general stream of experience from other experiences. A piece of work is finished in a way that is satisfactory; a problem receives its solution; a game is played through; a situation, whether that of eating a meal, playing a game of chess, carrying on a conversation, writing a book, or taking part in a political campaign, is so rounded out that its close is a consummation and not a cessation. Such an experience is a whole and carries with it its own individualizing quality and self-sufficiency. It is *an* experience.

Philosophers, even empirical philosophers, have spoken for the most part of experience at large. Idiomatic speech, however, refers to experiences each of which is singular, having its own beginning and end. For life is no uniform uninterrupted march or flow. It is a thing of histories, each with its own plot, its own inception and movement toward its close, each having its own particular rhythmic movement; each with its own unrepeated quality pervading it throughout. A flight of stairs, mechanical as it is, proceeds by individualized steps, not by undifferentiated progression, and an inclined plane is at least marked off from other things by abrupt discreteness.

Experience in this vital sense is defined by those situations and episodes that we spontaneously refer to as being 'real experiences'; those things of which we say in recalling them, 'that *was* an experience.' It may have been something of tremendous importance—a quarrel with one who was once an intimate, a catastrophe finally averted by a hair's breadth. Or it may have been something that in comparison was slight—and which perhaps because of its very slightness illustrates all the better what is to be an experience. There is that meal in a Paris restaurant of which one says 'that *was* an experience.' It stands out as an enduring memorial of what food may be. Then there is that storm one went through in crossing the Atlantic—the storm that seemed in its fury, as it was experienced, to sum up in itself all that a storm can be, complete in itself, standing out because marked out from what went before and what came after.

In such experiences, every successive part flows freely, without seam and without unfilled blanks, into what ensues. At the same time there is no sacrifice of the self-identity of the parts. A river, as distinct from a pond, flows. But its flow gives a definiteness and interest to its successive portions greater than exist in the homogeneous portions of a pond. In an experience, flow is from something to something. As one part leads into another and as one part carries on what went before, each gains distinctness in itself. The enduring whole is diversified by successive phases that are emphases of its varied colors.

Because of continuous merging, there are no holes, mechanical junctions, and dead centers when we have *an* experience. There are pauses, places of rest, but they punctuate and define the quality of movement. They sum up what has been undergone and prevent its dissipation and idle evaporation. Continued acceleration is breathless and prevents parts from gaining distinction. In a work of art, different acts, episodes, occurrences melt and fuse into unity, and yet do not disappear and lose their own character as they do so— just as in a genial conversation there is a continuous interchange and blending, and yet each speaker not only retains his own character but manifests it more clearly than is his wont.

An experience has a unity that gives it its name, *that* meal, that storm, that rupture of friendship. The existence of this unity is constituted by a single *quality* that pervades the entire experience in spite of the variation of its constituent parts. This unity is neither emotional, practical, nor intellectual, for these terms name distinctions that reflection can make within it. In discourse *about* an experience, we must make use of these adjectives of interpretation. In going over an experience in mind *after* its occurrence, we may find that one property rather than another was sufficiently dominant so that it characterizes the experience as a whole. There are absorbing inquiries and speculations which a scientific man and philosopher will recall as 'experiences' in the emphatic sense. In final import they are intellectual. But in their actual occurrence they were emotional as well; they were purposive and volitional. Yet the experience was not a sum of these different characters; they were lost in it as distinctive traits. No thinker can ply his occupation save as he is lured and rewarded by total integral experiences that are intrinsically worth while. Without them he would never know what it is really to think and would be completely at a loss in distinguishing real thought from the spurious article. Thinking goes on in trains of ideas, but the ideas form a train only because they are much more than what an analytic psychology calls ideas. They are phases, emotionally and practically distinguished, of a developing underlying quality; they are its moving variations, not separate and independent like Locke's and Hume's so-called ideas and impressions, but are subtle shadings of a pervading and developing hue.

We say of an experience of thinking that we reach or draw a conclusion. Theoretical formulation of the process is often made in such terms as to conceal effectually the similarity of 'conclusion' to the consummating phase of every developing integral experience. These formulations apparently take their cue from the separate propositions that are premises and the proposition that is the conclusion as they appear on the printed page. The impression is derived that there are first two independent and ready-made entities that are then manipulated so as to give rise to a third. In fact, in an experience of thinking, premisses emerge only as a conclusion becomes manifest. The experience, like that of watching a storm reach its height and gradually subside, is one of continuous movement of subject-matters. Like the ocean in the storm, there are a series of waves; suggestions reaching out and being broken in a clash, or being carried onwards by a coöperative wave. If a conclusion is reached, it is that of a movement of anticipation and cumulation, one that finally comes to completion. A 'conclusion' is no separate and independent thing; it is the consummation of a movement.

Hence *an* experience of thinking has its own esthetic quality. It differs from those experiences that are acknowledged to be esthetic, but only in its materials. The material of the fine arts consists of qualities; that of experience having intellectual conclusion are signs or symbols having no intrinsic quality of their own, but standing for things that may in another experience be qualitatively experienced. The difference is enormous. It is one reason why the strictly intellectual art will never be popular as music is popular. Nevertheless, the experience itself has a satisfying emotional quality because it possesses internal integration and fulfillment reached through ordered and organized movement. This artistic structure may be immediately felt. In so far, it is esthetic. What is even more important is that not only is this quality a significant motive in undertaking intellectual inquiry and in keeping it honest, but that no intellectual activity is an integral event (is *an* experience), unless it is rounded out with this quality. Without it, thinking is inconclusive. In short, esthetic cannot be sharply marked off from intellectual experience since the latter must bear an esthetic stamp to be itself complete.

The same statement holds good of a course of action that is dominantly practical, that is, one that consists of overt doings. It is possible to be efficient in action and yet not have a conscious experience. The activity is too automatic to permit of a sense of what it is about and where it is going. It comes to an end but not to a close or consummation in consciousness. Obstacles are overcome by shrewd skill, but they do not feed experience. There are also those who are wavering in action, uncertain, and inconclusive like the shades in classic literature. Between the poles of aimlessness and mechanical efficiency, there lie those courses of action in which through successive deeds there runs a sense of growing meaning conserved and accumulating toward an end that is felt as accomplishment of a process. Successful politicians and generals who turn statesmen like Caesar and Napoleon have something of the showman about them. This of itself is not art, but it is, I think, a sign that interest is not exclusively, perhaps not mainly, held by the result taken by itself (as it is in the case of mere efficiency), but by it as the outcome of a process. There is interest in completing an experience. The experience may be one that is harmful to the world and its consummation undesirable. But it has esthetic quality. [...]

A generalized illustration may be had if we imagine a stone, which is rolling down hill, to have an experience. The activity is surely sufficiently 'practical.' The stone starts from somewhere, and moves, as consistently as conditions permit, toward a place and state where it will be at rest—toward an end. Let us add, by imagination, to these external facts, the ideas that it looks forward with desire to the final outcome; that it is interested in the things it meets on its way, conditions that accelerate and retard its movement with respect to their bearing on the end; that it acts and feels toward them according to the hindering or helping function it attributes to them; and that the final coming to rest is related to all that went before as the culmination of a continuous movement. Then the stone would have an experience, and one with esthetic quality.

If we turn from this imaginary case to our own experience, we shall find much of it is nearer to what happens to the actual stone than it is to anything that fulfills the conditions fancy just laid down. For in much of our experience we are not concerned with the connection of one incident with what went before and what comes after. There is no interest that controls attentive rejection or selection of what shall be organized into the developing experience. Things happen, but they are neither definitely included nor decisively excluded; we drift. We yield according to external pressure, or evade and compromise. There are beginnings and cessations, but no genuine initiations and concludings. One thing replaces another, but does not absorb it and carry it on. There is experience, but so slack and discursive that it is not *an* experience. Needless to say, such experiences are anesthetic.

Thus the non-esthetic lies within two limits. At one pole is the loose succession that does not begin at any particular place and that ends—in the sense of ceasing—at no particular place. At the other pole is arrest, constriction, proceeding from parts having only a mechanical connection with one another. There exists so much of one and the other of these two kinds of experience that unconsciously they come to be taken as norms of all experience. Then, when the esthetic appears, it so sharply contrasts with the picture that has been formed of experience, that it is impossible to combine its special qualities with the features of the picture and the esthetic is given an outside place and status. The account that has been given of experience dominantly intellectual and practical is intended to show that there is no such contrast involved in having an experience; that, on the contrary, no experience of whatever sort is a unity unless it has esthetic quality.

The enemies of the esthetic are neither the practical nor the intellectual. They are the humdrum; slackness of loose ends; submission to convention in practice and intellectual procedure. Rigid abstinence, coerced submission, tightness on one side and dissipation, incoherence and aimless indulgence on the other, are deviations in opposite directions from the unity of an experience. Some such considerations perhaps induced Aristotle to invoke the 'mean proportional' as the proper designation of what is distinctive of both virtue and the esthetic. He was formally correct. 'Mean' and 'proportion' are, however, not self-explanatory, nor to be taken over in a prior mathematical sense, but are properties belonging to an experience that has a developing movement toward its own consummation. [...]

I have spoken of the esthetic quality that rounds out an experience into completeness and unity as emotional. The reference may cause difficulty. We are given to thinking of emotions as things as simple and compact as are the words by which we name them. Joy, sorrow, hope, fear, anger, curiosity, are treated as if each in itself were a sort of entity that enters full-made upon the scene, an entity that may last a long time or a short time, but whose duration, whose growth and career, is irrelevant to its nature. In fact emotions are qualities, when they are significant, of a complex experience that moves and changes. I say, when they are *significant*, for otherwise they are but the outbreaks and eruptions of a disturbed infant. All emotions are qualifications of a drama and they change as the drama develops. Persons are sometimes said to fall in love at first sight. But what they fall into is not a thing of that instant. What would love be were it compressed into a moment in which there is no room for cherishing and for solicitude? The intimate nature of emotion is manifested in the experience of one watching a play on the stage or reading a novel. It attends the development of a plot; and a plot requires a stage, a space, wherein to develop and time in which to unfold. Experience is emotional but there are no separate things called emotions in it.

By the same token, emotions are attached to events and objects in their movement. They are not, save in pathological instances, private. And even an 'objectless' emotion demands something beyond itself to which to attach itself, and thus it soon generates a delusion in lack of something real. Emotion belongs of a certainty to the self. But it belongs to the self that is concerned in the movement of events toward an issue that is desired or disliked. We jump instantaneously when we are scared, as we blush on the instant when we are ashamed. But fright and shamed modesty are not in this case emotional states. Of themselves they are but automatic reflexes. In order to become emotional they must become parts of an inclusive and enduring situation that involves concern for objects and their issues. The jump of fright becomes emotional fear when there is found or thought to exist a threatening object that must be dealt with or escaped from. The blush becomes the emotion of shame when a person connects, in thought, an action he has performed with an unfavorable reaction to himself of some other person.

Physical things from far ends of the earth are physically transported and physically caused to act and react upon one another in the construction of a new object. The miracle of mind is that something similar takes place in experience without physical transport and assembling. Emotion is the moving and cementing force. It selects what is congruous and dyes what is selected with its color, thereby giving qualitative unity to materials externally disparate and dissimilar. It thus provides unity in and through the varied parts of an experience. When the unity is of the sort already described, the experience has esthetic character even though it is not, dominantly, an esthetic experience. [. . .]

There are, therefore, common patterns in various experiences, no matter how unlike they are to one another in the details of their subject matter. There are conditions to be met without which an experience cannot come to be. The outline of the common pattern is set by the fact that every experience is the result of interaction between a live creature and some aspect of the world in which he lives. [. . .]

Experience is limited by all the causes which interfere with perception of the relations between undergoing and doing. There may be interference because of excess on the side of doing or of excess on the side of receptivity, of undergoing. Unbalance on either side blurs the perception of relations and leaves the experience partial and distorted, with scant or false meaning. Zeal for doing, lust for action, leaves many a person, especially in this hurried and impatient human environment in which we live, with experience of an almost incredible paucity, all on the surface. No one experience has a chance to complete itself because something else is entered upon so speedily. What is called experience becomes so dispersed and miscellaneous as hardly to deserve the name. Resistance is treated as an obstruction to be beaten down, not as an invitation to reflection. An individual comes to seek, unconsciously even more than by deliberate choice, situations in which he can do the most things in the shortest time.

Experiences are also cut short from maturing by excess of receptivity. What is prized is then the mere undergoing of this and that, irrespective of perception of any meaning. The crowding together of as many impressions as possible is thought to be 'life,' even though no one of them is more than a flitting and a sipping. The sentimentalist and the day-dreamer may have more fancies and impressions pass through their consciousness than has the man who is animated by lust for action. But his experience is equally distorted, because nothing takes root in mind when there is no balance between doing and receiving. Some decisive action is needed in order to establish contact with the realities of the world and in order that impressions may be so related to facts that their value is tested and organized.

Because perception of relationship between what is done and what is undergone constitutes the work of intelligence, and because the artist is controlled in the process of his work by his grasp of the connection between what he has already done and what he is to do next, the idea that the artist does not think as intently and penetratingly as a scientific inquirer is absurd. A painter must consciously undergo the effect of his every brush stroke or he will not be aware of what he is doing and where his work is going. Moreover, he has to see each particular connection of doing and undergoing in relation to the whole that he desires to produce. To apprehend such relations is to think, and is one of the most exacting modes of thought. The difference between the pictures of different painters is due quite as much to differences of capacity to carry on this thought as it is to differences of sensitivity to bare color and to differences in dexterity of execution. As respects the basic quality of pictures, difference depends, indeed, more upon the quality of intelligence brought to bear upon perception of relations than upon anything else— though of course intelligence cannot be separated from direct sensitivity and is connected, though in a more external manner, with skill.

Any idea that ignores the necessary rôle of intelligence in production of works of art is based upon identification of thinking with use of one special kind of material, verbal signs and words. To think effectively in terms of relations of qualities is as severe a demand upon thought as to think in terms of symbols, verbal and mathematical. Indeed, since words are easily manipu-lated in mechanical ways, the production of a work of genuine art probably demands more intelligence than does most of the so-called thinking that goes on among those who pride themselves on being 'intellectuals.'

I have tried to show [. . .] that the esthetic is no intruder in experience from without, whether by way of idle luxury or transcendent ideality, but that it is the clarified and intensified development of traits that belong to every normally complete experience. This fact I take to be the only secure basis upon which esthetic theory can build. It remains to suggest some of the implications of the underlying fact.

We have no word in the English language that unambiguously includes what is signified by the two words 'artistic' and 'esthetic.' Since 'artistic' refers primarily to the act of production and 'esthetic' to that of perception and enjoyment, the absence of a term designating the two processes taken together is unfortunate. Sometimes, the effect is to separate the two from each other, to regard art as something superimposed upon esthetic material, or, upon the other side, to an assumption that, since art is a process of creation, perception and enjoyment of it have nothing in common with the creative act. In any case, there is a certain verbal awkwardness in that we are compelled sometimes to use the term 'esthetic' to cover the entire field and sometimes to limit it to the receiving perceptual aspect of the whole opera-tion. I refer to these obvious facts as preliminary to an attempt to show how the conception of conscious experience as a perceived relation between doing and undergoing enables us to understand the connection that art as produc-tion and perception and appreciation as enjoyment sustain to each other.

Art denotes a process of doing or making. This is as true of fine as of technological art. Art involves molding of clay, chipping of marble, casting of bronze, laying on of pigments, construction of buildings, singing of songs, playing of instruments, enacting rôles on the stage, going through rhythmic movements in the dance. Every art does something with some physical material, the body or something outside the body, with or without the use of intervening tools, and with a view to production of something visible, audible, or tangible. So marked is the active or 'doing' phase of art, that the dictionaries usually define it in terms of skilled action, ability in execution. The Oxford Dictionary illustrates by a quotation from John Stuart Mill: 'Art is an endeavour after perfection in execution' while Matthew Arnold calls it 'pure and flawless workmanship.'

The word 'esthetic' refers, as we have already noted, to experience as appreciative, perceiving, and enjoying. It denotes the consumer's rather than the producer's standpoint. It is Gusto, taste; and, as with cooking, overt skillful action is on the side of the cook who prepares, while taste is on the side of the consumer, as in gardening there is a distinction between the gardener who plants and tills and the householder who enjoys the finished product.

These very illustrations, however, as well as the relation that exists in having an experience between doing and undergoing, indicate that the distinction between esthetic and artistic cannot be pressed so far as to become a separation. Perfection in execution cannot be measured or defined in terms of execution; it implies those who perceive and enjoy the product that is executed. The cook prepares food for the consumer and the measure of the value of what is prepared is found in consumption. Mere perfection in execution, judged in its own terms in isolation, can probably be attained better by a machine than by human art. [. . .]

In short, art, in its form, unites the very same relation of doing and undergoing, outgoing and incoming energy, that makes an experience to be an experience. Because of elimination of all that does not contribute to mutual organization of the factors of both action and reception into one another, and because of selection of just the aspects and traits that contribute to their interpretation of each other, the product is a work of esthetic art. Man whittles, carves, sings, dances, gestures, molds, draws and paints. The doing or making is artistic when the perceived result is of such a nature that *its* qualities *as perceived* have controlled the question of production. The act of producing that is directed by intent to produce something that is enjoyed in the immediate experience of perceiving has qualities that a spontaneous or uncontrolled activity does not have. The artist embodies in himself the attitude of the perceiver while he works.

Suppose, for the sake of illustration, that a finely wrought object, one whose texture and proportions are highly pleasing in perception, has been believed to be a product of some primitive people. Then there is discovered evidence that proves it to be an accidental natural product. As an external thing, it is now precisely what it was before. Yet at once it ceases to be a work of art and becomes a natural 'curiosity.' It now belongs in a museum of natural history, not in a museum of art. And the extraordinary thing is that the difference that is thus made is not one of just intellectual classification. A difference is made in appreciative perception and in a direct way. The esthetic experience—in its limited sense—is thus seen to be inherently connected with the experience of making.

The sensory satisfaction of eye and ear, when esthetic, is so because it does not stand by itself but is linked to the activity of which it is the consequence.

[. . .]

The process of art in production is related to the esthetic in perception organically—as the Lord God in creation surveyed his work and found it good. Until the artist is satisfied in perception with what he is doing, he continues shaping and reshaping. The making comes to an end when its result is experienced as good—and that experience comes not by mere intellectual and outside judgment but in direct perception. An artist, in comparison with his fellows, is one who is not only especially gifted in powers of execution but in unusual sensitivity to the qualities of things. This sensitivity also directs his doings and makings.

As we manipulate, we touch and feel, as we look, we see; as we listen, we hear. The hand moves with etching needle or with brush. The eye attends and reports the consequence of what is done. Because of this intimate connection, subsequent doing is cumulative and not a matter of caprice nor yet of routine. In an emphatic artistic-esthetic experience, the relation is so close that it controls simultaneously both the doing and the perception. Such vital intimacy of connection cannot be had if only hand and eye are engaged. When they do not, both of them, act as organs of the whole being, there is but a mechanical sequence of sense and movement, as in walking that is automatic. Hand and eye, when the experience is esthetic, are but instruments through which the entire live creature, moved and active throughout, operates. Hence the expression is emotional and guided by purpose.

[*Art as Experience* (New York: G. Putnam's Sons, 1934), 13, 16–17, 35–50.]

I. b. Many Aesthetics

KAKUZO OKAKURA

6 The Tea-Room

To European architects brought up on the traditions of stone and brick construction, our Japanese method of building with wood and bamboo seems scarcely worthy to be ranked as architecture. [...] Such being the case as regards our classic architecture, we could hardly expect the outsider to appreciate the subtle beauty of the tea-room, its principles of construction and decoration being entirely different from those of the West.

The tea-room (the Sukiya) does not pretend to be other than a mere cottage,—a straw hut, as we call it. The original ideographs for Sukiya mean the Abode of Fancy. Latterly the various tea-masters substituted various Chinese characters according to their conception of the tea-room, and the term Sukiya may signify the Abode of Vacancy or the Abode of the Unsymmetrical. It is an Abode of Fancy inasmuch as it is an ephemeral structure built to house a poetic impulse. It is an Abode of Vacancy inasmuch as it is devoid of ornamentation except for what may be placed in it to satisfy some aesthetic need of the moment. It is an Abode of the Unsymmetrical inasmuch as it is consecrated to the worship of the Imperfect, purposely leaving some thing unfinished for the play of the imagination to complete. The ideals of Teaism have since the sixteenth century influenced our architecture to such a degree that the ordinary Japanese interior of the present day, on account of the extreme simplicity and chasteness of its scheme of decoration, appears to foreigners almost barren.

The first independent tea-room was the creation of Sen-no-Sōeki, commonly known by his later name of Rikyu, the greatest of all tea-masters, who, in the sixteenth century, under the patronage of Taikō Hideyoshi, instituted and brought to a high state of perfection the formalities of the Tea-ceremony. The proportions of the tea-room had been previously determined by Shō-Ō,—a famous tea-master of the fifteenth century. The early tea-room consisted merely of a portion of the ordinary drawing-room partitioned off by screens for the purpose of the tea-gathering. The portion partitioned off was called the Kakoi (enclosure), a name still applied to those tea-rooms which are built into a house and are not independent constructions. The Sukiya consists of the tea-room proper, designed to accommodate not more than five persons, a number suggestive of the saying 'more than the Graces and less than the Muses,' an anteroom (mizuya) where the tea-utensils are washed *owing to the simple complexity (oxymoron?)*

and arranged before being brought in, a portico (machiai) in which the guests wait until they receive the summons to enter the tea-room, and a garden path (the rōji) which connects the machiai with the tea-room. The tea-room is unimpressive in appearance. It is smaller than the smallest of Japanese houses, while the materials used in its construction are intended to give the suggestion of refined poverty. Yet we must remember that all this is the result of profound artistic forethought, and that the details have been worked out with care perhaps even greater than that expended on the building of the richest palaces and temples. A good tea-room is more costly than an ordinary mansion, for the selection of its materials, as well as its workmanship, requires immense care and precision. Indeed, the carpenters employed by the tea-masters form a distinct and highly honoured class among artisans, their work being no less delicate than that of the makers of lacquer cabinets.

The tea-room is not only different from any production of Western architecture, but also contrasts strongly with the classical architecture of Japan itself. Our ancient noble edifices, whether secular or ecclesiastical, were not to be despised even as regards their mere size. The few that have been spared in the disastrous conflagrations of centuries are still capable of awing us by the grandeur and richness of their decoration. Huge pillars of wood, from two to three feet in diameter and from thirty to forty feet high, supported, by a complicated network of brackets, the enormous beams which groaned under the weight of the tile-covered slanting roofs. The material and mode of construction, though weak against fire, proved itself strong against earthquakes, and was well suited to the climatic conditions of the country. In the Golden Hall of Horyuji and the Pagoda of Yakushiji, we have noteworthy examples of the durability of our wooden architecture. These buildings have practically stood intact for nearly twelve centuries. The interior of the old temples and palaces was profusely decorated. In the Hōōdo temple at Uji, dating from the tenth century, we can still see the elaborate canopy and gilded baldachinos, many-coloured and inlaid with mirrors and mother-of-pearl, as well as remains of the paintings and sculpture which formerly covered the walls. Later, at Nikko and in the Nijo castle in Kyoto, we see structural beauty sacrificed to a wealth of ornamentation which in colour and exquisite detail equals the utmost gorgeousness of Arabian or Moorish effort.

The simplicity and purism of the tea-room resulted from emulation of the Zen monastery. A Zen monastery differs from those of other Buddhist sects inasmuch as it is meant only to be a dwelling place for the monks. Its chapel is not a place of worship or pilgrimage, but a college room where the students congregate for discussion and the practice of meditation. The room is bare except for a central alcove in which, behind the altar, is a statue of Bodhidharma, the founder of the sect, or of Sakyamuni attended by Kasyapa and Ananda, the two earliest Zen patriarchs. On the altar, flowers and incense are offered up in memory of the great contributions which these sages made to Zen. We have already said that it was the ritual instituted by the Zen monks of successively drinking tea out of a bowl before the image of Bodhidharma, which laid the foundations of the tea-ceremony. We might add here that the altar of the Zen chapel was the prototype of the Tokonoma,—the place of honour in a Japanese room where paintings and flowers are placed for the edification of the guests.

All our great tea-masters were students of Zen and attempted to introduce the spirit of Zennism into the actualities of life. Thus the room, like the other equipments of the tea-ceremony, reflects many of the Zen doctrines. The size of the orthodox tea-room, which is four mats and a half, or ten feet square, is determined by a passage in the Sutra of Vikramaditya. In that interesting work, Vikramaditya welcomes the Saint Manjusri and eighty-four thousand disciples of Buddha in a room of this size,—an allegory based on the theory of the non-existence of space to the truly enlightened. Again the rōji, the garden path which leads from the machiai to the tea-room, signified the first stage of meditation,—the passage into self-illumination. The rōji was intended to break connection with the outside world, and to produce a fresh sensation conducive to the full enjoyment of aestheticism in the tea-room itself. One who has trodden this garden path cannot fail to remember how his spirit, as he walked in the twilight of evergreens over the regular irregularities of the stepping stones, beneath which lay dried pine needles, and passed beside the moss-covered granite lanterns, became uplifted above ordinary thoughts. One may be in the midst of a city, and yet feel as if he were in the forest far away from the dust and din of civilisation. Great was the ingenuity displayed by the tea-masters in producing these effects of serenity and purity. The nature of the sensations to be aroused in passing through the rōji differed with different tea-masters. [. . .]

Thus prepared the guest will silently approach the sanctuary, and, if a samurai, will leave his sword on the rack beneath the eaves, the tea-room being preëminently the house of peace. Then he will bend low and creep into the room through a small door not more than three feet in height. This proceeding was incumbent on all guests,—high and low alike,—and was intended to inculcate humility. The order of precedence having been mutually agreed upon while resting in the machiai, the guests one by one will enter noiselessly and take their seats, first making obeisance to the picture or flower arrangement on the tokonoma. The host will not enter the room until all the guests have seated themselves and quiet reigns with nothing to break the silence save the note of the boiling water in the iron kettle. The kettle sings well, for pieces of iron are so arranged in the bottom as to produce a peculiar melody in which one may hear the echoes of a cataract muffled by clouds, of a distant sea breaking among the rocks, a rainstorm sweeping through a bamboo forest, or of the soughing of pines on some faraway hill.

Even in the daytime the light in the room is subdued, for the low eaves of the slanting roof admit but few of the sun's rays. Everything is sober in tint from the ceiling to the floor; the guests themselves have carefully chosen garments of unobtrusive colours. The mellowness of age is over all, everything suggestive of recent acquirement being tabooed save only the one note of contrast furnished by the bamboo dipper and the linen napkin, both immaculately white and new. However faded the tea-room and the tea-equipage may seem, everything is absolutely clean. Not a particle of dust will be found in the darkest corner, for if any exists the host is not a tea-master. One of the first requisites of a tea-master is the knowledge of how to sweep, clean, and wash, for there is an art in cleaning and dusting. A piece of antique metalwork must not be attacked with the unscrupulous zeal of the Dutch housewife. Dripping water from a flower vase need not be wiped away, for it may be suggestive of dew and coolness. *ritualistic*

In this connection there is a story of Rikyu which well illustrates the ideas of cleanliness entertained by the tea-masters. Rikyu was watching his son Sho-an as he swept and watered the garden path. 'Not clean enough,' said Rikyu, when Sho-an had finished his task, and bade him try again. After a weary hour the son turned to Rikyu: 'Father, there is nothing more to be done. The steps have been washed for the third time, the stone lanterns and the trees are well sprinkled with water, moss and lichens are shining with a fresh verdure; not a twig, not a leaf have I left on the ground.' 'Young fool,' chided the tea-master, 'that is not the way a garden path should be swept.' Saying this, Rikyu stepped into the garden, shook a tree and scattered over the garden gold and crimson leaves, scraps of the brocade of autumn! What Rikyu demanded was not cleanliness alone, but the beautiful and the natural also.

The name, Abode of Fancy, implies a structure created to meet some individual artistic requirement. The tea-room is made for the tea-master, not the tea-master for the tea-room. It is not intended for posterity and is therefore ephemeral. [. . .]

Zennism, with the Buddhist theory of evanescence and its demands for the mastery of spirit over matter, recognised the house only as a temporary refuge for the body. The body itself was but as a hut in the wilderness, a flimsy shelter made by tying together the grasses that grew around,—when these ceased to be bound together they again became resolved into the original waste. In the tea-room fugitiveness is suggested in the thatched roof, frailty in the slender pillars, lightness in the bamboo support, apparent carelessness in the use of commonplace materials. The eternal is to be found only in the spirit which, embodied in these simple surroundings, beautifies them with the subtle light of its refinement.

That the tea-room should be built to suit some individual taste is an enforcement of the principle of vitality in art. Art, to be fully appreciated, must be true to contemporaneous life. It is not that we should ignore the claims of posterity, but that we should seek to enjoy the present more. It is not that we should disregard the creations of the past, but that we should try to assimilate them into our consciousness. Slavish conformity to traditions and formulas fetters the expression of individuality in architecture. We can but weep over those senseless imitations of European buildings which one beholds in modern Japan. We marvel why, among the most progressive Western nations, architecture should be so devoid of originality, so replete with repetitions of obsolete styles. Perhaps we are now passing through an age of democratisation in art, while awaiting the rise of some princely master who shall establish a new dynasty. Would that we loved the ancients more and copied them less! It has been said that the Greeks were great because they never drew from the antique.

The term, Abode of Vacancy, besides conveying the Taoist theory of the all-containing, involves the conception of a continued need of change in decorative motives. The tea-room is absolutely empty, except for what may be placed there temporarily to satisfy some aesthetic mood. Some special art object is brought in for the occasion, and everything else is selected and arranged to enhance the beauty of the principal theme. One cannot listen to different pieces of music at the same time, a real comprehension of the beautiful being possible only through concentration upon some central motive. Thus it will be seen that the system of decoration in our tea-rooms is opposed to that which obtains in the West, where the interior of a house is often converted into a museum. To a Japanese, accustomed to simplicity of ornamentation and frequent change of decorative method, a Western interior permanently filled with a vast array of pictures, statuary, and bric-à-brac gives the impression of mere vulgar display of riches. It calls for a mighty wealth of appreciation to enjoy the constant sight of even a masterpiece, and limitless indeed must be the capacity for artistic feeling in those who can exist day after day in the midst of such confusion of colour and form as is to be often seen in the homes of Europe and America.

The 'Abode of the Unsymmetrical' suggests another phase of our decorative scheme. The absence of symmetry in Japanese art objects has been often commented on by Western critics. This, also, is a result of a working out through Zennism of Taoist ideals. Confucianism, with its deep-seated idea of dualism, and Northern Buddhism with its worship of a trinity, were in no way opposed to the expression of symmetry. As a matter of fact, if we study the ancient bronzes of China or the religious arts of the T'ang dynasty and the Nara period, we shall recognise a constant striving after symmetry. The decoration of our classical interiors was decidedly regular in its arrangement. The Taoist and Zen conception of perfection, however, was different. The dynamic nature of their philosophy laid more stress upon the process through which perfection was sought than upon perfection itself. True beauty could be discovered only by one who mentally completed the incomplete. The virility of life and art lay in its possibilities for growth. In the tea-room it is left for each guest in imagination to complete the total effect in relation to himself. Since Zennism has become the prevailing mode of thought, the art of the extreme Orient has purposely avoided the symmetrical as expressing not only completion, but repetition. Uniformity of design was considered as fatal to the freshness of imagination. Thus, landscapes, birds, and flowers became the favourite subjects for depiction rather than the human figure, the latter being present in the person of the beholder himself. We are often too much in evidence as it is, and in spite of our vanity even self-regard is apt to become monotonous.

In the tea-room the fear of repetition is a constant presence. The various objects for the decoration of a room should be so selected that no colour or design shall be repeated. If you have a living flower, a painting of flowers is not allowable. If you are using a round kettle, the water pitcher should be angular. A cup with a black glaze should not be associated with a tea-caddy of black lacquer. In placing a vase on an incense burner on the tokonoma, care should be taken not to put it in the exact centre, lest it divide the space into equal halves. The pillar of the tokonoma should be of a different kind of wood from the other pillars, in order to break any suggestion of monotony in the room.

Here again the Japanese method of interior decoration differs from that of the Occident, where we see objects arrayed symmetrically on mantelpieces and elsewhere. In Western houses we are often confronted with what appears to us useless reiteration. We find it trying to talk to a man while his full-length portrait stares at us from behind his back. We wonder which is real, he of the picture or he who talks, and feel a curious conviction that one of them must be fraud. Many a time have we sat at a festive board contemplating, with a secret shock to our digestion, the representation of abundance on the dining-room walls. Why these pictured victims of chase and sport, the elaborate carvings of fishes and fruit? Why the display of family plates, reminding us of those who have dined and are dead?

The simplicity of the tea-room and its freedom from vulgarity make it truly a sanctuary from the vexation of the outer world. There and there alone can one consecrate himself to undisturbed adoration of the beautiful. In the sixteenth century the tea-room afforded a welcome respite from labour to the fierce warriors and statesmen engaged in the unification and reconstruction of Japan. In the seventeenth century, after the strict formalism of the Tokugawa rule had been developed, it offered the only opportunity possible for the free communion of artistic spirits. Before a great work of art there was no distinction between daimyo, samurai, and commoner. Nowadays industrialism is making true refinement more and more difficult all the world over. Do we not need the tea-room more than ever?

[*The Book of Tea*, ed. Everett F. Bleiler (New York: Dover; 1964), 30–41.]

7 In Praise of Shadows

There are those who hold that to quibble over matters of taste in the basic necessities of life is an extravagance, that as long as a house keeps out the cold and as long as food keeps off starvation, it matters little what they look like. And indeed for even the sternest ascetic the fact remains that a snowy day is cold, and there is no denying the impulse to accept the services of a heater if it happens to be there in front of one, no matter how cruelly its inelegance may shatter the spell of the day. But it is on occasions like this that I always think how different everything would be if we in the Orient had developed our own science. Suppose for instance that we had developed our own physics and chemistry: would not the techniques and industries based on them have taken a different form, would not our myriads of everyday gadgets, our medicines, the products of our industrial art—would they not have suited our national temper better than they do? In fact our conception of physics itself, and even the principles of chemistry, would probably differ from that of Westerners; and the facts we are now taught concerning the nature and function of light, electricity, and atoms might well have presented themselves in different form.

Of course I am only indulging in idle speculation; of scientific matters I know nothing. But had we devised independently at least the more practical sorts of inventions, this could not but have had profound influence upon the conduct of our everyday lives, and even upon government, religion, art, and business. The Orient quite conceivably could have opened up a world of technology entirely its own.

To take a trivial example near at hand: I wrote a magazine article recently comparing the writing brush with the fountain pen, and in the course of it I remarked that if the device had been invented by the ancient Chinese or Japanese it would surely have had a tufted end like our writing brush. The ink would not have been this bluish color but rather black, something like India ink, and it would have been made to seep down from the handle into the brush. And since we would have then found it inconvenient to write on Western paper, something near Japanese paper—even under mass production, if you will—would have been most in demand. Foreign ink and pen would not be as popular as they are; the talk of discarding our system of writing for Roman letters would be less noisy; people would still feel an affection for the old system. But more than that: our thought and our literature might not be imitating the West as they are, but might have pushed forward into new regions quite on their own. An insignificant little piece of writing equipment, when one thinks of it, has had a vast, almost boundless, influence on our culture.

But I know as well as anyone that these are the empty dreams of a novelist, and that having come this far we cannot turn back. I know that I am only grumbling to myself and demanding the impossible. If my complaints are taken for what they are, however, there can be no harm in considering how unlucky we have been, what losses we have suffered, in comparison with the Westerner. The Westerner has been able to move forward in ordered steps, while we have met superior civilization and have had to surrender to it, and we have had to leave a road we have followed for thousands of years. The missteps and inconveniences this has caused have, I think, been many. If we had been left alone we might not be much further now in a material way than we were five hundred years ago. Even now in the Indian and Chinese countryside life no doubt goes on much as it did when Buddha and Confucius were alive. But we would have gone only in a direction that suited us. We would have gone ahead very slowly, and yet it is not impossible that we would one day have discovered our own substitute for the trolley, the radio, the airplane of today. They would have been no borrowed gadgets, they would have been the tools of our own culture, suited to us.

One need only compare American, French, and German films to see how greatly nuances of shading and coloration can vary in motion pictures. In the photographic image itself, to say nothing of the acting and the script, there somehow emerge differences in national character. If this is true even when identical equipment, chemicals, and film are used, how much better our own photographic technology might have suited our complexion, our facial features, our climate, our land. And had we invented the phonograph and the radio, how much more faithfully they would reproduce the special character of our voices and our music. Japanese music is above all a music of reticence, of atmosphere. When recorded, or amplified by a loudspeaker, the greater part of its charm is lost. In conversation, too, we prefer the soft voice, the understatement. Most important of all are the pauses. Yet the phonograph and radio render these moments of silence utterly lifeless. And so we distort the arts themselves to curry favor for them with the machines. These machines are the inventions of Westerners, and are, as we might expect, well suited to the Western arts. But precisely on this account they put our own arts at a great disadvantage.

Paper, I understand, was invented by the Chinese; but Western paper is to us no more than something to be used, while the texture of Chinese paper and Japanese paper gives us a certain feeling of warmth, of calm and repose. Even the same white could as well be one color for Western paper and another for our own. Western paper turns away the light, while our paper seems to take it in, to envelop it gently, like the soft surface of a first snowfall. It gives off no sound when it is crumpled or folded, it is quiet and pliant to the touch as the leaf of a tree.

As a general matter we find it hard to be really at home with things that shine and glitter. The Westerner uses silver and steel and nickel tableware, and polishes it to a fine brilliance, but we object to the practice. While we do sometimes indeed use silver for teakettles, decanters, or saké cups, we prefer not to polish it. On the contrary, we begin to enjoy it only when the luster has worn off, when it has begun to take on a dark, smoky patina. Almost every householder has had to scold an insensitive maid who has polished away the tarnish so patiently waited for. [. . .]

I possess no specialized knowledge of architecture, but I understand that in the Gothic cathedral of the West, the roof is thrust up and up so as to place its pinnacle as high in the heavens as possible—and that herein is thought to lie its special beauty. In the temples of Japan, on the other hand, a roof of heavy tiles is first laid out, and in the deep, spacious shadows created by the eaves the rest of the structure is built. Nor is this true only of temples; in the palaces of the nobility and the houses of the common people, what first strikes the eye is the massive roof of tile or thatch and the heavy darkness that hangs beneath the eaves. Even at midday cavernous darkness spreads over all beneath the roof's edge, making entryway, doors, walls, and pillars all but invisible. The grand temples of Kyoto—Chion'in, Honganji—and the farm-houses of the remote countryside are alike in this respect: like most buildings of the past their roofs give the impression of possessing far greater weight, height, and surface than all that stands beneath the eaves.

In making for ourselves a place to live, we first spread a parasol to throw a shadow on the earth, and in the pale light of the shadow we put together a house. There are of course roofs on Western houses too, but they are less to keep off the sun than to keep off the wind and the dew; even from without it is apparent that they are built to create as few shadows as possible and to expose the interior to as much light as possible. If the roof of a Japanese house is a parasol, the roof of a Western house is no more than a cap, with as small a visor as possible so as to allow the sunlight to penetrate directly beneath the eaves. There are no doubt all sorts of reasons—climate, building materials— for the deep Japanese eaves. The fact that we did not use glass, concrete, and bricks, for instance, made a low roof necessary to keep off the driving wind and rain. A light room would no doubt have been more convenient for us, too, than a dark room. The quality that we call beauty, however, must always grow from the realities of life, and our ancestors, forced to live in dark rooms, presently came to discover beauty in shadows, ultimately to guide shadows towards beauty's ends.

And so it has come to be that the beauty of a Japanese room depends on a variation of shadows, heavy shadows against light shadows—it has nothing else. Westerners are amazed at the simplicity of Japanese rooms, perceiving in them no more than ashen walls bereft of ornament. Their reaction is understandable, but it betrays a failure to comprehend the mystery of shadows. Out beyond the sitting room, which the rays of the sun can at best but barely reach, we extend the eaves or build on a veranda, putting the sunlight at still greater a remove. The light from the garden steals in but dimly through paper-paneled doors, and it is precisely this indirect light that makes for us the charm of a room. We do our walls in neutral colors so that the sad, fragile, dying rays can sink into absolute repose. The storehouse, kitchen, hallways, and such may have a glossy finish, but the walls of the sitting room will almost always be of clay textured with fine sand. A luster here would destroy the soft fragile beauty of the feeble light. We delight in the mere sight of the delicate glow of fading rays clinging to the surface of a dusky wall, there to live out what little life remains to them. We never tire of the sight, for to us this pale glow and these dim shadows far surpass any ornament. And so, as we must if we are not to disturb the glow, we finish the walls with sand in a single neutral color. The hue may differ from room to room, but the degree of difference will be ever so slight; not so much a difference in color as in shade, a difference that will seem to exist only in the mood of the viewer. And from these delicate differences in the hue of the walls, the shadows in each room take on a tinge peculiarly their own.

Of course the Japanese room does have its picture alcove, and in it a hanging scroll and a flower arrangement. But the scroll and the flowers serve not as ornament but rather to give depth to the shadows. We value a scroll above all for the way it blends with the walls of the alcove, and thus we consider the mounting quite as important as the calligraphy or painting. Even the greatest masterpiece will lose its worth as a scroll if it fails to blend with the alcove, while a work of no particular distinction may blend beautifully with the room and set off to unexpected advantage both itself and its surroundings. Wherein lies the power of an otherwise ordinary work to produce such an effect? Most often the paper, the ink, the fabric of the mounting will possess a certain look of antiquity, and this look of antiquity will strike just the right balance with the darkness of the alcove and room. [. . .]

I am aware of and most grateful for the benefits of the age. No matter what complaints we may have, Japan has chosen to follow the West, and there is nothing for her to do but move bravely ahead and leave us old ones behind. But we must be resigned to the fact that as long as our skin is the color it is the loss we have suffered cannot be remedied. I have written all this because I have thought that there might still be somewhere, possibly in literature or the arts, where something could be saved. I would call back at least for literature this world of shadows we are losing. In the mansion called literature I would have the eaves deep and the walls dark, I would push back into the shadows the things that come forward too clearly, I would strip away the useless decoration. I do not ask that this be done everywhere, but perhaps we may be allowed at least one mansion where we can turn off the electric lights and see what it is like without them.

[*In Praise of Shadows*, trans. Thomas J. Harper and Edward G. Seidensticker (Stony Creek, Conn.: Leete's Island Books, Inc., 1977), 7–10, 17–19, 42. First published in 1933/4.]

FRIEDRICH NIETZSCHE

8 The Dionysian

Already in the preface addressed to Richard Wagner,[1] art, and *not* morality, is presented as the truly *metaphysical* activity of man. In the book itself the suggestive sentence is repeated several times, that the existence of the world is *justified* only as an aesthetic phenomenon. Indeed, the whole book knows only an artistic meaning and crypto-meaning behind all events—a 'god,' if you please, but certainly only an entirely reckless and amoral artist-god who wants to experience, whether he is building or destroying, in the good and in the bad, his own joy and glory—one who, creating worlds, frees himself from the *distress* of fullness and *overfullness* and from the *affliction* of the contradictions compressed in his soul. The world—at every moment the *attained* salvation of God, as the eternally changing, eternally new vision of the most deeply afflicted, discordant, and contradictory being who can find salvation only in *appearance*: you can call this whole artists' metaphysics arbitrary, idle, fantastic; what matters is that it betrays a spirit who will one day fight at any risk whatever the *moral* interpretation and significance of existence. Here, perhaps for the first time, a pessimism 'beyond good and evil' is suggested. Here that 'perversity of mind' gains speech and formulation against which Schopenhauer never wearies of hurling in advance his most irate curses and thunderbolts: a philosophy that dares to move, to demote, morality into the realm of appearance—and not merely among 'appearances' or phenomena (in the sense assigned to these words by Idealistic philosophers), but among 'deceptions,' as semblance, delusion, error, interpretation, contrivance, art.

Perhaps the depth of this *antimoral* propensity is best inferred from the careful and hostile silence with which Christianity is treated throughout the whole book—Christianity as the most prodigal elaboration of the moral theme to which humanity has ever been subjected. In truth, nothing could be more opposed to the purely aesthetic interpretation and justification of the world which are taught in this book than the Christian teaching, which is, and wants to be, *only* moral and which relegates art, *every* art, to the realm of *lies*; with its absolute standards, beginning with the truthfulness of God, it negates, judges, and damns art. Behind this mode of thought and valuation, which must be hostile to art if it is at all genuine, I never failed to sense a *hostility to life*—a furious, vengeful antipathy to life itself: for all of life is based on semblance, art, deception, points of view, and the necessity of perspectives and error. Christianity was from the beginning, essentially and fundamentally, life's nausea and disgust with life, merely concealed behind, masked by, dressed up as, faith in 'another' or 'better' life. Hatred of 'the world,' condemnations of the passions, fear of beauty and sensuality, a beyond invented the better to slander this life, at bottom a craving for the nothing, for the end, for respite, for 'the sabbath of sabbaths'—all this always struck me, no less than the unconditional will of Christianity to recognize *only* moral values, as the most dangerous and uncanny form of all possible forms of a 'will to decline'—at the very least a sign of abysmal sickness, weariness, discouragement, exhaustion, and the impoverishment of life. For, confronted with morality (especially Christian, or unconditional, morality), life *must* continually and inevitably be in the wrong, because life *is* something essentially amoral—and eventually, crushed by the weight of contempt and the eternal No, life *must* then be felt to be unworthy of desire and altogether worthless. Morality itself—how now? might not morality be 'a will to negate life,' a secret instinct of annihilation, a principle of decay, diminution, and slander— the beginning of the end? Hence, the danger of dangers?

It was *against* morality that my instinct turned with this questionable book, long ago; it was an instinct that aligned itself with life and that discovered for itself a fundamentally opposite doctrine and valuation of life—purely artistic and *anti-Christian*. What to call it? As a philologist and man of words I baptized it, not without taking some liberty—for who could claim to know the rightful name of the Antichrist?—in the name of a Greek god: I called it Dionysian.

['Attempt at a Self-Criticism', in *The Birth of Tragedy and the Case of Wagner*, trans. Walter Kaufmann (New York: Random House, 1967), 22–4. First published in 1886.]

JOSHUA C. TAYLOR
....

9 Art and the Ethnological Artifact

As some artists discovered early in the century, there is a particular pleasure and stimulation to be derived from works of art created by cultures untouched by our own traditions of form. In part this is probably a delight in exoticism, in being away from home, and in part it possibly is our sentiment for cultures we look on as traditional, in a Jungian sense, or primitive in their unquestioning allegiance to simple cultural necessity. But more significantly, without indulging in philosophical or anthropological speculation, we are forced, in looking at such objects as these elegantly designed boxes and bowls, to revise our visual thinking, our assumptions about unity and grace.

Of course, at this point in history, when we have trained ourselves to respond to, or at least accept, all manner of forms and harmonies, and even to search for nonform and harmonic chaos, there is always the danger of losing that sense of ritual upon which any formal harmony is based. For anyone so threatened, a study of such objects as the boxes and bowls from the Northwest Coast Indian cultures, with their deftly chiseled forms contrasting an inner life with an outward austerity, should serve as a helpful restorative.

How to talk about such objects, however, is a nice problem. For the last one hundred or so years they have been collected as artifacts, and although since the 1930s they have found their way into museum collections as objects of art, the language by which they have been expertly catalogued and described remains that of the ethnologist and anthropologist. Although the critical language of art has changed much over the years, keeping pace at its best with new concepts in art that have broken with nineteenth-century norms of imitation and formal composition, the new critical disciplines have made little inroad into archaeology or anthropology. If indeed we are dealing with works of art, there seems little reason for closing off those sensibilities that have proved fruitful in revealing meaning in other reaches of art from these objects simply because they were collected for another purpose. No matter how objective the archaeologist or anthropologist feels himself to be, he is making critical judgments in his descriptions and should have not only the courage to face up to the fact but the critical awareness to recognize the sources of his own tradition.

Most of Western design has been based on the interplay or opposition of two compositional principles: the proportional relationship of clearly defined forms of a relatively simple geometric sort, or a continuity of line or form in which one shape flows into the next with little concern for beginnings and endings. These have been characterized by theorists in many different ways over the years, sometimes on the basis of large cultural schemes (note, e.g., Worringer's *Abstraction and Empathy*), sometimes in terms of individual response. But we have learned to accept these modes as such, no matter what the rationale, as part of our visual stock in trade.

This handy distinction in formal order is little help in looking at these containers from the Northwest Coast. In the first place, they seem always to be made up both of distinct formal entities arranged in nice symmetry, and of continuities. Every line is polished in contour until it moves, even when it encloses what otherwise would be a discrete and static shape. As a result the eye confronts a continuously ambivalent situation, having to choose between simply looking at a form—and many forms have the unnerving habit of looking back—and joining a rhythm that leads to something else. Which does one choose? Both, of course. It is a bit like staying in one place and going somewhere else at the same time. In art, however, the awarenesses of being

FIG. 1 End of a Haida relief-carved argillite chest, collected by James G. Swan (October 1883), National Collection of Fine Arts.

and becoming can live quite happily together, and these active though static compositions effectively demonstrate the fact.

The result of this somewhat wrenching experience, in which one is invited to join the lively movement and identify himself with the rhythm of the lines, only to be expelled from this empathetic union by the tightly integrated nature of the forms, is to recognize a kind of hypnotic power that surrounds these objects. And we need not be a believer in any particular mythological scheme to sense it. Worringer's distinction of cultures on the basis of abstraction or empathy would not work convincingly here because abstract distance and empathetic identity coexist, as if we were both participating in the work and looking on as observers. A universe is suggested that is part and parcel of ourselves, yet embodies an inner mystery that remains aloof.

Any insistence on distinguishing between the animate and the inanimate in these objects is bound to lead to frustration, chiefly because such a distinction is irrelevant. In a sense, every object or form that is kindled to life in the mind of the observer is animate and has to be dealt with as a separate personality. This is not an easy concept for one trained in the Western traditions in which to distinguish between animal, mineral, and humankind is a mark of sophistication. The idea that an identifiable, clearly dimensioned appearance is the only true reality dies hard, even though artists ceased trying to distinguish between objective and subjective a good many years ago. To attempt, in this case, to determine whether a bowl was made to look like an animal or the animal was distorted to become a bowl is a fruitless task. They grow together: the bowl became animate and its animation gave reason for its being a bird as well as a bowl. This is a very different situation from a Victorian soup tureen that looks like a sitting hen. The bowl does not have the form, the external appearance, but the spirit of a living thing, evoked not by likeness but by a compelling liveness of form. We tend to attribute organic life to a form if it eludes our imposition of geometrical order, or simple recognition as thing, but seems to proceed in accordance with an inner volition of its own. As in an early Chou bronze from China or a Zapotec design from Mexico, the flattened curves and elongated shapes of the Northwest Coast designs do just that. One can look in vain for circular arcs and spiral curves. For all their adherence to type, the lines of the carved designs are to be understood only in the act of following them, not by matching them to an established object or a geometrical concept.

All of this underscores the fact that these are not decorated objects in the usual Western sense. In sorting out their ideas about design in the general scheme of things, theorists in the middle of the last century made clear that decoration of an object must be adornment beyond the dictates of use if it were to be of value. Its intricacy and costliness made clear that the owner was not bound, by taste or pocket, to the restrictions of utility. A countertendency took shape later in the century which insisted that decoration, if used at all, should be related to the structure itself. And finally came the moral dictum that there should be no decoration; structure was all and austerity was good.

None of these approaches to design is helpful in getting at the character of our boxes and bowls because all such concepts are based on a series of isolated qualities such as utility, decoration, aesthetic structure, and a kind of symbolic morality. They all belong to a world of pragmatic values and are the product of deliberate analysis. To the Indian carver, decoration had meaning, not simply by virtue of its historical or sociological reference, although traditional mythological inferences were doubtless important, but because it effectively blurred precisely that difference between object and mind, the outer and inner, which has been so dear to the tradition of Western thought. Furthermore, the 'inner' was not simply the expression of animal spirit, as sometimes seems to be the case in what we regard as primitive art, but that which maintained a quality of mystery, of an order beyond calculation or sense.

Quite possibly, then, the revision of our way of looking, dictated by such designs as these, goes rather further than simply adding another flavor to our repertory of aesthetic tastes. If we, too, even though uninformed of the mythological systems and cultural mores of the people who created these objects, can sense this combination of vitality and wonder that the carvings evoke, then our estrangement from the world is not so complete as some popular philosophies would have us believe. We rarely talk of magic as a function of our present art, but of course it is. Art serves to kindle into meaning aspects of our perception that would otherwise remain external to our minds. To be sure the Northwest Indians organized a culture far different from our own, but we can sense a bond of sympathy in their art that goes well beyond a respect for craftsmanship. Exotic distance drops away under the impact of a shared human awareness.

['Two Visual Excursions', *Critical Inquiry*, 1 (Sept. 1974), 91–7.]

LINDA NOCHLIN

10 Women, Art, and Power

In this essay, I shall be investigating the relationships existing among women, art, and power in a group of visual images from the late eighteenth through the twentieth centuries. These visual images have been chosen for the most part because they represent women in situations involving power—most usually its lack. It is obvious that the story or content or narratives of these images—what art historians call their 'iconography'—will be an important element for analysis in this project: the story of the Horatii represented by David [and] that of the death of Sardanapalus depicted by Delacroix. [. . .]

Yet what I am really interested in are the operations of power on the level of ideology, operations which manifest themselves in a much more diffuse, more absolute, yet paradoxically more elusive sense, in what might be called the discourses of gender difference. I refer, of course, to the ways in which representations of women in art are founded upon and serve to reproduce indisputably accepted assumptions held by society in general, artists in particular, and some artists more than others about men's power over, superiority to, difference from, and necessary control of women, assumptions which are manifested in the visual structures as well as the thematic choices of the pictures in question. Ideology manifests itself as much by what is unspoken—unthinkable, unrepresentable—as by what is articulated in a work of art. Insofar as many of the assumptions about women presented themselves as a complex of commonsense views about the world, and were therefore assumed to be self-evident, they were relatively invisible to most contemporary viewers, as well as to the creators of the paintings. Assumptions about women's weakness and passivity; her sexual availability for men's needs; her defining domestic and nurturing function; her identity with the realm of nature; her existence as object rather than creator of art; the patent ridiculousness of her attempts to insert herself actively into the realm of history by means of work or engagement in political struggle—all of these notions, themselves premised on an even more general, more all-pervasive certainty about gender difference itself—all of these notions were shared, if not uncontestedly, to a greater or lesser degree by most people of our period, and as such constitute an ongoing subtext underlying almost all individual images involving women. Yet perhaps the term 'subtext' is misleading in view of my intentions. It is not a *deep* reading I am after; this is not going to be an attempt to move *behind* the images into some realm of more profound truth lurking beneath the surface of the various pictorial texts. My attempt to investigate the triad woman–art–power should rather be thought of as an effort to disentangle various discourses about power related to gender difference existing simultaneously with—as much surface as substratum—the master discourse of the iconography or narrative.

It is important to keep in mind that one of the most important functions of ideology is to veil the overt power relations obtaining in society at a particular moment in history by making them appear to be part of the natural, eternal order of things. It is also important to remember that symbolic power is invisible and can be exercised only with the complicity of those who fail to recognize either that they submit to it or that they exercise it. Women artists are often no more immune to the blandishments of ideological discourses than their male contemporaries, nor should dominant males be envisioned as conspiratorially or even consciously forcing their notions upon women. Michel Foucault has reflected that power is tolerable 'only on the condition that it mask a considerable part of itself.'[1] The patriarchal discourse of power over women masks itself in the veil of the natural—indeed, of the logical.

Strength and weakness are understood to be the natural corollaries of gender difference. Yet it is more accurate to say, in a work like David's *Oath of the Horatii*, that it is the representation of gender differences—male versus female—that immediately establishes that opposition between strength and weakness which is the point of the picture.

In the *Horatii*, the notion of woman's passivity—and her propensity to give in to personal feeling—would appear to have existed for the artist as an available element of a visual *langue* upon which the high intelligibility of this specific pictorial *parole* depends.[2] It is important to realize that the particular narrative incident represented here—the moment when the three brothers, the Horatii, take a patriotic oath of allegiance to Rome on swords held before them by their father in the presence of the women and children of the family—is not to be found in Classical or post-Classical texts, but is in essence a Davidian invention, arrived at after many other explorations of potential subjects from the story.[3] It is an invention which owes its revolutionary clarity precisely to the clear-cut opposition between masculine strength and feminine weakness offered by the ideological discourse of the period. The striking effectiveness of the visual communication here depends in the most graphic way possible upon a universal assumption: it is not something that needs to be thought about. The binary division here between male energy, tension, and concentration as opposed to female resignation, flaccidity, and relaxation is as clear as any Lévi-Straussian diagram of a native village; it is carried out in every detail of pictorial structure and treatment, is inscribed on the bodies of the protagonists in their poses and anatomy, and is even evident in the way that the male figures are allotted the lions' share of the architectural setting, expanding to fill it, whereas the women, collapsed in upon themselves, must make do with a mere corner. [. . .]

In the middle of the nineteenth century, in Victorian England, woman's passivity, her defining inability to defend herself against physical violence, would appear to have been such an accepted article of faith that the poses which had signified weakness—the very opposite of heroism in David's *Horatii*—could now, with a bit of neck straightening and chin stiffening, in the case of British ladies, be read as heroism itself. Indeed, Sir Joseph Noel Paton, the author of such a work, which appeared in the 1858 Royal Academy show under the title *In Memoriam* (the original has disappeared), dedicated it 'to Commemorate the Christian Heroism of the British Ladies in India during the Mutiny of 1857.' It must be added parenthetically that the figures entering so energetically from the rear were originally not the Scottish rescuers we see in the engraving after the painting, but rather those of bloodthirsty Sepoys, the Indian rebels, which were altered because the artist felt their presence created 'too painful an impression.'[4] The heroism of British ladies would seem to have consisted of kneeling down and allowing themselves and their children to be atrociously raped and murdered, dressed in the most unsuitably fashionable but flattering clothes possible, without lifting a finger to defend themselves. Yet to admiring spectators of the time, tranquility and the Bible, rather than vigorous self-defense, were precisely what constituted heroism for a lady. Said the reviewer in the *Art Journal* of the time: 'The spectator is fascinated by the sublimely calm expression of the principal head—hers is more than Roman virtue; her lips are parted in prayer; she holds the Bible in her hand, and that is her strength.'[5] Now there are at least two discourses articulated in this image. One is the overt story of heroic British ladies and their children during the Sepoy mutiny, fortifying themselves with prayer as they are about to be assaulted by savage, and presumably lustful, natives. The other discourse, less obvious, is the patriarchal and class-defined one which stipulates the appropriate behavior for the lady, and it implies that no lady will ever unsex herself by going so far as to raise a hand in physical violence, even in defense of her children. Such a notion about ladylike or 'womanly' behavior had of course some but not necessarily a great deal of relationship to how women, British ladies during the Sepoy mutiny included, have actually acted under similar circumstances. Goya's women, in the etching *And They Are Like Wild Beasts* from the 'Disasters of War' series (Fig. 1), though obviously not ladies, are shown behaving quite differently from those in *In Memoriam*, although the fact that these peasant women resort to violence itself functions as a sign of the extremity of the situation. The Spanish mothers who fight so desperately to defend their children, it is implied, are something other than women: they 'are like wild beasts.'[6]

[...] Victorian assumptions about ladylike behavior are premised on the kinds of threats that, although rarely mentioned, lie in store for those who

FIG. 2 *And They Are Like Wild Beasts*, Francisco Goya Lucientes (c. 1810–20)

call them into question: the woman who goes so far as to rely on physical force or independent action is no longer to be considered a lady. It then follows that because women are so naturally defenseless and men so naturally aggressive, real ladies must depend not on themselves but on male defenders—as in *In Memoriam*, the Scottish troops, to protect them from (similarly male) attackers, the (overpainted) Sepoy mutineers.

That these views were held to be self-evident by both men and women at the time goes without saying: ideology is successful precisely to the degree that its views are shared by those who exercise power and those who submit to it. But there is a corollary to the assumptions underlying the visual text here which would have been more available to men than to women: what one might call its fantasy potential—a discourse of desire—the imaginative construction of a sequel to *In Memoriam*: something like *The Rape and Murder of the British Women During the Indian Mutiny*, a subject current in the popular press of the period. It is this aspect of the painting, its hint of 'unspeakable things to come,' delicately referred to in the contemporary review as 'those fiendish artocities [which] cannot be borne without a shudder,'[7] which must have in part accounted for its popularity with the public.

This sort of sequel does, of course, exist, although it predates *In Memoriam* and was painted in France rather than in England: Delacroix's *Death of Sardanapalus* [. . .] [I]n power dreams begin—dreams of still greater power, in this case, fantasies of men's limitless power to enjoy, by destroying them, the bodies of women. Delacroix's painting cannot, of course, be reduced to a mere pictorial projection of the artist's sadistic fantasies under the guise of exoticism. Yet one must keep in mind that subtending the vivid turbulence of the text of Delacroix's story—the story of the ancient Assyrian ruler Sardanapalus, who, upon hearing of his incipient defeat, had all his precious possessions, including his women, destroyed, and then went up in flames with them in his palace—lies the more mundane assumption, shared by men of Delacroix's class, that they were naturally 'entitled' to desire, to possess, and to control the bodies of women. If the men were artists, it was assumed that they had more or less unlimited access to the bodies of the women who worked for them as models. In other words, Delacroix's private fantasy exists not in a vacuum but in a particular social context, granting permission as well as establishing boundaries for certain kinds of behavior. It is almost impossible to imagine a *Death of Cleopatra*, say, with nude male slaves being put to death by women servants, painted by a *woman* artist of this period. In the sexual power system of patriarchy, transgression is not merely that which violates understood codes of thought and behavior: it is, even more urgently, that which marks their farthest boundaries. Sexual transgression may be understood as a *threshold* of permissible behavior—actual, imaginary—rather than as its opposite. The true site of opposition is marked by gender difference. [. . .]

By no stretch of the imagination can one envisage a woman artist of the nineteenth century interpreting her role, as did her male counterparts quite freely and naturally, in terms of free access to the naked bodies of the opposite sex. Gérôme, on the contrary, in his self-portrait *The Artist's Model* has simply depicted himself in one of the most conventionally acceptable and, indeed, self-explanatory narrative structures for the self-representation of the artist. The topos of the artist in his studio assumes that being an artist has to do with man's free access to naked women. Art-making, the very creation of beauty itself, was equated with the representation of the female nude. Here, the very notion of the originary power of the artist, his status as creator of unique and valuable objects, is founded on a discourse of gender difference as power.

This assumption is presented quite overtly, although with a certain amount of tactful, naturalistic hedging, in *The Artist's Model*. The artist does not represent himself touching the *living woman* on her thigh, but only her plaster representation, with gloved hands; and the artist himself is (conveniently for the purposes of the painting) white-haired and venerable rather than young and lusty. He may remind us more of a doctor than an artist, and he keeps his eyes modestly lowered on his work, rather than raising them to confront the naked woman. The overt iconography here is the perfectly acceptable theme of the artist in his studio, industriously and single-mindedly engaging in creative activity, surrounded by testimonials to his previous achievements. Assumptions about masculine power are perfectly and disarmingly justified by the noble purposes which this power serves: although the naked model may indeed serve the purposes of the artist, he in turn is merely the humble servant of a higher cause, that of Beauty itself. This complex of beliefs involving male power, naked models, and the creation of art receives its most perfect rationalization in the ever-popular nineteenth-century representation of the Pygmalion myth: stone beauty made flesh by the warming glow of masculine desire. [. . .]

What of women as spectators or consumers of art? The acceptance of woman as object of the desiring male gaze in the visual arts is so universal that for a woman to question, or to draw attention to this fact, is to invite derision, to reveal herself as one who does not understand the sophisticated strategies of high culture and takes art 'too literally,' and is therefore unable to respond to aesthetic discourses. This is of course maintained within a world— a cultural and academic world—which is dominated by male power and, often unconscious, patriarchal attitudes. In Utopia—that is to say, in a world in which the power structure was such that both men and women equally could be represented clothed or unclothed in a variety of poses and positions without any implications of domination or submission—in a world of total and, so to speak, unconscious equality, the female nude would not be problematic. In our world, it is. As Laura Mulvey has pointed out in her often-cited article 'Visual Pleasure and Narrative Cinema,' there are two choices open to the woman spectator: either to take the place of the male or to accept the position of male-created seductive passivity and the questionable pleasure of masochism—lack of power to the nth degree.[8] This positioning of course offers an analogue to the actual status of women in the power structure of the art world—with the exception of the privileged few. To turn from the world of theory to that of mundane experience: I was participating as a guest in a college class on contemporary realism, when my host flashed on the screen the close-up image of a woman's buttocks in a striped bikini, as a presumed illustration of the substitution of part for whole in realist imagery, or perhaps it was the decorative impulse in realism. I commented on the overtly sexual—and sexist—implications of the image and the way it was treated. My host maintained that he 'hadn't thought of that' and that he 'had simply not been aware of the subject.' It was impossible for any woman in the class 'not to think of that' or for any man in the class to miss its crudely degrading implications. In a university art class, one is not supposed to speak of such things; women, like men, are presumably to take crudely fetishized motifs as signifiers of a refreshing liberatedness about sexual—and artistic— matters. My host insisted on the purely decorative, almost abstract, as he termed it, implications of the theme. But such abstraction is by no means a neutral strategy, as Daumier discovered when he transformed the recognizable head of Louis-Philippe into a neutral still-life object in his 'La Poire' series. For women, the sexual positioning of the female in visual representation obtrudes through the apparently neutral or aesthetic fabric of the art work. [. . .]

There is an analogy between women's compromised ability—her lack of self-determining power—in the realm of the social order and her lack of power to articulate a negative critique in the realm of pictorial representation. In both cases, her rejection of patriarchal authority is weakened by accusations of prudery or naïveté. Sophistication, liberation, belonging are equated with acquiescence to male demands; women's initial perceptions of oppression, of outrage, of negativity are undermined by authorized doubts, by the need to please, to be learned, sophisticated, aesthetically astute—in male-defined terms, of course. And the need to comply, to be inwardly at one with the patriarchal order and its discourses is compelling, inscribing itself in the deepest level of the unconscious, marking the very definitions of the self-as-woman in our society—and almost all others that we know of. I say this despite—indeed, because of—the obvious manifestations of change in the realm of women's power, position, and political consciousness brought about by the women's movement and more specifically by feminist criticism and art production over the last fifteen years. It is only by breaking the circuits, splitting apart those processes of harmonizing coherence that, to borrow the words of Lisa Tickner, 'help secure the subject to and in ideology,'[9] by fishing in those invisible streams of power and working to demystify the discourses of visual imagery—in other words, through a politics of representation and its institutional structures—that change can take place.

[*Women, Art, and Power and Other Essays* (New York: Harper & Row, 1988), 1–10, 17–19, 29–33.]

MICHAEL ROEMER

11   The Surfaces of Reality

As Siegfried Kracauer effectively demonstrates, the camera photographs the skin; it cannot function like an X-ray machine and show us what is underneath. This does not mean, however, that the film-maker has no control over the surfaces rendered by his camera. On the contrary, he *chooses* his surfaces for their content, and through their careful selection and juxtaposition builds a structure of feeling and meaning that are the core of his work.

There are times in the history of the medium when story, treatment and performance drift so far into a studio never-never land that we cannot help but make a virtue of 'pure' reality, as free from interference on the part of the film-maker as possible—even at the risk of creating something shapeless. This should not, however, obscure the fact that a film, like a poem or painting, is basically an artifact.

The assertion that film is nothing more than a documentary recording of reality undoubtedly stems from the fact that the medium must render all meaning in physical terms. This affinity for real surfaces, combined with great freedom of movement both in time and space, brings film closer than any other medium to our own random experience of life. Even the realistic playwright, who—until the advent of the camera—came closest to rendering the appearance of reality, is often forced in his structure to violate the very sense of life he is trying to create. But the film-maker can use the flexible resources at his command to approximate the actual fabric of reality. Moreover, he need not heighten his effects in order to communicate, for he can call on the same sensibilities in his audience that we use in life itself.

All of us bring to every situation, whether it be a business meeting or a love affair, a social and psychological awareness which helps us understand complex motivations and relationships. This kind of perception, much of it nonverbal and based on apparently insignificant clues, is not limited to the educated or gifted. We all depend on it for our understanding of other people and have become extremely proficient in the interpretation of subtle signs—a shading in the voice, an averted glance. This nuanced awareness, however, is not easily called upon by the arts, for it is predicated upon a far more immediate and total experience than can be provided by literature and the theatre, with their dependence on the word, or by the visual arts—with their dependence on the image. Only film renders experience with enough immediacy and totality to call into play the perceptual processes we employ in life itself.

The fact that film exercises this sort of perceptual capacity is, I believe, one of its chief appeals to us. It gives us practice in the delicate and always somewhat uncertain skill of finding out what is going on. As an extreme example, take these lines from *Marty*. They are spoken in a dance hall during the first encounter between a lonely man and a lonely girl. She says: 'I'm twenty-nine years old. How old are you?' And he answers: 'Thirty-six.'

On the stage or the printed page these lines would fall ludicrously flat. But on the screen, when spoken by performers who can make every detail yield a wealth of meaning, they instantly convey—as they would in life itself—a complex web of feeling: the girl's fear that she might be too old for the man, her need to come right to the point, her relief when he turns out to be older, and finally a mutual delight that their relationship has crossed its first hurdle.

Film thrives on this kind of intimate detail, for the camera reports it so closely that nothing essential is lost to the eye or ear. The camera makes it possible to use the stuff of life itself, without amplification or overstatement and without any loss in dramatic value. What is achieved in a large action or an explicit moment on the stage can be rendered just as dramatically on the screen in small and *implicit* terms, for it is not the magnitude of a gesture that makes it dramatic but its meaning and intention.

This is *not* to say that the medium is most aptly used on the kind of everyday story told in *Marty*, or that low-key dialogue without conflict or strong feeling is always effective on the screen. I quote the scene merely as an example of the medium's capacity for finding meaning in the detail of everyday life and would like to suggest that out of such detail, out of the ordinary surfaces of life, the film-maker can structure *any* kind of situation and story— lyrical or dramatic, historical or contemporary.

Like so many films that deal with the past, Dreyer's *Passion de Jeanne d'Arc* might well have been filled with violent action and theatrical confrontations. Instead the story is told in terms of mundane detail. Thus Jeanne is betrayed at a critical moment by a priest who averts his eyes when she turns to him for help. There is no call for anything more explicit. The betrayal is what matters, and the camera renders it far more credibly and forcefully in a mundane detail than it would be in a highly dramatized gesture.

In *Rashomon* and *The Seven Samurai* Kurosawa deals with events of the thirteenth and sixteenth centuries in the most everyday terms. He knows that our basic daily experience of reality has not changed much over the centuries: a war between bandits and samurai in a feudal Japanese village was as full of mud and rain, as gritty and as grotesque as a twentieth-century skirmish. Film at its best uses the language of ordinary experience—but uses it subtly and artfully.[. . .]

This use of ordinary surfaces requires great skill and discipline since the audience can sense every false move and movement, every false note in the dialogue, every unsubstantiated relationship. The very thing that works *for* the film-maker if he can master it—reality—can quickly turn against him, so that the most ordinary moment becomes utterly unreal. Not surprisingly most directors avoid the challenge and set their stories in unfamiliar parts, among unusual people and in unusual circumstances.

Because most good films use the language of the commonplace, they tend to have an unassuming appearance, whereas films that make a large claim— that speak nobly and poetically about life, love and death—almost invariably prove to be hollow. A good film is concrete: it creates a sequence of objective situations, actual relationships between people, between people and their circumstances. Thus each moment becomes an objective correlative; that is, feeling (or meaning) rendered in actual, physical terms: objectified.

By contrast, most movies are a series of conventional communicative gestures, dialogues, and actions. Most movie-makers *play* on the feelings of their audience by setting up a sequence of incidents that have a proven effect. The events are not rendered; they are merely *cited*. The films do not use the vocabulary of actuality but rather a second-hand language that has proven effective in other films—a language that is changed only when the audience no longer responds.

This language of conventions gives most pictures the appearance of ludicrous unreality fifteen or twenty years after they have been acclaimed as masterpieces. The dramatic conventions of the 1940's are recognized as a system of hollow clichés by the sixties. When *The Best Years of Our Lives* was first shown, references to the war were enough to make an audience feel strongly about a situation or character without any substantiation whatever; there were feelings abroad which, when touched, produced the desired effect. By 1964 this is no longer true and the tissue of the film disintegrates.

Audiences can be 'played' by a skillful movie-maker with a fair amount of predictability, so that even discriminating audiences are easily taken in. At the beginning of Bergman's *Wild Strawberries* Professor Borg dreams that he is on a deserted street with all its doors and windows shuttered tight. He looks up at a clock that has no hands and pulls out his own watch only to find that its hands are missing also. A man appears on the corner with his head averted; when he turns, he has no face and his body dissolves into a pool on the side- walk. A glass hearse comes down the street and spills a coffin that opens. Borg approaches and discovers his own body in the coffin. The corpse comes to life and tries to pull him in.

The nightmare quality in this sequence is derivative. The deserted, shut- tered street, the clock and watch without hands, the glass hearse, the faceless man are all conventions familiar to surrealist painting and literature. Bergman uses them skillfully and with conviction to produce an effect in the audience, but they are not true film images, derived from life and rendered in concrete, physical terms.

There is a similar nightmare in Dreyer's *Vampire*. A young man dreams that he has entered a room with an open coffin in it. He approaches and discovers that he himself is the corpse. The camera now assumes the point-of-view of the dead man: we look up at the ceiling. Voices approach and two carpenters appear in our field of vision. They close the coffin with a lid but we continue to look out through a small glass window. Talking indistinctly, they nail down the lid and plane the edges of the wood. The shavings fall onto the window. One of them has put a candle down on the glass and wax drips onto it. Then the coffin is lifted up and we pass close under the ceiling, through the doorway, beneath the sunlit roofs and the church steeple of a small town—out into the open sky.

Here the detail is concrete: an experience is rendered, not cited; the situation is objective and out of it emerges, very powerfully, the feeling that Dreyer is after: a farewell to life, a last confined look at the earth before the coffin is lowered into the grave. Once again we note that the unassuming detail can render a complex feeling (or meaning) which eludes the more obviously ambitious but abstract statement.

Good film dialogue, too, has this concrete quality. Like the speech of everyday life, it does not tell you *directly* what is felt or meant. One might call it symptomatic dialogue: symptomatic because it is a surface manifestation of what is going on inside the person. The dialogue in most films is, of course, the opposite: a direct statement of feeling or meaning: 'I love you'; 'I am so happy'; 'You are this'; 'I am that.' But just as the action should be a physical or surface correlative that permits the audience to discover for itself the implicit meaning, so the dialogue should be a *surface* that renders its content by implication—not directly. The two lines quoted from *Marty* are good film dialogue. In contrast, here is an incident from Bergman's *The Seventh Seal*.

Shortly before his death the knight Antonius Block shares a meal with a young couple in front of their covered wagon. 'I shall always remember this moment,' he says. 'The silence, the twilight, the bowls of strawberries and milk, your faces in the evening light. Mikhael sleeping, Jof with his lyre. I'll try to remember what we have talked about. I'll carry this moment between my hands as carefully as if it were a bowl filled to the brim with fresh milk. And it will be an adequate sign—it will be enough for me.'

Without this lengthy and explicit verbalization, one would have little insight into the feelings of Antonius Block. The situation itself does not communicate them and Bergman uses dialogue as a way of getting us to understand and feel something the film itself does not render. In Kurosawa's *Ikiru*, a petty official who is dying of cancer and trying desperately to give meaning to his life by pushing a playground project through the sterile bureaucracy, stops on his way home from work to look at the evening sky. 'It's beautiful,' he says to his companion, 'but I have no time.' Here the dialogue is part of the objective situation. No direct statement is needed since the man and his feelings are clear.

What is true for dialogue is equally true for performance. A good film performance is a carefully integrated sequence of concrete actions and reactions that render the feelings and thoughts of a character. It is not a system of hollow gestures that, like bad dialogue, *tell* the audience what is going on. Most film performances are drawn from the vast repertory of acting conventions. Conversely, the good film actor—whether trained in the Method or not—tries to render feelings through the use of surface correlatives. He is not concerned with the demonstration of feeling but with the symptom of feeling.

Chaplin's best work is continuously physical and concrete. If his performance in *The Gold Rush* had been generalized (or conventionalized) the scene in which he boils and eats his shoe would have become preposterous. He executes it, however, in the most careful physical detail. While the shoe is cooking, he pours water over it as if he were basting a bird. He carves and serves it with meticulous care, separating the uppers from the sole as though boning a fish. Then he winds the limp laces around his fork like spaghetti and sucks each nail as if it were a delicate chicken bone. Thus a totally incongruous moment is given an absolute, detailed physicality; the extraordinary is made ordinary, credible—and therefore funny.

It must be noted again that while the screen exceeds all other media in verisimilitude, its reality is nevertheless a *mode*. We appear to be looking at reality but are actually looking at a representation of it that may be as carefully structured as a still-life by Cézanne. The film-maker uses the surfaces of life itself—literal photographic images and accurately reproduced sounds. But the arrangement of these images and sounds is totally controlled. Each moment, each detail is carefully co-ordinated into the structure of the whole—just like the details in a painting or poem. By artfully controlling his images, the film-maker presents an unbroken realistic surface; he preserves the appearance of reality.

This means that he should at no time interpose himself between audience and action. He must be absent from the scene. An example of this is the use of the camera. In the standard film the camera is often editorial; the director uses it to *point out* to the audience what he wants them to see. Imagine a scene between husband and wife: we see them in a medium-shot, talking; then we cut to a close-up of the woman's hand and discover that she is slipping her wedding ring off and on. The director has made his point: we now know that she is unhappily married. But by artificially lifting the detail out of context and bringing it to our attention, the autonomous reality of the scene is violated and the audience becomes aware of the film-maker. Of course a good director may also be said to use the camera editorially—to point out what he wants us to see. But he never seems to be doing so; he preserves the appearance of an autonomous reality on the screen. The moment with the ring would have been incidental to the scene—for the camera must follow the action, not lead it.

Since the process of editing is an obvious and continued intrusion by the film-maker on the material, an editor tries to make most of his cuts in such a way that the cut itself will be obscured. In order to cut from a medium-shot to a close-up of a man, he will probably use a moment when the man rises from a chair or turns rapidly. At such a time the audience is watching the action and is unaware of the jump; once again, the effort is to preserve an apparently autonomous reality.

At the end of *Notti di Cabiria* the girl and the man she has just married are sitting in a restaurant. We see her from the back, talking. Then Fellini cuts to a shot from the front and we see that she has taken out a large wad of bank notes—her savings. We immediately realize, with something of a shock, that the man is after her money. If Fellini had actually *shown* us Cabiria taking the money out of her pocketbook, the moment would have become self-conscious and overloaded with meaning; we would have had too much time to get the point. By jumping the moment and confronting us suddenly with the money, Fellini renders the meaning *and* preserves the apparent autonomy of the situation.

Spontaneity, the sense that what is happening on the screen is happening for the first time and without plan or direction, is an essential factor in establishing a reality. It is also extremely difficult to achieve, since a huge industry has sprung up around the medium, putting enormous financial and technical pressure on the moment before the camera. Years of routine and a high degree of established skill in every department of film-making all conspire against it. From writing and casting to the angles of the camera a monstrous if unintended predictability crushes all life. Even a strong director is often helpless against the machinery; and even location shooting, which should be a liberating force, turns into a dead-end when a huge crew descends on the place, seals it off hermetically and effectively turns it into a studio. The channels have been set up too long and too well; all vision is trapped into standardized imagery and the living moment cannot survive. [. . .]

Our sense of reality is so delicately attuned that certain moments are better left off the screen or the situation is destroyed. This is especially true for violence and death. When someone's head is cut off in a fiction film we know perfectly well that a trick is employed and unless a scene of this kind is handled with great care, it ends up being incredible or even funny. Similarly, when someone dies on the screen and remains in full view, many of us cannot resist watching for the slightest sign of life in the supposed corpse. We are pitting our own sense of reality against the movie-maker's; needless to say, *we* come out on top and the scene is destroyed.

In Dreyer's unproduced script on the life of Christ he describes the crucifixion by showing us the back of the cross, with the points of the nails splintering through the wood. On the screen these would be undeniably real nails going through real wood, and the authenticity of the moment would not be challenged. If, however, Dreyer had chosen to show us the cross from the front we would know absolutely that the nails going through the *flesh* are a deception—and the suffering figure would turn into a performer.

The nail splintering through the wood forces us to use our imagination— forces us to visualize what is happening on the other side of the cross. This involves us in a far deeper participation than could be achieved by the spurious horror of a nail going through the flesh of an actor.

There is something to be learned here about the entire process of perception in film. If we are explicitly told something, as we are in most pictures, we remain passive and essentially outsiders. If, however, we have to draw our *own* conclusions on the basis of evidence presented, as we do in life itself, we cannot help but participate. We become actively involved. When we are told something explicitly, we are in a sense deprived of the experience. It has been digested for us and we are merely informed of the results, or the meaning. But it is *experience* we are after, even if it remains vicarious experience.

This brings us to another characteristic of the medium—one that is profoundly related to our previous discussion. Although the experience of the motion-picture audience remains essentially vicarious, film comes closer than any other medium to giving us the illusion of a *primary* experience. This has been studied by psychologists who have found that the dark theatre, the bright hypnotic screen, the continuous flow of images and sounds, and the large anonymous audience in which we are submerged all contribute to a suspension of self-awareness and a total immersion in the events on the screen.

Beyond this, however, the medium itself encourages the illusion of a primary participation. The camera can induce an almost physical response—so that when Chaplin sits on a hypodermic needle in the lair of a dope fiend, or when Dreyer's Jeanne d'Arc has her head shaved and some of the hair falls onto her lip, the sensation produced in us is almost physical. Moreover, this physical participation is not limited to sharp sensory detail; it extends to the realm of movement.

Most directors think of the screen as of a *picture frame* within which each shot is carefully composed. They emphasize the *pictorial* quality of film. But while the medium is visual, it is not pictorial in the conventional sense. A sequence of beautifully composed shots tends to leave the audience outside the frame—spectators who are continually aware of the director's fine eye for composition. A good director tries to eliminate this distance between audience and action, to destroy the screen as a picture frame, and to drag the audience *through* it into the reality of the scene. That is the function of the running shots in *Rashomon* and of the extraordinarily emphatic camerawork of Fellini, who leans subtly into every movement and propels us into the action kinesthetically. By contrast, we have the autonomous camera motion and stiff pictorial composition of most films.

Images of movement rather than beautifully composed shots are at the heart of the medium, and significantly some of the most haunting moments in film derive their effect from motion. In Vigo's *L'Atalante*, a bride on her wedding night, still dressed in her white gown, walks along the deck of a moving barge. The barge moves forward, she is walking toward the stern, and the camera is set on the edge of the canal, so that there is a dark stationary line in the foreground. The combination of the silent forward gliding of the barge with the backward motion of the girl, whose gown and veil are streaming in the wind, has a profound emotional impact; it renders perfectly both her feelings and our own.

At the end of *Ikiru* the dying bureaucrat has succeeded in building the playground. It is a winter night; the camera moves slowly past a jungle-gym; beyond it we see the old man, swaying to and fro on a child's swing and singing to himself under the falling snow. The various components of this scene are hard to separate: the hoarse, cracked voice of the dying man; his happiness; the song itself. But the motion of the camera, the falling snow, and the slow movement of the swing certainly contribute to the extraordinary sense of peace and reconciliation that is communicated by the image. [. . .]

Film can further strengthen the illusion of a primary experience by using a subjective point-of-view. In the ancient and Elizabethan theatres, while we remain in objective possession of the entire stage, the poetry and particularly the soliloquy can focus our attention on one person and shift it to his point-of-view. At any given moment the world can be seen through his eyes, subjectively. In the realistic theatre, with its fidelity to the surfaces of everyday life, this has become difficult if not impossible. We *know* how Ibsen's Nora sees the world but except for rare moments do not *experience* it from her point-of-view. She cannot, as it were, reach out and envelop us in her vision—as Hamlet and Lear can.

On the screen it again becomes possible to shift from an objective vision of a person to a vision of what *he* sees. This is done continually, often with little understanding or control. We see a girl enter a room in an objective shot. Then the camera renders what *she* sees: there is a party and her husband is talking to another woman. The next moment might be objective again, or it might be seen from the husband's point-of-view. Montage makes it possible to shift from objective to subjective, or from one subjective point-of-view to another. Film can render a place, a person, or a situation not just as they are but in the context of the protagonist's experience—*as* his experience. A point-of-view can be so carefully articulated that we comprehend every object, every passing figure, every gesture and mood in terms of the protagonist. The medium thus extends the meaning of realistic surfaces beyond their objective value; it renders them in their subjective context as well.

This brings us to an apparent paradox, for we have insisted throughout that film is at its best when rendering an objective situation. It is true, of course, that a moment can be rendered subjectively on the screen and still retain its objective reality. When the girl sees her husband talking to another woman, we see them through her eyes and so become privy to a subjective state. But the husband and the other woman are *in themselves* rendered objectively: they look no different; they are not affected by the point-of-view. The basic language of the medium, the realistic surface, has not been violated. The same may be said of most flash-backs: a subjective recollection is rendered—but in objective, undistorted terms. [. . .]

By and large the language of the medium remains the surface of reality, and there seem to be few experiences that cannot be rendered in this language. Moreover, there is a great challenge in making the commonplaces of life, that have so long eluded art, yield up their meaning and take their rightful place in the larger patterns of existence. Film is indeed, as Kracauer put it, the redemption of physical reality. For we are finally able to use the much-despised and ephemeral detail of everyday life, the common physical dross, and work it into the gold of art.

['The Surfaces of Reality', *Film Quarterly*, 18 (Autumn 1964), 15–22.]

Section II

Why Identify Anything as Art?

INTRODUCTION

Whoever raises questions about what fine art is, either generally or for a given people or time, employs a term with a history. How old is that history, and how does that history bear on the present meaning of the term 'art'? Emphasizing that the arts themselves are 'certainly as old as human civilization', Paul Oskar Kristeller argues from historical sources that the grouping of 'the fine arts' was not fully formed until the latter part of the eighteenth century in Europe, was not formed by artists themselves, and was not widely accepted until the next century (points underscored in a remarkable passage by Goethe). Kristeller argues that the idea of fine arts had, of course, important antecedents. These include the ancient ideas of craft and 'mimesis', the medieval grouping of liberal and mechanical arts, and the Renaissance grouping of 'arts of *disegno*'. The merging of aspects of these traditions into 'the fine arts' was partly occasioned by an increasing separation of arts and sciences through the progress of sciences and technology in the seventeenth century. But, according to Kristeller, the shift in patronage due to growth of secular, urban audiences, and, 'above all ... the rise of an amateur public to which art collections and exhibitions, concerts as well as opera and theatre performances were addressed, must be considered as important factors' in the grouping.' Sections IV and V illustrate, among other things, how this modern point of view of the spectator characterizes subsequent conceptions of fine art.

At issue here is more than a taxonomy of productive processes. As Kristeller says, not just the arts but their 'modern system' represents an important part of a 'scheme of life and of culture'. An excerpt from the eighteenth-century Abbé Batteux's treatise that, according to Kristeller, took '[t]he decisive step toward a system of the fine arts', presents not only the general system of arts as we know it, but the main conceptions under which we have continued to understand artistic matters. In producing 'a single principle' for fine or 'beaux' arts, Batteux uses four ideas whose influences are to be found in all controversies since: skill, genius, representation, and beauty. A fine art is a craft or skill, in the sense of principled knowledge, whose application requires 'genius'. What it produces is mimesis, 'imitation' or representation, of 'beautiful nature'. Mimesis, Kristeller observes, was the available cord with which Batteux bound together a wide variety of talent-assisted productive skills.

Jean le Rond d'Alembert's introduction to Diderot's influential *Encyclopédie* shows the consolidation and spread of these ideas and attitudes about the arts expressed by Batteux. For d'Alembert, pleasure and beauty are separated from 'necessities'. Representation, 'distance', nature, taste, and genius are all introduced in accord with the prevailing psychology of the three 'mental faculties' of reason, memory, and imagination. Art is understood in terms of beauty, and beauty is fatefully taken by d'Alembert, as by Batteux and others of the time, in terms of spectators' pleasures and luxury—conceptions that are directly challenged in other excerpts.

Clifford Geertz gives us access to several very broad, contrasting cultural backgrounds to consider why works of art 'seem important—that is, as affected with import—to those who make or possess them'. His answer is always culturally specific: 'what art is . . . is just not the same thing' from culture to culture. Still, Geertz finds artistic commonality in an account that is, broadly speaking, aesthetic, in that it is perceptual and non-utilitarian. Common to the art forms of all cultures, he holds, is the impulse to produce designs that make a culture's values perceptible to the senses and emotions: artworks of any culture 'materialize a way of experiencing'. Of a culture's many forms of expression, the artistic are those that display to the senses that culture's 'form of life'. Such expressive forms may be as seemingly simple as a cut or an inscribed line.

Mark Sagoff, like Geertz, is interested in the value of art as an institution (the value 'of having any art at all'). He suggests that anthropologists (like Geertz) are in a better position than philosophers to explicate the importance of art within a society. Sagoff compares the economic value of what are recognized as the finest artworks, or masterpieces, with their value 'as art' (which he calls 'aesthetic value'). The principles employed in arriving at the economic value of the finest artworks, he suggests, reveal that they function not merely as commodities but as 'totems' (a term borrowed from anthropologists) with which one identifies one's clan or culture.

If artworks do hold a special status as monuments and symbols of a culture, we should ask whose work is taken to define and represent a culture. A short selection from Whitney Chadwick explains how the institutions of painting in eighteenth-century England virtually prevented women from being recognized as great artists. Griselda Pollock argues that class, gender, and economic factors often restrict who can be participants in culturally significant practices. As a case in point, she shows how the paradigms for what we call 'modernist painting' involve subject matter that would not have been available to women to paint: for example, bars, brothel scenes, and cityscapes. Hers is only one set of examples of how 'ways of seeing' (as well as 'ways of describing') employ paradigms that reflect and reinforce positions of power and privilege within a culture.

Kristeller finds the historical origin of the idea of fine arts in 'collections and exhibitions, concerts [and] performances'. In many 'scheme[s] of life and culture' there are no such presentations. Kathleen Higgins calls our attention to many types of music, not only 'classical' music, but also folk-songs, jazz, rock and roll, rap, tunes from Broadway musicals, Latin samba music, African polyrhythms, Indian ragas, and the fado, many of which do not have performance settings designed for listening, but are performed for dancing, or not performed for an audience at all but constitute informal activity (e.g. folk-songs) or the formal activity of ceremony (e.g. African polyrhythms). According to Higgins, 'the search for a common denominator' that identifies all these as music, or as included within 'the fine arts', is likely to be fruitless. She nevertheless proposes that it is important to recognize all the above as music, in part because they suggest ethical possibilities and reflect society's ethical values.

The public art museum conceived as a site for 'collections and exhibitions' developed in Europe at about the time the concept of the 'beaux arts' was itself being defined in its modern sense. Yet today, objects produced in cultures that do not employ a concept similar to the Western idea of the fine arts are often displayed in art museums, a practice that many say is a manifestation of cultural imperialism. The museum appropriates artefacts from other cultures, and assimilates them into the culture that supports the museum. Removing an object from its place of origin and context of use will necessarily misrepresent it to at least some degree. Ivan Karp describes the option of assimilation—which, he holds, is often based on spurious assumptions of commonality between the museum world and the world of the original artefact—and the option of exoticizing, which, in emphasizing how different the objects and people who produce them are from the culture of the museum, can end up with caricatures and stereotypes.

II.a. Ideas of Art

PAUL OSKAR KRISTELLER

12 The Modern System of the Arts

The fundamental importance of the eighteenth century in the history of aesthetics and of art criticism is generally recognized. To be sure, there has been a great variety of theories and currents within the last two hundred years that cannot be easily brought under one common denominator. Yet all the changes and controversies of the more recent past presuppose certain fundamental notions which go back to that classical century of modern aesthetics. It is known that the very term 'Aesthetics' was coined at that time, and, at least in the opinion of some historians, the subject matter itself, the 'philosophy of art,' was invented in that comparatively recent period and can be applied to earlier phases of Western thought only with reservations. It is also generally agreed that such dominating concepts of modern aesthetics as taste and sentiment, genius, originality and creative imagination did not assume their definite modern meaning before the eighteenth century. Some scholars have rightly noticed that only the eighteenth century produced a type of literature in which the various arts were compared with each other and discussed on the basis of common principles, whereas up to that period treatises on poetics and rhetoric, on painting and architecture, and on music had represented quite distinct branches of writing and were primarily concerned with technical precepts rather than with general ideas. Finally, at least a few scholars have noticed that the term 'Art,' with a capital A and in its modern sense, and the related term 'Fine Arts' (Beaux Arts) originated in all probability in the eighteenth century.

In this paper, I shall take all these facts for granted, and shall concentrate instead on a much simpler and in a sense more fundamental point that is closely related to the problems so far mentioned, but does not seem to have received sufficient attention in its own right. Although the terms 'Art,' 'Fine Arts' or 'Beaux Arts' are often identified with the visual arts alone, they are also quite commonly understood in a broader sense. In this broader meaning, the term 'Art' comprises above all the five major arts of painting, sculpture, architecture, music and poetry. These five constitute the irreducible nucleus of the modern system of the arts, on which all writers and thinkers seem to agree. On the other hand, certain other arts are sometimes added to the scheme, but with less regularity, depending on the different views and interests of the authors concerned: gardening, engraving and the decorative arts, the dance and the theatre, sometimes the opera, and finally eloquence and prose literature.

The basic notion that the five 'major arts' constitute an area all by themselves, clearly separated by common characteristics from the crafts, the sciences and other human activities, has been taken for granted by most writers on aesthetics from Kant to the present day. It is freely employed even by those critics of art and literature who profess not to believe in 'aesthetics'; and it is accepted as a matter of course by the general public of amateurs who assign to 'Art' with a capital A that ever narrowing area of modern life which is not occupied by science, religion, or practical pursuits.

It is my purpose here to show that this system of the five major arts, which underlies all modern aesthetics and is so familiar to us all, is of comparatively recent origin and did not assume definite shape before the eighteenth century, although it has many ingredients which go back to classical, medieval and Renaissance thought. I shall not try to discuss any metaphysical theories of beauty or any particular theories concerning one or more of the arts, let alone their actual history, but only the systematic grouping together of the five major arts. This question does not directly concern any specific changes or achievements in the various arts, but primarily their relations to each other and their place in the general framework of Western culture. [. . .]

The Greek term for Art ($\tau \acute{\epsilon} \chi \nu \eta$) and its Latin equivalent (*ars*) do not specifically denote the 'fine arts' in the modern sense, but were applied to all kinds of human activities which we would call crafts or sciences. Moreover, whereas modern aesthetics stresses the fact that Art cannot be learned, and thus often becomes involved in the curious endeavor to teach the unteachable, the ancients always understood by Art something that can be taught and learned. Ancient statements about Art and the arts have often been read and understood as if they were meant in the modern sense of the fine arts. This may in some cases have led to fruitful errors, but it does not do justice to the original intention of the ancient writers. When the Greek authors began to oppose Art to Nature, they thought of human activity in general. When Hippocrates contrasts Art with Life, he is thinking of medicine, and when his comparison is repeated by Goethe or Schiller with reference to poetry, this merely shows the long way of change which the term Art had traversed by 1800 from its original meaning. Plato puts art above mere routine because it proceeds by rational principles and rules, and Aristotle, who lists Art among the so-called intellectual virtues, characterizes it as a kind of activity based on knowledge, in a definition whose influence was felt through many centuries. The Stoics also defined Art as a system of cognitions, and it was in this sense that they considered moral virtue as an art of living.

The other central concept of modern aesthetics also, beauty, does not appear in ancient thought or literature with its specific modern connotations.

The Greek term καλόν and its Latin equivalent (*pulchrum*) were never neatly or consistently distinguished from the moral good. When Plato discusses beauty in the *Symposium* and the *Phaedrus*, he is speaking not merely of the physical beauty of human persons, but also of beautiful habits of the soul and of beautiful cognitions, whereas he fails completely to mention works of art in this connection. An incidental remark made in the *Phaedrus* and elaborated by Proclus was certainly not meant to express the modern triad of Truth, Goodness and Beauty. When the Stoics in one of their famous statements connected Beauty and Goodness, the context as well as Cicero's Latin rendering suggest that they meant by 'Beauty' nothing but moral goodness, and in turn understood by 'good' nothing but the useful. Only in later thinkers does the speculation about 'beauty' assume an increasingly 'aesthetic' significance, but without ever leading to a separate system of aesthetics in the modern sense. [. . .] Plotinus in his famous treatises on beauty is concerned primarily with metaphysical and ethical problems, but he does include in his treatment of sensuous beauty the visible beauty of works of sculpture and architecture, and the audible beauty of music. Likewise, in the speculations on beauty scattered through the works of Augustine there are references to the various arts, yet the doctrine was not primarily designed for an interpretation of the 'fine arts.' Whether we can speak of aesthetics in the case of Plato, Plotinus or Augustine will depend on our definition of that term, but we should certainly realize that in the theory of beauty a consideration of the arts is quite absent in Plato and secondary in Plotinus and Augustine.

Let us now turn to the individual arts and to the manner in which they were evaluated and grouped by the ancients. Poetry was always most highly respected, and the notion that the poet is inspired by the Muses goes back to Homer and Hesiod. The Latin term (*vates*) also suggests an old link between poetry and religious prophecy, and Plato is hence drawing upon an early notion when in the *Phaedrus* he considers poetry one of the forms of divine madness. However, we should also remember that the same conception of poetry is expressed with a certain irony in the *Ion* and the *Apology* and that even in the *Phaedrus* the divine madness of the poet is compared with that of the lover and of the religious prophet. There is no mention of the 'fine arts' in this passage, and it was left to the late sophist Callistratus to transfer Plato's concept of inspiration to the art of sculpture.

Among all the 'fine arts' it was certainly poetry about which Plato had most to say, especially in the *Republic*, but the treatment given to it is neither systematic nor friendly, but suspiciously similar to the one he gives to rhetoric in some of his other writings. Aristotle, on the other hand, dedicated a whole treatise to the theory of poetry and deals with it in a thoroughly systematic and constructive fashion. The *Poetics* not only contains a great number of specific ideas which exercised a lasting influence upon later criticism; it also established a permanent place for the theory of poetry in the philosophical encyclopaedia of knowledge. [. . .]

Music also held a high place in ancient thought; yet it should be remembered that the Greek term μουσική, which is derived from the Muses, originally comprised much more than we understand by music. Musical education, as we can still see in Plato's *Republic*, included not only music, but also poetry and the dance. Plato and Aristotle, who also employ the term music in the more specific sense familiar to us, do not treat music or the dance as separate arts but rather as elements of certain types of poetry, especially of lyric and dramatic poetry. There is reason to believe that they were thus clinging to an older tradition which was actually disappearing in their own time through the emancipation of instrumental music from poetry. On the other hand, the Pythagorean discovery of the numerical proportions underlying the musical intervals led to a theoretical treatment of music on a mathematical basis, and consequently musical theory entered into an alliance with the mathematical sciences which is already apparent in Plato's *Republic*, and was to last far down into early modern times.

When we consider the visual arts of painting, sculpture and architecture, it appears that their social and intellectual prestige in antiquity was much lower than one might expect from their actual achievements or from occasional enthusiastic remarks which date for the most part from the later centuries. [. . .]

If we want to find in classical philosophy a link between poetry, music and the fine arts, it is provided primarily by the concept of imitation (μίμησις). Passages have been collected from the writings of Plato and Aristotle from which it appears quite clearly that they considered poetry, music, the dance, painting and sculpture as different forms of imitation. This fact is significant so far as it goes, and it has influenced many later authors, even in the eighteenth century. But aside from the fact that none of the passages has a systematic character or even enumerates all of the 'fine arts' together, it should be noted that the scheme excludes architecture, that music and the dance are treated as parts of poetry and not as separate arts, and that on the other hand the individual branches or subdivisions of poetry and of music seem to be put on a par with painting or sculpture. Finally, imitation is anything but a laudatory category, at least for Plato. [. . .] Moreover, Aristotle's distinction between the arts of necessity and the arts of pleasure is quite incidental and does not identify the arts of pleasure with the 'fine' or even the imitative arts, and when it is emphasized that he includes music and drawing in his scheme of education in the *Politics*, it should be added that they share this place with grammar (writing) and arithmetic.

The final ancient attempts at a classification of the more important human arts and sciences were made after the time of Plato and Aristotle. They were due partly to the endeavors of rival schools of philosophy and rhetoric to organize secondary or preparatory education into a system of elementary disciplines (τὰ ἐγκύκλια). This system of the so-called 'liberal arts' was subject to a number of changes and fluctuations, and its development is not known in all of its earlier phases. Cicero often speaks of the liberal arts and of their mutual connection, though he does not give a precise list of these arts, but we may be sure that he did not think of the 'fine arts' as was so often believed in modern times. The definitive scheme of the seven liberal arts is found only in Martianus Capella: grammar, rhetoric, dialectic, arithmetic, geometry, astronomy, and music. [. . .] If we compare Capella's scheme of the seven liberal arts with the modern system of the 'fine arts,' the differences are obvious. Of the fine arts only music, understood as musical theory, appears among the liberal arts. Poetry is not listed among them, yet we know from other sources that it was closely linked with grammar and rhetoric. The visual arts have no place in the scheme, except for occasional attempts at inserting them. [. . .] On the other hand, the liberal arts include grammar and logic, mathematics and astronomy, that is, disciplines we should classify as sciences.

The same picture is gained from the distribution of the arts among the nine Muses. It should be noted that the number of the Muses was not fixed before a comparatively late period, and that the attempt to assign particular arts to individual Muses is still later and not at all uniform. However, the arts listed in these late schemes are the various branches of poetry and of music, with eloquence, history, the dance, grammar, geometry and astronomy. In other words, just as in the schemes of the liberal arts, so in the schemes for the Muses poetry and music are grouped with some of the sciences, whereas the visual arts are omitted. Antiquity knew no Muse of painting or of sculpture; they had to be invented by the allegorists of the early modern centuries. And the five fine arts which constitute the modern system were not grouped together in antiquity, but kept quite different company: poetry stays usually with grammar and rhetoric; music is as close to mathematics and astronomy as it is to the dance, and poetry; and the visual arts, excluded from the realm of the Muses and of the liberal arts by most authors, must be satisfied with the modest company of the other manual crafts.

Thus classical antiquity left no systems or elaborate concepts of an aesthetic nature, but merely a number of scattered notions and suggestions that exercised a lasting influence down to modern times but had to be carefully selected, taken out of their context, rearranged, reemphasized and reinterpreted or misinterpreted before they could be utilized as building materials for aesthetic systems. We have to admit the conclusion, distasteful to many historians of aesthetics but grudgingly admitted by most of them, that ancient writers and thinkers, though confronted with excellent works of art and quite susceptible to their charm, were neither able nor eager to detach the aesthetic quality of these works of art from their intellectual, moral, religious and practical function or content, or to use such an aesthetic quality as a standard for grouping the fine arts together or for making them the subject of a comprehensive philosophical interpretation. [. . .]

Musical theory retained during the Renaissance its status as one of the liberal arts, and the author of an early treatise on the dance tries to dignify his subject by the claim that his art, being a part of music, must be considered as a liberal art. It seems that the practice of the Improvvisatori as well as the reading of classical sources suggested to some humanists a closer link between music and poetry than had been customary in the preceding period. This tendency received a new impetus by the end of the sixteenth century, when the program of the Camerata and the creation of the opera brought about a reunion of the two arts. It would even seem that some of the features of Marinismo and baroque poetry that were so repulsive to classicist critics were due to the fact that this poetry was written with the intention of being set to music and sung.

Still more characteristic of the Renaissance is the steady rise of painting and of the other visual arts that began in Italy with Cimabue and Giotto and reached its climax in the sixteenth century. An early expression of the increasing prestige of the visual arts is found on the Campanile of Florence, where painting, sculpture, and architecture appear as a separate group between the liberal and the mechanical arts. What characterizes the period is not only the quality of the works of art but also the close links that were established between the visual arts, the sciences and literature. The appearance of a distinguished artist who also was a humanist and writer of merit, such as Alberti, was no coincidence in a period in which literary and classical learning began, in addition to religion, to provide the subject matter for painters and sculptors. When a knowledge of perspective, anatomy, and geometrical proportions was considered necessary for the painter and sculptor, it was no wonder that several artists should have made important contributions to the various sciences. [. . .]

[T]he claim of Renaissance writers on painting to have their art recognized as liberal, however weakly supported by classical authority, was significant as an attempt to enhance the social and cultural position of painting and of the other visual arts, and to obtain for them the same prestige that music, rhetoric, and poetry had long enjoyed. And since it was still apparent that the liberal arts were primarily sciences or teachable knowledge, we may well understand why Leonardo tried to define painting as a science and to emphasize its close relationship with mathematics.

The rising social and cultural claims of the visual arts led in the sixteenth century in Italy to an important new development that occurred in the other European countries somewhat later: the three visual arts, painting, sculpture and architecture, were for the first time clearly separated from the crafts with which they had been associated in the preceding period. The term *Arti del disegno*, upon which 'Beaux Arts' was probably based, was coined by Vasari, who used it as the guiding concept for his famous collection of biographies. And this change in theory found its institutional expression in 1563 when in Florence, again under the personal influence of Vasari, the painters, sculptors and architects cut their previous connections with the craftsmen's guilds and formed an Academy of Art (*Accademia del Disegno*), the first of its kind that served as a model for later similar institutions in Italy and other countries. The Art Academies followed the pattern of the literary Academies that had been in existence for some time, and they replaced the older workshop tradition with a regular kind of instruction that included such scientific subjects as geometry and anatomy.

The ambition of painting to share in the traditional prestige of literature also accounts for the popularity of a notion that appears prominently for the first time in the treatises on painting of the sixteenth century and was to retain its appeal down to the eighteenth: the parallel between painting and poetry. Its basis was the *Ut pictura poesis* of Horace, as well as the saying of Simonides reported by Plutarch, along with some other passages in Plato, Aristotle and Horace. [. . .]

During the first half of the eighteenth century the interest of amateurs, writers and philosophers in the visual arts and in music increased. The age produced not only critical writings on these arts composed by and for laymen, but also treatises in which the arts were compared with each other and with poetry, and thus finally arrived at the fixation of the modern system of the fine arts. Since this system seems to emerge gradually and after many fluctuations in the writings of authors who were in part of but secondary importance, though influential, it would appear that the notion and system of the fine arts may have grown and crystallized in the conversations and discussions of cultured circles in Paris and in London, and that the formal writings and treatises merely reflect a climate of opinion resulting from such conversations. [. . .]

The decisive step toward a system of the fine arts was taken by the Abbé Batteux in his famous and influential treatise, *Les beaux arts réduits à un même principe* (1746). It is true that many elements of his system were derived from previous authors, but at the same time it should not be overlooked that he was the first to set forth a clearcut system of the fine arts in a treatise devoted exclusively to this subject. This alone may account for his claim to originality as well as for the enormous influence he exercised both in France and abroad, especially in Germany. Batteux codified the modern system of the fine arts almost in its final form, whereas all previous authors had merely prepared it. He started from the poetic theories of Aristotle and Horace, as he states in his preface, and tried to extend their principles from poetry and painting to the other arts. In his first chapter, Batteux gives a clear division of the arts. He separates the fine arts which have pleasure for their end from the mechanical arts, and lists the fine arts as follows: music, poetry, painting, sculpture and the dance. He adds a third group which combines pleasure and usefulness and puts eloquence and architecture in this category. In the central part of his treatise, Batteux tries to show that the 'imitation of beautiful nature' is the principle common to all the arts, and he concludes with a discussion of the theatre as a combination of all the other arts. The German critics of the later eighteenth century, and their recent historians, criticized Batteux for his theory of imitation and often failed to recognize that he formulated the system of the arts which they took for granted and for which they were merely trying to find different principles. They also overlooked the fact that the much maligned principle of imitation was the only one a classicist critic such as Batteux could use when he wanted to group the fine arts together with even an appearance of ancient authority. For the 'imitative' arts were the only authentic ancient precedent for the 'fine arts,' and the principle of imitation could be replaced only after the system of the latter had been so firmly established as no longer to need the ancient principle of imitation to link them together. Diderot's criticism of Batteux has been emphasized too much, for it concerned only the manner in which Batteux defined and applied his principle, but neither the principle itself, nor the system of the arts for which it had been designed.

As a matter of fact, Diderot and the other authors of the *Encyclopédie* not only followed Batteux's system of the fine arts, but also furnished the final touch and thus helped to give it a general currency not only in France but also in the other European countries. [...]

Still more interesting is D'Alembert's famous *Discours préliminaire*. In his division of knowledge, purportedly based on Francis Bacon, D'Alembert makes a clear distinction between philosophy, which comprises both the natural sciences and such fields as grammar, eloquence, and history, and 'those cognitions which consist of imitation,' listing among the latter painting, sculpture, architecture, poetry and music. He criticizes the old distinction between the liberal and mechanical arts, and then subdivides the liberal arts into the fine arts which have pleasure for their end, and the more necessary or useful liberal arts such as grammar, logic and morals. He concludes with a main division of knowledge into philosophy, history and the fine arts. This treatment shows still a few signs of fluctuation and of older notions, but it sets forth the modern system of the fine arts in its final form, and at the same time reflects its genesis. The threefold division of knowledge follows Francis Bacon, but significantly d'Alembert speaks of the five fine arts where Bacon had mentioned only poetry. D'Alembert is aware that the new concept of the fine arts is taking the place of the older concept of the liberal arts which he criticizes, and he tries to compromise by treating the fine arts as a subdivision of the liberal arts, thus leaving a last trace of the liberal arts that was soon to disappear. Finally, he reveals his dependence on Batteux in certain phrases and in the principle of imitation, but against Batteux and the classical tradition he now includes architecture among the imitative arts, thus removing the last irregularity which had separated Batteux's system from the modern scheme of the fine arts. Thus we may conclude that the *Encyclopédie*, and especially its famous introduction, codified the system of the fine arts after and beyond Batteux and through its prestige and authority gave it the widest possible currency all over Europe. [. . .]

Having followed the French development through the eighteenth century, we must discuss the history of artistic thought in England. The English writers were strongly influenced by the French down to the end of the seventeenth century and later, but during the eighteenth century they made important contributions of their own and in turn influenced continental thought, especially in France and Germany. Interest in the arts other than poetry began to rise slowly in the English literature of the seventeenth century. [. . .] Early in the eighteenth century, Jonathan Richardson was praising painting as a liberal art, and John Dennis in some of his critical treatises on poetics stressed the affinity between poetry, painting and music.

Of greater importance were the writings of Anthony, Earl of Shaftesbury, one of the most influential thinkers of the eighteenth century, not only in England but also on the continent. His interest and taste for literature and the arts are well known, and his writings are full of references to the various arts and to the beauty of their works. The ideal of the *virtuoso* which he embodied and advocated no longer included the sciences, as in the seventeenth century, but had its center in the arts and in the moral life. Since Shaftesbury was the first major philosopher in modern Europe in whose writings the discussion of the arts occupied a prominent place, there is some reason for considering him as the founder of modern aesthetics. Yet Shaftesbury was influenced primarily by Plato and Plotinus, as well as by Cicero, and he consequently did not make a clear distinction between artistic and moral beauty. His moral sense still includes both ethical and aesthetic objects. Moreover, although references to the particular arts are frequent in his writings, and some of his works are even entirely devoted to the subjects of painting or of poetry, the passages in which he mentions poetry, the visual arts and music together are not too frequent, and do not contain any more specific notions than may be found in earlier authors. Poetry, especially, appears still in the company not only of eloquence but also of history, thus reflecting the Renaissance tradition of the *Studia humanitatis*. Almost equally influential in England as well as on the continent, at least in literary circles, was Joseph Addison. His famous essays on imagination, which appeared in the *Spectator* in 1712, are remarkable not merely for their early emphasis on that faculty, but also for the manner in which he attributes the pleasures of the imagination to the various arts as well as to natural sights. Without ever giving a definite system, he constantly refers to gardening and architecture, painting and sculpture, poetry and music, and makes it quite clear that the pleasures of the imagination are to be found in their works and products.

The philosophical implications of Shaftesbury's doctrine were further developed by a group of Scottish thinkers. Francis Hutcheson, who considered himself Shaftesbury's pupil, modified his doctrine by distinguishing between the moral sense and the sense of beauty. This distinction, which was adopted by Hume and quoted by Diderot, went a long ways to prepare the separation of ethics and aesthetics, although Hutcheson still assigned the taste of poetry to the moral sense. [...]

In the decades after 1760, the interest in the new field of aesthetics spread rapidly in Germany. Courses on aesthetics were offered at a number of universities after the example set by Baumgarten and Meier, and new tracts and textbooks, partly based on these courses, appeared almost every year. These authors have been listed, but their individual contributions remain to be investigated. The influence of the great *Encyclopédie* is attested by a curious engraving printed in Weimar in 1769 and attached to a famous copy of the *Encyclopédie*. It represents the tree of the arts and sciences as given in the text of D'Alembert's *Discours*, putting the visual arts, poetry and music with their subdivisions under the general branch of imagination. [...]

It is interesting to note the reaction to this aesthetic literature of the leaders of the younger generation, especially of Goethe and of Herder. Goethe in his early years published a review of Sulzer which was quite unfavorable. Noticing the French background of Sulzer's conception, Goethe ridicules the grouping together of all the arts which are so different from each other in their aims and means of expression, a system which reminds him of the old-fashioned system of the seven liberal arts, and adds that this system may be useful to the amateur but certainly not to the artist.[1] This reaction shows that the system of the fine arts was something novel and not yet firmly established, and that Goethe, just like Lessing, did not take an active part in developing the notion that was to become generally accepted. Toward the very end of his life, in the *Wanderjahre*, Goethe shows that he had by then accepted the system of the fine arts, for he assigns a place to each of them in his pedagogical province. Yet his awareness of the older meaning of art is apparent when in a group of aphorisms originally appended to the same work he defines art as knowledge and concludes that poetry, being based on genius, should not be called an art. [...]

I should like to conclude this survey with Kant, since he was the first major philosopher who included aesthetics and the philosophical theory of the arts as an integral part of his system. Kant's interest in aesthetic problems appears already in his early writing on the beautiful and sublime, which was influenced in its general conception by Burke. [. . .] [I]n his *Critique of Judgment*, which constitutes the third and concluding part of his philosophical system, the larger of its two major divisions is dedicated to aesthetics, whereas the other section deals with teleology. The system of the three *Critiques* as presented in this last volume is based on a threefold division of the faculties of the mind, which adds the faculty of judgment, aesthetic and teleological, to pure and practical reason. Aesthetics, as the philosophical theory of beauty and the arts, acquires equal standing with the theory of truth (metaphysics or epistemology) and the theory of goodness (ethics).

[. . .] [N]either Descartes nor Spinoza nor Leibniz nor any of their ancient or medieval predecessors had found a separate or independent place in their system for the theory of the arts and of beauty, though they had expressed occasional opinions on these subjects. If Kant took this decisive step after some hesitation, he was obviously influenced by the example of Baumgarten and by the rich French, English, and German literature on the arts his century had produced, with which he was well acquainted. In his critique of aesthetic judgment, Kant discusses also the concepts of the sublime and of natural beauty, but his major emphasis is on beauty in the arts, and he discusses many concepts and principles common to all the arts. [. . .] [S]ince Kant aesthetics has occupied a permanent place among the major philosophical disciplines, and the core of the system of the fine arts fixed in the eighteenth century has been generally accepted as a matter of course by most later writers on the subject, except for variations of detail or of explanation.

We shall not attempt to discuss the later history of our problem after Kant, but shall rather draw a few general conclusions from the development so far as we have been able to follow it. The grouping together of the visual arts with poetry and music into the system of the fine arts with which we are familiar did not exist in classical antiquity, in the Middle Ages or in the Renaissance. However, the ancients contributed to the modern system the comparison between poetry and painting, and the theory of imitation that established a kind of link between painting and sculpture, poetry and music. The Renaissance brought about the emancipation of the three major visual arts from the crafts, it multiplied the comparisons between the various arts, especially between painting and poetry, and it laid the ground for an amateur interest in the different arts that tended to bring them together from the point of view of the reader, spectator and listener rather than of the artist. The seventeenth century witnessed the emancipation of the natural sciences and thus prepared the way for a clearer separation between the arts and the sciences. Only the early eighteenth century, especially in England and France, produced elaborate treatises written by and for amateurs in which the various fine arts were grouped together, compared with each other and combined in a systematic scheme based on common principles. The second half of the century, especially in Germany, took the additional step of incorporating the comparative and theoretical treatment of the fine arts as a separate discipline into the system of philosophy. The modern system of the fine arts is thus pre-romantic in its origin, although all romantic as well as later aesthetics takes this system as its necessary basis.

It is not easy to indicate the causes for the genesis of the system in the eighteenth century. The rise of painting and of music since the Renaissance, not so much in their actual achievements as in their prestige and appeal, the rise of literary and art criticism, and above all the rise of an amateur public to which art collections and exhibitions, concerts as well as opera and theatre performances were addressed, must be considered as important factors. The fact that the affinity between the various fine arts is more plausible to the amateur, who feels a comparable kind of enjoyment, than to the artist himself, who is concerned with the peculiar aims and techniques of his art, is obvious in itself and is confirmed by Goethe's reaction. The origin of modern aesthetics in amateur criticism would go a long way to explain why works of art have until recently been analyzed by aestheticians from the point of view of the spectator, reader and listener rather than of the producing artist. [. . .]

Another observation seems to impose itself as a result of our study. The various arts are certainly as old as human civilization, but the manner in which we are accustomed to group them and to assign them a place in our scheme of life and of culture is comparatively recent. This fact is not as strange as may appear on the surface. In the course of history, the various arts change not only their content and style, but also their relations to each other, and their place in the general system of culture, as do religion, philosophy or science. Our familiar system of the five fine arts did not merely originate in the eighteenth century, but it also reflects the particular cultural and social conditions of that time. If we consider other times and places, the status of the various arts, their associations and their subdivisions appear very differ-ent. There were important periods in cultural history when the novel, instrumental music, or canvas painting did not exist or have any importance. On the other hand, the sonnet and the epic poem, stained glass and mosaic, fresco painting and book illumination, vase painting and tapestry, bas relief and pottery have all been 'major' arts at various times and in a way they no longer are now. Gardening has lost its standing as a fine art since the eight-eenth century. On the other hand, the moving picture is a good example of how new techniques may lead to modes of artistic expression for which the aestheticians of the eighteenth and nineteenth century had no place in their systems. The branches of the arts all have their rise and decline, and even their birth and death, and the distinction between 'major' arts and their subdivisions is arbitrary and subject to change. There is hardly any ground but critical tradition or philosophical preference for deciding whether engraving is a separate art (as most of the eighteenth-century authors believed) or a subdivision of painting, or whether poetry and prose, dramatic and epic poetry, instrumental and vocal music are separate arts or subdivisions of one major art.

As a result of such changes, both in modern artistic production and in the study of other phases of cultural history, the traditional system of the fine arts begins to show signs of disintegration. Since the latter part of the nineteenth century, painting has moved further away from literature than at any previous time, whereas music has at times moved closer to it, and the crafts have taken great strides to recover their earlier standing as decorative arts. A greater awareness of the different techniques of the various arts has produced dissatisfaction among artists and critics with the conventions of an aesthetic system based on a situation no longer existing, an aesthetics that is trying in vain to hide the fact that its underlying system of the fine arts is hardly more than a postulate and that most of its theories are abstracted from particular arts, usually poetry, and more or less inapplicable to the others. The excesses of aestheticism have led to a healthy reaction which is yet far from universal. The tendency among some contemporary philosophers to consider Art and the aesthetic realm as a pervasive aspect of human experience rather than as the specific domain of the conventional fine arts also goes a long way to weaken the latter notion in its traditional form. All these ideas are still fluid and ill defined, and it is difficult to see how far they will go in modifying or undermining the traditional status of the fine arts and of aesthetics. In any case, these contemporary changes may help to open our eyes to an understanding of the historical origins and limitations of the modern system of the fine arts. Conversely, such historical understanding might help to free us from certain conventional preconceptions and to clarify our ideas on the present status and future prospects of the arts and of aesthetics.

['The Modern System of the Arts', as reprinted in Kristeller, *Renaissance Thought and the Arts* (New York: Harper & Row, 1965), 163–9, 171–4, 180–3, 196, 199–200, 202–9, 220–7.]

ABBÉ BATTEUX

13 The Fine Arts Reduced to a Single Principle

Part I: *Wherein it is established that the nature of the arts depends on the nature of the genius that creates them.*

Here we need not begin by praising the arts in general. They declare their own benefits sufficiently well. They are seen clearly throughout the whole world. It is they that build towns, bring together widely dispersed people, make them polite, civilized, capable of living in society. Some destined to serve us, others to delight us, still others to both serve and charm, they have become for us to some extent a second order of elements, whose creation nature had reserved for our efforts.

General definition, classification, and origin of the arts.

In general, an art is a collection or assemblage of rules for doing well what can be done well or badly, because what can only be done well or done badly has no need of art. These rules are only general principles, drawn from specific observations, repeated several times and verified by repetition. For example, it has been observed that an orator antagonized his audience, when at the beginning he showed haughtiness, impudence. That led to the general rule that all beginnings be modest. Thus every observation includes a precept, and all precepts are born from observations.

The prime inventor of the arts is need, the most ingenious of all masters, the one whose lessons are best heeded. Cast at birth, as Lucretius and Pliny say, naked on a naked earth, having outside cold, heat, damp, the impact of other bodies, and inside hunger, thirst, which warned man urgently to think of remedies, man could not remain long in inactivity. Feeling forced to seek solutions, he found some. When he found them, he perfected them, to make them of greater, surer, more complete use, whenever the need rose again. Thus whenever he felt, for example, the inconvenience of rain, he sought shelter. If that was a leafy tree, he got the idea before long, to better assure protection, to fit together branches, to intertwine them, to join together those of several trees, so as to provide a broader, surer roof, more convenient for his family, for his food, for his flocks. Increasing his observations, ingenuity and taste, having from day to day added something new to his first attempts, either to strengthen the structure or to adorn it, he formed with time the succession of precepts that were called architecture, and which is the art of making well-built, comfortable, and proper dwellings. He made the same observations in all other areas that relate to the conservation of life, to make it richer and more pleasant: that is how the arts of necessity and convenience came into being.

When necessity and convenience are provided for, it is only a short step to arrive at pleasure, which is a third order of need for sensitive people. Convenience, occupying a middle ground between necessity and what is true pleasure, leads from one to the other; since convenience is nothing but an easy necessity, and on the other hand pleasure seems only to be an additional degree of convenience.

Thus we can distinguish three sorts of arts with regard to the purpose proposed. For some, their purpose is the basic needs of mankind: nature, which has exposed us to a thousand difficulties and seems to abandon us to ourselves from the moment of birth, insists that remedies and protection be the price of our invention and work. Thus the mechanical arts were born. The object of the others is pleasure. They were born only in the womb of joy and of feelings that plenty and tranquillity produce: these are called the fine arts par excellence. Such are music, poetry, painting, drama, and the art of gesture or dance. The third category includes the arts that are both useful and agreeable: these include eloquence and architecture. Need brought them into being, taste perfected them: they occupy a middle position between the two other types. With those they share what is agreeable and what is useful.

Arts of the first category use nature just as she is, solely for practical use and work. The third type use her, polishing her for work and pleasure. Fine arts do not use her, rather they imitate her, each in their own fashion, something that needs to be explained. [. . .] Thus nature alone is the object of all the arts. She contains all our needs, all our pleasures; the mechanical arts and the fine arts are created only to be developed out of nature.

We will speak here only of the fine arts, that is to say, of the arts whose purpose is to please: and in order to know them better, let us go back to the cause which created them. It is people who have created the arts, created them for themselves. Bored with too uniform an enjoyment of the objects nature by itself offered them, and finding themselves, moreover, in a suitable situation to feel pleasure, they had recourse to their genius to seek a new order of ideas and emotions, which awakened their minds and stimulated their tastes. But what could this genius do, limited as it was in its creativity and in its views, which could not be extended any further than nature? and being obliged to work for those whose faculties were as limited as their own? All these efforts had necessarily to be limited to choosing among the most beautiful parts of nature, to make of them a beautiful whole, which is more perfect than nature herself, without, however, ceasing to be natural. That is the principle on which must have been drawn up, of necessity, the funda-mental program for the arts, and which great artists have followed in all the ages. From which I conclude: first, that genius, which is the father of the arts, should imitate nature. Second, that it should not imitate nature as it ordinarily is, as it ordinarily is presented to us all the time. Third, that taste, for which the arts are done, and which is their judge, should be satisfied when nature is well selected from and well imitated by them. Thus, all our proofs necessarily lead to recognizing the imitation of *la belle nature*—proofs based on the very nature of the genius that produces the arts, on the nature of taste, which is their arbiter, and on the practice of excellent artists.

[*Les Beaux Arts Réduits à un Même Principe*, trans. Robert L. Walters. First published in Paris, 1746.]

Since the first operation of reflection consists in drawing together and uniting direct notions, we of necessity have begun this Discourse by looking at reflection from that point of view and reviewing the different sciences that result from it. But the notions formed by the combination of primitive ideas are not the only ones of which our minds are capable. There is another kind of reflective knowledge, and we must turn to it now. It consists of the ideas which we create for ourselves by imagining and putting together beings similar to those which are the object of our direct ideas. This is what we call the imitation of Nature, so well known and so highly recommended by the ancients. Since the direct ideas that strike us most vividly are those which we remember most easily, these are also the ones which we try most to reawaken in ourselves by the imitation of their objects. Although pleasant objects [of reality] have a greater impact on us because they are real rather than mere imitations, we are somewhat compensated for that loss of attractiveness by the pleasure which results from imitation. As for the objects which, when real, excite only sad or tumultuous sentiments, imitation of them is more pleasing than the objects themselves, because it places us at precisely that distance where we experience the pleasure of the emotion without feeling its disturbance. That imitation of objects capable of exciting in us lively, vivid, or pleasing sentiments, whatever their nature may be, constitutes in general the imitation of *la belle Nature*, about which so many authors have written without presenting a clear idea of it. They fail to do so either because *la belle Nature* can be perceived by only an extremely delicate sensitivity, or perhaps also because in this matter the limits which distinguish the arbitrary from the true are not yet well defined and leave some area open to opinion.

Painting and Sculpture ought to be placed at the head of that knowledge which consists of imitation, because it is in those arts above all that imitation best approximates the objects represented and speaks most directly to the senses. Architecture, that art which is born of necessity and perfected by luxury, can be added to those two. Having developed by degrees from cottages to palaces, in the eyes of the philosopher it is simply the embellished mask, so to speak, of one of our greatest needs. The imitation of *la belle Nature* in Architecture is less striking and more restricted than in Painting or Sculpture. The latter express all the parts of *la belle Nature* indifferently and without restriction, portraying it as it is, uniform or varied; while Architecture, combining and uniting the different bodies it uses, is confined to imitating the symmetrical arrangement that Nature observes more or less obviously in each individual thing, and that contrasts so well with the beautiful variety of all taken together.

Poetry, which comes after Painting and Sculpture, and which imitates merely by means of words disposed according to a harmony agreeable to the ear, speaks to the imagination rather than to the senses. In a touching and vivid manner it represents to the imagination the objects which make up this universe. By the warmth, the movement, and the life which it is capable of giving, it seems rather to create than to portray them. Finally, music, which speaks simultaneously to the imagination and to the senses, holds the last place in the order of imitation—not that its imitation is less perfect in the objects which it attempts to represent, but because until now it has apparently been restricted to a smaller number of images. This should be attributed less to its nature than to the lack of sufficient inventiveness and resourcefulness in most of those who cultivate it. It will not be useless to make some reflections on this subject. In its origin music perhaps was intended only to represent noise. Little by little it has become a kind of discourse, or even language, through which the different sentiments of the soul, or rather its different passions, are expressed. But why reduce this kind of expression to passions alone, and why not extend it as much as possible to the sensations themselves? Although the perceptions that we receive through various organs differ among themselves as much as their objects, we can nevertheless compare them according to another point of view which is common to them: that is, by the pleasurable or disquieting effect they have upon our soul. A frightening object, a terrible noise, each produces an emotion in us by which we can bring them somewhat together, and we can often designate both of these emotions either by the same name or by synonymous names. Thus, I do not see why a musician who had to portray a frightening object could not succeed in doing so by seeking in nature the kind of sound that can produce in us the emotion most resembling the one excited by this object. I say the same of agreeable sensations. To think otherwise would be to wish to restrict the limits of art and of our pleasures. I confess that the kind of depiction of which we are speaking here demands a subtle and profound study of the shadings which differentiate our sensations; thus it is not to be hoped that these shadings will be distinguished by an ordinary talent. Grasped by the man of genius, perceived by the man of taste, understood by the man of intelligence, they are lost on the multitude. Any music that does not portray something is only noise; and without that force of habit which denatures everything, it would hardly create more pleasure than a sequence of harmonious and sonorous words stripped of order and connection. It is true that a musician desirous of portraying everything would in many circumstances give us scenes of harmony which would not be grasped by vulgar senses. But all that can be concluded from this is that after having created an art of learning music one ought also to create an art of listening to it.

We will stop enumerating the principal parts of our knowledge here. If one now looks at them all together and attempts to find some general points of view which can serve to differentiate them, one finds that some which are purely practical in nature [arts] have as their aim the execution of something. Others of a purely speculative nature [sciences] are limited to the examination of their object and the contemplation of its properties. Finally, still others derive practical use from the speculative study of their object. Speculation and practice constitute the principal difference that distinguishes the *Sciences* from the *Arts*, and it is more or less according to this concept that we have given one or another name to each of the parts of our knowledge. [. . .]

In general the name *Art* may be given to any system of knowledge which can be reduced to positive and invariable rules independent of caprice or opinion. In this sense it would be permitted to say that several of our sciences are arts when they are viewed from their practical side. But just as there are rules for the operations of the mind or soul, there are also rules for those of the body: that is, for those operations which, applying exclusively to external bodies, can be executed by hand alone. Such is the origin of the differentiation of the arts into liberal and mechanical arts, and of the superiority which we accord to the first over the second. That superiority is doubtless unjust in several respects. Nevertheless, none of our prejudices, however ridiculous, is without its reason, or to speak more precisely, its origin, and although philosophy is often powerless to correct abuses, it can at least discern their source. After physical force rendered useless the right of equality possessed by all men, the weakest, who are always the majority, joined together to check it. With the aid of laws and different sorts of governments they established an 'inequality of convention' in which force ceased to be the defining principle. [. . .] The mechanical arts, which are dependent upon manual operation and are subjugated (if I may be permitted this term) to a sort of routine, have been left to those among men whom prejudices have placed in the lowest class. Poverty has forced these men to turn to such work more often than taste and genius have attracted them to it. Subsequently it became a reason for holding them in contempt—so much does poverty harm everything that accompanies it. With regard to the free operations of the mind, they have been apportioned to those who have believed themselves most favored of Nature in this respect. However, the advantage that the liberal arts have over the mechanical arts, because of their demands upon the intellect and because of the difficulty of excelling in them, is sufficiently counterbalanced by the quite superior usefulness which the latter for the most part have for us. It is this very usefulness which reduced them perforce to purely mechanical operations in order to make them accessible to a larger number of men. But while justly respecting great geniuses for their enlightenment, society ought not to degrade the hands by which it is served. [. . .]

Among the liberal arts that have been reduced to principles, those that undertake the imitation of Nature have been called the Fine Arts because they have pleasure for their principal object. But that is not the only characteristic distinguishing them from the more necessary or more useful liberal arts, such as Grammar, Logic, and Ethics. The latter have fixed and settled rules which any man can transmit to another, whereas the practice of the Fine Arts consists principally in an invention which takes its laws almost exclusively from genius. The rules which have been written concerning these arts are, properly speaking, only the mechanical part. Their effect is somewhat like that of the telescope; they only aid those who see.

From everything we have said heretofore it follows that the different ways in which our mind operates on objects and also the different uses which it derives from these objects are the first available means of generally distinguishing the various parts of knowledge from one another. Everything is related to our needs, whether from absolute necessity, or from convenience and pleasure, or even from custom and caprice. The more the needs are remote or difficult to satisfy, the slower the knowledge intended to satisfy them will be in making its appearance. Think of the progress Medicine would have made at the expense of the purely speculative sciences if it were as certain as Geometry. But there are still other very marked characteristics in the way our knowledge affects us and in the different judgments that our soul makes of ideas. These judgments are designated by the words evidence, certitude, probability, feeling, and taste.

Evidence properly pertains to the ideas whose connection the mind perceives immediately. Certitude pertains to those whose connection can be known only by the aid of a certain number of intermediate ideas, or, what is the same thing, to propositions whose identity with a self-evident principle can be discovered only by a circuit of greater or lesser length. [. . .] Feeling is of two sorts. The one concerned with moral truths is called conscience. It is a result of natural law and of our conception of good and evil. One could call it evidence of the heart, for, although it differs greatly from the evidence of the mind which concerns speculative truths, it subjugates us with the same force. The other sort of feeling pertains in particular to the imitation of la belle Nature and to what we call beauties of expression. It grasps sublime and striking beauties with rapture, subtly discerns hidden beauties, and proscribes those that merely feign their appearance. Often, indeed, it pronounces severe judgments without bothering to describe in detail the motives for them, because these motives depend upon a multitude of ideas that are difficult to expound all at once and still more difficult to transmit to others. It is to this kind of feeling that we owe taste and genius, which are distinguished from one another in that genius is the feeling that creates and taste the feeling that judges.

[*Preliminary Discourse to the Encyclopedia of Diderot*, trans. Richard N. Schwab (Indianapolis: Bobbs-Merrill Company, Inc., 1963), 36–45. First published in 1751.]

15 Art as a Cultural System

Art is notoriously hard to talk about. It seems, even when made of words in the literary arts, all the more so when made of pigment, sound, stone, or whatever in the non-literary ones, to exist in a world of its own, beyond the reach of discourse. It not only is hard to talk about it; it seems unnecessary to do so. It speaks, as we say, for itself: a poem must not mean but be; if you have to ask what jazz is you are never going to get to know.

Artists feel this especially. Most of them regard what is written and said about their work, or work they admire as at best beside the point, at worst a distraction from it. [. . .] But anyone at all responsive to aesthetic forms feels it as well. Even those among us who are neither mystics nor sentiment-alists, nor given to outbursts of aesthetic piety, feel uneasy when we have talked very long about a work of art in which we think we have seen some-thing valuable. The excess of what we have seen, or imagine we have, over the stammerings we can manage to get out concerning it is so vast that our words seem hollow, flatulent, or false. After art talk, 'whereof one cannot speak, thereof one must be silent,' seems like very attractive doctrine.

But, of course, hardly anyone, save the truly indifferent, is thus silent, artists included. On the contrary, the perception of something important in either particular works or in the arts generally moves people to talk (and write) about them incessantly. Something that meaningful to us cannot be left just to sit there bathed in pure significance, and so we describe, analyse, compare, judge, classify; we erect theories about creativity, form, perception, social function. [. . .] The surface bootlessness of talking about art seems matched by a depth necessity to talk about it endlessly. And it is this peculiar state of affairs that I want here to probe, in part to explain it, but even more to determine what difference it makes.

To some degree art is everywhere talked about in what may be called craft terms—in terms of tonal progressions, color relations, or prosodic shapes. This is especially true in the West where subjects like harmony or pictorial composition have been developed to the point of minor sciences, and the modern move toward aesthetic formalism, best represented right now by structuralism. But the craft approach to art talk is hardly confined to either the West or the modern age, as the elaborate theories of Indian musicology, Javanese choreography, Arabic versification, or Yoruba embossment remind us. Even the Australian aborigines, everybody's favorite example of primitive peoples, analyze their body designs and ground paintings into dozens of isolable and named formal elements, unit graphs in an iconic grammar of representation.[1]

But what is more interesting and I think more important is that it is perhaps only in the modern age and in the West that some men (still a small minority, and destined, one suspects, to remain such) have managed to convince themselves that technical talk about art, however developed, is sufficient to a complete understanding of it; that the whole secret of aesthetic power is located in the formal relations among sounds, images, volumes, themes, or gestures. Everywhere else—and, as I say, among most of us as well—other sorts of talk, whose terms and conceptions derive from cultural concerns art may serve, or reflect, or challenge, or describe, but does not in itself create, collects about it to connect its specific energies to the general dynamic of human experience. 'The purpose of a painter,' Matisse, who can hardly be accused of undervaluing form, wrote, 'must not be conceived as separate from his pictorial means, and these pictorial means must be more complete (I do not mean more complicated) the deeper his thought. I am unable to distinguish between the feeling I have for life and my way of expressing it.'[2]

The feeling an individual, or what is more critical, because no man is an island but a part of the main, the feeling a people has for life appears, of course, in a great many other places than in their art. It appears in their religion, their morality, their science, their commerce, their technology, their politics, their amusements, their law, even in the way they organize their everyday practical existence. The talk about art that is not merely technical or a spiritualization of the technical—that is, most of it—is largely directed to placing it within the context of these other expressions of human purpose and the pattern of experience they collectively sustain. No more than sexual passion or contact with the sacred, two more matters it is difficult to talk about, but yet somehow necessary, can confrontation with aesthetic objects be left to float, opaque and hermetic, outside the general course of social life. They demand to be assimilated.

What this implies, among other things, is that the definition of art in any society is never wholly intra-aesthetic, and indeed but rarely more than marginally so. The chief problem presented by the sheer phenomenon of aesthetic force, in whatever form and in result of whatever skill it may come, is how to place it within the other modes of social activity, how to incor-porate it into the texture of a particular pattern of life. And such placing, the giving to art objects a cultural significance, is always a local matter; what art is in classical China or classical Islam, what it is in the Pueblo southwest or highland New Guinea, is just not the same thing, no matter how universal the intrinsic qualities that actualize its emotional power (and I have no desire to deny them) may be. The variety that anthropologists have come to expect in the spirit beliefs, the classification systems, or the kinship structures of different people, and not just in their immediate shapes but in the way of being-in-the-world they both promote and exemplify, extends as well to their drummings, carvings, chants, and dances.

It is the failure to realize this on the part of many students of non-western art, and particularly of so-called 'primitive art,' that leads to the oft-heard comment that the peoples of such cultures don't talk, or not very much, about art—they just sculpt, sing, weave, or whatever; silent in their expertise. What is meant is that they don't talk about it the way the observer talks about it—or would like them to—in terms of its formal properties, its symbolic content, its affective values, or its stylistic features, except laconically, cryptically, and as though they had precious little hope of being understood.

But, of course, they do talk about it, as they talk about everything else striking, or suggestive, or moving, that passes through their lives—about how it is used, who owns its, when it is performed, who performs or makes it, what role it plays in this or that activity, what it may be exchanged for, what it is called, how it began, and so forth and so on. But this tends to be seen not as talk about art, but about something else—everyday life, myths, trade, or whatever. To the man who may not know what he likes but knows what art is, the Tiv, aimlessly sewing raffia onto cloth prior to resist dyeing it (he will not even look at how the piece is going until it is completely finished), who told Paul Bohannan, 'if the design does not turn out well, I will sell it to the Ibo; if it does, I will keep it; if it comes out extraordinarily well, I shall give it to my mother-in-law,' seems not to be discussing his work at all, but merely some of his social attitudes.[3] The approach to art from the side of Western aesthetics (which, as Kristeller has reminded us, only emerged in the mid-eighteenth century, along with our rather peculiar notion of the 'fine arts'), and indeed from any sort of prior formalism, blinds us to the very existence of the data upon which a comparative understanding of it could be built. And we are left, as we used to be in studies of totemism, caste, or bridewealth—and still are in structuralist ones—with an externalized conception of the phenomenon supposedly under intense inspection but actually not even in our line of sight.

For Matisse, as is no surprise, was right: the means of an art and the feeling for life that animates it are inseparable, and one can no more understand aesthetic objects as concatenations of pure form than one can understand speech as a parade of syntactic variations, or myth as a set of structural transformations. Take, as an example, a matter as apparently transcultural and abstract as line, and consider its meaning, as Robert Faris Thompson brilliantly describes it, in Yoruba sculpture.[4] Linear precision, Thompson says, the sheer clarity of line, is a major concern of Yoruba carvers, as it is of those who assess the carvers' work, and the vocabulary of linear qualities, which the Yoruba use colloquially and across a range of concerns far broader than sculpture, is nuanced and extensive. It is not just their statues, pots, and so on that Yoruba incise with lines: they do the same with their faces. [. . .]

The intense concern of the Yoruba carver with line, and with particular forms of line, stems therefore from rather more than a detached pleasure in its intrinsic properties, the problems of sculptural technique, or even some generalized cultural notion one could isolate as a native aesthetic. It grows out of a distinctive sensibility the whole of life participates in forming—one in which the meanings of things are the scars that men leave on them.

This realization, that to study an art form is to explore a sensibility, that such a sensibility is essentially a collective formation, and that the foundations of such a formation are as wide as social existence and as deep, leads away not only from the view that aesthetic power is a grandiloquence for the pleasures of craft. [...] Nothing very measurable would happen to Yoruba society if carvers no longer concerned themselves with the fineness of line, or, I daresay, even with carving. Certainly, it would not fall apart. Just some things that were felt could not be said—and perhaps, after awhile, might no longer even be felt—and life would be the greyer for it. Anything may, of course, play a role in helping society work, painting and sculpting included; just as anything may help it tear itself apart. But the central connection between art and collective life does not lie on such an instrumental plane, it lies on a semiotic one. Matisse's color jottings (the word is his own) and the Yoruba's line arrangements don't, save glancingly, celebrate social structure or forward useful doctrines. They materialize a way of experiencing; bring a particular cast of mind out into the world of objects, where men can look at it.

The signs or sign elements—Matisse's yellow, the Yoruba's slash—that make up a semiotic system we want, for theoretical purposes, to call aesthetic are ideationally connected to the society in which they are found, not mechanically. They are, in a phrase of Robert Goldwater's, primary documents. [...]

To develop the point more concretely [...] we can look for a moment at some aspects of one of the few other discussions of tribal art that manages to be sensitive to semiotic concerns without disappearing into a haze of formulas: Anthony Forge's analysis of the four-color flat painting of the Abelam people of New Guinea.[6] The group produces, in Forge's phrase, 'acres of painting,' on flat sheets of sago spathe, all done in cult situations of one sort or another. [...] But what is of immediate interest is the fact that, although Abelam painting ranges from the obviously figurative to the totally abstract (a distinction which, as their painting is declamatory, not descriptive, has no meaning to them), it is mainly connected to the wider world of Abelam experience by means of an almost obsessively recurrent motif, a pointed oval, representing, and called, the belly of a woman. The representation is, of course, at least vaguely iconic. But the power of the connection for the Abelam lies less in that, hardly much of an achievement, than in the fact that they are able with it to address a burning preoccupation of theirs in terms of color-shapes (in itself, line here hardly exists as an aesthetic element; while paint has a magical force)—a preoccupation they address in somewhat different ways in work, in ritual, in domestic life: the natural creativity of the female.

The concern for the difference between female creativity, which the Abelam see as pre-cultural, a product of woman's physical being, and therefore primary, and male creativity, which they see as cultural, dependent upon men's access to supernatural power through ritual, and therefore derivative, runs through the whole of their culture. [...]

[...] One could as well argue that the rituals, or the myths, or the organization of family life, or the division of labor enact conceptions evolved in painting as that painting reflects the conceptions underlying social life. All these matters are marked by the apprehension of culture as generated in the womb of nature as man is in the belly of woman, and all of them give it a specific sort of voice. Like the incised lines on Yoruba statues, the color-ovals in Abelam paintings are meaningful because they connect to a sensibility they join in creating—here, one where, rather than scars signing civilization, pigment signs power:

In general colour (or strictly paint) words are applied only to things of ritual concern. This can be seen very clearly in the Abelam classification of nature. Tree species are subject to an elaborate classification, but . . . the criteria used are seed and leaf shapes. Whether the tree has flowers or not, and the colour of flowers or leaves are rarely mentioned as criteria. Broadly speaking, the Abelam had use only for the hibiscus and a yellow flower, both of which served as [ritual] decorations for men and yams. Small flowering plants of any colour were of no interest and were classified merely as grass or undergrowth. Similarly with insects: all those that bite or sting are carefully classified, but butterflies form one huge class regardless of size or colour. The words for the four colours are . . . really words for paints. Paint is an essentially powerful substance and it is perhaps not so surprising that the use of colour words is restricted to those parts of the natural environment that have been selected as ritually relevant . . .

The association between colour and ritual significance can also be seen in Abelam reactions to European importations. Coloured magazines sometimes find their way into the village and occasionally pages are torn from them and attached to the matting at the base of the ceremonial house façade . . . The pages selected were brightly coloured, usually food advertisements . . . [and] the Abelam had no idea of what was represented but thought that with their bright colours and incomprehensibility the selected pages were likely to be European [sacred designs] and therefore powerful.[7]

So in at least two places, two matters on the face of them as self-luminous as line and color draw their vitality from rather more than their intrinsic appeal, as real as that might be. Whatever the innate capacities for response to sculptile delicacy or chromatic drama, these responses are caught up in wider concerns, less generic and more contentful, and it is this encounter with the locally real that reveals their constructive power. The unity of form and content is, where it occurs and to the degree it occurs, a cultural achievement, not a philosophical tautology. If there is to be a semiotic science of art it is that achievement it will have to explain. And to do so it will have to give more attention to talk, and to other sorts of talk but the recognizably aesthetic, than it has usually been inclined to give.

A common response to this sort of argument, especially when it comes from the side of anthropologists, is to say, that may be all well and good for primitives, who confuse the realms of their experience into one large, un-reflective whole, but it doesn't apply to more developed cultures where art emerges as a differentiated activity responsive mainly to its own necessities. And like most such easy contrasts between peoples on different sides of the literacy revolution, it is false, and in both directions: as much in under-estimating the internal dynamic of art in—what shall I call them? unlettered societies?—as in over-estimating its autonomy in lettered ones. I will set aside the first sort of error here—the notion that Yoruba and Abelam type art traditions are without a kinetic of their own—perhaps to come back to it on a later occasion. For the moment I want to scotch the second by looking briefly at the matrix of sensibility in two quite developed, and quite different, aesthetic enterprises: quattrocento painting and Islamic poetry.

For Italian painting, I will mainly rely on Michael Baxandall's recent book, *Painting and Experience in Fifteenth Century Italy,* which takes precisely the sort of approach I here am advocating.[8] Baxandall is concerned with defining what he calls 'the period eye'—that is, 'the equipment that a fifteenth-century painter's public [i.e., other painters and "the patronizing classes"] brought to complex visual stimulations like pictures.'[9] A picture, he says, is sensitive to the kinds of interpretive skill—patterns, categories, inferences, analogies—the mind brings to it:

A man's capacity to distinguish a certain kind of form or relationship of forms will have consequences for the attention with which he addresses a picture. For instance, if he is skilled in noting proportional relationships, or if he is practiced in reducing complex forms to compounds of simple forms, or if he has a rich set of categories for different kinds of red and brown, these skills may well lead him to order his experience of Piero della Francesca's *Annunciation* differently from people without these skills, and much more sharply than people whose experience has not given them many skills relevant to the picture. For it is clear that some perceptual skills are more relevant to any one picture than others: a virtuosity in classifying the ductus of flexing lines—a skill many Germans, for instance, possessed in this period . . . would not find much scope on the *Annunciation*. Much of what we call 'taste' lies in this, the conformity between discriminations demanded by a painting and skills of discrimination pos-sessed by the beholder.[10]

But what is even more important, these appropriate skills, for both the beholder and the painter, are for the most part not built in like retinal sensitivity for focal length but are drawn from general experience, the experience in this case of living a quattrocento life and seeing things in a quattrocento way:

... some of the mental equipment a man orders his visual experience with is variable, and much of this variable equipment is culturally relative, in the sense of being determined by the society which has influenced his experience. Among these variables are categories with which he classified his visual stimuli, the knowledge he will use to supplement what his immediate vision gives him, and the attitude he will adopt to the kind of artificial object seen. The beholder must use on the painting such visual skills as he has, very few of which are normally special to painting, and he is likely to use those skills his society esteems highly. The painter responds to this; his public's visual capacity must be his medium. Whatever his own specialized professional skills, he is himself a member of the society he works for and shares its visual experience and habit.[11]

The first fact (though, as in Abelam, only the first) to be attended to in these terms is, of course, that most fifteenth-century Italian paintings were religious paintings, and not just in subject matter but in the ends they were designed to serve. Pictures were meant to deepen human awareness of the spiritual dimensions of existence; they were visual invitations to reflections on the truths of Christianity. Faced with an arresting image of The Annunciation, The Assumption of the Virgin, The Adoration of the Magi, The Charge to St Peter, or The Passion, the beholder was to complete it by reflecting on the event as he knew it and on his personal relationship to the mysteries it recorded. 'For it is one thing to adore a painting,' as a Dominican preacher defending the virtuousness of art, put it, 'but it is quite another to learn from a painted narrative what to adore.'[12]

Yet the relation between religious ideas and pictorial images (and this I think is true for art generally) was not simply expositive; they were not Sunday school illustrations. The painter, or at least the religious painter, was concerned with inviting his public to concern themselves with first things and last, not with providing them with a recipe or a surrogate for such concern, nor with a transcription of it. His relation, or more exactly, the relations of his painting, to the wider culture was interactive or, as Baxandall puts it, complementary. [. . .] The public does not need, as Baxandall remarks, what it has already got. What it needs is an object rich enough to see it in; rich enough, even, to, in seeing it, deepen it. [. . .]

The capacity, variable among peoples as it is among individuals, to perceive meaning in pictures (or poems, melodies, buildings, pots, dramas, statues) is, like all other fully human capacities, a product of collective experience which far transcends it, as is the far rarer capacity to put it there in the first place. It is out of participation in the general system of symbolic forms we call culture that participation in the particular we call art, which is in fact but a sector of it, is possible. A theory of art is thus at the same time a theory of culture, not an autonomous enterprise. [. . .]

There is hardly a better example of the fact that an artist works with signs which have a place in semiotic systems extending far beyond the craft he practices than the poet in Islam. A Muslim making verses faces a set of cultural realities as objective to his intentions as rocks or rainfall, no less substantial for being non-material, and no less stubborn for being man-made. He operates, and alway has operated, in a context where the instrument of his art, language, has a peculiar, heightened kind of status, as distinctive a significance, and as mysterious, as Abelam paint. Everything from metaphysics to morphology, scripture to calligraphy, the patterns of public recitation to the style of informal conversation conspires to make of speech and speaking a matter charged with an import if not unique in human history, certainly extraordinary. The man who takes up the poet's role in Islam traffics, and not wholly legitimately, in the moral substance of his culture.

In order even to begin to demonstrate this it is of course necessary first to cut the subject down to size. It is not my intention to survey the whole course of poetic development from the Prophecy forward; but just to make a few general, and rather unsystematic, remarks about the place of poetry in traditional Islamic society—most particularly Arabic poetry; most particularly in Morocco. [. . .]

There are, from this perspective, three dimensions of the problem to review and interrelate. The first, as always in matters Islamic is the peculiar nature and status of the Quran, 'the only miracle in Islam.' The second is the performance context of the poetry, which, as a living thing, is as much a musical and dramatic art as it is a literary one. And the third, and most difficult to delineate in a short space, is the general nature—agonistic, as I will call it—of interpersonal communication in Moroccan society. Together they make of poetry a kind of paradigmatic speech act, an archetype of talk, which it would take, were such a thing conceivable, a full analysis of Muslim culture to unpack.

But as I say, wherever the matter ends it starts with the Quran. The Quran (which means neither 'testament' nor 'teaching' nor 'book,' but 'recitation') differs from the other major scriptures of the world in that it contains not reports about God by a prophet or his disciples, but His direct speech, the syllables, words, and sentences of Allah. Like Allah, it is eternal and uncreated, one of His attributes, like Mercy or Omnipotence, not one of his creatures, like man or the earth. [. . .] [T]he point is that he who chants Quranic verses—Gabriel, Muhammad, the Quran-reciters, or the ordinary Muslim, thirteen centuries further along the chain—chants not words about God, but of Him, and indeed, as those words are His essence, chants God himself. The Quran, as Marshall Hodgson has said, is not a treatise, a statement of facts and norms, it is an event, an act:

It was never designed to be read for information or even for inspiration, but to be recited as an act of commitment in worship . . . What one did with the Qur'ân was not to peruse it but to worship by means of it; not to passively receive it but, in reciting it, to reaffirm it for oneself: the event of revelation was renewed every time one of the faithful, in the act of worship, relived [that is, respoke] the Qur'ânic affirmation.[13]

Now, there are a number of implications of this view of the Quran— among them that its nearest equivalent in Christianity is not the Bible but Christ—but for our purposes the critical one is that its language, seventh- century Meccan Arabic, is set apart as not just the vehicle of a divine message, like Greek, Pali, Aramaic, or Sanskrit, but as itself a holy object. Even an individual recitation of the Quran, or portions of it, is considered an uncre- ated entity, something which puzzles a faith centered on divine persons, but to an Islamic one, centered on divine rhetoric, signifies that speech is sacred to the degree that it resembles that of God. [. . .]

[. . .] [P]oetry lies in between the divine imperatives of the Quran and the rhetorical thrust and counter-thrust of everyday life, and it is that which gives it its uncertain status and strange force. On the one hand, it forms a kind of para-Quran, sung truths more than transitory and less than eternal in a language style more studied than the colloquial and less arcane than the classical. On the other, it projects the spirit of everyday life into the realm of, if not the holy, at least the inspired. Poetry is morally ambiguous because it is not sacred enough to justify the power it actually has and not secular enough for that power to be equated to ordinary eloquence. The Moroccan oral poet inhabits a region between speech types which is at the same time a region between worlds, between the discourse of God and the wrangle of men. And unless that is understood neither he nor his poetry can be under- stood, no matter how much ferreting out of latent structures or parsing of verse forms one engages in. Poetry, or anyway this poetry, constructs a voice out of the voices that surround it. If it can be said to have a 'function,' that is it.

'Art,' says my dictionary, a usefully mediocre one, is 'the conscious produc- tion or arrangement of colors, forms, movements, sounds or other elements in a manner that affects the sense of beauty,' a way of putting the matter which seems to suggest that men are born with the power to appreciate, as they are born with the power to see jokes, and have only to be provided with the occasions to exercise it. As what I have said here ought to indicate, I do not think that this is true (I don't think that it is true for humor either); but, rather, that 'the sense of beauty,' or whatever the ability to respond intelli- gently to face scars, painted ovals, domed pavillions, or rhymed insults should be called, is no less a cultural artifact than the objects and devices concocted to 'affect' it. The artist works with his audience's capacities—capacities to see, or hear, or touch, sometimes even to taste and smell, with understand- ing. And though elements of these capacities are indeed innate—it usually helps not to be color blind—they are brought into actual existence by the experience of living in the midst of certain sorts of things to look at, listen to, handle, think about, cope with, and react to; particular varieties of cabbages, particular sorts of kings. Art and the equipment to grasp it are made in the same shop.

For an approach to aesthetics which can be called semiotic—that is, one concerned with how signs signify—what this means is that it cannot be a formal science like logic or mathematics, but must be a social one like history or anthropology. [. . .] This is not a plea [. . .] for the neglect of form, but for seeking the roots of form not in some updated version of faculty psychology but in what I have called elsewhere 'the social history of the imagination'— that is, in the construction and deconstruction of symbolic systems as individuals and groups of individuals try to make some sense of the profusion of things that happen to them. When a Bamileke chief took office, Jacques Maquet informs us, he had his statue carved; 'after his death, the statue was respected, but it was slowly eroded by the weather as his memory was eroded in the minds of the people.'[14] Where is the form here? In the shape of the statue or the shape of its career? It is, of course, in both. But no analysis of the statue that does not hold its fate in view, a fate as intended as is the arrangement of its volume or the gloss of its surface, is going to understand its meaning or catch its force.

It is, after all, not just statues (or paintings, or poems) that we have to do with but the factors that cause these things to seem important—that is, affected with import—to those who make or possess them, and these are as various as life itself. If there is any commonality among all the arts in all the places that one finds them (in Bali they make statues out of coins, in Australia drawings out of dirt) that justifies including them under a single, Western-made rubric, it is not that they appeal to some universal sense of beauty. That may or may not exist, but if it does it does not seem, in my experience, to enable people to respond to exotic arts with more than an ethnocentric sentimentalism in the absence of a knowledge of what those arts are about or an understanding of the culture out of which they come. (The Western use of 'primitive' motifs, its undoubted value in its own terms aside, has only accentuated this; most people, I am convinced, see African sculpture as bush Picasso and hear Javanese music as noisy Debussy.) If there is a commonality it lies in the fact that certain activities everywhere seem specifically designed to demonstrate that ideas are visible, audible, and—one needs to make a word up here—tactible, that they can be cast in forms where the sense, and through the senses the emotions, can reflectively address them. The variety of artistic expression stems from the variety of conceptions men have about the way things are, and is indeed the same variety.

['Art as a Cultural System', *Modern Language Notes*, 91 (1974), 1473–83, 1488–90, 1497–9.]

MARK SAGOFF

16 On the Aesthetic and Economic Value of Art

That no necessary connection exists between the aesthetic and economic values of art is a commonplace everyone understands. Fine works of art, especially at the time they are created, often must be given away, while mediocre works draw huge prices. Yet not everyone who buys art does so merely as an investment; people pay high prices, in part, at least, because they believe a work is aesthetically valuable. The astounding sums now paid for famous works of art suggest that people are willing to gamble much to possess a first-rate work. Why? What does the enormous economic value of certain works tell us, if not about the aesthetic value of these paintings, then about the way we value art in general?

What does the price tag tell us?

I

As to what is meant by *aesthetic* value I believe I can state my position very briefly. I can state it, indeed, in three words—*I don't know*. I do not know why art is valuable as art; I do not know what aesthetic value consists in. That is one reason I want to see if any light can be shed on the concept of aesthetic value by an examination of the economic value of art.

I think that there is no shame, incidentally, in knowing nothing about the concept of aesthetic value. Those who have pretended to know something have shown, on the contrary, that they too know little or nothing. Some—those who follow Clive Bell, for example—say things like this: 'A good work of visual art carries a person who is capable of appreciating it out of life and into ecstasy. . . . Art transforms us from the world of man's activity to a world of aesthetic exaltation'.[1] They speak about art in the same breathless terms that users of drugs sometimes speak about marijuana or cocaine.

I worry whenever someone tells me a thing is valuable because it gives pleasure. Many contemptible and worthless things, after all, are pleasant to many people, things such as pornography, violence on television, and prostitution. The fact that you enjoy these things does not make them better; it only makes you worse. A sense of pleasure does not catapult these diversions into the realm of value occupied by art. Why should we think, then, that the value of art consists in the pleasure it may produce?

It seems to me that any sound cost-benefit study will reveal, moreover, that the pleasures of art are small when compared with those, say, of the gambling den or the massage parlour. (Evolution, after all, has used pleasure to promote procreation, not painting.) The pleasures of art, in sheer fire-power, are of very low wattage, in relation to their costs. Why, then, do so many of us—especially struggling young painters—make such sacrifices in the name of art? Surely these are not sacrifices made merely for the sake of pleasure—for pleasure may be had in many easier, cheaper, and more certain ways.

People have said that art is good because it causes a pleasure or communicates an emotion or some other excitement or passion. But what is *good* about any of these things? When I was an adolescent I loved stimulation, as it were, for its own sake; I would say things like 'Oh, wow!' So I did appreciate it. When someone passes the age of thirty-five, however, he or she begins to lose interest in emotion, passion, or pleasure for its own sake. You value nothing so much as quiet and peace of mind. You become, shall I say, reflective. You value emotions or pleasures not for their own sake but only in relation to their cause. You take pleasure in things because you find or know that they are good; you do not find them to be good because you take pleasure in them. [. . .]

II

In order to get some purchase on the notion of aesthetic value, I shall discuss something we contrast with it, namely, economic or monetary value. Money is always interesting even if one can only talk about it. It is particularly interesting to me because we all go to great pains to distinguish the value of art as art from the value of art as an investment. By 'art', incidentally, I mean to include, in this discussion, not only paintings and sculptures but other prime objects one might find in a museum, such as antiques, and even ephemera, such as old advertisements, handbills and documents.

E.L. Doctorow's novel *Ragtime* has a scene in which J. P. Morgan purchases, at bargain-basement prices, great works of art from the nobility of Europe. The nobles offer to sell Morgan their daughters at the same time. It comes to the same thing. Any society that would sell off its masterpieces for a few thousand dollars must also be willing to sell its children into bondage. The nobles, in this situation, were reduced to savagery by the onset of World War One. What they did not sell to the Americans they thought the Germans would take for nothing.

Suppose I told you that, fifty years from now, the great museums of America and Europe would offer their collections for sale for a few dollars or a few bags of wheat or rice. You would read the message clearly: some catastrophe, probably a nuclear holocaust, had reduced us all to savagery, and ended our social order. Nothing else would make sense of the low prices charged for great works of art.

Now, suppose I told you that in fifty years gold would bring very low prices. One ounce may purchase a loaf of bread or a bottle of milk. You *might* think that a catastrophe had occurred; but there are other explanations. Gold is a speculative commodity. A rush to sell or the discovery of massive quantities in the ground could severely alter its price.

I believe that an important law governs the sale of all prime objects of art—all objects, that is to say, which are widely regarded as among the finest examples of painting, sculpture, antique furniture, or whatever. The iron law is this: the prices of these things always go up, never down. Imagine a Leonardo, Rembrandt or Turner selling for a hundred dollars. You shudder to think of what would reduce society to such a savage state.

timeless value

A powerful social expectation exists that accepted or established masterpieces of art will never lose their economic value; minor pieces, when fully entrenched in catalogue and collection, similarly never decline in worth. I think that there is a concomitant expectation about the aesthetic value of these objects. Tastes may change, of course; people may prefer one museum to another; they may like the Impressionists one year and prefer the Old Masters the next. The aesthetic value of these works, however, does not change, or, if it does, it increases. The aesthetic value of the 'truly great', like its price, never diminishes. One must always find *more* in a masterpiece; never *less*.

More, Never less

The iron law that prices for prime art objects increase has a number of corollaries. These are related, I believe, to conceptual or analytic truths about aesthetic value. I have space here to mention five or six of the principles I have in mind.

III

First Principle: Works of art endure for the foreseeable future; they have no natural life-span; they are assumed never to perish.

John Keats has written: 'A thing of beauty is a joy for ever…' [...] If art were not assumed to last 'for ever'—or at least to last through the foreseeable future—we should not be able to support the iron law of increasing price. This is true, first, because the price would plummet as the work approached its demise. No one would pay very much even for a Rembrandt if it had only a few more months to survive. Works which are new would have an advantage over those which are old. This would severely inhibit the expectation that prices paid for an art work always increase.

Deterioration is also an important factor. If art works were allowed or perceived greatly to deteriorate over time (which, of course, many do), then, one would expect, the prices would have to decline, because of the condition of the object. In order to prevent this, an enormous industry has developed to conserve, restore, repair and protect works of art against the inevitable ravages of time.

Where conservation and restoration fail, aesthetic perception makes up the difference. Critics and connoisseurs tell us, with much truth, that even wholesale damage to a work of art can be aesthetically less intrusive than a smug or unsatisfactory retouching. What is more, deterioration—the crackle of paint, patina on sculpture—is thought to add to the aesthetic experience. Once a work has found an established place in the world of art it can survive even as a fragment without losing aesthetic importance and value. Without this commitment to the aesthetic integrity of worn and damaged work we should have to say that art *has* a lifespan, and for many masterpieces, it is long past.

IV

Second Principle: The vast majority of art objects must be kept out of circulation.

An enormous number of art works exist. Small towns in Italy sometimes contain enough prized works to occupy tourists for weeks; in America, many middle-sized cities have established large-size collections. The sheer amount of significant art is staggering. It is also growing—since, as I have argued, art, once established, cannot be destroyed. While the supply of art grows, however, the demand does not. People are not rushing in great numbers to buy significant works of art. It seems to ordinary observation that the supply of art, then, greatly exceeds demand. Why, then, are higher prices consistently paid?

The answer is given in the second principle. Very few art objects are offered for sale. This does not mean, however, that the vast majority are kept off the market to await a higher price. Most established art works, on the contrary, are locked away in public and private collections, often legally bound to remain where they are. Were art works regarded as objects of speculation, were they held primarily for purposes of investment, then the iron law of prices could not hold. Paintings, antiques, or other objects would flood the market when prices are high and thus would lower them.

The iron law requires, then, that art objects must *not* be treated as items for speculation or investment. The vast majority of them must be regarded, rather, as *priceless* and never offered for sale. An art work, in other words, is to be considered an object of *love* or *respect* or *esteem*; it cannot function as a consumer product, bestowing some sort of 'satisfaction'. For then we would trade works of art for other consumer goods—and the prices would come tumbling down.

The idea that the value of a work of art is 'above all price' finds support in aesthetic theory. Philosophers may not have a developed theory of aesthetic value; they tend, nevertheless, sharply to distinguish aesthetic from economic worth. They argue or indeed assume, as a rule, that we are not to regard art as a commodity, the value of which is measured by a market price. We do not draw indifference curves between Picassos and potatoes. Art, on the contrary, is celebrated as a monument of the unaging intellect, an expression or intuition of the eternal, an insight into the meaning of things; and, therefore,

The way that classic art works are treated in the marketplace contributes to their esteemed economic value

art is to be valued 'for its own sake'. This kind of thinking, whether it means anything definite or not, I suspect, is necessary if we are to keep the vast majority of art works out of circulation. And this, in turn, is required to ensure that ever higher prices will be paid for those works which do come up for sale.

The question arises whether higher and higher prices are paid because art is regarded as priceless or whether, on the contrary, art is regarded as priceless in order to protect or increase the prices that in fact are paid for it. How would you answer the question?

The question is not as foolish as it first might seem. It need not suggest in any way a conspiracy among philosophers and auction houses to inflate the price of art. What it suggests is this: for reasons we have yet to explore, it is very important for society that the monuments and symbols of its history should not sell so cheaply that just anybody could control them. It is important to the structure of society that significant art works should be controlled by the appropriate *caste*; this, then, is guaranteed, in part, by the iron law of increasing price.

Is this intentional? It's society's way to protect the aesthetic experience

V

Third Principle: Forgeries, except in very special cases, are worthless, no matter how perfect they may be.

I once attended an auction at which a reproduction Queen Anne sofa was offered for sale. Nobody bid. No one wished to be embarrassed, even among strangers, by bidding for something which was inauthentic. The sofa, incidentally, was a magnificent recreation; no expense had been spared in craftsmanship or in materials. A dealer friend of mine, sitting next to me, bent towards me, screwing his face into a hideous scowl. 'It's *new*', he whispered, with utter contempt. *We protect the "realness" of the aesthetic experience*

No auction house with any self-respect handles fakes; the best houses always guarantee authenticity. This has nothing to do with how a chair, buffet, painting, or sculpture *looks*. It is a question of what the object *is*. *That* is what makes it authentic; *that* is necessary for its having value. A severely worn painting or vase from a particular period or artist may bring an astounding price; a copy which looks much better will not attract a bid.

The iron law of increasing price plainly requires that all forgeries—with the exception of a few special instances—have no value. Were the copy valued as highly as the original for the mere reason that it *looks* equally well or even better (even *more* authentic), we should have chaos. [...] Monuments of cultural history might roll over the block at prices usually paid for colour televisions and naugahide chairs.

Can we justify, on aesthetic grounds, the way collectors scorn imitations? It is hard to answer this question in the absence of a general conception or theory of aesthetic value. Nevertheless, many philosophers agree on at least one explanation of the preference we share for authentic works of art. This explanation posits on what seem *a priori* grounds that some small, yet crucial, difference must exist in the appearance of the authentic and the inauthentic work of art.

This approach can best be understood within what we may call the 'stimulus-response' model of aesthetic experience. The idea is that a painting creates a stimulus causing, in the informed observer, a response of some elevated, intense, or otherwise desirable kind. (It is this response, incidentally, which is supposed, on this model, to be valuable. The object has value only as a cause.) On this approach, a forgery, if it caused precisely the same response, would have the same aesthetic value as the original work of art.

We all know stories about eminent connoisseurs and critics who have been taken in by forgeries. How do philosophers deny, then, that the forgery causes the same response, and therefore has the same aesthetic value, as the authentic work? Philosophers tend to explain this by proposing that when the critic knows which work is authentic and which is the forgery he or she is able to discern differences. These differences, moreover, inform future perception. Critics may be wrong occasionally; what counts, however, is that they learn from their mistakes.

The problem with this explanation is this. While minute, yet important, differences may be assumed to exist between originals and reproductions, these differences are likely to favour the copy. The reason is the one we noted: old paintings deteriorate; a forgery, therefore, may look more like the original looked at its creation than the original now resembles its former self. People who do aesthetics tell all kinds of stories about the beauty of deterioration or about the irrelevance of deterioration; but the problem is hard to solve. We tend to impeach forgeries on *empirical* grounds, claiming that, *in fact*, they are rarely or never as good as originals. We 'prove' this by noticing differences which show the inferiority of *whichever* work we identify as the fake. The thesis, then, is really an *a priori* assumption which, in principle, can never be given an empirical disproof.

VI

I shall mention briefly another two related principles. They are:

Fourth Principle: Art objects have no practical function or use.

Fifth Principle: Enduring art works, with few and special exceptions, cannot be created directly; they must be 'found' or 'discovered' long after they have been rejected or thrown out.

In his excellent study, *Rubbish Theory* (London: 1979), Michael Thompson writes:

Symbolism over practicality

I know of a family that owns a very large Turner which they were considering having made into a dining room table. I was disappointed to hear that, rather than eating straight off the oil-painted surface, they planned to protect it beneath a sealed glass frame and that they abandoned the whole project when they found that this could not be done in such a way as to guarantee that the painting survive unaltered—proof that one cannot have one's art-cake and eat off it.   (p. 119)

[. . .] An art object, once it has established itself in that status, never goes back to any earlier use it might have had, even if it was first intended, e.g., as a sofa, bureau, sailor's box, or scrap of advertising. Once an object 'moves up' into the durable category it functions as a symbol and has meaning of some kind; it has no other primary function. Why is this? One reason is plain: use would cause deterioration. A man does not drive his Model T, then, except on ceremonial occasions or in dire emergencies. Driving it might wear it out.

I believe, however, there may be a deeper explanation. The economic worth the object has, or could have, if it were regarded and traded as an object of use would be minimal. Nobody would want an antique car *as a car*; just think of the problem of spare parts. Similarly, people buy antiques for their homes in order to fill their living rooms not *with furniture* but *with meanings*. The Queen Anne sofa is to be perceived as a symbol. Were it merely to function as furniture, a reproduction would do as well, and a contemporary piece probably better. The antique could not command *as furniture* a price commensurate with its status *as art*.   Boundaries

It should be plain that an important boundary—a social boundary—exists between objects we view as symbols and as parts of our heritage, to be preserved from the past and transferred to the future, and articles which we merely use, and which, therefore, wear out or have a 'natural' life. The distinction between objects of art and objects of use, in our society, marks and protects this crucial cultural boundary.

Aesthetic theory similarly insists upon this distinction. Were an aesthetic object judged according to a purpose, it would have only the economic value attaching to whatever met that need; accordingly, one could not distinguish the aesthetic from the economic, and thus give it a status which is above all price.

Let me now turn to the final principle [. . .]. This is the rule that art objects achieve that status only if they have been 'discovered' after having been rejected and thrown out. The increasing prices paid for established art objects and the effort of restoration lavished upon them, indeed, may be seen as a continuous ritual effort to reclaim these things from the dustbin. [. . .]

The rule applies with almost no exception to antiques, that is, to objects which are created for economic use, and are later received or perceived primarily in aesthetic terms, as symbols. Antiques are, literally, yesterday's rubbish: the things we value as symbols of our common heritage are the objects our great-grandparents were glad to be rid of. Oddly enough, in cherishing these objects, I choose, as it were, my great-grandparents. In filling my home with, say, colonial pieces, I exchange my natural origin (Russian) for an adopted one (English-American). I trace my common ancestry to the same forebears as my neighbour, who has also gentrified a house, and put up a Georgian door. The fact that he is second generation Italian makes no difference: now we are both children of Adams.

That art objects have to go through a waiting-period is easily explained on the principle that ever-increasing prices must be paid for them once they come into their own. Otherwise, too many people have a key, as it were, to the bank door. A very long-lived painter, like Picasso, who manages to achieve a position of historical importance, suggests the dimensions of the problem. The usual course, then, must be to wait until almost all the examples of a period or style have passed out of existence or have been taken out of circulation. When objects are suitably rare, and no more can be produced, it is possible to collect them for their meaning or for their significance as symbols. One does not then put too much pressure on the rule of increasing price.

An amusing example of this comes to mind. The cars which have appeared most recently in the antique class are the Ford Edsel and the 1965 Corvair. Other automobiles have to wait thirty years or more before being allowed antique or classic status by clubs and by motor vehicle authorities. But not these cars. Why? The answer is that they were rejected as junk almost upon manufacture. The Edsel was discontinued, virtually the day it was first marketed, because of poor design; Corvair is the one Ralph Nader described in his book *Unsafe at Any Speed*. The fact that these cars were certified as undrivable and unsaleable within a year or two of manufacture paved the way for their early retirement as 'priceless' antiques, with prices that always increase.

VII

I have now put forward five principles which, as I have argued, are true to the phenomenology of our experience of art. These were: (1) Art works are not transient but endure; (2) Most art is kept out of circulation and not exchanged; (3) Forgeries are worthless; (4) Art has no practical purpose or economic use; (5) Works of art must pass through the wastebasket, in most instances. I have tried to relate these generalizations to traditional views in philosophical aesthetics.

Now the question which arises is: why have I done this? Ostensibly, I have been showing that all these principles derive from what I have called the 'iron rule' of increasing prices. My proposal seems to be, then, that many of our basic aesthetic boundaries and commitments are entailed, or at least explained, by the rule that higher prices for art must always be paid.

Plainly, however, this is a ridiculous thesis. It seems to lack philosophic seriousness. Why, then, have I suggested it?

I do not regard the iron rule of increasing prices as important. I regard it, rather, as trivial. I have only used it as a foil for presenting the other principles. If we consider the 'iron rule', however, as a *sixth* principle, it may lead us to a significant thesis about the relation of the value of art to its history, or, to be more pointed, to *our* history. (For to experience an object as art is, in some ways, to perceive and share in a history.) The six principles together also suggest a rather obvious approach to a theory of aesthetic value.

One reason why art works, including antiques, draw ever increasing prices may be this: they confer on their owners status as being protectors and preservers of the past. They assure us in our status of maintaining our cultural heritage and passing it on to our children improved or at least unimpaired. (This is the reason that the owners of the Turner decided against the table; the painting would be permanently damaged.) What more can we do than pass on to our children what we ourselves have inherited? What higher status can one have than to be one who conserves and presides over that heritage?

Two subsidiary points come to mind. The rapid discovery of new art works, for example, in the gentrification of slum housing into monuments of our glorious past, is essentially egalitarian, in so far as more of us join the ranks of the very few who, formerly, could claim 'historical' or 'landmark' status. Even more socially important may be the sudden and enormous interest in ephemera, which may include anything which has been purified or purged of its usefulness by having spent at least a few years in the wastebasket. Items which were discarded in the Fifties—old advertisements, for example—may have a historical meaning today. And by collecting these objects, we join a select but growing caste of those charged with the discovery and maintenance of the past.

My second subsidiary point is this: it is fair to say that many environmentalists have come to see the earth as part of our shared heritage, in other words, as having a historical and authentic character which must be preserved, as a symbol, or for its meaning. Environmentalists of this persuasion tend not to see their natural surroundings primarily in economic terms. They do not argue merely that we ought to leave enough and as good resources to the future. They seem to regard nature, rather, as a historical artifact, which should be cherished, preserved, and passed on more or less as found. [. . .]

To conclude, I shall indicate the direction in which I think the principles I mentioned lead us in thinking about the value of art as art. They lead us, I believe, to a distinction between two kinds of value. We may think, first, about the value of art as an institution; the value, in other words, of having any art at all. We may ask, then, what would be missing in a society which had no art, or what function art and its preservation plays within our larger world of individual value. We may be concerned, second, about the relative worth of individual works. Then we would ask what makes one painting or antique or whatever better than another.

I can frame this distinction by referring back to the problem of forgeries. People who ask whether forgeries are 'as good as' the originals they copy tend to think in terms of the relative worth of the individual works. I believe that the problem with forgeries, however, arises at the first level, in relation to the general value or cultural and social purpose of having art. I believe that this purpose, in part, is to allow us to choose and to be in touch with our past or pasts; it allows us to constitute from bits and pieces of paint, paper, and stone a collective heritage, to identify ourselves as part of that tradition, and to link ourselves through it to the future. Forgeries simply have no place in this process. The question of comparing the qualities of forgeries to those of authentic works, therefore, is an issue that need not and should not arise.

To discover the value or function served in general by art, one may think of primitive or older societies, to see what analogy exists between their respect and esteem for art and ours. Primitive peoples may not have paid for art at auction; they did all they could to preserve and defend it, however, and surrounded it with ceremonies and rituals of respect which equal or outdo our practices today. Although the word 'totem' was used only by the Ojibway, an Algonquin tribe, to describe their ornamental poles, early ethnographers, including Frazer, Boas, and Durkheim, extended the term to cover any art or ceremonial object with which an individual tribesman identifies his group or clan. The totem, among many or most tribes, is supposed to contain, or have some contact with, the souls of the ancestors of the tribe. A totem is kept, as a sacred trust, by the present generation, and handed on to the next. When the totem is abandoned—as the European nobles were willing (in Doctorow's novel) to abandon both their art and their children—a clan, society, or civilization is at an end.

We do not have to look far to see why philosophers have not told us how or why art is valuable as art. The question is not answered by philosophers because it has little to do with logic or with conceptual analysis. The question might better be presented to anthropologists. It is, perhaps, a question for philosophical anthropology. Kant would have done wonders with it. The value and function of art in civilization, perhaps, has not changed, in principle, from the time of the Ojibways. Their totems had the same value to them as our artistic tradition has to us. The function of the symbol is essentially the same. The difference between the aesthetic and the economic value of art, then, may be simply explained. It is the difference between the sacred and the profane.

['On the Aesthetic and Economic Value of Art', *British Journal of Aesthetics*, 21 (Autumn, 1981), 318–29.]

17 Women Artists and the Institutions of Art

Among the founding members of the British Royal Academy in 1768 were two women, Angelica Kauffmann and Mary Moser. The fact that both were the daughters of foreigners, and that both were active in the group of male painters instrumental in forming the Royal Academy, no doubt facilitated their membership. Kauffmann, elected to the prestigious Academy of Saint Luke in Rome in 1765, was hailed as the successor to Van Dyke on her arrival in London in 1766. The foremost painter associated with the decorative and romantic strain of classicism, she was largely responsible for the spread of the Abbé Winckelmann's aesthetic theories in England and was credited, along with Gavin Hamilton and Benjamin West, with popularizing Neoclassicism there. Moser, whose reputation then rivalled Kauffmann's, was the daughter of George Moser, a Swiss enameller who was the first Keeper of the Royal Academy. A fashionable flower painter patronized by Queen Charlotte, she was one of only two floral painters accepted into the Academy. Yet when Johann Zoffany's group portrait celebrating the newly founded Royal Academy, *The Academicians of the Royal Academy* (1771–72) [Fig. 1] appeared, Kauffmann and Moser were not among the artists casually grouped around the male models. There is no place for the two female academicians in the discussion about art which is taking place here. Women were barred from the study of the nude model which formed the basis for academic training and representation from the sixteenth to the nineteenth centuries. After Kauffmann and Moser, they were barred from membership in the Royal Academy itself, until Annie Louise Swynnerton became an Associate Member in 1922 and Laura Knight was elected to full membership in 1936. Zoffany, whose painting is as much about the ideal of the academic artist as it is about the Royal Academicians, has included painted busts of the two women on the wall behind the model's platform. Kauffmann and Moser have become the objects of art rather than its producers; their place is with the bas-reliefs and plaster casts that are the objects of contemplation and inspiration for the male artists. They have become *representations*, a term used today to denote not just painting and sculpture, but a wide range of imagery drawn from popular culture, media and photography, as well as the so-called fine arts.

Zoffany's painting, like many other works of art, conforms to widely held cultural assumptions about women which have subsumed women's interests under those of men and structured women's access to education and public life according to beliefs about what is 'natural.' It reiterates the marginal role traditionally ascribed to women artists in the history of painting and sculpture and affirms the female image as an object of male contemplation

FIG. 1 *The Academicians of the Royal Academy,* Johann Zoffany (1771–2)

in a history of art commonly traced through 'Old Masters' and 'master-pieces.'

[*Women, Art, and Society* (London: Thames & Hudson, 1990), 7–8.]

18 Modernity and the Spaces of Femininity

The schema which decorated the cover of Alfred H. Barr's catalogue for the exhibition *Cubism and Abstract Art* at the Museum of Modern Art, New York, in 1936 is paradigmatic of the way modern art has been mapped by modernist art history (Fig. 1). Artistic practices from the late nineteenth century are placed on a chronological flow chart where movement follows

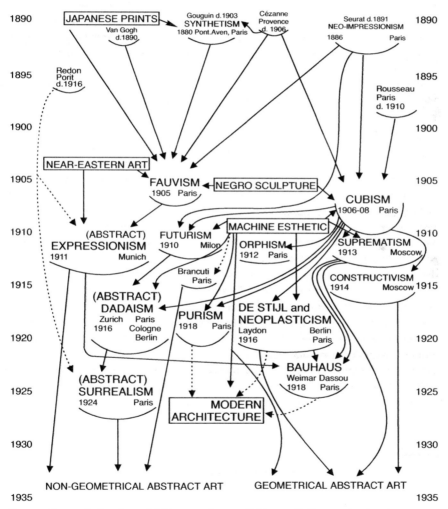

FIG. 1. Cover design for exhibition catalogue, *Cubism and Abstract Art* (1936)

movement connected by one-way arrows which indicate influence and reaction. Over each movement a named artist presides. All those canonized as the
initiators of modern art are men. Is this because there were no women
involved in early modern movements? No. Is it because those who were,
were without significance in determining the shape and character of modern
art? No. Or is it rather because what modernist art history celebrates is a
selective tradition which normalizes, as the *only* modernism, a particular and
gendered set of practices? I would argue for this explanation. As a result
any attempt to deal with artists in the early history of modernism who are
women necessitates a deconstruction of the masculinist myths of modernism.

These are, however, widespread and structure the discourse of many
counter-modernists, for instance in the social history of art. The recent
publication *The Painting of Modern Life: Paris in the Art of Manet and his
Followers*, by T. J. Clark,[1] offers a searching account of the social relations
between the emergence of new protocols and criteria for painting—modernism—and the myths of modernity shaped in and by the new city of Paris
remade by capitalism during the Second Empire. Going beyond the commonplaces about a desire to be contemporary in art, 'il faut être de son temps',[2]
Clark puzzles at what structured the notions of modernity which became the
territory for Manet and his followers. He thus indexes the impressionist
painting practices to a complex set of negotiations of the ambiguous and
baffling class formations and class identities which emerged in Parisian
society. Modernity is presented as far more then a sense of being 'up to
date'—modernity is a matter of representations and major myths—of a new
Paris for recreation, leisure and pleasure, of nature to be enjoyed at weekends
in suburbia, of the prostitute taking over and of fluidity of class in the popular
spaces of entertainment. The key markers in this mythic territory are leisure,
consumption, the spectacle and money. And we can reconstruct from Clark a
map of impressionist territory which stretches from the new boulevards via
Gare St Lazare out on the suburban train to La Grenouillère, Bougival or
Argenteuil. In these sites, the artists lived, worked and pictured themselves.
But in two of the four chapters of Clark's book, he deals with the problematic
of sexuality in bourgeois Paris and the canonical paintings are *Olympia* (1863,
Paris, Musée du Louvre) and *A bar at the Folies-Bergère* (1881–2, London,
Courtauld Institute of Art).

It is a mighty but flawed argument on many levels but here I wish to attend
to its peculiar closures on the issue of sexuality. For Clark the founding fact is
class. Olympia's nakedness inscribes her class and thus debunks the mythic
classlessness of sex epitomized in the image of the courtesan.[3] The fashion-
ably blasé barmaid at the Folies evades a fixed identity as either bourgeois or
proletarian but none the less participates in the play around class that
constituted the myth and appeal of the popular.[4]

Although Clark nods in the direction of feminism by acknowledging that these paintings imply a masculine viewer/consumer, the manner in which this is done ensures the normalcy of that position leaving it below the threshold of historical investigation and theoretical analysis. To recognize the gender specific conditions of these paintings' existence one need only imagine a female spectator and a female producer of the works. How can a woman relate to the viewing positions proposed by either of these paintings? Can a woman be offered, in order to be denied, imaginary possession of Olympia or the barmaid? Would a woman of Manet's class have a familiarity with either of these spaces and its exchanges which could be evoked so that the painting's modernist job of negation and disruption could be effective? Could Berthe Morisot have gone to such a location to canvass the subject? Would it enter her head as a site of modernity as she experienced it? Could she as a woman experience modernity as Clark defines it at all?

For it is a striking fact that many of the canonical works held up as the founding monuments of modern art treat precisely with this area, sexuality, and this form of it, commercial exchange. I am thinking of innumerable brothel scenes through to Picasso's *Demoiselles d'Avignon* or that other form, the artist's couch. The encounters pictured and imagined are those between men who have the freedom to take their pleasures in many urban spaces and women from a class subject to them who have to work in those spaces often selling their bodies to clients, or to artists. Undoubtedly these exchanges are structured by relations of class but these are thoroughly captured within gender and its power relations. Neither can be separated or ordered in a hierarchy. They are historical simultaneities and mutually inflecting.

So we must enquire why the territory of modernism so often is a way of dealing with masculine sexuality and its sign, the bodies of women—why the nude, the brothel, the bar? What relation is there between sexuality, modernity and modernism. If it is normal to see paintings of women's bodies as the territory across which men artists claim their modernity and compete for leadership of the avant-garde, can we expect to rediscover paintings by women in which they battled with their sexuality in the representation of the male nude? Of course not; the very suggestion seems ludicrous. But why? Because there is a historical asymmetry—a difference socially, economically, subjectively between being a woman and being a man in Paris in the late nineteenth century. This difference—the product of the social structuration of sexual difference and not any imaginary biological distinction—determined both what and how men and women painted.

I have long been interested in the work of Berthe Morisot (1841–96) and Mary Cassatt (1844–1926), two of the four women who were actively involved with the impressionist exhibiting society in Paris in the 1870s and 1880s who were regarded by their contemporaries as important members of the artistic group we now label the Impressionists.[5] But how are we to study the work of artists who are women so that we can discover and account for the specificity of what they produced as individuals while also recognizing that, as women, they worked from different positions and experiences from those of their colleagues who were men?

Analysing the activities of women who were artists cannot merely involve mapping women on to existing schemata even those which claim to consider the production of art socially and address the centrality of sexuality. We cannot ignore the fact that the terrains of artistic practice and of art history are structured in and structuring of gender power relations.

As Roszika Parker and I argued in *Old Mistresses: Women, Art and Ideology* (1981), feminist art history has a double project. The historical recovery of data about women producers of art coexists with and is only critically possible through a concomitant deconstruction of the discourses and practices of art history itself.

Historical recovery of women who were artists is a prime necessity because of the consistent obliteration of their activity in what passes for art history. We have to refute the lies that there were no women artists, or that the women artists who are admitted are second-rate and that the reason for their indifference lies in the all-pervasive submission to an indelible femininity—always proposed as unquestionably a disability in making art. But alone historical recovery is insufficient. What sense are we to make of information without a theorized framework through which to discern the particularity of women's work? This is itself a complicated issue. To avoid the embrace of the feminine stereotype which homogenizes women's work as determined by natural gender, we must stress the heterogeneity of women's art work, the specificity of individual producers and products. Yet we have to recognize what women share—as a result of nurture not nature, i.e. the historically variable social systems which produce sexual differentiation.

This leads to a major aspect of the feminist project, the theorization and historical analysis of sexual difference. Difference is not essential but understood as a social structure which positions male and female people asymmetrically in relation to language, to social and economic power and to meaning. Feminist analysis undermines one bias of patriarchal power by refuting the myths of universal or general meaning. Sexuality, modernism or modernity cannot function as given categories to which we add women. That only identifies a partial and masculine viewpoint with the norm and confirms women as other and subsidiary. Sexuality, modernism or modernity are organized by and organizations of sexual difference. To perceive women's specificity is to analyse historically a particular configuration of difference.

This is my project here. How do the socially contrived orders of sexual difference structure the lives of Mary Cassatt and Berthe Morisot? How did that structure what they produced? The matrix I shall consider here is that of space.

Space can be grasped in several dimensions. The first refers us to spaces as locations. What spaces are represented in the paintings made by Berthe Morisot and Mary Cassatt? And what are not? A quick list includes:

dining-rooms
drawing-rooms
bedrooms
balconies/verandas
private gardens.

The majority of these have to be recognized as examples of private areas or domestic space. But there are paintings located in the public domain, scenes for instance of promenading, driving in the park, being at the theatre, boating. They are the spaces of bourgeois recreation, display and those social rituals which constituted polite society, or Society, *Le Monde*. In the case of Mary Cassatt's work, spaces of labour are included, especially those involving child care. In several examples, they make visible aspects of working-class women's labour within the bourgeois home.

I have previously argued that engagement with the impressionist group was attractive to some women precisely because subjects dealing with domestic social life hitherto relegated as mere genre painting were legitimized as central topics of the painting practices.[6] On closer examination it is much more significant how little of typical impressionist iconography actually reappears in the works made by artists who are women. They do not represent the territory which their colleagues who were men so freely occupied and made use of in their works, for instance bars, cafés, backstage and even those places which Clark has seen as participating in the myth of the popular—such as the bar at the Folies Bergère or even the Moulin de la Galette. A range of places and subjects was closed to them while open to their male colleagues who could move freely with men and women in the socially fluid public world of the streets, popular entertainment and commercial or casual sexual exchange.

The second dimension in which the issue of space can be addressed is that of the spatial order within paintings. Playing with spatial structures was one of the defining features of early modernist painting in Paris, be it Manet's witty and calculated play upon flatness or Degas's use of acute angles of vision, varying viewpoints and cryptic framing devices. With their close personal contacts with both artists, Morisot and Cassatt were no doubt party to the conversations out of which these strategies emerged and equally subject to the less conscious social forces which may well have conditioned the predisposition to explore spatial ambiguities and metaphors. Yet although there are examples of their using similar tactics, I would like to suggest that spatial devices in the work of Morisot and Cassatt work to a wholly different effect.

A remarkable feature in the spatial arrangements in paintings by Morisot is the juxtaposition on a single canvas of two spatial systems—or at least of two compartments of space often obviously boundaried by some device such as a balustrade, balcony, veranda or embankment whose presence is underscored by facture. In *The harbour at Lorient*, 1869, Morisot offers us at the left a landscape view down the estuary represented in traditional perspective while in one corner, shaped by the boundary of the embankment, the main figure is seated at an oblique angle to the view and to the viewer. A comparable composition occurs in *On the terrace*, 1874, where again the foreground figure is literally squeezed off-centre and compressed within a box of space marked by a heavily brushed-in band of dark paint forming the wall of the balcony on the other side of which lies the outside world of the beach. In *On the balcony*, 1872 (Fig. 2), the viewer's gaze over Paris is obstructed by the figures who are none the less separated from that Paris as they look over the balustrade from the Trocadéro, very near to her home. The point can be underlined by contrasting the painting by Monet, *The garden of the princess*, 1867, where the viewer cannot readily imagine the point from which the painting has been made, namely a window high in one of the new apartment buildings, and instead enjoys a fantasy of floating over the scene. What Morisot's balustrades demarcate is not the boundary between public and private but between the spaces of masculinity and of femininity inscribed at the level of both what spaces are open to men and women and what relation a man or woman has to that space and its occupants.

In Morisot's paintings, moreover, it is as if the place from which the painter worked is made part of the scene creating a compression or immediacy in the foreground spaces. This locates the viewer in that same place, establishing a notional relation between the viewer and the woman defining the foreground, therefore forcing the viewer to experience a dislocation between her space and that of a world beyond its frontiers. [. . .]

The spaces of femininity operated not only at the level of what is represented, the drawing-room or sewing-room. The spaces of femininity are those from which femininity is lived as a positionality in discourse and social practice. They are the product of a lived sense of social locatedness, mobility and visibility, in the social relations of seeing and being seen. Shaped within the sexual politics of looking they demarcate a particular social organization of the gaze which itself works back to secure a particular social ordering of sexual difference. Femininity is both the condition and the effect.

How does this relate to modernity and modernism? As Janet Wolff has convincingly pointed out, the literature of modernity describes the experience of men.[7] It is essentially a literature about transformations in the public world and its associated consciousness. It is generally agreed that modernity as a nineteenth-century phenomenon is a product of the city. It is a response

FIG. 2. *On the balcony,* Berthe Morisot (1872)

in a mythic or ideological form to the new complexities of a social existence passed amongst strangers in an atmosphere of intensified nervous and psychic stimulation, in a world ruled by money and commodity exchange, stressed by competition and formative of an intensified individuality, publicly defended by a blasé mask of indifference but intensely 'expressed' in a private, familial context.[8] Modernity stands for a myriad of responses to the vast increase in population leading to the literature of the crowds and masses, a speeding up of the pace of life with its attendant changes in the sense and regulation of time and fostering that very modern phenomenon, fashion, the shift in the character of towns and cities from being centres of quite visible activities—

manufacture, trade, exchange—to being zoned and stratified, with production becoming less visible while the centres of cities such as Paris and London become key sites of consumption and display producing what Sennett has labelled the spectacular city.[9]

All these phenomena affected women as well as men, but in different ways. What I have described above takes place within and comes to define the modern forms of the public space changing as Sennett argues in his book significantly titled *The Fall of Public Man* from the eighteenth century formation to become more mystified and threatening but also more exciting and sexualized. One of the key figures to embody the novel forms of public experience of modernity is the flâneur or impassive stroller, the man in the crowd who goes, in Walter Benjamin's phrase, 'botanizing on the asphalt'.[10] The flâneur symbolizes the privilege or freedom to move about the public arenas of the city observing but never interacting, consuming the sights through a controlling but rarely acknowledged gaze, directed as much at other people as at the goods for sale. The flâneur embodies the gaze of modernity which is both covetous and erotic.

But the flâneur is an exclusively masculine type which functions within the matrix of bourgeois ideology through which the social spaces of the city were reconstructed by the overlaying of the doctrine of separate spheres on to the division of public and private which became as a result a gendered division. In contesting the dominance of the aristocratic social formation they were struggling to displace, the emergent bourgeoisies of the late eighteenth century refuted a social system based on fixed orders of rank, estate and birth and defined themselves in universalistic and democratic terms. The pre-eminent ideological figure is MAN which immediately reveals the partiality of their democracy and universalism. The rallying cry, liberty, equality and fraternity (again note its gender partiality) imagines a society composed of free, self-possessing male individuals exchanging with equal and like. Yet the economic and social conditions of the existence of the bourgeoisie as a class are structurally founded upon inequality and difference in terms both of socio-economic categories and of gender. The ideological formations of the bourgeoisie negotiate these contradictions by diverse tactics. One is the appeal to an imaginary order of nature which designates as unquestionable the hierarchies in which women, children, hands and servants (as well as other races) are posited as naturally different from and subordinate to white European man. Another formation endorsed the theological separation of spheres by fragmentation of the problematic social world into separated areas of gendered activity. This division took over and reworked the eighteenth-century compartmentalization of the public and private. The public sphere, defined as the world of productive labour, political decision, government, education, the law and public service, increasingly became exclusive to men. The private sphere was the world, home, wives, children and servants. As Jules Simon, moderate republican politician, explained in 1892:

What is man's vocation? It is to be a good citizen. And woman's? To be a good wife and a good mother. One is in some way called to the outside world, the other is *retained* for the interior.[11] (my italics)

Woman was defined by this other, non-social space of sentiment and duty from which money and power were banished.[12] Men, however, moved freely between the spheres while women were supposed to occupy the domestic space alone. Men came home to be themselves but in equally constraining roles as husbands and fathers, to engage in affective relationships after a hard day in the brutal, divisive and competitive world of daily capitalist hostilities. We are here defining a mental map rather than a description of actual social spaces. [. . .]

As both ideal and social structure, the mapping of the separation of the spheres for women and men on to the division of public and private was powerfully operative in the construction of a specifically bourgeois way of life. It aided the production of the gendered social identities by which the miscellaneous components of the bourgeoisie were helped to cohere as a class, in difference from both aristocracy and proletariat. Bourgeois women, however, obviously went out in public, to promenade, go shopping, or visiting or simply to be on display. And working-class women went out to work, but that fact presented a problem in terms of definition as woman. For instance Jules Simon categorically stated that a woman who worked ceased to be a woman.[13] Therefore, across the public realm lay another, less often studied map which secured the definitions of bourgeois womanhood—femininity—in difference from proletarian women. [. . .]

In the diaries of the artist Marie Bashkirtseff, who lived and worked in Paris during the same period as Morisot and Cassatt, the following passage reveals some of the restraints:

What I long for is the freedom of going about alone, of coming and going, of sitting in the seats of the Tuileries, and especially in the Luxembourg, of stopping and looking at the artistic shops, of entering churches and museums, of walking about old streets at night; that's what I long for; and that's the freedom without which one cannot become a real artist. Do you imagine that I get much good from what I see, chaperoned as I am, and when, in order to go to the Louvre, I must wait for my carriage, my lady companion, my family?[14]

These territories of the bourgeois city were however not only gendered on a male / female polarity. They became the sites for the negotiation of gendered class identities and class gender positions. The spaces of modernity are where class and gender interface in critical ways, in that they are the spaces of sexual exchange. The significant spaces of modernity are neither simply those of masculinity, nor are they those of femininity which are as much the spaces of modernity for being the negative of the streets and bars. They are, as the canonical works indicate, the marginal or interstitial spaces where the fields of the masculine and feminine intersect and structure sexuality within a classed order. [...]

To enter such spaces as the masked ball or the café-concert constituted a serious threat to a bourgeois woman's reputation and therefore her femininity. The guarded respectability of the lady could be soiled by mere visual contact for seeing was bound up with knowing. This other world of encounter between bourgeois men and women of another class was a no-go area for bourgeois women. It is the place where female sexuality or rather female bodies are bought and sold, where woman becomes both an exchangeable commodity and a seller of flesh, entering the economic domain through her direct exchanges with men. Here the division of the public and private mapped as a separation of the masculine and feminine is ruptured by money, the ruler of the public domain, and precisely what is banished from the home.

Femininity in its class-specific forms is maintained by the polarity virgin/whore which is mystifying representation of the economic exchanges in the patriarchal kinship system. In bourgeois ideologies of femininity the fact of the money and property relations which legally and economically constitute bourgeois marriage is conjured out of sight by the mystification of a one-off purchase of the rights to a body and its products as an effect of love to be sustained by duty and devotion.

Femininity should be understood therefore not as a condition of women but as the ideological form of the regulation of female sexuality within a familial, heterosexual domesticity which is ultimately organized by the law. The spaces of femininity—ideologically, pictorially—hardly articulate female sexualities. That is not to accept nineteenth-century notions of women's asexuality but to stress the difference between what was actually lived or how it was experienced and what was officially spoken or represented as female sexuality.

In the ideological and social spaces of femininity, female sexuality could not be directly registered. This has a crucial effect with regard to the use artists who were women could make of the positionality represented by the gaze of the flâneur—and therefore with regard to modernity. The gaze of the flâneur articulates and produces a masculine sexuality which in the modern sexual economy enjoys the freedom to look, appraise and possess, in deed or in fantasy. [...]

It is not the public realm simply equated with the masculine which defines the flâneur/artist but access to a sexual realm which is marked by those interstitial spaces, the spaces of ambiguity, defined as such not only by the relatively unfixed or fantasizable class boundaries Clark makes so much of but because of cross-class sexual exchange. Women could enter and represent selected locations in the public sphere—those of entertainment and display. But a line demarcates not the end of the public/private divide but the frontier of the spaces of femininity. Below this line lies the realm of the sexualized and commodified bodies of women, where nature is ended, where class, capital and masculine power invade and interlock. It is a line that marks off a class boundary but it reveals where new class formations of the bourgeois world restructured gender relations not only between men and women but between women of different classes.

[*Vision and Difference: Femininity, Feminism and the Histories of Art* (London: Routledge, 1988), 50–6, 62–3, 66–70, 78–9.]

KATHLEEN MARIE HIGGINS

19 The Music of Our Lives

Music, to most of us, would seem to be an unproblematic term. We know it when we hear it, and that seems sufficient for most purposes. But the persuasiveness of the claim that music bears a relationship to ethics depends on what is meant by *music*. And when a definition is demanded, the term turns out to be anything but clear. In setting out to discuss music, we must immediately confront the problem: what is music and what is it not?

How can we define music? The compositions of Bach, Beethoven, and Brahms certainly count as music. Presumably, the works of the Beatles and the Rolling Stones do, too. But does everything that the Sex Pistols, or even Lou Reed, have recorded count as music? And what about John Cage's notorious '4′33″,' a 'composition' that consists of four minutes, thirty-three seconds of silence? Can silence count as music? Does the term *music* imply a certain level of quality? Is it appropriate for someone to say of trivial background music, 'That isn't really music'? Does music have to be produced by human beings? Is birdsong music? Is the howling of wolves? What about whalesong, or music produced by machines? [...]

The idea that music consists of definite tonal structures, for instance, would make little sense to members of the Basongye tribe of the Congo. The Basongye do not conceive of musical intervals as absolute distances; some of our distinct intervals are not distinguished in their musical practice. They treat major and minor seconds more or less interchangeably, for instance, and the same is true for major and minor thirds.[1]

The idea that music has emotional impact, although common to a number of cultures, is far from universal. The Navajo consider the impact of music to be medicinal, not emotional. Music is good if it cures the patient; bad if it does not.[2]

The Western idea that music is an object of aesthetic contemplation is not extended to all sorts of music in the West (even when this term is taken to apply only to Europe and most of North America). Jazz is an obvious example of music that most Westerners take to be participatory. Another is rock 'n' roll (in that appropriate response involves at least moving to the beat). Rock is not primarily seen as a phenomenon for contemplation (hence the oddity of rock magazines, which Frank Zappa describes as interviews with those who can't talk by those who can't write for those who can't read). Neither are hymns in church or the songs performed at sing-alongs.

If we look farther across the world, we find that music has a wide variety of functions. Alan Merriam notes ten such functions (including 'symbolic representation of other things, ideas, and behaviors' and 'enforcing conformity to social norms'), only one of which is directly linked to aesthetic value; and he is hesitant to claim that all cultures consider music to be an object of aesthetic enjoyment. He concludes that while many societies may view music as an object of aesthetic enjoyment in our Western sense, it is clear that some do not. The literature of ethnomusicology, moreover, is replete with examples of societies that do not share another assumption Westerners often make about art: that good art is a product of special talent, not common to everyone. In many societies, the ability to make music is considered a universal human capacity.[3]

Nettl's use of the plural term *musics* suggests a difficulty in our task of defining *music* that may not have occurred to many of us. We tend to think of music as all of a piece, even as 'the universal language,' but the evidence of ethnomusicology suggests that music is not a single, natural kind. Even if the use of musical instruments seems to be common around the world, the significance of their use may vary considerably. As Sparshott puts it, 'Who is to say that all pipings belong together, much less that all pipings belong with all drummings?'[4]

An account of music's ethical character must address this difficulty. Indeed, the ethical dimension of music for many cultures depends on a paradigm of music different from the one we are accustomed to in the West. And the West's recent disinterest in music's ethical dimension is related to its own conception of music. How we construe the term *music* determines our ability to see it as ethically relevant.

The Western classical tradition is unique in taking the paradigm of music to be a musical *work* that endures over time, and whose existence is established once it is notated, whether or not it is ever performed. This tendency of the Western classical tradition, developed over the past several centuries, allows us to think of music unproblematically as a natural kind. In Jan Broeckx's words, we identify 'the concept of "music" with the totality of all actual and conceivable musical works—and nothing but that.'[5]

[. . .]

Even on first inspection, the characterization of 'music' in terms of 'works of music' is obviously faulty, or at least incomplete, for it does not apply to all music. The music of the world does not all conform to the Western model of the 'separate, identifiable, coherent, intentionally developed and individually composed' work. Even a significant percentage of Western music fails to match this description. Broeckx cites four major categories of music that resist it:

(A) Musical products, lacking a preconceived, written composition: e.g.: Improvisations and Tape-Music (= sonorous compositions, directly planned and realized on tape); (B) Musical products of non-individual authorship (or products the authorship of which is either uncertain or of which the impact on the ultimate, sonorous result is indeterminable: Multi-individual and Collective products in Avant-garde Music, in Jazz-Music and in Folk-Music; Quotation-Music and Traditional liturgical Repertories (e.g. Gregorian Chants); (C) Musical products of non-autonomous function and character: Film-Music and some types of Incidental Music; (D) Musical products without fixed beginning and termination, with indetermined course and variable extent and with heterogenous contents: Full Aleatory Music and Background-Sounds.[6]

We could resign ourselves, in our quest for a definition of music, to a set of disjunctive characterizations, each of which describes music as conceived by a particular culture or group of cultures. But the applicability of Broeckx's categories to many instances of music in our own culture suggests that there may not be a single conception of music reigning even within a given culture at a given time. And clearly different conceptions of music reign within a culture at different times. Full aleatory (that is, 'random') music may be acknowledged as music by most serious present-day musicians in the West, but it would not have been considered music by the musically literate contemporaries of Beethoven.

That a single conception of music may not be common even to the members of a single society is further supported by the range of cultural characterizations of music studied by ethnomusicologists. Many cultures do not have a term equivalent to our term *music*. Our term describes a wide collection of phenomena; and while other cultures might have similar phenomena, they often categorize these phenomena differently than we do. Nettl observes, for instance, that the Iranian singing of the Koran is not considered music by Iranians. The phenomenon primarily identified by the term most similar to our *music* (*mūsīqī*) is instrumental music. The distinction grounds an important difference in status. The singing of the Koran is a valued religious practice, while *musiqi* is 'in certain ways an undesirable and even sinful activity' that must, as a concept, 'be kept separate from religion.' Philip Gbeho similarly notes that African Gold Coast 'music' is understood to include 'drumming, dancing, and singing,' which are 'all the same thing, and must not be separated.' The Navajo have no word for music at all, while the Blackfoot use their term for 'dance' to include music used for dancing (but no other music).[7]

But is there really no common denominator among the various phenomena in the world that we might describe as 'music'? Perhaps we are seeking too much detail in our definition and ignoring obvious basics. Charles Culver suggests a candidate for a common denominator when he observes that we in the West tend to distinguish musical from nonmusical sounds on the basis of acoustic criteria. Music involves 'sounds with regular and periodic vibrations.'[8]

But this fails as a universal criterion. Scraping sounds are considered musical in some cultures if they are so designated by context. Merriam observes that this is true for certain African tribes, and Steven Feld notes that scraping sounds are frequently an element in women's work songs among the Kaluli tribe of Papua, New Guinea. The Japanese folk music of the Ainu people of Hokkaido Island includes a form called *upopo* ('sitting song'), which is 'noted for its polyphonic texture produced by imitative group singing and the beating of chest lids (*hokai*) by the singers.' Haydn's 'Toy Symphony' is a Western example in which traditionally 'unmusical' sounds are employed. And countless others can be found in recent Western popular music (for example, Kate Bush's use of whalesong in her song 'Moving').[9]

Nettl observes that the phenomena that we colloquially include in our category 'music' are rather arbitrarily chosen: 'Birds sing, we say, but not donkeys and dogs.... The sound of a machine is not music unless it is produced in a concert with a program that lists its "composer" and with an audience which applauds (or at least boos).'[10] Many theorists would disagree that our description of birds 'singing' is evidence that we believe birds to be making music. Moreover, Westerners typically consider music to be something produced by human beings, and, indeed, this might be considered essential to a definition of music. (Computer music poses a problem for this criterion, but presumably it could be described as ultimately a human product, albeit a highly mediated one, in that humans have constructed the computer's compositional program.) John Blacking does loosely define music as 'humanly organized sound.'

But the demand that music be made by human beings is not universal. The nightingale's songs are considered musical models by classical Iranian musicians. And the Kaluli tribe of Papua New Guinea interprets forest sounds as musical in an even stronger sense. The Kaluli themselves make duets with birds, cicadas, and other forest sounds; and they often sing when near a waterfall, for they consider the waterfall to be a desirable musical accompaniment. When Plato's Socrates in the *Phaedrus* tells the story of the cicadas being granted the Muses' favor because of their constant singing, we might consider this to be metaphorical 'singing.' But contemporary American philosopher Charles Hartshorne considers many animals to be literally 'music-making,' among these not only songbirds but also the gibbon ape and the humpback whale. And Hartshorne does not use the term *music* metaphorically in this context. He argues that some species of songbirds have 'a primitive aesthetic musical sense' that is not only biologically useful but motivated by 'an innate capacity to enjoy the making and hearing of musical songs,' and that 'the song of birds...has (in many cases at least) a definite musically analyzable structure.'[11]

Regarding a definition of music, Nettl concludes, 'If music can be defined, it cannot easily be circumscribed, its boundaries are unclear.'[12] As recordings of the world's range of music become increasingly available to us in the West, this conclusion seems unavoidable. A strict definition of music can be maintained only at the price of excluding many phenomena that one could and might want to call 'music.' [. . .] Nevertheless, we need a working description of our subject matter. I use the word *music* as a category term identifying a broad and open-ended range of intentionally produced auditory phenomena. Although Western classical music occupies an important part of this range, popular music, non-Western music, and even what is often dismissed as 'background music' are also among the phenomena I mean to examine. [. . .]

Music is, first of all, an experience. Celebration calls for music in every culture known to anthropology. People make music to mark the most important events and turning points in their lives. Music is a vital part of most marriages, ceremonies of initiation, and commemorations of important events in the lives of individuals and of civic and religious communities. Describing the range of human uses of music, Merriam observes, 'There is probably no other human cultural activity which is so all-pervasive and which reaches into, shapes, and often controls so much of human behavior.' What American birthday party would be complete without an often cacophonous rendition of 'Happy Birthday to You'? And what American shopping mall would forgo the opportunity to immerse its shoppers in musical gestures toward the 'Christmas spirit' as soon as Thanksgiving is past (or even before)? [. . .]

The thought that musical listening is a social phenomenon may seem out of date. In contemporary American society, it is only in the aberrant case that one experiences music in a live, group format. Our primary mode of musical production is recording technology (whether broadcast or personally employed). And through our use of such technology, our culture has become both predominantly passive and individualistic with respect to music. Passivity is encouraged by the fact that, although music is an accompaniment of the typical waking day, much of it is inflicted on us by someone else (a boss, a store manager, or a restaurant owner, for example). And while we choose our own radio stations when we drive, we still rely on stations and disc jockeys to tell us what is worth hearing.

Other features of our everyday experience encourage the impression that music is a matter of individual consumption. The availability of recorded music has made possible the development of a historically novel use of music: individual self-assertion, often in aggressive opposition to others. Such assertions are common in all walks of life. The person who accompanies his or her walking with a boom-box, the driver who blasts his radio station into the surrounding countryside, and the undergraduate who positions stereo speakers in a dormitory window are aggressively foisting their tastes on others. Each is using music for asocial, if not antisocial, ends. And most of us have been irritated at one time or another by the similarly asocial Walkman phenomenon, which enables people to appear in the midst of public bustle with their auditory capacities channeled into an entirely different world. Bloom casts the teenager with the Walkman as an icon of declining Western culture. I think he overstates the point; but the Walkman-wired cyclist I recently saw tying a shoe in front of oncoming traffic surely represents some kind of communicative breakdown.

With such conspicuous uses of music to tune out the immediate social environment, it is no wonder that many Americans besides philosophers do not consider music a particularly communal phenomenon. And yet it is not so many years since Woodstock, which reminded at least one generation that music can create a community, even if a short-lived one. Events like Woodstock, even the well-attended local concert (of whatever musical discourse), make it obvious that a communal dimension of music is still evident to Americans who seek it out.

Furthermore, although our society's appropriation of music disguises its social dimension, this dimension remains inevitably a part of our awareness when we experience music. Music is, by its very nature, a social activity. Even the music heard through the earphones of a Walkman sounds like it comes from external reality. In fact it does come from outside the individual listener. A social relationship between those who produce it and the listener still occurs, albeit a highly mediated one. But in addition, I believe that most listeners experience music, even that which comes to them through earphones, as a kind of communication between themselves and other human beings.

When one identifies with the gait and emotion suggested by music, one senses that one is joining an experience that others share. Even such intimate expressions of the longing individual soul as one hears in Bach's partitas for solo violin admit the listener into a communion of one soul with another. If only in a semiconscious way, one is aware of music as a shared experience—and of its potential to be shared by other listeners as well.

Usually it is not perversity or showing off when, in our society, the owner of records, tapes, or compact discs wants to play them for friends and acquaintances. The typical motivation is to share an experience. And when music is used to encourage a particular mood in guests, the host or hostess is also immersing him- or herself in a musical experience with them. Again, when one hears music that inspires foot-tapping or the desire to dance, one is at least quasi-consciously motivated to put one's entire body into a context of social celebration.

Music is perhaps the most open medium of socially shared experience available in our culture. Contemporary American society has an impoverished range of social rituals, and most are linked to specific group memberships. Even worship services and baseball games typically involve reinforced awareness that one supports one doctrine or team as opposed to others. But although music can be employed to urge solidarity within a faction, it is almost uniquely suited to incite a sense of community among people who have little else in common besides appreciating it. [. . .]

[Alan] Lomax has developed a scheme of categorizing various musics in terms of a small number of basic variables, a method that he terms 'cantometrics.'[13] [. . .] He uses them to construct 'cantometric profiles,' which he correlates with modes of social organization. The parallels, he observes, are striking. For example, he observes that Pygmy singing style, which emphasizes group participation and enjoyment in group production of counterpoint and involves a shift of leadership from one singer to another, reflects the cooperative cultural style of Pygmy social interaction. The idiosyncratic yodeling style of Pygmy singing, which 'in the estimation of laryngologists, is produced by the voice in its most relaxed state,' also reflects cultural conditions: 'This extraordinary degree of vocal relaxation, which occurs rarely in the world as an over-all vocal style, seems to be a psycho-physiological set, which symbolizes openness, nonrepressiveness, and an unconstructed approach to the communication of emotion.'[14] Recognizing these characteristics of Pygmy social interaction and style of living, we are likely to notice that our own society has different characteristics and that ours are not the only human possibilities.

Listening to the music of other cultures also gives us more immediate insight into our own social nature. Because the listener typically identifies with the act of music-making, listening involves an imaginative projection of oneself into the matrix of social interaction that is heard in the music. In this respect, music yields intuitions of what it is like to interact with other human beings in particular configurations that may or may not resemble those of one's usual musical experience.

When I listen to Michael (Babatunde) Olatunji's 'Flirtation Dance,' for example, I project myself into a situation in which a group composed of all members of one sex flirtatiously confronts all members of the other sex. Such group confrontation of the two sexes differs strikingly from any situation that I have practically encountered in my own society, where flirtation is extremely individualistic. In my society, instead, any imagined group confrontation between the sexes is almost always portrayed as a battle. David Byrne's 'Women vs. Men,' which depicts a war with trivial motives but no end in sight, is a musical reflection of this idea.[15]

I think that in both cases, listener self-projection sheds light on social experience. Of course, I probably cannot fully get inside the mindset that conditions Nigerian experience. But consideration of alternative ways of relating to other human beings assists one's understanding of the way one actually does interact with others. What about our society makes the situation to which Olatunji's music belongs so unimaginable for us? Could the 'Women vs. Men' mindset be modified by considering the whole conjunction of social male–female attractions as jubilant and something worth celebrating with dance? Precisely because Olatunji's music suggests situations foreign to my own experience, I find my imagination stirred to seek answers to such questions as 'Who are the people making this music?' and 'Who am I?'

More fundamentally, the open-ended sociability of music puts us in touch with what is common to human beings across societies. The capacity to feel and to respond to musical stimuli is not limited to a particular group of people. By reminding us of our common human makeup, music serves a universal human function. Music locates us first within the human community, and only second and in some cases within our particular society.

Music—both our own and that of other societies—clarifies our place in the world by allowing us to explore different human ways of encountering it. The musics of different societies focus on different features of that place and underscore different ways of understanding it. One society may focus, in its construction and appropriation of music, on human beings' relationship to the supernatural, as Nettl suggests. In another society, one may engage with music as an individual with a certain social role to fulfill. Our classical tradition, by encouraging 'disinterested' listening, may obscure this function of music. But it, too, gives us a sense of who we are in the world—most commonly a sense of ourselves as capable of empathy with the range of human emotional experience, unimpeded by personal motive.

Understanding one's place within the world—and particularly within the social world—is important to ethical living. Ethics concerns thought-mediated behavior, and a large extent of the mediation that thought provides is shaped by one's sense of self in relation to others. Music's contribution to this sense makes it ethically important. This role of music also helps make the ideal of harmonious living with others seem both coherent and delightful.

[*The Music of Our Lives* (Philadelphia: Temple University Press, 1991), 10, 12–16, 138–9, 150–1, 172–4.]

Toward the end of President Reagan's tenure, the *Miami News* published a remarkable cartoon by Don Wright, which showed silhouettes of Ronald and Nancy Reagan in grass skirts dancing around what appears to be a sacrificial shrine (Fig. 1). Ronald holds a goat over his head, Nancy a chicken in each hand. Ronald says, 'What's the astrologer say to do next, Nancy?' Answer: 'Sacrifice the goat, singe the chickens and pound the lizard to powder!'

The cartoon's images of the Reagans echo, quite deliberately, the popular imagery of the witch doctor. Herbert Ward's 1890 Victorian travel book *Five Years with Congo Cannibals* contains a strikingly similar illustration, though drawn without the same satirical intent (Fig. 2). It portrays a so-called witch doctor, similarly clothed in sketchy costume, dancing around a fire and holding over his head a fetish figure.

I do not suggest the cartoonist was copying Ward, but both draw upon a stock of deeply held and patently enduring cultural imagery about the 'other'—the generalized conception of people on the losing side of the colonial and imperial encounter. Both the figures of the Reagans and the Ward witch doctor, for example, are depicted in classic ballet positions, a similarity that helps exemplify the paradox of representing the other: Difference can only be communicated in terms that are familiar.

Two strategies are used when representing other cultures or their works of art. Exoticizing showcases the differences between the cultural group being displayed and the cultural group doing the viewing, while assimilating highlights the similarities. Whether we are describing a text or an exhibition, otherness is either made strange by exoticizing or made familiar by assimilating.[1]

In exoticizing, the differences of the other are portrayed as an absence of qualities the dominant, often colonizing, cultural groups possess. In the cartoon and engraving, three features of civilized man are missing in the witch doctor character: rationality, symbolic (as opposed to true) animal sacrifice, and an orderly bourgeois sense of propriety. Imagine what little effect the *Miami News* cartoon would have had if the Reagans were dressed in vestments and placed primly behind a lectern with a holy book, 'sacrificing' only bread and wine.

Both the editorial cartoon and the engraving represent so-called savages as controlled by emotions and unable to calculate rationally. Myth making here is not isolated from real life; it is part of the process whereby our beliefs about other people are shaped. Radio and television news, for example, report that black South Africans belong to tribes when they are in conflict with each other and to political parties when they dispute with the white regime.

FIG. 1. Don Wright's cartoon published in the *Miami News*, 1988

FIG. 2. *Antics of the Charm Dancer*, S. Northcote
(published 1890)

Likewise, journalists refer to the leaders of Columbia's Medellin cartel of cocaine dealers as part of a clan of closely knit persons who act in concert. If the other is different from us, one feature of that difference is his identification with social groups that claim his loyalties in ways that impede rational calculation.

Conversely, otherness can also be positively valued. Recent writings about American Indians or definitions of Afrocentricity often romanticize minority and Third World cultures as possessing a less aggressive attitude toward nature and a more group-oriented attitude toward social life. Yet these assertions still embody a depressingly familiar set of beliefs: The other lacks the rationality of modern man, or the other's thought process is circular rather than linear. These images of the other are turned not so much on their head as on their side. Assigning positive values to the other may be novel, but the racial and ethnic stereotypes used to arrive at these conclusions are shockingly familiar.

The image of the other is derived not only from assertions about cultural differences. The use of a ballet pose to portray the Reagans and the African witch doctor was probably not consciously intended; neither was it accidental. Negative images need positive associations to make them work. If familiar devices were not used, the consumers of the image would have nothing onto which to graft cultural, racial, or ethnic differences. The politics of producing the image of the other requires a poetics of difference *and* similarity. The familiar becomes the bridge through which we understand the exotic. [. . .]

Exoticizing often works by inverting the familiar—showing how a well-known practice takes an inverted form among other peoples. The common belief that Africans practice animism is an example. The anthropomorphic tendency of most Western religious belief is inverted, thus creating the notion that there is a class of people who worship beings created not in their own image, but in the image of nature. That such beliefs have never been documented in a non-Western religion has not stopped legions of writers from describing Africans as animists.

Assimilating strategies are less easy to read. They appeal to the audience's sense of the familiar and natural. They don't stop exhibit goers in their tracks with such thoughts as 'What in the world is that?' Assimilating is inherently a more subtle exhibiting strategy than exoticizing. In the so-called primitive or tribal exhibits in fine art museums, art objects are usually isolated from any sort of context. Encased in a vitrine, they are provided with a label that reveals more about the collectors who donated them than about their maker, their iconography, or their history.[2] The governing assumptions behind these displays are that primitive objects mysteriously embody the same aesthetics as modern art forms and that curators and museum audiences are able to appreciate such objects because they are the heirs to a familiar aesthetic tradition whose history encompasses the primitives who make primitive art.

What they truly inherit is a capitalist world system that has acquired things from other peoples and transformed them into objects of modern art.

The controversial 1984 MOMA exhibition ' "Primitivism" in 20th Century Art' provides us with a classic example of the assimilating strategy.[3] Objects were brought together either because they were known to provide models for modern artists or because they were known to exhibit perceived affinities. For William Rubin, the curator of the exhibition, affinities exist because artists working independently on similar formal problems arrive at similar solutions. This is a pure structuralist interpretation. Considerations of content, such as iconography, or questions about intention and purpose, such as the religious role of an object, or even the examination of the contexts of production and use are omitted as possible factors that influence the final form of the object. History is omitted from consideration. Objects are defined as the products of individuals who accidentally derive their work from a limited stock of available forms. The result is assimilating because cultural and historical differences are obliterated from the exhibiting record. Rubin's exhibit turns the African, American Indian, and Pacific makers of the objects displayed in his exhibition into modern artists who lack only the individual identity and history of modern art.[4] Given the curator's insistence that context is absolutely irrelevant to the exhibition of affinities between the primitive and the modern, the only place in history allowed for the artists of other cultures and their works is as a footnote to the development of art in the West. [. . .]

The Pompidou Center's answer to MOMA's 'Primitivism' exhibition, the 1989 'Magiciens de la Terre' consisted of two entire halls of artworks derived from vastly different cultural traditions, yet the master narrative for the whole exhibition asserted a fundamental underlying similarity in spirit and intent among the producers of such disparate works of art.[5] In this sense, the curators of 'Magiciens de la Terre' did no better than the curator of 'Primitivism.' By juxtaposing a work by Richard Long with a sand drawing by Australian aboriginal artists, the curators conflated Long's attempt to return to the elemental with the Australian re-creation of an alternative universe— the 'dream time' in which the cultural world was wrested from nature. Given the audience's lack of familiarity with Australian cosmology and art, the act of conflation becomes an act of assimilation: the Australian artists become echoes of Long. As Yogi Berra once said, 'It's déjà vu all over again.' There is, in effect, no substantial difference between the 'Magiciens' exhibition's juxtaposition of Long's work with the Australian aborigines' sand drawing and the 'Primitivism' show's juxtaposition of Kenneth Noland's Circle painting with a New Guinea shield exhibiting concentric motifs.[6]

Nevertheless, the curators of 'Magiciens' could be seen as more egalitarian than the curator of 'Primitivism.' They deny that Third World artists and contemporary artists differ in self-consciousness. All, in their view, are equally conscious about the sources and meanings of the art they create; perhaps it would be fairer to say that all are equally naive about the magical and elemental sources of their art. The cost of this egalitarian strategy of assimilation, however, is the elimination of cultural context, motives, and resources from the record. [. . .]

No genre of museum has been able to escape the problems of exoticizing and assimilating inherent in exhibiting other cultures. That includes museums that restrict themselves to examining diversity within their own societies. The same museums that make the products of others into a minor digression in the history of modern art also treat the art and artists of their own traditions the same way. What happens to an artist who moves outside of the Paris–New York orbit? How do so-called 'regional' traditions get created in the stories curators tell in exhibitions? Cultural centers and peripheries are determined by museums, not by nature. The only hope is to develop more reflective exhibitions that question their own assumptions. This would have its parallel in the new research in anthropology and history, in what is coming to be called the 'History of the Other' or the 'Anthropology of the Imaginary,' which is less about the examination of people's everyday lives than an examination of how images and ideas about imaginary and unknown worlds come to appear real and even effect what is real. This new field demonstrates how the image of the other is formed partly from images of class, ethnicity, and gender in Western cultures, partly from negation and inversion of Western self-images, and partly from images transmitted by explorers, colonials, and other occupants of cultural and imperial frontiers.[7]

The solution will not be to invent new tropes of representation or new exhibiting devices for museum displays. Every venture into the unknown is based on an analogy with the known. Exoticizing and assimilating are all we have to reach out to the unknown. At best, they enable us to approximate other experiences and to appreciate new forms of art; at worst, they prevent us from truly learning about other cultures and their works of art. The error is not in using these strategies, but in failing to reflect on our own work when making analogies with the other and in treating our works as if they were naturally occurring—as if they did not also carry the unacknowledged baggage of other associations.[8]

['How Museums Define Other Cultures', *American Art*, 5 (1991), 10–15.]

Section III

What Do Artists Do?

INTRODUCTION

'I make paintings as a poet composes poems, simply to recite my feelings and to express my nature.' These words might be those of many Western artists of the nineteenth or twentieth centuries. They are in fact the words of Li Kung-li, an eleventh century Chinese scholar-official of the Sung Dynasty (trans. Susan Bush). Such ideas have emerged in different cultures at different ages. Indeed, while the idea and the institutions of 'the fine arts' in the West may have been fashioned from the point of view of the spectator, the idea came increasingly to represent the point of view of the artist. Thus a common understanding of the word 'art' would be of artists' self-expression of feeling and 'creativity'.

For example, early in the nineteenth century, J. S. Mill, by use of emotional self-expression, sharply distinguishes not only poetry but 'the poetic' in all the arts from the eighteenth century's skills of narrative representation, which were aimed at audience effect. Poetry, for Mill, is what he calls a kind of 'soliloquy'. By the end of the nineteenth century Leo Tolstoy's arguments against aesthetic conceptions of art as expressions of the tastes of the dominant classes show how for him the question 'what is art?' matters only when it means, 'why is art important?' For Tolstoy, however, emotional self-expression, though necessary for art, is not enough. By means of two analogies (nutrition and verbal communication), Tolstoy argues that art is a basic human need: essential, indeed, for the solidarity of any society, through communal sharing of feelings, rather than a matter of habituated desires for aesthetic pleasures. By his emphasis on community, Tolstoy indicates a large, important realm of expression in art beyond that of an individual's emotions.

Clive Bell ventures the hypothesis that shapes, lines, and colour in works of art are aesthetically moving because they express the feelings of the artist. Artists, he suggests, feel aesthetic emotion in response to significant form in natural objects, whereas non-artists can feel that emotion only in relation to art. A distinctive aspect of his view is that these psychological hypotheses about why we respond to significant form have nothing to do with the value of either—the arts or aesthetic experience—while others have held self-expression and communal sharing of feelings to be fundamental to the value of the arts.

Against self-expression theories sceptical aesthetic-based arguments have often been raised. John Hospers voices the widely shared misgiving that ideas about the artists' self-expression draw attention away from the characteristics that artworks actually present to us—characteristics that are usually 'aesthetic' or immediately perceptual. According to Hospers, the very idea of self-expression in art should be replaced by the idea of 'expressiveness'—an artistically important characteristic of works of art, but one that would most usefully be explained without reference to artists' or audiences' feelings. 'How can a work of art before us be "itself" so full of feeling and yet that feeling be an internal state of the artist?', sceptics like Hospers ask. On the other hand, how the depth and range of feeling apparent in all the arts can be explained in terms of perceptual characteristics of what Hospers calls 'the work itself' poses a riddle that has perplexed many—notably those who write in appreciation of music. As an issue about interpreting art, this contested topic will be taken up again by several authors in Section IV.

It is usual to identify the romanticism of early nineteenth-century Europe with the development of the idea of the arts as the self-expression of feeling. But even 'romanticism' stands for a more inclusive set of issues concerning liberty and self-identity, for communities, as well as for individuals: this is the focus of Section III. b. Such freedoms include social and political freedom, as well as the mind's freedom from nature's determinations—of which feelings, individual or communal, are important but far from isolated aspects. As this idea of art became increasingly connected with the idea of 'creativity', art became the exemplar of many sorts of liberty. Indeed the very words 'artist' and 'art' have come to be their emblem.

This does not mean that such ideas were entirely peculiar to European romanticism. To begin with, previous ages of the West had well prepared the way for developments there. In an introduction to Denis Diderot's ideas, Meyer Schapiro explains how the idea of art's expressive freedom was present from the eighteenth century, when those skills requiring more of what was commonly called 'genius' were specially marked out. Even then the general sentiment was far from new. In the fourteenth century Boccaccio had quoted Cicero's comment: 'while other arts are matters of science and formula and technique, poetry depends solely upon an inborn faculty, is evoked by a purely mental activity, and is infused with a strange supernatural inspiration.' Modern Western aesthetics is distinguished by systematic attempts to account for artistic genius through new theories of mind, often focused on 'imagination'. The most influential of these theories is due to Immanuel Kant.

Kant approaches the established themes of craft and fine art, aesthetic matters, the mental 'faculties', and freedom, and, in reconsidering them, interrelates them in depth. Kant works progressively through degrees of mental freedom, beginning from the idea of art or craft, through the free playfulness of humour, to the fine arts which, alone, he calls the arts of 'genius'. Fine art is the product of the mental faculty of genius, or spirit, which is the power to produce what Kant calls imaginative 'aesthetic ideas'. These are unparaphrasable sensuous syntheses of ideas that are free, not only from formative rules, but of subsequent explanation: also free from imitation. Kant's account of these 'ideas' resonates through artistic movements of later eras, and sets out important issues about meaning, metaphorical thought, and symbolic content. For example, Coleridge argued for creative imagination against the eighteenth-century idea of wit and fancy; Baudelaire is representative of a wide symbolist movement in the arts, whose influence stretches through artistic practice, teaching, and theory to the present time.

Not long after Kant, Hegel develops the theme of freedom in two historically important ways. First, he opposes the aesthetic approach to art, which closely relates art to natural beauty. Second, the 'need' for any art or craft, Hegel argues, is the need for active self-consciousness, asserting ourselves against our subjection to nature. Furthermore, as Hegel attempts to illustrate by reference to Dutch painting, a people realizes its spirit, its identity, through its artistic expression, as well as through its languages, customs, politics, religious life—its sense of its own history.

Although sharp distinctions between skill, talent, and genius are often associated with romanticism, an account of traditional conceptions of the Gola people of Liberia and extracts from classic Chinese sources combine with excepts in Sections I and II to show that these general conceptions apply, not only to different epochs, but to many kinds of societies. Warren d'Azevedo portrays the conceptions of artistry among the Gola. By describing in detail their traditional belief-system and vocabulary, their occupational roles, and their attitudes toward artistic products, d'Azevedo provides a case study of how broadly the roots of conceptions of art and artistry run through particular cultures. On the theme of liberty, d'Azevedo's comments about the relative social freedom of Gola artists, against the demands of their intimate guiding spirits, should be recognizable in other traditions.

The Chinese readings introduce the concept of 'spirit resonance', which is central to Taoist philosophy. In sixth-century China, Hsieh Ho provided the foundation for theories of painting with a famous set of 'six rules', which, far from being formulas that could be followed mechanically, require special insight. These canons have themselves a history of interpretation. Notably, Su Shih, leader of a group of eleventh-century scholar painters, proposes the first rule, of 'spirit resonance', as the most important. Poetry is not a vehicle for the expression of personal, idiosyncratic feelings, but a means to express this spirit of the subject, such as bamboo or a mountain. To do this the poet or painter needs to adopt or become the spirit of the bamboo, or the mountain, so that it becomes part of oneself. Wang Ch'in ch'en urged that what is common to poetry and painting is the Tao, not a set of rules but a spirit, a way of approaching life. A poem by Su Shih succinctly captures the idea that different painters are better with respect to one or another of the six rules for painting, though it takes a genius to follow them all.

Views about artistic creation in China have also connected it with social and political freedom. During the Yuan Dynasty, China was ruled by a foreign people, the Mongols. Professional painters, following traditional styles requiring much training and skill, were employed by the court. In defiance of the court and its profession a group of amateur painters developed the theory of *wen ren* painting that promotes an intentionally 'naïve' or 'primitive' style. Painting *style* thus becomes a mode of political resistance. The amateur painters also believed, some what like Tolstoy, that the best painting comes from the noblest minds. Since these amateur painters held that moral and political judgements about the painter are relevant to judgements about the quality of the painting, they have a theoretical basis for condemning the work of those with those political views they disagree, in this case, those who capitulate to foreign rule.

The continuing debate between conceptions of the arts as groupings of traditional, principled, teachable, productive skills, and as powers that surpass rules, is carried forward by selections from Edgar Allan Poe and Robin Collingwood. Poe describes the process of writing his well-known and widely enjoyed poem, 'The Raven', as a matter of figuring out what means suffice to produce the kinds of effects he desired to evoke in his readers. The process that Poe describes is what Collingwood would call a craft, whereas creating art, for him, is a process of clarifying and coming to know one's feelings: an exploration of one's own mind. Collingwood continues the Western tradition of developing a theory of art through theories of mind and imagination.

III.a. Expression

CLIVE BELL

21 The Metaphysical Hypothesis

I want now to consider that metaphysical question—'Why do certain arrangements and combinations of form move us so strangely?' [. . .]

It seems to me possible, though by no means certain, that created form moves us so profoundly because it expresses the emotion of its creator. Perhaps the lines and colours of a work of art convey to us something that the artist felt. If this be so, it will explain that curious but undeniable fact, to which I have already referred, that what I call material beauty (e.g. the wing of a butterfly) does not move most of us in at all the same way as a work of art moves us. It is beautiful form, but it is not significant form. It moves us, but it does not move us aesthetically. It is tempting to explain the difference between 'significant form' and 'beauty'—that is to say, the difference between form that provokes our aesthetic emotions and form that does not—by saying that significant form conveys to us an emotion felt by its creator and that beauty conveys nothing.

For what, then, does the artist feel the emotion that he is supposed to express? Sometimes it certainly comes to him through material beauty. The contemplation of natural objects is often the immediate cause of the artist's emotion. Are we to suppose, then, that the artist feels, or sometimes feels, for material beauty what we feel for a work of art? Can it be that sometimes for the artist material beauty is somehow significant—that is, capable of provoking aesthetic emotion? And if the form that provokes aesthetic emotion be form that expresses something, can it be that material beauty is to him expressive? Does he feel something behind it as we imagine that we feel something behind the forms of a work of art? Are we to suppose that the emotion which the artist expresses is an aesthetic emotion felt for something the significance of which commonly escapes our coarser sensibilities? All these are questions about which I had sooner speculate than dogmatise.

Let us hear what the artists have got to say for themselves. We readily believe them when they tell us that, in fact, they do not create works of art in order to provoke our aesthetic emotions, but because only thus can they materialise a particular kind of feeling. What, precisely, this feeling is they find it hard to say. One account of the matter, given me by a very good artist, is that what he tries to express in a picture is 'a passionate apprehension of form.' [. . .]

Occasionally when an artist—a real artist—looks at objects (the contents of a room, for instance) he perceives them as pure forms in certain relations to each other, and feels emotion for them as such. These are his moments of inspiration: follows the desire to express what has been felt. The emotion that the artist felt in his moment of inspiration he did not feel for objects seen as means, but for objects seen as pure forms—that is, as ends in themselves. [. . .]

Now to see objects as pure forms is to see them as ends in themselves. For though, of course, forms are related to each other as parts of a whole, they are related on terms of equality; they are not a means to anything except emotion. But for objects seen as ends in themselves, do we not feel a profounder and a more thrilling emotion than ever we felt for them as means? All of us, I imagine, do, from time to time, get a vision of material objects as pure forms. We see things as ends in themselves, that is to say; and at such moments it seems possible, and even probable, that we see them with the eye of an artist. Who has not, once at least in his life, had a sudden vision of landscape as pure form? For once, instead of seeing it as fields and cottages, he has felt it as lines and colours. In that moment has he not won from material beauty a thrill indistinguishable from that which art gives? And, if this be so, is it not clear that he has won from material beauty the thrill that, generally, art alone can give, because he has contrived to see it as a pure formal combination of lines and colours? May we go on to say that, having seen it as pure form, having freed it from all casual and adventitious interest, from all that it may have acquired from its commerce with human beings, from all its significance as a means, he has felt its significance as an end in itself?

What is the significance of anything as an end in itself? What is that which is left when we have stripped a thing of all its associations, of all its significance as a means? What is left to provoke our emotion? What but that which philosophers used to call 'the thing in itself' and now call 'ultimate reality'? Shall I be altogether fantastic in suggesting, what some of the profoundest thinkers have believed, that the significance of the thing in itself is the significance of Reality? Is it possible that the answer to my question, 'Why are we so profoundly moved by certain combinations of lines and colours?' should be, 'Because artists can express in combinations of lines and colours an emotion felt for reality which reveals itself through line and colour'?

If this suggestion were accepted it would follow that 'significant form' was form behind which we catch a sense of ultimate reality. There would be good reason for supposing that the emotions which artists feel in their moments of inspiration, that others feel in the rare moments when they see objects artistically, and that many of us feel when we contemplate works of art, are the same in kind. All would be emotions felt for reality revealing itself through pure form.

[*Art* (London and New York: Chatto & Windus/G. P. Putnam's Sons, 1958), 43–6. First published in 1914.]

22 | What is Poetry?

That, [...] the word 'poetry' *does* import something quite peculiar in its nature, something which may exist in what is called prose as well as in verse, something which does not even require the instrument of words, but can speak through those other audible symbols called musical sounds, and even through the visible ones, which are the language of sculpture, painting, and architecture; all this, as we believe, is and must be felt, though perhaps indistinctly, by all upon whom poetry in any of its shapes produces any impression beyond that of tickling the ear. To the mind, poetry is either nothing, or it is the better part of all art whatever, and of real life too; and the distinction between poetry and what is not poetry, whether explained or not, is felt to be fundamental.

Where everyone feels a difference, a difference there must be. All other appearances may be fallacious, but the appearance of a difference is itself a real difference. Appearances too, like other things, must have a cause, and that which can *cause* anything, even an illusion, must be a reality. And hence, while a half-philosophy disdains the classifications and distinctions indicated by popular language, philosophy carried to its highest point may frame new ones, but never sets aside the old, content with correcting and regularizing them. It cuts fresh channels for thought, but it does not fill up such as it finds ready made, but traces, on the contrary, more deeply, broadly, and distinctly, those into which the current has spontaneously flowed.

Let us then attempt, in the way of modest inquiry, not to coerce and confine nature within the bounds of an arbitrary definition, but rather to find the boundaries which she herself has set, and erect a barrier round them; not calling mankind to account for having misapplied the word 'poetry,' but attempting to clear up to them the conception which they already attach to it, and to bring before their minds as a distinct *principle* that which, as a vague *feeling*, has really guided them in their actual employment of the term.

The object of poetry is confessedly to act upon the emotions; and therein is poetry sufficiently distinguished from what Wordsworth affirms to be its logical opposite, namely, not prose, but matter of fact or science. The one addresses itself to the belief, the other to the feelings. The one does its work by convincing or persuading, the other by moving. The one acts by presenting a proposition to the understanding, the other by offering interesting objects of contemplation to the sensibilities.

This, however, leaves us very far from a definition of poetry. We have distinguished it from one thing, but we are bound to distinguish it from everything. To present thoughts or images to the mind for the purpose of acting upon the emotions, does not belong to poetry alone. It is equally the province (for example) of the novelist: and yet the faculty of the poet and the faculty of the novelist are as distinct as any other two faculties; as the faculty of the novelist and of the orator, or of the poet and the metaphysician. The two characters may be united, as characters the most disparate may; but they have no natural connection.

Many of the finest poems are in the form of novels, and in almost all good novels there is true poetry. But there is a radical distinction between the interest felt in a novel as such, and the interest excited by poetry; for the one is derived from *incident*, the other from the representation of *feeling*. In one, the source of the emotion excited is the exhibition of a state or states of human sensibility; in the other, of a series of states of mere outward circumstances. Now, all minds are capable of being affected more or less by representations of the latter kind, and all, or almost all, by those of the former; yet the two sources of interest correspond to two distinct and (as respects their greatest development) mutually exclusive characters of mind. So much is the nature of poetry dissimilar to the nature of fictitious narrative, that to have a really strong passion for either of the two, seems to presuppose or to superinduce a comparative indifference to the other.

[. . .] The sort of persons whom not merely in books but in their lives, we find perpetually engaged in hunting for excitement from without, are invariably those who do not possess, either in the vigor of their intellectual powers or in the depth of their sensibilities, that which would enable them to find ample excitement nearer at home. The same persons whose time is divided between sight-seeing, gossip, and fashionable dissipation, take a natural delight in fictitious narrative; the excitement it affords is of the kind which comes from without. Such persons are rarely lovers of poetry, though they may fancy themselves so, because they relish novels in verse. But poetry, which is the delineation of the deeper and more secret workings of the human heart, is interesting only to those to whom it recalls what they have felt, or whose imagination it stirs up to conceive what they could feel, or what they might have been able to feel, had their outward circumstances been different. [. . .]

All this is no bar to the possibility of combining both elements, poetry and narrative or incident, in the same work, and calling it either a novel or a poem; but so may red and white combine on the same human features, or on the same canvas; and so may oil and vinegar, though opposite natures, blend together in the same composite taste. There is one order of composition which requires the union of poetry and incident, each in its highest kind—the dramatic. Even there the two elements are perfectly distinguishable, and may exist of unequal quality, and in the most various proportion. The incidents of a dramatic poem may be scanty and ineffective, though the delineation of passion and character may be of the highest order; as in Goethe's glorious *Torquato Tasso*; or again, the story as a mere story may be well got up for effect, as is the case with some of the most trashy productions of the Minerva press: it may even be, what those are not, a coherent and probable series of events, though there be scarcely a feeling exhibited which is not exhibited falsely, or in a manner absolutely commonplace. The combination of the two excellencies is what renders Shakespeare so generally acceptable, each sort of readers finding in him what is suitable to their faculties. To the many he is great as a storyteller, to the few as a poet.

In limiting poetry to the delineation of states of feeling, and denying the name where nothing is delineated but outward objects, we may be thought to have done what we promised to avoid—to have not *found*, but *made* a definition, in opposition to the usage of the English language, since it is established by common consent that there is a poetry called *descriptive*. We deny the charge. Description is not poetry because there is descriptive poetry, no more than science is poetry because there is such a thing as a didactic poem; no more, we might almost say, than Greek or Latin is poetry because there are Greek and Latin poems. But an object which admits of being described, or a truth which may fill a place in a scientific treatise, may *also* furnish an occasion for the generation of poetry, which we thereupon choose to call descriptive or didactic. The poetry is not in the object itself, nor in the scientific truth itself, but in the state of mind in which the one and the other may be contemplated. The mere delineation of the dimensions and colors of external objects is not poetry, no more than a geometrical ground plan of St Peter's or Westminster Abbey is painting. Descriptive poetry consists, no doubt, in description, but in description of things as they appear, not as they *are*; and it paints them not in their bare and natural lineaments, but arranged in the colors and seen through the medium of the imagination set in action by the feelings. If a poet is to describe a lion, he will not set about describing him as a naturalist would, nor even as a traveler would, who was intent upon stating the truth, the whole truth, and nothing but the truth. He will describe him by *imagery*, that is, by suggesting the most striking likenesses and contrasts which might occur to a mind contemplating the lion, in the state of awe, wonder, or terror, which the spectacle naturally excites, or is, on the occasion, supposed to excite. Now this is describing the lion professedly, but the state of excitement of the spectator really. The lion may be described falsely or in exaggerated colors, and the poetry be all the better; but if the human emotion be not painted with the most scrupulous truth, the poetry is bad poetry, i.e., is not poetry at all, but a failure. [. . .]

Poetry and eloquence are both alike the expression or uttering forth of feeling. But if we may be excused the seeming affectation of the antithesis, we should say that eloquence is *heard*, poetry is *over*heard. Eloquence supposes an audience; the peculiarity of poetry appears to us to lie in the poet's utter unconsciousness of a listener. Poetry is feeling confessing itself to itself, in moments of solitude, and bodying itself forth in symbols which are the nearest possible representations of the feeling in the exact shape in which it exists in the poet's mind. Eloquence is feeling pouring itself forth to other minds, courting their sympathy, or endeavoring to influence their belief, or move them to passion or to action.

All poetry is of the nature of soliloquy. It may be said that poetry, which is printed on hot-pressed paper, and sold at a bookseller's shop, is a soliloquy in full dress, and upon the stage. But there is nothing absurd in the idea of such a mode of soliloquizing. What we have said to ourselves, we may tell to others afterwards; what we have said or done in solitude, we may voluntarily reproduce when we know that other eyes are upon us. But no trace of consciousness that any eyes are upon us must be visible in the work itself. The actor knows that there is an audience present; but if he act as though he knew it, he acts ill. A poet may write poetry with the intention of publishing it; he may write it even for the express purpose of being paid for it; that it should *be* poetry, being written under any such influences, is far less probable; not, however, impossible; but not otherwise possible than if he can succeed in excluding from his work every vestige of such lookings-forth into the out-ward and everyday world, and can express his feelings exactly as he has felt them in solitude, or as he feels that he should feel them, though they were to remain forever unuttered. But when he turns round and addresses himself to another person; when the act of utterance is not itself the end, but a means to an end,—viz., by the feelings he himself expresses to work upon the feelings, or upon the belief, or the will of another,—when the expression of his emotions, or of his thoughts, tinged by his emotions, is tinged also by that purpose, by that desire of making an impression upon another mind, then it ceases to be poetry, and becomes eloquence.

Poetry, accordingly, is the natural fruit of solitude and meditation; elo-quence, of intercourse with the world. The persons who have most feeling of their own, if intellectual culture have given them a language in which to express it, have the highest faculty of poetry; those who best understand the feelings of others, are the most eloquent. The persons, and the nations, who commonly excel in poetry, are those whose character and tastes render them least dependent for their happiness upon the applause, or sympathy, or concurrence of the world in general. [...]

If the above be, as we believe, the true theory of the distinction commonly admitted between eloquence and poetry; or though it be not *that*, yet if, as we cannot doubt, the distinction above stated be a real *bona fide* distinction, it will be found to hold, not merely in the language of words, but in all other language, and to intersect the whole domain of art.

Take, for example, music: we shall find in that art, so peculiarly the expression of passion, two perfectly distinct styles; one of which may be called the poetry, the other the oratory of music. This difference being seized would put an end to much musical sectarianism. There has been much contention whether the character of Rossini's music—the music, we mean, which is characteristic of that composer—is compatible with the expression of passion. Without doubt, the passion it expresses is not the musing, meditative tenderness, or pathos, or grief of Mozart, the great poet of his art. Yet it is passion, but *garrulous* passion—the passion which pours itself into other ears; and therein the better calculated for *dramatic* effect, having a natural adaptation for dialogue. Mozart also is great in musical oratory; but his most touching compositions are in the opposite style—that of soliloquy. Who can imagine 'Dove sono' *heard*? We imagine it *over* heard. [...]

In the arts which speak to the eye, the same distinctions will be found to hold, not only between poetry and oratory, but between poetry, oratory, narrative, and simple imitation or description.

Pure *description* is exemplified in a *mere* portrait or a *mere* landscape—productions of art, it is true, but of the mechanical rather than of the fine arts, being works of simple imitation, not *creation*. We say, a *mere* portrait, or a *mere* landscape, because it is possible for a portrait or a landscape, without ceasing to be such, to be also a *picture*. A portrait by Lawrence, or one of Turner's views, is not a mere copy from nature: the one combines with the given features that particular expression (among all good and pleasing ones) which those features are most capable of wearing, and which, therefore, in combination with them, is capable of producing the greatest positive beauty. Turner, again, unites the objects of the given landscape with whatever sky, and whatever light and shade, enable those particular objects to impress the imagination most strongly. In both, there is *creative* art—not working after an actual model, but realizing an idea.

Whatever in painting or sculpture expresses human feeling, or *character*, which is only a certain state of feeling grown habitual, may be called, according to circumstances, the poetry or the eloquence of the painter's or the sculptor's art; the poetry, if the feeling declares itself by such signs as escape from us when we are unconscious of being seen; the oratory, if the signs are those we use for the purpose of voluntary communication.

The poetry of painting seems to be carried to its highest perfection in the *Peasant Girl* of Rembrandt, or in any Madonna or Magdalen of Guido; that of sculpture, in almost any of the Greek statues of the gods; not considering these in respect to the mere physical beauty, of which they are such perfect models, nor undertaking either to vindicate or to contest the opinion of philosophers, that even physical beauty is ultimately resolvable into expression; we may safely affirm, that in no other of man's works did so much of soul ever shine through mere inanimate matter.

The narrative style answers to what is called historical painting, which it is the fashion among connoisseurs to treat as the climax of the pictorial art. That it is the most difficult branch of the art, we do not doubt, because, in its perfection, it includes, in a manner, the perfection of all the other branches. As an epic poem, though, in so far as it is epic (i.e., narrative), it is not poetry at all, is yet esteemed the greatest effort of poetic genius, because there is no kind whatever of poetry which may not appropriately find a place in it. But an historical picture, as such, that is, as the representation of an incident, must necessarily, as it seems to us, be poor and ineffective. The narrative powers of painting are extremely limited. Scarcely any picture, scarcely any series even of pictures, which we know of, tells its own story without the aid of an interpreter; you must know the story beforehand; *then*, indeed, you may see great beauty and appropriateness in the painting. But it is the single figures which, to us, are the great charm even of a historical picture. It is in these that the power of the art is really seen: in the attempt to *narrate*, visible and permanent signs are far behind the fugitive audible ones which follow so fast one after another, while the faces and figures in a narrative picture, even though they be Titian's, stand still. [. . .]

There are some productions of art which it seems at first difficult to arrange in any of the classes above illustrated. The direct aim of art as such, is the production of the *beautiful*; and as there are other things beautiful besides states of mind, there is much of art which may seem to have nothing to do with either poetry or eloquence as we have defined them. Take for instance a composition of Claude, or Salvator Rosa. There is here *creation* of new beauty: by the grouping of natural scenery, conformably indeed to the laws of outward nature, but not after any actual model; the result being a beauty more perfect and faultless than is perhaps to be found in any actual landscape. Yet there is a character of poetry even in these, without which they could not be so beautiful. The unity, and wholeness, and aesthetic congruity of the picture still lies in singleness of expression; but it is expression in a different sense from that in which we have hitherto employed the term. The objects in an imaginary landscape cannot be said, like the words of a poem or the notes of a melody, to be the actual utterance of a feeling; but there must be some feeling with which they harmonize, and which they have a tendency to raise up in the spectator's mind. They must inspire a feeling of grandeur, a loveliness, a cheerfulness, a wildness, a melancholy, a terror. The painter must surround his principal objects with such imagery as would spontaneously arise in a highly imaginative mind, when contemplating those objects under the impression of the feelings which they are intended to inspire. This, if it be not poetry, is so nearly allied to it, as scarcely to require being distinguished.

In this sense we may speak of the poetry of architecture. All architecture, to be impressive, must be the expression or symbol of some interesting idea; some thought, which has power over the emotions. The reason why modern architecture is so paltry, is simply that it is not the expression of any idea; it is a mere parroting of the architectural tongue of the Greeks, or of our Teutonic ancestors, without any conception of a meaning.

To confine ourselves, for the present, to religious edifices: these partake of poetry, in proportion as they express, or harmonize with, the feelings of

devotion. But those feelings are different according to the conception entertained of the beings, by whose supposed nature they are called forth. To the
Greek, these beings were incarnations of the greatest conceivable physical
beauty, combined with supernatural power: and the Greek temples express
this, their predominant character being graceful strength; in other words,
solidity, which is power, and lightness which is also power, accomplishing
with small means what seemed to require great; to combine all in one word,
majesty. To the Catholic, again, the Deity was something far less clear and
definite; a being of still more resistless power than the heathen divinities;
greatly to be loved; still more greatly to be feared; and wrapped up in
vagueness, mystery, and incomprehensibility. A certain solemnity, a feeling
of doubting and trembling hope, like that of one lost in a boundless forest
who thinks he knows his way but is not sure, mixes itself in all the genuine
expressions of Catholic devotion. This is eminently the expression of the pure
Gothic cathedral; conspicuous equally in the mingled majesty and gloom of
its vaulted roofs and stately aisles, and in the 'dim religious light' which steals
through its painted windows.

There is no generic distinction between the imagery which is the *expression*
of feeling and the imagery which is felt to *harmonize* with feeling. They are
identical. The imagery in which feeling utters itself forth from within, is also
that in which it delights when presented to it from without. All art, therefore,
in proportion as it produces its effects by an appeal to the emotions partakes
of poetry, unless it partakes of oratory, or of narrative. And the distinction
which these three words indicate, runs through the whole field of the fine
arts.

The above hints have no pretension to the character of a theory. They are
merely thrown out for the consideration of thinkers, in the hope that if they
do not contain the truth, they may do somewhat to suggest it. Nor would they,
crude as they are, have been deemed worthy of publication, in any country but
one in which the philosophy of art is so completely neglected, that whatever
may serve to put any inquiring mind upon this kind of investigation, cannot
well, however imperfect in itself, fail altogether to be of use.

['What is Poetry?', in *Mill's Essays on Literature and Society*, ed. J. B. Schneewind (New York:
Collier Books, 1965), 103–17. First published in the *Monthly Repository*, 7 (1833), 714–24.
Published with additions and alterations as 'Poetry and Its Varieties'.]

LEO TOLSTOY

23 What is Art?

[T]here are (and it could not be otherwise) only two definitions of beauty: the
one objective, mystical, merging this conception into that of the highest

mystical vs. tangible pleasure (More)

perfection, God—a fantastic definition, founded on nothing; the other, on the contrary, a very simple and intelligible subjective one, which considers beauty to be that which pleases (I do not add to the word 'pleases' the words 'without the aim of advantage,' because 'pleases' naturally presupposes the absence of the idea of profit). [. . .]   *All subjective*

There is no objective definition of beauty. The existing definitions (both the metaphysical and the experimental) amount only to one and the same subjective definition, which (strange as it seems to say so) is that art is that which makes beauty manifest, and beauty is that which pleases (without exciting desire). Many aestheticians have felt the insufficiency and instability of such a definition, and, in order to give it a firm basis, have asked themselves why a thing pleases. And they have converted the discussion on beauty into a question concerning taste, as did Hutcheson, Voltaire, Diderot, and others. But all attempts to define what taste is must lead to nothing, as the reader may see both from the history of aesthetics and experimentally. There is and can be no explanation of why one thing pleases one man and displeases another, or vice versa. So that the whole existing science of aesthetics fails to do what we might expect from it, being a mental activity calling itself a science; namely, it does not define the qualities and laws of art or of the beautiful (if that be the content of art), or the nature of taste (if taste decides the question of art and its merit), and then, on the basis of such definitions, acknowledge as art those productions which correspond to these laws and reject those which do not come under them. But this science of aesthetics consists in first acknowledging a certain set of productions to be art (because they please us), and then framing such a theory of art that all those productions which please a certain circle of people should fit into it. There exists an art canon according to which certain productions favored by our circle are acknowledged as being art—Phidias, Sophocles, Homer, Titian, Raphael, Bach, Beethoven, Dante, Shakespeare, Goethe, and others—and the aesthetic laws must be such as to embrace all these productions. In aesthetic literature you will incessantly meet with opinions on the merit and importance of art, founded not on any certain laws by which this or that is held to be good or bad, but merely on the consideration whether this art tallies with the art canon we have drawn up. [. . .]

All the existing aesthetic standards are built on this plan. Instead of giving a definition of true art and then deciding what is and what is not good art by judging whether a work conforms or does not conform to the definition, a certain class of works which for some reason please a certain circle of people is accepted as being art, and a definition of art is then devised to cover all these productions. [. . .] No matter what insanities appear in art, when once they find acceptance among the upper classes of our society a theory is quickly invented to explain and sanction them, just as if there had never been periods in history when certain special circles of people recognized and approved false, deformed, and insensate art which subsequently left no trace and has been utterly forgotten. And to what lengths the insanity and deformity of art may go, especially when, as in our days, it knows that it is considered infallible, may be seen by what is being done in the art of our circle today.

So the theory of art founded on beauty, expounded by aesthetics, and in dim outline professed by the public, is nothing but the setting up as good of that which has pleased and pleases us, i.e., pleases a certain class of people.

In order to define any human activity it is necessary to understand its sense and importance. And in order to do that it is primarily necessary to examine that activity in itself, in its dependence on its causes and in connection with its effects, and not merely in relation to the pleasure we can get from it.

If we say that the aim of any activity is merely our pleasure, and define it solely by that pleasure, our definition will evidently be a false one. But this is precisely what has occurred in the efforts to define art. Now, if we consider the food question it will not occur to anyone to affirm that the importance of food consists in the pleasure we receive when eating it. Everyone understands that the satisfaction of our taste cannot serve as a basis for our definition of the merits of food, and that we have therefore no right to presuppose that the dinners with cayenne pepper, Limburg cheese, alcohol, etc., to which we are accustomed and which please us, form the very best human food.

And in the same way, beauty, or that which pleases us, can in no sense serve as the basis for the definition of art; nor can a series of objects which afford us pleasure serve as the model of what art should be. [. . .]

Just as people who conceive the aim and purpose of food to be pleasure cannot recognize the real meaning of eating, so people who consider the aim of art to be pleasure cannot realize its true meaning and purpose because they attribute to an activity the meaning of which lies in its connection with other phenomena of life, the false and exceptional aim of pleasure. People come to understand that the meaning of eating lies in the nourishment of the body only when they cease to consider that the object of that activity is pleasure. And it is the same with regard to art. People will come to understand the meaning of art only when they cease to consider that the aim of that activity is beauty, i.e., pleasure. The acknowledgment of beauty (i.e., of a certain kind of pleasure received from art) as being the aim of art not only fails to assist us in finding a definition of what art is, but, on the contrary, by transferring the question into a region quite foreign to art (into metaphysical, psychological, physiological, and even historical discussions as to why such a production pleases one person, and such another displeases or pleases someone else), it renders such definition impossible. And since discussions as to why one man likes pears and another prefers meat do not help toward finding a definition of what is essential in nourishment, so the solution of questions of taste in art (to which the discussions on art involuntarily come) not only does not help to make clear in what this particular human activity which we call art really consists, but renders such elucidation quite impossible until we rid ourselves of a conception which justifies every kind of art at the cost of confusing the whole matter.

To the question, what is this art to which is offered up the labor of millions, the very lives of men, and even morality itself? we have extracted replies from the existing aesthetics, which all amount to this: that the aim of art is beauty, that beauty is recognized by the enjoyment it gives, and that artistic enjoyment is a good and important thing because it *is* enjoyment. In a word, enjoyment is good because it is enjoyment. Thus what is considered the definition of art is no definition at all, but only a shuffle to justify existing art. Therefore, however strange it may seem to say so, in spite of the mountains of books written about art no exact definition of art has been constructed., And the reason for this is that the conception of art has been based on the conception of beauty. [...] His argument...

In order correctly to define art, it is necessary, first of all, to cease to consider it as a means to pleasure and to consider it as one of the conditions of human life. Viewing it in this way we cannot fail to observe that art is one of the means of intercourse between man and man.

Every work of art causes the receiver to enter into a certain kind of relationship both with him who produced, or is producing, the art, and with all those who, simultaneously, previously, or subsequently, receive the same artistic impression. Analogy to speech!

Speech, transmitting the thoughts and experiences of men, serves as a means of union among them, and art acts in a similar manner. The peculiarity of this latter means of intercourse, distinguishing it from intercourse by means of words, consists in this, that whereas by words a man transmits his thoughts to another, by means of art he transmits his feelings.

The activity of art is based on the fact that a man, receiving through his sense of hearing or sight another man's expression of feeling, is capable of experiencing the emotion which moved the man who expressed it. To take the simplest example: one man laughs, and another who hears becomes merry; or a man weeps, and another who hears feels sorrow. A man is excited or irritated, and another man seeing him comes to a similar state of mind. By his movements or by the sounds of his voice, a man expresses courage and determination or sadness and calmness, and this state of mind passes on to others. A man suffers, expressing his sufferings by groans and spasms, and this suffering transmits itself to other people; a man expresses his feeling of admiration, devotion, fear, respect, or love to certain objects, persons, or phenomena, and others are infected by the same feelings of admiration, devotion, fear, respect, or love to the same objects, persons, and phenomena.

And it is upon this capacity of man to receive another man's expression of feeling and experience those feelings himself, that the activity of art is based.

If a man infects another or others directly, immediately, by his appearance or by the sounds he gives vent to at the very time he experiences the feeling; if he causes another man to yawn when he himself cannot help yawning, or to laugh or cry when he himself is obliged to laugh or cry, or to suffer when he himself is suffering—that does not amount to art.

Art begins when one person, with the object of joining another or others to himself in one and the same feeling, expresses that feeling by certain external indications. To take the simplest example: a boy, having experienced, let us say, fear on encountering a wolf, relates that encounter; and, in order to evoke in others the feeling he has experienced, describes himself, his condition before the encounter, the surroundings, the wood, his own lightheartedness, and then the wolf's appearance, its movements, the distance between himself and the wolf, etc. All this, if only the boy, when telling the story, again experiences the feelings he had lived through and infects the hearers and compels them to feel what the narrator had experienced, is art. If even the boy had not seen a wolf but had frequently been afraid of one, and if, wishing to evoke in others the fear he had felt, he invented an encounter with a wolf and recounted it so as to make his hearers share the feelings he experienced when he feared the wolf, that also would be art. And just in the same way it is art if a man, having experienced either the fear of suffering or the attraction of enjoyment (whether in reality or in imagination), expresses these feelings on canvas or in marble so that others are infected by them. And it is also art if a man feels or imagines to himself feelings of delight, gladness, sorrow, despair, courage, or despondency and the transition from one to another of these feelings, and expresses these feelings by sounds so that the hearers are infected by them and experience them as they were experienced by the composer.

The feelings with which the artist infects others may be most various—very strong or very weak, very important or very insignificant, very bad or very good: feelings of love for one's own country, self-devotion and submission to fate or to God expressed in a drama, raptures of lovers described in a novel, feelings of voluptuousness expressed in a picture, courage expressed in a triumphal march, merriment evoked by a dance, humor evoked by a funny story, the feeling of quietness transmitted by an evening landscape or by a lullaby, or the feeling of admiration evoked by a beautiful arabesque—it is all art.

If only the spectators or auditors are infected by the feelings which the author has felt, it is art.

To evoke in oneself a feeling one has once experienced, and having evoked it in oneself, then, by means of movements, lines, colors, sounds, or forms expressed in words, so to transmit that feeling that others may experience the same feeling—this is the activity of art.

What happens when the spectators have different feelings? Is that NOT art?

Art is a human activity consisting in this, that one man consciously, by means of certain external signs, hands on to others feelings he has lived through, and that other people are infected by these feelings and also experience them.

Art is not, as the metaphysicians say, the manifestation of some mysterious Idea of beauty or God; it is not, as the aesthetical physiologists say, a game in which man lets off his excess of stored-up energy; it is not the expression of man's emotions by external signs; it is not the production of pleasing objects; and, above all, it is not pleasure; but it is a means of union among men, joining them together in the same feelings, and indispensable for the life and progress toward well-being of individuals and of humanity. *Thesis*

As, thanks to man's capacity to express thoughts by words, every man may know all that has been done for him in the realms of thought by all humanity before his day, and can in the present, thanks to this capacity to understand the thoughts of others, become a sharer in their activity and can himself hand on to his contemporaries and descendants the thoughts he has assimilated from others, as well as those which have arisen within himself; so, thanks to man's capacity to be infected with the feelings of others by means of art, all that is being lived through by his contemporaries is accessible to him, as well as the feelings experienced by men thousands of years ago, and he has also the possibility of transmitting his own feelings to others.

If people lacked this capacity to receive the thoughts conceived by the men who preceded them and to pass on to others their own thoughts, men would be like wild beasts, or like Kaspar Hauser.

And if men lacked this other capacity of being infected by art, people might be almost more savage still, and, above all, more separated from, and more hostile to, one another.

And therefore the activity of art is a most important one, as important as the activity of speech itself and as generally diffused.

We are accustomed to understand art to be only what we hear and see in theaters, concerts, and exhibitions, together with buildings, statues, poems, novels. . . . But all this is but the smallest part of the art by which we communicate with each other in life. All human life is filled with works of art of every kind—from cradlesong, jest, mimicry, the ornamentation of houses, dress, and utensils, up to church services, buildings, monuments, and triumphal processions. It is all artistic activity. So that by art, in the limited sense of the word, we do not mean all human activity transmitting feelings, but only that part which we for some reason select from it and to which we attach special importance.

This special importance has always been given by all men to that part of this activity which transmits feelings flowing from their religious perception, and this small part of art they have specifically called art, attaching to it the full meaning of the word.

[*What Is Art?*, trans. Aylmer Maude (Indianapolis: Bobbs-Merrill Company, Inc., 1960), 42–53. First published in 1898.]

[Handwritten annotations: "this is awesome!"; "thesis"; "Tolstoy's definition of art expands the # and type of objects that other theorist might not have considered art"]

24 Art as Expression

Most philosophers and critics of art have not been formalists, although many of them agree that the emphasis on formalism has been a healthy one, in that it has served the useful purpose of directing our attention toward the work of art itself—that is, on what it presents, rather than what it represents. These critics hold that art has other values to offer us, but that these must emerge through the form and cannot be apprehended without close attention to the form. In this respect they have agreed with the emphasis on form, but have not agreed that the form deserves exclusive emphasis. Specifically, many critics have held that in addition to satisfying formal requirements, a work of art must in some way be expressive, especially of human feeling. This view is chiefly exemplified in the expression theory of art.

'Art is an expression of human feeling' is a stock formula, and most students of art respond to it at once. However, philosophers must ask what it means to say this. Like many terms that can refer both to a process and to the product resulting from that process, the term 'expression' (and the related term 'expressive') can refer both to a process engaged in by the artist and to a feature of the product of that process.

Traditionally, the expression theory of art has been a theory concerning what the artist experiences and undergoes when he creates a work of art. Eugène Véron, Tolstoy, Benedetto Croce, R. G. Collingwood, and a host of other writers have in one way or another promulgated this formula, and the general public still responds to the formula 'art is expression' more favorably than to any other. A typical statement of the view, which is to be found in Collingwood's *The Principles of Art*, describes the artist as being stimulated by an emotional excitement whose nature and source he does not know until he can find some form of expressing it, which involves bringing it before his conscious mind. This process is accompanied by feelings of release and new understanding. The main question is whether this process is relevant to aesthetic theory, or whether it is concerned rather with psychology—the psychology of artistic creation.

Has anything been said about the work of art itself, as opposed to the conditions under which it was created? Even if we are considering not the art product but rather the process of its creation, the question arises, What is the connection between the expression theory's description of the creative process and the creation of works of art? One would have thought that the creation of works of art implies at least that the artist is working with materials *in a medium*—that is, he is exploring new combinations of elements in a given medium. Indeed, this constitutes his creative activity as an artist. Where is the transition from the emotions which animate or inspire the artist, and which in some way he is supposed to 'express,' and the medium in which he is working? Suppose we agree that a certain musical composition is a great one and learn subsequently that the composer felt no emotions whatever while he was composing it (Richard Strauss, for example, said 'I work very coldly, without agitation, without emotion even; one must be completely master of oneself to organize that changing, moving, flowing chessboard, orchestration'). Must we then conclude that the work of art was not as good as we thought it was when we heard it without having this knowledge?

Whether or not the artist has in some sense expressed his own feelings in creating the work of art is, it would seem, irrelevant to the question of what, if anything, the work of art is expressive *of*. 'The music expresses sadness' does not mean the same as 'The composer expressed his own feelings of sadness when he wrote his music.' If the music is sad, it is so regardless of how the composer felt when he wrote it.

But what does it mean to say that the music is sad or expresses sadness? Clearly it is a metaphor, for in the literal sense only sentient beings capable of emotion can be sad. How can music be sad, or have or contain any other feeling quality?

One answer to this question—an extremely simple one, but quite surely mistaken—is that 'The music is sad' means 'The music makes me (or other listeners, or most listeners, or a selected group of listeners) feel sad when they hear it.' But if this is what is meant, we already have a perfectly satisfactory word for it, namely, *evocation*—'The music evokes sadness in me (or in most listeners).' But this is a most unsatisfactory analysis. A person can recognize certain melodies as being sad without feeling sad himself. If hearing the music really made him feel sad, as a person does when he feels sad at the loss of a dear one, he would probably not wish to repeat the experience. In any case, the recognition of the quality of the melody is quite distinct from the emotions a person feels when he hears it. One may hear happy music and be bored by it. What a person feels and what quality he attributes to the music are two different things. The sadness of the music is phenomenally objective (that is, felt as being 'in the music'), whereas a person's sadness when he hears it (if such sadness occurs) is quite distinguishable from the sadness of the music; it is felt as being 'phenomenally subjective,' belonging to him and not to the music, and only evoked by the music. There is no reason why the two phenomena should even accompany each other. To say, then, that the music expresses sadness, or simply that it is sad, is to say something about a felt quality of the music itself, rather than about how it makes listeners feel.

But what is this quality which inheres in, is embodied in, or is in some way contained in or a property of the music? It is difficult to explicate what it means to say that a work of art contains emotional properties. The andante is not sad in the same sense in which it is so many notes long or has certain rising and falling rhythms. If a disagreement arises concerning its expressive quality, how is one to defend one's position?

Perhaps the most satisfactory approach is to analyze the most basic sense of the term 'expression,' namely, that of outer behavior manifesting or reflecting inner states. When people feel sad they exhibit certain types of behavior: they move slowly, they tend to talk in hushed tones, their movements are not jerky and abrupt or their tones strident and piercing. Now music can be said to be sad when it exhibits these same properties: sad music is normally slow, the intervals between the tones are small, the tones are not strident but hushed and soft. In short, the work of art may be said to have a specific feeling property when it has features that human beings have when they feel the same or similar emotion, mood, etc. This is the bridge between musical qualities and human qualities, which explains how music can possess properties that are literally possessed only by sentient beings.

The same considerations apply to the other arts. We can claim that a line in a painting is graceful because it possesses similarities to the contour of the limbs of human and animal bodies when they are said to be graceful. The horizontal line is restful (as opposed to vertical or jagged lines) because the human being in a horizontal position is in a situation of rest and sleep and is in a secure position from which he cannot fall. The horizontal line is not intrinsically restful and secure, but is so for creatures subject to gravitation, for whom the natural position of rest is horizontal. For human beings, at any rate, the connection is a universal one, not subject to individual variation or even to cultural relativity. If a horizontal line had one effect on one individual and an entirely different effect on another, how could the creative artist rely on the effect of his work upon other human beings? Moreover, such claims can be put to a test. If someone were to insist that a fast sprightly waltz was really sad or melancholy, we would refer him to the behavioral features of sad people and show him that when people are in that state they do exhibit the qualities in question (i.e., the qualities of sad music), rather than speed or sprightliness.

Works of art, then, can be expressive of human qualities: one of the most characteristic and pervasive features of art is that percepts (lines, colors, progressions of musical tones) can be and are suffused with affect. Hence, this claim of the expression theory seems quite certainly to be true. The work of art can properly be said to contain or embody feeling qualities. A piece of music is sad; it does not merely evoke sadness. The formalists' objections to seeking emotional effects from works of art is, at least in part, based upon the mistaken belief that the only sense in which a work of art can 'be emotional' is for it to evoke emotions, whereas in fact (in the sense just explained) the feeling quality is a genuine quality of the work of art.

In conclusion, we may note that in presenting and defending its claim, the expression theory has in a sense made itself unnecessary. It is no longer necessary to say that the work of art is expressive of feeling qualities; it is only necessary to say that it *has* them—that it *is* sad or *embodies* sadness as a property.

['Aesthetics, Problems of', in Paul Edwards (ed.), *The Encyclopedia of Philosophy* (New York: Macmillan Publishing Co. and The Free Press, 1967), i. 46–8.]

III. b. Artistic Freedom and Creativity

MEYER SCHAPIRO

25 Diderot on the Artist and Society

Diderot wrote on the artist in response to a situation that seemed to him universal, as if at all times the power of patrons and the constraining nature of society imperiled the artist's liberty. In this general view I believe he was mistaken; yet much that he said about artists of his time is relevant to our own. [...]

The problems treated by Diderot with his engaging directness are those of freedom, considered in its inner and outer circumstances. It was Diderot's great merit that he saw in freedom both an individual and a social aspect and that he recognized the connections between them. The same polar concepts of impulse and control, of the personal and the social, appear often in critical discussion today in more dogmatic forms.

For Diderot, the artist's inner freedom is the impulsive, unaccountable flow of the pencil and brush, of images and ideas; verve, enthusiasm, spontaneity, and naturalness are its outward signs. Without that flow there is no authentic art. Even a disciplined classic style needs a source of artistic ideas, a continuously renewed energy of conception—otherwise this art is a sterile routine.

What conditions are most favorable to the life-giving flow in art? They are not only a matter of temperament; they are also social. If, as the poet Young remarked before Diderot, we are all born originals and die copies, there is in society a power that makes for dullness. The artist, passionate by nature, is hampered and denatured by imposed tasks. The tyranny of patronage, however disguised by gracious manners and rewards, enslaves art. Practical aims, rules, methods, fixed notions of style, are obstacles to enthusiasm.

Besides, the character of society apart from the pressure of individual patrons, may be more or less favorable to spontaneity in art. The painter's integrity will be corrupted by his accommodation to a worldly way of life. On the other hand, a society dominated by economic calculations must discourage art as something superfluous and wasteful. The pin-maker has seemed to an economist more worthy than Raphael. Yet in Diderot's strong plea for the artist's freedom, which is required by the inner laws governing artistic production, is there not some affinity with the Physiocrats' idea of economic *laissez-faire*?

Diderot must have known the complaint of the ancient author, Longinus, living under Roman imperial rule, who like himself praised enthusiasm and imagination as roots of art and denounced in his own time 'that half-heartedness in which the life of all of us with few exceptions is passed.' In his treatise on the sublime in art, Longinus speaks of the constraining effects of political servitude on art—'slavery takes away half of our manhood'—and of the debasement of art in a society pervaded by the love of money, luxury, and pleasure.

In his vigorous attack on the despotism of patronage which sets the artist's task, intervenes in details of his work, and judges its worth, Diderot ignored the achievements of older times when art was subject to such controls. He could hardly have known that in Egypt, Greece, Rome, medieval Europe, Byzantium, Persia, India and China, most art was made to order with a prescribed content and that even forms were sometimes dictated by authority. Even in the Renaissance, as the contracts show, the painter and sculptor carried out the minutely detailed stipulations of a patron. This state of affairs does not seem to have choked inspiration, though artists of that time have left us reports of their uneasiness. Many great works were made to satisfy a command. And nearer to home, societies like the Dutch and the Venetian, dominated by the merchant, were able to produce a high art.

How limited was Diderot's horizon of art may be judged from his example of China as an empire where utility stifled art and enthusiasm. He would have been amazed—and delighted, too, I think—to learn that in the China of the seventeenth and eighteenth centuries, as well as of earlier times, artistic spontaneity was held in honor and that there existed in the Far East under despotic regimes a class of independent literate artists who painted and wrote poetry for themselves and each other, with exacting standards of perfection. A colophon by the painter Wu Li (1632–1718) quotes a Sung artist: 'I write in order to express my heart, I paint in order to comfort my mind. I may wear rough clothes and eat coarse food, but I would not ask support from others.' And the same Wu Li said of the old artists: 'Neither kings nor dukes or nobles could command these painters; they were unattainable by worldly honors.'

The relations between social life and the artist's creativeness are clearly more complex than Diderot suspected. Yet he seems to us right in criticizing patronage and practicality as constraints on art in his own time. He saw correctly that in his culture—which is still ours—such control is in the long run incompatible with high accomplishment.

Why does his view apply to us and not to the past? How could the spontaneity of the old artists survive the restricting conditions of work?

To the old painter, as to any artisan, an assigned task did not appear as an infringement of his freedom. It was rather an opportunity to apply the skills of hand and mind that were his surest ground of self-esteem. To be an artist meant to serve the powerful. Those who commissioned a work—and it generally embodied their ideas—respected the artist's judgement. And as long as he held to the beliefs and practices that maintained the ruling institutions, the artist was unlikely to judge in a critical spirit the tasks to which his art was adapted.

It was in the course of a long process of social development, during which the aristocracy and church lost their authority and the middle class assumed the leading role, that the artist's work became increasingly secular and intimate in the choice of themes and freer and more open to everyday experience in the forms. As the ideas of the old social powers ceased to appear self-evident, they no longer nourished the imagination of artists. Even in the Royal courts, the most original art reflected in certain features the outlook of the middle class. The concept of a freely created art, of artists responsible to themselves alone, like the concept of intellectual freedom, was an outcome of the situation of society as a whole. Then the dependence on a commanding patron seemed degrading and incompatible with the artist's dignity.

Perhaps it is wrong to speak of the old employers of artists as patrons in the modern sense, just as we do not think of industry and government today as patrons of the engineers and other experts whom they hire for definite tasks. The patron in Diderot's time was something more: a wealthy noble or bourgeois who in commanding a work wished to associate himself with the arts as critic or connoisseur. The mid-eighteenth century was a time of struggle between the artists and the high-placed or journalistic dictators of fashion and opinion in art. We sense behind Diderot's polemic against the patron something of that conflict and the need of artists to defend their professional authority.

In the eighteenth century, the leading artists were often middle-class intellectuals who engaged in public discussion of art, asserting their personal views against the ideas of patronizing amateurs, critics, and officials of the schools. They displayed in their writings the independence of thought and the bold polemical style of the most advanced minds in their milieu.

Ever since then, culture in our society has been founded on free choice and individuality, less on institutions. The creation of art has rested on the activity of self-directed men who regard their work as a free expression of their natures. The arts have established a place for themselves as a field of individual imagination open to the most daring and fanciful forms. The state can purchase works of art and provide means for the practice and exhibition of art as a public interest; it is unable, as in the past, to prescribe its content and style without risking a degraded art. The attempts to reverse history by restoring the old servile relationships in art have been part of a program of more general constraints on freedom and have failed to stimulate good art. The story of dictated art in Russia and Nazi Germany has made this clear. Occasional works of value have been created to order for a democratic regime or a patron who respected the artist's conception. They have not affected the general principle: art in modern society requires for its life the artist's spontaneity, as Diderot saw in his own time. The painters he admired most—Chardin, La Tour, Greuze—were men who determined their own subjects outside any institutional frame and pursued a personal ideal, in which we discern, however, typical values of their age. And if La Tour's art was still attached in its theme to a command, it was a theme that suited perfectly the developing ethos of personal liberty: the intimate portrayal of living men and women who seem in these pictures to breathe in every feature the open spirit of the Enlightenment. In painting them, the artist expressed his own dignity as a conversing equal, a frank but affable observer confronting his fellow human beings.

It is a surprise then, after we have read Diderot's brilliant pages on spontaneity, to come upon his demand for a moral content in art. While defending with passion the artist's independence, Diderot wishes him to be a moral and civic agent in his work. He could therefore applaud the stagey tableaux of Greuze, with their cold artifice of sentimental gesture, as high works of art with a noble lesson. Building on an older concept of didactic religious art, he helped to form, with perfect good will, the secular substitute which in our time could become an instrument of despotism and a support of mediocrity.

How has he come to this contradiction?

Diderot was too reactive and passionate a thinker to present his views in systematic form; he wrote down his acute observations as they occurred. Attentive in turn to painters of different temperament and to different sides of art according to his momentary interest, he celebrates at times the impulsive and barbaric in art, at other times the rational and refined. After having preached spontaneity, he lays down a program of style and subject matter that could please a pontiff of academic art. He is able with good conscience to advocate an inner despotism of form as a necessary discipline, though he knows very well that those who constrain themselves are also apt to constrain others.

His contradictions arise perhaps from the fact that he has lived through the turn from rococo to neo-classic forms in the 1760s and '70s and has felt deeply the human situation from which the new art drew its support. It is from the rococo that Diderot learned to appreciate the sketch, the lively stroke, the qualities of verve and enthusiasm in painting. The rococo was an art of feeling and virtuoso brushwork which satisfied a taste sensitive to the grace of the body and the charms of color and texture; while the classicist tendency, aiming at naturalness, simplicity, and the noble, introduced rules, ancient models, and a serious moral content. The canons of ideal art could be seen also as principles of conduct. The personal freedom which is called inspiration or enthusiasm required then self-control, reflection, and order for the work to be more than a pleasing sketch. Genius was a happy conjunction of verve and judgment, a fusion of the inspired and the rational. In the context of rococo art, which was identified with the manners and life of the court though created by artists of the middle class, the revival of antique art appeared as a reaction against a depraved aristocratic taste and possessed a social value. The moralism of Greuze was for Diderot an implicit critique of egoistic indulgence. Beside the looseness of the rococo brush, which once seemed the natural expression of an artist's vitality, the style of Greuze in his scenes of lower-class family life appeared austere in drawing, the carrier of an ethical norm. At this moment Diderot looked for a Spartan principle in art; his writings seem to foretell a Jacobin style like David's.

One should note, too, that in advocating the new moral content and classic form, he was not imposing an art from above. It was an ideal that had originated among the artists themselves and had found a prepared supporter in the passionate moralist who responded intensely to the events of his time. From his other writings and from the books of his philosopher-friends, we know how urgent for them was the promotion of an ethics of altruism, based on the rational social nature of man. Having rejected the authority of religion, he proposed like other generous radical minds a secular morality grounded in universal human nature and necessary for individual well-being.

While praising in Greuze's pictures the moral content, Diderot could also praise Chardin and LaTour, of whose art he speaks as directed only to the beautiful and true. Yet what he admired in Chardin—truth, patient skill, simplicity, and honesty—were also moral qualities. In condemning Boucher, after having long enjoyed his spontaneity and color, he observed with distaste that not only was his art frivolous, untrue, corrupt, lacking integrity and innocence; it was filled with figures incapable of work.

Insisting now on the artist's autonomy and now on a content through which the artist could reach the moral conscience of his public, Diderot anticipates a dilemma of artists today. They wish to be free creators, unconfined by any goal external to art; but they wish to participate in the most advanced consciousness of their society and to influence it by their work. Diderot's own writing was a spontaneous expression of his vitality and a daring critical engagement with the actualities of social life. In both he felt equally free. Whether delighting the reader with his verve and imagination or challenging him by paradoxical ideas, Diderot addresses the whole human being; in appealing to the reader's aesthetic sense, he cannot overlook his moral nature.

Diderot is so intensely concerned with artists not simply because he loves their paintings or sculptures. The artist is for him an example par excellence of the free man. As a producer he works from inner necessity; art is his life and in this work he appears as his own master, creating from impulse but guided by an ideal of truth, and correcting himself for the perfection of the result and not from fear of others. What Diderot says about the artist's freedom can be applied to the freedom of the citizen, which is a condition of the latter's dignity. In his warmth and spontaneity the artist is a model of the natural, productive, self-fulfilling man. Feeling and thought are equally active in him and joined to a truly social nature. Through this freedom and full individuality he serves others, including a future mankind. If the artist must work in solitude, like the poet and thinker, it is for the good of society; his withdrawal is a first step towards that creative independence which has its own laws and self-imposed controls. [. . .]

[As reprinted, 'Diderot on the Artist and Society', *Theory and Philosophy of Art: Style, Artist, and Society: Selected Papers* (New York: George Braziller, Inc., 1994), 201–7.]

IMMANUEL KANT

26 Art and Genius

§ 43 *Art in general*

(1.) *Art* is distinguished from *nature* as making (*facere*) is from acting or operating in general (*agere*), and the product or the result of the former is distinguished from that of the latter as *work (opus)* from operation (*effectus*).

By right it is only production through freedom, i.e. through an act of will that places reason at the basis of its action, that should be termed art. For, although we are pleased to call what bees produce (their regularly constructed cells) a work of art, we only do so on the strength of an analogy with art; that is to say, as soon as we call to mind that no rational deliberation forms the basis of their labour, we say at once that it is a product of their nature (of instinct), and it is only to their Creator that we ascribe it as art.

If, as sometimes happens, in a search through a bog, we light on a piece of hewn wood, we do not say it is a product of nature but of art. Its producing cause had an end in view to which the object owes its form. Apart from such cases, we recognize an art in everything formed in such a way that its actuality must have been preceded by a representation of the thing in its cause (as even in the case of the bees), although the effect could not have been *thought* by the cause. But where anything is called absolutely a work of art, to distinguish it from a natural product, then some work of man is always understood.

(2.) *Art*, as human skill, is distinguished also from *science* (as *ability* from *knowledge*), as a practical from a theoretical faculty, as technic from theory (as the art of surveying from geometry). For this reason, also, what one *can* do the moment one only *knows* what is to be done, hence without anything more than sufficient knowledge of the desired result, is not called art. To art that alone belongs for which the possession of the most complete knowledge does not involve one's having then and there the skill to do it. *Camper* describes very exactly how the best shoe must be made, but he, doubtless, was not able to turn one out himself.[1]

(3.) *Art* is further distinguished from *handicraft*. The first is called *free*, the other may be called *industrial art*. We look on the former as something which could only prove final (be a success) as play, i.e. an occupation which is agreeable on its own account; but on the second as labour, i.e. a business, which on its own account is disagreeable (drudgery), and is only attractive by means of what it results in (e.g. the pay), and which is consequently capable of being a compulsory imposition. Whether in the list of arts and crafts we are to rank watchmakers as artists, and smiths on the contrary as craftsmen, requires a standpoint different from that here adopted—one, that is to say, taking account of the proportion of the talents which the business undertaken in either case must necessarily involve. Whether, also, among the so called seven free arts some may not have been included which should be reckoned as sciences, and many, too, that resemble handicraft, is a matter I will not discuss here. It is not amiss, however, to remind the reader of this: that in all free arts something of a compulsory character is still required, or, as it is called, a *mechanism*, without which the *soul*, which in art must be *free*, and which alone gives life to the work, would be bodyless and evanescent (e.g. in the poetic art there must be correctness and wealth of language, likewise prosody and metre). For not a few leaders of a newer school believe that the best way to promote a free art is to sweep away all restraint, and convert it from labour into mere play.

§ 44   *Fine art*

There is no science of the beautiful, but only a Critique. Nor, again, is there an elegant (*schöne*) science, but only a fine (*schöne*) art. For a science of the beautiful would have to determine scientifically, i.e. by means of proofs, whether a thing was to be considered beautiful or not; and the judgement upon beauty, consequently, would, if belonging to science, fail to be a judgement of taste. As for a beautiful science—a science which, as such, is to be beautiful, is a nonentity. For if, treating it as a science, we were to ask for reasons and proofs, we would be put off with elegant phrases (*bons mots*). What has given rise to the current expression *elegant sciences* is, doubtless, no more than this, that common observation has, quite accurately, noted the fact that for fine art, in the fulness of its perfection, a large store of science is required, as, for example, knowledge of ancient languages, acquaintance with classical authors, history, antiquarian learning, &c. Hence these historical sciences, owing to the fact that they form the necessary preparation and groundwork for fine art, and partly also owing to the fact that they are taken to comprise even the knowledge of the products of fine art (rhetoric and poetry), have by a confusion of words, actually got the name of elegant sciences.

Where art, merely seeking to actualize a possible object to the *cognition* of which it is adequate, does whatever acts are required for that purpose, then it is *mechanical*. But should the feeling of pleasure be what it has immediately in view it is then termed *aesthetic* art. As such it may be either *agreeable* or *fine* art. The description 'agreeable art' applies where the end of the art is that the pleasure should accompany the representations considered as mere *sensations*, the description 'fine art' where it is to accompany them considered as *modes of cognition*.

Agreeable arts are those which have mere enjoyment for their object. Such are all the charms that can gratify a dinner party: entertaining narrative, the art of starting the whole table in unrestrained and sprightly conversation, or with jest and laughter inducing a certain air of gaiety. Here, as the saying goes, there may be much loose talk over the glasses, without a person wishing to be brought to book for all he utters, because it is only given out for the entertainment of the moment, and not as a lasting matter to be made the subject of reflection or repetition. (Of the same sort is also the art of arranging the table for enjoyment, or, at large banquets, the music of the orchestra—a quaint idea intended to act on the mind merely as an agreeable noise fostering a genial spirit, which, without any one paying the smallest attention to the composition, promotes the free flow of conversation between guest and guest.) In addition must be included play of every kind which is attended with no further interest than that of making the time pass by unheeded.

Fine art, on the other hand, is a mode of representation which is intrinsically final, and which, although devoid of an end, has the effect of advancing the culture of the mental powers in the interests of social communication.

The universal communicability of a pleasure involves in its very concept that the pleasure is not one of enjoyment arising out of mere sensation, but must be one of reflection. Hence aesthetic art, as art which is beautiful, is one having for its standard the reflective judgement and not organic sensation. [. . .]

§ 46   *Fine art is the art of genius*

Genius is the talent (natural endowment) which gives the rule to art. Since talent, as an innate productive faculty of the artist, belongs itself to nature, we may put it this way: *Genius* is the innate mental aptitude (*ingenium*) *through which* nature gives the rule to art.

Whatever may be the merits of this definition, and whether it is merely arbitrary, or whether it is adequate or not to the concept usually associated with the word *genius* (a point which the following sections have to clear up), it may still be shown at the outset that, according to this acceptation of the word, fine arts must necessarily be regarded as arts of *genius*.

For every art presupposes rules which are laid down as the foundation which first enables a product, if it is to be called one of art, to be represented as possible. The concept of fine art, however, does not permit of the judgement upon the beauty of its product being derived from any rule that has a *concept* for its determining ground, and that depends, consequently, on a concept of the way in which the product is possible. Consequently fine art cannot of its own self excogitate the rule according to which it is to effectuate its product. But since, for all that, a product can never be called art unless there is a preceding rule, it follows that nature in the individual (and by virtue of the harmony of his faculties) must give the rule to art, i.e. fine art is only possible as a product of genius.

From this it may be seen that genius (1) is a *talent* for producing that for which no definite rule can be given: and not an aptitude in the way of cleverness for what can be learned according to some rule; and that consequently *originality* must be its primary property. (2) Since there may also be original nonsense, its products must at the same time be models, i.e. be *exemplary*; and, consequently, though not themselves derived from imitation, they must serve that purpose for others, i.e. as a standard or rule of estimating. (3) It cannot indicate scientifically how it brings about its product, but rather gives the rule as *nature*. Hence, where an author owes a product to his genius, he does not himself know how the *ideas* for it have entered into his head, nor has he it in his power to invent the like at pleasure, or methodically, and communicate the same to others in such precepts as would put them in a position to produce similar products. (Hence, presumably, our word *Genie* is derived from *genius*, as the peculiar guardian and guiding spirit given to a man at his birth, by the inspiration of which those original ideas were obtained.) (4) Nature prescribes the rule through genius not to science but to art, and this also only in so far as it is to be fine art.

§ 47   *Elucidation and confirmation of the above explanation of genius*

Every one is agreed on the point of the complete opposition between genius and the *spirit of imitation*. Now since learning is nothing but imitation, the greatest ability, or aptness as a pupil (capacity), is still, as such, not equivalent to genius. Even though a man weaves his own thoughts or fancies, instead of merely taking in what others have thought, and even though he go so far as to bring fresh gains to art and science, this does not afford a valid reason for calling such a man of *brains*, and often great brains, a *genius*, in contradistinction to one who goes by the name of *shallow-pate*, because he can never do more than merely learn and follow a lead. For what is accomplished in this way is something that *could* have been learned. Hence it all lies in the natural path of investigation and reflection according to rules, and so is not specifically distinguishable from what may be acquired as the result of industry backed up by imitation. So all that *Newton* has set forth in his immortal work on the Principles of Natural Philosophy may well be learned, however great a mind it took to find it all out, but we cannot learn to write in a true poetic vein, no matter how complete all the precepts of the poetic art may be, or however excellent its models. The reason is that all the steps that Newton had to take from the first elements of geometry to his greatest and most profound discoveries were such as he could make intuitively evident and plain to follow, not only for himself but for every one else. On the other hand no *Homer* or *Wieland* can show how his ideas, so rich at once in fancy and in thought, enter and assemble themselves in his brain, for the good reason that he does not himself know, and so cannot teach others. In matters of science, therefore, the greatest inventor differs only in degree from the most laborious imitator and apprentice, whereas he differs specifically from one endowed by nature for fine art. No disparagement, however, of those great men, to whom the human race is so deeply indebted, is involved in this comparison of them with those who on the score of their talent for fine art are the elect of nature. The talent for science is formed for the continued advances of greater perfection in knowledge, with all its dependent practical advantages, as also for imparting the same to others. Hence scientists can boast a ground of considerable superiority over those who merit the honour of being called geniuses, since genius reaches a point at which art must make a halt, as there is a limit imposed upon it which it cannot transcend. This limit has in all probability been long since attained. In addition, such skill cannot be communicated, but requires to be bestowed directly from the hand of nature upon each individual, and so with him it dies, awaiting the day when nature once again endows another in the same way—one who needs no more than an example to set the talent of which he is conscious at work on similar lines.

Seeing, then, that the natural endowment of art (as fine art) must furnish the rule, what kind of rule must this be? It cannot be one set down in a formula and serving as a precept—for then the judgement upon the beautiful would be determinable according to concepts. Rather must the rule be gathered from the performance, i.e. from the product, which others may use to put their own talent to the test, so as to let it serve as a model, not for *imitation*, but for *following*. The possibility of this is difficult to explain. The artist's ideas arouse like ideas on the part of his pupil, presuming nature to have visited him with a like proportion of the mental powers. For this reason the models of fine art are the only means of handing down this art to posterity. This is something which cannot be done by mere descriptions (especially not in the line of the arts of speech), and in these arts, furthermore, only those models can become classical of which the ancient, dead languages, preserved as learned, are the medium.

Despite the marked difference that distinguishes mechanical art, as an art merely depending upon industry and learning, from fine art, as that of genius, there is still no fine art in which something mechanical, capable of being at once comprehended and followed in obedience to rules, and consequently something *academic* does not constitute the essential condition of the art. For the thought of something as end must be present, or else its product would not be ascribed to an art at all, but would be a mere product of chance. But the effectuation of an end necessitates determinate rules which we cannot venture to dispense with. Now, seeing that originality of talent is one (though not the sole) essential factor that goes to make up the character of genius, shallow minds fancy that the best evidence they can give of their being full-blown geniuses is by emancipating themselves from all academic constraint of rules, in the belief that one cuts a finer figure on the back of an ill-tempered than of a trained horse. Genius can do no more than furnish rich *material* for products of fine art; its elaboration and its *form* require a talent academically trained, so that it may be employed in such a way as to stand the test of judgement. But, for a person to hold forth and pass sentence like a genius in matters that fall to the province of the most patient rational investigation, is ridiculous in the extreme. One is at a loss to know whether to laugh more at the impostor who envelops himself in such a cloud—in which we are given fuller scope to our imagination at the expense of all use of our critical faculty,—or at the simpleminded public which imagines that its inability clearly to cognize and comprehend this masterpiece of penetration is due to its being invaded by new truths *en masse*, in comparison with which, detail, due to carefully weighed exposition and an academic examination of root-principles, seems to it only the work of a tyro.

§ 48 *The relation of genius to taste*

For *estimating* beautiful objects, as such, what is required is *taste*; but for fine art, i.e. the *production* of such objects, one needs *genius*.

If we consider genius as the talent for fine art (which the proper sig-nification of the word imports), and if we would analyse it from this point of view into the faculties which must concur to constitute such a talent, it is imperative at the outset accurately to determine the difference between beauty of nature, which it only requires taste to estimate, and beauty of art, which requires genius for its possibility (a possibility to which regard must also be paid in estimating such an object).

A beauty of nature is a *beautiful thing*; beauty of art is a *beautiful representa-tion* of a thing.

To enable me to estimate a beauty of nature, as such, I do not need to be previously possessed of a concept of what sort of a thing the object is intended to be, i.e. I am not obliged to know its material finality (the end), but, rather, in forming an estimate of it apart from any knowledge of the end, the mere form pleases on its own account. If, however, the object is presented as a product of art, and is as such to be declared beautiful, then, seeing that art always presupposes an end in the cause (and its causality), a concept of what the thing is intended to be must first of all be laid at its basis. And, since the agreement of the manifold in a thing with an inner character belonging to it as its end constitutes the perfection of the thing, it follows that in estimating beauty of art the perfection of the thing must be also taken into account—a matter which in estimating a beauty of nature, as beautiful, is quite irrel-evant.—It is true that in forming an estimate, especially of animate objects of nature, e.g. of a man or a horse, objective finality is also commonly taken into account with a view to judgement upon their beauty; but then the judgement also ceases to be purely aesthetic, i.e. a mere judgement of taste. Nature is no longer estimated as it appears like art, but rather in so far as it actually *is* art, though superhuman art; and the teleological judgement serves as basis and condition of the aesthetic, and one which the latter must regard. In such a case, where one says, for example, 'that is a beautiful woman,' what one in fact thinks is only this, that in her form nature excellently portrays the ends present in the female figure. For one has to extend one's view beyond the mere form to a concept, to enable the object to be thought in such manner by means of an aesthetic judgement logically conditioned.

Where fine art evidences its superiority is in the beautiful descriptions it gives of things that in nature would be ugly or displeasing. The Furies, diseases, devastations of war, and the like, can (as evils) be very beautifully described, nay even represented in pictures. One kind of ugliness alone is incapable of being represented conformably to nature without destroying all aesthetic delight, and consequently artistic beauty, namely, that which excites *disgust*. For, as in this strange sensation, which depends purely on the imagina-tion, the object is represented as insisting, as it were, upon our enjoying it, while we still set our face against it, the artificial representation of the object is no longer distinguishable from the nature of the object itself in our sensation, and so it cannot possibly be regarded as beautiful. The art of sculpture, again, since in its products art is almost confused with nature, has excluded from its creations the direct representation of ugly objects, and, instead, only sanctions, for example, the representation of death (in a beautiful genius), or of the warlike spirit (in Mars), by means of an allegory, or attributes which wear a pleasant guise, and so only indirectly, through an interpretation on the part of reason, and not for the pure aesthetic judgement.

So much for the beautiful representation of an object, which is properly only the form of the presentation of a concept, and the means by which the latter is universally communicated. To give this form, however, to the product of fine art, taste merely is required. By this the artist, having practised and corrected his taste by a variety of examples from nature or art, controls his work and, after many, and often laborious, attempts to satisfy taste, finds the form which commends itself to him. Hence this form is not, as it were, a matter of inspiration, or of a free swing of the mental powers, but rather of a slow and even painful process of improvement, directed to making the form adequate to his thought without prejudice to the freedom in the play of those powers.

Taste is, however, merely a critical, not a productive faculty; and what conforms to it is not, merely on that account, a work of fine art. It may belong to useful and mechanical art, or even to science, as a product following definite rules which are capable of being learned and which must be closely followed. But the pleasing form imparted to the work is only the vehicle of communication and a mode, as it were, of execution, in respect of which one remains to a certain extent free, notwithstanding being otherwise tied down to a definite end. So we demand that table appointments, or even a moral dissertation, and, indeed, a sermon, must bear this form of fine art, yet without its appearing *studied*. But one would not call them on this account works of fine art. A poem, a musical composition, a picture-gallery, and so forth, would, however, be placed under this head; and so in a would-be work of fine art we may frequently recognize genius without taste, and in another taste without genius.

§ 49   *The faculties of the mind which constitute genius*

Of certain products which are expected, partly at least, to stand on the footing of fine art, we say they are *soulless*; and this, although we find nothing to censure in them as far as taste goes. A poem may be very pretty and elegant, but is soulless. A narrative has precision and method, but is soulless. A speech on some festive occasion may be good in substance and ornate withal, but may be soulless. Conversation frequently is not devoid of enter-tainment, but yet soulless. Even of a woman we may well say, she is pretty, affable, and refined, but soulless. Now what do we here mean by 'soul'?

'Soul' (*Geist*) in an aesthetical sense, signifies the animating principle in the mind. But that whereby this principle animates the psychic substance (*Seele*)— the material which it employs for that purpose—is that which sets the mental powers into a swing that is final, i.e. into a play which is self-maintaining and which strengthens those powers for such activity.

Now my proposition is that this principle is nothing else than the faculty of presenting *aesthetic ideas*. But, by an aesthetic idea I mean that representation of the imagination which induces much thought, yet without the possibility of any definite thought whatever, i.e. *concept*, being adequate to it, and which language, consequently, can never get quite on level terms with or render completely intelligible.—It is easily seen, that an aesthetic idea is the counterpart (pendant) of a *rational idea*, which, conversely, is a concept, to which no *intuition* (representation of the imagination) can be adequate.

The imagination (as a productive faculty of cognition) is a powerful agent for creating, as it were, a second nature out of the material supplied to it by actual nature. It affords us entertainment where experience proves too commonplace; and we even use it to remodel experience, always following, no doubt, laws that are based on analogy, but still also following principles which have a higher seat in reason (and which are every whit as natural to us as those followed by the understanding in laying hold of empirical nature). By this means we get a sense of our freedom from the law of association (which attaches to the empirical employment of the imagination), with the result that the material can be borrowed by us from nature in accordance with that law, but be worked up by us into something else—namely, what surpasses nature.

Such representations of the imagination may be termed *ideas*. This is partly because they at least strain after something lying out beyond the confines of experience, and so seek to approximate to a presentation of rational concepts (i.e. intellectual ideas), thus giving to these concepts the semblance of an objective reality. But, on the other hand, there is this most important reason, that no concept can be wholly adequate to them as internal intuitions. The poet essays the task of interpreting to sense the rational ideas of invisible beings, the kingdom of the blessed, hell, eternity, creation, &c. Or, again, as to things of which examples occur in experience, e.g. death, envy, and all vices, as also love, fame, and the like, transgressing the limits of experience he attempts with the aid of an imagination which emulates the display of reason in its attainment of a maximum, to body them forth to sense with a completeness of which nature affords no parallel; and it is in fact precisely in the poetic art that the faculty of aesthetic ideas can show itself to full advantage. This faculty, however, regarded solely on its own account, is properly no more than a talent (of the imagination).

If, now, we attach to a concept a representation of the imagination belonging to its presentation, but inducing solely on its own account such a wealth of thought as would never admit of comprehension in a definite concept, and, as a consequence, giving aesthetically an unbounded expansion to the concept itself, then the imagination here displays a creative activity, and it puts the faculty of intellectual ideas (reason) into motion—a motion, at the instance of a representation, towards an extension of thought, that, while germane, no doubt, to the concept of the object, exceeds what can be laid hold of in that representation or clearly expressed.

Those forms which do not constitute the presentation of a given concept itself, but which, as secondary representations of the imagination, express the derivatives connected with it, and its kinship with other concepts, are called (aesthetic) *attributes* of an object, the concept of which, as an idea of reason, cannot be adequately presented. In this way Jupiter's eagle, with the lightning in its claws, is an attribute of the mighty king of heaven, and the peacock of its stately queen. They do not, like *logical attributes*, represent what lies in our concepts of the sublimity and majesty of creation, but rather something else—something that gives the imagination an incentive to spread its flight over a whole host of kindred representations that provoke more thought than admits of expression in a concept determined by words. They furnish an *aesthetic idea*, which serves the above rational idea as a substitute for logical presentation, but with the proper function, however, of animating the mind by opening out for it a prospect into a field of kindred representations stretching beyond its ken. But it is not alone in the arts of painting or sculpture, where the name of attribute is customarily employed, that fine art acts in this way; poetry and rhetoric also derive the soul that animates their works wholly from the aesthetic attributes of the objects—attributes which go hand in hand with the logical, and give the imagination an impetus to bring more thought into play in the matter, though in an undeveloped manner, than allows of being brought within the embrace of a concept, or, therefore, of being definitely formulated in language.—For the sake of brevity I must confine myself to a few examples only. When the great king expresses himself in one of his poems by saying:

> Oui, finissons sans trouble, et mourons sans regrets,
> En laissant l'Univers comblé de nos bienfaits.
> Ainsi l'Astre du jour, au bout de sa carrière,
> Répand sur l'horizon une douce lumière,
> Et les derniers rayons qu'il darde dans les airs
> Sont les derniers soupirs qu'il donne à l'Univers;[2]

he kindles in this way his rational idea of a cosmopolitan sentiment even at the close of life, with the help of an attribute which the imagination (in remembering all the pleasures of a fair summer's day that is over and gone—a memory of which pleasures is suggested by a serene evening) annexes to that representation, and which stirs up a crowd of sensations and secondary representations for which no expression can be found. On the other hand, even an intellectual concept may serve, conversely, as attribute for a representation of sense, and so animate the latter with the idea of the supersensible; but only by the aesthetic factor subjectively attaching to the consciousness of the supersensible being employed for the purpose. So, for example, a certain poet says in his description of a beautiful morning: 'The sun arose, as out of virtue rises peace.' The consciousness of virtue, even where we put ourselves only in thought in the position of a virtuous man, diffuses in the mind a multitude of sublime and tranquillizing feelings, and gives a boundless outlook into a happy future, such as no expression within the compass of a definite concept completely attains.[3]

In a word, the aesthetic idea is a representation of the imagination, annexed to a given concept, with which, in the free employment of imagination, such a multiplicity of partial representations are bound up, that no expression indicating a definite concept can be found for it—one which on that account allows a concept to be supplemented in thought by much that is indefinable in words, and the feeling of which quickens the cognitive faculties, and with language, as a mere thing of the letter, binds up the spirit (soul) also.

The mental powers whose union in a certain relation constitutes *genius* are imagination and understanding. Now, since the imagination, in its employment on behalf of cognition, is subjected to the constraint of the understanding and the restriction of having to be conformable to the concept belonging thereto, whereas aesthetically it is free to furnish of its own accord, over and above that agreement with the concept, a wealth of undeveloped material for the understanding, to which the latter paid no regard in its concept, but which it can make use of, not so much objectively for cognition, as subjectively for quickening the cognitive faculties, and hence also indirectly for cognitions, it may be seen that genius properly consists in the happy relation, which science cannot teach nor industry learn, enabling one to find out ideas for a given concept, and, besides, to hit upon the *expression* for them—the expression by means of which the subjective mental condition induced by the ideas as the concomitant of a concept may be communicated to others. This latter talent is properly that which is termed soul. For to get an expression for what is indefinable in the mental state accompanying a particular representation and to make it universally communicable—be that expression in language or painting or statuary—is a thing requiring a faculty for laying hold of the rapid and transient play of the imagination, and for unifying it in a concept (which for that very reason is original, and reveals a new rule which could not have been inferred from any preceding principles or examples) that admits of communication without any constraint of rules.

If, after this analysis, we cast a glance back upon the above definition of what is called *genius*, we find: *First*, that it is a talent for art—not one for science, in which clearly known rules must take the lead and determine the procedure. *Secondly*, being a talent in the line of art, it presupposes a definite concept of the product—as its end. Hence it presupposes understanding, but, in addition, a representation, indefinite though it be, of the material, i.e. of the intuition, required for the presentation of that concept, and so a relation of the imagination to the understanding. *Thirdly*, it displays itself, not so much in the working out of the projected end in the presentation of a definite *concept*, as rather in the portrayal, or expression of *aesthetic ideas* containing a wealth of material for effecting that intention. Consequently the imagination is represented by it in its freedom from all guidance of rules, but still as final for the presentation of the given concept. *Fourthly*, and lastly, the unsought and undesigned subjective finality in the free harmonizing of the imagination with the understanding's conformity to law presupposes a proportion and accord between these faculties such as cannot be brought about by any observance of rules, whether of science or mechanical imitation, but can only be produced by the nature of the individual.

Genius, according to these presuppositions, is the exemplary originality of the natural endowments of an individual in the *free* employment of his cognitive faculties. On this showing, the product of a genius (in respect of so much in this product as is attributable to genius, and not to possible learning or academic instruction), is an example, not for imitation (for that would mean the loss of the element of genius, and just the very soul of the work), but to be followed by another genius—one whom it arouses to a sense of his own originality in putting freedom from the constraint of rules so into force in his art, that for art itself a new rule is won—which is what shows a talent to be exemplary. Yet, since the genius is one of nature's elect—a type that must be regarded as but a rare phenomenon—for other clever minds his example gives rise to a school, that is to say a methodical instruction according to rules, collected, so far as the circumstances admit, from such products of genius and their peculiarities. And, to that extent, fine art is for such persons a matter of imitation, for which nature, through the medium of a genius, gave the rule.

But this imitation becomes *aping* when the pupil *copies* everything down to the deformities which the genius only of necessity suffered to remain, because they could hardly be removed without loss of force to the idea. This courage has merit only in the case of a genius. A certain *boldness* of expression, and, in general, many a deviation from the common rule becomes him well, but in no sense is it a thing worthy of imitation. On the contrary it remains all through intrinsically a blemish, which one is bound to try to remove, but for which the genius is, as it were, allowed to plead a privilege, on the ground that a scrupulous carefulness would spoil what is inimitable in the impetuous ardour of his soul. *Mannerism* is another kind of aping—an aping of *peculiarity* (originality) in general, for the sake of removing oneself as far as possible from imitators, while the talent requisite to enable one to be at the same time *exemplary* is absent.—There are, in fact, two modes (*modi*) in general of arranging one's thoughts for utterance. The one is called a *manner* (*modus aestheticus*), the other a *method* (*modus logicus*). The distinction between them is this: the former possesses no standard other than the *feeling* of unity in the presentation, whereas the latter here follows definite *principles*. As a consequence the former is alone admissible for fine art. It is only, however, where the manner of carrying the idea into execution in a product of art is *aimed at* singularity instead of being made appropriate to the idea, that *mannerism* is properly ascribed to such a product. The ostentatious (*précieux*), forced, and affected styles, intended to mark one out from the common herd (though soul is wanting), resemble the behaviour of a man who, as we say, hears himself talk, or who stands and moves about as if he were on a stage to be gaped at—action which invariably betrays a tyro.

§ 50   *The combination of taste and genius in products of fine art*

To ask whether more stress should be laid in matters of fine art upon the presence of genius or upon that of taste, is equivalent to asking whether more turns upon imagination or upon judgement. Now, imagination rather entitles an art to be called an *inspired* (*geistreiche*) than a *fine* art. It is only in respect of judgement that the name of fine art is deserved. Hence it follows that judgement, being the indispensable condition (*conditio sine qua non*), is at least what one must look to as of capital importance in forming an estimate of art as fine art. So far as beauty is concerned, to be fertile and original in ideas is not such an imperative requirement as it is that the imagination in its freedom should be in accordance with the understanding's conformity to law. For in lawless freedom imagination, with all its wealth, produces nothing but nonsense; the power of judgement, on the other hand, is the faculty that makes it consonant with understanding.

Taste, like judgement in general, is the discipline (or corrective) of genius. It severely clips its wings, and makes it orderly or polished; but at the same time it gives it guidance, directing and controlling its flight, so that it may preserve its character of finality. It introduces a clearness and order into the plenitude of thought, and in so doing gives stability to the ideas, and qualifies them at once for permanent and universal approval, for being followed by others, and for a continually progressive culture. And so, where the interests of both these qualities clash in a product, and there has to be a sacrifice of something, then it should rather be on the side of genius; and judgement, which in matters of fine art bases its decision on its own proper principles, will more readily endure an abatement of the freedom and wealth of the imagination, than that the understanding should be compromised.

The requisites for fine art are, therefore, *imagination, understanding, soul*, and *taste*.[4]

[*Critique of Judgement*, trans. James Creed Meredith (Oxford: Clarendon Press, 1952), 162–83. First published in 1790.]

G. W. F. HEGEL

27   Art, Nature, Freedom

What is man's *need* to produce works of art? On the one hand, this production may be regarded as a mere play of chance and fancies which might just as well be left alone as pursued; for it might be held that there are other and even better means of achieving what art aims at and that man has still higher and more important interests than art has the ability to satisfy. On the other hand, however, art seems to proceed from a higher impulse and to satisfy higher needs,—at times the highest and absolute needs since it is bound up with the most universal views of life and the religious interests of whole epochs and peoples.—This question about the non-contingent but absolute need for art, we cannot yet answer completely, because it is more concrete than an answer could turn out to be at this stage. Therefore we must content ourselves in the meantime with making only the following points.

The universal and absolute need from which art (on its formal side) springs has its origin in the fact that man is a *thinking* consciousness, i.e. that man draws out of himself and puts *before himself* what he is and whatever else is. Things in nature are only *immediate* and *single*, while man as spirit *duplicates* himself, in that (i) he *is* as things in nature are, but (ii) he is just as much *for* himself; he sees himself, represents himself to himself, thinks, and only on the strength of this active placing himself before himself is he spirit. This consciousness of himself man acquires in a twofold way: *first, theoretically*, in so far as inwardly he must bring himself into his own consciousness, along with whatever moves, stirs, and presses in the human breast; and in general he must see himself, represent himself to himself, fix before himself what thinking finds as his essence, and recognize himself alone alike in what is summoned out of himself and in what is accepted from without. *Secondly*, man brings himself before himself by *practical* activity, since he has the impulse, in whatever is directly given to him, in what is present to him externally, to produce himself and therein equally to recognize himself. This aim he achieves by altering external things whereon he impresses the seal of his inner being and in which he now finds again his own characteristics. Man does this in order, as a free subject, to strip the external world of its inflexible foreignness and to enjoy in the shape of things only an external realization of himself. Even a child's first impulse involves this practical alteration of external things; a boy throws stones into the river and now marvels at the circles drawn in the water as an effect in which he gains an intuition of something that is his own doing. This need runs through the most diversi-form phenomena up to that mode of self-production in external things which is present in the work of art. And it is not only with external things that man proceeds in this way, but no less with himself, with his own natural figure which he does not leave as he finds it but deliberately alters. This is the cause of all dressing up and adornment, even if it be barbaric, tasteless, completely disfiguring, or even pernicious like crushing the feet of Chinese ladies, or slitting the ears and lips. For it is only among civilized people that alteration of figure, behaviour, and every sort and mode of external expression proceeds from spiritual development.

The universal need for art, that is to say, is man's rational need to lift the inner and outer world into his spiritual consciousness as an object in which he recognizes again his own self. The need for this spiritual freedom he satisfies, on the one hand, within by making what is within him explicit to himself, but correspondingly by giving outward reality to this his explicit self, and thus in this duplication of himself by bringing what is in him into sight and knowledge for himself and others. This is the free rationality of man in which all acting and knowing, as well as art too, have their basis and necessary origin. [. . .]

In the opposition between nature and art there are the following general points:

The purely formal ideality of the work of art. Poetry in general, as the very word indicates, is something made, produced by a man who has taken it into his imagination, pondered it, and issued it by his own activity out of his imagination.

(α) Here the subject-matter may be quite indifferent to us or may interest us, apart from the artistic presentation, only incidentally, for example, or momentarily. In this way Dutch painting, for example, has recreated, in thousands and thousands of effects, the existent and fleeting appearance of nature as something generated afresh by man. Velvet, metallic lustre, light, horses, servants, old women, peasants blowing smoke from cutty pipes, the glitter of wine in a transparent glass, chaps in dirty jackets playing with old cards—these and hundreds of other things are brought before our eyes in these pictures, things that we scarcely bother about in our daily life, for even if we play cards, drink wine, and chat about this and that, we are still engrossed by quite different interests. But what at once claims our attention in matter of this kind, when art displays it to us, is precisely this pure shining and appearing of objects as something produced by the *spirit* which transforms in its inmost being the external and sensuous side of all this material. For instead of real wool and silk, instead of real hair, glass, flesh, and metal, we see only colours; instead of all the dimensions requisite for appearance in nature, we have just a surface, and yet we get the same impression which reality affords.

(β) In contrast to the prosaic reality confronting us, this pure appearance, produced by the spirit, is therefore the marvel of ideality, a mockery, if you like, and an ironical attitude to what exists in nature and externally. For think what arrangements nature and man must make in ordinary life, what countless means of the most varied kind they must use, in order to produce things like those depicted; what resistance the material exerts here, e.g. a metal, when it is to be worked upon! On the other hand, the imagination, out of which art creates, is a pliant, simple element which easily and flexibly draws from its inner being everything on which nature, and man in his natural existence, have to work hard. Even so the objects represented and the ordinary man are not of an inexhaustible richness, but have their limitations: precious stones, gold, plants, animals, etc., have in themselves only this bounded existence. But man as creative artist is a whole world of matter which he filches from nature and, in the comprehensive range of his ideas and intuitions, has accumulated a treasure which he now freely disgorges in a simple manner without the far-flung conditions and arrangements of the real world.

In this ideality, art is the middle term between purely objective indigent existence and purely inner ideas. It furnishes us with the things themselves, but out of the inner life of mind; it does not provide them for some use or other but confines interest to the abstraction of the ideal appearance for purely contemplative inspection.

(γ) Now, consequently, through this ideality, art at the same time *exalts* these otherwise worthless objects which, despite their insignificant content, it fixes and makes ends in themselves; it directs our attention to what otherwise we would pass by without any notice. The same result art achieves in respect of time, and here too is ideal. What in nature slips past, art ties down to permanence: a quickly vanishing smile, a sudden roguish expression in the mouth, a glance, a fleeting ray of light, as well as spiritual traits in human life, incidents and events that come and go, are there and are then forgotten— anything and everything art wrests from momentary existence, and in this respect too conquers nature.

But in this formal ideality of art it is not the subject-matter which principally makes a claim on us but the satisfaction which comes from what the *spirit* has produced. The artistic presentation must appear here as natural, yet it is not the natural there as such but that making, precisely the extinction of the sensuous material and external conditions, which is the poetic and the ideal in a formal sense. We delight in a manifestation which must appear as if nature had produced it, while without natural means it has been produced by the spirit; works of art enchant us, not because they are so natural, but because they have been *made* so natural. [. . .]

The Dutch have selected the content of their artistic representations out of their own experience, out of their own life in the present, and to have actualized this present once more through art too is not to be made a reproach to them. What the contemporary world has brought before our vision and our spirit must also belong to that world if it is to claim our whole interest. In order to ascertain what engrossed the interest of the Dutch at the time of these paintings, we must ask about Dutch history. The Dutch themselves have made the greatest part of the land on which they dwell and live; it has continually to be defended against the storms of the sea, and it has to be maintained. By resolution, endurance, and courage, townsmen and countrymen alike threw off the Spanish dominion of Philip II, son of

Charles V (that mighty King of the World), and by fighting won for themselves freedom in political life and in religious life too in the religion of freedom. This citizenship, this love of enterprise, in small things as in great, in their own land as on the high seas, this painstaking as well as cleanly and neat well-being, this joy and exuberance in their own sense that for all this they have their own activity to thank, all this is what constitutes the general content of their pictures. This is no vulgar material and stuff which, it is true, is not to be approached by a man of high society who turns up his nose at it, convinced of the superiority of courts and their appendages. Fired by a sense of such vigorous nationality, Rembrandt painted his famous Night Watch, now in Amsterdam, Van Dyck so many of his portraits, Wouwerman his cavalry scenes, and even in this category are those rustic carousels, jovialities, and convivial merriments.

To cite a contrast, we have, for example, good *genre* paintings in our exhibition this year too, but in skill of representation they fall far below the Dutch pictures of the same kind, and even in content they cannot rise to freedom and joyfulness like that of the Dutch. For example, we see a woman going into an inn to scold her husband. Here we have nothing but a scene of snarling and vicious people. On the other hand, with the Dutch in their taverns, at weddings and dances, at feasting and drinking, everything goes on merrily and jovially, even if matters come to quarrels and blows; wives and girls join in and a feeling of freedom and gaiety animates one and all. This spiritual cheerfulness in a justified pleasure, which enters even pictures of animals and which is revealed as satisfaction and delight—this freshly awakened spiritual freedom and vitality in conception and execution—constitutes the higher soul of pictures of this kind.

In the like sense the beggar boys of Murillo [. . .] are excellent too. Abstractly considered, the subject-matter here too is drawn from 'vulgar nature': the mother picks lice out of the head of one of the boys while he quietly munches his bread; on a similar picture two other boys, ragged and poor, are eating melon and grapes. But in this poverty and semi-nakedness what precisely shines forth within and without is nothing but complete absence of care and concern—a Dervish could not have less—in the full feeling of their well-being and delight in life. This freedom from care for external things and the inner freedom made visible outwardly is what the Concept of the Ideal requires. In Paris there is a portrait of a boy by Raphael: his head lies at rest, leaning on an arm, and he gazes out into the wide and open distance with such bliss of carefree satisfaction that one can scarcely tear oneself away from gazing at this picture of spiritual and joyous well-being. The same satisfaction is afforded by those boys of Murillo. We see that they have no wider interests and aims, yet not at all because of stupidity; rather do they squat on the ground content and serene, almost like the gods of Olympus; they do nothing, they say nothing; but they are people all of one piece without any surliness or discontent; and since they possess this foundation of all excellence, we have the idea that anything may come of these youths.

[*Aesthetics: Lectures on Fine Art*, trans. T. M. Knox (Oxford: Clarendon Press, 1975), i. 30–2, 162–4, 169–70. First published in 1835.]

WARREN L. D'AZEVEDO

28 Sources of Gola Artistry

There are among the Gola of Liberia many persons who as woodcarvers, singers, dancers, musicians, storytellers, and other specialists are recognized within the culture as representing a mode of conduct, a type of personality, and a set of life-experiences relatively distinct from those of other persons. These individuals fit into a broad category in Gola culture roughly equivalent to that suggested by our concept of 'the creative personality,' and some of them are artists. Though I know of no clearly equivalent Gola term or concept for the artist as we apply it to the role and status of certain persons in our society, I will show in this paper that there is a type of person engaged in activities among the Gola for which our concepts are applicable.

The fact that the Gola do not have a distinct term for artist or art, as we conceive it, or that they may categorize roles somewhat differently than do we, should not prevent us from differentiating activities and values in their culture which seem similar if not identical to certain phenomena that we can find in our own. I know, for example, a Liberian ethnographer who enjoys the interpretive exercises of categorizing European or American acquaintances into 'dreamers' and 'non-dreamers,' very much as he would do in evaluating certain kinds of orientations and behavior of persons in his own culture. Though these particular categories may seem alien to us, it is not long before one can perceive what is meant. Moreover, the designations begin to strike one as specially apt and strangely familiar.

Among the Gola, just as in our own society, not everyone who carves wood, tells stories, plays an instrument, or decorates something is included in a category that implies specially creative persons, or those whom we would call artists. As with us, certain activities of this sort are stereotyped so that anyone who engages in them to any extent is suspected of having all the other characteristics of the type as well. A child who plays more than casually at carving wood, singing, story-telling, or mimicry is observed intently by adults. Consequently, many details of his general behavior which might ordinarily have gone unnoticed begin to be interpreted as signs of his life's orientation. Just as parents of an odd but intriguing child in our own society might anxiously ponder whether he will turn out to be either a ne'er-do-well or a great inventor, so Gola parents might express mixed admiration and weary exasperation by declaring, 'he is just like those woodcarvers,' or 'this child knows the days of my life!'

The last statement is much the same as our 'he'll be the death of me,' but the Gola are much more literal than we. The strange child is an immediate as well as a potential danger to his family and fellows. He may be the agent of malevolent forces which bring sickness and death. He may be in league with an angry ancestor or a subversive soul from a rival lineage or chiefdom. Sorrow and fear surround such persons, and they may die young through the violence of some supernatural agency or of the righteous community itself. At the same time, the ambivalent attitude toward the unusual child includes the possibility that he may bring gifts of greatness and power to his family and society. [. . .] The extraordinary individual of this kind is considered to be in constant and precarious struggle with mysterious forces which seek to alienate him from society. If he achieves a degree of success in the world, and brings honor to his family and community, it is believed that he has mastered these forces and turned them to benevolent ends. But if he dies in youth or lives to become a person of wealth and power through disloyalty and trickery, it is said that he was ruled by evil powers.

The Gola concept of the extraordinary person is, therefore, more concretely rationalized than our notion of the creative person or genius. But the characteristics of this type of person also constitute an archetype in the culture which is applied to explanations about individuals performing many kinds of activities. Among these are persons whose roles and specific productive activities would fit our designations of artist and art. Entertainers, sculpturers, and other skilled producers of aesthetic objects are subject to evaluation and interpretation in terms of the archetypical criteria. They are, in fact, set apart as a distinct subcategory of persons, though such distinctions are not easily discovered by the investigator from another culture.

The discussion which follows is a presentation of materials concerning a particular type of individual among the Gola who is immediately recognizable in terms of our concept of the artist. [. . .]

Talent, Virtuosity, and Genius

Gola attitudes concerning exceptional skills are permeated with the idea of supernatural power and guidance. A clear distinction is made between those pedestrian abilities which many persons may achieve through careful observation and practice, and those which give evidence of unique gifts which compel an individual to concentration and excellence in a line of work. This is even true of such basic and generalized activities as farming and other subsistence tasks. If a person pursues any activity with intensive interest and becomes known for a degree of superiority in performance, spiritual guidance is suspected. The degree of full-time specialization or professionalism is not a decisive factor in these judgments. Many successful professionals might be excluded from the category of exceptional persons, while certain part-time or casual specialists are held up as prime examples.

The Gola believe that there are sentient spirits behind all natural phenomena. These are classed into three general categories: the *jina* who are the spirits of sky, forests, mountains, and waters; the *anyun fa* who are the ancestral spirits; and *esē* ('witches') who are the spirits of evil persons, rejected by the world of the living and of the ancestors alike, wandering endlessly about doing terrible deeds. The various spirits of the world live in communities of their own in places under the earth, in the sky, or in distant forests and mountains. But all of them carry on commerce with human beings and concern themselves with human affairs. The ancestors, in particular, watch over the activities of their descendents, and their anger or pleasure has an immediate impact upon the living. [. . .] It is possible for individual human beings and individual *jina* to form alliances which are known as 'friendships.' In fact, every human being has such a potential 'friend' even though he may not know of it or may have scrupulously avoided it. Some persons are born with a friend that has joined them in their mother's womb, or who was inherited from a relative who passed on the friendship to the beloved descendent after death. Others 'discover' their spiritual friends later in life in the most unpredictable circumstances. [. . .]

These beliefs, validated by myth and expressed in on-going social relations, are a profoundly significant aspect of Gola life. The potential spiritual friends of human beings are known as *neme* (literally, 'the thing found'). They are usually of the opposite sex, and the relationship can be so intense as to overshadow all others. To the Gola, the concept of the *neme* as a powerful tutelary spirit provides explanation for a wide range of human conduct and, particularly, for the exceptional person. Every human being is considered to be born with his own individual character involving a degree of inherited talent or *emɔnə* ('sense' or 'wits'). Or it may be said of a person *wo na bene* (he is very able), implying much the same as our word 'talented.' But without 'luck' (*ké du*), which comes through the gift of power (*egòò*) granted by a *neme*, a personal talent may never bring greatness or success in life. Though each person has certain innate abilities and an individual way of thinking (*edí ne suwa*—'what is inside the head,' the 'inner mind'), it is the *neme* which guides one to special knowledge (*na jikea je*—'new thoughts,' or 'ideas') and gives one an advantage over other persons. This knowledge comes through dream or vision (*egwa*), which creates the condition for communication between 'friends.' A person reflects the character of his *neme* and shares its thoughts and powers. This is referred to as *anyun gbı iyáigba yi gwá gó ne suwa* (every man is different in his own way of dreaming). [. . .]

The private *neme* relationship is thought to be varied in quality and fraught with dangers for the individual as well as the community. The *neme* is selfish and is concerned with its own mysterious, nonhuman ends. It promises success to its human friend, but always at great cost. The cost is in the form of some personal sacrifice—restrictive rules of personal conduct, physical impairment, the death of one's beloved relatives, or something as crucial as childlessness. The most desirable *neme* is one which had a former friendship with an ancestor and represents the class of *neme* shared by other members of one's kinship group. Such a *neme* has learned to respect one's family and to consider its interests as well as that of its friend. [. . .] It is said that 'without *neme* one can be happy and live a good life, but one will never be truly great among men.' There are many other persons who have no recollection of having been aware of *neme*. It is said of them that they 'do not know themselves,' or that they 'would not feel a cow fly's bite.'

Two terms which denote exceptional persons of the genius type among the Gola are *yun edi* (a person of special mind) and *yun gò gwá* (a dreamer). These are persons whose character and works reveal the spiritual source of their powers. They may be found in all walks of life and in all circumstances. They are usually specialists of one kind or another, but not necessarily full-time professionals. Certain vocations are, because of their nature, predominantly represented by persons of this type. Most diviners, curers, sorcerers, and other manipulators of magic are considered, by virtue of the requirements of these practices, to be *anyun edi* under the guidance of *neme*. Some herbalists, however, and other makers of medicinal potions need not be guided directly by spirit powers but may have learned certain techniques from another who is. In all special activities the Gola make a distinction of this kind between the skills which ordinary persons may attain in accordance with their various talents, and those which are clearly extraordinary and proof of supernatural support.

The title *zo* is conferred on individuals who have demonstrated a high degree of disciplined skill in certain vocations over a substantial portion of their lifetimes. It denotes a respected person of wisdom of a particular kind, an expert, or more specifically, a master. A *zo* is one who has become a virtuoso in some field of specialization and who has earned the trust and admiration of the entire community. Not all persons referred to as *ma zonya* (plural) are *anyun edi* or *anyun go gwa*. They may be merely individuals who have performed exceptional services to the community and who are custodians of a body of knowledge and technical procedures that can be taught to others. They are, therefore, exemplars of proper conduct, of the rewards of rigorous training, and of the ideal relationship between the individual and society. [. . .]

A *zo* with *neme* has proven by his life's work that the spiritual powers derived from the relationship have been channeled into service of family and public ends rather than to private and selfish advantage. Thus, the *zo* is the laureate, the exceptionally talented person whom the elders and ancestors have singled out as most worthy of their special regard. [. . .]

Qualities of Aesthetic Expressive Roles

A common Gola allusion to the behavior believed to be associated with certain vocations is made by the comment that a person is 'acting like' a storyteller, a singer, or a woodcarver. It has much the same significance that references to minstrels, actors, or hippies have had in our own culture. Older people frequently admonish the young by warning them that they may turn out to be like such persons. Any behavior which is particularly expressive or intent upon public display is referred to jokingly or contemptuously in this way. It includes any concentration of interests in recreative activities such as games, dancing and music, or time spent in making of non-utilitarian things for pleasure or for diversion.

The general terms which denote activities of this kind are *e fɔwɔ* (play) and *wō dá* (festivity or feasting). Both carry the connotation of 'pastime,' or 'fun' as well. Thus a person who spends an inordinate amount of time and effort in such pursuits is *wo máné fɔwɔ ziŋgbe* (one who likes play too much) or *wo máné dá gbe* (one who likes feasts or good times). The Gola concept of play subsumes all activities and objects that are taken as ends in themselves. Funeral wakes (*é ziava*), for example, are sometimes alluded to as *é ziava fɔwɔ* (a mourning play), and the professional woman mourner who puts more than the required amount of zeal into her work is said to be 'making a play.' This in no way implies dissembling, but merely that a spectacle is being presented and that both performer and observers are intent upon the creative act and appreciation. Any elaborate decoration or personal adornment (*e kpa*), or anything that is kept because it is novel or attractive, may be referred to as *ne fɔwɔ* (a plaything) or *ne ma dí* (a thing for entertainment—usually in connection with dancing and singing). [. . .]

The above concepts apply primarily to recreation and entertainment where pleasurable experience is the focus of activity. Persons who either informally or professionally give emphasis to such activities are known as *anyun fɔwɔ* (literally, the players), or *anyun ma dí* (the entertainers). Though these terms are used loosely to denote any persons who are celebrating, gambling, or playing games, they also have specific reference to semiprofessional and professional performers in the various categories of entertainment.

Another term which is important for the analysis of the concept of artistry among the Gola is *ne fɔno* (something imitated or portrayed). This denotes a photograph, a drawing, a sculpture, a shadow, or a reflection in the water. Mimicry or a dramatic performance may also be referred to by this term. It connates something *created* either by man or supernatural agents and that it is a likeness taken from an original model. The term comes closest to designating the objects and activities we associate with the graphic or plastic arts. A woodcarver or painter of wall murals may be referred to as *yun fɔno ne* (a maker of images or representations).

These terms and their uses provide evidence that the Gola do conceptualize a category of persons who are performers and artisans of a special kind. Play, festiveness, display, and the making of images are activities which, when focused in a specialization or vocation, constitute for the Gola most of the qualities which we associate with the concept of the artist's role.

The Gola word *e sié* is the equivalent of our word beautiful, but it applies to anything which is good, fine, or attractive (also *na tévi*—good to look at). The emphasis, however, is upon the remarkable or the wondrous. Something marvelous or fascinating is described by the superlatives *e sié sié* or *e sié ziŋgbe*. But it may be set apart from ordinary goodness, truth, or propriety, and may detract one from these verities. Intensity of feeling and the giving way to spontaneous enjoyment also may be conditions produced by the bad or ugly (*e siè*). The interplay of revulsion and attraction is recognized, for example, in the response to certain masks, spirit impersonations, natural phenomena, or human behaviors which verge on the morally reprehensible, the overwhelming, or the unusual. One is caught up in contradictory emotions, but is made almost powerless to escape the entrancement. Such things may be *e siè*, as well, and not merely the simple opposite of what is ordinarily good or beautiful. One may speak of such a thing as though it represents all facets of terribleness or of badness, but in the tone of immense admiration and pleasure, much like the French '*il est formidable*' or the current American idiom 'it is *too* much.'

Profound reflection, *gongo súwá* ('inside thought' or, literally, the thought of the stomach), and a state of awe or dread (*e jul*), are connected with remarkable things. [. . .] Feelings of this kind are aroused by behavior and objects which give hint of hidden meanings or which present exaggerated versions of reality. People who skillfully do and make things of this kind do so by means of unnatural skill and knowledge. They are ambitious to prove their powers by putting what they have dreamed into visible or audible form.

These interrelated qualities of personality, social orientation, and certain material objects are focal aspects of those roles in Gola culture which symbolize values that are distinct from the ideal norms of the society. The model of such roles springs from concepts of traditional Gola culture which provide rationalization for certain forms of deviancy and privatized motivation. The cultural roots are the same as for all supernaturally endowed specialists, including the sorcerer or the opportunistic upstart pledged to an unprincipled tutelary. But artistry differs from these in the kind of activity performed, its function within society, in the orientation of its values and in its products. [. . .]

Singing as a vocation offers opportunity for a high degree of professionalization. Singers (*anyun gbemgbe*) are in constant demand for entertainment at funeral feasts and village festivals. They are required at all receptions in honor of important persons and in the traveling retinue of chiefs and other leading persons. Most professional singers are women, though professional male storytellers are also expected to be accomplished singers. Great female singers are renowned throughout many chiefdoms for their youth, beauty, and songs. [. . .] In a culture where everyone has learned to sing and dance as part of early socialization and secret society training, there is intense appreciation for virtuoso performance. The renowned professional singers are clearly distinguished from the numerous semi- or nonprofessional local singers who competently perform in secret society ritual or informal village 'plays.' Their way of life and their excellence surround them with an aura of glamor and legend similar to that of some popular entertainers in our own culture. Moreover, there is the factor of supernatural endowment. Beauty and success in youth are among the gifts which famous singers have gained from their *neme*. They also have been given the ability to invent new songs spontaneously during performance and to remember a repertoire of hundreds of songs accurately. Their wit and daring in song texts and their talent for eulogy are especially admired. They are also admired for endurance, for singers will compete with one another in festivals by continuing day and night without rest or sleep. It is said that they are driven to excess by their desire to please the crowd and their fear of the deep sense of loss and unhappiness which they experience when such events have come to an end. It is also believed that the *neme* of each singer is jealous of competition and wants its human companion to achieve fame above all others. [. . .]

Professional women singers are said to enjoy the adoration of all men, but they are inconstant and distressing wives or lovers. Their real lovers are their spiritual guardians, and in many cases, they have sacrificed their ability to have children in exchange for beauty, voice, and songs. They can cause men to love them above all women, but they are fickle and prefer to go from one man to another. They are proud and will show humility to no one. In this they do not behave as the ideal Gola woman should, but their powers protect them, and their abilities bring such enjoyment that they are allowed to be as they are. There are some older women who are professional singers, but it is an arduous and dangerous life. Most professional women singers give up the work when their beauty fades. Some become despondent and die; others marry and bring prestige to the households of wealthy families.

Dancing is also a generalized activity among the Gola. All ritual and festival involves mass participation in both singing and dancing. But again, it is virtuoso dancing which attracts special interest. There are very few professional dancers (*anyun yiva*) as such, though they are said to have been numerous in former times. Virtuoso dancing by both men and women is actually a related skill of other performing vocations such as those of the professional singers, storytellers, acrobats, and musicians. Gola secret societies (*Poro* and

Sande) are known by surrounding tribes as 'dancing societies.' Great stress is placed on dance as part of ritual and training of youth. [. . .]

Gola virtuoso dancing is quite different in style and form from group dancing in which everybody participates. The latter is slow, somnambulistic, and intent upon collective response to music and traditional public choreography. Virtuoso dancing is highly individualized with emphasis upon difficult, even acrobatic, movement which is intended to awe the beholder. Agility and dexterity are the predominant qualities. The performing role of the professional dancer [and the] [. . .] personal qualities attributed to these individuals is similar to that of the singer. [. . .]

[. . .] [T]he role of the artist emerges most clearly among the Gola in connection with vocations or statuses which are not embedded in the structure of local institutions. The special titles and ranks which are conferred on exemplary officials of tribal government, of the secret societies, or of the learned professions of curing, divining, and master blacksmithing are seldom if ever conferred on those who are primarily engaged in specializations of artistry. The ideal communal values of Gola culture are focused in official roles, and incumbents are selected and evaluated with reference to rigorously prescribed criteria of lineage rank, personality, and evidence of social responsibility.

The role of the artist, however, is associated with values that underscore particularly individualized, subjective, and expressive qualities of Gola behavior. It represents achievement and success with relative independence from the ideal communal requirements and sanctions of the local group. In this sense it provides a mirror for the ambivalence and tensions in the Gola value system. As in our own society, a high degree of voluntarism is attributed to the artist as well as a certain invulnerability with regard to sanctions for deviance. The sources of motivation and ability of the artist are considered to be more remote from common scrutiny than they are for most other activities. [. . .]

The archetypical Gola artist is one who 'dreams,' and whose [. . .] work in life is focused on activities that express the quality of the *neme* friendship not only in his personal behavior but in the creation of external forms that project the 'ideas' given to him by his spiritual companion. In this the artist may be distinguished to some degree from certain sorcerers, diviners, heroic warriors, *zonya*, and other remarkable persons who are *anyun gò gwá* (dreamers). The latter are engaged in activities which may be considered oriented to the practical on-going business of the world, and success is attributed to an essentially pragmatic and impersonal exchange of services between human and nonhuman agents. But the artist reveals by his behavior that he is preoccupied by a profound absorption in a relationship of love. He appears to be concerned seriously with little else than the 'gift' he has received from his lover and is intent upon transforming its essence into forms that can be presented for the admiration of others. [. . .]

The artist's product is seen, from the point of view of the archetype, as an objectification of a way of life and the embodiment of specific values manipulated by him under spiritual guidance. All that is artist and artistry in Gola terms is congealed in the artist's product. It at once personifies his own unique qualities as a person, the qualities of his spiritual counterpart, and reflects what he believes to be important in the world. Once completed, it can never be considered apart from him, but must be respected as a part of himself consecrated by the power of a spiritual benefactor. Even when the original producer is unknown or forgotten, an object whose qualities are such that it gives every evidence of having been produced under these conditions is dealt with in the context of presentation. It cannot be handled or exchanged in an impersonal way. It moves in the sphere of gifts and ritual. This is true of all goods and services involving the concept of unusual creative power. [...]

The artistic product associated with the archetype acquires its qualities not only from the conditions of its creation, but also from the fact of creation itself. For the average Gola the processes of artistry that occur between the initial inspiration of the artist and the public presentation of his result are only vaguely perceived. Matters of skill and technology are not part of the discourse between the artist and the public and remain mysteries of creation shared only among the producers or held as the cryptic property of an individual. Thus to the public the product of the archetypical artist is miraculous, and the artist is viewed essentially as a daring entrepreneur in exchanges of gifts between human society and a special supernatural realm. The years of training and arduous application of the artist are seen as tasks imposed upon him by his tutelary for whom he is a passive instrument.

I have shown that this is not the way the artist views his relation with *neme*, but that to some degree it provides him with the desired insulation from public scrutiny and control. He encourages the illusion of spontaneous creation and presents his results as a gift of spirit. The product, therefore, is not perceived by others so much as an embodiment of the intention of the artist as it is of the intention of a supernatural personality.

The effect of the artistic object is profoundly enhanced by this concept of creativity. It qualifies all response to innovations, novelties, and special interpretations of traditional forms presented by the players and makers of images in Gola culture. The awe which surrounds them involves ambivalent reference to deviant human behavior supported by extraordinary access to supernatural power. [...] The artist has established a personal contact with a spiritual agent outside of the sphere of communal supervision of such relations. His products, like his person, represent qualities which are both heroic and eccentric. As the child of society his work is a kind of eternal 'play' but his playthings are the more-than-lifelike symbols which awaken disturbing thoughts and values which lie for the most part dormant in culture.

['Sources of Gola Artistry', in Warren L. d'Azevedo (ed.), *The Traditional Artist in African Societies* (Bloomington, Ind.: Indiana University Press, 1973), 282–4, 291, 294–7, 304, 306–7, 311–13, 334–7.]

XIE-HE (HSIEH HO)

29 Six Canons of Painting

Now by classification of painters is meant the relative superiority and inferiority of all painters. As for painters, there is not one who does not illustrate some exhortation or warning, or show the rise and fall [in man's affairs]. The solitudes and silences of a thousand years may be seen as in a mirror by merely opening a scroll.

Even though painting has its Six Elements [or Laws], few are able to combine them thoroughly, and from ancient times until now each painter has excelled in one particular branch. What are these Six Elements? First, Spirit Resonance which means vitality; second, Bone Method which is [a way of] using the brush; third, Correspondence to the Object which means the depicting of forms; fourth, Suitability to Type which has to do with the laying on of colors; fifth, Division and Planning, that is, placing and arrangement; and sixth, Transmission by Copying, that is to say the copying of models.

[*Ku hua-p'in lu*, trans. James Cahill; repr. in Susan Bush and Hsio-yen Shih (eds.), *Early Chinese Texts on Painting* (Cambridge, Mass.: Harvard University Press, 1985), 39–40.]

SU SHIH

30 Painting Bamboo

When Wen T'ung painted bamboo,
He saw bamboo and not himself.
Not simply unconscious of himself,
Trance-like, he left his body behind.
His body was transferred into bamboo,
Creating inexhaustible freshness.
Chuang-tzu is no longer in this world,
So who can understand such concentration?

[*Early Chinese Texts on Painting*, ed. Susan Bush and Hsio-yen Shih (Cambridge, Mass.: Harvard University Press, 1985), 212.]

SU SHIH

31 Genius

> If anyone discusses painting in terms of formal likeness,
> His understanding is close to that of a child.
> If someone composing a poem must have a certain poem,
> Then he is definitely not a man who knows poetry.
> There is one basic rule in poetry and painting;
> Natural genius and originality...

[*Early Chinese Texts on Painting*, ed. Susan Bush and Hsio-yen Shih (Cambridge, Mass.: Harvard University Press, 1985), 224.]

FIG. 1. *Fishermen*, Xu Daoning (1049–52)

WANG CH'IN-CH'EN

32 Spiritual Excellence

We know, indeed, that spiritual excellence is not easy to describe.
But if one's heart is in accord with the Tao, one can know how to do it.

There is surely a single principle in literature, calligraphy, and painting.
Have we not heard of Wang Wei's 'In a former life I must have been a Painting
   Master'.

[*Early Chinese Texts on Painting*, ed. Susan Bush and Hsio-yen Shih (Cambridge, Mass.:
Harvard University Press, 1985), 209.]

EDGAR ALLAN POE

33   The Philosophy of Composition

Nothing is more clear than that every plot, worth the name, must be
elaborated to its *dénouement* before anything be attempted with the pen. It
is only with the *dénouement* constantly in view that we can give a plot its
indispensable air of consequence, or causation, by making the incidents, and
especially the tone at all points, tend to the development of the intention.

There is a radical error, I think, in the usual mode of constructing a
story. Either history affords a thesis—or one is suggested by an incident of
the day—or, at best, the author sets himself to work in the combination
of striking events to form merely the basis of his narrative—designing,
generally, to fill in with description, dialogue, or authorial comment, whatever crevices of fact, or action, may, from page to page, render themselves
apparent.

I prefer commencing with the consideration of an *effect*. Keeping originality *always* in view—for he is false to himself who ventures to dispense with
so obvious and so easily attainable a source of interest—I say to myself, in the
first place, 'Of the innumerable effects, or impressions, of which the heart,
the intellect, or (more generally) the soul is susceptible, what one shall I,
on the present occasion, select?' Having chosen a novel, first, and secondly a
vivid effect, I consider whether it can be best wrought by incident or tone—
whether by ordinary incidents and peculiar tone, or the converse, or by
peculiarity both of incident and tone—afterward looking about me (or rather
within) for such combinations of event, or tone, as shall best aid me in the
construction of the effect.

I have often thought how interesting a magazine paper might be written by
any author who would—that is to say who could—detail, step by step, the
processes by which any one of his compositions attained its ultimate point of
completion. Why such a paper has never been given to the world, I am much
at a loss to say—but, perhaps, the authorial vanity has had more to do with
the omission than any one other cause. Most writers—poets in especial—
prefer having it understood that they compose by a species of fine frenzy—an
ecstatic intuition—and would positively shudder at letting the public take a
peep behind the scenes, at the elaborate and vacillating crudities of thought—

at the true purposes seized only at the last moment—at the innumerable glimpses of idea that arrived not at the maturity of full view—at the fully matured fancies discarded in despair as unmanageable—at the cautious selections and rejections—at the painful erasures and interpolations—in a word, at the wheels and pinions—the tackle for scene-shifting—the step-ladders and demon-traps—the cock's feathers, the red paint and the black patches, which, in ninety-nine cases out of the hundred, constitute the properties of the literary *histrio*.

I am aware, on the other hand, that the case is by no means common, in which an author is at all in condition to retrace the steps by which his conclusions have been attained. In general, suggestions, having arisen pell-mell, are pursued and forgotten in a similar manner.

For my own part, I have neither sympathy with the repugnance alluded to nor, at any time the least difficulty in recalling to mind the progressive steps of any of my compositions; and, since the interest of an analysis, or reconstruction, such as I have considered a *desideratum*, is quite independent of any real or fancied interest in the thing analyzed, it will not be regarded as a breach of decorum on my part to show the *modus operandi* by which some one of my own works was put together. I select 'The Raven,' as most generally known. It is my design to render it manifest that no one point in its composition is referrible either to accident or intuition—that the work proceeded, step by step, to its completion with the precision and rigid consequence of a mathematical problem.

Let us dismiss, as irrelevant to the poem, *per se*, the circumstance—or say the necessity—which, in the first place, gave rise to the intention of composing *a* poem that should suit at once the popular and the critical taste.

We commence, then, with this intention.

The initial consideration was that of extent. If any literary work is too long to be read at one sitting, we must be content to dispense with the immensely important effect derivable from unity of impression—for, if two sittings be required, the affairs of the world interfere, and every thing like totality is at once destroyed. But since, *ceteris paribus*, no poet can afford to dispense with *any thing* that may advance his design, it but remains to be seen whether there is, in extent, any advantage to counterbalance the loss of unity which attends it. Here I say no, at once. What we term a long poem is, in fact, merely a succession of brief ones—that is to say, of brief poetical effects. It is needless to demonstrate that a poem is such, only inasmuch as it intensely excites, by elevating, the soul; and all intense excitements are, through a psychal necessity, brief. For this reason, at least one half of the *Paradise Lost* is essentially prose—a succession of poetical excitements interspersed, *inevitably,* with corresponding depressions—the whole being deprived, through the extremeness of its length, of the vastly important artistic element, totality, or unity, of effect.

It appears evident, then, that there is a distinct limit, as regards length, to all works of literary art—the limit of a single sitting—and that, although in certain classes of prose composition, such as *Robinson Crusoe*, (demanding no unity), this limit may be advantageously overpassed, it can never properly be overpassed in a poem. Within this limit, the extent of a poem may be made to bear mathematical relation to its merit—in other words, to the excitement or elevation—again in other words, to the degree of the true poetical effect which it is capable of inducing; for it is clear that the brevity must be in direct ratio of the intensity of the intended effect:—this, with one proviso—that a certain degree of duration is absolutely requisite for the production of any effect at all.

Holding in view these considerations, as well as that degree of excitement which I deemed not above the popular, while not below the critical, taste, I reached at once what I conceived the proper *length* for my intended poem—a length of about one hundred lines. It is, in fact, a hundred and eight.

My next thought concerned the choice of an impression, or effect, to be conveyed: and here I may as well observe that, throughout the construction, I kept steadily in view the design of rendering the work *universally* appreciable. I should be carried too far out of my immediate topic were I to demonstrate a point upon which I have repeatedly insisted, and which, with the poetical, stands not in the slightest need of demonstration—the point, I mean, that Beauty is the sole legitimate province of the poem. A few words, however, in elucidation of my real meaning, which some of my friends have evinced a disposition to misrepresent. That pleasure which is at once the most intense, the most elevating, and the most pure, is, I believe, found in the contemplation of the beautiful. When, indeed, men speak of Beauty, they mean, precisely, not a quality, as is supposed, but an effect—they refer, in short, just to that intense and pure elevation of *soul*—*not* of intellect, or of heart—upon which I have commented, and which is experienced in consequence of contemplating 'the beautiful.' Now I designate Beauty as the province of the poem, merely because it is an obvious rule of Art that effects should be made to spring from direct causes—that objects should be attained through means best adapted for their attainment—no one as yet having been weak enough to deny that the peculiar elevation alluded to is *most readily* attained in the poem. Now the object, Truth, or the satisfaction of the intellect, and the object Passion, or the excitement of the heart, are, although attainable, to a certain extent, in poetry, far more readily attainable in prose. Truth, in fact, demands a precision, and Passion a *homeliness* (the truly passionate will comprehend me) which are absolutely antagonistic to that Beauty which, I maintain, is the excitement, or pleasurable elevation, of the soul. It by no means follows from any thing here said, that passion, or even truth, may not be introduced, and even profitably introduced, into a poem—for they may serve in elucidation, or aid the general effect, as do discords in music, by contrast—but the true artist will always contrive first, to tone them into proper subservience to the predominant aim, and, secondly, to enveil them, as far as possible, in that Beauty which is the atmosphere and the essence of the poem.

Regarding, then, Beauty as my province, my next question referred to the *tone* of its highest manifestation—and all experience has shown that this tone is one of *sadness*. Beauty of whatever kind, in its supreme development, invariably excites the sensitive soul to tears. Melancholy is thus the most legitimate of all the poetical tones.

The length, the province, and the tone, being thus determined, I betook myself to ordinary induction, with the view of obtaining some artistic piquancy which might serve me as a key-note in the construction of the poem—some pivot upon which the whole structure might turn. In carefully thinking over all the usual artistic effects—or more properly *points*, in the theatrical sense—I did not fail to perceive immediately that no one had been so universally employed as that of the *refrain*. The universality of its employment sufficed to assure me of its intrinsic value, and spared me the necessity of submitting it to analysis. I considered it, however, with regard to its susceptibility of improvement, and soon saw it to be in a primitive condition. As commonly used, the *refrain*, or burden, not only is limited to lyric verse, but depends for its impression upon the force of monotone—both in sound and thought. The pleasure is deduced solely from the sense of identity—of repetition. I resolved to diversify, and so heighten, the effect, by adhering, in general, to the monotone of sound, while I continually varied that of thought: that is to say, I determined to produce continuously novel effects, by the variation of *the application* of the *refrain*—the *refrain* itself remaining, for the most part, unvaried.

These points being settled, I next bethought me of the *nature* of my *refrain*. Since its application was to be repeatedly varied, it was clear that the *refrain* itself must be brief, for there would have been an insurmountable difficulty in frequent variations of application in any sentence of length. In proportion to the brevity of the sentence, would, of course, be the facility of the variation. This led me at once to a single word as the best *refrain*.

The question now arose as to the *character* of the word. Having made up my mind to a *refrain*, the division of the poem into stanzas was, of course, a corollary: the *refrain* forming the close of each stanza. That such a close, to have force, must be sonorous and susceptible of protracted emphasis, admitted no doubt: and these considerations inevitably led me to the long *o* as the most sonorous vowel, in connection with *r* as the most producible consonant.

The sound of the *refrain* being thus determined, it became necessary to select a word embodying this sound, and at the same time in the fullest possible keeping with that melancholy which I had predetermined as the tone of the poem. In such a search it would have been absolutely impossible to overlook the word 'Nevermore.' In fact, it was the very first which presented itself.

The next *desideratum* was a pretext for the continuous use of the one word 'nevermore.' In observing the difficulty which I at once found in inventing a sufficiently plausible reason for its continuous repetition, I did not fail to perceive that this difficulty arose solely from the pre-assumption that the word was to be so continuously or monotonously spoken by a *human* being— I did not fail to perceive, in short, that the difficulty lay in the reconciliation of this monotony with the exercise of reason on the part of the creature repeating the word. Here, then, immediately arose the idea of a *non*-reasoning creature capable of speech; and, very naturally, a parrot, in the first instance, suggested itself, but was superseded forthwith by a Raven, as equally capable of speech, and infinitely more in keeping with the intended *tone*.

I had now gone so far as the conception of a Raven—the bird of ill omen— monotonously repeating the one word, 'Nevermore,' at the conclusion of each stanza, in a poem of melancholy tone, and in length about one hundred lines. Now, never losing sight of the object *supremeness*, or perfection, at all points, I asked myself—'Of all melancholy topics, what, according to the *universal* understanding of mankind, is the *most* melancholy?' Death—was the obvious reply. 'And when,' I said, 'is this most melancholy of topics most poetical?' From what I have already explained at some length, the answer, here also, is obvious—'When it most closely allies itself to *Beauty*: the death, then, of a beautiful woman is, unquestionably, the most poetical topic in the world—and equally is it beyond doubt that the lips best suited for such topic are those of a bereaved lover.'

I had now to combine the two ideas, of a lover lamenting his deceased mistress and a Raven continuously repeating the word 'Nevermore.'—I had to combine these, bearing in mind my design of varying, at every turn, the *application* of the word repeated; but the only intelligible mode of such combination is that of imagining the Raven employing the word in answer to the queries of the lover. And here it was that I saw at once the opportunity afforded for the effect on which I had been depending—that is to say, the effect of the *variation of application*. I saw that I could make the first query propounded by the lover—the first query to which the Raven should reply 'Nevermore'—that I could make this first query a commonplace one—the second less so—the third still less, and so on—until at length the lover, startled from his original *nonchalance* by the melancholy character of the word itself—by its frequent repetition—and by a consideration of the omin- ous reputation of the fowl that uttered it—is at length excited to superstition, and wildly propounds queries of a far different character—queries whose solution he has passionately at heart—propounds them half in super- stition and half in that species of despair which delights in self-torture— propounds them not altogether because he believes in the prophetic or demoniac character of the bird (which, reason assures him, is merely repeating a lesson learned by rote) but because he experiences a phrenzied pleasure in so modeling his questions as to receive from the *expected* 'Nevermore' the most delicious because the most intolerable of sorrow. Perceiving the opportunity thus afforded me—or, more strictly, thus forced upon me in the progress of the construction—I first established in mind the climax, or concluding query—that query to which 'Nevermore' should be in the last place an answer—that in reply to which this word 'Nevermore' should involve the utmost conceivable amount of sorrow and despair.

Here then the poem may be said to have its beginning—at the end, where all works of art should begin—for it was here, at this point of my preconsiderations, that I first put pen to paper in the composition of the stanza:

> 'Prophet,' said I, 'thing of evil! prophet still if bird or devil!
> By that heaven that bends above us—by that God we both adore,
> Tell this soul with sorrow laden, if within the distant Aidenn,
> It shall clasp a sainted maiden whom the angels name Lenore—
> Clasp a rare and radiant maiden whom the angels name Lenore.'
>   Quoth the raven 'Nevermore.'

I composed this stanza, at this point, first that, by establishing the climax, I might the better vary and graduate, as regards seriousness and importance, the preceding queries of the lover—and, secondly, that I might definitely settle the rhythm, the metre, and the length and general arrangement of the stanza—as well as graduate the stanzas which were to precede, so that none of them might surpass this in rhythmical effect. Had I been able, in the subsequent composition, to construct more vigorous stanzas, I should, without scruple, have purposely enfeebled them, so as not to interfere with the climacteric effect. [...]

The next point to be considered was the mode of bringing together the lover and the Raven—and the first branch of this consideration was the *locale*. For this the most natural suggestion might seem to be a forest, or the fields—but it has always appeared to me that a close *circumscription of space* is absolutely necessary to the effect of insulated incident:—it has the force of a frame to a picture. It has an indisputable moral power in keeping concentrated the attention, and, of course, must not be confounded with mere unity of place.

I determined, then, to place the lover in his chamber—in a chamber rendered sacred to him by memories of her who had frequented it. The room is represented as richly furnished—this in mere pursuance of the ideas I have already explained on the subject of Beauty, as the sole true poetical thesis.

The *locale* being thus determined, I had now to introduce the bird—and the thought of introducing him through the window, was inevitable. The idea of making the lover suppose, in the first instance, that the flapping of the wings of the bird against the shutter, is a 'tapping' at the door, originated in a wish to increase, by prolonging, the reader's curiosity, and in a desire to admit the incidental effect arising from the lover's throwing open the door, finding all dark, and thence adopting the half-fancy that it was the spirit of his mistress that knocked.

I made the night tempestuous, first, to account for the Raven's seeking admission, and secondly, for the effects of contrast with the (physical) serenity within the chamber.

I made the bird alight on the bust of Pallas, also for the effect of contrast between the marble and the plumage—it being understood that the bust was absolutely *suggested* by the bird—the bust of *Pallas* being chosen, first, as most in keeping with the scholarship of the lover, and, secondly, for the sonorousness of the word, Pallas, itself. [. . .]

With the *dénouement* proper—with the Raven's reply, 'Nevermore,' to the lover's final demand if he shall meet his mistress in another world—the poem, in its obvious phase, that of a simple narrative, may be said to have its completion. So far, every thing is within the limits of the accountable—of the real. A raven, having learned by rote the single word 'Nevermore,' and having escaped from the custody of its owner, is driven at midnight, through the violence of a storm, to seek admission at a window from which a light still gleams—the chamber-window of a student, occupied half in poring over a volume, half in dreaming of a beloved mistress deceased. The casement being thrown open at the fluttering of the bird's wings, the bird itself perches on the most convenient seat out of the immediate reach of the student, who, amused by the incident and the oddity of the visitor's demeanor, demands of it, in jest and without looking for a reply, its name. The raven addressed, answers with its customary word, 'Nevermore'—a word which finds immediate echo in the melancholy heart of the student, who, giving utterance aloud to certain thoughts suggested by the occasion, is again startled by the fowl's repetition of 'Nevermore.' The student now guesses the state of the case, but is impelled, as I have before explained, by the human thirst for self-torture, and in part by superstition, to propound such queries to the bird as will bring him, the lover, the most of the luxury of sorrow, through the anticipated answer 'Nevermore.' With the indulgence, to the extreme, of this self-torture, the narration, in what I have termed its first or obvious phase, has a natural termination, and so far there has been no overstepping of the limits of the real.

But in subjects so handled, however skilfully, or with however vivid an array of incident, there is always a certain hardness or nakedness, which repels the artistical eye. Two things are invariably required—first, some amount of complexity, or more properly, adaptation; and, secondly, some amount of suggestiveness—some under-current, however indefinite, of meaning. [. . .]

It will be observed that the words, 'from out my heart,' involve the first metaphorical expression in the poem. They, with the answer, 'Nevermore,' dispose the mind to seek a moral in all that has been previously narrated. The reader begins now to regard the Raven as emblematical—but it is not until the very last line of the very last stanza, that the intention of making him emblematical of *Mournful and Never-ending Remembrance* is permitted distinctly to be seen:

> And the Raven, never flitting, still is sitting, still is sitting,
> On the pallid bust of Pallas, just above my chamber door;
> And his eyes have all the seeming of a demon's that is dreaming,
> And the lamplight o'er him streaming throws his shadow on the floor;
> And my soul *from out that shadow* that lies floating on the floor
> Shall be lifted—nevermore.

['The Philosophy of Composition', 1846.]

R. G. COLLINGWOOD

34 Art and Craft

The first sense of the word 'art' to be distinguished from art proper is the obsolete sense in which it means what in this book I shall call craft. This is what *ars* means in ancient Latin, and what τέχνη means in Greek: the power to produce a preconceived result by means of consciously controlled and directed action. In order to take the first step towards a sound aesthetic, it is necessary to disentangle the notion of craft from that of art proper. In order to do this, again, we must first enumerate the chief characteristics of craft.

1. Craft always involves a distinction between means and end, each clearly conceived as something distinct from the other but related to it. The term 'means' is loosely applied to things that are used in order to reach the end, such as tools, machines, or fuel. Strictly, it applies not to the things but to the actions concerned with them: manipulating the tools, tending the machines, or burning the fuel. These actions (as implied by the literal sense of the word means) are passed through or traversed in order to reach the end, and are left behind when the end is reached. [. . .]

2. It involves a distinction between planning and execution. The result to be obtained is preconceived or thought out before being arrived at. The craftsman knows what he wants to make before he makes it. This foreknowledge is absolutely indispensable to craft: if something, for example stainless steel, is made without such foreknowledge, the making of it is not a case of craft but an accident. Moreover, this fore knowledge is not vague but precise. If a person sets out to make a table, but conceives the table only vaguely, as

somewhere between two by four feet and three by six, and between two and three feet high, and so forth, he is no craftsman.

3. Means and end are related in one way in the process of planning; in the opposite way in the process of execution. In planning the end is prior to the means. The end is thought out first, and afterwards the means are thought out. In execution the means come first, and the end is reached through them.

4. There is a distinction between raw material and finished product or artifact. A craft is always exercised upon something, and aims at the trans-formation of this into something different. That upon which it works begins as raw material and ends as finished product. The raw material is found ready made before the special work of the craft begins.

5. There is a distinction between form and matter. The matter is what is identical in the raw material and the finished product; the form is what is different, what the exercise of the craft changes. To describe the raw material as raw is not to imply that it is formless but only that it has not yet the form which it is to acquire through 'transformation' into finished product.

6. There is a hierarchical relation between various crafts, one supplying what another needs, one using what another provides. [. . .]

Without claiming that these features together exhaust the notion of craft, or that each of them separately is peculiar to it, we may claim with tolerable confidence that where most of them are absent from a certain activity that activity is not a craft, and, if it is called by that name, is so called either by mistake or in a vague and inaccurate way. [. . .]

The central and primary characteristic of craft is the distinction it involves between means and end. If art is to be conceived as craft, it must likewise be divisible into means and end. [. . .] [I]t is not so divisible; but we have now to ask why anybody ever thought it was. What is there in the case of art which these people misunderstood by assimilating it to the well-known distinction of means and end? [. . .]

1. This, then, is the first point we have learnt from our criticism: that there is in art proper a distinction resembling that between means and end, but not identical with it.

2. The element which the technical theory calls the end is defined by it as the arousing of emotion. The idea of arousing (i.e. of bringing into existence, by determinate means, something whose existence is conceived in advance as possible and desirable) belongs to the philosophy of craft, and is obviously borrowed thence. But the same is not true of emotion. This, then, is our second point. Art has something to do with emotion; what it does with it has a certain resemblance to arousing it, but is not arousing it. [. . .]

Out first question is this. Since the artist proper has something to do with emotion, and what he does with it is not to arouse it, what is it that he does?. [. . .] Nothing could be more commonplace that to say he expresses them.

[...] When a man is said to express emotion, what is being said about him comes to this. At first, he is conscious of having an emotion, but not conscious of what this emotion is. All he is conscious of is a perturbation or excitement, which he feels going on within him, but of whose nature he is ignorant. While in this state, all he can say about his emotion is: 'I feel...I don't know what I feel.' From this helpless and oppressed condition he extricates himself by doing something which we call expressing himself. This is an activity which has something to do with the thing we call language: he expresses himself by speaking. It has also something to do with consciousness: the emotion expressed is an emotion of whose nature the person who feels it is no longer unconscious. It has also something to do with the way in which he feels the emotion. As unexpressed, he feels it in what we have called a helpless and oppressed way; as expressed, he feels it in a way from which this sense of oppression has vanished. His mind is somehow lightened and eased.

This lightening of emotions which is somehow connected with the expression of them has a certain resemblance to the 'catharsis' by which emotions are earthed through being discharged into a make-believe situation; but the two things are not the same. Suppose the emotion is one of anger. If it is effectively earthed, for example by fancying oneself kicking some one down stairs, it is thereafter no longer present in the mind as anger at all: we have worked it off and are rid of it. If it is expressed, for example by putting it into hot and bitter words, it does not disappear from the mind; we remain angry; but instead of the sense of oppression which accompanies an emotion of anger not yet recognized as such, we have that sense of alleviation which comes when we are conscious of our own emotion as anger, instead of being conscious of it only as an unidentified perturbation. This is what we refer to when we say that it 'does us good' to express our emotions.

The expression of an emotion by speech may be addressed to some one; but if so it is not done with the intention of arousing a like emotion in him. If there is any effect which we wish to produce in the hearer, it is only the effect which we call making him understand how we feel. But, as we have already seen, this is just the effect which expressing our emotions has on ourselves. It makes us, as well as the people to whom we talk, understand how we feel. A person arousing emotion sets out to affect his audience in a way in which he himself is not necessarily affected. He and his audience stand in quite different relations to the act, very much as physician and patient stand in quite different relations towards a drug administered by the one and taken by the other. A person expressing emotion, on the contrary, is treating himself and his audience in the same kind of way; he is making his emotions clear to his audience, and that is what he is doing to himself.

It follows from this that the expression of emotion, simply as expression, is not addressed to any particular audience. It is addressed primarily to the speaker himself, and secondarily to any one who can understand. Here again, the speaker's attitude towards his audience is quite unlike that of a person desiring to arouse in his audience a certain emotion. If that is what he wishes to do, he must know the audience he is addressing. He must know what type of stimulus will produce the desired kind of reaction in people of that particular sort; and he must adapt his language to his audience in the sense of making sure that it contains stimuli appropriate to their peculiarities. If what he wishes to do is to express his emotions intelligibly, he has to express them in such a way as to be intelligible to himself; his audience is then in the position of persons who overhear him doing this. Thus the stimulus-and-reaction terminology has no applicability to the situation.

The means-and-end, or technique, terminology too is inapplicable. Until a man has expressed his emotion, he does not yet know what emotion it is. The act of expressing it is therefore an exploration of his own emotions. He is trying to find out what these emotions are. There is certainly here a directed process: an effort, that is, directed upon a certain end; but the end is not something foreseen and preconceived, to which appropriate means can be thought out in the light of our knowledge of its special character. Expression is an activity of which there can be no technique.

Expressing an emotion is not the same thing as describing it. To say 'I am angry' is to describe one's emotion, not to express it. The words in which it is expressed need not contain any reference to anger as such at all. Indeed, so far as they simply and solely express it, they cannot contain any such reference. The curse of Ernulphus, as invoked by Dr Slop on the unknown person who tied certain knots, is a classical and supreme expression of anger; but it does not contain a single word descriptive of the emotion it expresses.

This is why, as literary critics well know, the use of epithets in poetry, or even in prose where expressiveness is aimed at, is a danger. If you want to express the terror which something causes, you must not give it an epithet like 'dreadful'. For that describes the emotion instead of expressing it, and your language becomes frigid, that is inexpressive, at once. A genuine poet, in his moments of genuine poetry, never mentions by name the emotions he is expressing.

Some people have thought that a poet who wishes to express a great variety of subtly differentiated emotions might be hampered by the lack of a vocabulary rich in words referring to the distinctions between them; and that psychology, by working out such a vocabulary, might render a valuable service to poetry. This is the opposite of the truth. The poet needs no such words at all; the existence or non-existence of a scientific terminology describing the emotions he wishes to express is to him a matter of perfect indifference. If such a terminology, where it exists, is allowed to affect his own use of language, it affects it for the worse.

The reason why description, so far from helping expression, actually damages it, is that description generalizes. To describe a thing is to call it a thing of such and such a kind: to bring it under a conception, to classify it. Expression, on the contrary, individualizes. The anger which I feel here and now, with a certain person, for a certain cause, is no doubt an instance of anger, and in describing it as anger one is telling truth about it; but it is much more than mere anger: it is a peculiar anger, not quite like any anger that I ever felt before, and probably not quite like any anger I shall ever feel again. To become fully conscious of it means becoming conscious of it not merely as an instance of anger, but as this quite peculiar anger. Expressing it, we saw, has something to do with becoming conscious of it; therefore, if being fully conscious of it means being conscious of all its peculiarities, fully expressing it means expressing all its peculiarities. The poet, therefore, in proportion as he understands his business, gets as far away as possible from merely labelling his emotions as instances of this or that general kind, and takes enormous pains to individualize them by expressing them in terms which reveal their difference from any other emotion of the same sort.

This is a point in which art proper, as the expression of emotion, differs sharply and obviously from any craft whose aim it is to arouse emotion. The end which a craft sets out to realize is always conceived in general terms, never individualized. However accurately defined it may be, it is always defined as the production of a thing having characteristics that could be shared by other things. A joiner, making a table out of these pieces of wood and no others, makes it to measurements and specifications which, even if actually shared by no other table, might in principle be shared by other tables. A physician treating a patient for a certain complaint is trying to produce in him a condition which might be, and probably has been, often produced in others, namely, the condition of recovering from that complaint. So an 'artist' setting out to produce a certain emotion in his audience is setting out to produce not an individual emotion, but an emotion of a certain kind. It follows that the means appropriate to its production will be not individual means but means of a certain kind: that is to say, means which are always in principle replaceable by other similar means. As every good craftsman insists, there is always a 'right way' of performing any operation. A 'way' of acting is a general pattern to which various individual actions may conform. In order that the 'work of art' should produce its intended psychological effect, therefore, whether this effect be magical or merely amusing, what is necessary is that it should satisfy certain conditions, possess certain characteristics: in other words be, not this work and no other, but a work of this kind and of no other. [. . .]

Art proper, as expression of emotion, has nothing to do with all this. The artist proper is a person who, grappling with the problem of expressing a certain emotion, says, 'I want to get this clear.' It is no use to him to get something else clear, however like it this other thing may be. Nothing will serve as a substitute. He does not want a thing of a certain kind, he wants a certain thing. This is why the kind of person who takes his literature as psychology, saying 'How admirably this writer depicts the feelings of women, or bus-drivers, or homosexuals . . .', necessarily misunderstands every real work of art with which he comes into contact, and takes for good art, with infallible precision, what is not art at all.

[*The Principles of Art* (New York: Oxford University Press, 1958), 15–17, 108–15.
First published in 1938.]

Can we ever Understand an Artwork?

Section III explored the conception of art as self-expression and freedom, and considered the extent to which the production of art may be subject to rules of craft. As we return to what Dewey called the spectator's standpoint, familiar questions arise. What difference does it make to the perceiver whether art is self-expression or whether there are rules for creating art? Should perceivers try to understand what processes went through the artist's mind during creation? Is knowledge about the psychological origins of a work relevant to understanding (and appreciating) it? Or should perceivers remove such preconceptions from their minds in order to experience 'the work itself'? However one answers these questions—whether one holds that a perceiver should acquire or ignore certain ideas and information—a perceiver will have to *do* something to understand a work. One cannot expect understanding to flow automatically, without becoming involved and engaged with the work in some way. Selections in this section and the next present a rich diversity of views and considerations regarding what cognitive and emotional involvement is typically required.

Monroe Beardsley distinguishes between causes of the work (psychological processes of the artist) and qualities of a work when viewed as an aesthetic object. He makes the general claim that 'Characteristics of an aesthetic object [include] *no* characteristics . . . that depend upon knowledge of their causal conditions, whether physical or psychological'. He defends this principle for all types of art; the selection here discusses literature and music. On the other hand, Stephen Davies holds that because at least some intentions of a composer are crucial to establishing what a work *is*, they should affect how it is performed. Parallel issues arise for performances of theatrical works, for dance, and also for technological enhancements of musical recordings and motion pictures.

Regarding the visual arts, do we understand a work better when we perceive or experience it as it was intended to be experienced? Richard Wollheim uses the word 'criticism' to indicate the *process* of coming to understand a work of art. Viewers, he holds, should reconstruct the creative process *as it is realized in the work* so they can see the work in light of the artist's productive process, and he defends his position by criticizing what he considers to be its likely rivals. How often is the information that Wollheim asks for available to us? Understanding can be difficult, for example, if one is not a member of the community or culture within which the work was produced. As Michael Baxandall writes, 'The participant understands and knows his culture with an immediacy and spontaneity the observer does not share.' Baxandall recommends that interpreters, 'observers' of the work of a culture which is not their own, reconstruct categories for perceiving that would have been operative at the time the work was created.

On the other hand, interpretations of artworks often appeal to theories or systems of thought that are not available to the community in which the work is made. Some examples would be a Freudian account of a Leonardo portrait, a Marxist account of Renaissance altarpieces, or a feminist analysis of how Titian's nudes reinforce thinking about women as objects of sexual attention. In her well-known essay 'Against Interpretation', Susan Sontag deplores such purported attempts at 'understanding' an artwork. Since art is to be perceived—it is to be sensed and experienced, related to the body and not (merely) the mind—such theorizing constitutes, she says, 'the revenge of the intellect upon art'. On her view, such interpretation is a cerebral 'translation' of the work into intellectual terms, rather than a passionate, lived experience.

Arthur Danto takes a different position on what he calls 'deep interpretation', where the objective is to reveal meanings that are 'more than the speaker realizes'. Surface interpretations require understanding the ways the artist intended a work to be perceived, but deep interpretations do not. Danto argues that some meanings *have* to be hidden (deep) for a work to mean what it does. Sounding a theme that has appeared throughout his work, he provides different surface interpretations, reflecting different intentions, for two visually indistinguishable objects.

The hypothetical possibility of having two objects which are perceptually indistinguishable suggests the idea that one may be a forgery. If one cannot detect, just by looking, whether a work is an original or a forgery, why should its being a forgery make any aesthetic difference? But as we have seen all along, how something looks depends on beliefs and experiences one brings to it: the same object may look very different to different people, and it may look different to the same person at different times. Nelson Goodman shows why these differences are so important by placing the problem in the context of understanding art in general: artworks should not be thought of as separate and isolated from other artworks (or from nature or other artefacts).

Roland Barthes celebrates the plurality of meanings of what he calls 'a text'. A *work* is the work of someone, the artist; a text is not someone's (completed) work, but an opportunity for the *activity* of extracting meaning. Beardsley's anti-intentionalism was founded on a belief that meaning resided in 'the work itself'. Barthes's anti-intentionalism (he is, after all, responsible for the phrase 'the death of the author') is founded on his belief that texts are resistant to interpretation, so that understanding never achieves closure. Thus, Barthes places the responsibility on readers of texts (whether the texts be verbal, visual, auditory, or whatever) for creating meaning rather than seeing it as fixed by some supposed objective properties of 'the work itself'.

35 The Artist's Intention

The things that naturally come to mind when we think of works of art are the products of deliberate human activity, sometimes long and arduous—think of the Ceiling of the Sistine Chapel, *Elegy in a Country Churchyard*, *Wozzeck*, and the Cathedral at Chartres. To put it another way, these things were *intended* by someone, and no doubt they are largely what they were intended to be by those who made them.

The artist's intention is a series of psychological states or events in his mind: what he wanted to do, how he imagined or projected the work, before he began to make it and while he was in the process of making it. Something was going on in Chaucer's mind when he was planning *The Canterbury Tales* and in Beethoven's mind when he was considering various possible melodies for the choral finale of his *D Minor Symphony* (*No. 9*). And these happenings were no doubt among the factors that caused those works to come into being. One of the questions we can ask about any work, but probably not with much hope of a conclusive answer, is: What was its *cause*? And of course a good deal of writing about works of art consists in describing the historical situation, the social, economic and political conditions, under which they were produced—including the domestic affairs and physical health of the artist—in an attempt to explain, if possible, why they were created, and why they turned out the way they did. [...]

[T]hough I think there are good reasons to be doubtful of many explanations of particular works of art, or of general movements such as Romanticism, Impressionism, or the Baroque, this is presumably due to the complexity of the thing to be explained and to the scarcity of available evidence. It is a great field for half-baked speculation, which can often not be disproved and is thus allowed to stand. And perhaps this is why more critics concern themselves, not with the remoter antecedents of the work, but with its proximate or immediate cause in the mind of the artist. These are the critics who are fond of inquiring after the artist's *intention*.

Two sets of problems appear when we consider the connection between the aesthetic object and the artist's intention. One set of problems concerns the role of intention in *evaluating* the object; [...] The other concerns the role of intention in *describing* and *interpreting* the object: these we shall consider here. It is the simple thesis of this section that we must distinguish between the aesthetic object and the intention in the mind of its creator.

When you state the distinction that way, it seems harmless enough, and perfectly acceptable. Yet there are some rather serious and interesting difficulties about it, and we shall have to look into them. [...]

[. . .] [I]n the case of aesthetic object and intention, we have direct evidence of each: we discover the nature of the object by looking, listening, reading, etc., and we discover the intention by biographical inquiry, through letters, diaries, workbooks—or, if the artist is alive, by asking him. But also what we learn about the nature of the object itself is indirect evidence of what the artist intended it to be, and what we learn about the artist's intention is indirect evidence of what the object became. Thus, when we are concerned with the object itself, we should distinguish between internal and external evidence of its nature. Internal evidence is evidence from direct inspection of the object; external evidence is evidence from the psychological and social background of the object, from which we may infer something about the object itself.

Where internal and external evidence go hand in hand—for example, the painter writes in an exhibition catalogue that his painting is balanced in a precise and complicated way, and we go to the painting and see that it *is* so balanced—there is no problem. But where internal and external evidence conflict, as when a painter tells us one thing and our eyes tell us another, there is a problem, for we must decide between them. The problem is how to make this decision. If we consider the 'real' painting to be that which the painter projected in his mind, we shall go at it one way; if we consider the 'real' painting to be the one that is before us, open to public observation, we shall go at it another way.

We generally do not hesitate between these alternatives. As long as we stick to the simplest descriptive level, we are in no doubt; if a sculptor tells us that his statue was intended to be smooth and blue, but our senses tell us it is rough and pink, we go by our senses. We might, however, be puzzled by more subtle qualities of the statue. Suppose the sculptor tells us his statue was intended to be graceful and airy. We might look at it carefully and long, and not find it so. If the sculptor insists, we will give it a second look. But if we still cannot see those qualities, we conclude that they are not there; it would not occur to us to say they must be there, merely because the sculptor is convinced that he has put them there. Yet it is well known that our perceptions can be influenced by what we expect or hope to see, and especially by what we may be socially stigmatized for not seeing. Though no doubt the sculptor cannot talk us into perceiving red as blue, if his words have prestige—if we are already disposed to regard his intention as a final court of appeal—his words may be able to make us see grace where we would otherwise not see it, or a greater airiness than we would otherwise see. If this works on everyone, then everyone will see these qualities in the statue, and for all practical purposes they will be in the statue. Thus the intention, or the announcement of it, actually brings something to pass; what the statue is cannot be distinguished from what it is intended to be. So the argument might go.

But it is precisely this argument that presents a strong reason for not making intention the final court of appeal. [. . .] If a quality can be seen in a statue *only* by someone who already believes that it was intended by the sculptor to be there, then that quality is not in the statue at all. For what can be seen only by one who expects and hopes to see it is what we would call illusory by ordinary standards—like the strange woman in the crowd who momentarily looks like your wife.

When it comes to *interpreting* the statue, the situation is more complicated. Suppose the sculptor says his statue symbolizes Human Destiny. It is a large, twisted, cruller-shaped object of polished teak, mounted at an oblique angle to the floor. We look at it, and see in it no such symbolic meaning, even after we have the hint. Should we say that we have simply missed the symbolism, but that it must be there, since what a statue symbolizes is precisely what its maker makes it symbolize? Or should we say, in the spirit of Alice confronting the extreme semantical conventionalism of Humpty Dumpty, that the question is whether that object can be made to mean Human Destiny? If we take the former course, we are in effect saying that the nature of the object, as far as its meaning goes, cannot be distinguished from the artist's intention; if we take the latter course, we are saying it can. But the former course leads in the end to the wildest absurdity: anyone can make anything symbolize anything just by saying it does, for another sculptor could copy the same object and label it 'Spirit of Palm Beach, 1938.' [. . .]

This distinction [between aesthetic object and artist's intention] may seem oversubtle, but we shall find it of the highest importance, especially for those arts in which the distinction between object and intention seems most difficult, that is, the verbal arts. In literature, the distinction is most often erased by a principle that is explicitly defended by many critics, and tacitly assumed by many more: since a poem, in a sense, is what it means, to discover what the *poem* means is to discover what the *poet* meant. [. . .] At present we are concerned only with the possibility of the distinction between what words mean and what people mean.

Suppose someone utters a sentence. We can ask two questions: (1) What does the *speaker* mean? (2) What does the *sentence* mean? Now, if the speaker is awake and competent, no doubt the answers to these two questions will turn out to be the same. And for practical purposes, on occasions when we are not interested in the sentence except as a clue to what is going on in the mind of the speaker, we do not bother to distinguish the two questions. But suppose someone utters a particularly confused sentence that we can't puzzle out at all—he is trying to explain income tax exemptions, or the theory of games and economic behavior, and is doing a bad job. We ask him what he meant, and after a while he tells us in different words. Now we can reply, 'Maybe that's what you meant but it's not what you said,' that is, it's not what the sentence meant. And here we clearly make the distinction.

For what the sentence means depends not on the whim of the individual, and his mental vagaries, but upon public conventions of usage that are tied up with habit patterns in the whole speaking community. It is perhaps easy to see this in the case of an ambiguous sentence. A man says, 'I like my secretary better than my wife'; we raise our eyebrows, and inquire: 'Do you mean that you like her better than you like your wife?' And he replies, 'No, you misunderstand me; I mean I like her better than my wife does.' Now, in one sense he has cleared up the misunderstanding, he has told us what he meant. Since what he meant is still not what the first sentence succeeded in meaning, he hasn't made the original sentence any less ambiguous than it was; he has merely substituted for it a better, because unambiguous, one.

Now let us apply this distinction to a specific problem in literary criticism. On the occasion of Queen Victoria's Golden Jubilee, A. E. Housman published his poem '1887.' The poem refers to celebrations going on all over England. 'From Clee to Heaven the beacon burns,' because 'God has saved the Queen.' It recalls that there were many lads who went off to fight for the Empire, who 'shared the work with God,' but 'themselves they could not save,' and ends with the words,

> Get you the sons your fathers got,
> And God will save the Queen.[1]

Frank Harris quoted the last stanza to Housman, in a bitterly sarcastic tone, and praised the poem highly: 'You have poked fun at the whole thing and made splendid mockery of it.' But this reading of the poem, especially coming from a radical like Harris, made Housman angry:

I never intended to poke fun, as you call it, at patriotism, and I can find nothing in the sentiment to make mockery of: I meant it sincerely; if Englishmen breed as good men as their fathers, then God will save the Queen. I can only reject and resent your—your truculent praise.[2]

We may put the question, then, in this form: Is Housman's poem, and particularly its last stanza, ironic? The issue can be made fairly sharp. There are two choices: (1) We can say that the meaning of the poem, including its irony or lack of it, is precisely what the author intended it to be. Then any evidence of the intention will automatically be evidence of what the poem is: the poem is ironic if Housman says so. He is the last court of appeal, for it is his poem. (2) Or we can distinguish between the meaning of the poem and the author's intention. Of course, we must admit that in many cases an author may be a good reader of his own poem, and he may help us to see things in it that we have overlooked. But at the same time, he is not necessarily the best reader of his poem, and indeed he misconstrues it when, as perhaps in Housman's case, his unconscious guides his pen more than his consciousness can admit. And if his report of what the poem is intended to mean conflicts with the evidence of the poem itself, we cannot allow him to *make* the poem mean what he wants it to mean, just by fiat. So in this case we would have the poem read by competent critics, and if they found irony in it, we should conclude that it is ironical, no matter what Housman says.

[*Aesthetics: Problems in the Philosophy of Criticism* (New York: Harcourt, Brace & World, 1958), 17–21, 24–6.]

STEPHEN DAVIES

36 Authenticity in Musical Performance

In this paper I discuss musical performances and their authenticity with respect to the independently identifiable musical pieces of which they are performances. I intend my account to be descriptive rather than prescriptive (but I appreciate that, where intuitions clash, it is the location of the border between description and prescription which is at issue).

The adjective 'authentic' has a number of meanings which no doubt are related. But I am not here interested in the unity of the concept, nor with the relative primacy of these different meanings. Nor shall I discuss one familiar notion of musical authenticity—that in which a performance is authentic with respect to a style or *genre*. My limited interest is in the authenticity of musical performances *as* performances of particular compositions (which are independently identified with event-specifications which, in the case of the Western cultural tradition on which I shall concentrate, take the form of musical scores). That is, if I talk of the authenticity of a performance of Beethoven's Fifth Symphony, I am interested in its authenticity as a member of the class of performances recognizable as performance of Beethoven's Fifth Symphony and not with it as a member of other classes of performances to which it may also belong, such as nineteenth-century symphony.

The view for which I argue characterizes authenticity in musical performance as follows: a performance which aims to realize the composer's score faithfully in sound may be judged for authenticity. A performance of X is more rather than less authentic the more faithful it is to the intentions publicly expressed in the score by the composer (where those intentions are determinative and not merely recommendatory of performance practice). Because the composer's score under-determines the sound of a faithful performance, the authenticity of any particular performance is judged against (the appropriate member/s of) a set of ideally faithful performances. As a commendatory term 'authentic' is used to acknowledge the creative role of the performer in realizing faithfully the composer's specifications. [. . .]

In this first section I argue that the pursuit of authenticity involves the attempt to produce musical *sounds* as opposed to the social *milieu* within which those sounds originally were created.

Over the past fifty years there has been a growing interest in authenticity in musical performance. The same period also has seen a developing interest in the performance of pre-modern music. These parallel developments probably are related. Where modern music is written for modern instruments and notated in the standard fashion, a high degree of authenticity will be achieved in performance by a competent musician. But the more foreign the styles of performance and the more unfamiliar the instruments employed, the harder will it be for musicians to produce authentic performances without the benefit of scholarly advice and instruction.

A moment's reflection shows that the pursuit of authenticity in musical performance has been highly selective. The price of admission, the dress of the audience, the method by which the programme is printed—each of these and much else in the context in which music is performed is decidedly modern. The search for musical authenticity takes a very particular direction. A highly authentic performance is likely to be one in which instruments contemporary to the period of composition (or replicas of such instruments) are used in its performance, in which the score is interpreted in the light of stylistic practices and performance conventions of the time when the work was composed, in which ensembles of the same size and disposition as accord with the composer's specification are employed, and so forth.

The selectivity displayed in the search for authenticity in musical performance has been systematic in a way which suggests that the quest may be characterized as aiming at the production of a particular *sound*, rather than at the production of, for example, the social ambience within which the music would or could be presented by the composer's contemporaries. This point is effectively illustrated as follows: orchestral music composed in the latter half of the eighteenth century might standardly have been performed in wood-panelled rooms. Nowadays such works would be performed in concert halls. Modern concert halls are designed with modifiable acoustics, the adjustments being made by the use of baffles etc. In performing music of the period in question, the acoustics of the concert hall would be set with a reverberation period such as one might find in a wood-panelled room containing a small audience. Although the music now is performed in a large hall in front of a large audience, the acoustic properties of the modern building are so arranged that they duplicate the acoustic properties of the sort of room in which the music would have been performed in the composer's day. Now, whilst one might prefer the intimacy of music performed in salons I take it that it will be accepted that the use of concert halls which reproduce the acoustic properties of wood-panelled rooms would be considered not *merely* as an adequate compromise between the demands of authenticity and, say, economic considerations, but, instead, would be accepted as a full-blooded attempt at authentic performance.[1] That modern acoustic technology might serve the aim of authenticity in this way suggests strongly that musical authenticity aims at the creation of a particular sound and not at the production of a particular visual, social, or other effect.

Some performances are less authentic for being given in buildings other than that for which the work was written, but this is true only of performances of works written with an ear to the unique acoustic properties of a particular building. That is, it is true of performances of Stravinsky's *Canticum Sacrum* and of many works by Andrea and Giovanni Gabrieli which were written for San Marco in Venice, and it is not true of Verdi's *Aïda* which was written for the opera house in Cairo, because, whereas the acoustics of the opera house in Cairo are not distinctively different from those of other opera houses, the acoustics of San Marco are unlike those of other buildings. These examples do not count against the point that a concern with the authenticity of a performance is a concern with its sound.

In this second section I suggest that one might best hope to make a performance authentic by recreating the musical sound of a performance which might have been heard by the composer's contemporaries. (Why this is a formula for success is a matter considered in the next section.) I also argue that the sound to which an authentic performance aspires is that of a possible, rather than an actual, performance; that is, authenticity in musical performance is judged against an ideal.

So far I have said that a performance is more or less authentic in a way which depends upon its sound. One might ask—the sound of what? A musical work comprises notes and relationships between them, so an authentic performance of a given work must be a performance which concerns itself with producing the notes which comprise the work. The sound of an authentic performance will be the sound of those notes.

But it is not easy to specify the set of notes which comprise a given work. The notes recorded in the score often are not the notes which the performer should play; frequently there are conventions known both to composers and performers governing the ways in which the written notes are to be modified (for example by accidentals or embellishment). So an interest in discrepancies between that which is written and that which is conventionally to be played is of practical and not merely scholarly significance. Debates about the problems of *musica ficta* in music written pre-1600 reflect strongly a desire to achieve authentic performances of the music in question.

Even where the conventions by which the score is to be read are known, it is not a straightforward matter always to say which notes should be played. Consider music written at about the end of the seventeenth century when pitches were as much as a minor third lower than now. The modern performer might play the work at the modern pitch level, but vocal and wind parts will then sound strained even if sung or played brilliantly and correctly. Or the performer might tune down modern instruments, as a result of which their tone will suffer, or transpose orchestral parts, in which case the sound is affected by alterations in fingerings and *embouchure*, by changes in register, by shifts to harmonics etc. In view of such difficulties it is understandable that performers have turned to the use of instruments from the period of composition, or to replicas of such instruments, so that vocal and instrumental parts 'lie' comfortably to the voice and hands. The use of such instruments is justified ultimately by the resulting sound of the performance.

However, despite the use of instruments and the appeal to musical conventions from the time of composition, clearly it is inadequate to characterize authenticity in musical performance in terms of the sound heard by the composer's contemporaries. His or her contemporaries could perform the work in question in ways which were relatively inauthentic. Typically this would occur where the performance contained wrong notes or where the composer's specifications were misrepresented in some other way. Probably the musicians who sight-read the overture to *Don Giovanni* from orchestral parts on which the ink was still wet gave a performance which was not as authentic as it could have been. Since the performances heard by the composer's contemporaries often were less authentic than was possible, authenticity in musical performance cannot be defined in terms of the sounds actually heard by the composer's contemporaries. This suggests that, in striving for authenticity, the performer aims at an *ideal* sound rather than at the sound of some actual, former performance.

In this third section I consider the relevance of the composer's intentions in an assessment of the authenticity of a performance of the composer's work. I suggest that only those intentions which conventionally are accepted as determinative are relevant to judgements of authenticity; other of the composer's intentions or wishes might be ignored in an ideally authentic performance. Because the composer's determinative intentions under-determine the sound of an ideally authentic performance of his or her work, there is a set of ideal performances (and not any single ideal performance) in terms of which the relative authenticity of actual performances is judged.

There are conventions in terms of which musical scores are to be read. The composer is able to express his or her intentions in a musical notation only because the conventions for realizing in sound that notation are known both to the composer and to the performer of the day. Those conventions provide not only a vehicle for, but also a limitation on, the intentions which may be expressed in the score. Not all of the intentions which the conventions allow to be expressed are determinative of that which can be required in the name of authenticity. Non-determinative intentions (as expressed in the score or in other ways) have the status of recommendations. I take it that exact metronome indications are non-determinative in that tempo may be varied to suit the performance conditions. Both the composer and the performing musician who is his or her contemporary are familiar with the conventions usually and know which of the expressed intentions are determinative and which are not determinative of that at which an authentic performance must aim.

The conventions by which musical scores are to be read change over time in ways which affect that which the composer may determine with respect to the performer's attempt to produce an authentic performance. Phrasing was not notationally determined in the early seventeenth century, but was notationally determined by the nineteenth century. At some time, before the convention was established, composers notated phrasings which would have been understood rightly as recommendations for, rather than as determinative of, what should be played. At that time the composer's indications of phrasing might be disregarded without any diminution in the authenticity of the performance (although the performance may have been less good as a result on other grounds). (Sometimes these changes in convention arise from composers' rebelling against the existing conventions, but such rebellions reject only a few conventions at any one time and do so against a wider background of accepted conventions.) Because conventions of determinativeness change through time, the conventions appropriate to the authentic performance of a score are those with which the composer would have taken musicians *of the day* to be familiar. It is this fact which explains that which I have emphasized in the previous section—that an attempt at an authentic performance is likely to be successful by aiming to recreate the sound of an accurate performance by the composer's contemporaries.

Sometimes it is possible to infer from what is written in the score that the composer would have preferred to write something else had the instruments or the performers been capable of accommodating his or her intentions. For example, a sequential pattern might be interrupted by an octave transposition where a continuation of the pattern would have exceeded the singer's or the instrument's range. In these cases it is appropriate to talk of the composer's wishes (rather than intentions). Sometimes nowadays, with the wider range of some instruments and the greater proficiency of many musicians, these wishes could be realized and there would be a musical point to doing so. However, such wishes have no more a bearing on the authenticity of a performance than do the composer's non-determinative intentions. Both the work and the performance may be better for the modification, but not because the alteration makes the performance more authentic. If it were accepted that mere wishes could set the standards of authenticity, it would also be accepted that many works could not have been performed authentically by the composer's contemporaries and some could not be performed authentically at all.

Clearly, in taking the line that I have, I must deny that authenticity in musical performance is judged against the *sound* of some particular performance which was envisaged by the composer. I have said that not all of the composer's expressed intentions are determinative of that which must be accurately rendered in an ideally authentic performance, in which case I must also hold that the sound of an ideally authentic performance is underdetermined by the intentions in terms of which its authenticity is judged. The way in which we talk of authenticity favours my view, I claim, rather than the view that authenticity is measured against the *sound* of a performance which the composer had in mind. First, in reaching judgments about the authenticity of performances we do not seem to face the epistemological difficulties which would inevitably arise if the standard for authenticity was a sound which may never have been realized. Second, rather than taking composers' performances as definitive models which performers are obliged to copy slavishly, we take them to be revealing of what we expect to be an interesting interpretation. In a performance the composer may make his or her intentions as regards the *sound* of a performance more explicit than could be done in the score, but that which is made explicit is not thereby made definitive. Other performers are left with the job of interpreting the score for themselves. Third, we would not (as we do) accept that *different-sounding* performances of a single work might be equally and ideally authentic if authenticity were judged against the sound of a *particular* performance imagined by the composer. It is (a member of) a *set* of ideal performances against which the authenticity of an actual performance is judged.

This last point deserves emphasis. Because an ideally authentic performance faithfully preserves the composer's determinative intentions, and because those intentions under-determine the sound of a faithful performance, different-sounding performances may be equally and ideally authentic. [. . .] As long as two performances are faithful to the score and are consistent with the performance practices in terms of which it is to be rendered, they may be equally authentic whilst sounding different. Compare, for example, performances of Beethoven's symphonies as conducted by Klemperer and Toscanini, both of whom have been praised as interpreters of the works. Klemperer tends to take the pieces at the slowest tempo consistent with Beethoven's instructions and he emphasizes the structural qualities of the music so that, for example, climaxes at relatively weak structural points receive less weight than do those in structurally important places, even where the dynamics are the same in both places. Toscanini takes the works at a brisk tempo and concentrates on the drama or beauty of each individual passage, investing every note and phrase with its full potential of power. Without Klemperer's staid approach, the grandeur and architectonic qualities of Beethoven's music could not be presented. Without Toscanini's volatile approach, the dynamism and verve of Beethoven's music could not be appreciated. So, the ideally authentic performance has no *particular* sound because it is no *particular* performance. Rather, the standard against which the authenticity of performances of a work is judged comprises a *set* of perform-ances each of which is faithful to the composer's determinative intentions.

In view of the above I offer the following account: a performance will be more rather than less authentic if it successfully (re)creates the sound of a performance of the work in question as could be given by good musicians playing good instruments under good conditions (of rehearsal time etc.), where 'good' is relativized to the best of what was known by the composer to be available at the time, whether or not those resources were available for the composer's use. [. . .]

In this fifth section I consider the way in which authenticity in musical performance is valued. I suggest that, although such authenticity would not be valued were it not a means to an independently valued end—the end of presenting the composer's interesting musical ideas—nevertheless, authenti-city in musical performance is not valued *as* a means to this end.

Beyond the level of an acceptably competent performance, authenticity is value-conferring. That is, a musical performance is better for its being more authentic (other things being equal). Because we have an aesthetic concern with the musical interest of the composer's ideas, and because those musical ideas must be mediated by performance, we value authenticity in perform-ance for the degree of faithfulness with which the performance realizes the composer's musical conception as recorded in the score. I am not maintaining that authenticity in performance takes its value from the worth of the musical content contributed by the composer. Rather, my point is this: were it not for the fact that composers set out to write aesthetically rewarding works, and were it not for the fact that they are usually successful in this, we would not value authenticity in musical performances as we do. But, in any particular instance, authenticity in performance is valued independently and irrespec-tive of the aesthetic value of the work itself. A performance is better for a higher degree of authenticity (other things being equal) *whatever* the merits of the composition itself. A performance praiseworthy for its authenticity may make evident that the composer wrote a work with little musical interest or merit. It is the creative skill required of the performer in faithfully interpret-ing the composer's score which is valued in praising the authenticity of performances of that score.

Of course, authenticity is not the only quality for which a performance might be valued. Where a relatively inauthentic performance is highly valued, it is valued *in spite of* its inauthenticity. Thus Schnabel's recorded perform-ances of the Beethoven sonatas are well regarded despite the wrong notes that they contain.

['Authenticity in Musical Performance', *British Journal of Aesthetics*, 27 (1987), 39–45, 47.]

37 Criticism as Retrieval

It is a deficiency of at least the English language that there is no single word, applicable over all the arts, for the process of coming to understand a particular work of art. To make good this deficiency I shall appropriate the word 'criticism', but in doing so I know that, though this concurs with the way the word is normally used in connection with, say, literature, it violates usage in, at any rate, the domain of the visual arts, where 'criticism' is the name of a purely evaluative activity.

The central question to be asked of criticism is, What does it do? How is a piece of criticism to be assessed, and what determines whether it is adequate? To my mind the best brief answer, of which this essay will offer an exposition and a limited defence, is, Criticism is *retrieval*. The task of criticism is the reconstruction of the creative process, where the creative process must in turn be thought of as something not stopping short of, but terminating on, the work of art itself. The creative process reconstructed, or retrieval complete, the work is then open to understanding.

To the view advanced, that criticism is retrieval, several objections are raised.

1. The first objection is that, by and large, this view makes criticism impossible: and this is so because, except in exceptional circumstances, it is beyond the bounds of practical possibility to reconstruct the creative process.

Any argument to any such conclusion makes use of further premises either about the nature of knowledge and its limits, or about the nature of the mind and its inaccessibility—and the character of these further premises comes out in the precise way the conclusion is formulated or how it is qualified. For, though an extreme form of the objection would be that the creative process can never be reconstructed, the conclusion is likelier to take some such form as that criticism is impossible unless the critic and the artist are one and the same person, or the work was created in the ambience of the critic, or the creative process was fully, unambiguously, and contemporaneously documented by the artist. This is not the place to assess the general philosophical theses of scepticism or solipsism, or their variants, but it is worth observing that these theses ought not to be credited with greater force outside general philosophy than they are inside it. The observation is called for, because traditionally philosophers of art permit the creative process, or, more broadly, the mental life of artists, to give rise to epistemological problems of an order that they would not sanction in inquiry generally.

These difficulties apart, the objection in its present form offers a persuasive rather than a conclusive argument against the retrieval view. For maybe the truth is that criticism *is* a practical impossibility, or is so outside very favoured circumstances. But sometimes the objection is stated to stronger effect, and then an incompatibility is asserted between the sceptical or solipsistic premisses, however framed, and not just the practice of criticism as retrieval but the view that criticism is retrieval.

A step further, and [. . .] an alternative view of criticism follows. This alternative view may be expressed as, Criticism is *revision*, and it holds that the task of criticism is so to interpret the work that it says most to the critic there and then. Assuming the critical role, we must make the work of art speak 'to us, today'.

[. . .] One thing seems certain, though it is often ignored by adherents of the revisionary view, and that is this: If criticism is justifiably revision when we lack the necessary evidence for reconstructing the creative process, then it must also be revision when we have, if we ever do, adequate evidence for retrieval. We cannot as critics be entitled to make the work of art relate to us when we are in a state of ignorance about its history without our having an obligation to do so, and this obligation must continue to hold in the face of knowledge. Otherwise revision is never a critical undertaking: it is only, sometimes, a *pis-aller*, or a second best to criticism. Indeed, the strongest case for the revisionary view of criticism draws support from a thesis which appears to dispense with scepticism or, at any rate, cuts across it.

The thesis I have in mind, which is generally called 'radical historicism' and is best known through the advocacy of Eliot, holds that works of art actually change their meaning over history. On this thesis the task of the critic at any given historical moment is not so much to impose a new meaning upon, as to extract the new meaning from, the work of art. That works of art are semantically mobile in this way is to be explained not simply—to take the case of a literary work—by reference to linguistic change or to shifts in the meaning of words and idioms, but, more fundamentally, more radically, by appeal to the way in which every new work of art rewrites to some degree or other every related, or maybe every known, work of art in the same tradition. To this central contention the thesis adds the corollary that, as some particular meaning of a work of art becomes invalid or obsolete, it also becomes inaccessible: it ceases to be a possible object of knowledge.

Radical historicism is a doctrine, like the Whorfian thesis about the non-intertranslatability of natural languages, with which indeed it has much in common, that has its greatest appeal when it gets us to imagine something which on reflection turns out to be just what it asserts is unimaginable. So, for instance, under the influence of radical historicism (or so it seems) we start to imagine how a contemporary of Shakespeare's would find the inherited reading of Chaucer's *Troilus* dull or dead, and we find ourselves readily sympathizing with his preference for a new revitalized reading inspired by *Troilus and Cressida*. And then we reflect that, if radical historicism is indeed true, just such a comparison was not open to one of Shakespeare's contemporaries, and is even less so to us. To him only one term to the comparison was accessible: to us neither is.

2. A second objection to the retrieval view of criticism goes deeper in that it concentrates upon the view itself and not merely upon its consequences. According to this objection, retrieval is, from the critical point of view, on any given occasion either misleading or otiose. From the outset the objection contrasts retrieval with its own favoured view of criticism, which may be expressed as, Criticism is *scrutiny*—scrutiny of the literary text, of the musical score, of the painted surface—and it holds that retrieval is misleading when its results deviate from the findings of scrutiny and it is otiose when its results concur with the findings of scrutiny. [. . .]

[. . .] Suppose we confine ourselves [. . .] to that part of the creative process which is realized in the work of art. It becomes clear that there is something that reconstruction of this part of the process can bring to light which scrutiny of the corresponding part of the work cannot. It can show that that part of the work which came about through design did indeed come about through design and not through accident or error. Scrutiny, which *ex hypothesi* limits itself to the outcome, cannot show this. (A parallel in the philosophy of action: If an action is intentional, then, it might be thought, reconstruction of the agent's mental process will not tell us more about it than we could learn from observation of the action: but we can learn this from observation of the action only if we already or independently know that the action is intentional.) Accordingly—and as yet the point can be made only hypothetically—if criticism is concerned to find out not just what the work of art is like but what the work is like by design, then, contrary to what the objection asserts, scrutiny, to be a source of knowledge, must presuppose retrieval. [. . .]

[. . .] [T]he objection, in claiming that scrutiny can establish everything that at one and the same time is critically relevant and can be established by retrieval, totally misconceives the nature of the interest that criticism might take in the creative process and, therefore, what it stands to gain from reconstructing it. For the objection appears to assume that, if the critic is interested in the creative process, this is because, or is to be accounted for by the degree to which, it provides him with good evidence for the character of the work. The critic seeks to infer from how the work was brought about how it is. Now, of course, if this were so, then there would, on the face of it at any rate, be reason to think that retrieval was at best a detour to a destination to which scrutiny could be a short cut. But that this is a misconception is revealed by the fact that the critic committed to retrieval is not committed to any assumptions about the likely degree of match between the creative process and the resultant work and he will continue to be interested in the creative process even in the case when he knows that there is a mismatch between the two. The critic who tries to reconstruct the creative process has a quite different aim from that which the objection to the retrieval view assumes. He does so in order to understand the work of art—though it would be wrong to say, as some philosophers of art tend to, that he seeks understanding rather than description. Understanding is reached through description, but through profound description, or description profounder than scrutiny can provide, and such description may be expected to include such issues as how much of the character of the work is by design, how much has come about through changes of intention, and what were the ambitions that went to its making but were not realized in the final product. [. . .]

Crucially the view that criticism is scrutiny is seriously under-defined until an answer is given to the question, Scrutiny by whom? The following cases illustrate the problem: The listener who is ignorant of the mission of Christ will miss much of the pathos in the St Matthew Passion: a viewer who has not gathered that Bernini's mature sculpture requires a frontal point of view, as opposed to the multiple viewpoint against which it reacted, will fail to discern the emotional immediacy it aims at: a reader's response to Hardy's 'At Castle Boterel' will be modified when he learns that the poet's wife had just died, and then it will be modified again as he learns how unhappy the marriage had been: the spectator who is made aware that in the relevant panel of the S. Francesco altarpiece Sassetta uses to paint the cloak that the Saint discards, thereby renouncing his inheritance, the most expensive and most difficult pigment available will come to recognize a drama first in the gesture, then in the picture as a whole, of which he had been previously ignorant. With any form of perception—and scrutiny is a form of perception—what is perceptible is always dependent not only upon such physical factors as the nature of the stimulus, the state of the organism, and the prevailing local conditions, but also upon cognitive factors. Accordingly, the scrutiny view needs to be filled out by a definition of the person whose scrutiny is authoritative, or 'the ideal critic', and any such definition must be partly in terms of the cognitive stock upon which the critic can draw. There are a number of possible definitions, for each of which the appeal of the scrutiny view, as well as its right to go by that name, will vary.

A heroic proposal, deriving from Kant, the aim of which is to ensure the democracy of art, is to define the ideal critic as one whose cognitive stock is empty, or who brings to bear upon the work of art zero knowledge, beliefs, and concepts. The proposal has, however, little to recommend it except its aim. It is all but impossible to put into practice, and, if it could be, it would lead to critical judgments that would be universally unacceptable. [. . .]

[Another] proposal is to define the cognitive stock on which the ideal critic is entitled to draw by reference not to its source of origin but to its function. Whether or not the beliefs have been derived, or could have been derived, from scrutiny is now reckoned immaterial, and the requirement is only that they should contribute to scrutiny. Now, it is true that most beliefs capable of modifying our perception of a work of art are beliefs that, given appropriate

background beliefs, could have been derived from perception of the work—
or, at any rate, of some other related work by the same artist. Nevertheless,
there are some beliefs of this kind that could not have been, they need to be
acquired independently, and the novelty of the present proposal is that it says
that these too are available to the ideal critic. Examples of beliefs that could
not be gleaned from, yet could contribute to, perception of works of art are
the following: That Palladio believed that the ancient temple evolved from
the ancient house and therefore thought temple fronts appropriate facades for
private villas; that Mozart's favourite instruments were the clarinet and the
viola; that Franz Hals was destitute and in a state of total dependence upon
the Regents and Regentesses of the Old Men's Almshouses in Haarlem when
he painted their two great group-portraits; that the Athenian Geometric vase-
painters who introduced lions on to their pots could never have seen such an
animal; and that Titian painted the altar piece of *St Peter Martyr* in competition with Pordenone and wanted to outdo him in dramatic gesture.

However it is important to see that a shift has just occurred in the
argument. It is not plausible to regard the new proposal as, like the first two,
operating within the scope of the scrutiny view in that it imposes a substantive restriction upon the cognitive stock that the critic may draw upon in
scrutiny. For that a belief on which criticism is based should be capable of
modifying perception is a minimal condition if the resultant criticism is to
count as scrutiny. Accordingly, we need another way of taking the proposal,
and one that suggests itself is to see it as proposing scrutiny as a restriction
upon retrieval. In other words, reconstruction of the creative process is
admitted as the, or at least a, central task of criticism, but it must have a
purpose in mind, and that purpose is that its findings should be put to use in
scrutinizing the work. Retrieval is legitimate because, but only in so far as,
through its findings it contributes to perception.

But with this change in direction the question must be asked: Is this new
thesis legitimate? Does it impose an acceptable constraint upon retrieval? Are
the only facts about a work of art that are critically relevant those which
modify, or could modify, our perception of it?

Standardly this question is raised, and the thesis tested, in a special and
highly artificial context, and, unless great care is taken, the very artificiality of
the context can seriously distort the answer we give. The context is that of the
'perfect forgery'. Let us suppose that there are two paintings, one by
Rembrandt, the other a forgery of it, and they are perceptually indistinguishable. Now, *ex hypothesi* the facts of authorship cannot modify our perception
of either painting. In this case, are they not critically irrelevant, and critically
irrelevant for just this reason?

[. . .] Is it so clear that in such a case the belief that one painting is a forgery
of the other cannot modify our perception of either? What the supposition of
the perfect forgery brings out is an important ambiguity in the thesis under

test. For there are two different ways in which an item in a critic's cognitive stock could be said to influence his perception of a work of art. It could affect what he perceives in a work—belief might make him sensitive to something he would otherwise have missed, like the anamorphic skull in Holbein's *Ambassadors*, or the use that Manet makes of the man's reflection in the *Bar aux Folies-Bergères* to inculpate the spectator in the man's sexual advances—or it could affect how he perceives the work. Consideration suggests that it cannot be only the first way that secures critical relevance for a belief: the second way must too. Part of coming to understand a work of art is learning how to perceive it, where this is over and above taking perceptual account of everything that is there to see. Now, there is nothing in the supposition of the perfect forgery to eliminate *ex hypothesi* influence of the critic's belief about the authorship of the paintings upon how he sees the two paintings. All that the supposition eliminates is the influence of this belief—indeed of any belief—upon what he sees in the paintings: because there is nothing to be seen in the paintings which corresponds directly to the difference of author-ship or to the fact that one is a forgery of the other. [. . .]

But there is a more fundamental objection to the thesis under test, and this the supposition does not bring out. Indeed, it helps to obscure it. For what the thesis presupposes is an unduly atomistic conception of criticism. Certainly, in seeking to understand a particular work of art, we try to grasp it in its particularity, and so we concentrate on it as hard as we can: but at the same time we are trying to build up an overall picture of art, and so we relate the work to other works and to art itself. Nearly everything that we learn about the work that is critically relevant contributes to both projects. But there could be some information about a work that is of critical value but con-tributes only to the second project. It is arguable that, if the supposition of the perfect forgery has any theoretical value, just what it should show us is that there are concepts which have a fundamental role to play in organizing our experience of art—in this case, the concepts of autograph and forgery—but which might, in certain special and altogether insulated circumstances, have no influence upon our perception of individual works of art. [. . .]

All objections apart, and I shall consider no more, the retrieval view invites, in one significant respect, clarification. For the arguments that I have been considering for and against the view that the creative process is the proper critical object bear a close resemblance to arguments advanced of recent years for and against the critical relevance of the artist's intentions. It, therefore, seems appropriate to ask, How are the creative process (as I have introduced it) and the artist's intention (as it figures in recent debate) related?

The creative process, as I envisage it, is a more inclusive phenomenon than the artist's intentions, and in two ways. In the first place, the creative process includes the various vicissitudes to which the artist's intentions are subject. Some of these will be themselves intentional—change of mind—but some will be chance or uncontrolled. Secondly, the creative process includes the many background beliefs, conventions, and modes of artistic production against which the artist forms his intentions: amongst these will be current aesthetic norms, innovations in the medium, rules of decorum, ideological or scientific world-pictures, current systems of symbolism or prosody, physiognomic conventions, and the state of the tradition.

A consequence follows which is of major importance for the process of retrieval. In recording an artist's intention the critic must state it from the artist's point of view or in terms to which the artist could give conscious or unconscious recognition. The critic must concur with the artist's intentionality. But the reconstruction of the creative process is not in general similarly restrained. The critic must certainly respect the artist's intentionality, but he does not have to concur with it. On the contrary he is justified in using both theory and hindsight unavailable to the artist if thereby he can arrive at an account of what the artist was doing that is maximally explanatory. Retrieval, like archaeology, and archaeology provides many of the metaphors in which retrieval is best thought about, is simultaneously an investigation into past reality and an exploitation of present resources. Anachronism arises not when the critic characterizes the past in terms of his own day, but only when in doing so he falsifies it. There is no anachronism involved in tracing the *Virgin and Child with St Anne* to Leonardo's Oedipal strivings, or in describing Adolf Loos as bridging the gap between C. F. A. Voysey and Le Corbusier—if, that is, both these statements are true. In *Art and Its Objects*, I have said that the constant possibility of reinterpretation is one of the sources of art's continuing interest for us, and I stand by this. [...]

A question remains: Is a limit set to retrieval? Obviously where evidence is lacking, our understanding stops short. The 30,000 years or so of Palaeolithic art must remain ultimately a mystery to us, short of a landslide victory for archaeology. We shall probably never know the authentic rhythm or phrasing of medieval plainsong. But are there cases where both retrieval is impossible (or barely possible—for it must be conceded that, like the creative process itself, reconstruction of the creative process is realizable to varying degrees) and the explanation lies in a radical difference of perspective between the artist and us, the interpreters?

I suspect that there are, and an analogy gives us an insight into the situation. For an outward parallel to the reconstruction of the creative process is provided, at any rate in the case of the visual arts, by the physical restoration of the work of art. Admirers of French romanesque architecture, well aware that originally a great deal of the sculpture that adorns such buildings would have been brightly painted, are nevertheless likely, when confronted with attempts to restore it to its original condition—for instance, the historiated capitals at Issoire—to deplore the result. The heavy hand of the restorer is partly to blame, but not totally. For the modern spectator there seems to be no way of getting anything like the original colours to make anything like the intended impact upon him. We might restate the point in terms of the present discussion and say that he seems powerless to reconstruct the creative process in a way that at once meets the demands of internal coherence and seems naturally to terminate on the work before him. Maybe he can do so computationally but he cannot internalize the result, and the consequence is that here we may have reached the limits of retrieval.

In such an eventuality the restorer may resort to a compromise. He may hit on a colour scheme that is acceptable to our eyes and is functionally equivalent to the original scheme. Similarly a musicologist may orchestrate Monteverdi's madrigals for modern instruments and we may listen to them in a comfortable concert hall. Or a clever modern producer may present Antigone as a political drama about women's rights, or relate *The Merchant of Venice* to twentieth-century central European anti-Semitic rhetoric. Any such attempt will be to varying degrees anachronistic. Some of the great art of the past is accessible to us, some is not. When it is accessible, we should, surely, wish to retrieve it. But when it is not, or when it is retrievable only to an inadequate degree, we may be wise to settle for a counterpart. Either way round, it is better that we know what we are doing.

['Criticism as Retrieval', in *Art and its Objects*, 2nd edn. (Cambridge: Cambridge University Press, 1980), 185–95, 197–204.]

MICHAEL BAXANDALL

38 Truth and Other Cultures

1. *Cultural Difference*

For some time two related issues have been hanging around this discussion of intention. One is the question of how far we are really going to penetrate into the intentional fabric of painters living in cultures or periods remote from our own. The other is the question of whether we can in any sense or degree verify or validate our explanations. I shall discuss these in order. But it will be better to work to an example culturally more distant from us than Picasso or even Chardin, and I shall return now to Piero della Francesca's *Baptism of Christ*. This is the central panel, five and a half feet high, from a fairly small altarpiece now dispersed. It was painted for a church in Borgo Sansepolcro, Piero's native town, around 1450, plus or minus a dozen years. Most, not all, experts have dated it on the basis of style early in Piero's career, not long after 1440; I agree with them, but it need not become a matter for debate here.

What is obvious is that the broad Brief Piero della Francesca took from mid-fifteenth-century Sansepolcro was [...] a Brief to address [...] central

Italian painting of about 1425–50. [. . .] Piero painted such pictures to order, within the terms of a legal contract, and he painted them for men with complicated fifteenth-century needs embodied in subtly and implicitly defined fifteenth-century genres. The generic demands in 1450 were very different. Not to multiply too much, the picture falls into three preliminary main classes: (1) it is an altarpiece picture; (2) it is a picture of the Baptism of Christ; (3) it is a picture by Piero della Francesca. All three would have been stipulated by the client. The contract for this picture does not survive, but that for a similar format picture by Piero contracted for in Sansepolcro in 1445 does, and it is specific about the painting being an altarpiece, that the subject-matter agreed is to be followed by Piero, and that no painter may put his hand to the brush other than Piero himself.

To take at this point only the first—'altarpiece'—it is not, in the sense it had then, a category of our own time. What did it mean? It meant, first, a religious image—a sensitive class of thing that had three canonical functions: to narrate scripture clearly, to arouse appropriate feeling about the narrated matter, and to impress that matter on the memory. But an altarpiece is a specialized religious image: it stands on the altar, the table of the Lord. It is very immediately present at the administration of the Mass and dignifies the Mensa on which the sacrament is conducted. It has less freedom than some picture in a fresco cycle on a chapel wall or in a devotional book and it is present as a focus for the mind at the most important moment of devotion. Yet it can also have a secular tinge. An altarpiece of the moderate size of this panel would have been on a side-altar in a church, furnished by some individual parishioner or family or confraternity. There are many indications that such donors wanted their gifts to God to be publicly worthy of them, as well as of God. Indeed, one reason for stipulating that the picture be by Piero della Francesca, the best-known painter of the town, would be the desire to be done proud. For the moment, to summarize, let us say simply that it is implicit in the genre 'altarpiece' that the picture be among other things a clear, moving, memorable, sacramental, creditable representation of its subject.

But if we posit cultural difference with any seriousness at all, we are likely to go beyond the Brief and postulate basic differences in cognitive and reflective disposition: it is to be supposed that both Piero and his customers perceived pictures and thought about pictures differently from us, in that their culture equipped them with different visual experience and skill and different conceptual structures. What was offered to Piero *en troc* was a range of facilities different from those offered in Paris in 1730 or 1910, or in London or Berkeley now.

Cultures do not impose uniform cognitive and reflective equipment on individuals. People differ in occupational experiences, for example. A medical man perceives a human body differently from the rest of us: he has learned certain kinds of alertness and discrimination and he has terms and categories to help him with many of them. The Paduan doctor Michele Savonarola, a contemporary of Piero, observed particularly the proportions of human bodies depicted by various painters—he names Giotto, Jacopo Avanzi of Bologna, Giusto de' Menabuoi, Altichiero and Guariento—and noted that they vary in this. Medical men then attended closely to human proportion for Aristotelian purposes of diagnosis, and under certain circumstances such a professional disposition and skill would transfer to other situations, such as the judgement of painting. At any time painters have special occupational ways of seeing too, and these are obviously powerfully in play in pictures. But cultures also facilitate certain kinds of cognitive development in large classes of their members. Living in a culture, growing up and learning to survive in it, involves us in a special perceptual training. It endows us with habits and skills of discrimination that affect the way we deal with the new data that sensation offers the mind. And because the trick of pictures—that is, marking a flat plane to suggest the three-dimensional—puts a premium on expectation and visual inference, it is sensitive to otherwise marginal differences in the beholder's equipment.

One aspect of Piero della Francesca's way of painting represents both a culture making a skill available and an individual electing to take it up. Fifteenth-century Italy was a culture in which a distinctive sort of commercial mathematics was highly developed, energetically taught in the schools, and widely known. A certain kind of geometry was learned for gauging barrels and packs, and a certain kind of proportional arithmetic was learned for calculating such things as partnership dues and rates of exchange. Both were almost fetish skills of the time and they provided a resource for both painters and their middle-class public. Seeing was 'theory-laden'. Piero is a man who stands for the continuity between the merchants and the painters in this: he wrote treatises both on commercial mathematics and on pictorial perspective (using the geometry) and proportion (using the arithmetic). Perspective, proportion and the Euclidean analysis of forms are very conspicuous in his painting, registering this element in the culture. Both he and his clients were differently equipped from us. But it was Piero who chose to take this resource up; there were other painters who did so much less.

This was a matter of a skill and disposition of visual perception; it involved concepts like 'pyramid' and 'proportion', but these had fairly direct visual application. Other intellectual dispositions offered by the culture might be less visual and more external but still were relevant to reflection on pictures. To take an instance that gets very near our knuckle, educated fifteenth-century people had a rather different equipment from us for thinking about the causes of things, including the causes of pictures: the structure of explanation was different, not least in relation to purpose and intention. To simplify: a picture could have been seen as the product of two main kinds of cause, efficient cause and final cause. The efficient causes were persons or things which by their agency produced effects—pictures being among other things effects. The final causes were the ends to which activity was directed. In this causal structure the client was more broadly causal of a picture than was the painter. The client who ordered the *Baptism of Christ* was an efficient cause of it in that he effected that Piero should make the picture; he was also a final cause of it in that the picture was made for him, for his use or at least disposal. Piero was also an efficient cause of the *Baptism of Christ*—as were his brushes and assistants—his activity producing the picture as an effect; but, since the picture was not destined for him, he was not a final cause of it— except in rather elaborate and extended senses fifteenth-century people did not think about. And if one wanted to characterize the picture as registering the personality of Piero, rather than of the client who willed it for a purpose of his own, then one would do it mainly by drawing up a balance sheet of his relative competences as an *efficient* in the different departments of his art— 'colour' and 'design' and 'composition' and so on. Or if one were very educated one might think of Piero as pursuing an 'idea' in the *Baptism of Christ*—a sense of intention even more remote from problem-solution. The fifteenth-century style of thinking about the causes of the *Baptism of Christ*, and so fifteenth-century expectations of the *Baptism of Christ*, and so also Piero's notion of what he was doing in the *Baptism of Christ*, were all rather different formally from our style of explanation.

So how far do we reconstruct the intention of Piero della Francesca, a man culturally different from us in his knowledge of pictures, in his assumptions about what his pictures are for, in his perceptual skills and dispositions, and even in his thinking about causes and about intention itself?

2. Knowledge of Other Cultures: Participant's Understanding and Observer's Understanding

It is best, first, to be clear about our investigative purpose and posture: it is peculiar and limited. We are interested in the intention of pictures and painters as a means to a sharper perception of the pictures, for us. It is the picture as covered by a description *in our terms* that we are attempting to explain; the explanation itself becomes part of a larger description of the picture, again in our terms. The account of intention is not a narrative of what went on in the painter's mind but an analytical construct about his ends and means, as we infer them from the relation of the object to identifiable circumstances. It stands in an ostensive relation to the picture itself.

It is usual, when discussing the 'understanding' of other cultures and actors in them—an issue discussed a great deal—to start from a distinction between *participants'* understanding and *observers'* understanding. The participant understands and knows his culture with an immediacy and spontaneity the observer does not share. He can act within the culture's standards and norms without rational self-consciousness, often indeed without having formulated standards as standards. He does not, for example, have to list to himself five requirements of altarpiece paintings: he has internalized an expectation about these over a period of experience of altarpieces. He moves with ease and delicacy and creative flexibility within the rules of his culture. His culture, for him, is like the language he has learned, informally, since infancy: indeed his language is one large articulating part of his culture. The observer does not have this kind of knowledge of the culture. He has to spell out standards and rules, making them explicit and so making them also coarse, rigid and clumsy. He lacks the participant's pure tact and fluid sense of the complexities. On the other hand, what the observer may have is a perspective—precisely that perspective being one of the things that bars him from the native's internal stance: the burghers of Sansepolcro in 1450, to make a particular point which is important for us, had not seen the painting of Chardin and Picasso. The observer typically works from comparisons not made by participants to generalizations participants would find offensively crude and crisp. Moreover he will give special prominence to certain elements in the life of the culture because, from his comparative stance, they seem special to the culture: the participant is not likely to have the same sense of some institutions in his life being constants of human society and others—intensive education in a certain kind of commercial mathematics, for instance—being local peculiarities of his time and place. Yet again, he would be contemptuous of the simplistic and tactless account the observer would offer of them. Any burgher of Sansepolcro in 1450, if he heard what I have said about the culture of fifteenth-century Italy so far, would just laugh, or shake his hand with exasperation—itself a very cultural thing to do. [. . .] So, cheerfully agreeing that we are observers, not participants, in what we say and think of the intention of the picture, let us proceed.

3. Commensurazione—an Old Word

Having said this, I shall now do something that may seem to go against it. I shall use a participant's concept and say:—The *Baptism of Christ* is remarkable for its *commensurazione*. The first thing is to give *commensurazione* a sense—one additional to the element of ostensive definition implicit in using it with reference to the *Baptism of Christ*.

Piero himself offered a formal definition in the context of a division of the art of painting into three parts at the beginning of his book on perspective:

Painting consists of three principal parts, which we call *disegno, commensuratio* and *colorare*. By *disegno* we mean profiles and contours which enclose objects. By *commensuratio* we mean the profiles and contours set in their proper places in proportion. By *colorare* we mean how colours show themselves on objects—lights and darks as the lighting changes them.

This is interesting, but short formal definitions in limited contexts have limitations, and the sense of *commensurazione* is larger and richer than Piero covers here.

Its origin is as a post-classical Latin translation of the Greek word *symmetria* (a word, as Petrarch noted, the classical Romans lacked) and the Latin translation of Aristotle gave it currency by using it for this purpose: for instance, 'Beauty of the parts of a body seems to be a certain *commensuratio*.' It was also used in musical theory. In fifteenth-century vernacularized uses— and it is not a vastly common word—it seems to mean something near proportion or proportionality itself. For instance, the Platonizing philosopher Ficino criticized the Aristotelian conception of beauty thus: 'There are people who are of the opinion [*wrongly*] that beauty is a certain placing of all parts of a body, or *commensurazione* and proportion between them, along with a pleasantness of colour.'

But in Piero it takes on a special accent from its introduction in this context of painting's three principal parts. Earlier in the century it had been usual to consider painting as having two parts, *disegno* and *colore*: Cennino Cennini's treatise, for instance, states this a generation or two before Piero. Looking at fifteenth-century painting, one can see why just two parts might come to seem inadequate, and in 1435 the humanist art critic Alberti had taken the step towards a part of painting that would give some account of how outlines and colours are arranged within the picture as a whole: he brought in *compositio* (Latin) or *compositione* (Italian) as a third part. It is to this that Piero's *commensurazione* broadly corresponds in the triplet. But there is an important difference between *composizione* and *commensurazione*. Alberti's concept is a metaphor from our use of language: it sees the picture as a hierarchy of bodies, members of bodies, and planes, corresponding to the hierarchy of clauses, phrases and words in a sentence. Piero's concept is a term from numerical analysis. He replaces the model of language with the model of mathematics, and it is clear that for Piero mathematics had the same paradigmatic authority as language had, in this respect, for Alberti—who was himself, it should be said, a very numerate man and an exponent of perspective and proportion. In the book from which I took the division and definition, the treatise on perspective, it is specifically geometrical linear perspective that Piero is denoting by *commensurazione*; but it seems that *commensurazione* normally extended out to cover more than just setting contours in their proper places by perspective method. It is an expansionist concept, and its range is quite well caught by Piero's own pupil Luca Pacioli, even though the term he is using, because of *his* context, is *proportion*:

You will find that proportion is the queen and mother of all, and that without her nothing can be carried through. Perspective proves that in pictures. In pictures, if one does not give the size of a human figure its proper bigness in the eyes of a beholder, it never answers well. Again, the painter never prepares his colours well if he does not attend to the strength of this one and that one; I mean that in painting a figure's flesh, for instance, so much white or black or yellow and so on need so much red and so on. Then in the planes, too, where the painters have to place the figure, it is very important that they should have a care to set it with a proper proportion of distance. ... And so it is too with all the other lineaments and dispositions of any painted figure. As confirmation of all this—in order that painters should know how to arrange things—the sublime painter Piero de li Franceschi (still living in our own time and like myself a man of Sansepolcro) wrote not long ago a worthy book on just this 'Perspective'. . . . In that book nine out of ten words are about proportion.

Commensurazione's reference can be taken as to a general mathematics-based alertness in the total arrangement of a picture, in which what we call proportion and perspective are keenly felt as interdependent and interlocking.

4. *Three Functions of Old Words: Necessity, Strangeness and Superostensivity*

Why should one go to this much effort only to half-retrieve a participant's category of visual interest? It would be bad to revert to the ambition to reproduce the intentional workings of Piero's mind in a narrative mode. In fact, the inferential critic's taste for using participant's terms is often mis-understood in this sense: people insist on reminding us yet again that it is *not* possible to enter into other-cultural minds and indeed that if we go on trying we may do ourselves harm. It had better be justified, then, and [. . .] there seem [to be] three main justifications.

The first and most obvious is that we now have no category or concept quite like *commensurazione*. Here one must tread carefully, for it is not true to say that we share no categories with fifteenth-century Italy: Euclid stands through time and so does a verbal concept like 'proportion', even if they spelled and spoke them differently then or even used a word of quite differ-ent form. The concepts are, if not universal, shared by many cultures and periods. [. . .]

But what we are interested in is particular quality: our aim is to differenti-ate and so to de-generalize or qualify 'proportion'. It is the distinctive colour of proportionality in Piero we are after, and this is likely to mean that we are going to need to move down the order of generality to categories that are less persistent and more bound to a particular culture—whether ours or theirs. Our culture does not offer a word with this particular meaning. *Commensur-azione* takes much of its meaning from the history of use I have sketched: translation from the Greek, and Aristotelian beauty, the stealing of aspects of Cennini's *disegno* and *colore*, the mathematical term ousting Alberti's language-model term *compositio*, 'perspective' and 'proportion' interlocked. These are not weak associative meanings of *commensurazione*, though its affective value may have been strong: they are a part of a conceptual range established in use, a distinctive sector and arrangement of experience. We need the word to group a set of related qualities in Piero.

The second justification is that *commensurazione* helps to make Piero and his picture 'strange'. Many pictures, including the *Baptism of Christ*, are enclosed in a terrible varnish or carapace of false familiarity which, when we think about them, is difficult to break through. [...] A first task in the historical perception of a picture is therefore often that of working through to a realization of quite how alien it and the mind that made it are; only when one has done this is it really possible to move to a genuine sense of its human affinity with us. [...]

In this process alien concepts like *commensurazione* have an important part not only because we apprehend historical distance in the course of learning them but because, in the texture of our conceptualization about the picture, they stand for the contrast between those people and us. In a way they are a declaration precisely of our inability fully to re-enact. [...]

The third justification harks back yet again to my starting-point in the language of art criticism, so I will indicate it briefly only. I suggested then that the relation between concepts and picture was a reciprocal one: we use the concept to point in a differentiating way at a picture, and its meaning is sharpened for us by the relation between it and the painting we perceive. This process is good for us: we have to work at it and this work leads us to a closer perception of the picture. In this respect concepts like *commensurazione* are exceptionally stimulating. Because our hold on them is not a relaxed and internalized one, we have to work hard between them and the picture.

[*Patterns of Intention: On the Historical Explanation of Pictures* (New Haven: Yale University Press, 1985), 105–16.]

SUSAN SONTAG

39 Against Interpretation

> It is only shallow people who do not judge by appearances. The mystery
> of the world is the visible, not the invisible.
>
> Oscar Wilde, *in a Letter*

[...]

2 None of us can ever retrieve that innocence before all theory when art knew no need to justify itself, when one did not ask of a work of art what it *said* because one knew (or thought one knew) what it *did*. From now to the end of consciousness, we are stuck with the task of defending art. We can only quarrel with one or another means of defense. Indeed, we have an obligation to overthrow any means of defending and justifying art which

becomes particularly obtuse or onerous or insensitive to contemporary needs and practice.

This is the case, today, with the very idea of content itself. Whatever it may have been in the past, the idea of content is today mainly a hindrance, a nuisance, a subtle or not so subtle philistinism.

Though the actual developments in many arts may seem to be leading us away from the idea that a work of art is primarily its content, the idea still exerts an extraordinary hegemony. I want to suggest that this is because the idea is now perpetuated in the guise of a certain way of encountering works of art thoroughly ingrained among most people who take any of the arts seriously. What the overemphasis on the idea of content entails is the perennial, never consummated project of *interpretation*. And, conversely, it is the habit of approaching works of art in order to *interpret* them that sustains the fancy that there really is such a thing as the content of a work of art.

3 Of course, I don't mean interpretation in the broadest sense, the sense in which Nietzsche (rightly) says, 'There are no facts, only interpretations.' By interpretation, I mean here a conscious act of the mind which illustrates a certain code, certain 'rules' of interpretation.

Directed to art, interpretation means plucking a set of elements (the X, the Y, the Z, and so forth) from the whole work. The task of interpretation is virtually one of translation. The interpreter says, Look, don't you see that X is really—or, really means—A? That Y is really B? That Z is really C?

What situation could prompt this curious project for transforming a text? History gives us the materials for an answer. Interpretation first appears in the culture of late classical antiquity, when the power and credibility of myth had been broken by the 'realistic' view of the world introduced by scientific enlightenment. Once the question that haunts post-mythic consciousness—that of the *seemliness* of religious symbols—had been asked, the ancient texts were, in their pristine form, no longer acceptable. Then interpretation was summoned, to reconcile the ancient texts to 'modern' demands. Thus, the Stoics, to accord with their view that the gods had to be moral, allegorized away the rude features of Zeus and his boisterous clan in Homer's epics. What Homer really designated by the adultery of Zeus with Leto, they explained, was the union between power and wisdom. In the same vein, Philo of Alexandria interpreted the literal historical narratives of the Hebrew Bible as spiritual paradigms. The story of the exodus from Egypt, the wandering in the desert for forty years, and the entry into the promised land, said Philo, was really an allegory of the individual soul's emancipation, tribulations, and final deliverance. Interpretation thus presupposes a discrepancy between the clear meaning of the text and the demands of (later) readers. It seeks to resolve that discrepancy. The situation is that for some reason a text has become unacceptable; yet it cannot be discarded. Interpretation is a radical strategy for conserving an old text, which is thought too precious to repudiate, by revamping it. The interpreter, without actually erasing or rewriting the text, *is* altering it. But he can't admit to doing this. He claims to be only making it intelligible, by disclosing its true meaning. However far the interpreters alter the text (another notorious example is the Rabbinic and Christian 'spiritual' interpretations of the clearly erotic Song of Songs), they must claim to be reading off a sense that is already there.

Interpretation in our own time, however, is even more complex. For the contemporary zeal for the project of interpretation is often prompted not by piety toward the troublesome text (which may conceal an aggression), but by an open aggressiveness, an overt contempt for appearances. The old style of interpretation was insistent, but respectful; it erected another meaning on top of the literal one. The modern style of interpretation excavates, and as it excavates, destroys; it digs 'behind' the text, to find a sub-text which is the true one. The most celebrated and influential modern doctrines, those of Marx and Freud, actually amount to elaborate systems of hermeneutics, aggressive and impious theories of interpretation. All observable phenomena are bracketed, in Freud's phrase, as *manifest content*. This manifest content must be probed and pushed aside to find the true meaning—the *latent content*—beneath. For Marx, social events like revolutions and wars; for Freud, the events of individual lives (like neurotic symptoms and slips of the tongue) as well as texts (like a dream or a work of art)—all are treated as occasions for interpretation. According to Marx and Freud, these events only *seem* to be intelligible. Actually, they have no meaning without interpretation. To understand *is* to interpret. And to interpret is to restate the phenomenon, in effect to find an equivalent for it.

Thus, interpretation is not (as most people assume) an absolute value, a gesture of mind situated in some timeless realm of capabilities. Interpretation must itself be evaluated, within a historical view of human consciousness. In some cultural contexts, interpretation is a liberating act. It is a means of revising, of transvaluing, of escaping the dead past. In other cultural contexts, it is reactionary, impertinent, cowardly, stifling.

4 Today is such a time, when the project of interpretation is largely reactionary, stifling. Like the fumes of the automobile and of heavy industry which befoul the urban atmosphere, the effusion of interpretations of art today poisons our sensibilities. In a culture whose already classical dilemma is the hypertrophy of the intellect at the expense of energy and sensual capability, interpretation is the revenge of the intellect upon art.

Even more. It is the revenge of the intellect upon the world. To interpret is to impoverish, to deplete the world—in order to set up a shadow world of 'meanings.' It is to turn *the* world into *this* world. ('This world'! As if there were any other.)

The world, our world, is depleted, impoverished enough. Away with all duplicates of it, until we again experience more immediately what we have.

5 In most modern instances, interpretation amounts to the philistine refusal to leave the work of art alone. Real art has the capacity to make us nervous. By reducing the work of art to its content and then interpreting *that*, one tames the work of art. Interpretation makes art manageable, comformable.

This philistinism of interpretation is more rife in literature than in any other art. For decades now, literary critics have understood it to be their task to translate the elements of the poem or play or novel or story into something else. Sometimes a writer will be so uneasy before the naked power of his art that he will install within the work itself—albeit with a little shyness, a touch of the good taste of irony—the clear and explicit interpretation of it. Thomas Mann is an example of such an overcooperative author. In the case of more stubborn authors, the critic is only too happy to perform the job.

The work of Kafka, for example, has been subjected to a mass ravishment by no less than three armies of interpreters. Those who read Kafka as a social allegory see case studies of the frustrations and insanity of modern bureaucracy and its ultimate issuance in the totalitarian state. Those who read Kafka as a psychoanalytic allegory see desperate revelations of Kafka's fear of his father, his castration anxieties, his sense of his own impotence, his thralldom to his dreams. Those who read Kafka as a religious allegory explain that K. in *The Castle* is trying to gain access to heaven, that Joseph K. in *The Trial* is being judged by the inexorable and mysterious justice of God. . . . Another *oeuvre* that has attracted interpreters like leeches is that of Samuel Beckett. Beckett's delicate dramas of the withdrawn consciousness—pared down to essentials, cut off, often represented as physically immobilized—are read as a statement about modern man's alienation from meaning or from God, or as an allegory of psychopathology.

Proust, Joyce, Faulkner, Rilke, Lawrence, Gide . . . one could go on citing author after author; the list is endless of those around whom thick encrustations of interpretation have taken hold. But it should be noted that interpretation is not simply the compliment that mediocrity pays to genius. It is, indeed, *the* modern way of understanding something, and is applied to works of every quality. Thus, in the notes that Elia Kazan published on his production of *A Streetcar Named Desire*, it becomes clear that, in order to direct the play, Kazan had to discover that Stanley Kowalski represented the sensual and vengeful barbarism that was engulfing our culture, while Blanche Du Bois was Western civilization, poetry, delicate apparel, dim lighting, refined feelings and all, though a little the worse for wear to be sure. Tennessee

Williams' forceful psychological melodrama now became intelligible: it was *about* something, about the decline of Western civilization. Apparently, were it to go on being a play about a handsome brute named Stanley Kowalski and a faded mangy belle named Blanche Du Bois, it would not be manageable.

6 It doesn't matter whether artists intend, or don't intend, for their works to be interpreted. Perhaps Tennessee Williams thinks *Streetcar* is about what Kazan thinks it to be about. It may be that Cocteau in *The Blood of a Poet* and in *Orpheus* wanted the elaborate readings which have been given these films, in terms of Freudian symbolism and social critique. But the merit of these works certainly lies elsewhere than in their 'meanings.' Indeed, it is precisely to the extent that Williams' plays and Cocteau's films do suggest these portentous meanings that they are defective, false, contrived, lacking in conviction.

From interviews, it appears that Resnais and Robbe-Grillet consciously designed *Last Year at Marienbad* to accommodate a multiplicity of equally plausible interpretations. But the temptation to interpret *Marienbad* should be resisted. What matters in *Marienbad* is the pure, untranslatable, sensuous immediacy of some of its images, and its rigorous if narrow solutions to certain problems of cinematic form.

Again, Ingmar Bergman may have meant the tank rumbling down the empty night street in *The Silence* as a phallic symbol. But if he did, it was a foolish thought. ('Never trust the teller, trust the tale,' said Lawrence.) Taken as a brute object, as an immediate sensory equivalent for the mysterious abrupt armored happenings going on inside the hotel, that sequence with the tank is the most striking moment in the film. Those who reach for a Freudian interpretation of the tank are only expressing their lack of response to what is there on the screen.

It is always the case that interpretation of this type indicates a dissatisfaction (conscious or unconscious) with the work, a wish to replace it by something else.

Interpretation, based on the highly dubious theory that a work of art is composed of items of content, violates art. It makes art into an article for use, for arrangement into a mental scheme of categories.

7 Interpretation does not, of course, always prevail. In fact, a great deal of today's art may be understood as motivated by a flight from interpretation. To avoid interpretation, art may become parody. Or it may become abstract. Or it may become ('merely') decorative. Or it may become non-art.

The flight from interpretation seems particularly a feature of modern painting. Abstract painting is the attempt to have, in the ordinary sense, no content; since there is no content, there can be no interpretation. Pop Art works by the opposite means to the same result; using a content so blatant, so 'what it is,' it, too, ends by being uninterpretable.

A great deal of modern poetry as well, starting from the great experiments of French poetry (including the movement that is misleadingly called Symbolism) to put silence into poems and to reinstate the *magic* of the word, has escaped from the rough grip of interpretation. The most recent revolution in contemporary taste in poetry—the revolution that has deposed Eliot and elevated Pound—represents a turning away from content in poetry in the old sense, an impatience with what made modern poetry prey to the zeal of interpreters. [. . .]

8 What kind of criticism, of commentary on the arts, is desirable today? For I am not saying that works of art are ineffable, that they cannot be described or paraphrased. They can be. The question is how. What would criticism look like that would serve the work of art, not usurp its place?

What is needed, first, is more attention to form in art. If excessive stress on *content* provokes the arrogance of interpretation, more extended and more thorough descriptions of *form* would silence. What is needed is a vocabulary—a descriptive, rather than prescriptive, vocabulary—for forms. The best criticism, and it is uncommon, is of this sort that dissolves considerations of content into those of form. On film, drama, and painting respectively, I can think of Erwin Panofsky's essay, 'Style and Medium in the Motion Pictures,' Northrop Frye's essay 'A Conspectus of Dramatic Genres,' Pierre Francastel's essay 'The Destruction of a Plastic Space.' Roland Barthes' book *On Racine* and his two essays on Robbe-Grillet are examples of formal analysis applied to the work of a single author. (The best essays in Erich Auerbach's *Mimesis*, like 'The Scar of Odysseus,' are also of this type.) An example of formal analysis applied simultaneously to genre and author is Walter Benjamin's essay, 'The Story Teller: Reflections on the Works of Nicolai Leskov.'

Equally valuable would be acts of criticism which would supply a really accurate, sharp, loving description of the appearance of a work of art. This seems even harder to do than formal analysis. Some of Manny Farber's film criticism, Dorothy Van Ghent's essay 'The Dickens World: A View from Todgers', Randall Jarrell's essay on Walt Whitman are among the rare examples of what I mean. These are essays which reveal the sensuous surface of art without mucking about in it.

9 *Transparence* is the highest, most liberating value in art—and in criticism—today. Transparence means experiencing the luminousness of the thing in itself, of things being what they are. This is the greatness of, for example, the films of Bresson and Ozu and Renoir's *The Rules of the Game*.

Once upon a time (say, for Dante), it must have been a revolutionary and creative move to design works of art so that they might be experienced on several levels. Now it is not. It reinforces the principle of redundancy that is the principal affliction of modern life.

Once upon a time (a time when high art was scarce), it must have been a revolutionary and creative move to interpret works of art. Now it is not. What we decidedly do not need now is further to assimilate Art into Thought, or (worse yet) Art into Culture.

Interpretation takes the sensory experience of the work of art for granted, and proceeds from there. This cannot be taken for granted, now. Think of the sheer multiplication of works of art available to every one of us, superadded to the conflicting tastes and odors and sights of the urban environment that bombard our senses. Ours is a culture based on excess, on overproduction; the result is a steady loss of sharpness in our sensory experience. All the conditions of modern life—its material plenitude, its sheer crowdedness—conjoin to dull our sensory faculties. And it is in the light of the condition of our senses, our capacities (rather than those of another age), that the task of the critic must be assessed.

What is important now is to recover our senses. We must learn to *see* more, to *hear* more, to *feel* more.

Our task is not to find the maximum amount of content in a work of art, much less to squeeze more content out of the work than is already there. Our task is to cut back content so that we can see the thing at all.

The aim of all commentary on art now should be to make works of art—and, by analogy, our own experience—more, rather than less, real to us. The function of criticism should be to show *how it is what it is*, even *that it is what it is*, rather than to show *what it means*.

10 In place of a hermeneutics we need an erotics of art.

['Against Interpretation', in *Against Interpretation and Other Essays* (New York: Farrar, Straus & Giroux, 1961), 13–23.]

> But if you were to hide the world in the world so that nothing could get
> away, this would be the final reality of the constancy of things.
>
> Chuang Tzu (Burton Watson, tr.)

Understanding what an author as agent and authority at once could have meant is central to [an] order of interpretation that *for just this reason*, must be distinguished from the sort of interpretation, hermeneutic or what I shall designate *deep* interpretation, which I want to examine here. It is deep precisely because there is not that reference to authority which is a conceptual feature of what we may as well term *surface* interpretation. There is not because the level of explanation referred to in deep interpretation is not a level on which a participant in a form of action can as such occupy a position of authority. [. . .]

Perhaps a differentiation may be eked out as follows. The distinction between depth and surface cuts at right angles across the philosophically more commonplace distinction between inner and outer. It is difficult to draw the inner-outer distinction without begging every question in the philosophies of mind and knowledge, but surface interpretation undertakes to characterize the external behavior of an agent with reference to the internal representation of it presumed to be the agent's, and the agent is in some privileged position with regard to what his representations are. Or at least what his surface representations are. With regard to his deep representations, he has no privilege, hence no authority, for he must come to know them in ways no different from those imposed upon others: they are at least cognitively external to him, even if part of his character and personality, and with regard to them he is, as it were, an Other Mind to himself.

The operation known as *Verstehen* [empathy], in which we seek to interpret through vicarious occupation of the agent's own point of view, though certainly a flawed conception, is at least a possible theory of how the Outer traverses the dark boundaries that separate him from Inner, if we grant that Inner has no need or use for *Verstehen* as applied to himself, the point of view being his. But it is not a possible theory of how we arrive at a deep interpretation, if only because Inner is cut off from his own depths for reasons different from those that cut Outer off from Inner. It has been said that part of what makes a reason an unconscious one is that it would not be a reason for him whose action it explains if it were conscious. It would not in part because the beliefs that would justify it if conscious are alien to the system of beliefs which the agent would invoke. So it is part of something being deep that it is hidden, as much from him whose depth is in question as from anyone else.

We may never—and bats may always—know what it is like to be a bat; but bats, if they have depths, are no better situated than we for knowing what it deeply is to be a bat. And perhaps the very notion of what it is to be something implies just that sort of consciousness which has no more application than the concept of authority to the depths. In the depths there is nothing that counts as being there.

Deep interpretation, all this having been said, cannot altogether dispense with those representations with reference to the accessibility of which we mark the difference between Inner and Outer. It cannot because, in pretending to give a deep interpretation of what persons do, it takes it for granted that it is known what in fact persons do, and this may require reference precisely to those representations. Indeed, what deep interpretation undertakes is a kind of understanding of the complex consisting of representations together with the conduct they, at the surface level, enable us to understand; so surface interpretation, when successfully achieved, gives us the interpretanda for deep interpretation, the interpretantia for which are to be sought in the depths. [. . .]

Surface interpretation, which we are all obliged in the course of socialization to become masters of, has been extensively discussed by philosophers in the theory of action and in the analysis of other languages and other minds. But deep interpretation has been scarcely discussed at all. Yet because it is practiced by the humansciences, the theories it presupposes are presupposed by them, and their viability depends upon its viability. I should like therefore to give some examples of deep interpretation and to sketch some problems it gives rise to in at least some of those examples. And I should like to dissipate certain confusions which come about, especially in the philosophy of art, when the claims of deep and surface interpretation are not kept isolated. Depth, needless to say, has little to do with profundity. But I have no analysis of 'deep' in the sense of profound readings of texts to offer.

Of the forms of divination anciently practiced by the Greeks, one in particular has a curious pertinence to our topic. This was divination *dia kleodon*, exercised upon the casual utterances of men. The message-seeker pressed a coin into the hand of a certain statue of Hermes, whispered his query in the idol's ear, blocked his own ears—and the answer would be contained in the first human words he heard upon unblocking them. Needless to say, interpretation of these would be required, supposing, as altogether likely, the words did not transparently reveal the message. [. . .] More likely a passerby mumbled something about the price of olive oil while the message-seeker wished to know whether Daphne (or was it Ion?) really cared. And an interpreter as middleman would be called upon to map interpretandum onto interpretans. The automatic writing from which the Surrealists sought to elicit astounding insights belongs to the same general sort of undertaking.

In view of the god's identity, we have an archeohermeneutical practice here, which pivots upon interpreting utterances 'that mean more than the speaker realises,' which is the English definition of the Greek work *kledon*, herewith introduced as an English word in its own right. Divination, like oracles and auguries generally, has fallen into disuse, but kledons and the form of interpretation they exemplify play a considerable role in modern hermeneutic theory, where we deal with symbols that Ricoeur, somewhat gnomically, tells us 'say more than they say.' It is a kledon, then, when in saying *a* a speaker says *b* (or when, in performing a meaningful action *c* an agent does *d*), but where the ordinary structures for understanding *a* would not disclose to a hearer that *b* is also being said: nor is the speaker at all aware that he is saying *b*, meaning as he does only to be saying *a* (speakers have no authority over what they are saying when they voice kledons). In one of his novels, Vonnegut portrays a radio announcer in Nazi Germany who manages to alert the Allies to important military movements in Germany through messages coded into the anti-Semitic utterances his audience believes it is listening to. He happens to know he is doing this, which puts him in a difficult moral posture that would not be altered were he merely the writer of military intelligence embedded invisibly in bigoted discourse, delivered by a staff announcer who, unaware of hidden messages, would only be doing his job of filling the air with banal evil. Like his ancient counterpart who was an unwitting *porte-parole* of hermetic communication, this announcer would be kledonizing and, given his presumed values, would not transmit the concealed message if he knew he was doing it; so what he is *deeply* doing is not only unintentional, it is (almost dialectically) counterintentional. From the perspective of the surface of discourse, the status as kledon of what he says is inscrutable, and the meaning of what he says in saying what he would suppose himself (only) to be saying is not really his. Much as in one sense the child born to the Virgin is not really *hers*. Had the identity of the child not been somehow *revealed*, there would be no way of knowing that a god had been born into history. It takes a prophet to reveal the divine overcharge on ordinary communication. Without these revelations, life would have gone on in both instances with no way of knowing that kledons were being transmitted into the unheeding air. What makes kledons so interesting is that they supervene upon forms of life and discourse that are already, as it were, under surface interpretation complete as they are. It is like the world being hidden in the world.

Now the interesting question is why the meanings are hidden. We can of course understand it when the secret agent uses the airwaves to disguise subversive intelligence, but why must Hermes graft his tidings onto inadvertent hosts instead of speaking directly? Well, why must Jupiter have recourse to bolts of lightning and flights of birds to communicate matters it would not have been thought beyond divine power to lay upon us directly, without the mediation of interpreters? There is a cynical answer. If there were direct communication, the interpreters would suffer technological unemployment. So in order to secure their economic position, they claim semantical monopoly over crucial urgent messages that only they can make out. I have no idea whether this cynical answer is true, but it illustrates a kind of low-level deep interpretation in its own right, in that the divinators are in fact maintaining their own position in the world through the fact that their clients believe them to be discharging an important, though in truth it is an epiphenomenal, function. The deep reasons governing these transactions, and in the light of which we are enabled to say what really is happening, are hidden from interpreter and consumer alike, and the surface practice would not survive if the deep reasons for it were known: it would not exist if it were *not* hidden. Its being hidden from the client could be put down as priestly fourberie but for the fact that it is hidden from the priests themselves: which is what makes the mechanisms of concealment philosophically interesting.

I have archeologized this long-abandoned practice to bring to prominence a structure of action in which, when *a* is done, there is a description of *a*, call it *b*, such that in doing *a*, one is really doing *b* in the sense that *a* is done in order that *b* be done—which distinguishes *b* from the countless many other descriptions of *a* recognized in the theory of action—and where it is hidden from the *a*-doer that he is a *b*-doer. A deep interpretation of *a* identifies it as *b*. Surface interpretation, as we saw, is with reference to the agent's reasons, though not his deep reasons, and though he may have difficulty in saying what his reasons are, this will not be because they are hidden. Its being hidden is a special kind of reason for not being able to make something out. But let me now give some examples, most of them familiar, where it seems to me this structure occurs.

Marxist Theories

Marx and Engels do not accept at face value the descriptions and explanations men spontaneously give of their own actions. In every instance this side of the classless society, in doing *a*, whatever it may be, they are doing something else, call it *b*, which must be understood in terms of their class location. Marx explained the repeal of the Corn Laws, under the ideological leadership of Cobden and the political leadership of Peel, which *they* explained as done in order that the working man should pay less for bread, as *really* to be explained as done so that the industrialist should pay less for the working man. Peel and Cobden, both Free Traders, vested their actions (sincerely) in humanitarian terms, but really were advancing the interests of their class, just as their opponents were expressing the interests of theirs. Peel was politically and

Cobden economically ruined, but they were but the kledons of their class, instruments of the forces of history in the dramatical interplay of which classes are the true agents. A parallel sort of theory explains the sacrifice of the male insect in the rage of reproduction in terms of the interests of the species. [...]

Psychoanalytical Theories

[...] The distance between a commonplace and a kledonic reading of an action or an utterance could scarcely have been more surprising under divination *dia kleodon* than the distance between the manifest thought or conduct of a person and its redescription with reference to its latent form as revealed by psychoanalytical interpretation. The Ratman jogs furiously after meals, 'in order,' he would rationalize, patting a surprisingly flat stomach, 'to eliminate *Dick*.' *Dick*, which is thickness in the Ratman's native language, German, happens also to be the name of his lady-love's American suitor, whose elimination the Ratman deeply intends. Obviously, jogging cannot remotely be a means for eliminating rivals, and 'eliminating Dick' would not be a reason for running were it conscious. So the acceptable reason, 'in order to eliminate *Dick*,' only rationalizes a reason the Ratman cannot acceptably act on and connects with this deep reason via a punning transformation; and the deep reason is hidden from him, though not from his interpreter (Freud), for whatever reason the unconscious itself is hidden. The example is far from atypical, and the type is found broadcast through Freud's collected works.

Structuralisms

Puns plan transformative roles in Freud's great hermeneutical works, which may explain, if those works are sound, why puns are socially so offensive (why do they meet with groans, why are they classed the 'lowest form of humor,' why does the leading French philosogist, who has made punning the principal feature of his mythod, get rejected for positions in his ungrateful land?), and certainly explains, since puns are native to the language they occur in, why they cannot be translated. So interpretation, rather than translation or even paraphrase, connects the speech and actions of the neuropath to the Language of his Unconscious. Indeed it is just because the symptom is a pun on the psychic pathogen that Lacan postulates his hasty theory that the structure of the unconscious must be the structure of a language. Psychoanalysis as practiced by Lacan consists precisely in identifying what the symptom says— or better, what a piece of behavior says when treated as a symptom, where symptoms are treated as a discourse hidden, as it were, on the surface of conduct, as the purloined letter is hidden in full sight of those who seek it. But the theory of the linguistic unconscious generates a wide class of theories— e.g., Lévi-Strauss' witty thought that marriage is a kind of language, or at least a form of communication, if we can construe, as he sees no obstacle to doing, the exchange of women as a kind of exchange of words. Now the reasons Elizabeth may give for marrying Paul are rationalizations of the interests of clans she is *really* advancing, whatever *she* may think. Dinners at the Douglases', cockfights at the Geertzes', are other examples of conduct in which whatever we think we are doing, we are doing something else, deep interpretation telling us what.

Philosophies of History

It is Hegel who lays upon us the alarming thought that 'Reason is the sovereign of the world,' and that 'the history of the world, therefore [*sic*], presents us with a rational process.' So, however chaotic it may appear, Reason is in some way to be interpreted as acting through the actions of men to achieve ends, or an end, which can come about in no other way, even though the secondary agents of historical realization are totally unaware of the grand scheme in which they figure. What Hegel speaks of as Reason is close to what Vico speaks of as Providence, which exploits human intentions in order to subvert them and bring about states of affairs ironically opposite to what those who act on those intentions envision. Through 'ferocity, arrogance, and ambition . . . the three great vices that could destroy mankind on the face of the earth' are generated 'soldiers, merchants, and rulers,' through the civilizing conduct of whom social happiness prevails. The kledonic meaning of actions under the interpretational schemes of philosophical history are hidden from agents for whatever reason the future is hidden. [. . .]

In view of the fact that any work of art you choose can be imagined matched by a perceptually congruent counterpart which, though not a work of art, cannot be told apart from the artwork by perceptual differentia, the major problem in the philosophy of art consists in identifying what the difference then consists in between works of art and mere things. Consider thus the corpus of Leonardo's frescoes viewed in the light of a curious bit of advice he offered fellow painters as a stimulant to invention. He urges them to equip themselves with a wall spotted with stains. Then, whatever they intend to paint, they will find pictorial adumbrations of it on the smudged wall. 'You will see in it a resemblance to various landscapes, adorned with mountains, rivers, rocks, trees, plains, wide valleys, and various groups of hills. You will also be able to see divers combats and figures in quick movement and strange expressions of faces and outlandish costumes, and an infinite number of things you can reduce into separate and well-conceived forms.' (Leonardo observes that similarly every tune can be heard in pealing bells, and I am certain that there is a literary equivalent where every story can be read from a patch of spotted prose.) There are sheets of Leonardo's sketches that may have been generated by just such transfigurative vision, and it is always fascinating to speculate over which of his great works may have been provoked into artistic existence by this prosthetic of painterly vision. But this suggests an obverse exercise—to try to see, through an act of deliberate *disinvention*, a divine landscape, such as the one against which la Gioconda is set, or for that matter La Gioconda herself, as so much stain-splotched expanse. Nature and a certain surprising casualness regarding the material bases of his craft have helped turn certain of Leonardo's works into what looks like stains to the casual eye. His *intonacco* for the *Battle of Anghiari* was, Vasari tells us, so coarse that the legendary composition sank into the wall; and though recent projects have thought of locating it by means of sonar and thus bringing a lost masterpiece to light, it is conceivable that the wall was stuccoed over in the first place because it looked more and more as though it were attacked by mildew. The rough napoleonic troops who occupied the refectory in Milan where the *Last Supper* is painted are often impugned as barbarians for the brutal way they treated that priceless wall, but since it takes strenuous curatorial intervention even today to prevent the painting from subsiding into stains, it is feasible that the soldiers only saw it as so much fungus and damp. To be sure, there may here to there have been seen a surprising form—an eye, a finger—but that might itself be of the same playful order as seeing the profile of Talleyrand in a lombardian cloud or, more likely in terms of soldierly fantasy, two hills as *des tetons*.

So imagine that on a forgotten wall in the sacristy of the Chiesa of Santo Leone Pietromontana, Leonardo depicted a Last Judgement that has, alas, reverted to a set of stains so as to be indiscernible from the very wall in Leonardo's studio from which his fancy projected and realized those great works, including, of course, the Last Judgement itself. Both have a certain art-historical interest. Owning the wall in the studio would be like owning Leonardo's palette, or better, his *camera obscura*. It would be owning a bit of remarkable gear. Owning the other wall, by contrast, would be owning a work of art in a sad state of degradation, worth, even so, plenty of millions if only the *Patrimonio Nazionale* would permit it to be moved to Düsseldorf or Houston. Knowing it to be a work of art, we must interpret those stains and mottles, an operation having no application to the counterpart, though we may use the latter just as Leonardo did, to excite the visual imagination. To interpret means in effect an imaginative restoration, to try to find the identity of areas gone amorphous through chemistry and time. It would be helpful to have a sketch, a contemporary copy, a description—anything to help with recovering Leonardo's intentions. There are many Last Judgements, but how much really will they help us? Will this one possess the celebrated moral diagonal the Vatican guides never tire of tracing for the edification of tourists who learned about it through popular lectures on Michelangelo? Will there even be a Christ figure? Perhaps Leonardo absented Him from a scene defined by His traditionally heavy presence. Or perhaps a certain blob is all that remains of a remarkable Christ, originally tiny in proportion to the dimension of the tableau, one more anticipation to Leonardo's credit, this time to manneristic optics. Interpretations are endless, but only because knowledge is unattainable. The right sort of knowledge gives the work its identity, and *surface* interpretation has done its work. What remains is responding to the work, so far as this is possible in its sad state. We have an aesthetic for ruins, even for faded photographs, but not quite for ruined paintings. But such matters must be mooted elsewhere.

Deep interpretation supposes surface interpretation to have done its work, so that we know what has been done and why. Now we look for the deep determinates of da vincian action. Appeal to his intentions only individuates the interpretandum for a deep interpretation, but the interpretantia refer us to Leonardo's kinky unconscious, his economic locus, and to the semiotics of embellishment in Florentine culture—what the Medici went in for instead of cockfights—and on and on and on. There is no end to deep interpretation, perhaps because there is no end to science, not even humanscience, and who knows what deep structures the future will reveal? The artist's intentions have nothing to do with these. Surface interpretation must be scrupulously histor-ical, and refer only to possibilities Leonardo could have acknowledged with-out attributing to him knowledge of the humansciences of the future. He could not have known of Eisler's book, nor the theory Eisler used. But that requires no references to the artist's authority. Deep interpretation, finally, admits a certain overdetermination—the work can mean many different things under deep interpretation without being rendered the least indeter-minate under surface interpretation. Like philosophy, in a way, deep interpretation leaves the world as it finds it. Nor does knowledge of it enter into response, except to the degree that response itself is given deep inter-pretation.

It is deep interpretation which those who speak out against interpretation speak out against, in urging that we allow the works to speak for themselves. They hardly can be speaking out against surface interpretation, inasmuch as we cannot so much as identify the work, let alone allow it to speak, save against an assumption of achieved interpretation. Without surface interpreta-tion, the artworld lapses into so much ruined canvas, and so many stained walls.

Of course it is irresistible to ponder what need for ritual purification it must have been that drove Leonardo to transcend stains and transfigure them into works of art—to ask what the stains *meant*—and to contrast his achievement with that of the American painter Morris Louis, in whose works stains remain stains, resist transfiguration even into veils, showing, perhaps, a hatred for fat? a need to soil? a wish for pushing off the white radiance of eternity? . . . This is to treat works of art as Leonardo treated his spotted wall, as an occasion for critical invention which knows no limit, the deep play of departments of literature and hermeneutics.

['Deep Interpretation', in *The Philosophical Disenfranchisement of Art* (New York: Columbia University Press, 1986), 50–60, 63–7.]

NELSON GOODMAN

41   **Art and Authenticity**

> . . . the most tantalizing question of all: If a fake is so expert that even after the most thorough and trustworthy examination its authenticity is still open to doubt, is it or is it not as satisfactory a work of art as if it were unequivocally genuine?
>
> Aline B. Saarinen[1]

Forgeries of works of art present a nasty practical problem to the collector, the curator, and the art historian, who must often expend taxing amounts of time and energy in determining whether or not particular objects are genuine. But the theoretical problem raised is even more acute. The hardheaded question why there is any aesthetic difference between a deceptive forgery and an original work challenges a basic premiss on which the very functions of collector, museum, and art historian depend. A philosopher of art caught without an answer to this question is at least as badly off as a curator of paintings caught taking a Van Meegeren for a Vermeer.

The question is most strikingly illustrated by the case of a given work and a forgery or copy or reproduction of it. Suppose we have before us, on the left, Rembrandt's original painting *Lucretia* and, on the right, a superlative imitation of it. We know from a fully documented history that the painting on the left is the original; and we know from X-ray photographs and microscopic examination and chemical analysis that the painting on the right is a recent fake. Although there are many differences between the two—e.g., in authorship, age, physical and chemical characteristics, and market value—we cannot see any difference between them; and if they are moved while we sleep, we cannot then tell which is which by merely looking at them. Now we are pressed with the question whether there can be any aesthetic difference between the two pictures; and the questioner's tone often intimates that the answer is plainly *no*, that the only differences here are aesthetically irrelevant.

We must begin by inquiring whether the distinction between what can and what cannot be seen in the pictures by 'merely looking at them' is entirely clear. We are looking at the pictures, but presumably not 'merely looking' at them, when we examine them under a microscope or fluoroscope. Does merely looking, then, mean looking without the use of any instrument? This

seems a little unfair to the man who needs glasses to tell
hippopotamus. But if glasses are permitted at all, how str
and can we consistently exclude the magnifying glass and
Again, if incandescent light is permitted, can violet-ray ligh.
And even with incandescent light, must it be of medium inten.
normal angle, or is a strong raking light permitted? All these c
covered by saying that 'merely looking' is looking at the picture:
use of instruments other than those customarily used in looking   ɯ
general. This will cause trouble when we turn, say, to certain miniature
illuminations or Assyrian cylinder seals that we can hardly distinguish from
the crudest copies without using a strong glass. Furthermore, even in our case
of the two pictures, subtle differences of drawing or painting discoverable
only with a magnifying glass may still, quite obviously, be aesthetic differences between the pictures. If a powerful microscope is used instead, this is
no longer the case; but just how much magnification is permitted? To specify
what is meant by merely looking at the pictures is thus far from easy; but for
the sake of argument, let us suppose that all these difficulties have been
resolved and the notion of 'merely looking' made clear enough.

Then we must ask who is assumed to be doing the looking. Our questioner
does not, I take it, mean to suggest that there is no aesthetic difference
between two pictures if at least one person, say a cross-eyed wrestler, can
see no difference. The more pertinent question is whether there can be any
aesthetic difference if nobody, not even the most skilled expert, can ever tell
the pictures apart by merely looking at them. *But notice now that no one can
ever ascertain by merely looking at the pictures that no one ever has been or will be
able to tell them apart by merely looking at them.* In other words, the question in
its present form concedes that no one can ascertain by merely looking at the
pictures that there is no aesthetic difference between them. This seems
repugnant to our questioner's whole motivation. For if merely looking can
never establish that two pictures are aesthetically the same, something that is
beyond the reach of any given looking is admitted as constituting an aesthetic
difference. And in that case, the reason for not admitting documents and the
results of scientific tests becomes very obscure.

The real issue may be more accurately formulated as the question whether
there is any aesthetic difference between the two pictures *for me* (or for x) if I
(or x) cannot tell them apart by merely looking at them. But this is not quite
right either. For I can never ascertain merely by looking at the pictures that
even I shall never be able to see any difference between them. And to concede
that something beyond any given looking at the pictures by me may constitute an aesthetic difference between them *for me* is, again, quite at odds
with the tacit conviction or suspicion that activates the questioner.

Thus the critical question amounts finally to this: is there any aesthetic
difference between the two pictures for x at t, where t is a suitable period of

$_{\nu}$ if x cannot tell them apart by merely looking at them at t? Or in other words, can anything that x does not discern by merely looking at the pictures at t constitute an aesthetic difference between them for x at t?

In setting out to answer this question, we must bear clearly in mind that what one can distinguish at any given moment by merely looking depends not only upon native visual acuity but upon practice and training. Americans look pretty much alike to a Chinese who has never looked at many of them. Twins may be indistinguishable to all but their closest relatives and acquaintances. Moreover, only through looking at them when someone has named them for us can we learn to tell Joe from Jim upon merely looking at them. Looking at people or things attentively, with the knowledge of certain presently invisible respects in which they differ, increases our ability to discriminate between them—and between other things or other people—upon merely looking at them. Thus pictures that look just alike to the newsboy come to look quite unlike to him by the time he has become a museum director.

Although I see no difference now between the two pictures in question, I may learn to see a difference between them. I cannot determine now by merely looking at them, or in any other way, that I *shall* be able to learn. But the information that they are very different, that the one is the original and the other the forgery, argues against any inference to the conclusion that I *shall not* be able to learn. And the fact that I may later be able to make a perceptual distinction between the pictures that I cannot make now constitutes an aesthetic difference between them that is important to me now.

Furthermore, to look at the pictures now with the knowledge that the left one is the original and the other the forgery may help develop the ability to tell which is which later by merely looking at them. Thus, with information not derived from the present or any past looking at the pictures, the present looking may have a quite different bearing upon future lookings from what it would otherwise have. The way the pictures in fact differ constitutes an aesthetic difference between them for me now because my knowledge of the way they differ bears upon the role of the present looking in training my perceptions to discriminate between these pictures, and between others.

But that is not all. My knowledge of the difference between the two pictures, just because it affects the relationship of the present to future lookings, informs the very character of my present looking. This knowledge instructs me to look at the two pictures differently now, even if what I see is the same. Beyond testifying that I may learn to see a difference, it also indicates to some extent the kind of scrutiny to be applied now, the comparisons and contrasts to be made in imagination, and the relevant associations to be brought to bear. It thereby guides the selection, from my past experience, of items and aspects for use in my present looking. Thus not only later but right now, the unperceived difference between the two pictures is a consideration pertinent to my visual experience with them.

In short, although I cannot tell the pictures apart merely by looking at them now, the fact that the left-hand one is the original and the right-hand one a forgery constitutes an aesthetic difference between them for me now because knowledge of this fact (1) stands as evidence that there may be a difference between them that I can learn to perceive, (2) assigns the present looking a role as training toward such a perceptual discrimination, and (3) makes consequent demands that modify and differentiate my present experience in looking at the two pictures.

Nothing depends here upon my ever actually perceiving or being able to perceive a difference between the two pictures. What informs the nature and use of my present visual experience is not the fact or the assurance that such a perceptual discrimination is within my reach, but evidence that it may be; and such evidence is provided by the known factual differences between the pictures. Thus the pictures differ aesthetically for me now even if no one will ever be able to tell them apart merely by looking at them.

But suppose it could be *proved* that no one ever will be able to see any difference? This is about as reasonable as asking whether, if it can be proved that the market value and yield of a given US bond and one of a certain nearly bankrupt company will always be the same, there is any financial difference between the two bonds. For what sort of proof could be given? One might suppose that if nobody—not even the most skilled expert—has ever been able to see any difference between the pictures, then the conclusion that I shall never be able to is quite safe; but, as in the case of the Van Meegeren forgeries (of which, more later), distinctions not visible to the expert up to a given time may later become manifest even to the observant layman. Or one might think of some delicate scanning device that compares the color of two pictures at every point and registers the slightest discrepancy. What, though, is meant here by 'at every point'? At no mathematical point, of course, is there any color at all; and even some physical particles are too small to have color. The scanning device must thus cover at each instant a region big enough to have color but at least as small as any perceptible region. Just how to manage this is puzzling since 'perceptible' in the present context means 'discernible by merely looking', and thus the line between perceptible and nonperceptible regions seems to depend on the arbitrary line between a magnifying glass and a microscope. If some such line is drawn, we can never be sure that the delicacy of our instruments is superior to the maximal attainable acuity of unaided perception. Indeed, some experimental psychologists are inclined to conclude that every measurable difference in light can sometimes be detected by the naked eye. And there is a further difficulty. Our scanning device will examine color—that is, reflected light. Since reflected light depends partly upon incident light, illumination of every quality, of every intensity, and from every direction must be tried. And for each case, especially since the paintings do not have a plane surface, a complete scanning must be made from every angle. But of course we cannot cover every variation, or even determine a single absolute correspondence, in even one respect. Thus the search for a proof that I shall never be able to see any difference between the two pictures is futile for more than technological reasons.

Yet suppose we are nevertheless pressed with the question whether, if proof *were* given, there would then be any aesthetic difference for me between the pictures. And suppose we answer this farfetched question in the negative. This will still give our questioner no comfort. For the net result would be that if no difference between the pictures can in fact be perceived, then the existence of an aesthetic difference between them will rest entirely upon what is or is not proved by means other than merely looking at them. This hardly supports the contention that there can be no aesthetic difference without a perceptual difference.

Returning from the realm of the ultra-hypothetical, we may be faced with the protest that the vast aesthetic difference thought to obtain between the Rembrandt and the forgery cannot be accounted for in terms of the search for, or even the discovery of, perceptual differences so slight that they can be made out, if at all, only after much experience and long practice. This objection can be dismissed at once; for minute perceptual differences can bear enormous weight. The clues that tell me whether I have caught the eye of someone across the room are almost indiscernible. The actual differences in sound that distinguish a fine from a mediocre performance can be picked out only by the well-trained ear. Extremely subtle changes can alter the whole design, feeling, or expression of a painting. Indeed, the slightest perceptual differences sometimes matter the most aesthetically; gross physical damage to a fresco may be less consequential than slight but smug retouching.

All I have attempted to show, of course, is that the two pictures can differ aesthetically, not that the original is better than the forgery. In our example, the original probably is much the better picture, since Rembrandt paintings are in general much better than copies by unknown painters. But a copy of a Lastman by Rembrandt may well be better than the original. We are not called upon here to make such particular comparative judgments or to formulate canons of aesthetic evaluation. We have fully met the demands of our problem by showing that the fact that we cannot tell our two pictures apart merely by looking at them does not imply that they are aesthetically the same—and thus does not force us to conclude that the forgery is as good as the original.

The example we have been using throughout illustrates a special case of a more general question concerning the aesthetic significance of authenticity. Quite aside from the occurrence of forged duplication, does it matter whether an original work is the product of one or another artist or school or period? Suppose that I can easily tell two pictures apart but cannot tell who painted either except by using some device like X-ray photography. Does the fact that the picture is or is not by Rembrandt make any aesthetic difference? What is involved here is the discrimination not of one picture from another but of the class of Rembrandt paintings from the class of other paintings. My chance of learning to make this discrimination correctly—of discovering projectible characteristics that differentiate Rembrandts in general from non-Rembrandts—depends heavily upon the set of examples available as a basis. Thus the fact that the given picture belongs to the one class or the other is important for me to know in learning how to tell Rembrandt paintings from others. In other words, my present (or future) inability to determine the authorship of the given picture without use of scientific apparatus does not imply that the authorship makes no aesthetic difference to me; for knowledge of the authorship, no matter how obtained, can contribute materially toward developing my ability to determine without such apparatus whether or not any picture, including this one on another occasion, is by Rembrandt.

Incidentally, one rather striking puzzle is readily solved in these terms. When Van Meegeren sold his pictures as Vermeers, he deceived most of the best-qualified experts; and only by his confession was the fraud revealed. Nowadays even the fairly knowing layman is astonished that any competent judge could have taken a Van Meegeren for a Vermeer, so obvious are the differences. What has happened? The general level of aesthetic sensibility has hardly risen so fast that the layman of today sees more acutely than the expert of twenty years ago. Rather, the better information now at hand makes the discrimination easier. Presented with a single unfamiliar picture at a time, the expert had to decide whether it was enough like known Vermeers to be by the same artist. And every time a Van Meegeren was added to the corpus of pictures accepted as Vermeers, the criteria for acceptance were modified thereby; and the mistaking of further Van Meegerens for Vermeers became inevitable. Now, however, not only have the Van Meegerens been subtracted from the precedent-class for Vermeer, but also a precedent-class for Van Meegeren has been established. With these two precedent-classes before us, the characteristic differences become so conspicuous that telling other Van Meegerens from Vermeers offers little difficulty. Yesterday's expert might well have avoided his errors if he had had a few known Van Meegerens handy for comparison. And today's layman who so cleverly spots a Van Meegeren may well be caught taking some quite inferior school-piece for a Vermeer.

In answering the questions raised above, I have not attempted the formidable task of defining 'aesthetic' in general, but have simply argued that since the exercise, training, and development of our powers of discriminating among works of art are plainly aesthetic activities, the aesthetic properties of a picture include not only those found by looking at it but also those that determine how it is to be looked at. This rather obvious fact would hardly have needed underlining but for the prevalence of the time-honored Tingle–Immersion theory,[2] which tells us that the proper behavior on encountering a work of art is to strip ourselves of all the vestments of knowledge and experience (since they might blunt the immediacy of our enjoyment), then submerge ourselves completely and gauge the aesthetic potency of the work by the intensity and duration of the resulting tingle. The theory is absurd on the face of it and useless for dealing with any of the important problems of aesthetics; but it has become part of the fabric of our common nonsense.

[*Languages of Art: An Approach to a Theory of Symbols*, 2nd edn. (Indianapolis: Hackett, 1976), 99–112.]

ROLAND BARTHES

42   From Work to Text

Over the past several years, a change has been taking place in our ideas about language and, as a consequence, about the (literary) work, which owes at least, its phenomenal existence to language. This change is obviously linked to current developments in, among other fields, linguistics, anthropology, Marxism, and psychoanalysis (the word 'link' is used here in a deliberately neutral fashion: it implies no decision about a determination, be it multiple and dialectical). The change affecting the notion of the work does not necessarily come from the internal renewal of each of these disciplines, but proceeds, rather, from their encounter at the level of an object that traditionally depends on none of them. *Interdisciplinary* activity, valued today as an important aspect of research, cannot be accomplished by simple confrontations between various specialized branches of knowledge. Interdisciplinary work is not a peaceful operation: it begins *effectively* when the solidarity of the old disciplines breaks down—a process made more violent, perhaps, by the jolts of fashion—to the benefit of a new object and a new language, neither of which is in the domain of those branches of knowledge that one calmly sought to confront.

It is precisely this uneasiness with classification that allows for the diagnosis of a certain mutation. The mutation that seems to be taking hold of the idea of the work must not, however, be overestimated: it is part of an epistemological shift rather than of a real break, a break of the kind which, as has often been remarked, supposedly occurred during the last century, with the appearance of Marxism and Freudianism. No new break seems to have occurred since, and it can be said that, in a way, we have been involved in repetition for the past hundred years. Today history, our history, allows only displacement, variation, going-beyond, and rejection. Just as Einsteinian science requires the inclusion of the *relativity of reference points* in the object studied, so the combined activity of Marxism, Freudianism, and structuralism requires, in the case of literature, the relativization of the *scriptor's*, the reader's, and the observer's (the critic's) relationships. In opposition to the notion of the *work*—a traditional notion that has long been and still is thought of in what might be called Newtonian fashion—there now arises a need for a new object, one obtained by the displacement or overturning of previous categories. This object is the *Text*. I realize that this word is fashionable and therefore suspect in certain quarters, but that is precisely why I would like to review the principal propositions at the intersection of which the Text is situated today. These propositions are to be understood as enunciations rather than arguments, as mere indications, as it were, approaches that 'agree' to remain metaphoric. Here, then, are those propositions: they deal with method, genre, the sign, the plural, filiation, reading (in an active sense), and pleasure.

1. The Text must not be thought of as a defined object. It would be useless to attempt a material separation of works and texts. [. . .] The difference is as follows: the work is concrete, occupying a portion of book-space (in a library, for example); the Text, on the other hand, is a methodological field. [. . .] While the work is held in the hand, the text is held in language: it exists only as discourse. The Text is not the decomposition of the work; rather it is the work that is the Text's imaginary tail. In other words, *the Text is experienced only in an activity, a production.* [. . .]

2. Similarly, the Text does not come to a stop with (good) literature; it cannot be apprehended as part of a hierarchy or even a simple division of genres. What constitutes the Text is, on the contrary (or precisely), its subversive force with regard to old classifications. [. . .]

If the Text raises problems of classification, that is because it always implies an experience of limits. Thibaudet used to speak (but in a very restricted sense) about limit-works (such as Chateaubriand's *Life of Rancé*, a work that today indeed seems to be a 'text'): the Text is that which goes to the limit of the rules of enunciation (rationality, readability, and so on). The Text tries to situate itself exactly *behind* the limit of *doxa* (is not public opinion—constitutive of our democratic societies and powerfully aided by mass communication—defined by its limits, its energy of exclusion, its *censorship?*). One could literally say that the Text is always *paradoxical*.

3. [. . .] The logic that governs the Text is not comprehensive (seeking to define 'what the work means') but metonymic; and the activity of associations, contiguities, and cross-references coincides with a liberation of symbolic energy. The work (in the best of cases) is moderately symbolic (its symbolism runs out, comes to a halt), but the Text is *radically* symbolic. *A work whose integrally symbolic nature one conceives, perceives, and receives is a text.* [. . .]

4. The Text is plural. This does not mean just that it has several meanings, but rather that it achieves plurality of meaning, an *irreducible* plurality. The Text is not coexistence of meanings but passage, traversal; thus it answers not to an interpretation, liberal though it may be, but to an explosion, a dissemination. [. . .]

Every text, being itself the intertext of another text, belongs to the intertextual, which must not be confused with a text's origins: to search for the 'sources of' and 'influence upon' a work is to satisfy the myth of filiation. The quotations from which a text is constructed are anonymous, irrecoverable, and yet *already read*: they are quotations without quotation marks. [. . .]

5. The work is caught up in a process of filiation. Three things are postulated here: a *determination* of the work by the outside world (by race, then by history), a *consecution* of works among themselves, and an *allocation* of the work to its author. The author is regarded as the father and the owner of his work; literary research therefore learns to *respect* the manuscript and the author's declared intentions, while society posits the legal nature of the author's relationship with his work (these are the 'author's rights,' which are actually quite recent; they were not legalized in France until the Revolution).

The Text, on the other hand, is read without the father's signature. The metaphor that describes the Text is also distinct from that describing the work. The latter refers to the image of an *organism* that grows by vital expansion, by 'development' (a significantly ambiguous word, both biological and rhetorical). The Text's metaphor is that of the *network*: if the Text expands, it is under the effect of a *combinatorial*, a *systematics* (an image which comes close to modern biology's views on the living being).

Therefore, no vital 'respect' is owed to the Text: it can be broken (this is exactly what the Middle Ages did with two authoritative texts, the Scriptures and Aristotle). The Text can be read without its father's guarantee: the restitution of the intertext paradoxically abolishes the concept of filiation. It is not that the author cannot 'come back' into the Text, into his text; however, he can only do so as a 'guest,' so to speak. If the author is a novelist, he inscribes himself in his text as one of his characters, as another figure sewn into the rug; his signature is no longer privileged and paternal, the locus of genuine truth, but rather, ludic. He becomes a 'paper author': his life is no longer the origin of his fables, but a fable that runs concurrently with his work. There is a reversal, and it is the work which affects the life, not the life which affects the work: the work of Proust and Genet allows us to read their lives as a text. The word 'bio-graphy' reassumes its strong meaning, in accordance with its etymology. At the same time, the enunciation's sincerity, which has been a veritable 'cross' of literary morality, becomes a false problem: the *I* that writes the text is never, itself, anything more than a paper *I*.

6. The work is ordinarily an object of consumption. I intend no demagoguery in referring here to so-called consumer culture, but one must

realize that today it is the work's 'quality' (this implies, ultimately, an appreciation in terms of 'taste') and not the actual process of reading that can establish differences between books. There is no structural difference between 'cultured' reading and casual subway reading. The Text (if only because of its frequent 'unreadability') decants the work from its consumption and gathers it up as play, task, production, and activity. This means that the Text requires an attempt to abolish (or at least to lessen) the distance between writing and reading, not by intensifying the reader's projection into the work, but by linking the two together in a single signifying process.

The distance separating writing from reading is historical: during the era of greatest social division (before the institution of democratic cultures), both reading and writing were class privileges. Rhetoric, the great literary code of those times, taught *writing* (even though speeches and not texts were generally produced). It is significant that the advent of democracy reversed the order: (secondary) school now prides itself on teaching how to *read* (well), and not how to *write*.

In fact, *reading* in the sense of *consuming* is not *playing* with the text. Here 'playing' must be understood in all its polysemy. The text itself *plays* (like a door on its hinges, like a device in which there is some 'play'); and the reader himself plays twice over: playing the Text as one plays a game, he searches for a practice that will re-produce the Text; but, to keep that practice from being reduced to a passive, inner mimesis (the Text being precisely what resists such a reduction), he also *plays* the Text in the musical sense of the term. The history of music (as practice, not as 'art') happens to run quite parallel to the history of the Text. There was a time when 'practicing' music lovers were numerous (at least within the confines of a certain class), when 'playing' and 'listening' constituted an almost undifferentiated activity. Then two roles appeared in succession: first, that of the *interpreter*, to whom the bourgeois public delegated its playing; second, that of the music lover who listened to music without knowing how to play it. Today, post-serial music has disrupted the role of the 'interpreter' by requiring him to be, in a certain sense, the coauthor of a score which he completes rather than 'interprets.'

The Text is largely a score of this new type: it asks the reader for an active collaboration. This is a great innovation, because it compels us to ask 'who *executes* the work?' (a question raised by Mallarmé, who wanted the audience to *produce* the book). Today only the critic *executes* the work (in both senses). The reduction of reading to consumption is obviously responsible for the 'boredom' that many people feel when confronting the modern ('unreadable') text, or the avant-garde movie or painting: to suffer from boredom means that one cannot produce the text, play it, open it out, *make it go*.

7. This suggests one final approach to the Text, that of pleasure. I do not know if a hedonistic aesthetic ever existed, but there certainly exists a pleasure associated with the work (at least with certain works). I can enjoy reading and

rereading Proust, Flaubert, Balzac, and even—why not?—Alexandre Dumas; but this pleasure, as keen as it may be and even if disengaged from all prejudice, remains partly (unless there has been an exceptional critical effort) a pleasure of consumption. If I can read those authors, I also know that I cannot *rewrite* them (that today, one can no longer write 'like that'); that rather depressing knowledge is enough to separate one from the production of those works at the very moment when their remoteness founds one's modernity (for what is 'being modern' but the full realization that one cannot begin to write the same works once again?). The Text, on the other hand, is linked to enjoyment, to pleasure without separation. Order of the signifier, the Text participates in a social utopia of its own: prior to history, the Text achieves, if not the transparency of social relations, at least the transparency of language relations. It is the space in which no one language has a hold over any other, in which all languages circulate freely.

These few propositions, inevitably, do not constitute the articulation of a theory of the Text. This is not just a consequence of the presenter's insufficiencies (besides, I have in many respects only recapitulated what is being developed around me); rather, it proceeds from the fact that a theory of the Text cannot be fully satisfied by a metalinguistic exposition. The destruction of metalanguage, or at least (since it may become necessary to return to it provisionally) the questioning of it, is part of the theory itself. Discourse on the Text should itself be only 'text,' search, and textual toil, since the Text is that *social* space that leaves no language safe or untouched, that allows no enunciative subject to hold the position of judge, teacher, analyst, confessor, or decoder. The theory of the Text can coincide only with the activity of writing.

['From Work to Text', in Josué V. Harari (ed.), *Textual Strategies: Perspectives in Post-Structuralist Criticism* (Ithaca, NY: Cornell University Press, 1979), 73–81.]

Why Respond Emotionally to Art?

Many people would say that art's main value lies with how it makes them feel: that is, because of their emotional responses to it. Many theorists, as well, have recognized that feelings and emotions are essential both to our appreciation of art and to why it is important to us. We have already seen that some are reluctant to inquire into a work's history, an artist's intentions, or other interpretative matters dealt with in the two previous sections, lest such 'intellectualization' interfere with their emotional responses. Some authors in the present section, on the contrary, explain how the emotional is not easily separated from the cognitive.

R. K. Elliott describes how an artwork may exploit our capacity for empathy, especially when it is experienced as the expression of a particular individual's feelings, ideas, or point of view. In such cases, Elliott holds, we experience the work 'from the inside'. We also experience works 'from the outside'. Doing so will not necessarily remove their emotional power, but the effects will be different, as Elliott attempts to show by discussion of examples drawn from poetry, music, and painting.

Kendall Walton's theory of representation does not wait for subtle or powerful emotional effects to address the issue of our active and affective engagement with works of art. Walton would root such participation in the simplest phenomena of picture perception—matters, he argues, that are literally child's play. Since, on this theory, to perceive something in a picture is already to be involved in a rich game of self imagination, rather than merely visual recognition, our emotional intimacy with works of art comes as no surprise. And, as Elliott writes of experiencing works of various media from the inside, Walton attributes much of the value of representational participation to empathetic feeling: the imagining of ourselves in another's position.

One art form which has a great deal of power to move us emotionally is theatre, and audiences have been enjoying that power for literally thousands of years. Writing nearly 2,500 years ago, Aristotle says that tragedy should generate the emotions of pity and fear. He holds that what we call different genres of writing are supposed to generate different kinds of emotions: comedies should amuse us, and tragedy (according to Aristotle) is supposed to produce pity and fear. Martha Nussbaum provides an explanation why these two emotions in particular should be so important for tragedy. One of the most important and difficult facts about human life is that one can be as good a person as one can reasonably be expected to be but still suffer overwhelming misfortune, due to factors beyond one's control. The appropriate feelings towards such a situation are pity (for suffering which is undeserved and beyond one's control) and fear (because the same could well happen to ourselves). Through our emotional responses to a dramatic work, we learn a fundamental fact about the human condition.

Since emotions are such an important part of our responses to art, we should ask what an emotion is. Aristotle is among the first philosophers credited with developing what has come to be known as a cognitive theory of emotion, where emotions such as pity and fear are not identified simply as feeling states, but as feelings accompanied by certain beliefs or thoughts. That is, each emotion has a specific sort of cognitive content that helps us distinguish one emotion from another. (Dewey, Nussbaum, Walton, and Levinson all endorse cognitive theories of emotion.) For example, to experience fear one must believe that one is in danger; to have pity for a character one must believe that the character has suffered undeserved misfortune.

If, as Aristotle asserts, we desire to learn, and learning gives pleasure, then he can answer another question about our emotional responses to art: why do we *enjoy* going to performances and movies that make us cry, that make us sad and melancholy, and where we pity the characters, or become angry with them, and fear for ourselves. Aristotle also says that imitation in itself gives us pleasure. (Some commentators have also thought that catharsis provides pleasure, but the idea of catharsis, so widely associated with Aristotle, is not developed explicitly or in detail by him.) Susan Feagin has another explanation for the pleasure we experience in viewing tragedies. Some of our 'direct' responses to tragedies are painful—sadness, pity, perhaps even anger and indignation. But we also have 'metaresponses', which can be responses to the fact that we respond in these ways. These metaresponses are pleasurable, especially if we are pleased to find ourselves to be the kind of people who are saddened and distressed by suffering, injustice, and other types of misfortune. Appreciating tragedy is thus seen as having a moral dimension insofar as it involves, as Aristotle himself might say, having the right kinds of responses at the right time to the right things.

If tragedy is supposed to generate pity and fear, jokes are supposed to generate laughter and amusement. Ted Cohen asks, 'What is the relation of the joke to the amusement?' Many jokes, to be successful, require the listener to have certain background beliefs or inclinations—even prejudices. Jokes can therefore create and reinforce a sense of community *and* a sense of exclusion for those who don't have the background to 'get' the joke, or who have interests or desires which prevent them from finding it funny.

Edmund Burke argues that there is a kind of experience, which he calls 'delight', that is different from both pleasure and pain. Delight, Burke says, is the reduction or cessation of pain, whereas pleasure is a positive feeling on its own. (It is interesting to note that the philosopher Arthur Schopenhauer had a contrary view: pain is a positive feeling on its own, and pleasure is simply the reduction of pain. Pleasure in art and beauty he considered a temporary respite from the pain of unfulfilled desire.) Burke proposes that painful responses—horror, fear, terror, astonishment—to tragedies, certain poetry, and even the vast ocean, are accompanied by delight (but not by pleasure), which is produced by our awareness that we are not actually in danger. Objects that produce pain and delight he calls 'sublime', a common term in the eighteenth century, though one that has fallen out of use. It is, however, a very useful term because the significance of certain works of art (and certain aspects of nature) is revealed in their capacity to move us in ways that are unpleasant and disturbing.

Emotional and other feeling responses to music raise a different set of challenges. Music does not typically have content, at least not with the richness and specificity that literature has, and hence, given the cognitive theory of emotions, it may seem puzzling how we could have *emotional* responses to music at all. Nevertheless, we certainly seem to have such responses, including such 'negative responses' as sadness and melancholy, which we would ordinarily want to avoid. Jerrold Levinson provides an account of the nature of these emotional responses and how they can arise in response to music, and offers several explanations for why we would seek out and enjoy having them.

For Expression Theory, in its classical or 'refined' form, the arousal of emotion as by the operation of a cause was a sign either of bad art or lack of taste. Aesthetic experience was not a matter of recognizing that the object possesses emotional (and other) qualities, but required the reader to transfer himself into the poet's mind, re-enact his creative expression and thereby allow his clarified emotion to be manifested in him. According to Gentile, in aesthetic experience every duality between ourselves and the poet is transcended; when we have entered into the poet's feeling we feel ourselves to be looking upon the same world as he looked upon, with the same heart and eyes.

The exaggerations of Expression Theory, especially the belief that in experiencing a poem aesthetically we reproduce in ourselves the creative activity of the poet, may have obscured its less spectacular but more genuine insight, namely, that some works of art are capable of being experienced as if they were human expression and that we do not experience expression exactly as we perceive objects or ordinary objective qualities. By 'expression' I mean only that expression which is perceived as qualifying or issuing from the person, especially gesture, speech and such internal activities as thinking and imagining. I do not intend the term to cover any object perceived as made by a person and existing independently of him. The Expression Theorists recognized that a poem can be perceived not as an object bearing an impersonal meaning but as if it were the speech or thought of another person and that it is possible for us to make this expression our own. A work may be experienced 'from within' or 'from without'. I cannot define these terms but hope that this paper will elucidate their meaning. So far as poetry and painting are concerned, experiencing a work from within is, roughly speaking, experiencing it as if one were the poet or the artist. If a work is experienced as expression, experiencing it from within involves experiencing this expression after a certain imaginative manner as one's own. Experiencing it from without is experiencing it as expression, but not experiencing this expression as if it were one's own. When I say that a work 'expresses emotion' I mean that if it is perceived as or as if it were expression, it may be perceived as or as if it were the expression of an emotion.

In so far as experiencing a lyric poem differs from hearing someone actually speaking to us, in general these differences make it easier rather than more difficult for us to experience the poem from within. The poet is not visibly before us as another individual; the poem itself may rapidly and lucidly acquaint us with all that is necessary for us to understand the situation in which the poet (*qua* 'speaker' of the poem) is represented as experiencing an emotion; and to experience the poem at all we have to give it a real or virtual reading in which we embody the poet's expression in our own voice. Consequently, the lyric 'I' functions as an invitation to the reader to place himself, in imagination, at the point from which the poet is related to the situation given in the poem. *Qua* maker, the poet may employ devices which tend to inhibit this communion, but in many cases the reader is able, eventually if not immediately, to take up the lyric 'I', invest himself imaginatively with the poet's situation, and experience the poet's expression and the emotion expressed from the place of the expressing subject rather than from the place of one who hears and understands the expression from without.

When we experience an emotion in this way, through an imaginative assumption of the expression and situation of another person (real or imaginary) we need not and commonly do not experience it as we would if the situation were unequivocally our own. In the *Lysis* Plato distinguishes between the ignorance which is both present in and predicable of a man and that which though it is present in him is not predicable of him. Emotion is subject to a similar distinction: the emotion that I feel in experiencing a work of art from within (and that which I feel as another person's in real life) may be present in me without being predicable of me. It is present in me because I do not merely recognize that the poet is expressing, for example, sadness, but actually feel this sadness; yet the emotion I feel is not predicable of me, i.e., it would be false to say that I *am* sad or even, unqualifiedly, that I feel sad. Edith Stein describes emotion felt in this way (in our experience of other persons) as 'primordial' for the other subject, 'non-primordial' for me: it is 'there for me in him'. The emotion expressed in a lyric poem may be 'there for me in the speaker of the poem', even if the speaker is a fiction and even if the emotion was never experienced by the historical poet.

In experiencing a poem from within, the reader keeps more or less explicit contact with the poet. Sometimes he seems to be there together with the poet, as if they inhabited the same body and as if the poet were speaking or thinking with the reader's voice; sometimes the reader seems to be there in place of the poet, expressing and experiencing the poet's emotion as it were on the poet's behalf; sometimes the reader seems even to have supplanted the poet, but still without experiencing the expressed emotion as the product of his own fantasy. On occasions, as Longinus recognized, the experience is so vivid that it seems almost as if the reader were actually in the poet's situation. He has to return to himself, rather as if he were waking from a dream. As a rule, however, the reader is aware of his ability to relinquish the imagined situation and break off his communion with the poet immediately and without effort. We rarely experience a poem entirely from within, but are drawn into the world of the poem at certain points and later once more experience it from without, usually without noticing these changes in our point of view.

I have spoken of 'experiencing' a poem from within and from without, but these are very like alternative manners of performing a work as well as alternative modes of experiencing it. The word 'poem' is correctly applied not only to the text but also to that which may be constructed and experienced on the basis of the text, rather as the musical work is both the score and that which is present for perception when the work is performed. A poem is 'realized' by a process in which understanding and imagination supplement and progressively correct each other. An initial understanding of the words of the text enables us to begin to represent the work in imagination, and these same words appear also in the imaginative representation. Through the representation which at this stage is the partial intuitive fulfilment of a meaning as yet only tentatively grasped, we become aware of new significances which lead in turn to the modification of the representation. This process continues indefinitely. Not every poem need be represented according to either of the modes that I have described, but where it is possible to experience a work according to these modes (i.e., when it can be experienced as expression) it is not immaterial which of them we adopt, for the perception of aesthetic qualities begins almost as soon as we begin to realize the poem and these qualities will differ according to the mode of representation. Two critics may find the same poem to be vivid and unified, but for one it has the vividness and unity of an observed event, for the other a vividness and unity more like those of an experience in which he actively participates. Even the aesthetic qualities of the rhythm and word-music will differ in some degree. Although for a particular poem one mode of representation may be more appropriate than the other, there is no ground for declaring either mode to be in general 'unaesthetic'. In so far as psychical distance is taken to be the absence of merely personal feeling and practical concern, it may be maintained or lost whichever mode is adopted. Each is a way of making the work available to aesthetic awareness. In one case the poem arises as a complex content entirely at the objective pole of consciousness; in the other it is realized as an experience the description of which involves a reference not simply to an objective content but also to the subject. In the first case aesthetic perception is awareness of certain qualities of an objective content; in the second it also includes a reflexive awareness of certain aspects of the experience as such.

It is difficult not to experience Donne's first *Holy Sonnet* ('Thou hast made me') from within. If after having experienced the poem in this way the reader were asked what his attention had been fixed upon, he could only answer that it had been fixed upon death and damnation—not upon death and damnation in general, however, nor his own, nor yet the poet's. He could not say exactly what it had been fixed upon unless he could describe his own situation relative to the poet and the world of the poem. If he is a person of critical temperament, the poem *qua* experience will become more and more com-

prehensively an object of reflection, so that at some stage it will be appropriate to say that he is related to the poem as to an objective content. But the
object so contemplated is one which cannot be described without reference
to the subject. So long as the full extent of the equivocality of 'work of art'
and of all its specifications is not clearly recognized, such assertions as
'Aesthetic experience is experience of the work' and 'The critic's task is to
talk about the work, not about himself' have the sort of ambivalence which
allows them to be misused as instruments of persuasion. Except in so far as he
reflects upon his own experience, a person who experiences a poem from
within does not concentrate his attention on any objective content which can
be identified with the poem *qua* aesthetic object. He does not even fix his
attention on the words of the poem, for when we speak or think from deep
feelings, although we are aware of our words, of their adequacy or the lack of
it, and even of the quality of their sound, it is scarcely correct to say that our
attention is concentrated upon them. When experiencing a poem from
within we do not fix our attention upon it but live it according to a certain
imaginative mode. This is not sufficient from the aesthetic point of view, but
it is not in any way aesthetically improper. [. . .] The inability to experience
such a poem from within is a deprivation for which no exquisiteness of taste
can compensate. When we experience Donne's poem *The Sunne Rising* from
without, we hear the poet, represented as lying in bed with his mistress,
address the sun with good-humoured but violently expressed contempt. We
are shocked by his impiety and impressed by the brilliance of his wit. When
we experience the poem from within, the poet's expression is reproduced in
us at a level which is prior to the distinction between what is spoken aloud
and what is merely thought. As a result the dramatic character of the poem is
appreciably softened, and what appeared from without as aggressively clever
conceit now seems at once more playful and more serious. The lyrical aspect
of the poem is experienced more convincingly, and we feel a sense of the
power and glory of sensual love—the same emotion which is experienced
with such splendour in the *Song of Solomon*. Now it seems to us that the poet
diminished the sun only to glorify a greater god, one whose power we
ourselves feel in experiencing the poem from within. But in this case the
understanding obtained through experiencing the poem from within does
not establish its authority absolutely. This poem has two faces, and the critic
must experience it according to both modes if he is to evaluate it justly.

There is a sense in which a poem can be said to provide an adequate
'objective correlative' of an emotion if the poem is experienced from within.
It does this to the extent that it displays or 'imitates' the emotion, and to the
extent to which it enables us to experience it when we realize the poem from
within. A poem like Hölderin's elegy *Homecoming* or Donne's *The Sunne
Rising* accomplishes this by deploying a situation around the reader as he
realizes the poem, by representing the structure of a developing mood, and

by enabling him to reproduce in imagination, from the place of the experiencing subject, modes of speech, changes in the direction, tempo and pressure
of thought, movements of fancy, and even the modifications of perception
through which the emotion manifests itself. The reader must himself contribute the appropriate feelings and emotional tone, but his feeling will be
appropriate not only to the imagined situation but also to the expression he
has made his own. Under this guidance the emotion comes into being in him.

In his article 'The Expression Theory of Art' Professor Bouwsma argues that
we can perceive or sense the sadness of sad music without feeling sad ourselves, and that to attempt to elucidate the application of 'emotional' predicates to music by reference to expression is only to invite confusion. When
we say 'The music is sad' we may mean that it makes us sad, but for the good
critic, at least, 'The music is sad' means that the form or *gestalt* character of
the music has a certain audible quality which we call 'sad' because the music
has some of the characteristics of sad persons. 'The sadness is to the music
rather like the redness to the apple, than it is like the burp to the cider.' We do
apply emotional predicates to sounds according to the two criteria Bouwsma
mentions, but we also apply them because we perceive sounds as or as if they
were expressing emotion. [. . .] We call some sounds 'happy' or 'merry' in this
way, because they have some of the characteristics of happy persons, and we
perceive these emotional qualities as *gestalt* characters without hearing the
sounds as if they were expression. But in such cases we have to judge that it is
appropriate to apply the emotional predicate. To perceive music as *expressing*
emotion we have to perceive the sounds *as if* they were expression. When I
watch the foliage of a tree blown hither and thither in a strong wind, at first I
see only a multiplicity of movements. Then this multitude becomes a unity,
and I see a restless and fearful agitation on the brink of frenzy. But to see the
foliage in this way is to see it as if it were a person and to grasp its movement
as if it were expression. If I am to continue perceiving this vividly explicit
fearfulness I must remain under the spell. As soon as I concentrate upon the
movements simply as movements, I cease to see the tree as if it were a person
and drop back into a more ordinary mode of perception. Similarly, the
humming of telegraph wires may be heard as the contented murmuring of
a number of 'voices', but if one concentrates upon the sound the voices
disappear and the inhuman noise of the wire returns. If I listen to a passage of
'sad' music to discover whether I perceive an emotional quality or an expression of sadness, I hear sounds with an emotional quality. But the conditions of
the experiment preclude me from hearing anything else. Music is eminently
expressive but the musical sounds are very different from the sound of the
human voice. Consequently, when attention is fixed on the sounds, one hears
something inhuman having an intense emotional quality. For it to be possible
for us to hear the music as expressing emotion, we must not be concentrating

too keenly upon the qualities of the sounds themselves but listening to the music in a more relaxed and 'natural' way. Then we find ourselves hearing some passage as if someone were expressing his emotion in and through the sounds as a person does in and through his voice; but although we hear the sounds rather as if they were a voice, in listening to pure music we seldom if ever hear them as the ordinary human voice. But there is a different manner in which we may hear the music as if it were expressing emotion, namely, by hearing it as our own expression. We value these experiences because the emotion in the music is realized most definitely and most vividly in these ways. Hearing the music as expressing emotion, whether from without or from within, is an instance of imaginatively enriched perception, one of many which we encounter in the experience of art.

That the expression and the emotion it expresses 'belong' to nobody is no more a hindrance to our understanding the expression and experiencing the emotion than it is with poetry. We sometimes attribute the expressed emotion to the composer, but very often we do not attribute it to anyone definite: it is merely 'his' emotion which is being expressed. On occasions, perhaps, although we hear the music as expression we do not attribute the expression to anyone at all, perceiving expression without an expressor, as no doubt we once did in early childhood. The emotion expressed in a song or aria is usually referred to the character the singer is personating. Perceiving anything as if it were expression of emotion involves a reference to feeling, but we can perceive the music as expressing sadness without being made sad by it. Whether we are made sad by it or not, experiencing it simply as the expression of someone else's sadness is experiencing it from without. Often, however, we are able to experience the music from within, in which case we experience it as if it were our own expression and may feel the expressed emotion non-primordially. The hearer does not have to perform the music as the reader has to perform the poem, but in a certain way he can appropriate the stream of musical sound as his own expression. An extreme experience of emotionally expressive music from within is very like a real-life experience of, say, joy, when the emotion has no definite object and when we express it by voice or gesture. In this case we begin by directing an ordinary attention on the musical sounds, but, as if in a single movement, the music is received by us and, as it were, reissues from us as if it were our own expression, not exactly as if it were our own voice but as a mode of expression *sui generis*. Once the mood or emotion is present in us the experience is usually extremely pleasing, for to the extent that emotion is not tied to any external state of affairs or dependent in any other way upon the subject's representing anything to himself by means of concepts, music is an incomparably lucid and powerful means of expression. It is as if in feeling joy or sadness we were at the same time conscious of an adequacy of expression far beyond anything we could have imagined.

Coming to understand a musical work is not simply a matter of frequently exercising concentration upon an object for the purpose of discerning its aesthetic qualities. In experiencing a work for the first time it appears to us chiefly, perhaps, as a sonorous object, but in places as someone else's expression. As we grow more familiar with it, however, some phrases and melodies no longer seem to be directed at us from a source outside us. We may not experience them as if they were issuing from us, on an analogy with the voice, but as coming into being in us, an analogy with a process of thought. We may become aware of this when at some time we feel ourselves to be inwardly articulating or 'containing' a passage which we remember had previously seemed to be directed at us from without. Slow reflective passages lend themselves readily to an appropriation of this sort; vehement passages may seem to be 'thought' by us or to issue from us as external expression. This is not *mere* familiarity with the work, for instead of causing our interest in the music to slacken it enables us to experience the mood or emotional tone rather than merely recognize its emotional quality. That is, having made the expression our own, we contribute the element of feeling, as we do in experiencing a lyric poem from within. When we seem to be expressing the music externally, it seems as if it is flowing forth from the mood, though often the mood seems inadequate to the expression—it may seem as if the expression were sustaining the mood, rather than vice versa. When we seem to be 'thinking' the music, it often seems as if we are at the same time feeling it. In many cases hearing the music from within *is* feeling the emotion or feeling expressed. Sometimes we find ourselves not only 'thinking' or otherwise 'expressing' the music, but thinking or expressing it powerfully, as if our own resources were equal to the music. It is firmly appropriated and we are expressing it as if from the heart. This is feeling the expressed emotion. [. . .]

Whether we experience some passages from within or from without or as pure sound may well make a difference to our evaluation of a musical work. Sometimes, when we fail to experience them as expression we regard the hearing as abortive and consider that the work's aesthetic qualities have not been properly experienced. In other cases we may value a work without having experienced certain passages from within, and one day be surprised to find that someone else values it, as we think, excessively, but gives very much the same reasons for its merit as we do. In extreme cases, there is complete aesthetic disagreement. This is understandable, since a passage which seems banal if it and other passages have been experienced as pure sound may seem almost unbearably poignant if it and certain earlier passages have been experienced as expression. A case in point is the 'hurdy gurdy' passage in the finale of Bartók's 5th String Quartet. Some critics value it for its expressiveness, others can see it only as an appalling error of judgement. Some passages in some of Wordsworth's poems present criticism with a similar problem, seeming on one reading wholly banal, on another wholly sublime. Where emotionally expressive music is found within a literary context, as in opera, the significance of the music may differ very considerably according to the mode of perception we adopt. There is a passage of presentation music in Bartók's opera *Bluebeard's Castle* which occurs when Bluebeard is showing Judith his vast domain, and we naturally experience this music as Bluebeard's expression. When we experience it from without, it gives an impression of vanity, even pomposity, in a character of great force; but we can hardly avoid experiencing it also from within, whereupon it seems to express a somewhat naïve pride and strength with which it is easy to sympathize. This ambivalence is in keeping with Bluebeard's character as we know it from the rest of the opera. The music is complex, and I suspect that some features are more prominent when it is experienced from without, others when it is experienced from within, and that this is enough to change the significance of the music as delineating Bluebeard's character. But like Donne's poem, this passage must be experienced according to both modes if one is to grasp its full significance.

There are many pictures before which ordinary aesthetic contemplation can be transformed into a mode of perception in which the percipient seems to see the reality of what is represented in the representation. A picture like Rouault's *Flight into Egypt* would be quite insignificant if it did not have the power suddenly to make it seem that we are actually there, in an unbounded landscape, with the sky extending over us in a chill dawn. Our point of view shifts spontaneously from a point outside the world of the work to a point within it. If we value a work because it offers us such an experience we may be inclined, for want of a better word, to call it 'vivid' or 'realistic', but the relevant aesthetic property cannot be adequately described except by reference to the shift in the subject's point of view. The movement from seeing the picture as representing a chill dawn to the imaginative experience of such a dawn as if real, is of the same kind as the movement from experiencing a lyric poem from without to experiencing it from within, for it is the assumption of 'the painter's' point of view and of his relation to his world. The historical painter may not have painted from life, as the historical poet may not have actually experienced the events he describes in his poem, but as the poem is given as verbal expression, so the representational picture is given as a visual field—that of an 'observer' who is analogous with the poet *qua* 'speaker' of the poem, and as it is possible to make the poet's expression one's own, so the picture may cease to be an object in the percipient's visual field, become itself the visual field, and be experienced as if the objects in it were real. Ordinarily we see the represented dawn as such, either simply as a represented dawn or as the representation of a dawn seen by Rouault. In the experience I am describing we are shifted suddenly from one of these more ordinary modes of perception to a mode which is like the extreme kind of poetic experience of which Longinus writes. Both in the experience of a poem and of a picture from within, an emotional character is realized through an imaginative response to the work, but in the experience of the picture this realization is accomplished rather through an imaginative extension and modification of what is actually seen than through what is merely imagined, so that the experience of the picture from within has an aspect of illusion. Nevertheless the difference between the poetic and pictural experiences is chiefly that between what activates imagination in each case, whether words or things seen. In neither case is what activates imagination transcended: the words are not superseded in the poetic experience, nor is perception supplanted by imagination in the experience of the picture. Words or things seen are taken up into a more comprehensive experience in the constitution of which imagination plays a vital part.

A perfect analogy between the experience of a picture and that of a lyric poem from within, has not yet been established, however, for it has not been shown that a picture, when experienced from within, can be an adequate 'objective correlative' of an emotion. Before Rouault's *Flight into Egypt* we experience 'the dawn-feeling', but the picture relies upon our providing a general human response and does little to determine this response any further. Here the painter is at a disadvantage. In experiencing a lyric poem it is normally quite easy to distinguish the objects of the poet's world from his attitude towards them: if he speaks of the sun as an officious court dignitary we do not have to imagine it as wearing a ruff or as appropriately grey-bearded. But whatever means the painter adopts to determine our attitude must be visible in the picture. If he distorts the image of the object of the emotion he wishes to communicate, it is this distorted image which we experience as if real when we experience the work from within its world, so that we respond not to the object of the emotion but rather to the emotion itself as objectified in the image. If on contemplating a picture of Rouault's I feel myself to be in the real presence of one of his monstrous judges, this experience will not directly deliver either the emotion that the artist intended to convey or its object. But if the painter does not obviously distort the image the percipient is left free to adopt what attitude he pleases: it is a matter of temperament whether he feels pity or contempt for the unattractive elder members of Goya's royal family. Yet in some pictures even this difficulty has been surmounted. One's first impressions of Bonnard's *Nude before a Mirror* are of its brilliant colour and of its decorative character. The nude is the centre of the picture-space and is more sharply and emphatically drawn than anything at the sides of the picture or in the background. All the rest is an extravagant *décor* for the central figure. The mirror, which occupies much of the left margin of the picture, reflects a curtain as a long narrow area of brilliantly coloured patches and spots. The window glistens. The corner of the bedspread in the right foreground is richly coloured and formally pleasing. One recognizes almost immediately that this is a good picture, but the judgement is made with reservations. The central figure seems a little awkwardly related to the background, the sensuous charm of which is perhaps excessive. But even while he is contemplating the picture in this way, the percipient's mode of perception may be transformed, and it is as if he were in the very room, looking at a real woman standing before a mirror, not with the neutral attitude of someone looking at something in a picture but with an affectionate, even a loving glance. It is as if he has assumed not only the artist's visual field but his very glance, and is gazing upon the same world with the same heart and eyes. He is no longer aware of the exaggerated colour or of the decorative aspect of the picture. It is as if these features had helped to create the attitude appropriate for the perception of the central figure—a technique common in religious painting—and in accomplishing this had given up their own prominence. I do not maintain that it is the function of painting to produce experiences of this kind, but it is in such experiences that Expression Theory's dream of a communion which is temporarily an identity seems most nearly to be realized. Less intense or less complete experiences of pictures from within, involving only a part of a picture or a momentary sense of the real presence of the object represented, are not uncommon. Imaginatively enhanced perception of these and other kinds have nothing to do with skill or taste, but this does not suffice to establish their irrelevance from the aesthetic point of view.

A somewhat clearer indication of what it means, in general, to experience a work 'from within' can now be given. Music is perceived as expression, but does not deliver a situation. Painting delivers a situation but is not perceived as expression. Poetry both delivers a situation and is perceived as expression. In each case there is the possibility of an imaginative movement whereby the percipient enters into a more intimate relation with the work, either by appropriating the musical expression, or by allowing the world of the picture to become as if it were his world instead of contemplating it as an object in his world, or by taking up the poetic expression and constructing the world of the poem as if it were his world. But expression and world are relative to a subject, and the percipient is often explicitly aware that the expression or world that he has made or allowed to become his is not in fact his own. Hence he may well feel a sense of identity or close communion with someone else, whom he is likely to identify as the artist. These, I believe, are the features of our experience of art which provide a certain limited justification for Expression Theory. At the same time they cast doubt on the adequacy of any exclusively objectivist aesthetic theory.

The theory I have been criticizing restricts the application of 'aesthetic' to one aspect or region of our experience of art, perhaps in the belief that this is necessary if aesthetic judgement is to have objective validity. By this impover-ishment of the concept of aesthetic experience Aesthetics becomes the philosophy of a scarcely practicable aestheticism which it has itself created.

Yet even the problem of the objectivity of aesthetic judgement could be clarified by a more catholic understanding of our actual experience of art, in particular of the creative contribution made by the subject. Our experience of art, like our religious or moral experience, has its own character but is not yet transparent to us. It is this, in all its variety and complexity and with all the problems it presents, that Aesthetics should exhibit and examine, not only for the sake of remaining in contact with ordinary lovers of art but in order that through Aesthetics we may attain a better understanding of ourselves. A version of aesthetic experience adapted in a comparatively simple manner to our intellectualist preferences is not an acceptable substitute.

['Aesthetic Theory and the Experience of Art', *Proceedings of the Aristotelian Society*, NS 67 (1966–7), 111–26.]

KENDALL L. WALTON

44   Make-Believe and the Arts

Make-believe is not just for children. Many adult activities are best understood as continuations of children's make-believe, and can be illuminated by comparing them with games of dolls, cops and robbers, and hobby horses. One adult activity that involves make-believe is that of making and looking at pictures.[1] What are pictures? How does a picture of a man differ from the word 'man'? In a nutshell, pictures are props in visual games of make-believe.[2]

In 'Meditations on a Hobby Horse', Ernst Gombrich compared pictures to a simple hobby horse, a stick—perhaps with a wooden 'head' attached, but perhaps just a plain stick—on which a child 'rides' around the house. Gombrich considered and rejected describing this stick as an 'image of a horse', an 'imitation of [a horse's] external form'. He also considered and rejected thinking of it as a sign that signifies or stands for or refers to a horse, or to the concept horse. Pictures also, he suggested, are not to be thought of in either of these ways. He proposed thinking of pictures and hobby horses, rather, as *substitutes*. A hobby horse substitutes for a horse; a picture of a man substitutes for a man.[3]

'Meditations on a Hobby Horse', famous though it is, has been largely ignored. It is fair to say that most discussions of pictorial representation during the last forty years have proceeded in one or the other of the two directions Gombrich advised against. There are resemblance theories of representation (some more sophisticated than others). And there are semiotic theories, such as that of Nelson Goodman, who declares flatly that 'denotation is the core of representation'.[4] Even Gombrich's own later work, including *Art and Illusion*, has been understood by some to advance the idea that pictures are imitations of the external forms of objects. Others find in it the conception of pictures as symbols or signs that signify or stand for what they are pictures of.[5] Neither interpretation is entirely without justice. But Gombrich's original characterization of pictures as substitutes, and his comparison of pictures with hobby horses, was on the right track.

Two central thoughts stand out in Gombrich's reflections on pictures and the hobby horse. First, he emphasizes that 'art is "creation" rather than "imitation"'. 'The child "makes" a train either of a few blocks or with pencil on paper', he observes—she doesn't *imitate* or *refer to* a train; she *makes* one.[6] 'All art is "image-making" and all image-making is rooted in the creation of substitutes.'[7] But is it mere substitutes that the image maker creates? Gombrich described the child as making a *train* out of blocks or on paper, not a substitute for a train. To cement the uncertainty he states: 'By its capacity to serve as a "substitute" the stick becomes a horse in its own right, it belongs in the class of "gee-gees" and may even merit a proper name of its own.'[8] What is it that the artist creates when she draws a man, a man or a substitute for a man?

The second central idea that Gombrich derives from the association of pictures with hobby horses is an emphasis on function rather than form. 'The "first" hobby horse was . . . just a stick which qualified as a horse because one could ride on it.' 'Any ridable object could serve as a horse.' A ball represents a mouse to a cat, he says. And to a baby, who sucks its thumb as if it were a breast, the thumb represents a breast. 'The ball has nothing in common with the mouse except that it is chasable. The thumb nothing with the breast except that it is suckable.'[9] Function rather than form.

But the distinction between function and form might seem to be just where hobby horses and pictures diverge. Yes, a mere stick with hardly any of the form of a horse, just enough to be 'ridable', serves as a horse. But pictures capture the *appearance* of the things they picture. One doesn't ride a picture of a horse; one looks at it. A single object can have more than one function, however. One function of a horse is to be ridden, but another function, which some horses have for some people, is to be looked at. Maybe pictures of horses substitute for horses as objects of seeing.

Much of what Gombrich said in spelling out the analogy between hobby horses and pictures is blatantly and straightforwardly false. (This might be one reason why his early essay was ignored.) The notion that the stick is (literally) a horse, or that a picture of a man is (literally) a man, is as blatant a falsehood as one can find. The stick is a stick and the picture is a picture. Nevertheless, as Gombrich observes, it is perfectly ordinary for perfectly sane people to point to a picture of a man and say, in all seriousness, 'That is a man.' It is also perfectly natural for a perfectly normal child to point to the stick and say, 'This is a horse.'

Are these just short ways of saying, 'That is a *substitute* man' or 'This is a *substitute* horse', it being understood that substitutes are not the real thing?

But the hobby horse is not much of a substitute for a horse. Had Paul Revere's horse been sick the night of the British attack, he could hardly have made do with a hobby horse borrowed from a neighborhood child. Not even a wonderfully realistic hobby horse with a carved head and carpet tacks for eyes would have enabled him to beat the British to Concord. Hobby horses are *not* ridable, not *really*, so they can't really substitute for actual horses. And if someone wants to look at a horse, a picture of a horse is not a very satisfactory replacement. To see a picture of a horse is not to see a horse, not really. And the viewer of the picture does not even enjoy an illusion of seeing a horse. In all but the rarest of cases it is perfectly obvious that what one is seeing is a flat surface with marks on it, not a horse. [. . .]

Children playing hobby horses establish a *fictional world*—the world of their game of make-believe. *Within this world* there are horses—real horses, not substitutes. Let's say that it is *fictional*, fictional in the world of make-believe, that there are real horses. Speaking in the real world, we must allow that the horses are *merely* fictional, 'real' *only* in the world of the game, that actually they are nothing but sticks. The children participating in the make-believe belong to the fictional world themselves, however, it is fictional, in their game, that they ride horses. And within the game they can say, pointing to the sticks, 'Those are real horses.' It is only when we stand outside the game, when parents are talking about the fun their children are having with their hobby horses, for instance, that 'That is a horse' is a blatant falsehood. Yes, Paul Revere cannot replace an ailing real horse with a hobby horse. But that is because the British attack comes in the real world. If the British attacked in the world of make-believe, a child might ride off on his hobby horse—on what in the world of the game is a real horse—to spread the alarm.

Spectators use pictures as props in games of make-believe. Normally we don't do anything with pictures as physical as riding them; museums have rules about not touching paintings. But we do *look* at them. When I look at Salvador Dali's etching *Don Quixote* in the normal manner it is fictional, in my world of make-believe, that I see Don Quixote astride his horse. And depending on the manner in which I examine the picture, it may be fictional that I notice the long shadow cast by a knight in the background or the mountains in the distance, or fail to notice them, that I examine the plants in the foreground, that I remark the jaunty attitude of the errant knight. (We are sometimes tempted to play more physical games with pictures. A portrait of a despised politician makes a wonderful prop in a game in which we, fictionally, throw darts at him.)

The world of make-believe is not, of course, to be identified with the world of the picture, although the two are closely related. The world of Dali's etching contains only Don Quixote and his horse, the plants and the mountains, etc.—not me, when I happen to be looking at the print. But in viewing the etching I engage in a game of make-believe, incorporating the picture world into a larger world of make-believe, a world that contains me as well as Don Quixote. When the hobby horse leans unused in the corner of a room, we can think of it as, by itself, establishing a fictional world something like the world of a picture (or a sculpture). There is a real horse in that world, but a child playing checkers on the other side of the room does not belong to it. When the child takes the stick and uses it as a prop in a game, the world of the hobby horse expands into a world of make-believe, and in *this* world the child rides the horse. The larger world is established by the prop, the stick, together with what the child does with it.

So I *can* say 'That is a man', while pointing to a mere picture of a man, provided that in saying this I am participating in the game of make-believe, speaking within the world of my game. Just as straddling a stick and jumping around introduces a fictional world in which one rides a horse, looking at a picture establishes a world in which one observes things of the kind the picture depicts.

We now have a better way of understanding what it means to call the stick or a picture a *substitute*. The stick is neither a real horse nor can it really be used as a horse; one can't ride it. But it can be used in a game of make-believe within which it *is* real and is really ridable. The picture is used in games in which it is fictional that one really sees a real man or a horse.

Games of make-believe are *imaginative* activities. The children playing hobby horses do not merely observe that it is fictional that they are riding horses, chasing bandits, and so forth. They also *imagine* all this to be true. A mere spectator of the game could imagine this as well, of course. So what is the advantage of *participating* in the game? In part, it is the fact that participants imagine about *themselves*. A child, let's call him Dan, imagines that *he* is riding a horse. But this is not all. He also imagines riding one. Imagining *doing* something or *experiencing* something is not the same as imagining *that* one is doing or experiencing it. . . . In imagining riding the horse, and chasing the band of desperadoes into the hills, Dan may achieve something of a sense of what it might be like to experience such adventures.

Children participate in games of make-believe, not only in the overt physical ways I have described, but also *verbally* and *psychologically.* Dan shouts 'Giddyup!' to spur his horse on. He really does utter that sound, and in doing so he makes it fictional that he shouts to his horse. He imagines of the noise he actually emits that it is addressed to his horse, and he imagines—as he races ahead—that the horse responds by breaking into a gallop.

Psychological participation is especially important. It is fictional that Dan is proud to belong to the sheriff's posse, and excited and nervous about pursuing the bandits. He knows, of course, that he is not really in a sheriff's posse and that he won't actually confront any bandits; he knows that he is only playing a game. But he does really experience a swelling sensation and he does feel genuine excitement and tension. It is partly these actual sensations that make it fictional that he swells with pride in the importance of his assignment, and fictional that he faces the dangers of the mission with some trepidation. Aware of his swelling sensations, he spontaneously imagines them to be swellings of pride in the responsibility he bears. And he imagines his actual sensations of tension to be feelings of nervousness about the dangers he will face in the hills. Where do his swelling sensations and feelings of tension come from? They result from his imaginings, from his imagining, vividly, being responsible for bringing the desperadoes to justice.

Compare a dream in which you are on your way to school, and the school bell rings while you are still two blocks away. This means a tardy slip and half an hour of detention at the end of the day. On waking from the dream, you realize that the school bell was really the sound of your alarm clock, and that you still have an hour before classes begin. The sound of the alarm was actual and you really did hear it while you were dreaming, but you 'interpreted' it in your dream as the school bell. You imagined hearing the school bell, and you imagined what actually was the hearing of the alarm to be your hearing of the school bell. [. . .]

In viewing a picture, one's imagination is engaged as one participates in the make-believe. But the viewer enjoys a visual as well as an imaginative experience, of course. She perceives the picture in a manner that is imbued with her imagining. Borrowing a phrase from Richard Wollheim, we can describe the experience as one of seeing a horse or a man in the picture.[10] More needs to be said about the nature of the perceiving and the imagining, and how they are related.

To see a horse in a picture is to imagine a horse, and to imagine *seeing* a horse, while one actually sees the picture. Furthermore, the viewer imagines her actual perceiving of the picture to be her act of perceiving a horse. Imagining seeing is imagining in a 'first person manner', not just imagining *that* one sees. It is also imagining 'from the inside'.[11] We should add that the spectator's imagining is not deliberate, but a spontaneous response to the marks on the canvas; she just finds herself imagining seeing a horse and imagining her actual seeing to be a seeing of a horse, as she looks at the picture. (Imagining is sometimes regarded as, necessarily, a deliberate act under the subject's control. This is a mistake. Dreams are obvious counter-examples, and so are many of the imaginings that make up daydreams.)

Finally, the viewer of the picture is best regarded, not as seeing the picture and *also* engaging, spontaneously, in the imaginings I described, but as enjoying a single experience that is both perceptual and imaginative; her perception of the picture is colored by the imagining. (Probably she enjoys a succession of experiences each of which is both perceptual and imaginative.)

The experience of recognizing an (actual) tree as a tree is not a *combination* of a pure perception, and a judgment that what one perceives is a tree. It is rather a perceptual experience that is also a cognitive one, one colored by the realization that what one is experiencing is a tree. Likewise, to see a horse in a design is to have a perceptual experience colored by imagining one's perception to be of a horse, a perceptual experience that is also an imaginative one. [. . .]

Whatever the exact nature of spectators' perceptual/imaginative participation in visual games of make-believe, it is crucial that we recognize that pictures are used as props in make-believe, and that there is a world of make-believe to which the spectator belongs. Most accounts of pictorial representation recognize only the world of the picture, and have the viewer standing outside that world and observing it. Theories differ as to the manner in which a picture picks out the propositions constituting its world. Some say it does so by virtue of resemblance or similarity; the picture resembles states of affairs of the kind the propositions it picks out express—a picture of a horse resembles or looks like a horse (or the state of affairs of there being a horse). Others say conventions of some sort are involved. (These correspond roughly to Gombrich's two rejected alternatives.) In either case, the viewer's job is, supposedly, to ascertain what propositions the picture picks out, what is 'true in the world of the picture', by noting the relevant resemblances or by adducing the relevant conventions.

Here is an example to demonstrate the inadequacy of understanding picture perception as merely a matter of ascertaining what is 'true in the picture'. Consider two films of a roller coaster ride. Both were made by a camera attached to the last car of the roller coaster. In one case, the camera is hung from a support in such a way that it remains aligned with the horizon even when the car rolls from side to side. In the other case the camera is attached rigidly to the roller coaster so as to tip back and forth as the car does. In the first film, the horizon remains horizontal on the screen, and one sees the roller coaster sway to the right and the left. In the second film, the image of the roller coaster remains upright on the screen, while the horizon tilts. Let's add that both films have circular rather than rectangular images on the screen. The two films contain exactly the same information; the world of the picture is the same in both cases. In fact, we could make a showing of one indistinguishable from the other just by rotating the projected image at the appropriate times.

But the viewer's experiences of the two films will be very different. The viewer of the one made by the rigidly attached camera has the impression of riding in the roller coaster, of swaying dangerously right and left as the car goes around turns. The viewer of the other film has the impression of watching the swaying roller coaster from a stable position outside of it. The viewer of the former is more likely than the viewer of the latter to feel sick.

The difference lies in the spectators' games of make-believe and their experiences of imagining seeing. The spectator of one film imagines seeing the roller coaster from a perspective fixed relative to the careering roller coaster. The spectator of the other film imagines seeing the same roller coaster careering in the same manner, but from a perspective fixed relative to the earth and detached from the roller coaster.

Words are not pictures. And the difference is much more fundamental than is suggested by saying merely that words and pictures are symbols of different kinds. Words do not essentially have anything to do with make-believe at all. If you tell me that San Antonio is the site of the battle of the Alamo, you are just conveying to me a piece of information. Your words do not call for imaginings on my part at all like the imaginings a child engages in when she 'rides' a hobby horse, or the imaginings of spectators when they look at pictures. When language is used fictionally, however, as it is in novels and stories and theater, it is used as a prop in games of make-believe. Spectators at a performance of *Romeo and Juliet* engage in make-believe in which they, fictionally, not only watch Juliet and Romeo but also listen to their words. And of course they are likely to participate psychologically. The spectators may shed tears, on learning of the tragic events on stage. The tears are actual, but they are not actually tears of grief for the characters, since the spectators fully realize that there is nobody really to grieve for. They 'interpret' their tears, in the make-believe, as tears of grief; they imaginatively grieve for Romeo and Juliet and imagine their actual tears to be tears of grief. Where did the tears come from in the first place? They flow as a result of the spectators' vivid imaginings of the sufferings endured by Romeo and Juliet. The vivacity of the imaginings depends to a considerable extent on the skill with which the actors portray the tragedy, of course. A bad performance will fail to elicit vivid imaginings and actual tears that can be imagined to be tears of grief.

Novels and stories are not usually props in *visual* games of make-believe. But we do use them in games that have psychological dimensions. The reader of *Anna Karenina* does not merely note that it is fictional that Anna is unfaithful to her husband, suffers the disapproval of society, and is finally driven to throw herself under the wheels of a train. It is fictional in the reader's game that he learns about all this, that he sympathizes with Anna, and suffers with her. He imagines learning about an actual Anna, and imagines sympathizing and grieving for her.

The words of many novels and stories are 'substitutes' not for people and events of the kinds they describe, but for serious reports about such events. We use the text of *Gulliver's Travels* in a game in which it is fictional that it is the text of the journal of a ship's physician, a certain Lemuel Gulliver. We imagine, of our actual reading of the novel, that it is a reading of such a journal, and we imagine learning from it about Gulliver's adventures in various exotic lands.

What is the point of all this make-believe? It consists largely in the imaginings props elicit in participants, especially in their imagining seeing, or reading about, or learning about, or knowing about, events of this or that sort, and imagining feeling one way or another about them. By engaging in these imaginings we enrich our understanding of the kinds of experiences we imagine having, and of the situations we imagine experiencing.[12]

It is usually *characters*, people *inside* pictures and novels, who have the interesting experiences. Appreciators just watch. It is a character who must choose between love and duty, or who is shipwrecked alone on a desert island, or who suffers bereavement. Appreciators, in the worlds of the games they play with the work, observe or read about or learn about the character's dilemma or his experiences on the desert island. In reading Yukio Mishima's 'Death in Midsummer' I imagine learning about the tragic drownings of three children and about how their parents respond to it. But the experience of reading the story does not help me to understand merely what it is or might be like to *learn about* such tragedies befalling other people; it is likely to give me insight into what it is or might be like to suffer such a tragedy oneself, to lose one's own children. How does this happen? A quick answer is that I *empathize* with the parents in the story. This empathy involves imagining myself in their shoes, imagining suffering bereavement myself, and responding as they do. But I imagine this, I empathize with them, as a result of imagining learning about *their* tragedy and noting how they deal with it.

Van Gogh's lithograph *Sorrow* (Fig. 1) is, in obvious respects, much less explicit and detailed than Mishima's story. We have no way of knowing why the woman is sorrowful. And the picture is more suggestive than explicit concerning her expressive behavior. We don't even see her face; all we have to go on is her hunched posture. Perhaps we 'empathize' with her, imagining ourselves to be sorrowful in the way we take her (fictionally) to be. But perhaps not. I am not sure that I actually imagine being sorrowful myself, when I contemplate the picture. I do imaginatively respond to the woman, however, in ways that are not easy to articulate. Understanding another person's feelings involves experiencing certain feelings oneself—feelings about the other person. By imagining feeling as I do toward the woman, I imaginatively understand her. And this imaginative experience gains for me an understanding of what a particular kind of sorrow is like.

All this began with the expansion of the picture world into a world of make-believe big enough to include the perceiver as well as the contents of the picture world. Rather than merely standing outside the picture and imagining

FIG. I *Sorrow*, Van Gogh (1882)

what it depicts, imagining a sorrowful woman sitting hunched with her head and arms resting on her knees, I imagine myself seeing her and observing her sorrow. This leads to imagining feeling about her and for her, and perhaps with her, in ways that enable me imaginatively to understand her sorrow. Thus I come to understand what it is like to feel this way. This would not be possible if pictures were merely imitations of visual forms, or if they were merely signs signifying or standing for things of the kind they represent—if they were not, like hobby horses, props in games of make-believe in which spectators participate visually, and also psychologically.

This is a modified version of 'Make-Believe, and its Role in Pictorial Representation and the Acquisition of Knowledge', *Philosophic Exchange* (1994), 81–95.

ARISTOTLE

45 The Emotions Proper to Tragedy

It is clear that the general origin of poetry was due to two causes, each of them part of human nature. Imitation is natural to man from childhood, one of his advantages over the lower animals being this, that he is the most imitative creature in the world, and learns at first by imitation. And it is also natural for all to delight in works of imitation. The truth of this second point is shown by experience: though the objects themselves may be painful to see, we delight to view the most realistic representations of them in art, the forms for example of the lowest animals and of dead bodies. The explanation is to be found in a further fact: to be learning something is the greatest of pleasures not only to the philosopher but also to the rest of mankind, however small their capacity for it; the reason of the delight in seeing the picture is that one is at the same time learning—gathering the meaning of things, e.g. that the man there is so-and-so; for if one has not seen the thing before, one's pleasure will not be in the picture as an imitation of it, but will be due to the execution or colouring or some similar cause. Imitation, then, being natural to us—as also the sense of harmony and rhythm, the metres being obviously species of rhythms—it was through their original aptitude, and by a series of improvements for the most part gradual on their first efforts, that they created poetry out of their improvisations. [. . .]

[L]et us proceed now to the discussion of Tragedy; before doing so, however, we must gather up the definition resulting from what has been said. A tragedy, then, is the imitation of an action that is serious and also, as having magnitude, complete in itself; in language with pleasurable accessories, each kind brought in separately in the parts of the work; in a dramatic, not in a narrative form; with incidents arousing pity and fear, wherewith to accomplish its catharsis of such emotions. Here by 'language with pleasurable accessories' I mean that with rhythm and harmony or song superadded; and by 'the kinds separately' I mean that some portions are worked out with verse only, and others in turn with song.

I. As they act the stories, it follows that in the first place the Spectacle (or stage-appearance of the actors) must be some part of the whole; and in the second Melody and Diction, these two being the means of their imitation. Here by 'Diction' I mean merely this, the composition of the verses; and by 'Melody', what is too completely understood to require explanation. But further: the subject represented also is an action; and the action involves agents, who must necessarily have their distinctive qualities both of character and thought, since it is from these that we ascribe certain qualities to their actions. There are in the natural order of things, therefore, two causes, Thought and Character, of their actions, and consequently of their success or failure in their lives. Now the action (that which was done) is represented in the play by the Fable or Plot. The Fable, in our present sense of the term, is simply this, the combination of the incidents, or things done in the story; whereas Character is what makes us ascribe certain moral qualities to the agents; and Thought is shown in all they say when proving a particular point or, it may be, enunciating a general truth. There are six parts consequently of every tragedy, as a whole (that is) of such or such quality, viz. a Fable or Plot, Characters, Diction, Thought, Spectacle, and Melody; two of them arising from the means, one from the manner, and three from the objects of the dramatic imitation; and there is nothing else besides these six. Of these, its formative elements, then, not a few of the dramatists have made due use, as every play, one may say, admits of Spectacle, Character, Fable, Diction, Melody, and Thought.

II. The most important of the six is the combination of the incidents of the story. Tragedy is essentially an imitation not of persons but of action and life, of happiness and misery. All human happiness or misery takes the form of action; the end for which we live is a certain kind of activity, not a quality. Character gives us qualities, but it is in our actions—what we do—that we are happy or the reverse. In a play accordingly they do not act in order to portray the Characters; they include the Characters for the sake of the action. So that it is the action in it, i.e. its Fable or Plot, that is the end and purpose of the tragedy; and the end is everywhere the chief thing. [. . .]

The next points after what we have said above will be these: (1) What is the poet to aim at, and what is he to avoid, in constructing his Plots? and (2) What are the conditions on which the tragic effect depends?

We assume that, for the finest form of Tragedy, the Plot must be not simple but complex; and further, that it must imitate actions arousing fear and pity, since that is the distinctive function of this kind of imitation. It follows, therefore, that there are three forms of Plot to be avoided. (1) A good man must not be seen passing from happiness to misery, or (2) a bad man from misery to happiness. The first situation is not fear-inspiring or piteous, but simply odious to us. The second is the most untragic that can be; it has no one of the requisites of Tragedy; it does not appeal either to the human feeling in us, or to our pity, or to our fears. Nor, on the other hand, should (3) an extremely bad man be seen falling from happiness into misery. Such a story may arouse the human feeling in us, but it will not move us to either pity or fear; pity is occasioned by undeserved misfortune, and fear by that of one like ourselves; so that there will be nothing either piteous or fear-inspiring in the situation. There remains, then, the intermediate kind of personage, a man not pre-eminently virtuous and just, whose misfortune, however, is brought upon him not by vice and depravity but by some error of judgement, of the number of those in the enjoyment of great reputation and prosperity; e.g. Oedipus, Thyestes, and the men of note of similar families. [. . .]

The tragic fear and pity may be aroused by the Spectacle: but they may also be aroused by the very structure and incidents of the play—which is the better way and shows the better poet. The Plot in fact should be so framed that, even without seeing the things take place, he who simply hears the account of them shall be filled with horror and pity at the incidents; which is just the effect that the mere recital of the story in *Oedipus* would have on one. To produce this same effect by means of the Spectacle is less artistic, and requires extraneous aid. Those, however, who make use of the Spectacle to put before us that which is merely monstrous and not productive of fear, are wholly out of touch with Tragedy; not every kind of pleasure should be required of a tragedy, but only its own proper pleasure.

The tragic pleasure is that of pity and fear, and the poet has to produce it by a work of imitation; it is clear, therefore, that the causes should be included in the incidents of his story. Let us see, then, what kinds of incident strike one as horrible, or rather as piteous. In a deed of this description the parties must necessarily be either friends, or enemies, or indifferent to one another. Now when enemy does it on enemy, there is nothing to move us to pity either in his doing or in his meditating the deed, except so far as the actual pain of the sufferer is concerned; and the same is true when the parties are indifferent to one another. Whenever the tragic deed, however, is done within the family— when murder or the like is done or meditated by brother on brother, by son on father, by mother on son, or son on mother—these are the situations the poet should seek after.

[*Poetics*, trans. Ingram Bywater, in *The Basic Works of Aristotle*, ed. Richard McKeon (New York: Random House, 1941), 1457–8, 1460–1, 1466–8.]

46   Emotions and Music

We accept the division of melodies proposed by certain philosophers into ethical melodies, melodies of action, and passionate or inspiring melodies, each having, as they say, a mode corresponding to it. But we maintain further that music should be studied, not for the sake of one, but of many benefits, that is to say, with a view to (1) education, (2) purgation (the word 'purgation' we use at present without explanation, but when hereafter we speak of poetry,[1] we will treat the subject with more precision); music may also serve (3) for intellectual enjoyment, for relaxation and for recreation after exertion. It is clear, therefore, that all the modes must be employed by us, but not all of them in the same manner. In education the most ethical modes are to be preferred, but in listening to the performances of others we may admit the modes of action and passion also. For feelings such as pity and fear, or, again, enthusiasm, exist very strongly in some souls, and have more or less influence over all. Some persons fall into a religious frenzy, whom we see as a result of the sacred melodies—when they have used the melodies that excite the soul to mystic frenzy—restored as though they had found healing and purgation. Those who are influenced by pity or fear, and every emotional nature, must have a like experience, and others in so far as each is susceptible to such emotions, and all are in a manner purged and their souls lightened and delighted. The purgative melodies likewise give an innocent pleasure to mankind. Such are the modes and the melodies in which those who perform music at the theatre should be invited to compete. But since the spectators are of two kinds—the one free and educated, and the other a vulgar crowd composed of mechanics, labourers, and the like—there ought to be contests and exhibitions instituted for the relaxation of the second class also. And the music will correspond to their minds; for as their minds are perverted from the natural state, so there are perverted modes and highly strung and unnaturally coloured melodies. A man receives pleasure from what is natural to him, and therefore professional musicians may be allowed to practise this lower sort of music before an audience of a lower type. But, for the purposes of education, as I have already said, those modes and melodies should be employed which are ethical, such as the Dorian, as we said before; though we may include any others which are approved by philosophers who have had a musical education.

[*Poetics*, trans. Benjamin Jowett, in *The Basic Works of Aristotle*, ed. Richard McKeon (New York: Random House, 1941), 1315–16.]

MARTHA C. NUSSBAUM

47 Luck and the Tragic Emotions

Aristotle, like Plato, believes that emotions are individuated not simply by the way they feel, but, more importantly, by the kinds of judgments or beliefs that are internal to each. A typical Aristotelian emotion is defined as a composite of a feeling of either pleasure or pain and a particular type of belief about the world. Anger, for example, is a composite of painful feeling with the belief that one has been wronged. The feeling and the belief are not just incidentally linked: the belief is the ground of the feeling. If it were found by the agent to be false, the feeling would not persist; or, if it did, it would no longer persist as a constituent in that emotion. If I discover that an imagined slight did not really take place, I can expect my painful angry feelings to go away; if some irritation remains, I will think of it as residual irrational *irritation* or excitation, not as *anger*. It is part of this same view that emotions may be assessed as either rational or irrational, 'true' or 'false', depending upon the nature of their grounding beliefs. If my anger is based upon a hastily adopted false belief concerning a wrong done me, it may be criticized as both irrational and 'false'. What I now want to do is to establish that the belief-structure internal to both pity and fear stands or falls with views about the importance of luck in human life that would be accepted by Aristotle and by most ordinary people, but rejected by his philosophical opponents, including Plato.

Pity, Aristotle tells us in the *Rhetoric*, is a painful emotion directed towards another person's pain or suffering (1385b13 ff.). It requires, then, the belief that the other person is really suffering, and, furthermore, that this suffering is not trivial, but something of real importance. [...] These sufferings he then divides into two groups: painful and injurious things, and substantial damages caused by luck. Representative examples of the former include: death, bodily assault, bodily ill-treatment, old age, illness, lack of food. Examples of the latter include: lack of *philoi*; having few *philoi*; being separated from your *philoi*; ugliness, weakness, being crippled, having your good expectations disappointed, having good things come too late, having no good things happen to you, or having them but being unable to enjoy them (1386a7–13). [. . .] In the *EN* [*Nicomachean Ethics*] examples from the two groups were brought together in the discussion of *tuchē* and external goods. We can see that there is a close connection between the listed occasions for pity and Aristotle's reflections about our vulnerability to the external in the ethical works; these happenings are prominent among the ways in which a good person can fall short of full *eudaimonia* [happiness].

Aristotle adds a further condition for pity, which he repeats and stresses in the *Poetics*. Pity, as response, is distinct from moral censure or blame: it requires the belief that the person did not deserve the suffering (*Po.* 1453a 3–5, *Rhet.* 1385a13 ff.). He claims, and I think correctly, that where we judge that the suffering is brought on by the agent's own bad choices, we (logically) do not pity: the structure of that emotion requires the opposing belief. In the *Rhetoric* he makes the interesting observation that the person who is too pessimistic about human nature will not feel pity at all—for he will believe that everyone deserves the bad things that happen to them (a remark pregnant with implications for the question of Christian tragedy). A dramatic story of such a *deserved* reversal, he tells us in the *Poetics*, will be benevolent and uplifting (*philanthrōpon*), but not tragic (1453a1 ff.).

Finally, he points out that pity is closely connected with the belief that you yourself are vulnerable in similar ways. If you believe that you are so badly off that nothing further could happen to you to make things worse, you will not be likely to be capable of pity for others because you will be looking at their plight from the very bottom, from the point of view of one whose sufferings are complete. On the other hand, if you believe yourself self-sufficient *vis-à-vis eudaimonia*, secure in your possession of the good life, you will suppose that what happens to others cannot possibly happen to you. This will put you in a state of bold assertiveness (*hubristikē diathesis*), in which the sufferings of others do not arouse pity (1565b19–24, 31–2). Pity then, evidently requires fellow feeling, the judgment that your possibilities are similar to those of the suffering object.

It is evident that this central tragic emotion depends on some controversial beliefs about the situation of human goodness in the world: that luck is seriously powerful, that it is possible for a good person to suffer serious and undeserved harm, that this possibility extends to human beings generally. Aristotle's philosophical opponents, however, insist that if a person's character is good, the person cannot be harmed in any serious way. So there is within their view no room, conceptually, for pity. It must be considered a thoroughly irrational and useless emotion, based upon false beliefs that ought to be rejected. We rationally must choose between the response of blame, if we judge that what has happened is the fault of the agent, and equanimity or dismissiveness about what has happened, if we judge that it is the fault of the world. Accordingly, Plato does, in fact, repudiate pity in the strongest terms. In the *Phaedo*, which is a clear case of Platonic anti-tragedy, there is repeated stress on the fact that Socrates' predicament is not an occasion for pity. The bad things are trivial, because they are happening only to his body; his soul is secure and self-sufficient. Accordingly, the dialogue's end replaces tragic pity with a praise of this good man's goodness. In *Republic* x, pity is again singled out for special abuse, in connection with the attack upon tragedy. Tragic poetry, Socrates says, does harm to practical rationality, in that 'after feeding fat the emotion of pity there, it is not easy to restrain it in our own experiences' (606B).

But if we should believe, with Aristotle, that being good is not sufficient for *eudaimonia*, for good and praiseworthy living, then pity will be an important and valuable human response. Through pity we recognize and acknowledge the importance of what has been inflicted on another human being similar to us, through no fault of his own. We pity Philoctetes, abandoned friendless and in pain on a desert island. We pity Oedipus, because the appropriate action to which his character led him was not the terrible crime that he, out of ignorance, committed. We pity Agamemnon because circumstances forced him to kill his own child, something deeply repugnant to his own and our ethical commitments. We pity Hecuba because circumstances deprived her of all the human relationships that had given meaning and value to her life. Through attending to our responses of pity, we can hope to learn more about our own implicit view of what matters in human life, about the vulnerability of our own deepest commitments.

We can say something similar about fear. The belief structure of fear is intimately connected with that of pity. Aristotle stresses repeatedly that what we pity when it happens to another we fear in case it might happen to ourselves (*Po.* 1453a4–5, *Rhet.* 1386a22–8). And since pity already, in his view, requires the perception of one's own vulnerability, one's similarity to the sufferer, then pity and fear will almost always occur together. Fear is defined as a painful emotion connected with the expectation of future harm or pain (1382a21 ff.). Aristotle adds that fear implies that these bad things are big or serious (1382a28–30), and that it is not in our power to prevent them. Thus we do not, he observes, in general fear that we will become unjust or slow-moving, presumably because we believe that that sort of change usually lies with us to control. Fear is above all connected with a sense of our passivity before events in the world—with 'the expectation of passively-suffering (*peisesthai*) some destructive affect' (*phthartikon pathos*, 1382b30–2); thus, those who believe they cannot passively-suffer anything will have no fears (1382b32–3).

For Aristotle's philosophical opponents, there will be little to fear. [. . .] The *Republic* [. . .] spends a long time criticizing and rejecting literary works that inspire fear. Plato's argument, repeatedly, is that correct beliefs about what is and is not important in human life remove our reasons for fear. The good person attaches no importance to any external loss, to any loss, that is, in a sphere of life that is beyond the control of the rational soul. But this means that he or she is in no way passive before nature, has nothing at all to fear. (We can see that the same would be true for Kant.) When we watch a tragic hero's downfall in the spirit of these philosophers, we will feel no fear for ourselves. For either our character and the hero's character are both good, in which case his difficulties give us nothing, really, to fear; or both characters need more work, in which case we had better get to work perfecting ours; or the hero's character is, after all, not similar to ours, in which case we will not be deeply moved in any way by his downfall. Nowhere is there the sense of vulnerability and passivity that gives rise to true fear. But in Aristotle's ethical universe there *are* serious things to fear, things of importance to *eudaimonia* itself. If, as Aristotle urges, we acknowledge the tragic characters as similar to us in their general goodness and their human possibilities, the tragedy as showing 'the sort of thing that might happen' to an aspiring person in human life generally, we will, with and in our fear, acknowledge their tragedy as a possibility for ourselves. And such a response will itself be a piece of learning concerning our human situation and our values.

Aristotle stresses, then, that central to our response to tragedy is a kind of identification with the suffering figure or figures depicted. They must, clearly, be good people, or we will not pity them. But the importance of identification imposes conditions on the ways in which they can be good. First of all, they must be good in a representative and not an idiosyncratic way. We can connect his demand for similarity between ourselves and the hero with his ranking of poetry above history as a source of wisdom. History, he points out, tells us what in fact happened; poetry 'the sort of thing that might happen' (1451b4–5). History tells us 'the particular, such as what Alcibiades did or suffered'; poetry 'the general, the sort of thing that happens to certain sorts of people' (1451b8–11). What he means here, I believe, is that often the events narrated by history are so idiosyncratic that they prevent identification. Because Alcibiades is such a unique and unusual figure, we do not regard what happens to him as showing a possibility for ourselves. [. . .] The tragic hero is not similarly idiosyncratic. He or she is seen by us to be a certain sort of good person, roughly similar to ourselves; for this reason we experience both pity and fear at his or her downfall.

Then again, if we are to see the hero as similar, he cannot be *too* perfectly good. Aristotle stresses that the tragic character, while he must indeed be good and while he must fall not through badness of character, must still not be 'one surpassing [perfect] in excellence and justice' (1453a8 ff.). He must be 'better rather than worse', and even 'better than us' (1453b16–17, 1454b8–9); but he must not be perfect. There are several points that Aristotle could be making here. [. . .] I believe [. . .] that he is making [the] [. . .] point [. . .] that imperfections in a hero enhance our identification. There is a kind of excellence that is so far beyond our grasp that we regard its possessor as being above and beyond our kind, not among us. This sort of excellence is discussed at the opening of *Nicomachean Ethics* vii under the name 'heroic' or 'divine' excellence, or 'the excellence that is above us' (1145a19–20). It is exemplified by a Homeric quotation telling us that a certain hero is 'not like the child of a mortal man but like the child of a god'. Aristotle is even inclined to say of such a divine figure that he is 'more honorable than human excellence'—i.e., he is not the kind of being to whom it makes sense to ascribe the ordinary virtues at all, his goodness is in an altogether different category from ours. I think that Aristotle's point in the *Poetics* is that if tragedy shows us heroes who are in this way divine, lacking the limitations of patience, vision, reflection, and courage that characterize even the best of human subjects, the sense of similarity that is crucial to tragic response will not develop. The tragic hero should not fall through wickedness; but his being less than perfectly good is important to our pity and fear. Thus Oedipus's shortness of temper is not the *cause* of his decline; but it is one thing about Oedipus that makes him a character with whom we can identify. It is not a 'tragic flaw'; but it is instrumental to the tragic response. So, indeed, are Philoctetes' self-pity, Creon's self-ignorance and his mistaken ambition, Antigone's relentless denial of the civic, Agamemnon's excessive boldness. So, above all, might be the attempts of so many tragic good characters to deny their own vulnerability to chance happenings, those avoidances of their own condition which we, so much of the time, share with them. Aristotle's claim is that none of these defects is sufficient to make the person a wicked person in underlying character: even Creon preserves, beneath his (blameworthy) ambition, a rich and basically balanced set of values and attachments, and the fact is extremely important in determining our response to him. He can claim with some justice that he is a victim of his self-ignorance, not a deliberate perpetrator of evil deeds (cf. *ouch hekōn*, 1340). Such people fall, therefore, not *from* wickedness, but from something more like a mistake or error, blameworthy or not. But the presence of imperfections (some, perhaps, somehow involved in the decline and some not) means that we will see and acknowledge them as like us in kind, though good and, perhaps, better.

We find, then, that for Aristotle the viewing of pitiable and fearful things, *and* our responses of pity and fear themselves, can serve to show us something of importance about the human good. [. . .] For Aristotle, pity and fear will be sources of illumination or clarification, as the agent, responding and attending to his or her responses, develops a richer self-understanding concerning the attachments and values that support the responses. For Aristotle's opponents, pity and fear can never be better than sources of delusion and obfuscation.

[*The Fragility of Goodness: Luck and Ethics in Greek Tragedy* (New York: Cambridge University Press, 1986), 383–8.]

SUSAN L. FEAGIN

48 The Pleasures of Tragedy

David Hume begins his little essay 'Of Tragedy' with the observation: 'It seems as unaccountable pleasure which the spectators of a well-written tragedy receive from sorrow, terror, anxiety, and other passions that are in themselves disagreeable and uneasy.' Here Hume addresses a paradox that has puzzled philosophers of art since Aristotle: tragedies produce, and are designed to produce, pleasure for the audience, without supposing any special callousness or insensitivity on its part (in fact, quite the opposite). I will introduce a distinction which enables us to understand how we can feel pleasure in response to tragedy, and which also sheds some light on the complexity of such responses. The virtues of this approach lie in its straightforward solution to the paradox of tragedy as well as the bridges the approach builds between this and some other traditional problems in aesthetics, and the promising ways in which we are helped to see their relationships. In particular, we are helped to understand the feeling many have had about the greatness of tragedy in comparison to comedy, and provided a new perspective from which to view the relationship between art and morality. The very close connection which is seen to hold here between pleasures from tragedy and moral feelings also gives rise to a potential problem, which is examined later in the paper.

Hume himself alleged that imagination, imitation, and expression are all 'naturally' pleasurable to the mind, and argued that when they 'predominate' over the unpleasant feelings the latter are 'converted' into the former. But it is not clear how the 'dominance' of imagination and expression is to be achieved. It is not insured by the fact that what is depicted is fictional, or even by our knowledge that it is fictional, since Hume discusses a play where the events depicted (even though fictional) are so gory that no amount of expression can 'soften' them into pleasure. More puzzling, however, is the process of 'conversion' which imagination performs on the unpleasant feelings (and which those feelings, when dominant, perform on the natural pleasantness of the imagination). Pains are not merely mitigated by the pleasure, but converted or transformed into something different. The mechanics of this conversion are never explained, and as long as they remain obscure, even if we accept other features of Hume's view, many of which are quite insightful, we have merely substituted one puzzle for another. [. . .]

Though my own discussion of the pleasures of tragedy does not utilize such notions as imagination and passion on which Hume depended, it does have its own special presuppositions. I shall speak of two kinds of responses to art: a direct response and a meta-response. A direct response is a response to the qualities and content of the work. A meta-response is a response to the direct response. The distinction is not one of epistemological or ontological status; I presuppose no view about sense data, epistemologically 'primitive' experiences, or incorrigibility of mental status. A direct response is direct only in the sense that it is a response to the qualities and content of the work of art. Of course, there are complex questions about what is 'in the work' and what constitutes the 'work itself,' but those need not be resolved for the purposes of this discussion. The important contrast is not between a direct response to the work as opposed to a direct response to what is not really in the work. The important contrast is between a direct response and a meta-response which is a response to the direct response: it is how one feels about and what one thinks about one's responding (directly) in the way one does to the qualities and content of the work. The meta-response is what Ryle called a 'higher order' operation: it depends on (and is partly a function of) another mental phenomenon, i.e., a direct response. Ideally, my remarks will be independent of any specific view of the 'logical category' of pleasure itself, and I fear perhaps the term 'response' may cause some unwarranted discomfort in that sphere. Let me therefore make the following caveats: (1) by calling pleasure a response I do not imply that it is not essentially connected to its source (what one finds pleasurable), i.e., it is not distinguishable as a response independently of what the pleasure is a pleasure in; (2) a response is not necessarily a mental episode or occurrence (*a fortiori* it is not necessarily a private mental episode) but it may turn out to be a mood or even a disposition or a change of disposition, or some other type of thing.

Both direct and meta-responses exist in ordinary life as well as in artistic contexts. For example, the remains of a spectacular car crash may titillate our curiosity, and we may feel disgusted with ourselves for being so morbid. On the other hand, we may enjoy the enticement of hawkers outside seamy strip joints, and be pleased with ourselves for having overcome a puritanical upbringing. We can be depressed at our failure to meet a challenge, impressed with our ability to rise to an occasion, disgusted with our lack of sympathy for a friend's bereavement, or pleased with the commitment we are inclined to make to help a neighbor. It should be noted that in ordinary as well as aesthetic contexts the two kinds of responses cannot be distinguished merely by what words are used to describe them. 'Pleasure,' 'shock,' 'melancholy,' and 'delight' may all describe direct or meta-responses, and the two are not always clearly distinguishable from each other. A blush of embarrassment may be intensified by embarrassment over the blush. That two things being distinguished cannot be infallibly distinguished, and that there are unclear cases of how and even whether the two are distinguishable, does not necessarily undermine the utility of the distinction.

A Solution

Direct responses to tragedy are responses to the unpleasantness of the work, and they are hence unpleasant experiences we would expect to have from works having unpleasant subject matter and/or unhappy endings. Direct responses draw on our feelings and sympathies: tear-jerkers jerk tears because of our sympathy with persons who are ill-treated or the victims of misfortune. Many people, in fact, dislike attending depressing plays and violent movies, or reading weighty books and poetry, precisely because these experiences are unpleasant and consequently depress and sadden them, making them too well aware of the evil of people and the perils of existence. These works of art, rather than being uplifting and inspiring, often instead produce feelings of torpor and futility as one is overwhelmed by the amount and variety of viciousness in the world. A dose of direct response unpleasantness is a good antidote to creeping misanthropy, as it feeds off of our concern for others. It is also, as John Stuart Mill discovered, a cure for ennui. Mill reported in his *Autobiography* (Sec. v) that it was his crying over the distressed condition of Marmontel as related in his memoirs that initially jogged Mill out of his 'mental crisis' by showing him that he did have feelings, concerns, and cares, and that he was not just 'a logic machine.'

It is the nature of these direct responses to tragedy which we expect and in fact receive which gives rise to the question in the first place, how do we derive pleasure from tragedy? Certainly the typical person who appreciates and enjoys such works of art doesn't feel the direct response any less poignantly than those described above who don't enjoy these works. Lovers of Dostoyevsky, Verdi, and Shakespeare, let us hope, are no more callous than those who find them too hard to take. But whence the pleasure? It is, I suggest, a meta-response, arising from our awareness of, and in response to, the fact that we do have unpleasant direct responses to unpleasant events as they occur in the performing and literary arts. We find ourselves to be the kind of people who respond negatively to villainy, treachery, and injustice. This discovery, or reminder, is something which, quite justly, yields satisfaction. In a way it shows what we care for, and in showing us we care for the welfare of human beings and that we deplore the immoral forces that defeat them, it reminds us of our common humanity. It reduces one's sense of aloneness in the world, and soothes, psychologically, the pain of solipsism.

Perhaps this is something like what Kant had in mind when he spoke in the *Critique of Judgment* of a 'common sense.' We derive pleasure from the communicability or 'shareability' of a response to a work of art: it is something which unites us with other people through feeling something which could, in principle, be felt by anyone. [. . .]

Tragedy and Comedy

The observation is often made that tragedies are much more important or significant artworks than comedies. The great works of Shakespeare are *Hamlet*, *King Lear*, and *Macbeth*, notwithstanding the brilliance of *Twelfth Night* and *As You Like It*. The greatest plays of antiquity are the Oedipus Trilogy and the *Oresteia*, despite the cunning wit of Aristophanes. The greatness of Voltaire's *Candide* is due more to his portrayal of the fate of humankind than his avowedly clever humor. There are great comedies, but the significance of the greatest is not thought to reach the significance of even less great tragedies. Why?

It is not due, as one might suppose on first blush, to some essential morbidity in the outlook of those who defend this judgment. If it were, the greatness of tragedy would be due to the simple truth of the basic picture drawn by tragedy of the nature of man's lot: doomed to suffer injustice, wage war, suffer defeat, and be overcome by conniving women, conniving men, mistakes in judgment, accidents of birth, ignorance, and foolish advice. Tragedy then would be taken to confirm, or at least to echo, one's solemn conviction in the nastiness of human life. The pleasure from tragedy would then also be a morbid one, like the evil-doer who, in his every act, enjoys providing more evidence against the existence of a benevolent god. Whether or not one does believe in the existence of such a god, the pleasure taken in providing evidence against its existence by performing acts of evil is undoubtedly a morbid one.

But the greatness of tragedy is not due to any supposed truth of 'profound' pictures such as these, and our pleasure in it is not therefore in recognizing this unpleasant truth. Tragedy is anything but morbid, for if people did not feel sympathy with their fellow human beings we would not have the initial negative responses we do to the tragic situation, the unpleasant direct responses. At the foundation of the aesthetic pleasure from tragedy is the same feeling which makes possible moral action: sympathy with, and a concern for, the welfare of human beings *qua* human beings, feelings which are increased if those human beings bear any special relationship to oneself such as friends or family, with an attendant increase in moral commitment to them. I do not wish to argue about the basis of morality, but I do wish to suggest that the basis for our judgments of the aesthetic *significance* of tragedy (as opposed to the lesser significance of comedy) can plausibly be its calling forth feelings which are also at the basis of morality. Judgments about tragedy's greatness derive from a recognition of the importance of morality to human life.

In comedy there must be a 'butt' of the joke. The pleasure from comedy, then, is generally a direct response to the failures, defects, or absurdities of whomever (or whatever) is the object of ridicule or fun. Of course not all laughing is laughing *at* people—there is also laughing *with* people—and the two kinds of responses also provide a means for explaining what this means. One laughs *with* people when one is among those being laughed at. Depending on the joke, one's own emotional reactions to parts of the work may be the object of fun, or perhaps what one remembers having done or imagines one would have done under circumstances presented in the work. The response has then become more complex, requiring a kind of self-awareness, much like the meta-response that pleasure from tragedy requires.

Moreover, responses to comedy are to failures or defects judged to be insignificant. This judgment is important because if the imperfections were thought to be of great significance, the work would then take on the air of tragedy rather than comedy, it would be saddening rather than amusing that people were subject to such flaws. The arrogance and pomposity of Trissotin in Molière's *The Learned Ladies* is comic because he is a parochial poet with little influence outside of an equally insignificant small circle of dotty old ladies. But the arrogance of Jason is of cosmic proportions: it ruins Medea, and she in turn destroys his children, his bride, his future father-in-law, and by that act unstabilizes the very order of society. Human foibles may be minor or major, and it is precisely the latter ones which tear at (rather than tickle) the hearts of an audience. Comedy, one might say, is skin deep: it generally goes no further than direct response, and requires that one's responses be to things which do not play major roles in maintaining the happiness and security of human life. Presuming an imperfection to be insignificant makes it possible to laugh at it, but believing it to be important makes one cry. The person who laughs at tragedy may justifiably be called 'callous,' and one might sensibly harbor serious doubts about that person's morality. [. . .]

A Potential Problem

Given that, on this analysis, the same feelings are at the base of both morality and aesthetic pleasure from tragedy, it is necessary to explain how, consistently with this, one might respond aesthetically and be, for all intents and purposes, an immoral person, and also how one might be morally very upright but aesthetically insensitive. The first is what John Ruskin calls somewhere the 'selfish sentimentalist.' One can weep, groan, and cringe over a novel or in the theater, but remain blasé if the fictional events were to occur in reality. The pride one feels in one's theater tears is a selfish pride, and has actually very little to do with any concern for human welfare, or, consequently, one's virtue (though it may have a lot to do with one's supposed virtue). Wouldn't such an account as mine have to suppose that the moral feelings exist when one is in the theater, but that they dissolve when one walks outside?

In *The Concept of Mind*, Gilbert Ryle says, 'Sentimentalists are people who indulge in induced feelings without acknowledging the fictitiousness of their agitations'.[1] Their agitations are not real since their concern is not: without a genuine desire for people's welfare there is no opposition between that desire and the fate that eventually befalls them. They pretend a concern for the poor devils, and then feel real distress when they suffer only because their pretense has been so effective. But then one wonders how people can feel real distress over pretended concerns.

There should be another way of explaining the situation which does not involve so much self-delusion. Indeed, there is. One might genuinely care for others but not nearly so much as for oneself. Hence, when there is no risk to oneself all the tears come pouring forth out of compassion: as a casual reader or theater-goer one is merely a witness to, and cannot be a participant in, the proceedings. That is one of the delights of fiction (even tragedy): one is free to feel as one wishes at no risk to oneself, incurring no obligation, requiring no money, time, or dirty fingernails. But once one gets outside, the situation changes, and one's concern for others may just not be strong enough to overcome self-interest. Concern for others does not miraculously disappear when one travels from the theater to the marketplace—it is overpowered by concern for self. And there is still another way to view the phenomenon, consistently with what I have said about sympathetic responses and meta-responses. Perhaps one identifies with the character in the novel, film, or play, and hence one's concern is self-interested in the sense that it exists *only* because of that identification. What one may never have learned to do is to be concerned about others even when one does *not* feel at one with them. In this case there is a genuine sympathetic response, but one's capacity for sympathy is limited. I, at least, would expect such individuals to show rather pronounced patterns of likes and dislikes with respect to fictional material: only characters with certain salient properties (divorced women, perhaps, or aristocrats, or characters plagued by self-doubt, etc.) would excite their compassion, while others (bachelors, immigrants, or the chronically self-assured, etc.) leave them cold. One of the things we generally expect from a good work of art is a capacity to evoke sympathetic feelings in us for some of its characters, and it is a measure of its goodness that it can melt the hearts even of those not disposed to any concern for others. Of course, there are 'cheap' ways of doing this which we all recognize: there are tools for manipulating an audience that practically no one can resist. One such tool is to introduce someone who is young, intelligent, and good, but dies an untimely death (*Love Story, Death Be Not Proud*), and another is to capitalize on adorable youngsters who have been wronged in all their innocence and goodness (Cio-Cio-San's child, Trouble, in *Madame Butterfly*). Both are effective in disturbing even the weakest sense of injustice.

The other side of the potential problem is the unimaginative moralist, whose behavior is always exemplary but who cannot get worked up over a fictional creation. Isn't it even more difficult to explain how such a person will not respond sympathetically to fiction although he or she will do so in reality? We certainly do not have a case here of one's sympathy being over-powered by self-interest. The key to the solution is that this moralist is unimaginative, for it takes *more* effort of imagination to respond to a work of art than it does to respond to real life. In art one has to overcome the conventions of the medium, contemplate counterfactuals, and make the appropriate inferences and elaborations on the basis of them. Perhaps this is why some have thought that developing an appreciation of appropriate works of art is a good ingredient of moral education: if one can learn to respond morally in the imagined case, then it will be even easier to do so in reality. Too little, it seems to me, has been written on the role of imagination in art appreciation. The discussion has instead focused on the role of belief, and how we can respond emotionally without believing (or suspending disbelief) in the reality of the characters and events. If we pursue the suggestion mentioned earlier that our responses to art are from entertaining counter-factuals, which, *qua* counterfactuals are *imagined* characters and events (not believed ones), then the way is opened for examining traits of imagination which are involved in doing this. It seems we *are* at last, led back to Hume and imagination, in a way which has more potential for understanding our responses to art than his notion of imagination did. But this is a matter for separate study. For these purposes, we can explain the unimaginative mor-alist's failure to respond to art by virtue of that person's being unimaginative in a way which is required in the aesthetic context but not required in the actual moral one.

Meta-Responses to Art and to Life

Given the nature of pleasure from tragedy as analyzed here, it is not surpris-ing to find philosophers alleging the existence of special 'aesthetic emotions,' unlike those which exist in real life. Indeed, we don't generally feel pleasure from our sympathetic responses to real tragedies, and there needs to be some explanation of why the pleasurable response is appropriate to fiction and not to reality. The fact about fiction which makes this so is that in it no one *really* suffers; the suffering is fictional, but the fact that perceivers feel genuine sympathy for this imagined suffering enables perceivers to examine their own feelings without regard for other people. In real life, the importance of human compassion is easily overshadowed by the pain of human suffering. It is not possible in real life to respond to the importance of human sympathy as a distinct phenomenon, since that sympathy depends on, one might even say 'feeds on,' human misery. It is not, in life, an unequivocal good. In art, however, one experiences real sympathy without there having been real suffering, and this is why it is appropriate to feel pleasure at our sympathetic responses to a work of art, whereas it is not appropriate to feel pleasure at our sympathetic responses in reality. There the sympathy comes at too great a cost.

In real life, it is more appropriate to feel satisfaction, pride, or even pleasure with what one has done rather than with what one has felt. Though one should have some caution in how one feels about what one has done (because of unforeseen consequences), 'caution' isn't the right word to describe the hesitation one should have in responding to how one felt. Actions can be completed so that one can respond to them in themselves in a way inappropriate with feelings. One can go to a funeral, and be glad, looking back on it, that one had the courage to do so, but sadness over the person's death has no determinate end. Feelings are not the sorts of things which can be completed; they are not tasks to be performed. Feelings reveal one's sensitivities, which can be revealed not only in first-hand experience but also when one simply thinks about or remembers a situation. In real life, to be pleased with the feelings one had reveals a smugness, self-satisfaction, and complacency with what one has already felt. To be pleased that one once was sensitive (though now insensitive), is to be (properly) pleased very little, because one is at best pleased that one *once* was a feeling person (and, as explained above, one is pleased—because one's sympathy exists—at the expense of other people's misfortune). One should be more displeased that one has lost the sensitivity one once had. Pleasurable meta-responses in real life are foreclosed by the continued call for direct (unpleasant) responses, even when one is confronted with just the idea or memory of the event.

But such is not the case with a work of art. The direct response is to the work of art as experienced in its totality, in the integration of all its sensuous elements. The direct response is possible only in the presence of the work; take away the work and one is left merely to memories and meta-responses. In this sense, a direct response to art has 'closure' (unlike feelings in real life and somewhat like actions) so that those responses can, without smugness, self-satisfaction, and complacency, themselves be singled out and responded to.

Though a meta-response of pleasure to sympathy felt in real life would reveal smugness and self-satisfaction, a meta-response of displeasure to one's lack of sympathy is appropriate and even laudable. This shows that it is not the case that meta-responses are always inappropriate (or impossible) in real life, but that it depends on the nature of the situation. Discomfort, disgust, or dissatisfaction with oneself is desirable because it shows that we are aware of defects in our character, which is a first step to self-improvement. It is courting temptation to concentrate on how well one has done, for this makes us inattentive to the ways in which we might do better. It is also true that when one doesn't 'reap the benefits' of, i.e., gain pleasure from, one's sympathy, we can be reasonably sure that it is genuine.

The differences between responses and meta-responses to real situations and to art have to do both with (1) the important role actions play in morality but not in our responses to art, and (2) the differing roles which emotions themselves play in the two cases. This latter, at least, turns out to be a very complicated matter, a complete examination of which would require an analysis of the importance of a first person, direct experience of a work of art for an appreciation of it (a phenomenon which I have suggested allows for 'closure' of feelings in response to art which is not present in real life). But, most fundamentally, the meta-response of pleasure to the sympathy we feel for other people is appropriate to art but not in life because in the former there is no real suffering to continue to weigh on our feelings. In the latter case, real suffering easily commands our attention, so that any desirability of sympathy is of miniscule importance in comparison with the perniciousness of the conditions which gave rise to it.

In summary, pleasures from tragedy are meta-responses. They are responses to direct responses to works of art, which are themselves painful or unpleasant. But given the basis for the direct response, sympathy, it gives us pleasure to find ourselves responding in such a manner. That is, it is a recognition that there can be a unity of feeling among members of humanity, that we are not alone, and that these feelings are at the heart of morality itself. [. . .] It is, of course, possible to respond appropriately to art, even when those responses require sympathy, and not with the appropriate sympathy in life, as it is also possible to be morally upstanding in life but insensitive to art. Explanations of these phenomena involve intricacies of their own, but they reinforce rather than resist the analysis given of pleasure from tragedy as a meta-response. The fact that pleasurable meta-responses to our sympathetic responses to tragedy are appropriate to art but not in life suggests one respect in which aesthetic emotions are different from emotions of life, and also has to do with the importance of direct experience of a work for an appreciation of it. The peculiarity of the responses hinges on the fact that what one initially responds to is *not* real, thus making continued sympathy idle, and allowing one to reflect on the sympathy one previously felt.

['The Pleasures of Tragedy', *American Philosophical Quarterly*, 20 (1983), 95, 97–9, 101–4.]

49 Jokes

The thesis of this paper is not that jokes are works of art, although I think that may be true, or at least that some of the value and significance of jokes and art may be the same. What I hope to show is that jokes and art have enough in common so that they might illuminate one another's most enigmatic characteristics. In particular, I shall begin to develop two subjects: (1) the relation of a joke to its proper effect, and (2) the question of why we occupy ourselves with jokes. The proper effect of a joke, in some sense, must be to amuse people, to make them laugh. My first question, then, is, What is the relation of the joke to the amusement? The second question is, Why do we care to amuse one another in this way?

I

If you hear a joke, then you laugh.

Perhaps it should be,

If you hear a good joke and understand it, then you laugh.

What relation is signaled by this 'If—then'? It certainly isn't implication, for you can understand a good joke but not laugh. You might be in a bad mood, or not like jokes of that kind, or not like the particular joke-teller. If we could rule out all these adversities we would have,

If you understand a good joke and nothing militates against its humor, then you laugh.

Is that true? Probably not: it seems possible to comprehend a joke without prejudice and not find it funny. There is ambiguity, however, in the phrase 'find it funny'. It may be that failing to find it funny means only that you don't laugh, or that you are not amused. But finding it funny can also mean finding the fun, in which case failing to find it funny means not detecting the funniness, and in that case it is a bit harder to credit you, after all, with comprehending the joke. If you don't find the fun, what reason have you for thinking it a joke? That someone told you it is a joke? That it is in a joke book? The issue surfaces, although not with perfect clarity, in the not uncommon complaint 'It is supposed to be a joke', which is not quite the same as 'It is supposed to be funny'.

Of course you might find the funniness and still not laugh. There is a difference between finding the funniness and sensing or feeling the funniness.[1] It is the latter which characteristically consists of laughter. What should we say about someone who didn't sense the fun, even when he could find it? It may help to turn to another kind of structure with a proper effect. [. . .]

*

If it is irrational to fail to be persuaded by a good argument, what is it to fail to be amused by a good joke? Not irrational, I think; certainly not in the same way. It is like being without taste. We will say 'irrational', I think, not only of someone unpersuaded by a good argument, but also of someone who is unable to see that it *is* a good argument if the form is plainly valid and the premises obviously true. And we will, I think, deny a sense of humor not only in someone who isn't amused by the funniness he sees, but also in someone who can't see the funniness when it is clearly there.[2]

What is a sense of humor? A capacity to be amused by the amusing, I suppose.[3] What makes this capacity remarkable is that it is not coerced into activity. You don't *have* to laugh. Your response is not compelled in the way that an argument compels belief. Your response is not arbitrary, however. We don't all just happen coincidentally to be laughing when we've heard a joke, as if we'd all simultaneously been tickled under the arms. [. . .]

What is wrong with you if you are not amused [. . .]? In escaping the proper response you are not so much wrong as different. It is not a trivial difference. It is a difference which leaves you outside a vital community, the community of those who feel this fun. It is a community which creates and acknowledges itself in the moment, and is powerless to conscript its membership. To fail to laugh at a joke is to remain outside that community. But you cannot will yourself in, any more than you can will yourself out.

II

A point in telling a joke is the attainment of community. There is special intimacy in shared laughter, and a mastering aim of joke-telling is the purveyance of this intimacy. The intimacy is most purified, refined, and uncluttered when the laughter is bound to the joke by the relation I have just been worrying over, a relation in which the laughter is not exacted but is nonetheless rendered fit. There are derivative forms of intimacy, in which the laughter is not so absolutely free. These obtain when the joke calls upon the background of the audience and uses this as a material condition for securing the effect. I think there are two main forms.

In the first form the joke is *hermetic*. It really makes sense only to those with special information, and the intimacy brought to those who qualify is bound up with a recognition—or re-recognition—that they do constitute an audience more select than humanity in general. The joke occasions the reconstitution of that select community. For an hermetic joke the required background may be very specific and decisive.

What is Sacramento?
It is the stuffing in a Catholic olive.[4]

Either you know about pimento and the Church and its sacraments, and you get this joke, or you don't know these things and the joke is opaque. In

America a very common device of this kind of joke is the incorporation of words or phrases in Yiddish. Appreciators of these jokes were once nearly restricted to certain Jews, but this has changed as an endless stream of Jewish comics forces more and more elements of Jewish humor, including vocabulary, on more and more of the general public.

Not every hermetic joke offers itself on this all-or-nothing basis. Some have depths which permit appreciation on different, if cumulative, levels.

One day Toscanini was rehearsing the NBC Symphony. He stopped the playing to correct the trumpet line only to discover that the first-chair trumpet had intended exactly what he had played, and disagreed with Toscanini over how it should go. There ensued a heated argument which ended only when the trumpeter stalked angrily off the stage. As he reached the wings he turned to Toscanini and said 'Schmuck!' The maestro replied, 'It's-a too late to apologize.'

If you know only the word 'Schmuck' you can manage this joke. In fact even if you don't know what it means you can sense enough from its phonetic quality to salvage the joke. But the more you know of professional musicians in New York, of Toscanini's ego and his peculiar approach to non-Roman language, and so on, the more you will make of the joke.

Here is a more intricate example of an hermetic joke.

A musician was performing a solo recital in Israel. When he ended the last selection, a thunderous response came from the audience, including many cries of 'Play it again.' He stepped forward, bowed, and said, 'What a wonderfully moving response. Of course I shall be delighted to play it again.' And he did. At the end, again there was a roar from the audience, and again many cries of 'Play it again.' This time the soloist came forward smiling and said, 'Thank you. I have never been so touched in all my concert career. I should love to play it again, but there is no time, for I must perform tonight in Tel Aviv. So, thank you from the bottom of my heart—and farewell.' Immediately a voice was heard from the back of the hall saying, 'You will stay here and play it again until you get it right.'[5]

This joke works with nearly any audience, but its total riches are available only to those who know the Jewish religious requirement that on certain occasions the appropriate portion of the Hebrew Bible be read out, that those present make known any errors they detect in the reading, and that the reader not only acknowledge these corrections but that he then go back and read out the text correctly. That audience—those entirely within the community of this joke—will not only be able to find this extra level, but they should also find it a better joke. For them there is a point in the story's being set in Israel, and if there were no point in that, the joke would do better to omit the geography altogether.

In the second derivative form of intimacy the joke is likely to be rather simple, although not necessarily, and the background required is not one of knowledge but one of attitude or prejudice. I call these *affective* jokes. The most common examples are probably what in America are called ethnic jokes. It is not necessary that one actually believe that Jews are immoral, or Poles inept, or Italians lascivious, or whatever: indeed, most appreciators known to me have the opposite beliefs. What's needed is not a belief but a predisposition to enjoy situations in which Jews, Poles, Blacks, or whoever are singled out.

A Special Case: The Genre Joke

Some of these, like the Irish jokes current in England, are both hermetic and affective. They are affective as all such 'ethnic' jokes are—Polish ones, Jewish ones, racist ones. The concern here, however, is with the respect in which they are hermetic. This respect is the need for prior acquaintance with jokes of the relevant type; that is, the need for an understanding of the form. Such a joke is hermetic because its full appreciation requires this understanding; but because that understanding is all that is required, the joke is marginally hermetic. We might say that it is intrinsically hermetic, and not extrinsically hermetic, because its requirement will be satisfied by the audience's exposure to jokes of the relevant type and no additional, extra information will be required. It is possible, of course, that any particular instance of the type will be extrinsically hermetic, but that is a different matter. It is a bit complicated to sort everything out, and it will help to have an example. Let us take as a genus, or genre or type, lightbulb-changing jokes.

If, say, lightbulb-changing jokes are good, and J is a lightbulb joke, then J will be a good, lightbulb joke; and that is a comma away from being a good lightbulb joke. There is also a kind of intermediate case likely to be missed. Suppose you like a joke which is a lightbulb joke, but you don't like it only because it's a lightbulb joke: you don't like all lightbulb jokes. It doesn't follow that your liking it and its being a lightbulb joke are unconnected. Its being a lightbulb joke might have almost everything to do with your liking it. You may well need considerable earlier acquaintance with lightbulb jokes in order to be able to find the humor in this one.

The first lightbulb joke I remember hearing was not really a lightbulb joke at all, at the time. It was one of a number of those dismal Polish jokes concerning how many Poles it takes to do this or that, and it was merely the one which happened to involve lightbulbs:

How many Poles does it take to change a lightbulb?

But by now the lightbulb motif is itself a form.

How many Southern Californians does it take to change a lightbulb?
Five. One to replace the bulb; four to share the experience.

How many WASPs does it take to change a lightbulb?
Two. One to mix martinis while the other calls the repairman.

How many psychiatrists does it take to change a lightbulb?
Variation 1: Only one; but he cannot do it until the lightbulb really wants to change.
Variation 2: It doesn't take any. The lightbulb must change itself, steadily but over a
            long time.

How many Zen Buddhists does it take to change a lightbulb?
Two. One to replace the bulb, and one not to replace the bulb.

The form acquires a second-stage development when the teller moves from questioning narrator to character himself.

How many New Yorkers does it take to change a lightbulb?
None of your damned business.

How many feminists does it take to change a lightbulb?
That's not funny.

A further possibility is that the answer come from a character who is not one of the maligned group.

How many Jewish sons does it take to change a lightbulb?
Only one. But it's all right; I can sit in the dark.

Each of these jokes is extrinsically hermetic, for one must be aware of commonplaces concerning Southern Californians, WASPs, feminists, *et al.* And some or all of them may be affective as well, for one may need something related to a prejudice in order to be amused by references to these commonplaces. But the only element with which I am concerned here is that special hermetic quality they possess as members of a genus. It adds considerably to the force of these jokes if they are grasped as instances of a type, for each has its *raison* in large part as a variation. This seems to me exactly how it is with art forms. The form itself induces particular expectations and forms of attention, and then the individual work moves with or against them. The work cannot get to you unless you can see it in its frame. In these jokes and in this art there operates a kind of principle which requires that the medium be exploited. In a very good joke every element in the story has a point. If the joke is of a type, then that generic feature is one of the elements most in need of being used, of being given a point. The lapse of most ethnic jokes consists exactly in the failure to *use* the ethnicity, to do anything with it besides using it as a code to establish a vague and general presumption that the main character is an oaf or ignoramus (as if Shylock were made a Jew only in order to signal that he will be mean and grasping). Perfectly suited to explain this is one of Aristotle's sharpest insights. If you write a tragedy, you are stuck with having a plot. (It is, he says, the *only* thing you are stuck with.) You had therefore better do something with the plot: how good the plot is will have more than anything else to do with how good the whole tragedy is. If you want to tell a really good joke, then don't let it be a Polish joke unless you can really make the Polishness count for something.

The Utility of Exegesis

With hermetic jokes the question arises whether the teller could supply the necessary information along with the joke. While this may be possible after a fashion with some jokes, in all cases there seems bound to be a loss. What will be lost, specifically, is the special way in which the participants in a joke transaction acknowledge their mutual membership in a community. When your hermetic joke works with me, in that moment we attain the intimacy of community. If you *first* instruct me in the background, knowledge of which constitutes the community's membership conditions, then the joke itself cannot be the occasion of the uncovering of our mutuality. And that is a loss which deprives the joke of its characteristic humanizing force.

With jokes in general, as also with metaphors and works of art, the question arises whether they can be supplanted or augmented by their exegetical descriptions. We are virtually all agreed that no description or explanation of an art work will do in place of the work, but we find it very difficult to say exactly why not. Two things become more tractable if we turn to simple jokes. First, the structure of the thing is unlikely to be very complex. Second, a reason for thinking that art works and jokes have no exact equivalents is that only the original seems able to get the relevant effect; and it is, at least initially, much easier to say what that effect is if the object is a joke. It's the laughter. It is because of these two things that our intuition about the irreplaceability of things may become clearer if we turn to jokes.

Some jokes seem to work by delivering a composite effect, by bringing things together all at once. That's how it is with 'What is Sacramento?', and that is how it is with very many children's jokes.

Where does the king keep his armies?
Up his sleevies.

Where does the Lone Ranger take his garbage?
To the dump, to the dump, to the dump, dump, dump.[6]

These jokes, many of them riddles, are somewhat like simultaneous equations in algebra. The solution requires delivering something that can do more than one thing at once. The explanation of a joke will necessarily be discursive. It will give the solution discretely, and that will prevent the magical all-at-once click. That is like art, but now there is a puzzling difference. Although exegesis won't do in place of either an art work or a joke, it can augment appreciation of art while it seems to destroy a joke altogether. If I do not get your joke you can explain it to me and then I shall understand it, but I shall now 'get it' only in a severely attenuated sense, an academic sense indeed. It can now never jolt me, snap my sensibilities together. But if I do not appreciate some art, you may well explain and describe it to me, eventually equipping me to appreciate it profoundly. Why is there this difference? Would the difference disappear if we turned from simple stories and children's riddles to more elaborate jokes? Let us have an example.

An old, childless, married couple live together in a tiny town so poverty-stricken, remote, and backward that no one in the town knows anything of modern conveniences. In fact no one has ever seen a mirror. One day the husband chances on a small piece of reflecting glass nearly buried in the dirt. He takes it home, carries it up to the attic loft in his cottage, and then cleans it and leans it against the wall. After looking into it intently for a long time he says 'Papa!' and then goes downstairs. During the next few weeks he takes every opportunity to go upstairs alone, where he spends long hours.

His wife becomes concerned, and she begins to worry that her always devoted husband may have found someone else. She waits until one day she is left alone at home with enough time to investigate, and then she fearfully climbs the stairs. Once inside the loft she immediately sees the mirror, gazes into it briefly, and then goes downstairs cheerfully, saying aloud to herself, 'Oh, I am relieved. He couldn't possibly be interested in anyone so wrinkled and worn-out as that. She looks old enough to be my mother.'

That story will bear a lot of analysis, especially if you like it nearly as much as I do.[7] Its charm, its good humor, its bitter humor, have deep sources. And talking about them does not seem to obliterate the joke. We might even have discussed these things before hearing the joke and then still found the joke effective. Does this show that a joke can bear analysis just as an art work can? I was once inclined to say that this joke just happens to be art as well, but now I think I missed the point. It is not a difference between jokes and art works, but a difference between a structure, joke or art, which can work only once, and one which can work again and again. If a joke or an art work can be truly effective only once, then it is smothered by its exegesis. The explanation seems to usurp the one chance the work had. But if the work has a multiple capacity, then exegesis can even be invigorating.

There is nothing whatever wrong with what we might call 'conditional' (or derivative) intimacy as such, in either of its two forms. Jokes which lead to it are among the finest ways we have of identifying others with whom we belong. You tell me such a joke in order to determine whether we have a sensibility in common, and when I work my way through, using my special background, which you are invoking, we earn the comfort of shared feeling. These jokes are the equivalent in mirth of what Kant calls the forms of dependent beauty. But there is also the joking relation I was working on earlier, and I think that is the hard one to understand. [...] [T]he joke elicits the unconditioned intimacy of free community. You are expected to understand the language, but that is all. Nothing else is presupposed concerning what you know or what you find funny. You just find the particular joke funny. This kind of laughter, which makes us freely one with all others (who find the funniness) is, I think, a unique way of coming out of oneself. It takes you out of yourself and out of your groups and makes you one with everyone. It is worth study in its own right, and that study may well have other benefits, for I think that one of the only other available experiences very much like this is the shared experience of art.

III

The little schematism I've sketched divides jokes into two kinds, the pure ones and the conditional ones. The conditional ones, the ones the success of which requires a special background in the audience, are again divisible into two kinds: the hermetic ones, whose presumed background is one of knowledge or belief, and the affective ones, which require of the audience a particular prejudice, or feeling, or disposition, or inclination. [. . .]

Let me note two excellent topics associated with the complexity of conditional jokes. First is the matter of active complicity. When your special background is called into play, your sensibility is galvanized. Something that sets you apart from just any person is brought into your apprehension and this adds to the quantity and alters the quality of the intimacy achieved. The point is like the one I think Aristotle has in mind when he declares the enthymeme the argument most suitable for certain kinds of persuasion. His idea is this: if you wish to set your audience in motion, especially with an eye toward provoking them to action, then you are well advised to induce them to supply the initial momentum themselves. You can do this by offering them an incomplete argument. They must then undertake a mental scramble in order to locate the premises necessary to render the argument valid. This scramble is a motion of the mind undertaken *before* the legitimate arrival of the conclusion, and that motion augments the persuasion implicit in the validity of the completed argument. So it is, approximately, with conditional jokes. The requirement of a special background is not stated explicitly. The audience discovers that and it also discovers that it can supply what's needed. It is further aware that not everyone can supply the background (unlike an enthymeme's audience which potentially includes everyone because minimal logical acuity is enough to formulate the implicated missing premiss). In doing this the audience collaborates in the success of the joke—the constitution of intimacy—just as the audience for an enthymeme collaborates in the construction of a valid argument, with the difference that the audience of the joke derives additional intensity of feeling from knowing that the success is due to them specifically, that other groups would fail.

A second good topic concerning conditional jokes is the means they afford to a kind of fakery. A conditional joke demands a special contribution from the audience, either cognitive or affective. What if the joke-teller himself cannot supply this special constituent? In the first case, where the implicated background is cognitive, the teller is like a parrot, and he cannot himself know (find) what fun there is in the joke. This charlatan resembles a musician who doesn't divine the sense of a piece but nonetheless bangs it out note for note, or a religious practitioner who reads out texts or prayers in Latin or Hebrew, perhaps even 'with feeling', but doesn't know what the words mean.

In the second case, where the requisite special contribution is a matter of feeling, the teller is more like a liar. He can, typically, find the fun—recognize it or identify it—but he cannot feel it. Perhaps the plainest examples of this insincerity are jokes told to groups of (say, racially) prejudiced people—genuine bigots, that is—by one who does not share the true depths of the bigotry but means to ingratiate himself with the group. This is a kind of fraudulence, like that of the man who says 'I apologize' without feeling sorry, of the artist who mimics unfelt forms, and of the performer who does not feel the passion in the scores he plays with mindless virtuosity.

The two kinds of fakery are different. The first is, mainly, simply bizarre. The second is more devious, even deceitful. In both, however, there is the fraudulence of emptiness, as both betray the commitment to intimacy I have characterized as a kind of generic aim of joke-telling. The teller of these jokes is inauthentic: he invites and even induces you into a putative community in which he himself has no place. Who is he to be issuing these invitations?

The difference between pure and conditional jokes corresponds to a difference in moral and religious conceptions. The idea of a pure joke rests on a conviction that at some level people are essentially the same and can all be reached by the same device. This is, perhaps, a fundamentally Christian idea. The denial of the possibility of a pure joke rests on a conviction that people are essentially different, or at least that they belong to essentially different groups. The idea that all jokes necessarily are conditional seems to me a kind of Jewish idea (not the only kind).

Those who believe only in conditional jokes will concede that it is possible to appreciate a joke whose community does not include oneself. How is this possible? It must be through an act of imagination which transports one into the relevant community. Thus I can appreciate jokes meant for women, Englishmen, and mathematicians, although I am none of those. There is a point, however, at which it becomes impossible for me to be amused. I reach that point sooner when the joke is anti-Jewish or anti-American than when it is anti-women or anti-English. And there is a point for any type of affective joke beyond which its instances are objectionable. They are in bad taste. If you think that lapses of 'taste' are always relatively innocuous, then I would insist that these jokes are in fact unacceptable—immoral. Why does this happen, and when?

I cannot give a complete answer, even in outline, because there is a fundamental question I do not know how to answer. Suppose that x is some real event, and that it is (morally) unacceptable to laugh at x. The question I cannot answer is, under what conditions is it wrong to laugh at a fictional report of x, and why? It may be that a heavy traffic of amusement in x-jokes creates or reinforces beliefs or attitudes that are themselves objectionable or that lead to intolerable acts. That answer is insufficient, for two reasons. First, there is little evidence to show that it is always true, and some indication that it is sometimes false. Second, it doesn't get to the heart of the evil, even if it is true, for even if it could be demonstrated that these jokes lead to no bad ends the jokes themselves would still be offensive. With no good answer to the question of why (and when) it is wrong to laugh at a story of something you shouldn't laugh at, I shall nevertheless go on to suggest how an answer—if we had one—might lead to an understanding of the unacceptability of some jokes.

Suppose that prejudice against P's is a bad thing, and that to be amused by an x-joke requires a disposition which is related to anti-P prejudice, although that disposition is not itself a prejudice. The joke will be accessible only to those who either have the disposition or can, in imagination, respond as if they had it. The joke is obviously conditional—it is affective; but it will also be fundamentally parochial (essentially conditional, one might say) if there are people who cannot find it accessible. What people will be in this position? P's, I think. Even the imagined possession of the disposition is in conflict with what makes these people P's. To appreciate the joke a P must disfigure himself. He must forsake himself. He should not do that. In fact he cannot do that while remaining a P. The rest of us, who are not P's, *should* not appreciate the joke although we *can* in this sense in which a P cannot. The joke is viciously exclusionary, and it should be resisted.

What this implies depends upon exactly what people essentially are. Are they essentially men or women, of some race, of some age, of some religion, of some profession, of some size? That is a fine question in the metaphysics of morality, and one I do not care to answer here. I offer this account of a kind of unacceptable joke as an explanation and justification of why some people find some jokes intolerable. A currently common exchange begins with a man telling a joke (involving women, typically) which a woman finds offensive. She objects and is told she has no sense of humor. Her reply could be that she cannot bring her sense of humor to that joke without imaginatively taking on a disposition which is incompatible with her conception of herself as a woman or a certain kind of woman. And if she is essentially a woman or a certain kind of woman, then she cannot reach the joke without a hideous cost.

Although the basis for a pure joke has an obvious moral flavor, akin to the idea of a universal human sameness, conditional jokes are also congenial to the serious idea of morality. Conditional jokes are related to the idea that we can respect and even appreciate one another while remaining irreducibly different. They carry a danger, however, for their parochialism easily becomes unbearably sectarian.

A final note about pure jokes. The major question, I suppose, is whether there are any. If there are, they will be jokes whose presumptive success depends on nothing whatever. The audience need no special background. They bring to the joke only their humanity. Now the question is, When you tell such a joke, upon what basis do you expect anyone else to be moved? The answer must be, Upon the fact that the joke moves you, plus your estimate that it moves you simply as a person and without regard to any idiosyncracy of yours. [...]

Is there [...] an argument for the postulation of a universal sense of humor? I do not know. Is the capacity to find a joke funny a basic, essential feature of our sensibility? It needn't seem entirely implausible that it is if we suppose it to be, minimally—and it is only its minimal presence that matters—the capacity to feel simultaneously the appropriateness and the absurdity of a punch line. It is like feeling the wonderful hopelessness of the world. (Or is it the hopeless wonder of the world?) But must every one of us have within himself the capacity for that feeling, however disfigured it may have become? God knows.

IV

The sudden click at the end of a certain kind of joke is its hallmark. There is an unexpected, an almost-but-not-quite-predicted coincidence of moments. And this is part of a marvelous reflexivity. Earlier I guessed that the whole joke relates to its effect in an enigmatic relation which renders that effect both unforced and fitting. The relation can be found again entirely within the joke. The joke itself has a beginning which leads to an end which is unforced (and so, unpredicted), but altogether right. In laughing we fit ourselves to a joke just as its punch line fits to its body, by this relation of self-warranting propriety. It is a kind of mirroring. We find ourselves reflected in a surface which mirrors our dearest and perhaps most human hope: to do well, but not under compulsion. A joke shows us that and shows us doing that. Anything which can show us that aspect of ourselves deserves fond and serious attention.

['Jokes', in Eva Schaper (ed.), *Pleasure, Preference and Value* (Cambridge: Cambridge, University Press, 1983), 120–1, 123–36.]

EDMUND BURKE

50 | The Sublime: Of Delight and Pleasure

But shall we therefore say, that the removal of pain or its diminution is always simply painful? or affirm that the cessation or the lessening of pleasure is always attended itself with a pleasure? by no means. What I advance is no more than this; first, that there are pleasures and pains of a positive and independent nature; and secondly, that the feeling which results from the ceasing or diminution of pain does not bear a sufficient resemblance to positive pleasure to have it considered as of the same nature, or to entitle it to be known by the same name; and thirdly, that upon the same principle the removal or qualification of pleasure has no resemblance to positive pain. It is certain that the former feeling (the removal or moderation of pain) has something in it far from distressing, or disagreeable in its nature. This feeling, in many cases so agreeable, but in all so different from positive pleasure, has no name which I know; but that hinders not its being a very real one, and very different from all others. [...] Whenever I have occasion to speak of this species of relative pleasure, I call it *Delight*; and I shall take the best care I can, to use that word in no other sense. I am satisfied the word is not commonly used in this appropriated signification; but I thought it better to take up a word already known, and to limit its signification, than to introduce a new one which would not perhaps incorporate so well with the language. I should never have presumed the least alteration in our words, if the nature of the language, framed for the purposes of business rather than those of philosophy, and the nature of my subject that leads me but of the common track of discourse, did not in a manner necessitate me to it. I shall make use of this liberty with all possible caution. As I make use of the word *Delight* to express the sensation which accompanies the removal of pain or danger; so when I speak of positive pleasure, I shall for the most part call it simply *Pleasure*.

Whatever is fitted in any sort to excite the ideas of pain, and danger, that is to say, whatever is in any sort terrible, or is conversant about terrible objects, or operates in a manner analogous to terror, is a source of the *sublime*; that is, it is productive of the strongest emotion which the mind is capable of feeling. ⟨I say the strongest emotion, because I am satisfied the ideas of pain are much more powerful than those which enter on the part of pleasure. Without all doubt, the torments which we may be made to suffer, are much greater in their effect on the body and mind, than any pleasures which the most learned voluptuary could suggest, or than the liveliest imagination, and the most sound and exquisitely sensible body could enjoy. [...] But as pain is stronger in its operation than pleasure, so death is in general a much more affecting idea than pain; because there are very few pains, however exquisite, which are not preferred to death; nay, what generally makes pain itself, if I may say so, more painful, is, that it is considered as an emissary of this king of terrors.⟩[1] When danger or pain press too nearly, they are incapable of giving any delight, and are simply terrible; but at certain distances, and with certain modifications, they may be, and they are delightful, as we every day experience. [...]

To examine [...] the effect of tragedy in a proper manner, we must previously consider, how we are affected by the feelings of our fellow creatures in circumstances of real distress. I am convinced we have a degree of delight, and that no small one, in the real misfortunes and pains of others; for let the affection be what it will in appearance, if it does not make us shun such objects, if on the contrary it induces us to approach them, if it makes us dwell upon them, in this case I conceive we must have a delight or pleasure of some species or other in contemplating objects of this kind. Do we not read the authentic histories of scenes of this nature with as much pleasure as romances or poems, where the incidents are fictitious? [. . .] Our delight in cases of this kind, is very greatly heightened, if the sufferer be some excellent person who sinks under an unworthy fortune. [. . .] [F]or terror is a passion which always produces delight when it does not press too close, and pity is a passion accompanied with pleasure, because it arises from love and social affection. Whenever we are formed by nature to any active purpose, the passion which animates us to it, is attended with delight, or a pleasure of some kind, let the subject matter be what it will; and as our Creator has designed we should be united by the bond of sympathy, he has strengthened that bond by a proportionable delight; and there most where our sympathy is most wanted, in the distresses of others. If this passion was simply painful, we would shun with the greatest care all persons and places that could excite such a passion; as, some who are so far gone in indolence as not to endure any strong impression actually do. But the case is widely different with the greater part of mankind; there is no spectacle we so eagerly pursue, as that of some uncommon and grievous calamity; so that whether the misfortune is before our eyes, or whether they are turned back to it in history, it always touches with delight. This is not an unmixed delight, but blended with no small uneasiness. The delight we have in such things, hinders us from shunning scenes of misery; and the pain we feel, prompts us to relieve ourselves in relieving those who suffer; and all this antecedent to any reasoning, by an instinct that works us to its own purposes, without our concurrence.

It is thus in real calamities. In imitated distresses the only difference is the pleasure resulting from the effects of imitation; for it is never so perfect, but we can perceive it is an imitation, and on that principle are somewhat pleased with it. And indeed in some cases we derive as much or more pleasure from that source than from the thing itself. But then I imagine we shall be much mistaken if we attribute any considerable part of our satisfaction in tragedy to a consideration that tragedy is a deceit, and its representations no realities. The nearer it approaches the reality, and the further it removes us from all idea of fiction, the more perfect is its power. But be its power of what kind it will, it never approaches to what it represents. Chuse a day on which to represent the most sublime and affecting tragedy we have; appoint the most favourite actors; spare no cost upon the scenes and decorations; unite the greatest efforts of poetry, painting and music; and when you have collected your audience, just at the moment when their minds are erect with expectation, let it be reported that a state criminal of high rank is on the point of being executed in the adjoining square; in a moment the emptiness of the theatre would demonstrate the comparative weakness of the imitative arts, and proclaim the triumph of the real sympathy. I believe that this notion of our having a simple pain in the reality, yet a delight in the representation, arises from hence, that we do not sufficiently distinguish what we would by no means chuse to do, from what we should be eager enough to see if it was once done. We delight in seeing things, which so far from doing, our heartiest wishes would be to see redressed. [...]

The second passion belonging to society is imitation, or, if you will, a desire of imitating, and consequently a pleasure in it. This passion arises from much the same cause with sympathy. For as sympathy makes us take a concern in whatever men feel, so this affection prompts us to copy whatever they do; and consequently we have a pleasure in imitating, and in whatever belongs to imitation merely as it is such, without any intervention of the reasoning faculty, but solely from our natural constitution, which providence has framed in such a manner as to find either pleasure or delight according to the nature of the object, in whatever regards the purposes of our being. It is by imitation far more than by precept that we learn every thing; and what we learn thus we acquire not only more effectually, but more pleasantly. This forms our manners, our opinions, our lives. It is one of the strongest links of society; it is a species of mutual compliance which all men yield to each other, without constraint to themselves, and which is extremely flattering to all. Herein it is that painting and many other agreeable arts have laid one of the principal foundations of their power. And since by its influence on our manners and our passions it is of such great consequence, I shall here venture to lay down a rule, which may inform us with a good degree of certainty when we are to attribute the power of the arts, to imitation, or to our pleasure in the skill of the imitator merely, and when to sympathy, or some other cause in conjunction with it. When the object represented in poetry or painting is such, as we could have no desire of seeing in the reality; then I may be sure that its power in poetry or painting is owing to the power of imitation, and to no cause operating in the thing itself. So it is with most of the pieces which the painters call still life. In these a cottage, a dunghill, the meanest and most ordinary utensils of the kitchen, are capable of giving us pleasure. But when the object of the painting or poem is such as we should run to see if real, let it affect us with what odd sort of sense it will, we may rely upon it, that the power of the poem or picture is more owing to the nature of the thing itself than to the mere effect of imitation, or to a consideration of the skill of the imitator however excellent. Aristotle has spoken so much and so solidly upon the force of imitation in his poetics, that it makes any further discourse upon this subject the less necessary.

To draw the whole of what has been said into a few distinct points. The passions which belong to self-preservation, turn on pain and danger; they are simply painful when their causes immediately affect us; they are delightful when we have an idea of pain and danger, without being actually in such circumstances; this delight I have not called pleasure, because it turns on pain, and because it is different enough from any idea of positive pleasure. Whatever excites this delight, I call *sublime*. The passions belonging to self-preservation are the strongest of all the passions.

[*A Philosophical Enquiry into the Origin of our Ideas of the Sublime and Beautiful*, ed. James T. Boulton (London: Routledge & Kegan Paul, 1958), 35–7, 39–40, 45–7, 49–51. First published in 1757.]

JERROLD LEVINSON

51   Music and Negative Emotion

A grown man, of sound mind and body, manipulates the controls of an electronic apparatus. He settles into an easy chair, full of expectancy. Then it begins. For the next hour or so this man is subjected to an unyielding bombardment of stimuli, producing in him a number of states which prima facie are extremely unpleasant, and which one would normally go to some lengths to avoid. He appears upset, pained, and at turns a small sigh or a shudder passes through his body. Yet at the end of this ordeal our subject seems pleased. He avers that the past hour and a half has been a highly rewarding one. He declares his intention to repeat this sort of experience in the near future.

What has our man been doing, and more interestingly, why has he been doing it? He has been listening to music—just that. It turns out that his fare on this occasion was the *Marcia Funebre* of Beethoven's *Eroica* Symphony, the Scriabin Étude op. 42, no. 5, the third movement of Brahms's Third Symphony, Mozart's Adagio and Fugue in C Minor, K. 546, and the opening of Mahler's Second Symphony, all neatly assembled, with suitable pauses, on a reel of recording tape. What he experienced can be described—at least *provisionally*—as intense grief, unrequited passion, sobbing melancholy, tragic resolve, and angry despair. But why would anyone in effect torture himself in this manner? What could induce a sane person to purposely arrange for himself occasions of ostensibly painful experience?

My object in this essay is to give a comprehensive answer to this query. The general question can be formulated thus: Why do many sensitive people find the experience of negative emotion through music a rewarding or valuable one, and, what is especially paradoxical, rewarding or valuable partly in itself? Not only do appreciators of music appear to regard such experiences as instrumentally good or worthwhile—which itself needs much explaining—but they standardly seek them out and relish them for their own sakes, enjoying them or pleasuring in them, if truth be told.

At this point many readers will have ready some favorite wand for dissolving this paradox with a wave of the hand. But I do not intend to encourage them. While admitting that my initial description of the phenomenon will need to be modified somewhat, I maintain that even when all niceties on the aesthetic and psychological fronts have been attended to, the phenomenon, in essence, remains.

In its general form, of course, the problem of the value and desirability of the negative or unpleasant in art is one of the hoariest in aesthetics. It is the problem Aristotle raises for the appreciation of tragedy, evocative of pity and terror, and which he answers with the doctrine of catharsis. It is the problem of the sublime in eighteenth- and nineteenth-century thought, the 'delightful horror' analyzed among others by Burke and Schopenhauer, which a spectator feels face to face with some threatening aspect of life as embodied in a work of art. But in the case of music the problem is generated in the absence of any representational content, and so answers to it must be framed accordingly. [. . .]

One hypothesis concerning the effect of music would, if accepted, neatly defuse the paradox which concerns us. This hypothesis, less popular today than at some earlier times, is that of a special 'aesthetic emotion,' totally different from the emotions of life and occasioned only by the perception of works of art. This view is identified with Clive Bell in its general form, but its foremost exponent with specific application to music is the English psychologist Edmund Gurney.[1] According to Gurney, there is a unique, sui generis 'musical emotion' that is raised in listeners by all pieces of 'impressive' (i.e., beautiful) music, and only by such. This unvarying effect of impressive music is either a kind of pleasure itself, or else something the experience of which is pleasurable. Clearly, if the chief result of music that was both impressive and, say, anguished was the arousal of such a 'musical emotion,' there would be little difficulty in understanding how such music could be enjoyable.

There is, however, little else to be said for the view that appreciative response to music consists of but one type of emotion, a music-specific, invariably pleasant one. The effects of different sorts of music are too different from one another, and too reminiscent of life emotions, for this view to carry much plausibility. Our manifest interest in a multiplicity of musical works and experiences begins to seem puzzling if the primary benefit to be derived from any or all of them is this selfsame 'musical emotion.' It just is not the case that all good or impressive music induces a single positive emotion in listeners.

This is not to say that there could not be something specifically musical, and perhaps unduplicatable, in the experience of a particular piece of music.

The total experience—perceptual, emotional, cognitive—of listening to a given work may indeed be unique to it, and this fact not without aesthetic relevance. But one can maintain that without adopting the hypothesis of an invariant and specifically musical emotional element in each such experience. [...]

In order to discuss certain other approaches to our problem we must pursue the analysis of emotion somewhat further. It is by now orthodoxy among philosophers of mind that emotions are more than simply states of inner feeling.[2] Although there is not absolute accord on what all the components of an emotion are, and on which, if any, are essential to the emotion, most writers agree at least that emotions contain a *cognitive* component in addition to an *affective* one. This may be expressed in the form of a belief, attitude, desire, or evaluation, focused on and identifying the *object* of the emotion. Thus, if one is afraid, one feels a certain (rather unpleasant) way, and feels that way *toward* some object that one believes to be dangerous and wants to avoid. If one hopes, one feels a certain (rather more pleasant) way, and feels that way *about* some situation that one believes may possibly obtain, and that one desires to obtain. The presence of an intentional object on which thought and feeling are directed, then, is taken as central to the paradigm of an emotion.

In addition to affective and cognitive components, a case can be made that emotions have *behavioral* and *physiological* components as well. Being afraid may typically involve cowering, shaking, or the like, and perhaps necessarily a tendency or disposition to flee in the presence of the feared object. Being afraid may require, in addition to anything one is subjectively experiencing, a certain state of the endocrine or circulatory systems.

Concerning the affective component—that part of an emotion which consists in what one *feels* in a narrow sense—there is some question as to how this should be conceived. On one view, the affective component of emotion consists in a certain overall coloring of consciousness, a certain quality of inner feeling, of which pleasurable/painful is an important, though not the only, dimension. On another view, the affective component is simply a set of internal sensations of bodily changes—e.g., sensations registering lumps in the throat, goosebumps on the skin, churnings in the stomach, and tension across muscles of the head. I am inclined to think that the feeling component of emotion is best understood as involving both sorts of things. I will accordingly refer to these, respectively, as the *phenomenological* and the *sensational* aspects of the affective (or feeling) component of an emotion.

It is time to say clearly that the standard emotional response to a musical work—e.g., what I have called a sadness-reaction—is not in truth a case of *full-fledged* emotion. This is mainly because music neither supplies an appropriate object for an emotion to be directed on, nor generates the associated beliefs, desires, or attitudes regarding an object which are essential to an emotion being what it is. When a symphonic adagio 'saddens' me, I am not sad at or about the music, nor do I regard the adagio as something I would wish to be otherwise. Furthermore, this weakening of the cognitive component in emotional response to music generally results in the inhibition of most characteristic behaviors and in the significant lessening of behavioral tendencies.

Yet the purely physiological and, more important, affective components are occasionally, it seems, retained in something like full force. If music inevitably fails to induce by itself a proper, contextually embedded *emotion* of sadness, still, some music appears fully capable of inducing at least the characteristic *feeling* of sadness. This is enough, I take it, for the problem of negative emotional response to music to resist complete solution by any of the proposals shortly to be considered. I shall have occasion to distinguish between *emotions* (including cognitive elements) and associated *feelings* (lacking cognitive elements) in what follows. And when I speak subsequently of 'emotional response' to music, this should be understood as an experience produced in a listener which is *at least* the characteristic feeling of some emotion, but which is short of a complete emotion per se.

I am going to assume for the purposes of this essay that the majority of common emotions have affective components (comprising both phenomenological and sensational aspects) which are more or less distinctive of them, apart from the cognitive components that are perhaps the logically distinctive ones. That is to say, I will assume there are introspectible differences between common emotions. Evidence for this is provided by cases in which persons suddenly realize that they are sad, happy, depressed, anxious, or in love without recognizing explicitly that they hold certain beliefs, desires, or evaluations, and thus apparently on the basis of quality of feeling. There is, granted, some psychological research that appears to suggest that common emotions are not much differentiated in inner feeling or affect, but this research strikes me as inconclusive and as somewhat questionable in its method. In any event, it is undeniable that negative affect is integrally involved in a number of emotional conditions, and that there is at least *some* range of qualitative difference in affect across the spectrum of negative emotions. The persistence of our problem and the viability of certain answers to it that we shall entertain actually require nothing more than that. [. . .]

I now describe more fully what I take the typical strong emotional response to music to consist in. Sketching the outline of this experience in greater detail will aid us in determining what value it has. [. . .]

I begin by stating the conditions of listening that conduce to a response of this kind. For clearly not every audition of an emotionally powerful work will affect a listener in that way, nor would one want it to. The first condition would seem to be that a work be in a familiar style, and that the work itself be rather familiar to the listener, so that its specific flow and character have been registered internally, but not so familiar that there is anything of boredom in hearing it unfold on the given occasion. This occurs when a piece is well known though not tiresome, when expectations are firmly aroused in the course of it but denouements remain uncertain.

The second condition is generally taken to be central to the 'aesthetic attitude' on any account of that frame of mind. And that is a mode of attention closely focused on the music, its structure, progression, and emergent character, with a consequent inattention to, or reduced consciousness of, the extramusical world and one's present situation in it.

A third condition is one of emotional openness to the content of music, as opposed to distant contemplation of the same. One must be willing to identify with music, to put oneself in its shoes. One must allow oneself to be moved in a receptive manner by the emotion one hears, as opposed to merely noting or even marveling at it.

Such a listener is not, however, moved straight into a slough of feelings and as a result into oblivion of the music itself. On the contrary, deep emotional response to music typically arises as a product of the most intense musical perception. It is generally in virtue of the *recognition* of emotions expressed in music, or of emotion-laden gestures embodied in musical movement, that an emotional reaction occurs. Usually what happens is of an *empathetic* or *mirroring* nature. When we identify with music that we are perceiving—or perhaps better, with the person whom we imagine owns the emotions or emotional gestures we hear in the music—we share in and adopt those emotions as our own, for the course of the audition. And so we end up feeling as, in imagination, the music does. The point to note here about this phenomenon is that cognition is central to it. If I don't perceive what emotions are in the music by attending to it intently, I have nothing to properly identify and empathize with.

Now, what I am maintaining is simply that when the three conditions indicated above are fulfilled, then for certain musical compositions there is often an empathetic emotional response that consists in something very like experience of the emotion expressed in the music. As noted earlier, this experience includes at its core the characteristic physiological disturbances of the emotion and its characteristic inner affect. The crucial falling off from bona fide emotion occurs in the cognitive dimension; music-emotions lack objects and associated thoughts about them.

This is not to say, however, that emotional responses to music have *no* cognitive (or thoughtlike) component. They do, but it is *etiolated* by comparison to that of real-life emotion. Say the emotion expressed in the music is sadness. Then in an empathetic response, in addition to physiological and affective elements, there is, in the first place, the general *idea* (or *concept*) of sadness. Since a listener is standardly made sad by apprehending and then identifying with sadness in the music, naturally the thought of that emotion is present to the mind concurrent with whatever is felt. In the second place, identifying with the music involves initially the cognitive act of imagining that the music is either *itself* a sad individual or else the *audible expression* of somebody's sadness. In the third place, such identification involves subsequently a cognitive act of imagining that one, too, is sad—that it is *one's own* sadness the music expresses—and thus, however amorphously, that one has something to be sad about.

Let us look at this last phase more closely. When one hears sad music, begins to feel sad, and imagines that one is actually sad, one must, according to the logic of the concept, be imagining that there is an object for one's sadness and that one holds certain evaluative beliefs (or attitudes) regarding it. The point, though, is that this latter imagining generally remains *indeterminate*. That is to say, one does not actually imagine a *particular* object for one's sadness and does not imaginarily hold beliefs about it. In imagining that I have actually become sad by virtue of hearing some music I allow only that my feeling has *some* focus, but without going on to specify this any further. In other words, the object of an empathetic sadness response to music is a largely formal one. When through identification with music I am saddened by the *poco allegretto* of Brahms's Third Symphony, my 'sadness' is not directed on the music, or on any real-life situation of concern to me, but instead on some featureless object posited vaguely by my imagination.

Summing up, then, empathetic emotional responses to music of the sort we are interested in—the sort that our anecdotal hero underwent at the beginning of this essay—typically comprise the following: physiological and affective components of the emotion that is embodied in the music; the thought or idea of this emotion; and the imagination, through identification with the music, of oneself as actually experiencing this emotion, though without the usual determinateness of focus.

We are now, I think, in a decent position to offer explanations of the appeal of negative emotional response to music, the nature of which I have been attempting to make clear. [...]

The first point to be noted in arriving at the more comprehensive solution we seek is that emotional response to music and emotion in ordinary life differ in one crucial and obvious respect, connected to the attenuation of cognitive content in the former. Emotional responses to music typically *have no life-implications*, in contrast to their real counterparts. The 'sadness' one may be made to feel by sympathetically attending to music has no basis in one's extramusical life, signals no enduring state of negative affect, indicates no problem requiring action, calls forth no persisting pattern of behavior, and in general bodes no ill for one's future. One does not really believe—though one may intermittently imagine—that one's sadness-response is objectively apt, that some situation exists in one's life which is to be bemoaned. On the other hand, if one is truly sad one must believe this, and will, accordingly, both expect one's feeling to persist until objective conditions are changed and be disposed to take action to remedy one's unhappy state. The person having a sadness-response to music is generally free, however, from this expectation and disposition. The experience of sadness from music consists primarily of a feeling under a conception, but bracketed from and unfettered by the demands and involvements of the corresponding emotion in life.

Since negative emotional response to music is devoid of the contextual implications of such as sadness, grief, anger, we are able to focus more fully on just the feeling involved in these emotions. This opens the way for three benefits which we may reap by allowing ourselves to mirror darkly emotional music. These are benefits of enjoyment, of understanding, and of self-assurance.

To make out the first requires a somewhat startling claim, but it is one without which we cannot, I think, wholly resolve the paradox we have been addressing. This claim is that emotive affect itself, divorced from all psychological and behavioral consequences, is in virtually all cases something that we are capable of taking satisfaction in. That is to say, the pure feeling component of just about any emotion—providing it is not too violent or intense—is something we can, on balance, enjoy experiencing.

When feelings are made available to us isolated, backgroundless, and inherently limited in duration—as they are through music—we can approach them as if we were wine tasters, sampling the delights of various vintages, or like Des Esseintes, the hero of Huysmans's *A Rebours*, reveling in the flavors conveyed by a mouth organ fitted with a variety of liqueurs. We become cognoscenti of feeling, savoring the qualitative aspect of emotional life for its own sake.

[. . .] The undistracted experience of affects of just about any sort, when free of practical consequence, appears to have intrinsic appeal for many of us. I will label this the reward of Savoring Feeling.

The second reward attaching to negative emotional response to music in virtue of its contextual freedom is that of greater understanding of the condition of feeling involved in some recognized emotion. It is notoriously difficult to say what the knowledge of how an emotion feels consists in, but I think it is clear that such knowledge, whatever it amounts to, can be augmented by emotional experiences during or after occasions of music listening. At such times we have an opportunity to introspectively scrutinize and ponder the inner affective dimension of an emotion—say, anguish— whose idea is before the mind, in a manner not open to the individual who is caught in the throes of real anguish. We can attain insight into what the feeling of anguish is *like*, not in the sense that we learn what it resembles, but in the sense that we perceive and register it more clearly. This in turn cashes out in an improved ability to recognize and to recollectively contemplate this feeling in future. One can deepen or reinforce one's image of what it is to feel melancholy by experiencing the *poco allegretto* of Brahms's Third, or of what it is to feel hopeless passion by responding to Scriabin's C-sharp Minor Étude. [...]

The third of the rewards announced above relates directly to a person's self-respect or sense of dignity as a human being. Central to most people's ideal image of themselves is the capacity to feel deeply a range of emotions. We like to think of ourselves as able to be stirred profoundly, and in various ways, by appropriate occurrences. The individual whose emotional faculty is inactive, shallow, or one-dimensional seems to us less of a person. Since music has the power to put us into the feeling state of a negative emotion without its unwanted life consequences, it allows us to partly reassure ourselves in a nondestructive manner of the depth and breadth of our ability to feel. Having a negative emotional response to music is like giving our emotional engines a 'dry run.' If there is something wrong with the plane it is better to find this out on the runway than in the air. Although one would not opt to try on real grief just to see if one were capable of it, confirmation of this of a sort can perhaps be had less riskily by involvement with music. Whether such confirmation can legitimately be had in this way is not clearly to the point; for even if it is epistemically flawed, its psychological effect is real enough. Furthermore, in exercising our feeling capacities on music we might be said to tone them up, or get them into shape, thus readying ourselves for intenser and more focused reactions to situations in life. It is worth noting that this reward of emotional response to music is more naturally associated with negative than with positive emotions. It is usually not emotions like joy, amusement, or excitement that we have a need of proving ourselves equal to and prepared for feeling, and it is generally not the ability to feel those emotions which has the most weight in the common idea of an emotionally developed individual. Call this the reward of Emotional Assurance.

So far we have reckoned up certain rewards of negative emotional response to music which accrue to it regarded as an experience of pure feeling concurrent with the mere idea of a corresponding emotion. We must now turn to the rewards of imagining, through identification, that one is in the full emotional condition, while knowing throughout that one is not.

These are collectively as important as the rewards already considered. There seem to be at least three of them, which I will address in turn. The first is of special relevance to the paradox we have been concerned with in that it, unlike any of the other rewards mentioned, attaches almost exclusively to negative as opposed to positive emotional response to music.

If I empathetically experience feelings of despair or anguish from a despairing or anguished piece of music and also regard the music as the unfolding expression of someone's despair or anguish, then I may begin to identify with that someone and consequently to imagine, in a fashion described earlier, that I am myself in actual despair or anguish. I may even have the impression that I am generating the music de profundis as an expression of the despair or anguish I imagine I am now experiencing. In any case, since my imagined emotion is one with that of the music's persona, it will partake in the destiny and vicissitudes of that emotion as conveyed by the development of the music.

Since I have identified my emotional state with that expressed in the music, I can feel that what seems to happen to that emotion in the course of the music is happening to me as well. And this, because of the way in which emotional content is carried by musical structure, is often a source of satisfaction, especially where unpleasant or difficult emotions are involved.

Emotions presented in and imaginatively experienced through music, unlike those encountered in real life, have a character of inevitability, purposiveness, and finality about them. This is undoubtedly because they seem so intimately connected with the progress of musical substance itself as to be inseparable from it. Thus what primarily or initially characterizes musical movement or development comes to seem as well an attribute of the emotional content it underpins. Emotion in a musical composition, because of its construction, so often strikes us as having been resolved, transformed, transfigured, or triumphed over when the music is done.

When the first section in C minor of Brahms's *poco allegretto* gives way smoothly to a trio in A-flat major, we can imagine our sobbing melancholy melting into a mood of hesitant gaiety. When the main material of the *Marcia Funebre* breaks at midpoint into a stately fugue on the same themes, we can imagine our bottomless grief as metamorphosed, diffracted into shining fragments of a more easily borne pathos. And when the extended musical logic of the finale of Dvořák's Seventh Symphony in D Minor eventuates in a dissonant though shortly resolved brass-dominated yawp in the final measures, one can share in its experience of stern tragedy culminating in hard-won, reluctant resignation. [. . .] Call this the reward of Emotional Resolution.

The second reward of identifying with music to the point of imagining oneself possessed of real negative emotion is simpler than and in a sense prior to that just discussed. If one begins to regard music as the expression of one's own current emotional state, it will begin to seem as if it issues from oneself, as if it pours forth from one's innermost being.[3] It is then very natural for one to receive an impression of expressive power—of freedom and ease in externalizing and embodying what one feels. The sense one has of the richness and spontaneity with which one's inner life is unfolding itself, even where the feelings involved are of the negative kind, is a source of undeniable joy. The unpleasant aspect of certain emotions we imagine ourselves to experience through music is balanced by the adequacy, grace, and splendor of the exposition we feel ourselves to be according that emotion. Of course we do not really have such expressive ability—that which we seem to ourselves to have while identifying with music is obviously founded in the musical abilities of the composer. But we are not actually deceiving ourselves. We do not literally believe we are creators of music. The composer's musical genius makes possible the imaginative experience described above, and we can remain aware of that throughout. But this does not take away the resulting satisfaction. The coat may be borrowed, but it is just as warm. Call this the reward of Expressive Potency.

The last reward of imagining negative emotion I will discuss arises most clearly when a listener is willing to entertain what I call the Expressionist assumption concerning the emotional content of what he is hearing. On the Expression theory of music, espoused by Tolstoy and Cooke among others, emotion heard in a sonata is always emotion experienced by the composer on an earlier occasion, which has now been transmuted into music. The sonata is a vehicle for conveying a particular sort of emotional experience from one person to another. Now, it seems that without subscribing to the obviously inadequate Expression theory itself, we may sometimes as listeners adopt the Expressionist assumption—that the emotion expressed in a particular piece belongs to its composer's biography—while imagining ourselves to be possessed of the full emotion whose feeling has been aroused within us. If we do so we are in effect imagining that we are sharing in the precise emotional experience of another human being, the man or woman responsible for the music we hear. This, as Tolstoy so well appreciated, carried with it a decided reward—the reward of intimacy—which accrues whether the emotion is positive or negative in tone. The sense of intimate contact with the mind and soul of another, the sense that one is manifestly not alone in the emotional universe, goes a long way toward counterbalancing the possibly distressing aspect of the grief, sorrow, or anger one imagines oneself to have. The emotional separateness and alienation which occur frequently in daily living are here miraculously swept aside in imaginative identification with the composer whose feelings are, on the Expressionist assumption, plainly revealed for any listener to hear and to mirror. Call this the reward of Emotional Communion. [. . .]

Have we now succeeded in rescuing the occupant of the musical 'electric chair' with which we began? I think so. We have suggested, first, that although this person is actually registering the feelings of some negative emotions this may, in the circumstances, itself afford a certain satisfaction, and second, that there are a number of more indirect rewards deriving from those feelings and the imagined emotions erected upon them, which more than compensate for what disagreeableness we may be inclined to ascribe to the conditions assumed in the course of listening. Those works of Beethoven, Mozart, Brahms, Scriabin, and Mahler do not constitute for aesthetic appreciation a bed of hot coals, to be sure, but neither do they present themselves as merely a display case of mineral specimens, mounted and remote. I hope in this essay to have avoided the errors of both images and to have presented a more balanced picture. Little short of the story I have told, I think, can fully account for why we often seek negative emotion from the art of sound rather than remaining content with mere perception, at arm's length, of its musical embodiment.

['Music and Negative Emotion', *Pacific Philosophical Quarterly*, 63 (1982); repr. Jerrold Levinson, *Music, Art, & Metaphysics* (Ithaca, NY: Cornell University Press, 1990), 306–7, 309–10, 312–15, 319–29, 332–3.]

Section VI

How Can we Evaluate Art?

INTRODUCTION

O ne of the most commonly asked questions about the arts is whether-value judgements about works of art are in some sense objective. Those who claim that the value of an artwork lies in how it affects a perceiver (the subject) and that any given work will affect different people in different ways are called 'subjectivists'. On the other hand, those who believe that the value of an artwork lies *in the object* are called 'objectivists'. Which side one takes on this debate has implications for whether it is possible to give reasons as logical support for a value judgement, and whether and what kind of social and cultural significance is attributed to the arts. The readings in Section II.b address how defining art in particular ways can have social and cultural significance. The readings in this section focus on the objectivity of value judgements and the possibility of defending them by giving reasons.

Curt Ducasse defends the view that aesthetic judgements are subjective. He proposes that there is no good taste or bad taste, but only different tastes, and that the only difference between experienced critics and amateurs is that critics understand *why* they like or dislike something and can explain the reasons for their likes and dislikes to others. It is interesting to note that Ducasse is making claims about aesthetic judgements. He distinguishes such judgements from extra-aesthetic appraisals of an object, and some of these extra-aesthetic judgements are about whether something is good as a work of *art* (e.g. whether a work expresses what the artist intended it to express). His distinction recalls the one drawn between the aesthetic and the arts in Sections I and II.

While not endorsing a subjectivist view, Meyer Schapiro describes how *difficult* it can be to perceive relevant qualities of a work. Not only do our perceptual abilities change and grow through time, but fresh points of view enable us to see new structures in a work. Evaluation of art rests on perception of it, Schapiro argues, and any given perception is of the nature of a hypothesis, based on previous experience, communal with the perceptions of others, and open to revision. On Schapiro's account the multiple aesthetics described in Section I.b and difficulties of understanding a work of art brought forward in Section IV coalesce to show how varied perceptions and experiences of a work might be.

In his classic essay 'Of the Standard of Taste', David Hume asks whether judgements of taste (that is, judgements that something is beautiful) are subjective or objective. In cases where it is difficult to decide on a work's merit, the subjectivist view that accepts an 'equality of taste' may seem appropriate. Yet, in other cases it would be absurd. For example, if someone claimed that Ogilby, an obscure British poet, was a better poet than John Milton, who is still regarded as one of the greatest poets ever, we would dismiss that person's judgement. Hume emphasizes that appreciators must prepare themselves for a work by developing relevant perceptual skills and freeing their minds from prejudices. Hume's view is thus neither completely objective nor completely subjective but intersubjective in that judgements of taste, he says, are based on features of a work that may in principle please anyone. Nevertheless, he states that there are some areas where there is no right or wrong taste, just different tastes.

Arnold Isenberg rejects the idea that reasons can be used logically to defend an evaluative judgement of a work, and hence rejects the idea that there are general principles or criteria that establish the relevance of reasons in defending a value judgement. He argues that reasons function in a different way: they establish 'communication at the level of the senses'. He agrees with Ducasse that critics do not give reasons to prove evaluative conclusions logically, by giving arguments, but rejects the view that the function of reasons is simply to explain the critic's response. According to Isenberg, the function of reasons is not logical but psychological: to enrich the ways one sees and hears.

John Berger's approach to critical evaluation introduces a political dimension. Like several other authors represented in this collection, he insists that the purpose of art is not to give pleasure but to improve humankind at personal, social, and political levels. Ideally, such improvement would not be confined to the artist's own culture but be of broader human significance. For example, in the suite of prints known as *The Disasters of War*, Francisco Goya depicts the agony and horrors suffered by Spaniards attempting to resist Napoleon's invasions. But, Berger says, he also protests the destruction of human potential anywhere, since when human beings—whether perpetrators or victims—either abandon voluntarily or are forced to abandon our greatest resource, the ability to reason, we are reduced to the level of beasts. In looking at Goya's prints, a perceiver may well feel those emotions of pity and terror which Edmund Burke describes in his account of the sublime.

A characteristic of modernism, which includes a tradition of thinking about art and the aesthetic inaugurated in western Europe in the eighteenth century, is that there is a universal basis for judgements of aesthetic quality. The concept of the aesthetic as divorced from personal and utilitarian interests (as in I.a) provided a foundation for such a claim. The postmodern, on the other hand, typically denies the existence of culturally transcendent standards, in part because (as Nietzsche proposed) it is not possible to eliminate the effects of one's own personal and cultural background on how one experiences a work. This (alleged) fact has significant implications for the aesthetic and artistic appreciation and evaluation of objects produced in other cultures and of objects produced by 'outsider' elements—those outside the educational institutions of the official artworld—of one's own culture. Anthony Appiah develops the idea that Western judges of Baule objects employ criteria of 'their own aesthetic tradition' just as the Baule do, and also illustrates how difficult it is to define what is and is not part of a culture. As he puts it, cultures are 'contaminated' by one another, creating points of commonality even among major differences.

Along various paths, all the readings have led up to the questions in this section. For, whether one should conclude that evaluations of artworks are objective depends on the relationship between art and 'the aesthetic' or 'an aesthetic'; the potential impact and importance of art and its various forms in society; whether art is a vehicle for personal expression, ideas, or emotions; to what extent it is possible to understand an artwork; and whether one's responses are of a sort that others may in principle share.

52 Criticism as Appraisal

[T]he word 'criticism' is equivocal—sometimes meaning scholarly discussion of historical or textual matters, or of matters of technique; and sometimes, on the other hand, meaning judgment as to the merits of given works. Let us now pass to criticism in this latter, more common, sense.

It might seem, as regards the merits of a given work, that there would be little more to say than that it is good or bad, or better or worse than certain others. A certain *prima facie* plausibility is given to this opinion by the fact that the number of adjectives—such as good, bad, beautiful, ugly, sublime, noble, and so on—that are adjectives specifically of *value* is very small as compared with the number of adjectives, ordinarily contrasted with them as simply *descriptive*, that signify characters other than values.

But when we turn to what is actually said about given works of art by persons who are critics in the sense that they judge the values, positive or negative, of those works, we find that value adjectives, such as just mentioned, are rather seldom used by them. How it is that their judgments are nevertheless judgments of value is, at first, something of a puzzle. But the puzzle is solved as soon as we notice that the very same statement can at one time be used to express a merely descriptive and purely objective judgment, and at another time to express in addition a judgment of value. Whether the statement does express a judgment of value or not on a given occasion depends on whether a certain assumption is or is not then being made. The statement that a given work possesses a certain objective characteristic expresses at the same time a judgment of value if the characteristic is one that the judging person approves or, as the case may be, disapproves; and is thus one that he regards as conferring, respectively, positive or negative value on any object of the given kind that happens to possess it. But if, on the contrary, the assumption that the given characteristic is a valued or disvalued one is not made, then the statement that the object has this characteristic is not evaluative but descriptive only.

For example, the statement that a given novel runs to half-a-million words is descriptive of a certain perfectly objective and verifiable character of it, and may be intended as purely descriptive. But it may be intended to express, in addition, an adverse comment on the given novel, under the tacit assumption that it is a *bad* thing in any novel to be as long as that. Again, the statement that the style of a certain author is repetitious may be intended as purely descriptive; but ordinarily it would be intended to convey, and would convey in addition, the judgment that, because of this, his style is tedious and therefore bad.

It should be noticed also that the very same adjective may express favorable evaluation when applied to things of a certain sort, but unfavorable when applied to things of certain other sorts. The adjective 'involved,' for instance, as applied to the plot of a mystery story, is a term of praise; but when applied to a piece of reasoning, it is a term of blame.

Evaluative criticism, thus, actually consists not so much in saying simply that a given work is good or bad, or better or worse than another, as in saying in effect that it is so in consequence of its possessing this or that specific feature, which the critic regards as a good or a bad one for a work of that kind to possess. The sorts of features that a given critic approves or disapproves of, for works of a given kind, constitute the *standards of criticism* which he uses for evaluation of works of that kind.

The great difference between the judgments of goodness and badness passed by a trained critic and those passed by the ordinary, unsophisticated consumer of art is that the critic traces his evaluation of the object he is judging to the specific features that make it for him predominantly pleasing or displeasing; whereas the unsophisticated amateur of art is pleased or displeased by the given object without knowing which, in particular, are the features that cause the pleasure or displeasure he finds in it. *That is, the ordinary amateur's judgment of value is wholesale, unanalytical; that of the critic, detailed, analytical.*

But the true amateur, who is not a mere echo, nevertheless has a taste of his own and knows whether it is being gratified or offended. This is true also of the critic; but the critic knows in addition, and is able to describe, what specific sorts of characters do gratify or offend his taste.

It is very important here, however, to guard against a certain widespread illusion concerning the critic's judgment, namely, the illusion that mention by him of the specific grounds of his approval or disapproval of a given work constitutes proof or evidence that his judgment of its value is true or right, and is authoritative over that of a person who is not similarly able to give the grounds of his likes and dislikes—so that the latter person is held not really qualified to judge; and if his judgment differs from that of the critic, it is held to be wrong and his taste bad. This is an opinion very common indeed not only, as one might expect, among critics, but also among ordinary amateurs of art, who in general are deplorably humble and easily awed. But it is nevertheless an error.

This becomes evident as soon as we notice what happens if the critic is challenged to say, not why he likes a given painting, for example, but why he likes those specific features of the painting that he gives as the basis for his approval. To make the matter concrete, let us suppose that, when asked why he judges a certain painting good, the critic answers that, for one thing, it is because the plastic qualities of the objects in it are adequately represented. Then, when asked further why this characteristic is a good one in a painting, he may reply that it is a characteristic distinctive of all painting that is genuinely art. But obviously this reply merely begs the question. It is an implicit and probably unconscious, but nevertheless arbitrary, proposal by him to set up as a standard of what is genuine art in painting that which he personally values so highly; and to label as irrelevant that, for instance, which he would call the narrative and sentimental aspects of the painting. But, of course, question-begging epithets prove nothing on either side.

The long and short of the situation is thus that the critic is personally much interested in plastic qualities and not interested, or less interested, in the other things that a painter may also or instead be interested in and be attempting to express. Accordingly, when our critic is challenged to justify his own high valuation of plastic qualities, there is in the end nothing he can say, except that they interest and delight *him*. [...]

The critic's evaluations [...] ultimately are just as purely matters of his individual taste as are those of the unsophisticated amateur. The great difference, even when both of them have the same tastes, is, as already pointed out, that the naïve amateur is pleased or displeased without knowing exactly why, whereas the critic does know what specific features are responsible for his own pleasure or displeasure in a given work of art. But in both cases the situation is in the end just the same as with, let us say, the taste of pineapple. Some persons like it, and others dislike it; but it would be absurd to say that it is *really* good, although some dislike it, or *really* bad, although some like it. For when the values concerned are not instrumental values but immediate values—whether of odors, of tastes, of sounds, of plastic qualities, or of facial expressions—then individual likes and dislikes constitute the only meaning of good and bad.

A person's tastes, thus—whether he be sophisticated critic or simple amateur—are ultimately at once incapable of justification and self-justifying. And therefore, in the matter of tastes, there can be no disputing but, as Oscar Wilde pointed out, only quarrelling. We can indeed apply epithets to persons whose taste differs from ours; we can despise them, howl them down, and ostracize them. But we cannot possibly prove that their taste is bad in any sense other than that it is *different* from ours, or different from that of a majority or of some other particular group to which we ourselves belong or would like to belong. There is no such thing as *objective* goodness or badness of taste, but only such a thing as my taste and your taste, the taste of this man and the taste of some other man, tastes shared by many or by few.

A person's taste may change, of course, but whether we call the change development or perversion depends solely on whether it changes in the direction of our own or away from it. A change in our own taste is for each of us, by definition, development—not perversion. [...]

That there is no such thing as goodness or badness of taste in an objective, universally valid sense is a fact that profoundly disturbs some persons when they first come up against it. It seems to them to make art criticism impossible. But so to conclude is to mistake the import of the fact. As pointed out above, art criticism in aesthetic terms actually consists in analysis, by the critic, of the features of a given work of art that determine his liking or disliking it. That his evaluation of these features themselves is a matter of his own taste or interests leaves criticism in that sense perfectly possible. What is taken away is only the illusion that such criticism proves something and is authoritative over the evaluations of less analytical persons. To lose this illusion, however, does not entail that one no longer has a taste of one's own. Rather, the realization that there are no authorities in matters of taste throws one back upon one's own taste, frees one from distrust of it, and enlivens it. But realization of this also gives one a sense of humor about one's taste. That is, it replaces, by a certain abstract tolerance, the sneers or even sometimes the fury that before would almost have denied the right to exist to persons whose taste shockingly diverged from ours.

What has been said so far concerns the evaluation of works of art in terms of beauty and ugliness—that is, in terms of the pleasure or displeasure caused by a work in a beholder who contemplates it aesthetically. But it must now be emphasized that evaluation of a work of art thus in aesthetic terms is far from being the only possible or legitimate type of evaluation. Indeed, aesthetic evaluation does not even have priority over other types of evaluation, except in the case of persons whose own interest in the given work is predominantly aesthetic. Evaluation of a painting or of a book in terms of, for instance, religious values, is possible and quite as legitimate; and, for persons interested primarily in such values, is more relevant. The example of Tolstoy comes to mind in this connection. This important fact will become more evident if mention is now made of some of the principal terms, other than aesthetic, in which works of art may be evaluated.

There is first of all the consideration in terms of which the artist himself, at each moment as he creates the work, evaluates and, if need be, corrects what he has done. This consideration might be, but except in works of decorative art usually is not, whether what he has done is beautiful or ugly. Rather, what he asks himself is whether what he has done does or does not adequately express what he is attempting to express. [. . .]

Another consideration in the light of which the artist may criticize a finished work of his own is whether what it expresses is something that, on reflection, he is willing to acknowledge as a part of himself. Our own moods, feelings, attitudes, and sentiments, like our own thoughts, are made clear to us if we succeed in expressing them objectively. The object created—whether it be a painting, a melody, or a sentence—is a mirror that reflects back to us the feeling or the thought we had within us, and allows us to scrutinize and evaluate it more carefully than we could before. And it may well be that we then disapprove of that aspect of ourself which the mirror exhibits to us. In such a case, we may reject the work we have created, not because it expresses inadequately what we had to express, but because what it does adequately express is something that indeed was, but is no longer, a part of ourself. We have transcended, and now disown, the feeling the work objectifies.

Again, a work of art may be evaluated, as Tolstoy proposed, in terms of its adequacy as an instrument for the transmission to other persons of the emotional experience its creator had to express. For it is conceivable that the work might express the artist's insight adequately, but in a code language, as it were, which other persons understand perhaps imperfectly or not at all. Adequacy of the work *qua* instrument for the communication to others of what the artist felt is a sort of merit that the artist himself, as a gregarious being, may desire; and is also something that a spectator may legitimately demand if what he is interested in is sharing the artist's emotional experience. Only rough tests of such adequacy are possible, however, since there is no way of comparing directly the feeling the artist seeks to express with the feeling the spectator obtains.

On the other hand, the spectator has a perfect right to evaluate, if he wishes, a work of art simply in terms of its emotional import to himself or to beholders in general, irrespective of whether this import is or is not the import the artist intended his work to have.

Indeed, *when a work of art is considered from the point of view of the consumer, the values in terms of which it may legitimately be appraised by him are of the most diverse sorts.* They may be aesthetic values; but they may equally well be moral, political, or even commercial value. Or, appraisal may be in terms of the educational value of the given work—in terms, that is to say, of its capacity to initiate the consumer into sentiments, attitudes, or moods hitherto unexperienced by him. Literature especially is susceptible of being evaluated by most varied standards, since often it is a 'mixed' art, in the sense that it aims to express not only feelings for their own sakes but also certain ideas. That is, these ideas are then not mere means used by the writer to the end of expressing certain feelings arousable only through ideas, but are ideas that he regards as objectively important and wishes to disseminate.

A book, accordingly, may be appraised in terms of its informativeness or in terms of its effectiveness as propaganda for a cause in which the reader is interested. Another book may be prized by some because it furnishes an agreeable escape from so-called reality, and yet condemned by others for the very same reason. Some will value a book on account of its vivid depiction of a certain stratum of society; others will be primarily concerned with beauty, or quaintness, or originality of style; others perhaps with philosophical profundity; and so on.

Of these various terms in which it is possible to appraise a book or some other work of art, none can be claimed to be *the* objectively right terms. Prospectors have a saying that 'gold is where you find it'; and we may say conversely that a given book or other work of art is genuinely a mine of whatever species of value somebody does, in fact, find in it. The claim that one *ought* to seek this or that particular sort of value in a given work is sheer dogmatism; it is but an instinctive attempt to make one's own angle of interest obligatory for everybody.

[*Art, the Critics, and You* (Indianapolis: Bobbs-Merrill, 1944), 115–27.]

MEYER SCHAPIRO

53 On Perfection and Coherence in Art

My aim in this paper is to examine the ascription of certain qualities to the work of art as a whole, the qualities of perfection, coherence, and unity of form and content, which are regarded as conditions of beauty. While rooted in an immediate intuition of the structure of the whole, the judgments of these qualities often change with continuing experience of the object. They are never fully confirmed, but are sometimes invalidated by a single new observation. As criteria of value they are not strict or indispensable; there are great works in which these qualities are lacking. Coherence, for example, will be found in many works that fail to move us, and a supreme work may contain incoherences. Order in art is like logic in science, a built-in demand, but not enough to give a work the distinction of greatness. There are dull and interesting orders, plain and beautiful ones, orders full of surprises and subtle relations, and orders that are pedestrian and banal.

The word perfection is often a rhetorical term expressing the beholder's feeling of rightness, his conviction that everything in the work is as it should be, that nothing can be changed without ruining the whole. Our perception of a work is not exhaustive, however. We see only some parts and aspects; a second look will disclose much that was not seen before. We must not confuse the whole in a large aspect, coextensive with the boundaries of the work, with the whole as the totality of the work. Expert scrutiny will discern in the acknowledged masterpieces not only details that were defective when the artist produced them, but changes brought about by others who have repaired the work. Few old paintings are today in their original state. Even acute observers will often fail to notice these changes. A painting that has seemed complete and perfectly proportioned will, like Rembrandt's *Night Watch*, turn out to have lost a considerable part. In Homer's *Iliad* numerous passages are later interpolations. Few visitors to the cathedral of Chartres can distinguish the original painted glass from the replacements made in the same windows in later and especially in modern times. The example of Chartres reminds us, too, that for the judgment of artistic greatness it is not necessary that a work be consistent in style or complete. Many architects, sculptors, and painters collaborated on this marvel. The varying capacities of these artists, their unlike styles, even their indifference to consistency with each other, have not kept generations of beholders from adoring this beautiful church as a supreme achievement. It is not a single work of art, but, like the Bible, a vast collection of works which we value as a single incomparable whole. If the Parthenon holds up artistically in its ruined state through the grandeur of its qualities in all that remains of the original, in Chartres we accept a whole in which very different conceptions of form have been juxtaposed. The two West towers, begun by two architects of the twelfth century, were completed at different times, one of them in the late Gothic period in a style that is opposed in principle to the rest of the façade. The great West portal, too, is not as it was originally designed; several sculptors of different temperament and capacity have worked together; and parts have been arbitrarily cut and displaced to adjust to a change in the construction.

Even where a single great artist has been responsible for a work one can detect inconsistencies brought about by a new conception introduced in the course of work. So in the Sistine ceiling, Michelangelo has changed the scale of the figures in mid-passage. One can recall other great works of literature, painting, and architecture that are incomplete or inconsistent in some respects. And one might entertain the thought that in the greatest works of all such incompleteness and inconsistency are evidences of the living process of the most serious and daring art which is rarely realized fully according to a fixed plan, but undergoes the contingencies of a prolonged effort. Perfection, completeness, strict consistency are more likely in small works than in large. The greatest artists—Homer, Shakespeare, Michelangelo, Tolstoy—present us with works that are full of problematic features. Samuel Johnson, in considering Shakespeare, drew up a list of weaknesses which, taken alone, would justify dismissing as inferior any other writer in whose poems they occurred. The power of Shakespeare, recognized by Johnson, is manifest in the ability to hold us and satisfy us in spite of these imperfections. [. . .]

It is clear from continued experience and close study of works that the judgment of perfection in art, as in nature, is a hypothesis, not a certitude established by an immediate intuition. It implies that a valued quality of the work of art, which has been experienced at one time, will be experienced as such in the future; and in so far as the judgment of perfection covers the character of the parts and their relation to the particular whole, it assumes that the quality found in parts already perceived and cited as examples of that perfection will be found in all other parts and aspects to be scrutinized in the future. There is, of course, the negative evidence from the absence of observable inconsistencies and weaknesses. But we have learned often enough how limited is our perception of such complex wholes as works of art. In a circle a very tiny break or dent will arouse our attention. But in an object as complex as a novel, a building, a picture, a sonata, our impression of the whole is a resultant or summation in which some elements can be changed with little apparent difference to our sense of the whole; perception of such complexities is rapid and tolerant, isolating certain features and passing freely over others, and admitting much vagueness for the sake of the larger effects. We cannot hold in view more than a few parts or aspects, and we are directed by a past experience, an expectation and a habit of seeing, which is highly selective even in close scrutiny of an object intended for the fullest, most attentive perception. The capacity of an expert to discern in a familiar work unnoticed details and relationships that point to its retouching by others is therefore so astonishing. Here the sensibility of the expert, trained and set for such investigation, is like the power of the microscope to disclose in a work features beyond ordinary sensitive vision.

But even the experts are often blind or mistaken. To see the work as it is, to know it in its fullness, is a goal of collective criticism extending over genera-tions. This task is sustained by new points of view that make possible the revelation of significant features overlooked by other observers. In all these successive judgments there is an appeal to the freshly seen structure and qualities of the work.

What I have said about the fallibility of judgments of coherence and completeness applies also to judgments of incoherence and incompleteness. These are often guided by norms of style which are presented as universal requirements of art and inhibit recognition of order in works that violate the canons of form in that style. The norms are constantly justified in practice by perceptions—supposedly simple unprejudiced apprehensions of a qual-ity—which are in fact directed by these norms. This is familiar enough from the charge of formlessness brought against modern works and espe-cially the Cubist paintings that were criticized later from another point of view as excessively concerned with form. It is clear that there are many kinds of order and our impression of order and orderliness is influenced by a model of the quality. For someone accustomed to classic design, symmetry and a legible balance are prerequisites of order. Distinctness of parts, clear group-ing, definite axes are indispensable features of a well-ordered whole. This canon excludes the intricate, the unstable, the fused, the scattered, the broken, in composition; yet such qualities may belong to a whole in which we can discern regularities if we are disposed to them by another aesthetic.
[. . .]

I have argued that we do not see all of a work when we see it as a whole. We strive to see it as completely as possible and in a unifying way, though seeing is selective and limited. Critical seeing, aware of the incompleteness of perception, is explorative and dwells on details as well as on the large aspects that we call the whole. It takes into account others' seeing; it is a collective and cooperative seeing and welcomes comparison of different perceptions and judgments. It also knows moments of sudden revelation and intense experience of unity and completeness which are shared in others' scrutiny.

['On Perfection, Coherence, and Unity of Form and Content', in Sidney Hook (ed.), *Art and Philosophy: A Symposium* (New York: New York University Press, 1966), 3–6, 15.]

DAVID HUME

54   Of the Standard of Taste

The great variety of Taste, as well as of opinion, which prevails in the world, is too obvious not to have fallen under every one's observation. Men of the most confined knowledge are able to remark a difference of taste in the narrow circle of their acquaintance, even where the persons have been educated under the same government, and have early imbibed the same prejudices. But those, who can enlarge their view to contemplate distant nations and remote ages, are still more surprized at the great inconsistence and contrariety. We are apt to call *barbarous* whatever departs widely from our own taste and apprehension: But soon find the epithet of reproach retorted on us. And the highest arrogance and self-conceit is at last startled, on observing an equal assurance on all sides, and scruples, amidst such a contest of sentiment, to pronounce positively in its own favour.

As this variety of taste is obvious to the most careless enquirer; so will it be found, on examination, to be still greater in reality than in appearance. The sentiments of men often differ with regard to beauty and deformity of all kinds, even while their general discourse is the same. There are certain terms in every language, which import blame, and others praise; and all men, who use the same tongue, must agree in their application of them. Every voice is united in applauding elegance, propriety, simplicity, spirit in writing; and in blaming fustian, affectation, coldness, and a false brilliancy: But when critics come to particulars, this seeming unanimity vanishes; and it is found, that they had affixed a very different meaning to their expressions. In all matters of opinion and science, the case is opposite: The difference among men is there oftener found to lie in generals than in particulars; and to be less in reality than in appearance. An explanation of the terms commonly ends the controversy; and the disputants are surprized to find, that they had been quarrelling, while at bottom they agreed in their judgment.

Those who found morality on sentiment, more than on reason, are inclined to comprehend ethics under the former observation, and to maintain, that, in all questions, which regard conduct and manners, the difference among men is really greater than at first sight it appears. It is indeed obvious, that writers of all nations and all ages concur in applauding justice, humanity, magnanimity, prudence, veracity; and in blaming the opposite qualities. Even poets and

other authors, whose compositions are chiefly calculated to please the imagination, are yet found, from Homer down to Fenelon, to inculcate the same
moral precepts, and to bestow their applause and blame on the same virtues
and vices. This great unanimity is usually ascribed to the influence of plain
reason; which, in all these cases, maintains similar sentiments in all men, and
prevents those controversies, to which the abstract sciences are so much
exposed. So far as the unanimity is real, this account may be admitted as
satisfactory: But we must also allow that some part of the seeming harmony
in morals may be accounted for from the very nature of language. The word
virtue, with its equivalent in every tongue, implies praise; as that of *vice* does
blame: And no one, without the most obvious and grossest impropriety, could
affix reproach to a term, which in general acceptation is understood in a good
sense; or bestow applause, where the idiom requires disapprobation. Homer's
general precepts, where he delivers any such, will never be controverted; but
it is obvious, that, when he draws particular pictures of manners, and
represents heroism in Achilles and prudence in Ulysses, he intermixes a much
greater degree of ferocity in the former, and of cunning and fraud in the latter,
than Fenelon would admit of. The sage Ulysses in the Greek poet seems to
delight in lies and fictions, and often employs them without any necessity or
even advantage: But his more scrupulous son, in the French epic writer,
exposes himself to the most imminent perils, rather than depart from the
most exact line of truth and veracity.

The admirers and followers of the Alcoran insist on the excellent moral
precepts interspersed throughout that wild and absurd performance. But it is
to be supposed, that the Arabic words, which correspond to the English,
equity, justice, temperance, meekness, charity, were such as, from the constant use of that tongue, must always be taken in a good sense; and it would
have argued the greatest ignorance, not of morals, but of language, to have
mentioned them with any epithets, besides those of applause and approbation. But would we know, whether the pretended prophet had really attained
a just sentiment of morals? Let us attend to his narration; and we shall soon
find, that he bestows praise on such instances of treachery, inhumanity,
cruelty, revenge, bigotry, as are utterly incompatible with civilized society.
No steady rule of right seems there to be attended to; and every action is
blamed or praised, so far only as it is beneficial or hurtful to the true believers.

The merit of delivering true general precepts in ethics is indeed very small.
Whoever recommends any moral virtues, really does no more than is implied
in the terms themselves. That people, who invented the word *charity*, and
used it in a good sense, inculcated more clearly and much more efficaciously,
the precept, *be charitable*, than any pretended legislator or prophet, who
should insert such a *maxim* in his writings. Of all expressions, those, which,
together with their other meaning, imply a degree either of blame or
approbation, are the least liable to be perverted or mistaken.

It is natural for us to seek a *Standard of Taste*; a rule, by which the various sentiments of men may be reconciled; at least, a decision, afforded, confirming one sentiment, and condemning another.

There is a species of philosophy which cuts off all hopes of success in such an attempt, and represents the impossibility of ever attaining any standard of taste. The difference, it is said, is very wide between judgment and sentiment. All sentiment is right; because sentiment has a reference to nothing beyond itself, and is always real, wherever a man is conscious of it. But all determinations of the understanding are not right; because they have a reference to something beyond themselves, to wit, real matter of fact; and are not always conformable to that standard. Among a thousand different opinions which different men may entertain of the same subject, there is one, and but one, that is just and true; and the only difficulty is to fix and ascertain it. On the contrary, a thousand different sentiments, excited by the same object, are all right: Because no sentiment represents what is really in the object. It only marks a certain conformity or relation between the object and the organs or faculties of the mind; and if that conformity did not really exist, the sentiment could never possibly have being. Beauty is no quality in things themselves: It exists merely in the mind which contemplates them; and each mind perceives a different beauty. One person may even perceive deformity, where another is sensible of beauty; and every individual ought to acquiesce in his own sentiment, without pretending to regulate those of others. To seek the real beauty, or real deformity, is as fruitless an enquiry, as to pretend to ascertain the real sweet or real bitter. According to the disposition of the organs, the same object may be both sweet and bitter; and the proverb has justly determined it to be fruitless to dispute concerning tastes. It is very natural, and even quite necessary, to extend this axiom to mental, as well as bodily taste; and thus common sense, which is so often at variance with philosophy, especially with the sceptical kind, is found, in one instance at least, to agree in pronouncing the same decision.

But though this axiom, by passing into a proverb, seems to have attained the sanction of common sense; there is certainly a species of common sense which opposes it, at least serves to modify and restrain it. Whoever would assert an equality of genius and elegance between Ogilby and Milton, or Bunyan and Addison, would be thought to defend no less an extravagance, than if he had maintained a mole-hill to be as high as Teneriffe, or a pond as extensive as the ocean. Though there may be found persons, who give the preference to the former authors; no one pays attention to such a taste; and we pronounce without scruple the sentiment of these pretended critics to be absurd and ridiculous. The principle of the natural equality of tastes is then totally forgot, and while we admit it on some occasions, where the objects seem near an equality, it appears an extravagant paradox, or rather a palpable absurdity, where objects so disproportioned are compared together.

It is evident that none of the rules of composition are fixed by reasonings *a priori*, or can be esteemed abstract conclusions of the understanding, from comparing those habitudes and relations of ideas, which are eternal and immutable. Their foundation is the same with that of all the practical sciences, experience; nor are they any thing but general observations, concerning what has been universally found to please in all countries and in all ages. Many of the beauties of poetry and even of eloquence are founded on falsehood and fiction, on hyperboles, metaphors, and an abuse or perversion of terms from their natural meaning. To check the sallies of the imagination, and to reduce every expression to geometrical truth and exactness, would be the most contrary to the laws of criticism; because it would produce a work, which, by universal experience, has been found the most insipid and disagreeable. But though poetry can never submit to exact truth, it must be confined by rules of art, discovered to the author either by genius or observation. If some negligent or irregular writers have pleased, they have not pleased by their transgressions of rule or order, but in spite of these transgressions: They have possessed other beauties, which were conformable to just criticism; and the force of these beauties has been able to overpower censure, and give the mind a satisfaction superior to the disgust arising from the blemishes. Ariosto pleases; but not by his monstrous and improbable fictions, by his bizarre mixture of the serious and comic styles, by the want of coherence in his stories, or by the continual interruptions of his narration. He charms by the force and clearness of his expression, by the readiness and variety of his inventions, and by his natural pictures of the passions, especially those of the gay and amorous kind: And however his faults may diminish our satisfaction, they are not able entirely to destroy it. Did our pleasure really arise from those parts of his poem, which we denominate faults, this would be no objection to criticism in general: It would only be an objection to those particular rules of criticism, which would establish such circumstances to be faults, and would represent them as universally blameable. If they are found to please, they cannot be faults; let the pleasure, which they produce, be ever so unexpected and unaccountable.

But though all the general rules of art are founded only on experience and on the observation of the common sentiments of human nature, we must not imagine, that, on every occasion, the feelings of men will be conformable to these rules. Those finer emotions of the mind are of a very tender and delicate nature, and require the concurrence of many favourable circumstances to make them play with facility and exactness, according to their general and established principles. The least exterior hindrance to such small springs, or the least internal disorder, disturbs their motion, and confounds the operation of the whole machine. When we would make an experiment of this nature, and would try the force of any beauty or deformity, we must choose with care a proper time and place, and bring the fancy to a suitable situation and disposition. A perfect serenity of mind, a recollection of thought, a due attention to the object; if any of these circumstances be wanting, our experiment will be fallacious, and we shall be unable to judge of the catholic and universal beauty. The relation, which nature has placed between the form and the sentiment, will at least be more obscure; and it will require greater accuracy to trace and discern it. We shall be able to ascertain its influence not so much from the operation of each particular beauty, as from the durable admiration, which attends those works, that have survived all the caprices of mode and fashion, all the mistakes of ignorance and envy.

The same Homer, who pleased at Athens and Rome two thousand years ago, is still admired at Paris and at London. All the changes of climate, government, religion, and language, have not been able to obscure his glory. Authority or prejudice may give a temporary vogue to a bad poet or orator; but his reputation will never be durable or general. When his compositions are examined by posterity or by foreigners, the enchantment is dissipated, and his faults appear in their true colours. On the contrary, a real genius, the longer his works endure, and the more wide they are spread, the more sincere is the admiration which he meets with. Envy and jealousy have too much place in a narrow circle; and even familiar acquaintance with his person may diminish the applause due to his performances: But when these obstructions are removed, the beauties, which are naturally fitted to excite agreeable sentiments, immediately display their energy; and while the world endures, they maintain their authority over the minds of men.

It appears then, that, amidst all the variety and caprice of taste, there are certain general principles of approbation or blame, whose influence a careful eye may trace in all operations of the mind. Some particular forms or qualities, from the original structure of the internal fabric, are calculated to please, and others to displease; and if they fail of their effect in any particular instance, it is from some apparent defect or imperfection in the organ. A man in a fever would not insist on his palate as able to decide concerning flavours; nor would one, affected with the jaundice, pretend to give a verdict with regard to colours. In each creature, there is a sound and a defective state; and the former alone can be supposed to afford us a true standard of taste and sentiment. If, in the sound state of the organ, there be an entire or a considerable uniformity of sentiment among men, we may thence derive an idea of the perfect beauty; in like manner as the appearance of objects in day-light, to the eye of a man in health, is denominated their true and real colour, even while colour is allowed to be merely a phantasm of the senses.

Many and frequent are the defects in the internal organs, which prevent or weaken the influence of those general principles, on which depends our sentiment of beauty or deformity. Though some objects, by the structure of the mind, be naturally calculated to give pleasure, it is not to be expected, that in every individual the pleasure will be equally felt. Particular incidents and situations occur, which either throw a false light on the objects, or hinder the true from conveying to the imagination the proper sentiment and perception.

One obvious cause, why many feel not the proper sentiment of beauty, is the want of that *delicacy* of imagination, which is requisite to convey a sensibility of those finer emotions. This delicacy every one pretends to: Every one talks of it; and would reduce every kind of taste or sentiment to its standard. But as our intention in this essay is to mingle some light of the understanding with the feelings of sentiment, it will be proper to give a more accurate definition of delicacy, than has hitherto been attempted. And not to draw our philosophy from too profound a source, we shall have recourse to a noted story in Don Quixote.

It is with good reason, says Sancho to the squire with the great nose, that I pretend to have a judgment in wine: This is a quality hereditary in our family. Two of my kinsmen were once called to give their opinion of a hogshead, which was supposed to be excellent, being old and of a good vintage. One of them tastes it; considers it; and after mature reflection pronounces the wine to be good, were it not for a small taste of leather, which he perceived in it. The other, after using the same precautions, gives also his verdict in favour of the wine; but with the reserve of a taste of iron, which he could easily distinguish. You cannot imagine how much they were both ridiculed for their judgment. But who laughed in the end? On emptying the hogshead, there was found at the bottom, an old key with a leathern thong tied to it.

The great resemblance between mental and bodily taste will easily teach us to apply this story. Though it be certain, that beauty and deformity, more than sweet and bitter, are not qualities in objects, but belong entirely to the sentiment, internal or external; it must be allowed, that there are certain qualities in objects, which are fitted by nature to produce those particular feelings. Now as these qualities may be found in a small degree, or may be mixed and confounded with each other, it often happens, that the taste is not affected with such minute qualities, or is not able to distinguish all the particular flavours, amidst the disorder, in which they are presented. Where the organs are so fine, as to allow nothing to escape them; and at the same time so exact as to perceive every ingredient in the composition: This we call delicacy of taste, whether we employ these terms in the literal or metaphorical sense. Here then the general rules of beauty are of use; being drawn from established models, and from the observation of what pleases or displeases, when presented singly and in a high degree: And if the same qualities, in a continued composition and in a smaller degree, affect not the organs with a sensible delight or uneasiness, we exclude the person from all pretensions to this delicacy. To produce these general rules or avowed patterns of composition is like finding the key with the leathern thong; which justified the verdict of Sancho's kinsmen, and confounded those pretended judges who had condemned them. Though the hogshead had never been emptied, the taste of the one was still equally delicate, and that of the other equally dull and languid: But it would have been more difficult to have proved the superiority of the former, to the conviction of every by-stander. In like manner, though the beauties of writing had never been methodized, or reduced to general principles; though no excellent models had ever been acknowledged; the different degrees of taste would still have subsisted, and the judgment of one man been preferable to that of another; but it would not have been so easy to silence the bad critic, who might always insist upon his particular sentiment, and refuse to submit to his antagonist. But when we show him an avowed principle of art; when we illustrate this principle by examples, whose operation, from his own particular taste, he acknowledges to be conformable to the principle; when we prove, that the same principle may be applied to the present case, where he did not perceive or feel its influence: He must conclude, upon the whole, that the fault lies in himself, and that he wants the delicacy, which is requisite to make him sensible of every beauty and every blemish, in any composition or discourse.

It is acknowledged to be the perfection of every sense or faculty, to perceive with exactness its most minute objects, and allow nothing to escape its notice and observation. The smaller the objects are, which become sensible to the eye, the finer is that organ, and the more elaborate its make and composition. A good palate is not tried by strong flavours; but by a mixture of small ingredients, where we are still sensible of each part, notwithstanding its minuteness and its confusion with the rest. In like manner, a quick and acute perception of beauty and deformity must be the perfection of our mental taste; nor can a man be satisfied with himself while he suspects, that any excellence or blemish in a discourse has passed him unobserved. In this case, the perfection of the man, and the perfection of the sense or feeling, are found to be united. A very delicate palate, on many occasions, may be a great inconvenience both to a man himself and to his friends: But a delicate taste of wit or beauty must always be a desirable quality; because it is the source of all the finest and most innocent enjoyments, of which human nature is susceptible. In this decision the sentiments of all mankind are agreed. Wherever you can ascertain a delicacy of taste, it is sure to meet with approbation; and the best way of ascertaining it is to appeal to those models and principles, which have been established by the uniform consent and experience of nations and ages.

But though there be naturally a wide difference in point of delicacy between one person and another, nothing tends further to encrease and improve this talent, than *practice* in a particular art, and the frequent survey or contemplation of a particular species of beauty. When objects of any kind are first presented to the eye or imagination, the sentiment, which attends them, is obscure and confused; and the mind is, in a great measure, incapable of pronouncing concerning their merits or defects. The taste cannot perceive the several excellences of the performance; much less distinguish the particular character of each excellency, and ascertain its quality and degree. If it pronounce the whole in general to be beautiful or deformed, it is the utmost that can be expected; and even this judgment, a person, so unpractised, will be apt to deliver with great hesitation and reserve. But allow him to acquire experience in those objects, his feeling becomes more exact and nice: He not only perceives the beauties and defects of each part, but marks the distinguishing species of each quality, and assigns it suitable praise or blame. A clear and distinct sentiment attends him through the whole survey of the objects; and he discerns that very degree and kind of approbation or displeasure, which each part is naturally fitted to produce. The mist dissipates, which seemed formerly to hang over the object: The organ acquires greater perfection in its operations; and can pronounce, without danger of mistake, concerning the merits of every performance. In a word, the same address and dexterity, which practice gives to the execution of any work, is also acquired by the same means, in the judging of it.

So advantageous is practice to the discernment of beauty, that, before we can give judgment on any work of importance, it will even be requisite, that that very individual performance be more than once perused by us, and be surveyed in different lights with attention and deliberation. There is a flutter or hurry of thought which attends the first perusal of any piece, and which confounds the genuine sentiment of beauty. The relation of the parts is not discerned: The true characters of style are little distinguished: The several perfections and defects seem wrapped up in a species of confusion, and present themselves indistinctly to the imagination. Not to mention, that there is a species of beauty, which, as it is florid and superficial, pleases at first; but being found incompatible with a just expression either of reason or passion, soon palls upon the taste, and is then rejected with disdain, at least rated at a much lower value.

It is impossible to continue in the practice of contemplating any order of beauty, without being frequently obliged to form *comparisons* between the several species and degrees of excellence, and estimating their proportion to each other. A man, who has had no opportunity of comparing the different kinds of beauty, is indeed totally unqualified to pronounce an opinion with regard to any object presented to him. By comparison alone we fix the epithets of praise or blame, and learn how to assign the due degree of each. The coarsest daubing contains a certain lustre of colours and exactness of imitation, which are so far beauties, and would affect the mind of a peasant or Indian with the highest admiration. The most vulgar ballads are not entirely destitute of harmony or nature; and none but a person, familiarized to superior beauties, would pronounce their numbers harsh, or narration uninteresting. A great inferiority of beauty gives pain to a person conversant in the highest excellence of the kind, and is for that reason pronounced a deformity:

As the most finished object, with which we are acquainted, is naturally supposed to have reached the pinnacle of perfection, and to be entitled to the highest applause. One accustomed to see, and examine, and weigh the several performances, admired in different ages and nations, can only rate the merits of a work exhibited to his view, and assign its proper rank among the productions of genius.

But to enable a critic the more fully to execute this undertaking, he must preserve his mind free from all *prejudice*, and allow nothing to enter into his consideration, but the very object which is submitted to his examination. We may observe, that every work of art, in order to produce its due effect on the mind, must be surveyed in a certain point of view, and cannot be fully relished by persons, whose situation, real or imaginary, is not conformable to that which is required by the performance. An orator addresses himself to a particular audience, and must have a regard to their particular genius, interests, opinions, passions, and prejudices; otherwise he hopes in vain to govern their resolutions, and inflame their affections. Should they even have entertained some prepossessions against him, however unreasonable, he must not overlook this disadvantage; but, before he enters upon the subject, must endeavour to conciliate their affection, and acquire their good graces. A critic of a different age or nation, who should peruse this discourse, must have all these circumstances in his eye, and must place himself in the same situation as the audience, in order to form a true judgment of the oration. In like manner, when any work is addressed to the public, though I should have a friendship or enmity with the author, I must depart from this situation; and considering myself as a man in general, forget, if possible, my individual being and my peculiar circumstances. A person influenced by prejudice, complies not with this condition; but obstinately maintains his natural position, without placing himself in that point of view, which the performance supposes. If the work be addressed to persons of a different age or nation, he makes no allowance for their peculiar views and prejudices; but, full of the manners of his own age and country, rashly condemns what seemed admirable in the eyes of those for whom alone the discourse was calculated. If the work be executed for the public, he never sufficiently enlarges his comprehension, or forgets his interest as a friend or enemy, as a rival or commentator. By this means, his sentiments are perverted; nor have the same beauties and blemishes the same influence upon him, as if he had imposed a proper violence on his imagination, and had forgotten himself for a moment. So far his taste evidently departs from the true standard; and of consequence loses all credit and authority.

It is well known, that in all questions, submitted to the understanding, prejudice is destructive of sound judgment, and perverts all operations of the intellectual faculties: It is no less contrary to good taste; nor has it less influence to corrupt our sentiment of beauty. It belongs to *good sense* to check its influence in both cases; and in this respect, as well as in many others, reason, if not an essential part of taste, is at least requisite to the operations of this latter faculty. In all the nobler productions of genius, there is a mutual relation and correspondence of parts; nor can either the beauties or blemishes be perceived by him, whose thought is not capacious enough to comprehend all those parts, and compare them with each other, in order to perceive the consistence and uniformity of the whole. Every work of art has also a certain end or purpose, for which it is calculated; and is to be deemed more or less perfect, as it is more or less fitted to attain this end. The object of eloquence is to persuade, of history to instruct, of poetry to please by means of the passions and the imagination. These ends we must carry constantly in our view, when we peruse any performance; and we must be able to judge how far the means employed are adapted to their respective purposes. Besides, every kind of composition, even the most poetical, is nothing but a chain of propositions and reasonings; not always, indeed, the justest and most exact, but still plausible and specious, however disguised by the colouring of the imagination. The persons introduced in tragedy and epic poetry, must be represented as reasoning, and thinking, and concluding, and acting, suitably to their character and circumstances; and without judgment, as well as taste and invention, a poet can never hope to succeed in so delicate an undertaking. Not to mention, that the same excellence of faculties which contributes to the improvement of reason, the same clearness of conception, the same exactness of distinction, the same vivacity of apprehension, are essential to the operations of true taste, and are its infallible concomitants. It seldom, or never happens, that a man of sense, who has experience in any art, cannot judge of its beauty; and it is no less rare to meet with a man who has a just taste without a sound understanding.

Thus, though the principles of taste be universal, and, nearly, if not entirely the same in all men; yet few are qualified to give judgment on any work of art, or establish their own sentiment as the standard of beauty. The organs of internal sensation are seldom so perfect as to allow the general principles their full play, and produce a feeling correspondent to those principles. They either labour under some defect, or are vitiated by some disorder; and by that means, excite a sentiment, which may be pronounced erroneous. When the critic has no delicacy, he judges without any distinction, and is only affected by the grosser and more palpable qualities of the object: The finer touches pass unnoticed and disregarded. Where he is not aided by practice, his verdict is attended with confusion and hesitation. Where no comparison has been employed, the most frivolous beauties, such as rather merit the name of defects, are the object of his admiration. Where he lies under the influence of prejudice, all his natural sentiments are perverted. Where good sense is wanting, he is not qualified to discern the beauties of design and reasoning, which are the highest and most excellent. Under some or other of these imperfections, the generality of men labour; and hence a true judge in the finer arts is observed, even during the most polished ages, to be so rare a character; Strong sense, united to delicate sentiment, improved by practice, perfected by comparison, and cleared of all prejudice, can alone entitle critics to this valuable character; and the joint verdict of such, wherever they are to be found, is the true standard of taste and beauty.

But where are such critics to be found? By what marks are they to be known? How distinguish them from pretenders? These questions are embarrassing; and seem to throw us back into the same uncertainty, from which, during the course of this essay, we have endeavoured to extricate ourselves.

But if we consider the matter aright, these are questions of fact, not of sentiment. Whether any particular person be endowed with good sense and a delicate imagination, free from prejudice, may often be the subject of dispute, and be liable to great discussion and enquiry: But that such a character is valuable and estimable will be agreed in by all mankind. Where these doubts occur, men can do no more than in other disputable questions, which are submitted to the understanding: They must produce the best arguments, that their invention suggests to them; they must acknowledge a true and decisive standard to exist somewhere, to wit, real existence and matter of fact; and they must have indulgence to such as differ from them in their appeals to this standard. It is sufficient for our present purpose, if we have proved, that the taste of all individuals is not upon an equal footing, and that some men in general, however difficult to be particularly pitched upon, will be acknowledged by universal sentiment to have a preference above others.

But in reality the difficulty of finding, even in particulars, the standard of taste, is not so great as it is represented. Though in speculation, we may readily avow a certain criterion in science and deny it in sentiment, the matter is found in practice to be much more hard to ascertain in the former case than in the latter. Theories of abstract philosophy, systems of profound theology, have prevailed during one age: In a successive period, these have been universally exploded: Their absurdity has been detected: Other theories and systems have supplied their place, which again gave place to their successors: And nothing has been experienced more liable to the revolutions of chance and fashion than these pretended decisions of science. The case is not the same with the beauties of eloquence and poetry. Just expressions of passion and nature are sure, after a little time, to gain public applause, which they maintain for ever. Aristotle, and Plato, and Epicurus, and Descartes, may successively yield to each other: But Terence and Virgil maintain an universal, undisputed empire over the minds of men. The abstract philosophy of Cicero has lost its credit: The vehemence of his oratory is still the object of our admiration.

Though men of delicate taste be rare, they are easily to be distinguished in society, by the soundness of their understanding and the superiority of their faculties above the rest of mankind. The ascendant, which they acquire, gives a prevalence to that lively approbation, with which they receive any productions of genius, and renders it generally predominant. Many men, when left to themselves, have but a faint and dubious perception of beauty, who yet are capable of relishing any fine stroke, which is pointed out to them. Every convert to the admiration of the real poet or orator is the cause of some new conversion. And though prejudices may prevail for a time, they never unite in celebrating any rival to the true genius, but yield at last to the force of nature and just sentiment. Thus, though a civilized nation may easily be mistaken in the choice of their admired philosopher, they never have been found long to err, in their affection for a favorite epic or tragic author.

But notwithstanding all our endeavours to fix a standard of taste, and reconcile the discordant apprehensions of men, there still remain two sources of variation, which are not sufficient indeed to confound all the boundaries of beauty and deformity, but will often serve to produce a difference in the degrees of our approbation or blame. The one is the different humours of particular men; the other, the particular manners and opinions of our age and country. The general principles of taste are uniform in human nature: Where men vary in their judgments, some defect or perversion in the faculties may commonly be remarked; proceeding either from prejudice, from want of practice, or want of delicacy; and there is just reason for approving one taste, and condemning another. But where there is such a diversity in the internal frame or external situation as is entirely blameless on both sides, and leaves no room to give one the preference above the other; in that case a certain degree of diversity in judgment is unavoidable, and we seek in vain for a standard, by which we can reconcile the contrary sentiments.

A young man, whose passions are warm, will be more sensibly touched with amorous and tender images, than a man more advanced in years, who takes pleasure in wise, philosophical reflections concerning the conduct of life and moderation of the passions. At twenty, Ovid may be the favourite author; Horace at forty; and perhaps Tacitus at fifty. Vainly would we, in such cases, endeavour to enter into the sentiments of others, and divest ourselves of those propensities, which are natural to us. We choose our favourite author as we do our friend, from a conformity of humour and disposition. Mirth or passion, sentiment or reflection; whichever of these most predominates in our temper, it gives us a peculiar sympathy with the writer who resembles us.

One person is more pleased with the sublime; another with the tender; a third with raillery. One has a strong sensibility to blemishes, and is extremely studious of correctness: Another has a more lively feeling of beauties, and pardons twenty absurdities and defects for one elevated or pathetic stroke. The ear of this man is entirely turned towards conciseness and energy; that man is delighted with a copious, rich, and harmonious expression. Simplicity is affected by one; ornament by another. Comedy, tragedy, satire, odes, have each its partizans, who prefer that particular species of writing to all others. It is plainly an error in a critic, to confine his approbation to one species or style of writing, and condemn all the rest. But it is almost impossible not to feel a predilection for that which suits our particular turn and disposition. Such preferences are innocent and unavoidable, and can never reasonably be the object of dispute, because there is no standard, by which they can be decided.

For a like reason, we are more pleased, in the course of our reading, with pictures and characters, that resemble objects which are found in our own age or country, than with those which describe a different set of customs. It is not without some effort, that we reconcile ourselves to the simplicity of ancient manners, and behold princesses carrying water from the spring, and kings and heroes dressing their own victuals. We may allow in general, that the representation of such manners is no fault in the author, nor deformity in the piece; but we are not so sensibly touched with them. For this reason, comedy is not easily transferred from one age or nation to another. A Frenchman or Englishman is not pleased with the Andria of Terence, or Clitia of Machiavel; where the fine lady, upon whom all the play turns, never once appears to the spectators, but is always kept behind the scenes, suitably to the reserved humour of the ancient Greeks and modern Italians. A man of learning and reflection can make allowance for these peculiarities of manners; but a common audience can never divest themselves so far of their usual ideas and sentiments, as to relish pictures which in no wise resemble them.

But here there occurs a reflection, which may, perhaps, be useful in examining the celebrated controversy concerning ancient and modern learning; where we often find the one side excusing any seeming absurdity in the ancients from the manners of the age, and the other refusing to admit this excuse, or at least, admitting it only as an apology for the author, not for the performance. In my opinion, the proper boundaries in this subject have seldom been fixed between the contending parties. Where any innocent peculiarities of manners are represented, such as those above mentioned, they ought certainly to be admitted; and a man, who is shocked with them, gives an evident proof of false delicacy and refinement. The poet's *monument more durable than brass*, must fall to the ground like common brick or clay, were men to make no allowance for the continual revolutions of manners and customs, and would admit of nothing but what was suitable to the prevailing fashion. Must we throw aside the pictures of our ancestors, because of their ruffs and fardingales? But where the ideas of morality and decency alter from one age to another, and where vicious manners are described, without being marked with the proper characters of blame and disapprobation; this must be allowed to disfigure the poem, and to be a real deformity. I cannot, nor is it proper I should, enter into such sentiments; and however I may excuse the poet, on account of the manners of his age, I never can relish the composition. The want of humanity and of decency, so conspicuous in the characters drawn by several of the ancient poets, even sometimes by Homer and the Greek tragedians, diminishes considerably the merit of their noble performances, and gives modern authors an advantage over them. We are not interested in the fortunes and sentiments of such rough heroes: We are displeased to find the limits of vice and virtue so much confounded: And whatever indulgence we may give to the writer on account of his prejudices, we cannot prevail on ourselves to enter into his sentiments, or bear an affection to characters, which we plainly discover to be blameable.

The case is not the same with moral principles, as with speculative opinions of any kind. These are in continual flux and revolution. The son embraces a different system from the father. Nay, there scarcely is any man, who can boast of great constancy and uniformity in this particular. Whatever speculative errors may be found in the polite writings of any age or country, they detract but little from the value of those compositions. There needs but a certain turn of thought or imagination to make us enter into all the opinions, which then prevailed, and relish the sentiments or conclusions derived from them. But a very violent effort is requisite to change our judgment of manners, and excite sentiments of approbation or blame, love or hatred, different from those to which the mind from long custom has been familiarized. And where a man is confident of the rectitude of that moral standard, by which he judges, he is justly jealous of it, and will not pervert the sentiments of his heart for a moment, in complaisance to any writer whatsoever.

Of all speculative errors, those, which regard religion, are the most excusable in compositions of genius; nor is it ever permitted to judge of the civility or wisdom of any people, or even of single persons, by the grossness or refinement of their theological principles. The same good sense, that directs men in the ordinary occurrences of life, is not hearkened to in religious matters, which are supposed to be placed altogether above the cognizance of human reason. On this account, all the absurdities of the pagan system of theology must be overlooked by every critic, who would pretend to form a just notion of ancient poetry; and our posterity, in their turn, must have the same indulgence to their forefathers. No religious principles can ever be imputed as a fault to any poet, while they remain merely principles, and take not such strong possession of his heart, as to lay him under the imputation of *bigotry* or *superstition*. Where that happens, they confound the sentiments of morality, and alter the natural boundaries of vice and virtue. They are therefore eternal blemishes, according to the principle above mentioned; nor are the prejudices and false opinions of the age sufficient to justify them.

It is essential to the Roman catholic religion to inspire a violent hatred of every other worship, and to represent all pagans, mahometans, and heretics as the objects of divine wrath and vengeance. Such sentiments, though they are in reality very blameable, are considered as virtues by the zealots of that communion, and are represented in their tragedies and epic poems as a kind of divine heroism. This bigotry has disfigured two very fine tragedies of the French theatre. Polieucte and Athalia; where an intemperate zeal for particular modes of worship is set off with all the pomp imaginable, and forms the predominant character of the heroes. 'What is this,' says the sublime Joad to Josabet, finding her in discourse with Mathan, the priest of Baal, 'Does the daughter of David speak to this traitor? Are you not afraid, lest the earth should open and pour forth flames to devour you both? Or lest these holy walls should fall and crush you together? What is his purpose? Why comes that enemy of God hither to poison the air, which we breathe, with his horrid presence?' Such sentiments are received with great applause on the theatre of Paris; but at London the spectators would be full as much pleased to hear Achilles tell Agamemnon, that he was a dog in his forehead, and a deer in his heart, or Jupiter threaten Juno with a sound drubbing, if she will not be quiet.

Religious principles are also a blemish in any polite composition, when they rise up to superstition, and intrude themselves into every sentiment, however remote from any connection with religion. It is no excuse for the poet, that the customs of his country had burthened life with so many religious ceremonies and observances, that no part of it was exempt from that yoke. It must for ever be ridiculous in Petrarch to compare his mistress Laura, to Jesus Christ. Nor is it less ridiculous in that agreeable libertine, Boccace, very seriously to give thanks to God Almighty and the ladies, for their assistance in defending him against his enemies.

[*Four Dissertations*, 1757.]

ARNOLD ISENBERG

55 Critical Communication

The following remarks are for the most part restricted to meeting such questions as: What is the content of the critic's argument? What claim does he transmit to us? How does he expect us to deal with this claim?

A good point to start from is a theory of criticism, widely held in spite of its deficiencies, which divides the critical process into three parts. There is the value judgment or *verdict* (V): 'This picture or poem is good—.' There is a particular statement or *reason* (R): '—because it has such-and-such a quality—' And there is a general statement or *norm* (N): '—and any work which has that quality is *pro tanto* good.'

V has been construed, and will be construed here, as an expression of feeling—an utterance manifesting praise or blame. But among utterances of that class it is distinguished by being in some sense conditional upon R. This is only another phrasing of the commonly noted peculiarity of aesthetic feeling: that it is 'embodied' in or 'attached' to an aesthetic content.

R is a statement describing the content of an art work; but not every such descriptive statement will be a case of R. The proposition, 'There are just twelve flowers in that picture' [...] is without critical relevance; that is, without any bearing upon V. The description of a work of art is seldom attempted for its own sake. It is controlled by some purpose, some interest; and there are many interests by which it might be controlled other than that of reaching or defending a critical judgment. The qualities which are significant in relation to one purpose—dating, attribution, archaeological reconstruction, clinical diagnosis, proving or illustrating some thesis in sociology— might be quite immaterial in relation to another. At the same time, we cannot be sure that there is any *kind* of statement about art, serving no matter what main interest, which cannot also act as R; or, in other words, that there is any *kind* of knowledge about art which cannot influence aesthetic appreciation.

V and R, it should be said, are often combined in sentences which are at once normative and descriptive. If we have been told that the colors of a certain painting are garish, it would be astonishing to find that they were all very pale and unsaturated; and to this extent the critical comment conveys information. On the other hand, we might find the colors bright and intense, as expected, without being thereby forced to admit that they are garish; and this reveals the component of valuation (that is, distaste) in the critic's remark. This feature of critical usage has attracted much notice and some study; but we do not discuss it here at all. We shall be concerned solely with the descriptive function of R.

Now if we ask what makes a description critically useful and relevant, the first suggestion which occurs is that it is *supported by N*. N is based upon an inductive generalization which describes a relationship between some aesthetic quality and someone's or everyone's system of aesthetic response. Notice: I do not say that N *is* an inductive generalization; for in critical evaluation N is being used not to predict or to explain anybody's reaction to a work of art but to vindicate that reaction, perhaps to someone who does not yet share it; and in this capacity N is a precept, a rule, a *generalized value statement*. But the *choice* of one norm, rather than another, when that choice is challenged, will usually be given some sort of inductive justification. We return to this question in a moment. I think we shall find that a careful analysis of N is unnecessary, because there are considerations which permit us to dismiss it altogether.

At this point it is well to remind ourselves that there is a difference between *explaining and justifying* a critical response. A psychologist who should be asked 'why X likes the object y' would take X's enjoyment as a datum, a fact to be explained. And if he offers as explanation the presence in y of the quality Q, there is, explicit or latent in this causal argument, an appeal to some generalization which he has reason to think is true, such as 'X likes any work which has that quality.' But when we ask X as a critic 'why he likes the object y,' we want him to give us some reason to like it too and are not concerned with the causes of what we may so far regard as his bad taste. This distinction between genetic and normative inquiry, though it is familiar to all and acceptable to most of us, is commonly ignored in the practice of aesthetic speculation; and the chief reason for this—other than the ambiguity of the question 'Why do you like this work?'—is the fact that some statements about the object will necessarily figure both in the explanation and in the critical defence of any reaction to it. Thus, if I tried to explain my feeling for the line

But musical as is Apollo's lute,

I should certainly mention 'the pattern of *u*'s and *l*'s which reinforces the meaning with its own musical quality'; for this quality of my sensations is doubtless among the conditions of my feeling response. And the same point would be made in any effort to convince another person of the beauty of the line. The remark which gives a reason also, in this case, states a cause. But notice that, though as criticism this comment might be very effective, it is practically worthless as explanation; for we have no phonetic or psychological laws (nor any plausible 'common-sense' generalization) from which we might derive the prediction that such a pattern of *u*'s and *l*'s should be pleasing to me. In fact, the formulation ('pattern of *u*'s and *l*'s,' etc.) is so vague that one could not tell just what general hypothesis it is that is being invoked or assumed; yet it is quite sharp enough for critical purposes. On the other hand, suppose that someone should fail to be 'convinced' by my argument in favor of Milton's line. He might still readily admit that the quality of which I have spoken might have something to do with *my* pleasurable reaction, given my peculiar mentality. Thus the statement which is serving both to explain and to justify is not equally effective in the two capacities; and this brings out the difference between the two lines of argument. Coincident at the start, they diverge in the later stages. A *complete* explanation of any of my responses would have to include certain propositions about my nervous system, which would be irrelevant in any critical argument. And a critically relevant observation about some configuration in the art object might be useless for explaining a given experience, if only because the experience did not yet contain that configuration.

Now it would not be strange if, among the dangers of ambiguity to which the description of art, like the rest of human speech, is exposed, there should be some which derive from the double purpose—critical and psychological— to which such description is often being put. And this is, as we shall see, the case.

The necessity for sound inductive generalizations in any attempt at aesthetic explanation is granted. We may now consider, very briefly, the parallel role in normative criticism which has been assigned to N. Let us limit our attention to those metacritical theories which *deny* a function in criticism to

N. I divide these into two kinds, those which attack existing standards and those which attack the very notion of a critical standard.

1. It is said that we know of no law which governs human tastes and preferences, no quality shared by any two works of art that makes those works attractive or repellent. The point might be debated; but it is more important to notice what it assumes. It assumes that if N *were* based on a sound induction, it would be (together with R) a real ground for the acceptance of V. In other words, it would be reasonable to accept V on the strength of the quality Q if it could be shown that works which possess Q tend to be pleasing. It follows that criticism is being held back by the miserable state of aesthetic science. This raises an issue too large to be canvassed here. Most of us believe that the idea of progress applies to science, does not apply to art, applies, in some unusual and not very clear sense, to philosophy. What about criticism? Are there 'discoveries' and 'contributions' in this branch of thought? Is it reasonable to expect better evaluations of art after a thousand years of criticism than before? The question is not a simple one: it admits of different answers on different interpretations. But I do think that some critical judgments have been and are every day being 'proved' as well as in the nature of the case they ever can be proved. I think we have already numerous passages which are not to be corrected or improved upon. And if this opinion is right, then it could not be the case that the validation of critical judgments waits upon the discovery of aesthetic laws. Let us suppose even that we had some law which stated that a certain color combination, a certain melodic sequence, a certain type of dramatic hero has everywhere and always a positive emotional effect. To the extent to which this law holds, there is of course that much less disagreement in criticism; but there is no better method for resolving disagreement. We are not more fully convinced in our own judgment because we know its explanation; and we cannot hope to convince an imaginary opponent by appeal to this explanation, which by hypothesis does not hold for him.

2. The more radical arguments against critical standards are spread out in the pages of Croce, Dewey, Richards, Prall, and the great romantic critics before them. They need not be repeated here. In one way or another they all attempt to expose the absurdity of presuming to judge a work of art, the very excuse for whose existence lies in its *difference* from everything that has gone before, by its degree of *resemblance* to something that has gone before; and on close inspection they create at least a very strong doubt as to whether a standard of success or failure in art is either necessary or possible. But it seems to me that they fail to provide a positive interpretation of criticism. Consider the following remarks by William James on the criticism of Herbert Spencer: 'In all his dealings with the art products of mankind he manifests the same curious dryness and mechanical literality of judgment.... Turner's

painting he finds untrue in that the earth-region is habitually as bright in tone as the air-region. Moreover, Turner scatters his detail too evenly. In Greek statues the hair is falsely treated. Renaissance painting is spoiled by unreal illumination. Venetian Gothic sins by meaningless ornamentation.' And so on. We should most of us agree with James that this is bad criticism. But *all* criticism is similar to this in that it cites, as reasons for praising or condemning a work, one or more of its qualities. If Spencer's reasons are descriptively true, how can we frame our objection to them except in some such terms as that 'unreal illumination does not make a picture bad'; that is, by attacking his standards? What constitutes the relevance of a reason but its correlation with a norm? It is astonishing to notice how many writers, formally committed to an opposition to legal procedure in criticism, *seem* to relapse into a reliance upon standards whenever they give reasons for their critical judgments. The appearance is inevitable; for as long as we have no alternative interpretation of the import and function of R, we must assume *either* that R is perfectly arbitrary *or* that it presupposes and depends on some general claim.

With these preliminaries, we can examine a passage of criticism. This is Ludwig Goldscheider on *The Burial of Count Orgaz*:

Like the contour of a violently rising and falling wave is the outline of the four illuminated figures in the foreground: steeply upwards and downwards about the grey monk on the left, in mutually inclined curves about the yellow of the two saints, and again steeply upwards and downwards about . . . the priest on the right. The depth of the wave indicates the optical centre; the double curve of the saints' yellow garments is carried by the greyish white of the shroud down still farther; in this lowest depth rests the bluish-grey armor of the knight.

This passage—which, we may suppose, was written to justify a favorable judgment on the painting—conveys to us the idea of a certain quality which, if we believe the critic, we should expect to find in a certain painting by El Greco. And we do find it: we can verify its presence by perception. In other words, there is a quality in the picture which agrees with the quality which we 'have in mind'—which we have been led to think of by the critic's language. But the same quality ('a steeply rising and falling curve,' etc.) would be found in any of a hundred lines one could draw on the board in three minutes. It could not be the critic's purpose to inform us of the presence of a quality as obvious as this. It seems reasonable to suppose that the critic is thinking of another quality, no idea of which is transmitted to us by his language, which he *sees* and which by his use of language he *gets us to see*. This quality is, of course, a wavelike contour; but it is not the quality designated by the *expression* 'wavelike contour.' Any object which has this quality will have a wavelike contour; but it is not true that any object which has a wavelike contour will have this quality. At the same time, the expression 'wavelike contour' *excludes* a great many things: if anything is a wavelike contour, it is not a color, it is not a mass, it is not a straight line. Now the critic, besides imparting to us the idea of a wavelike contour, gives us directions for perceiving, and does this *by means* of the idea he imparts to us, which narrows down the field of possible visual orientations and guides us in the discrimination of details, the organization of parts, the grouping of discrete objects into patterns. It is as if we found both an oyster and a pearl when we had been looking for a seashell because we had been told it was valuable. It *is* valuable, but not because it is a seashell.

I may be stretching usage by the senses I am about to assign to certain words, but it seems that the critic's *meaning* is 'filled in,' 'rounded out,' or 'completed' by the act of perception, which is performed not to judge the truth of his description but in a certain sense to *understand* it. And if *communication* is a process by which a mental content is transmitted by symbols from one person to another, then we can say that it is a function of criticism to bring about communication at the level of the senses; that is, to induce a sameness of vision, of experienced content. If this is accomplished, it may or may not be followed by agreement, or what is called 'communion'—a community of feeling which expresses itself in identical value judgments.

There is a contrast, therefore, between critical communication and what I may call normal or ordinary communication. In ordinary communication, symbols tend to acquire a footing relatively independent of sense-perception. It is, of course, doubtful whether the interpretation of symbols is at any time completely unaffected by the environmental context. But there is a difference of degree between, say, an exchange of glances which, though it means 'Shall we go home?' at one time and place, would mean something very different at another—between this and formal science, whose vocabulary and syntax have relatively fixed connotations. With a passage of scientific prose before us, we may be dependent on experience for the definition of certain simple terms, as also for the confirmation of assertions; but we are not dependent on experience for the interpretation of compound expressions. If we are, this exposes semantical defects in the passage—obscurity, vagueness, ambiguity, or incompleteness. (Thus: 'Paranoia is marked by a profound egocentricity and deep-seated feelings of insecurity'—the kind of remark which makes every student think he has the disease—is suitable for easy comparison of notes among clinicians, who know how to recognize the difference between paranoia and other conditions; but it does not explicitly set forth the criteria which they employ.) Statements about immediate experience, made in ordinary communication, are no exception. If a theory requires that a certain flame should be blue, then we have to report whether it is or is not blue—regardless of shades or variations which may be of enormous importance aesthetically. We are bound to the letters of our words. Compare with this something like the following:

'The expression on her face was delightful.'
'What was delightful about it?'
'Didn't you see that smile?'

The speaker does not mean that there is something delightful about smiles as such; but he cannot be accused of not stating his meaning clearly, because the clarity of his language must be judged in relation to his purpose, which in this case is the *evaluation* of the immediate experience; and for that purpose the reference to the smile will be sufficient if it gets people to feel that they are 'talking about the same thing.' There is understanding and misunderstanding at this level; there are marks by which the existence of one or the other can be known; and there are means by which misunderstanding can be eliminated. But these phenomena are not identical with those that take the same names in the study of ordinary communication.

Reading criticism, otherwise than in the presence, or with direct recollection, of the objects discussed is a blank and senseless employment—a fact which is concealed from us by the cooperation, in our reading, of many non-critical purposes for which the information offered by the critic is material and useful. There is not in all the world's criticism a single purely descriptive statement concerning which one is prepared to say beforehand, 'If it is true, I shall like that work so much the better'. [...] *The truth of R never adds the slightest weight to V,* because R does not designate any quality the perception of which might induce us to assent to V. But if it is not R, or what it designates, that makes V acceptable, then R cannot possibly require the support of N. The critic is not committed to the general claim that the quality named Q is valuable because he never makes the particular claim that a work is good in virtue of the presence of Q.

[...] [R]eturning to the passage I quoted from Goldscheider about the painting by El Greco [...] Imagine, then, that the painting should be projected on to a graph with intersecting co-ordinates. It would then be possible to write complicated mathematical expressions which would enable another person who knew the system to construct for himself as close an approximation to the exact outlines of the El Greco as we might desire. Would this be an advance towards precision in criticism? Could we say that we had devised a more specific terminology for drawing and painting? I think not, for the most refined concept remains a concept; there is no vanishing point at which it becomes a percept. It is the idea *of* a quality, it is not the quality itself. To render a critical verdict we should still have to perceive the quality; but Goldscheider's passage already shows it to us as clearly as language can. The idea of a new and better means of communication presupposes the absence of the sensory contents we are talking about; but criticism always assumes the presence of these contents to both parties; and it is upon this assumption that the vagueness or precision of a critical statement must be judged. Any further illustration of this point will have to be rough and hasty. For the last twenty or thirty years the 'correct' thing to say about the metaphysical poets has been this: They think with their senses and feel with their brains. One hardly knows how to verify such a dictum: as a psychological observation it is exceedingly obscure. But it does not follow that it is not acute criticism; for it increases our awareness of the difference between Tennyson and Donne. Many words—like 'subtlety,' 'variety,' 'complexity,' 'intensity'—which in ordinary communication are among the vaguest in the language have been used to convey sharp critical perceptions. And many expressions which have a clear independent meaning are vague and fuzzy when taken in relation to the content of a work of art. An examination of the ways in which the language of concepts mediates between perception and perception is clearly called for, though it is far too difficult to be attempted here.

['Critical Communication', *Philosophical Review*, 58 (1949), 330–40.]

56   Lessons of the Past

[For] proper criticism [. . .] you must answer the question: What can art serve here and now? Then you criticize according to whether the works in question serve that purpose or not. You must beware of believing that they can always do so directly. You are not simply demanding propaganda. But you need not fall over backwards in order to avoid being proved wrong by those who later take your place. You will make mistakes. You will miss perhaps the genius who finally vindicates himself. But if you answer your initial question with historical logic and justice, you will be helping to bring about the future from which people will be able to judge the art of your own time with ease.

The question I ask is: Does this work help or encourage men to know and claim their social rights? First let me explain what I do not mean by that. When I go into a gallery, I do not assess the works according to how graphically they present, for example, the plight of our old-age pensioners. Painting and sculpture are clearly not the most suitable means for putting pressure on the government to nationalize the land. Nor am I suggesting that the artist, when actually working, can or should be primarily concerned with the justice of a social cause. [. . .]

What I do mean is something less direct and more comprehensive. After we have responded to a work of art, we leave it, carrying away in our consciousness something which we didn't have before. This something amounts to more than our memory of the incident represented, and also more than our memory of the shapes and colours and spaces which the artist has used and arranged. What we take away with us—on the most profound level—is the memory of the artist's way of looking at the world. The representation of a recognizable incident (an incident here can simply mean a tree or a head) offers us the chance of relating the artist's way of looking to our own. The forms he uses are the means by which he expresses his way of looking. The truth of this is confirmed by the fact that we can often recall the experience of a work though we have forgotten both its precise subject and its precise formal arrangement.

Yet why should an artist's way of looking at the world have any meaning for us? Why does it give us pleasure? Because, I believe, it increases our awareness of our own potentiality. Not, of course, our awareness of our potentiality as artists ourselves. But a way of looking at the world implies a certain relationship with the world, and every relationship implies action. The kinds of action implied vary a great deal. A classical Greek sculpture increases our awareness of our own potential physical dignity; a Rembrandt, of our potential moral courage; a Matisse, of our potential sensual awareness. Yet each of these examples is too personal and too narrow to contain the whole truth of the matter. A work can, to some extent, increase an awareness of different potentialities in different people. The important point is that a valid work of art promises in some way or another the possibility of an increase, an improvement. Nor need the work be optimistic to achieve this; indeed, its subject may be tragic. For it is not the subject that makes the promise, it is the artist's way of viewing his subject. [. . .]

Goya's genius as a graphic artist was that of a commentator. I do not mean that his work was straightforward reportage—far from it—but that he was much more interested in events than states of mind. Each work appears unique not on account of its style but on account of the incident upon which it comments. At the same time, these incidents lead from one to another, so that their effect is climactic—almost like that of film shots. [. . .]

What was the nature of Goya's commentary? For despite the variety of the incidents portrayed, there is a constant underlying theme. His theme was the consequences of man's neglect—sometimes mounting to hysterical hatred— of his most precious faculty, Reason. But Reason in the eighteenth-century materialistic sense: Reason as a discipline yielding Pleasure derived from the Senses. In Goya's work the flesh is a battleground between ignorance, uncontrolled passion, and superstition on the one hand and dignity, grace, and pleasure on the other. The unique power of his work is due to the fact that he was so *sensuously* involved in the terror and horror of the betrayal of Reason.

In all Goya's works—except perhaps the very earliest—there is a strong sensual and sexual ambivalence. His exposure of physical corruption in his Royal portraits is well known. But the implication of corruption is equally there in his portrait of Doña Isabel. His Maja undressed, beautiful as she is, is *terrifyingly* naked. One admires the delicacy of the flowers embroidered on the stocking of a pretty courtesan in one drawing, and then suddenly, immediately, one foresees in the next the mummer-headed monster that, as a result of the passion aroused by her delicacy, she will bear as a son. A monk undresses in a brothel and Goya draws him, hating him, not in any way because he himself is a puritan, but because he senses that the same impulses that are behind this incident will lead in the Disasters of War to soldiers castrating a peasant and raping his wife. The huge brutal heads he put on hunchback bodies, the animals he dressed up in official robes of office, the way he gave to the cross-hatched tone on a human body the filthy implication of fur, the rage with which he drew witches—all these were protests against the abuse of human possibilities. And what makes Goya's protests so desperately relevant for us, after Buchenwald and Hiroshima, is that he knew that when corruption goes far enough, when the human possibilities are denied with sufficient ruthlessness, both ravager and victim are made bestial.

Then there is the argument about whether Goya was an objective or subjective artist; whether he was haunted by his own imaginings, or by what he saw of the decadence of the Spanish court, the ruthlessness of the Inquisition, and the horror of the Peninsular War. In fact, this argument is falsely posed. Obviously Goya sometimes used his own conflicts and fears as the starting point for his work, but he did so because he consciously saw himself as being typical of his time. The intention of his work was highly objective and social. His theme was what man was capable of doing to man. Most of his subjects involve action between figures. But even when the figures are single—a girl in prison, an habitual lecher, a beggar who was once 'somebody'—the implication, often actually stated in the title, is: 'Look what has been done to them.'

I know that certain other modern writers take a different view. Malraux, for instance, says that Goya's is 'the age-old religious accent of useless suffering rediscovered, perhaps for the first time, by a man who believed himself to be indifferent to God.' Then he goes on to say that Goya paints 'the absurdity of being human' and is 'the greatest interpreter of anguish the West has ever known.' The trouble with this view, based on hindsight, is that it induces a feeling of subjection much stronger than that in Goya's own work: only one more shiver is needed to turn it into a feeling of meaningless defeat. If a prophet of disaster is proved right by later events (and Goya was not only recording the Peninsular War, he was also prophesying), then that prophecy does not increase the disaster; to a very slight extent it lessens it, for it demonstrates that man can foresee consequences, which, after all, is the first step towards controlling causes. [. . .]

One of the most interesting confirmations that Goya's work was outward-facing and objective is his use of light. In his works it is not, as with all those who romantically frighten themselves, the dark that holds horror and terror. It is the light that discloses them. Goya lived and observed through something near enough to total war to know that night is security and that it is the dawn that one fears. The light in his work is merciless for the simple reason that it shows up cruelty. Some of his drawings of the carnage of the Disasters are like film shots of a flare-lit target after a bombing operation; the light floods the gaps in the same way.

Finally and in view of all this one tries to assess Goya. There are artists such as Leonardo or even Delacroix who are more analytically interesting than Goya. Rembrandt was more profoundly compassionate in his understanding. But no artist has ever achieved greater honesty than Goya: honesty in the full sense of the word, meaning facing the facts *and* preserving one's ideals. With the most patient craft Goya could etch the appearance of the dead and the tortured, but underneath the print he scrawled impatiently, desperately, angrily: 'Why?' 'Bitter to be present,' 'This is why you have been born,' 'What more can be done?' 'This is worse.' The inestimable importance of Goya for us now is that his honesty compelled him to face and to judge the issues that still face us.

[*Toward Reality: Lessons of the Past* (New York: Knopf, 1962), 5–7, 187–91, 192.]

KWAME ANTHONY APPIAH

57 **The Postcolonial and the Aesthetic**

In 1987 the Center for African Art in New York organized a show entitled *Perspectives: Angles on African Art.*[1] The curator, Susan Vogel, had worked with a number of 'cocurators,' whom I list in order of their appearance in the table of contents: Ekpo Eyo, quondam director of the Department of Antiquities of the National Museum of Nigeria; William Rubin, director of painting and sculpture at the Museum of Modern Art and organizer of its controversial Primitivism exhibit; Romare Bearden, African-American painter; Ivan Karp, curator of African ethnology at the Smithsonian; Nancy Graves, European-American painter, sculptor, and filmmaker; James Baldwin, who surely needs no qualifying glosses; David Rockefeller, art collector and friend of the mighty; Lela Kouakou, Baule artist and diviner, from Ivory Coast (this a delicious juxtaposition, richest and poorest, side by side); Iba N'Diaye, Senegalese sculptor; and Robert Farris Thompson, Yale professor and African and African-American art historian. Vogel describes the process of selection in her introductory essay. The one woman and nine men were each offered a hundred-odd photographs of 'African Art as varied in type and origin, and as high in quality, as we could manage' and asked to select ten for the show.[2] Or, I should say more exactly, that this is what was offered to eight of the men. For Vogel adds, 'In the case of the Baule artist, a man familiar only with the art of his own people, only Baule objects were placed in the pool of photographs.' At this point we are directed to a footnote to the essay, which reads:

Showing him the same assortment of photos the others saw would have been interesting, but confusing in terms of the reactions we sought here. Field aesthetic studies, my own and others, have shown that African informants will criticize sculptures from other ethnic groups in terms of their own traditional criteria, often assuming that such works are simply inept carvings of their own aesthetic tradition.

I shall return to this irresistible footnote in a moment. But let me pause to quote further, this time from the words of David Rockefeller, who would surely never 'criticize sculptures from other ethnic groups in terms of [his] own traditional criteria,' discussing what the catalog calls a 'Fante female figure':[3]

I own somewhat similar things to this and I have always liked them. This is a rather more sophisticated version than the ones that I've seen, and I thought it was quite beautiful . . . the total composition has a very contemporary, very Western look to it. It's the kind of thing that goes very well with contemporary Western things. It would look good in a modern apartment or house.

We may suppose that David Rockefeller was delighted to discover that his final judgment was consistent with the intentions of the sculpture's creators. For a footnote to the earlier 'Checklist' reveals that the Baltimore Museum of Art desires to 'make public the fact that the authenticity of the Fante figure in its collection has been challenged.' Indeed, work by Doran Ross suggests this object is almost certainly a modern piece introduced in my hometown of Kumasi by the workshop of a certain Francis Akwasi, which 'specializes in carvings for the international market in the style of traditional sculpture. Many of its works are now in museums throughout the West, and were published as authentic by Cole and Ross'[4] (yes, the same Doran Ross) in their classic catalog *The Arts of Ghana*.

But then it is hard to be *sure* what would please a man who gives as his reason for picking another piece (this time a Senufo helmet mask), 'I have to say I picked this because I own it. It was given to me by President Houphouet Boigny of Ivory Coast.'[5] Or one who remarks, 'concerning the market in African art':

The best pieces are going for very high prices. Generally speaking, the less good pieces in terms of quality are not going up in price. And that's a fine reason for picking the good ones rather than the bad. They have a way of becoming more valuable.

I like African art as objects I find would be appealing to use in a home or an office. . . . I don't think it goes with everything, necessarily—although the very best perhaps does. But I think it goes well with contemporary architecture.[6]

There is something breathtakingly unpretentious in Mr Rockefeller's easy movement between considerations of finance, of aesthetics, and of decor. In these responses we have surely a microcosm of the site of the African in contemporary—which is, then, surely to say, postmodern—America.

I have given so much of David Rockefeller not to emphasize the familiar fact that questions of what we call 'aesthetic' value are crucially bound up with market value; not even to draw attention to the fact that this is known by those who play the art market. Rather, I want to keep clearly before us the fact that David Rockefeller is permitted to say *anything at all* about the arts of Africa because he is a *buyer* and because he is at the *center*, while Lela Kouakou, who merely makes art and who dwells at the margins, is a poor African whose words count only as parts of the commodification[7]—both for those of us who constitute the museum public and for collectors, like Rockefeller—of Baule art. I want to remind you, in short, of how important it is that African art is a *commodity.*

But the cocurator whose choice will set us on our way is James Baldwin—the only cocurator who picked a piece that was not in the mold of the Africa of the exhibition Primitivism, a sculpture that will be my touchstone, a piece labeled by the museum *Yoruba Man with a Bicycle* [Fig. 1]. Here is some of what Baldwin said about it:

This is something. This has got to be contemporary. He's really going to town. It's very jaunty, very authoritative. His errand might prove to be impossible. He is challenging something—or something has challenged him. He's grounded in immediate reality by the bicycle. . . . He's apparently a very proud and silent man. He's dressed sort of polygot. Nothing looks like it fits him too well.

Baldwin's reading of this piece is, of course and inevitably, 'in terms of [his] own . . . criteria,' a reaction contextualized only by the knowledge that bicycles are new in Africa and that this piece, anyway, does not look anything like the works he recalls seeing from his earliest childhood at the Schomburg museum in Harlem. And his response torpedoes Vogel's argument for her notion that the only 'authentically traditional' African—the only one whose responses, as she says, could have been found a century ago—must be refused a choice among Africa's art cultures because he, unlike the rest of the cocurators, who are Americans and the European-educated Africans, will use his 'own . . . criteria.' This Baule diviner, this authentically African villager, the message is, does not know what *we*, authentic postmodernists, now know: that the first and last mistake is to judge the Other on one's own terms. And so, in the name of this, the relativist insight, we impose our judgment that Lela Kouakou may not judge sculpture from beyond the Baule culture zone because he will—like all the other African 'informants' we have met in the field—read them as if they were meant to meet those Baule standards.

Worse than this, it is nonsense to explain Lela Kouakou's responses as deriving from an ignorance of other traditions—if indeed he is, as he is no

FIG. 1 *Yoruba Man with a Bicycle*
(Yoruba, Nigeria twentieth century; wood and paint H. 35¾ in.)

doubt supposed to be, like most 'traditional' artists today, if he is like, for
example, Francis Akwasi of Kumasi. Kouakou may judge other artists by his
own standards (what on earth else could he, could anyone, do, save make no
judgment at all?), but to suppose that he is unaware that there are other
standards within Africa (let alone without) is to ignore a piece of absolutely
basic cultural knowledge, common to most precolonial as to most colonial
and postcolonial cultures on the continent—the piece of cultural knowledge
that explains why the people we now call 'Baule' exist at all. To be Baule, for
example, is, for a Baule, not to be a white person, not to be Senufo, not to be
French. The ethnic groups—Lele Kouakou's Baule 'tribe,' for example—
within which all African aesthetic life apparently occurs, are [. . .] the products
of colonial and postcolonial articulations. And someone who knows enough
to make himself up as a Baule for the twentieth century surely knows that
there are other kinds of art. [. . .]

I do not know when the *Yoruba Man with a Bicycle* was made or by whom;
African art has, until recently, been collected as the property of 'ethnic'

groups, not of individuals and workshops, so it is not unusual that not one of the pieces in the Perspectives show was identified in the 'Checklist' by the name of an individual artist, even though many of them are twentieth-century; (and no one will have been surprised, by contrast, that most of them *are* kindly labeled with the name of the people who own the largely private collections where they now live). As a result I cannot say if the piece is literally postcolonial, produced after Nigerian independence in 1960. But the piece belongs to a genre that has certainly been produced since then: the genre that is here called *neotraditional*. And, simply put, what is distinctive about this genre is that it is produced for the West.

I should qualify. Of course, many of the buyers of first instance live in Africa, many of them are juridically citizens of African states. But African bourgeois consumers of neotraditional art are educated in the Western style, and, if they want African art, they would often rather have a 'genuinely' traditional piece—by which I mean a piece that they believe to be made precolonially, or at least in a style and by methods that were already established precolonially. And these buyers are a minority. Most of this art, which is *traditional* because it uses actually or supposedly precolonial techniques, but is *neo* [. . .] because it has elements that are recognizably from the colonial or postcolonial in reference, has been made for Western tourists and other collectors.

The incorporation of these works in the West's world of museum culture and its art market has almost nothing, of course, to do with postmodernism. By and large, the ideology through which they are incorporated is modernist: it is the ideology that brought something called 'Bali' to Artaud, something called 'Africa' to Picasso, and something called 'Japan' to Barthes. (This incorporation as an official Other was criticized, of course, from its beginnings: Oscar Wilde once remarked that 'the whole of Japan is a pure invention. There is no such country, no such people.')[8] What *is* postmodernist is Vogel's muddled conviction that African art should not be judged 'in terms of [someone else's] traditional criteria.' For modernism, primitive art was to be judged by putatively *universal* aesthetic criteria, and by these standards it was finally found possible to value it. The sculptors and painters who found it possible were largely seeking an Archimedean point outside their own cultures for a critique of a Weberian modernity. For *post*moderns, by contrast, these works, however they are to be understood, cannot be seen as legitimated by culture- and history-transcending standards.

What is useful in the *neotraditional* object as a model—despite its marginality in most African lives—is that its incorporation in the museum world (while many objects made by the same hands—stools, for example—live peacefully in nonbourgeois homes) reminds one that in Africa, by contrast, the distinction between high culture and mass culture, insofar as it makes sense at all, corresponds by and large to the distinction between those with and those without Western-style formal education as cultural consumers.

The fact that the distinction is to be made this way—in most of sub-Saharan Africa excluding the Republic of South Africa—means that the opposition between high culture and mass culture is available only in domains where there is a significant body of Western formal training, and this excludes (in most places) the plastic arts and music. There are distinctions of genre and audience in African musics, and for various cultural purposes there is something that we call 'traditional' music that we still practice and value. But village and urban dwellers alike, bourgeois and nonbourgeois, listen, through discs and, more importantly, on the radio, to reggae, to Michael Jackson, and to King Sonny Adé. [. . .]

And I am grateful to James Baldwin for his introduction to the *Yoruba Man with a Bicycle*—a figure who is, as Baldwin so rightly saw, polyglot, speaking Yoruba and English, probably some Hausa and a little French for his trips to Cotonou or Cameroon; someone whose 'clothes do not fit him too well.' He and the other men and women among whom he mostly lives suggest to me that the place to look for hope is not just to the postcolonial novel—which has struggled to achieve the insights of a Ouologuem or Mudimbe—but to the all-consuming vision of this less-anxious creativity. It matters little who it was made *for;* what we should learn from is the imagination that produced it. The *Man with a Bicycle* is produced by someone who does not care that the bicycle is the white man's invention—it is not there to be Other to the Yoruba Self; it is there because someone cared for its solidity; it is there because it will take us further than our feet will take us; it is there because machines are now as African as novelists—and as fabricated as the kingdom of Nakem.

['The Postcolonial and the Postmodern', in *In My Father's House: Africa in the Philosophy of Culture* (New York: Oxford University Press, 1992), 137–9, 147–8, 157.]

Notes

Extract 1

CLIVE BELL: *The Aesthetic Hypothesis*

1. [...] When Mr Okakura, the Government editor of *The Temple Treasures of Japan*, first came to Europe, he found no difficulty in appreciating the pictures of those who from want of will or want of skill did not create illusions but concentrated their energies on the creation of form. He understood immediately the Byzantine masters and the French and Italian Primitives. In the Renaissance painters, on the other hand, with their descriptive preoccupations, their literary and anecdotic interests, he could see nothing but vulgarity and muddle. [...] It was not till he came on to Henri-Matisse that he again found himself in the familiar world of pure art. Similarly, sensitive Europeans who respond immediately to the significant forms of great Oriental art, are left cold by the trivial pieces of anecdote and social criticism so lovingly cherished by Chinese dilettanti. It would be easy to multiply instances did not decency forbid the labouring of so obvious a truth.

Extract 2

PAUL ZIFF: *Anything Viewed*

1. Perry B. Cott, *Leonardo Da Vinci Ginevra de' Benci* (Washington, DC: National Gallery of Art, March 1967).
2. Ibid.
3. Ibid.

Extract 3

ALLEN CARLSON: *Aesthetic Appreciation of the Natural Environment*

1. G. Santayana, *The Sense of Beauty: Being the Outline of an Aesthetic Theory* [1896] (Collier, 1961), 99.
2. P. Ziff, 'Reasons in Art Criticism', *Philosophical Turnings: Essays in Conceptual Appreciation* (Cornell, 1966), 71.
3. Ibid., 71.
4. See A. Danto, 'The Artistic Enfranchisement of Real Objects: The Artworld', *Journal of Philosophy* (1964), 571–84. On issues about turning objects into art, see the institutional theory of art; the classic account is G. Dickie, *Art and the Aesthetic: An Institutional Analysis* (Cornell, 1974).
5. See Y. Tuan, *Topophilia: A Study of Environmental Perception, Attitudes, and Values* (Prentice Hall, 1974), 132–3.
6. Thomas West, *Guide to the Lakes* [1778], quoted in J. T. Ogden, 'From Spatial to Aesthetic Distance in the Eighteenth Century', *Journal of the History of Ideas*, 35 (1974), 66–7.

7. R. Rees, 'The Taste for Mountain Scenery', *History Today*, 25 (1975), 312.

8. Rees, 'Mountain Scenery', 312. Ethical concerns are also expressed by Tuan, *Topophilia*, ch. 8, and R. A. Smith and C. M. Smith, 'Aesthetics and Environmental Education', *Journal of Aesthetic Education* (1970), 131–2. Smith and Smith find 'a special form of arrogance in experiencing nature strictly in the categories of art'.

9. R. W. Hepburn, 'Aesthetic Appreciation of Nature', in H. Osborne (ed.), *Aesthetics and the Modern World* (Thames & Hudson, 1968), 53.

10. R. Elliot, 'Faking Nature', *Inquiry*, 25 (1982), 90. The label is from D. Mannison, 'A Prolegomenon to a Human Chauvinistic Aesthetic', in D. Mannison, M. McRobbie, and R. Routley (eds.), *Environmental Philosophy* (Australian National University. 1980).

11. A. Berleant, 'The Aesthetics of Art and Nature', *The Aesthetics of Environment* (Temple, 1992), 169–70. See also Berleant's *Art and Engagement* (Temple, 1991).

12. For a powerful statement of the orthodox view, see P. Ziff, 'Anything Viewed', *Antiaesthetics: An Appreciation of the Cow with the Subtile Nose* (Dordrecht: Reidel, 1984), 129–39.

13. Tuan, *Topophilia*, 96.

14. For a subtle account of the role of classification in art appreciation, see K. Walton, 'Categories of Art', *Philosophical Review*, 79 (1970), 334–67.

15. Perhaps the paradigm exemplification of aesthetic appreciation enhanced by natural science is Aldo Leopold's *A Sand County Almanac* (Oxford, 1949). Leopold's aesthetic views are elaborated in J. B. Callicott. 'The Land Aesthetic', *Companion to A Sand County Almanac* (Wisconsin, 1987), 157–71.

16. Muir's view is well exemplified in his *Atlantic Monthly* essays collected in *Our National Parks* (Houghton Mifflin, 1916). For an introduction to his aesthetic views, see P. Terrie, 'John Muir on Mount Ritter: A New Wilderness Aesthetic', *Pacific Historian*, 31 (1987), 135–44.

Extract 8

FRIEDRICH NIETZSCHE: *The Dionysian*

1. Nietzsche is referring to his own preface to *The Birth of Tragedy out of the Spirit of Music*, published in 1872 and again in 1874. He added 'Attempt at a Self-Criticism' as a preface in 1886 after he came to see Wagner differently.

Extract 10

LINDA NOCHLIN: *Women, Art, and Power*

1. Michel Foucault, *The History of Sexuality, i. An Introduction*, (New York: Pantheon, 1978), 86.

2. The distinction between *langue* (language, the social system fixed collectively by speakers of a language) and *parole* (speech, the individual act of speaking) is found in Ferdinand de Saussure.

3. Robert Rosenblum has pointed out that David's theme may well have been the artist's own invention. See *Transformations in Late Eighteenth Century Art* (Princeton: Princeton University Press, 1967), 68–9 and n. 68.

4. For information about the change, see M. H. Noel-Patton, *Tales of a Granddaughter* (Elgin, Moray, Scotland: Moravian Press, 1970), 22.
5. See *Art Journal*, NS 4 (1858), 169, for a review of *In Memoriam*. The painting was No. 471 in the Royal Academy catalogue of that year.
6. The Spanish title of Goya's print is *Y son fieras*.
7. *Art Journal*, NS 4 (1858), 169.
8. Laura Mulvey, 'Visual Pleasure and Narrative Cinema', *Screen*, 16/3 (1975), 6–18. As Mulvey herself has later pointed out, this is perhaps too simple a conception of the possibilities involved. Nevertheless, it still seems to offer a good working conception for beginning to think about the position of the female spectator of the visual arts.
9. Lisa Tickner, 'Sexuality and/in Representation: Five British Artists', in *Difference: On Representation and Sexuality* (New York: New Museum of Contemporary Art, 1985), 20.

Extract 12

PAUL OSKAR KRISTELLER: *The Modern System of the Arts*

1. [In translation (by David Hills), part of Kristeller's quotation from Goethe's review of Sulzer's *The Fine Arts in Their Origins* (1772): 'There's nothing here for anyone except the schoolboy after rudiments and the easygoing dilettante after the day's fashions.... Here they [the fine arts] are united once more, related or not. What doesn't turn up in this encyclopedia, one entry after another? What can't be bundled together by such a philosophy? Painting and dance, eloquence and architecture, poetry and sculpture, all projected through the same hole onto the same white wall by the magic lantern light of philosophy. It occurred to someone, who reasoned rather poorly, that certain human pastimes and joys, which imitators devoid of genius had turned into toil and laboriousness, could be classified for purposes of theoretical trickery under the rubric "arts", "fine arts". And so they stand in the philosophical textbooks, but only out of laziness, being in fact no more closely related than the seven liberal arts of the old seminaries.']

Extract 15

CLIFFORD GEERTZ: *Art as a Cultural System*

1. N. D. Munn, *Walbiri Iconography: Graphic Representation and Cultural Symbolism in a Central Australian Society* (Ithaca, NY: Cornell University Press, 1973).
2. Quoted in R. Goldwater and M. Treves (eds.), *Artists on Art: From the XIV to the XX Century* (New York: Pantheon, 1945), 410.
3. P. Bohannan, 'Artist and Critic in an African Society', in C. M. Otten (ed.), *Anthropology and Art: Readings in Cross-Cultural Aesthetics* (New York: Natural History Press, 1971), 178.
4. R. F. Thompson, 'Yoruba Artistic Criticism', in W. L. d'Azevedo (ed.), *The Traditional Artist in African Societies* (Bloomington, Ind.: Indiana University Press, 1973), 19–61.
5. R. Goldwater, 'Art and Anthropology: Some Comparisons of Methodology', in A. Forge (ed.), *Primitive Art and Society* (London: Oxford University Press, 1973), 10.

6. A. Forge, 'Style and Meaning in Sepik Art', in Forge (ed.), *Primitive Art and Society*, 169–92. See also A. Forge, 'The Abelam Artist', in M. Freedman (ed.), *Social Organization: Essays Presented to Raymond Firth* (London: Cass, 1967), 65–84.

7. A. Forge, 'Learning to See in New Guinea', in P. Mayer (ed.), *Socialization, the Approach from Social Anthropology* (London: Tavistock, 1970), 184–6.

8. M. Baxandall, *Painting and Experience in Fifteenth Century Italy* (London: Oxford University Press, 1972).

9. Ibid. 38.

10. Ibid. 34.

11. Ibid. 40.

12. Ibid. 41.

13. M. G. S. Hodgson, *The Venture of Islam: Conscience and History in a World Civilization*, i. (Chicago: University of Chicago Press, 1974), 367.

14. J. Maquet, 'Introduction to Aesthetic Anthropology', *A Macaleb Module in Anthropology* (Reading, Mass., 1971), 14.

Extract 16

MARK SAGOFF: *On the Aesthetic and Economic Value of Art*

1. Clive Bell, *Art* (New York: Putnam, 1958), 27, 29.

Extract 18

GRISELDA POLLOCK: *Modernity and the Spaces of Femininity*

1. T. J. Clark, *The Painting of Modern Life: Paris in the Art of Manet and his Followers* (New York: Knopf, and London: Thames & Hudson, 1984).

2. George Boas, 'Il faut être de son temps', *Journal of Aesthetics and Art Criticism*, 1 (1940), 52–65; reprinted in *Wingless Pegasus: A Handbook for Critics* (Baltimore: Johns Hopkins University Press, 1950).

3. Clark, *The Painting of Modern Life*, 146.

4. Ibid. 253.

5. Tamar Garb, *Women Impressionists* (Oxford: Phaidon Press, 1987). The other two artists involved were Marie Bracquemond and Eva Gonzales.

6. Roszika Parker and Griselda Pollock, *Old Mistresses: Women, Art and Ideology* (London: Routledge & Kegan Paul, 1981), 38.

7. Janet Wolff, 'The Invisible Flâneuse; Women and the Literature of Modernity', *Theory, Culture and Society*, 2/3 (1985), 37–48.

8. See George Simmel, 'The Metropolis and Mental Life', in Richard Sennett (ed.), *Classic Essays in the Culture of the City* (New York: Appleton-Century-Crofts, 1969).

9. Richard Sennett, *The Fall of Public Man* (Cambridge: Cambridge University Press, 1977), 126.

10. Walter Benjamin, *Charles Baudelaire; Lyric Poet in the Era of High Capitalism* (London: New Left Books, 1973), ch. II, 'The Flâneur', 36.

11. Jules Simon, *La Femme au vingtième siècle* (Paris, 1892), 67.

12. A fascinating interpretation of this process is offered in Bonnie G. Smith, *Ladies of the Leisure Class: The Bourgeoises of Northern France in the Nineteenth Century* (Princeton: Princeton University Press, 1981). She documents the shift from married women's active involvement in family business and management of

financial affairs common in the early nineteenth century to the completed practice of domesticity, which involved total dissociation from family businesses and money, accomplished by the 1870s. See especially chs. 2–3.

13. Jules Simon, *La Femme*, quoted in John MacMillan, *From Housewife to Harlot: French Nineteenth-Century Women* (Brighton: Harvester Press, 1981), 9.

14. *The Journals of Marie Bashkirtseff* (1890), introduced by Rozsika Parker and Griselda Pollock (London: Virago Press, 1985), entry for 2 January 1879, 347.

Extract 19
KATHLEEN MARIE HIGGINS: *The Music of Our Lives*

1. Alan P. Merriam, *The Anthropology of Music* (Evanston, Ill.: Northwestern University Press, 1964), 120–1.

2. See ibid. 80, and David P. McAllester, *Enemy Way Music: A Study of Social and Esthetic Values as Seen in Navaho Music* (Cambridge: Peabody Museum of American Archaeology and Ethnology, Harvard University, 1954).

3. Merriam, *Anthropology of Music*, 222–7, 272, and John Blacking, *How Musical Is Man?* (Seattle: University of Washington Press, 1973), 7–9.

4. Bruno Nettl, *The Study of Ethnomusicology: Twenty-Nine Issues and Concepts* (Urbana: University of Illinois Press, 1983); Francis Sparshott, 'Aesthetics of Music: Limits and Grounds', in Philip Alperson (ed.), *What Is Music? An Introduction to the Philosophy of Music* (New York: Haven, 1988), 43.

5. Jan L. Broeckx, 'Works and Plays in Music', in *Contemporary Views on Musical Style and Aesthetics* (Antwerp: Metropolis, 1979), 126. Lydia Goehr points out that this notion of the musical work has been with us only since the eighteenth century. See Lydia Goehr, 'Being True to the Work', *Journal of Aesthetics and Art Criticism*, 47/1 (Winter 1989), 55–67. Goehr notes, for instance, that 'Bach did not think centrally in these terms; Beethoven did. Haydn marks the transition' (ibid. 56).

6. Broeckx, *Contemporary Views*, 126–7, 131.

7. Nettl, *Study of Ethnomusicology*, 20. Philip Gbeho is quoted in R. F. Thompson, *African Art and Motion* (Berkeley and Los Angeles: University of California Press, 1974), 242.

8. Charles A. Culver, *Musical Acoustics* (Philadelphia: Blakiston, 1941), 4–5.

9. See Merriam, *Anthropology of Music*, 66–7; Steven Feld, 'Aesthetics as Iconicity of Style (uptown title), or (downtown title) "Lift-Up-Over-Sounding": Getting into the Kaluli Groove', *Yearbook for Traditional Music*, 20 (1988), 80; 'East Asia', in *New Harvard Dictionary of Music*, ed. Don Randel (Cambridge, Mass.: Harvard University Press, 1986), 257; Kate Bush, 'Moving', on *The Kick Inside*, EMI SW-17003. Although current scholarship no longer attributes the Toy Symphony to him, I follow tradition in calling it 'Haydn's'.

10. Nettl, *Study of Ethnomusicology*, 21.

11. Merriam, *Anthropology of Music*, 65; Steven Feld, 'Sound Structure as Social Structure', *Ethnomusicology*, 28/3 (Sept. 1984), 395; Nettl, *Study of Ethnomusicology*, 21; Plato, *Phaedrus* 259; Charles Hartshorne, 'Metaphysics Contributes to Ornithology', *Theoria to Theory*, 13 (1979), 127–8, 131, 133; cf. Friedrich Schiller, *On the Aesthetic Education of Man, in a Series of Letters*, trans. Reginald Snell (New York: Ungar, 1954), 133.

12. Nettl, *Study of Ethnomusicology*, 23–4.
13. Alan Lomax, 'Song Structure and Social Structure', in David P. McAllester (ed.), *Readings in Ethnomusicology* (New York: Johnson Reprints, 1971), 227–9.
14. Ibid., 237–40.
15. Michael (Babatunde) Olatunji, 'Baba Jinde', on *Olatunji! Drums of Passion*, Columbia, #8210, 1960; David Byrne, 'Women vs. Men', on *Rei Momo*, Luka Bop/Sire Record Company, #9-25990-4, 1989.

Extract 20
IVAN KARP: *How Museums Define Other Cultures*

1. See, for example, the essays in *Writing Culture*, ed. James Clifford and George Marcus (Berkeley: University of California Press, 1986). For an excellent account of how European travel writing about the other uses imagery that defines cultures as primitive by reducing them to nature, see Mary Louise Pratt's essay 'Scratches on the Face of the Land; Or what Mr. Barrow saw among the Bushmen', ibid. 27–50.
2. For an insightful account of how the identity of the collector tends to dominate the presentation of primitive arts in fine art museums, see Sally Price, *Primitive Art in Civilized Places* (Chicago: University of Chicago Press, 1989).
3. See Rubin's introductory essay 'Modernist Primitivism', in William Rubin (ed.), *'Primitivism' in 20th Century Art: Affinity of the Tribal with the Modern* (New York: Museum of Modern Art, 1984), 1–84, esp. pp. 50–5.
4. My account of Rubin's interpretation of primitive artists shows why I prefer to use the term *similarity* rather than *identity*. Even assimilating strategies conclude that similarity, not identity, is modified by critical differences. Rubin's primitive artists, however, are 'identical' to modern artists except for those features of modern art they do not have. Thus, his initial assertion of identity concludes with a declaration of difference.
5. See the sumptuous catalogue for this exhibition, *Magiciens de La Terre* (Paris: Éditions du Centre Pompidou, 1989).
6. For a description of the *Circle* and New Guinea shield juxtaposition, see Karen Wilkin, 'Making Sport of Modern Art', *New Criterion*, 8 (Nov. 1990), 75.
7. See the meticulous research in Peter Mason, *Deconstructing America: Representations of the Other* (London: Routledge & Kegan Paul, 1990).
8. This column is developed from material originally published by the author in Ivan Karp and Steven D. Levine (eds.), *Exhibiting Cultures: The Poetics and Politics of Museum Displays* (Washington, DC: Smithsonian Institution Press, 1991).

Extract 26
IMMANUEL KANT: *Art and Genius*

1. In my part of the country, if you set a common man a problem like that of Columbus and his egg, he says, 'There is no art in that, it is only science': i.e. you *can* do it if you know *how*; and he says just the same of all the would-be arts of jugglers. To that of the tight-rope dancer, on the other hand, he has not the least compunction in giving the name of art.

2. Let us part from life without grumbling or regrets,
   Leaving the world behind filled with our good deeds. Thus the sun, his daily
     course completed,
   Spreads one more soft light over the sky;
   And the last rays that he sends through the air
   Are the last sighs he gives the world for its well-being.
                                                (Trans. Werner S. Pluhar)]

3. Perhaps there has never been a more sublime utterance, or a thought more
   sublimely expressed, than the well-known inscription upon the Temple of *Isis*
   (Mother *Nature*): 'I am all that is, and that was, and that shall be, and no mortal
   hath raised the veil from before my face.' *Segner* made use of this idea in a
   suggestive vignette on the frontispiece of his Natural Philosophy, in order to
   inspire his pupil at the threshold of that temple into which he was about to lead
   him, with such a holy awe as would dispose his mind to serious attention.

4. The first three faculties are first *brought into union* by means of the fourth. *Hume*, in
   his history, informs the English that although they are second in their works to no
   other people in the world in respect of the evidences they afford of the first three
   qualities *separately* considered, still in what unites them they must yield to their
   neighbours, the French.

Extract 35

MONROE BEARDSLEY: *The Artist's Intention*

1. From '1887', from *The Collected Poems of A. E. Housman*. Copyright, 1940, by Henry
   Holt and Company, Inc. Copyright, 1936, by Barclays Bank, Ltd. By permission of
   the publishers. Canadian Clearance by permission of the Society of Authors as
   the Literary Representative of the Trustees of the Estate of the late A. E. Housman,
   and Messrs Jonathan Cape Ltd., publishers of A. E. Housman's *Collected Poems*.

2. Frank Harris, *Latest Contemporary Portraits* (New York: Macaulay, 1927), 280.

Extract 36

STEPHEN DAVIES: *Authenticity in Musical Performance*

1. As implied here, the desirability of musical authenticity may sometimes be out-
   weighed by other factors—musical, pragmatic or even moral. (I assume that
   arguments against the use of trained *castrati* in *opera seria* are of the latter kind.)
   Of course, where the choice is between no performance at all and a less than
   ideally authentic performance, the latter may be preferable.

Extract 41

NELSON GOODMAN: *Art and Authenticity*

1. *New York Times Book Review*, 30 July 1961, p. 14.
2. Attributed to Immanuel Tingle and Joseph Immersion (c.1800).

Extract 44

KENDALL L. WALTON: *Make-Believe and the Arts*

1. This paper began as part of the Stieren Distinguished Lecture in the Arts at Trinity
   University in 1991, and was included in the first of three Hempel Lectures at

Princeton University the same year. The present essay is a much abbreviated and slightly reworked version of 'Make-Believe, and its Role in Pictorial Representation and the Acquisition of Knowledge', *Philosophic Exchange* (1994), 81–95, and it includes several sentences from 'Seeing-In and Seeing Fictionally', in *Mind, Psychoanalysis, and Art: Essays for Richard Wollheim*, ed. James Hopkins and Anthony Savile (Oxford: Blackwell, 1992), 281–91. A different abbreviation appeared earlier in *Art Issues*, 21 (Jan./Feb. 1992), as 'Make-Believe, and its Role in Pictorial Representation', 22–7.

2. I develop the theory of make-believe much more thoroughly in *Mimesis as Make-Believe* (Harvard University Press, 1990). For a more complete statement of my account of depiction, see *Mimesis as Make-Believe*, ch. 8, and 'Seeing-In and Seeing Fictionally.'

3. Ernst Gombrich, 'Meditations on a Hobby Horse', in *Meditations on a Hobby Horse and Other Essays* (London: Phaidon Press, 1963), 1–3.

4. Nelson Goodman, *Languages of Art*, 2nd edn. (Indianapolis: Hackett, 1976), 5.

5. See David Summers, 'Metaphor: Towards a Redefinition of the "Conceptual" Image', in Norman Bryson *et al.* (eds.), *Visual Theory: Painting and Interpretation* (New York: Harper Collins, 1991), 234–5.

6. Gombrich, 'Meditations', 3.

7. Ibid. 9.

8. Ibid. 2.

9. Ibid. 4.

10. Cf. Richard Wollheim, *Art and Its Objects*, 2nd edn. (Cambridge: Cambridge University Press, 1980) and *Painting as an Art* (Princeton: Princeton University Press, 1987). Wollheim does not explain the experience of seeing in the way I do.

11. I discuss what it is to imagine in a first person manner, and from the inside, in *Mimesis as Make-Believe*, sect. 1.4. More needs to be said about the nature of the relevant kind of imagining.

12. This participation amounts to what has recently been called *mental simulation*, and is valuable in the ways that simulation is. See, for example, the essays collected in Martin Davies and Tony Stone (eds.), *Mental Simulation: Evaluations and Applications* (Oxford: Blackwell, 1995).

Extract 46

ARISTOTLE: *Emotions and Music*

1. Cf. *Poetics* 1449b27, though the promise is really unfulfilled. The reference is probably to a lost part of the *Poetics*.

Extract 48

SUSAN L. FEAGIN: *The Pleasures of Tragedy*

1. Gilbert Ryle, *The Concept of Mind* (New York: Barnes & Noble, 1949), 107.

Extract 49

TED COHEN: *Jokes*

1. There is a similar distinction to be made, vital but hard to formulate, in discussing responses to art. There is a difference between knowing or seeing that a work is

good, and liking it. If we could explain, or even describe, the relation between understanding a work and responding to it (in some more or less specific way—say, by liking it), we would go far toward answering what ought to be an absolutely basic question in the philosophy of art: what is *appreciation*?

2. [. . .] [T]here is a parallel with art, [. . .] showing the difficulty in formulating the distinction [. . .] between understanding and liking. What is a person of taste? Someone who discerns all that is there, or someone who reacts to what is there by exhibiting a preference? Both? Imagine a master wine-taster who infallibly iden-tifies the date and source of what he tastes but himself is as happy with Ripple as with Château Rothschild. Would you say he has taste?

3. It is, perhaps, just the kind of thing Aristotle calls a virtue in the *Nicomachean Ethics*, a 'settled capacity', a *hexis*.

4. For the provenance of this rare example see my 'Metaphor and the Cultivation of Intimacy', *Critical Inquiry,* 5/1 (Autumn 1978), 8 and n. 6.

5. I owe the bases of both these musical jokes to Professor Peter Kivy, himself a New York musician as well as a scholar.

6. This was told to me in a bar in Tucson by Janet Casebier as she was recalling her days as a Girl Scout. Shoshannah Cohen, a person of exceptional wit, and the retailer of the first of these two jokes, has since persuaded me that every child in the world has either already heard the second joke or was born knowing it.

7. I owe this marvelous joke/parable to Edward and Martha Snyder, but I received it at second hand and I have altered it still more, and so I am not sure what is the canonical version. In telling the story I have noticed an illustration of Hume's conviction that no standard of taste can eradicate differences owing to age. Younger audiences often think the couple benighted, and that either seems funny or not. Older hearers know that there is nothing whatever the couple needs to learn.

In the work of this essay I have been helped by many people. I should acknowl-edge the students at Augustana College and the philosophers at the University of Wisconsin, all of whom forced me to try to describe the offense in some jokes; and the marvelously cordial members of the Thyssen Philosophy Group (England) who made me rethink everything, and one of whom, Hidé Ishiguro, showed me that my first idea of fraudulence was too simple.

Extract 50

EDMUND BURKE: *The Sublime: Of Delight and Pleasure*

1. The angle brackets indicate additions to the second edition published in 1759.

Extract 51

JERROLD LEVINSON: *Music and Negative Emotion*

1. His chief work, *The Power of Sound*, was published in 1880.

2. See the discussions in William Alston, 'Emotion and Feeling', in *The Encyclopedia of Philosophy,* ed. Paul Edwards (New York: Macmillan, 1967); Georges Rey, 'Func-tionalism and the Emotions', in Amelie O. Rorty (ed.), *Explaining Emotions* (Berkeley: University of California Press, 1980); Moreland Perkins, 'Emotions and Feeling', *Philosophical Review,* 75 (1966); Patricia S. Greenspan, 'Ambivalence and

the Logic of Emotion', in Rorty (ed.), *Explaining Emotions*; and Malcolm Budd, 'The Repudiation of Emotion: Hanslick on Music', *British Journal of Aesthetics*, 20 (1980). The first two essays include rather extended analysis of the concept of an emotion, and I am particularly indebted to them for some distinctions I employ in this essay.

3. Cf. R. K. Elliott, 'Aesthetic Theory and the Experience of Art', in Harold Osborne (ed.), *Aesthetics* (London: Oxford University Press, 1972) (and in this volume) on the experience of hearing music 'from within'.

Extract 57

KWAME ANTHONY APPIAH: *The Postcolonial and the Aesthetic*

1. Susan Vogel *et al.*, *Perspectives: Angles on African Art* (New York: The Center for African Art, 1987); by James Baldwin, Romare Bearden, Ekpo Eyo, Nancy Graves, Ivan Karp, Lela Kouakou, Iba N'Diaye, David Rockefeller, William Rubin, and Robert Farris Thompson, interviewed by Michael John Weber, with an introduction by Susan Vogel.
2. Ibid. 11.
3. Ibid. 138.
4. Ibid. 29.
5. Ibid. 143.
6. Ibid. 131.
7. I should insist this first time I use this word that I do not share the widespread negative evaluation of commodification: its merits, I believe, must be assessed case by case. Certainly critics such as Kobena Mercer (for example, in his 'Black Hair/ Style Politics', *New Formations*, 3 (Winter 1987), 33–54) have persuasively criticized any reflexive rejection of the commodity form, which so often reinstates the hoary humanist opposition between 'authentic' and 'commercial'. Mercer explores the avenues by which marginalized groups have manipulated commodified artifacts in culturally novel and expressive ways.
8. Oscar Wilde, 'The Decay of Lying: An Observation', in *Intentions* (New York: The Nottingham Society, 1909), 45.

Select Bibliography

GENERAL

BEARDSLEY, MONROE C., *Aesthetics from Classical Greece to the Present: A Short History* (Macmillan: New York, 1966).

BRAND, PEGGY ZEGLIN and KORSMEYER, CAROLYN (eds.), *Feminism and Tradition in Aesthetics* (Pennsylvania State University Press: University Park, Pa., 1995).

COOPER, DAVID (ed.), *A Companion to Aesthetics* (Blackwell: Oxford, 1992).

EATON, MARCIA MUELDER, *Basic Issues in Aesthetics* (Wadsworth: Belmont, Calif., 1988).

HIGGINS, KATHLEEN M., *Aesthetics in Perspective* (Harcourt Brace: Fort Worth, Tex., 1996).

KELLY, MICHAEL (ed.), *Encyclopedia of Aesthetics* (Oxford University Press: New York, forthcoming).

KOSTELANETZ, RICHARD, *Esthetics Contemporary*, rev. edn. (Buffalo: Prometheus Books, 1989).

MAST, GERALD, COHEN, MARSHALL, and BRAUDY, LEO, *Film Theory and Criticism*, 4th edn. (Oxford University Press: New York, 1992).

SECTION I. WHY DESCRIBE ANYTHING AS AESTHETIC?

I.a. *The Aesthetic*

BEARDSLEY, MONROE C., 'The Aesthetic Point of View', in Howard E. Kiefer and Milton K. Munitz (eds.), *Contemporary Philosophic Thought*, iii, (SUNY Press: Albany, NY, 1970).

BULLOUGH, EDWARD, ' "Psychical Distance" as a Factor in Art and as an Aesthetic Principle', *British Journal of Psychology*, 5 (1912).

DICKIE, GEORGE, 'The Myth of the Aesthetic Attitude', *American Philosophical Quarterly*, 1 (1964).

FRY, ROGER, 'An Essay in Aesthetics', in *Vision and Design* (World Publishing Co.: Cleveland, 1963; first publ. 1920).

SANTAYANA, GEORGE, *The Sense of Beauty, Being the Outlines of Aesthetic Theory* (Scribner's: New York, 1896).

SARTRE, JEAN PAUL, *Nausea*, trans. Lloyd Alexander (New Directions: New York, 1964).

STOLNITZ, JEROME, ' "Beauty": History of an Idea', *Journal of the History of Ideas*, 23 (1961),

—— 'On the Origins of "Aesthetic Disinterestedness" ', *Journal of Aesthetics and Art Criticism*, 20 (1961).

TUAN, YI-FU, *Topophilia: A Study of Environmental Perception, Attitudes and Values* (Prentice-Hall: Englewood Cliffs, NJ, 1974).

WILDE, OSCAR, 'The Importance of Being Earnest' in *The Complete Writings of Oscar Wilde*, ii (The Nottingham Society: New York, 1907).

ZIFF, PAUL, 'Reasons in Art Criticism', in *Philosophic Turnings: Essays in Conceptual Appreciation* (Cornell University Press: Ithaca, NY, 1966).

I.b. A Variety of Aesthetics

BINKLEY, TIMOTHY, 'Piece: Contra Aesthetics', *Journal of Aesthetics and Art Criticism*, 35 (1977).

BOAS, FRANZ, *Primitive Art* (New York: Dover Publications, 1955; first publ. 1927).

GOMBRICH, E. H., *In Search of Cultural History* (Oxford University Press: New York, 1969).

HEPBURN, RONALD, 'Aesthetic Appreciation of Nature', in H. Osborne (ed.), *Aesthetics and the Modern World* (Thames and Hudson: London, 1968).

HIPPLE, WALTER J., *The Beautiful, the Sublime, and the Picturesque in Eighteenth-Century British Aesthetic Theory* (Southern Illinois Press: Carbondale, Ill., 1946).

HUYSMANS, J.-K., *Against Nature*, trans. Robert Baldick (Penguin: Harmondsworth, 1959).

KORSMEYER, CAROLYN, 'Pleasure: Reflections on Aesthetics and Feminism', *Journal of Aesthetics and Art Criticism*, 51 (1993).

KUNDERA, MILAN, *Testaments Betrayed*, trans. Linda Asher (New York: Harper Collins, 1993).

LESSING, GOTTHOLD EPHRAIM, *Laöcoon: An Essay upon the Limits of Painting and Poetry*, trans. E. A. McCormick (publ. New York, 1962; first publ. 1766).

LONGINUS, *Dionysius or Longinus on the Sublime*, trans. W. Hamilton Fyfe (Harvard University Press: Cambridge, Mass.; Heinemann: London, 1939).

NIETZSCHE, FRIEDRICH, *The Birth of Tragedy and The Case Against Wagner*, trans. Walter Kaufmann (Random House: New York, 1967).

WORRINGER, WILHELM, *Abstraction and Empathy: A Contribution to the Psychology of Style*, trans. Michael Bullock (London: Routledge, 1953; first publ. 1907).

SECTION II: WHY IS IT IMPORTANT TO RECOGNIZE OBJECTS AS ART?

II.a. Developing a Theory of Fine Art

DANTO, ARTHUR C., 'The Artworld', *Journal of Philosophy*, 6 (1964).

—— *The Transfiguration of the Commonplace* (Harvard University Press: Cambridge, Mass., 1981).

—— *The Philosophical Disenfranchisement of Art* (Columbia University Press: New York, 1985).

DICKIE, GEORGE, *Art and the Aesthetic: An Institutional Analysis* (Cornell University Press: Ithaca, NY, 1974).

LEVINSON, JERROLD, 'Defining Art Historically', *British Journal of Aesthetics*, 19 (1990).

SPARSHOTT, FRANCIS, 'On the Question: "Why Do Philosophers Neglect the Dance"', *Dance Research Journal*, 15 (1982).

STECKER, ROBERT, *Artworks: Definition, Meaning, Value* (Penn. State Press: University Park, Pa., 1997).

WEITZ, MORRIS, 'The Role of Theory in Aesthetics', *Journal of Aesthetics and Art Criticism*, 15 (1956).

II.b. What is the Relation between Art and Society?

BENJAMIN, WALTER, 'The Work of Art in the Age of Mechanical Reproduction', in Hannah Arendt (ed.), *Illuminations*, trans. Henry Zohn (Harcourt Brace and World: New York, 1968).

BERGER, JOHN *Ways of Seeing* (Viking Press: New York, 1973).

MALRAUX, ANDRÉ, *Museum without Walls*, trans. Stuart Gilbert and Francis Price (New York: Doubleday & Co., 1967; first publ. 1965).

SCRUTON, ROGER, 'Musical Understanding and Musical Culture', in Philip Alperson (ed.), *What is Music? An Introduction to the Philosophy of Music* (Penn. State Press: University Park, Pa., 1994).

SECTION III: ART AS A VEHICLE FOR EXPRESSION, CREATIVITY, AND FREEDOM

III.a. Expression

GOMBRICH, E. H., 'Expression and Communication', in *Meditations on a Hobby Horse and Other Essays* (Phaidon Press: London, 1965).

HEPBURN, R. W., 'Emotions and Emotional Qualities', in M. Lipman (ed.), *Contemporary Aesthetics* (Allyn and Bacon: Boston, 1973).

KIVY, PETER, *Sound Sentiment: An Essay on the Musical Emotions* (Temple University Press: Philadelphia, Pa., 1989).

LANGER, SUZANNE, *Feeling and Form* (Scribner's: New York, 1953).

—— *Problems of Art* (Scribner's: New York, 1957).

SIRCELLO, GUY, 'Expressive Properties of Art', in *Mind and Art: An Essay on the Varieties of Expression* (Princeton University Press: Princeton, 1972).

WOLLHEIM, RICHARD, 'Correspondence, Projective Properties, and Expression in the Arts', in Ivan Gaskell and Salim Kemal (eds.), *The Language of Art History* (Cambridge University Press: Cambridge, 1991).

III.b. Self-Expression and Society

COLERIDGE, SAMUEL TAYLOR, *Biographia Literaria* (1817), chs. 4, 13, 14.

GAY, JOHN, *The Enlightenment: An Interpretation*, ii: *The Science of Freedom* (New York: Knopf, 1969)

GOMBRICH, E. H., *Art and Illusion: A Study in the Psychology of Pictorial Representation* (Princeton University Press: Princeton, 1960).

GUYER, PAUL, *Kant and the Claims of Taste* (Harvard University Press: Cambridge, Mass., 1979).

JAMES, HENRY, 'The Real Thing' in *The Short Stories of Henry James*, ed. Clifton Fadiman (Random House: New York, 1945).

MARITAIN, JACQUES, *Art and Scholasticism, with Other Essays*, trans. J. F. Scanlan (Sheed and Ward: London, 1933).

MARX, KARL, 'Economic and Philosophic Manuscripts of 1844', trans. Martin Milligan, in Robert C. Tucker (ed.), *The Marx–Engels Reader*, 2nd edn. (New York: Norton, 1978; first publ. 1844).

PLATO, *Republic*, Books II–III (376–412), IX–X (588–608).

—— *Ion* (530–42).

SCHILLER, FRIEDRICH, *On the Aesthetic Education of Man*, trans. Reginald Snell (Routledge and Kegan Paul: London; Yale University Press: New Haven, 1954).

SCHOPENHAUER, ARTHUR, *The World as Will and Idea*, i, trans. R. B. Haldane and J. Kemp (Scribner's: New York; Routledge & Kegan Paul: London, n.d.; first publ. 1883).

WILLIAMS, RAYMOND, *Culture and Society, 1780–1950* (London: Chatto & Windus, 1958), ch. 2, 'The Romantic Artist'.

SECTION IV: CAN WE EVER UNDERSTAND AN ARTWORK?

DUTTON, DENIS (ed.), *The Forger's Art: Forgery and the Philosophy of Art* (University of California Press: Berkeley, Calif., 1983).

GARCÍA MÁRQUEZ, GABRIEL, *Chronicle of a Death Foretold*, trans. Gregory Rabassa (Ballantine: New York, 1982).

HIRSCH, E. D. (tr.), *Validity in Interpretation* (Yale University Press: New Haven, 1967).

ISEMINGER, GARY (ed.), *Interpretation and Intention* (Temple University Press: Philadelphia, Pa., 1992).

LODGE, DAVID (ed.), *20th Century Literary Criticism: A Reader* (London: Longmans, 1972).

SACKS, SHELDON (ed.), *On Metaphor* (University of Chicago Press: Chicago, 1978).

WALTON, KENDALL, 'Categories of Art', *Philosophical Review*, 79 (1970).

WOLLHEIM, RICHARD, *Painting as an Art* (Princeton University Press: Princeton, 1987).

SECTION V: WHY IS IT IMPORTANT TO RESPOND EMOTIONALLY TO ART?

BUDD, MALCOLM, *Music and the Emotions* (Routledge & Kegan Paul: London, 1985).

CARROLL, NOEL, *The Philosophy of Horror, or Paradoxes of the Heart* (Routledge: New York, 1990).

FEAGIN, SUSAN L., *Reading with Feeling: The Aesthetics of Appreciation* (Cornell University Press: Ithaca, NY, 1996).

HUME, DAVID, 'Of Tragedy', in *Of the Standard and Taste and Other Essays*, ed. John W. Lenz (Indianapolis: Bobbs-Merrill, 1965).

LAMARQUE, PETER, *Fictional Points of View* (Cornell University Press: Ithaca, NY, 1996).

MORREALL, JOHN, 'Enjoying Negative Emotions in Fiction', *Philosophy and Literature*, 9 (1985).

RORTY, AMELIE OKSENBERG (ed.), *Explaining Emotions* (University of California Press: Berkeley, Calif., 1980).

SCHIER, FLINT, 'The Claims of Tragedy: An Essay in Moral Psychology and Aesthetic Theory', *Philosophical Papers*, 18 (1989).

WALTON, KENDALL L., *Mimesis as Make-Believe* (Harvard University Press: Cambridge, Mass., 1990), ch. 7. 3.

SECTION VI: HOW CAN WE EVALUATE ART?

GOLDMAN, ALAN H., *Aesthetic Value* (Westview Press: Boulder, Colo., 1995).

KANT, IMMANUEL, *Critique of Judgment* ('Critique of Aesthetic Judgment'), trans. James Creed Meredith (Oxford University Press: Oxford, 1928; first publ. 1790).

KEMAL, SALIM and GASKELL, IVAN (eds.), *Explanation and Value in the Arts*, Cambridge Studies in Philosophy and the Arts (Cambridge University Press: Cambridge, 1993).

RIDLEY, AARON, *Music, Value and the Passions* (Cornell University Press: Ithaca, NY, 1995).

SCHAPER, EVA (ed.), *Pleasure, Preference and Value* (Cambridge University Press: Cambridge, 1983).

STEINBERG, LEO, 'Other Criteria' in *Other Criteria: Confrontations with Twentieth Century Art* (Oxford University Press: London and New York, 1972).

Biographical Notes

D'ALEMBERT, J.   Named for the church of St Jean-Le-Rond, on whose steps he was a foundling, Jean le Rond d'Alembert became one of the finest mathematician-physicists of the age, applying his calculus of partial differences to vibrating chords, as well as making great contributions to fluid dynamics and calculating the precession of the equinox and the perturbation of planets, among other subjects, d'Alembert was for years co-editor with Diderot of the great *Encyclopédie*, for which his *Discours préliminaire des éditeurs*, extracted here, expressed his interest in the arts as part of his new systematization of knowledge, rejecting traditional ways of thinking. His philosophy of mathematics was empiricist and his ethics was based on sympathetic feelings.

APPIAH, K. A.   Having taught at Yale, Cornell, and Duke University, Kwame Anthony Appiah is now Professor of Afro-American Studies at Harvard University. He has written extensively on philosophy of language and cultural studies. *In My Father's House* deals with numerous issues surrounding questions of race, African philosophy, and politics and identity. It was a 1992 *New York Times* Notable Book of the Year.

ARISTOTLE.   Aside from studies of logic and method, Aristotle divided systematic investigation into the theoretical or speculative, whose purpose is knowledge, the practical, whose purpose is good action, and the productive, whose purpose is good production. Called 'the Philosopher' by medieval Islamic and Christian thinkers, 'the master of those who know' by Dante, the greatest of biologists by Darwin, and depicted with his *Ethics* by Raphael, as the greatest exemplar of 'Philosophy', Aristotle left in *Poetics* one of his few works on productive or *poietike* inquiry, a work that has had great influence since the sixteenth century.

D'AZEVEDO, W. L.   Warren L. d'Azevedo, Professor of Anthropology at the University of Nevada, Reno, has done extensive field work among West African peoples and among the Washo people of California and Nevada, in the Great Basin of North America.

BARTHES, R.   Roland Barthes (1915–80) was Professor of Semiology at the Collège de France. Early on he was involved with structuralism, which used Ferdinand de Saussure's linguistic model for understanding the structures of virtually any kind of social system or practice. The meaning of a text was held to be determined by structure rather than artist's intent. Virtually any social practice—such as clothing and cuisine—could be understood as a system of signs with a 'grammar'. By the time of the publication of *S/Z* he was committed to a poststructuralist deconstructionism, rejecting the distinction between the sign and signified, and introducing the concept of a 'writerly' reading wherein a reader creates rather than discovers meaning. Besides *S/Z* (1970), his best known works include the short essay 'The Death of the Author' (1968) and *The Pleasure of the Text* (1975).

BATTEUX, C.   Seventeenth-century scholar Abbé Charles Batteax taught philosophy at the Collège de France, Paris, and is best known for *Les Beaux-Arts*, which argued for the autonomy of the rules of the 'fine arts' from those of morals. Often cited but not translated, that book is excerpted here to make Batteaux's main ideas available, in a translation by Voltaire scholar Professor Robert Walters.

BAXANDALL, M.   Professor of the History of the Classical Tradition at the Warburg Institute, University of London, then Professor of Art History at the University of California at Berkeley, Michael Baxandall, publications include *Giotto and the Orators*, his influential *Painting and Experience in Fifteenth-Century Italy, Limewood Sculptors of Renaissance Germany, Patterns of Intention*, and *Shadows and Enlightenment. Patterns of Intention* is an expanded version of a set of public lectures in which he lays out various factors that enable us to explain a picture.

BEARDSLEY, M.   Professor Monroe Beardsley taught at Swarthmore College, then at Temple University, and, among several other books, was the author of two standards of recent philosophical aesthetics: *Aesthetics* and the compact history *Aesthetics from Classical Greece to the Present*. A collection of his papers is titled *The Aesthetic Point of View*.

BELL, C.   Clive Bell (1881–1954) was an art critic and member of the Bloomsbury Group, which also included Vanessa Bell, Virginia Woolf, Roger Fry, Lytton Strachey and J. M. Keynes. Reacting against the prescriptions for painting advanced by the Royal Academy, he is known for his defence of post-impressionist painting. His belief that aesthetic experience had intrinsic value was influenced by the theory of value elaborated in G. E. Moore's *Principia Ethica*.

BERGER, J.   John Berger began as a painter and teacher of drawing and was art critic for the *New Statesman* before his wider literary career as prize-winning scenario writer, translator of Brecht, Booker Prize winner for his novel *G*, author of *The Success and Failure of Picasso* and the televised *Ways of Seeing*, among a number of books and essay collections about visual art.

BURKE, E.   Born in Dublin, Edmund Burke (1729–97) moved to London and pursued a political career. While at Trinity College, Dublin, he wrote *A Philosophical Enquiry into the Origin of our Ideas of the Sublime and Beautiful* and revised it extensively about ten years later. He studied law in London and sat in the House of Commons from 1765 to 1794. His best known political writing is *Reflections on the Revolution in France* (1790), in which he espoused a conservative viewpoint.

CARLSON, A.   Professor of Philosophy at the University of Alberta. He researches mainly in environmental aesthetics, and has published extensively in philosophy, aesthetics, environmental, and planning and design periodicals.

CHADWICK, W.   Professor of Art History at San Francisco State University, Whitney Chadwick writes on the role of women in the history of art. *Women Artists and the Surrealist Movement* (1985) focuses on the important but generally neglected role women played in that movement, and *Women, Art, and Society* (1990) covers ten centuries of women's contributions to the arts. She co-authored, with Isabelle de Courtivron, *Significant Others: Creativity and Intimate Partnership* (1993).

COHEN, T.   Teaches in the Philosophy Department of the University of Chicago. Ted Cohen has published pieces on Kant's aesthetics, metaphor, television, jokes, and baseball; he was awarded the Pushcart XVI 'best of the small presses' prize for 'There Are No Ties at First Base'. He is also President of the American Society for Aesthetics.

COLLINGWOOD, R.   English philosopher (1889–1943) who also wrote on Roman history and the philosophy of history, taught at Pembroke College, Oxford, and became Waynflete professor at Oxford in 1934.

DANTO, A.   Johnsonian professor emeritus of philosophy at Columbia University, New York, Arthur Danto is a past president of the American Society for Aesthetics and the American Philosophical Association. He is well known both for his art criticism (he has served as art critic for the *Nation* magazine since 1984) and philosophical writings on art. His most famous essay, 'The Artworld', explains how a work of art can be visually indistinguishable from an ordinary real thing and yet be a work of art. He has also applied a Hegelian theory of history to the history of art, observing that art has transmuted into philosophy and hence reached an end.

DAVIES, S.   Senior Lecturer in the department of philosophy at the University of Auckland, Stephen Davies writes on philosophy of music and also more widely on issues in aesthetics including the relevance of an artist's intentions to interpreting and defining art. He is the author of *Definitions of Art* (1991) and *Musical Meaning and Expression* (1994), and the editor of *Art and Its Messages: Meaning Morality, and Society* (1997).

DEWEY, J.   Among the most famous and influential of American philosophers, John Dewey worked at liberal education, social, and political reforms, and published books and articles—now collected in thirty-seven volumes—for over seventy years. Dewey's aesthetics reflects his continuous systematic criticism of oppositions between knowing and doing, creature and environment, self and society, and so on. His general Pragmatist epistemology was again celebrated by philosophers near the end of the twentieth century, with the rise of naturalistic, social, and otherwise contextual construals of philosophy. This renewed appreciation includes Dewey's *Art as Experience*, once influential with twentieth-century abstract painters, and long a staple, sometimes as a target, for philosophical aesthetics in previous decades, as its denial of dualisms became more attractive.

DUCASSE, C.   Curt John Ducasse was born in France in 1881 and went to the United States in 1900. He taught philosophy at the University of Washington and Brown University. Ducasse wrote on a wide variety of philosophical topics including two books on philosophy of art, *The Philosophy of Art* (1929) and *Art, the Critics, and You* (1944).

ELLIOTT, R. K.   Professor and Head, History and Philosophy of Education Division, University of Birmingham, has contributed many essays to books and journals on art education and appreciation.

FEAGIN, S.   Professor of Philosophy at the University of Missouri at Kansas City. Susan Feagin has published on numerous topics in aesthetics, focusing especially on ways in which aesthetics intersects the philosophy of mind. *Reading with Feeling: The Aesthetics of Appreciation* was published in 1996.

GEERTZ, C.   Professor of Social Science at the Institute for Advanced Study in Princeton, Clifford Geertz is a distinguished cultural anthropologist whose studies include *The Interpretation of Cultures, Islam Observed, The Religion of Java, Works and Lives*, and *After the Fact: Two Countries, Four Decades, One Anthropologist*.

GOODMAN, N.   Professor Emeritus of Philosophy at Harvard University, Nelson Goodman is known mainly for his work in the philosophy of science and aesthetics. *Languages of Art* (1968) described the syntactic and semantic properties of symbol systems employed by various arts (such as music, dance, and painting).

HEGEL, G. W. F.   Georg Wilhelm Friedrich Hegel's systematic, difficult, paradoxical philosophy of epistemology, metaphysics, politics, religion, and history is especially notable for several features regarding the arts. Hegel's is the first major philosophical system to feature art as a central form of human experience, whereby it relates art essentially to the history of mind, disentangling it from aesthetics of nature. Also, Hegel's abstruse speculations contain imaginative, detailed perceptions of individual works of art as well as of kinds of art, which continue to inspire. Hegel's introductory lectures to his *Aesthetics*, given in Berlin in the 1820s, are available separately from the larger work.

HIGGINS, K. M.   Professor of philosophy at the University of Texas at Austin, Kathleen Marie Higgins's research is primarily in aesthetics (especially musical aesthetics) and nineteenth-century continental philosophy. She is the author of *Nietzsche's 'Zarathustra', The Music of Our Lives*, and (with Robert C. Solomon) *A Short History of Philosophy* and *A Passion for Wisdom*. She is also editor of *Aesthetics in Perspective* and co-editor (with Robert C. Solomon) of *Reading Nietzsche, The Philosophy of (Erotic) Love, The Routledge History of Philosophy*, vol. 6: *The German Idealists, From Africa to Zen*, and *World Philosophy: A Text with Readings*. She was a resident scholar at the Rockefeller Foundation's Bellagio Study and Conference Center in 1993, and at the Australian National University in 1997. She has also held visiting positions at the University of California, Riverside, and the University of Auckland.

HUME, D.   First fully appreciated by Kant, David Hume (1711–76) was a Scots philosopher and historian whose early *Treatise of Human Nature* was supplemented by classic essays on the nature and limits of the workings of the human mind, including knowledge and belief, as well as on the passions, morals, letters, society, and economics.

ISENBERG, A.   Arnold Isenberg taught at Cornell, Harvard, Queens College and Michigan State where he was teaching when he died in 1965. Interested primarily in ethics and aesthetics, 'Critical Communication' is his best-known essay.

KANT, I.   The three systematic 'critiques' by Immanuel Kant (1724–1804) of the grounds, limits, and presuppositions of human reason, rational action, and perceptual judgment reset the direction of modern philosophy's evolution out of traditional forms. As influential as his writing in *The Critique of Judgment* on aesthetic judgment is that on the mental power of genius, whereby law-governed nature comes into perfect harmony with freedom.

KARP, I.   Director of the Institute of African Studies at Emory University, Ivan Karp was formerly curator of African ethnology in the Department of Anthropology at the National Museum of Natural History, Smithsonian Institution. He is co-editor of several volumes on the African systems of thought and the theory and politics of museum display, including *Museums and Communities* (1990) and *Exhibiting Cultures* (1992).

KRISTELLER, P. O.   Deprived by Fascism of a scholarly career in Germany or Italy, Paul Oskar Kristeller taught philosophy at Columbia University for over three decades, where, as a leading researcher of Italian Renaissance thought, he became Frederick Woodbridge Professor. He is organizer of the Renaissance Society and of the International Federation of Renaissance Studies, and author of over twenty volumes in several languages, including *Renaissance Thought and the Arts*. He is a member of many international scholarly academies, and has won numerous awards, including those of the Newberry Library, the Bibliographic Society of London, the British Academy, the American Historical Association, and the order of merit from the Italian government. His 1976 festschrift is titled *Philosophy and Humanism*.

LEVINSON, J.   Professor of philosophy at the University of Maryland, College Park. He is the author of *Music, Art and Metaphysics* (1990), *The Pleasures of Aesthetics* (1996), and *Music in the Moment* (1997), and the editor of *Aesthetics and Ethics* (1998). Known mainly for his works on the philosophy of music and the definition of art, he also writes on film, interpretation, appreciation, and emotional responses to art.

LI KUNG-LIN   As part of the group of scholar-officials whose central member was Su Shih, Li (1049–1105) promoted new types of poetry, calligraphy, and painting.

MILL, J. S.   Best known as a nineteenth-century Utilitarian philosopher and philosopher of social science, Mill's views on poetry, first published in journals, with the sobriquet 'Antiquus', accord with the ideas about individualism in his famous 'On Liberty', and his progressive social ideas, which postulated mutual understanding among people assisted by education and imaginative, expressive art. Many of these views he attributed to the influence of Harriet Taylor, whom he married in 1851.

NIETZSCHE, F.   Friedrich Nietzsche (1844–1900), a student of classical philology, has had great influence on existentialism and postmodernism. His first book, *The Birth of Tragedy*, developed the distinction between the Apollonian and Dionysian. He is also known for *Thus Spake Zarathustra* and *Twilight of the Idols*, which praise personal style over the search for truth, individual will and desire over attempts to be rational. The variety, passion, and style of his works accommodate numerous interpretations, which are further complicated by his descent into madness, so that virtually any claim about the content of work is likely to be controversial.

NOCHLIN. I.   Lila Acheson Wallace Professor of Modern Art at the Institute of Fine Arts of New York University, and author of the groundbreaking, 'Why Have There Been No Great Women Artists?' (1971), Linda Nochlin has published widely on feminist art history and nineteenth-century European painting. *Representing Women* (1997) is her most recent collection of essays.

NUSSBAUM, M.   Ernst Freund Professor of Law and Ethics at the University of Chicago School of Law, Martha Nussbaum writes on multiple topics in philosophy, including ancient philosophy, philosophy of literature, philosophy of feminism, political philosophy, and philosophy of law. Her numerous books include *The Fragility of Goodness* (1986), *Love's Knowledge* (1990), *The Therapy of Desire* (1994), and several co-edited volumes on politics, patriotism, and the quality of life.

OKAKURA, K. Kakuzo Okakura (d. 1913) was Curator of Chinese and Japanese Art at the Boston Museum of Fine Arts and responsible for the tremendous growth and quality of its collections. He lectured and published widely on the arts of Japan and China to become one of the best known interpreters of Japanese customs to the West.

POE, E. A. Edgar Allan Poe's poetry and short stories were in the tradition of the European romantic tradition, with its emphasis on the gothic and grotesque. Despite the briefness of his life (1809–1849), he in turn had a major effect on the Symbolist tradition in France. 'The Fall of the House of Usher' influenced many artists as well, including the filmmaker Jean Epstein and the composer Debussy, who planned an opera based on it. In his native America, however, critics condemned his works for being 'too Germanic', despite their popularity. His own psychological torments have provided ideal opportunities for psychoanalytic interpretations of his work.

POLLOCK, G. Professor of the Social and Critical Histories of Art in the department of fine art at the University of Leeds, Griselda Pollock's feminist cultural analysis challenges traditional art-historical accounts of the formations of modernism in late nineteenth- and early twentieth-century Europe and America. Her books include *Vision and Difference* (1988), and (with Rozsika Parker), *Old Mistresses: Women, Art and Ideology* (1981).

ROEMER, M. Michael Roemer's motion picture and television writing, directing, and producing have won many prizes and honours. Since 1971 he has taught film-making and aesthetics at Yale University, where he is Professor of Film and American Studies. Roemer's 1995 treatise *Telling Stories* is a study of the practice of narrative in all artistic genres.

SAGOFF, M. Senior Research Scholar at the Institute for Philosophy and Public Policy in the School of Public Affairs, University of Maryland, Mark Sagoff is the author of *The Economy of the Earth* (1988). Pew Scholar in Conservation and the Environment and President of the International Society for Environmental Ethics, Sagoff has an AB from Harvard and Ph.D. (Philosophy) from Rochester, and has taught at Princeton, University of Pennsylvania, University of Wisconsin (Madison), and Cornell University.

SCHAPIRO, M. Scholar, teacher, and art critic of wide learning, Meyer Schapiro was professor of art history at Columbia University for many decades. He was Slade Professor of Art History at Oxford University and Charles Eliot Norton Professor at Harvard. He lectured for many years at the New School for Social Research, and, through his exposition and advocacy of the works of artists of the Abstract Expressionist movement and beyond, had much influence on the New York schools of painting. His main written works are collected in a four-volume series of lectures and essays, beginning from his early specialization in Romanesque art and extending to modern art and aesthetics.

SONTAG, S.   Susan Sontag took degrees in English literature and philosophy before becoming a leading essayist, from her *Against Interpretation* (1966) through *Styles of Radical Will*, to the prize-winning *On Photography* and *AIDS and Its Metaphors*. Editor of Artaud, Barthes, and Danilo Kis, Sontag is also a playwright and novelist, author of *Duet for Cannibals: A Screenplay* and *The Volcano Lover: A Romance*. Sontag has held numerous awards and grants, including Guggenheim, MacArthur and Rockefeller fellowships, and has been president of the American Center of PEN. She is an officer of the French order of arts and letters.

SU SHIH   Su (1037–1101) was a poet-painter-statesman considered to be the greatest Sung poet. Though for a time banished by the government for his beliefs, he remained gregarious and personable, and thus became a model for how to deal with adversity. He and other members of his group elevated painting to the status of poetry and calligraphy. They saw it as a vehicle for personal expression for scholars (as opposed to artisan painters who paint for a living) and as revealing the moral qualities of the artist.

TANIZAKI, J.   Jun'ichirō Tanizaki was an eminent and learned Japanese novelist with a writing career of over fifty years, and was witness to radical changes in his country. His achievements include translation into modern Japanese of the eleventh-century classic *Tale of Genji*, but few of his own many works are available in western languages. His house was among the cultural losses of the Kobe earthquake of 1995, thirty years after his death.

TAYLOR, J. C.   Professor of Art History at the University of Chicago, author of the introductory *Learning to Look*, and specialist in modern as well as in American art history, Joshua Charles Taylor became Director of the National Collection of Fine Arts at the Smithsonian Institution, where he published such works as *To See Is to Think: Looking at American Art*.

TOLSTOY, L.   Among the greatest of novelists, Count Leo Tolstoy was a forceful social reformer of the late nineteenth century, an inspiration to Gandhi and many others. The Aylmer Maude English translation of *What is Art?* not only appeared before the Russian version, *Chto Takoye Isskustvo?*, but was approved by Tolstoy as the better, uncensored version. Eccentric in many ways, that treatise nevertheless presents an unexcelled challenge to aestheticism and high culture, regarding the necessity of art for any human society.

WALTON, K.   James B. and Grace J. Nelson Professor of Philosophy at the University of Michigan, Ann Arbor, Kendall L. Walton has published extensively on philosophical aesthetics, especially regarding fiction, the representational arts, and music. His 1990 *Mimesis as Make-Believe* is the first full-length presentation of a theory of representation as it applies to all the arts.

WILDE, O.   Oscar Fingal O'Flahertie Wills Wilde (1854–1900) was born into a middle class Irish Protestant family. After winning the gold medal for Greek at Trinity College, Dublin, he went on to study with Ruskin and Pater at Oxford. He was at the centre of a movement called 'aestheticism' which praised form over content, clever talk over moral action, and the view that one should live one's life as a work of art. He is known primarily for two literary works, the play *The Importance of Being Earnest* and the novel *The Picture of Dorian Gray.*

WOLLHEIM, R.   Grote Professor at the University of London, later Mills Professor at the University of California at Berkeley (among many appointments), Richard Wollheim has lectured widely and published, as author and editor, numerous books and essays on philosophy, visual art, and psychology. These include *The Thread of Life*, based on his 1981 William James Lectures at Harvard, and *Painting as an Art*, from the 1984 Mellon Lectures at the National Gallery of Art, Washington, which presents a 'substantive' or applied development of his theories of artistic meaning to complement his *Art and Its Objects*.

XIE HE (Hsieh Ho)   A portrait painter (*c*.500-*c*.535) in China known primarily for his Six Laws of painting. The Six Laws, which have been the subject of reinterpretation through the centuries, came to have a major importance for ranking painters and assessing the quality of their work.

Source Acknowledgements

TEXTS

APPIAH, KWAME ANTHONY, 'The Postcolonial and the Aesthetic', in *In My Father's House: Africa in the Philosophy of Culture* (Oxford University Press, New York, 1992).

ARISTOTLE, 'The Emotions Proper to Tragedy', in Ingram Bywater (trans.) and R. McKeon (ed.), *The Basic Works of Aristotle* (Random House, New York, 1941).

ARISTOTLE, 'Emotions and Music', in Ingram Bywater (trans.) and R. McKeon (ed.), *The Basic Works of Aristotle* (Random House, New York, 1941).

BATTEUX, ABBÉ, 'The Fine Arts Reduced to a Single Principle' trans. Robert L. Walters; first published Paris, 1746.

BARTHES, ROLAND, 'From Work to Text' in J. V. Harari (trans.), *Textual Strategies* (Cornell University Press, Ithaca, NY, 1979, reprinted with permission Les Presses de la Cité, Paris).

BAXANDALL, MICHAEL, 'Truth and Other Cultures', in *Patterns of Intention: On the Historical Explanation of Pictures* (Yale University Press, New Haven, 1985).

BEARDSLEY, MONROE, 'The Artist's Intention', in *Aesthetics: Problems in the Philosophy of Criticism* (Harcourt Brace, New York 1958).

BELL, CLIVE, *The Aesthetic Hypothesis* (Chatto & Windus, London, 1914).

BELL, CLIVE, *The Metaphysical Hypothesis* from *Art* (Chatto & Windus, London, 1958).

BERGER, JOHN, 'Lessons of the Past', in *Toward Reality* (Copyright © 1962 by John Berger; reprinted by permission of Alfred A. Knopf Inc.).

CARLSON, A., 'Aesthetic Appreciation of the Natural Environment', *Journal of Aesthetics and Art Criticism*, 37 (University of Wisconsin Press, Madison, 1979).

CHADWICK, WHITNEY, 'Women Artists and the Institutions of Art', in *Women Art and Society* (Thames and Hudson, London, 1990).

CH'IN CH'EN, WANG, 'Spiritual Excellence', repr. by permission of the publisher from Susan Bush and Hsio-yen Shih (eds.), *Early Texts on Painting*, Harvard University Press, Cambridge, Mass. Copyright © 1985 by the Presidents and Fellows of Harvard College.

COHEN, TED, 'Jokes', in Eva Schaper (ed.), *Pleasure, Preference and Value* (Cambridge University Press, 1983, and kind permission of the author).

COLLINGWOOD, R. G., 'Art and Craft', in *The Principles of Art* (Oxford University Press, New York, 1958).

D'ALEMBERT, JEAN LE ROND, 'Preliminary Discourse', in *Preliminary Discourse to the Encyclopedia of Diderot*, trans. Richard N. Schwab (Bobbs-Merrill Co. Inc., 1963, repr. by permission of Prentice Hall, Inc.).

DANTO, ARTHUR, 'Deep Interpretation', in *The Philosophical Disenfranchisement of Art* (Columbia University Press, New York, 1986; copyright © 1986 by Arthur Danto; repr. by permission of Georges Borchardt, Inc., for the author).

DAVIES, Stephen, 'Authenticity in Musical Performance', *British Journal of Aesthetics*, 27 (Oxford University Press, Oxford, 1987).

D'AZEVEDO, WARREN, 'Sources of Gola Artistry', in *The Traditional Artist in African Societies* (Indiana University Press, Bloomington, 1973).

DEWEY, JOHN, 'Having an Aesthetic Experience', in *Art as Experience* (G. Putnam & Sons, New York, 1934; repr. by permission of the Putnam Publishing Group; copyright © 1934 by John Dewey; renewed © 1973 by the John Dewey Foundation).

DUCASSE, CURT, 'Criticism as Appraisal', in *Art, the Critics, and You* (Bobbs-Merrill Co. Inc., 1944, repr. by permission of Prentice Hall Inc.).

ELLIOTT, R. K., 'Aesthetic Theory and the Experience of Art', *Proceedings of the Aristotelian Society*, NS 67 (1966–7; repr. by courtesy of the Editor of the Aristotelian Society, © 1966/7).

FEAGIN, SUSAN, 'The Pleasures of Tragedy', *American Philosophical Quarterly*, 20 (1983).

GEERTZ, CLIFFORD, 'Art as a Cultural System', *Modern Language Notes*, 91 (1974; © the Johns Hopkins University Press).

GOODMAN, NELSON, 'Art and Authenticity', in *Languages of Art: An Approach to a Theory of Symbols*, 2nd edn. (Hackett Publishing Co., Indianapolis, 1976).

HEGEL, G. W. F., 'Art, Nature, Freedom', in T. M. Knox (trans.), *Aesthetics: Lectures on Fine Art* (Clarendon Press, Oxford, 1975).

HIGGINS, KATHLEEN, *The Music of Our Lives* (Temple University Press, Philadelphia, 1991).

HOSPERS, JOHN, 'Aesthetics, Problems of . . .', in Paul Edwards (ed. in chief), *The Encyclopedia of Philosophy*, i. 35–56 (excerpted with permission of Macmillan Library Reference USA, a Simon & Schuster Macmillan Company, copyright © 1967 by Macmillan, Inc.; copyright renewed © 1995).

ISENBERG, ARNOLD, 'Critical Communication', *Philosophical Review*, 58/4 (1949; copyright 1949, Cornell University, Ithaca, NY; repr. by permission of the publisher).

KANT, IMMANUEL, 'Art and Genius', in *Critique of Judgement*, trans. James Creed Meredith (Oxford: Clarendon Press, 1952).

KARP, IVAN, 'How Museums Define Other Cultures', *American Art* (Winter/Spring 1991; repr. by permission of the National Museum of American Art).

KRISTELLER, P. O., 'The Modern System of the Arts', in *Renaissance Thought and the Arts* (Harper & Row, New York, 1965).

LEVINSON, JERROLD, 'Music and Negative Emotion', from *Music, Art and Metaphysics, Pacific Philosophical Quarterly*, 63 (1982; University of Southern California, © Blackwell Publishers Ltd., Oxford).

NIETZSCHE, FRIEDRICH, 'In Praise of Shadows', in Walter Kaufman (trans.), *The Birth of Tragedy and the Case of Wagner* (Copyright © 1967 by Random House, Inc.; repr. by permission of Random House Inc.).

NOCHLIN, LINDA, *Women, Art, and Power and Other Essays* (Harper & Row, New York, 1988).

NUSSBAUM, MARTHA, 'Luck and the Tragic Emotion', in *The Fragility of Goodness: Luck and Ethics in Greek Tragedy* (Cambridge University Press, Cambridge, 1986, and with permission of the author).

OKAKURA, KAKUZO, 'The Tea Room', in E. F. Bleiler (ed.), *The Book of Tea* (Dover Publications, New York, 1964).

POLLOCK, GRISELDA, 'Modernity and the Spaces of Feminity', in *Vision and Difference: Feminity, Feminisms and the Histories of Art* (Routledge, London, 1988, and kind permission of the author).

ROEMER, MICHAEL, 'The Surfaces of Reality', *Film Quarterly*, 18/1 (Fall 1964; © 1964 by The Regents of the University of the University of California).

SAGOFF, MARK, 'On the Aesthetic and Economic Value of Art', *British Journal of Aesthetics*, 21 (1981; repr. by permission of Oxford University Press).

SCHAPIRO, MEYER, 'Diderot on the Artist and Society', in *Theory and Philosophy of Art: Style, Artist and Society: Selected Papers* (George Braziller Inc., New York, 1994).

SCHAPIRO, MEYER, 'On Perfection and Coherence in Art', in Sidney Hook (ed.), *Art and Philosophy: A Symposium* (New York University Press, 1966, © the author's estate).

SONTAG, SUSAN, 'Against Interpretation', in *Against Interpretation and Other Essays* (Farrar, Strauss, and Giroux, New York, 1961).

SU SHIH, 'Painting Bamboo', repr. by permission of the publisher from Susan Bush and Hsio-yen Shih (eds.), *Early Texts on Painting* (Harvard University Press, Cambridge, Mass.; copyright © 1985 by the Presidents and Fellows of Harvard College).

SU SHIH, 'Genius', repr. by permission of the publisher from Susan Bush and Hsio-yen Shih (eds.), *Early Texts on Painting* (Harvard University Press, Cambridge, Mass.; copyright © 1985 by the Presidents and Fellows of Harvard College).

TANIZAKI, JUN'ICHIRO, *In Praise of Shadows*, trans. Thomas J. Harper, and Edward G. Seidensticker (New Haven, Leete's Island Books Inc., 1977).

TAYLOR, JOSHUA, 'Art and the Ethnological Artifact', *Critical Inquiry*, 11 (Sept. 1974; University of Chicago Press, 1974).

TOLSTOY, LEO, 'What is Art?', in Aylmer Maude (trans.), *What is Art?* (Bobbs-Merrill Co. Inc., 1960, repr. by permission of Prentice Hall Inc.).

WALTON, KENDALL, 'Make-Believe and its Role in Pictorial Representation', *Journal of Aesthetics Education* (University of Illinois Press, 1991).

WOLLHEIM, RICHARD, 'Criticism as Retrieval', in *Art and Its Objects*, 2nd edn., (Cambridge University Press, Cambridge, 1980).

XIE-HE (Hsieh Ho), 'Six Canons of Painting', repr. by permission of the publisher from Susan Bush and Hsio-yen Shih (eds.), *Early Texts on Painting* (Harvard University Press, Cambridge, Mass.; copyright © 1985 by the Presidents and Fellows of Harvard College).

ZIFF, PAUL, 'Anything Viewed', in *Antiaesthetics: An Appreciation of the Cow with the Subtile Nose* (Reidel Publishing Company, Dordrecht, 1984; repr. by kind permission of Kluwer Academic Publishers, Dordrecht).

ILLUSTRATIONS

1. *End of Haida relief-carved argillite chest*, collected by James G. Swan (October 1883), reproduced by courtesy of Department of Anthropology, Smithsonian Institution, Washington DC (cat. no. 89000).

2. *And They Are Like Wild Beasts*, Francisco Goya y Lucientes, *c*.1812/15, etching 15.6 × 20.8 cm., no. 5 from the series *Los Desastres de la Guerra*; photograph: AKG, London.

Index

Note: Page numbers in *italics* indicate captions to illustrations. Most references are to visual arts, except where otherwise indicated.